T0339964

Elements of Information Organization and Dissemination

Elements of Information Organization and Dissemination

AMITABHA CHATTERJEE

AMSTERDAM • BOSTON • HEIDELBERG • LONDON
NEW YORK • OXFORD • PARIS • SAN DIEGO
SAN FRANCISCO • SINGAPORE • SYDNEY • TOKYO
Chandos Publishing is an imprint of Elsevier

CHANDOS
PUBLISHING

Chandos Publishing is an imprint of Elsevier
50 Hampshire Street, 5th Floor, Cambridge, MA 02139, United States
The Boulevard, Langford Lane, Kidlington, OX5 1GB, United Kingdom

Notices
Knowledge and best practice in this field are constantly changing. As new research and
experience broaden our understanding, changes in research methods, professional practices,
or medical treatment may become necessary.

Practitioners and researchers must always rely on their own experience and knowledge
in evaluating and using any information, methods, compounds, or experiments described
herein. In using such information or methods they should be mindful of their own safety
and the safety of others, including parties for whom they have a professional responsibility.

To the fullest extent of the law, neither the Publisher nor the authors, contributors, or
editors, assume any liability for any injury and/or damage to persons or property as a
matter of products liability, negligence or otherwise, or from any use or operation of any
methods, products, instructions, or ideas contained in the material herein.

British Library Cataloguing-in-Publication Data
A catalogue record for this book is available from the British Library

Library of Congress Cataloging-in-Publication Data
A catalog record for this book is available from the Library of Congress

ISBN: 978-0-08-102025-8 (print)
ISBN: 978-0-08-102026-5 (online)

For information on all Chandos Publishing
visit our website at https://www.elsevier.com

Working together
to grow libraries in
developing countries

www.elsevier.com • www.bookaid.org

Publisher: Jonathvan Simpson
Acquisition Editor: Glyn Jones
Editorial Project Manager: Ana Claudia Garcia
Production Project Manager: Debasish Ghosh
Cover Designer: Maria Inês Cruz

Typeset by MPS Limited, Chennai, India

To
My wife Kabita
in appreciation of her support and silent participation
in my professional and intellectual endeavors.

CONTENTS

PREFACE

More than 30 years ago, the author of this book brought out a textbook, *Elements of Documentation*, on the then emerging subject of documentation. The book became very popular among the Library and Information Science (LIS) students. The intervening period saw enormous changes in the field of LIS, specially due to ushering in of digital age. Though efforts were made to revise the book earlier, it did not materialize so long due to various reasons. When finally the revision work was taken up, it was realized that simple revision would not be sufficient and there was need to rewrite majority of the chapters. Not only that, many new chapters needed to be added to cover new developments. While doing so, almost a new textbook has emerged covering not only the earlier subject of documentation but also the entire gamut of information sources, systems, and services, which is now an essential part of the syllabus of almost every LIS school. The new book has been named *Elements of Information Organization and Dissemination*, the reason for which has been explained in the first chapter itself. The word 'Elements' which was prefixed to the title of the previous book, has been retained in the title of the new book too, as it seems to have become a buzzword, which was suggested by late Prof. P.N. Kaula, the first guru of the author in the field of LIS.

The author is greatly indebted to late Dr. S.R. Ranganathan, the doyen of library and information science in India, and Prof. Bimalendu Guha, former Professor and head of the Department of Library & Information Science, Banaras Hindu University, Varanasi, India, whose ideas had a profound impact on the author and whose writings have been profusely quoted by him in this book. He also places on record his gratitude to his guru late Prof. P.N. Kaula, who would have been one of the happiest persons to see this book in print. The author has received help from many of his colleagues and students in various ways in preparing the book. He thanks them all. He also thanks his former student, Mr. Somen Mondal, who ungrudgingly word-processed the initial text of this book. Last, but not book the least, the author also thanks his daughter Rima and son-in-law Sanjay for their help and encouragement during the long period of writing this book.

The author also sincerely thanks Mr. Jonathvan Simpson, Publisher, and other members of the production team, viz., Dr. Glyn Jones, Ms. Ana Claudia Garcia, Mr. Debasish Ghosh, Ms. Sheela Bernardine Josy and Ms. Maria Ines Criz for their valuable contribution in bringing out the book in an attractive format within a short time.

It is expected that the book will be able to satisfy the needs of the students while pursuing LIS courses as also while preparing themselves for jobs, and if that happens the author will feel his labor amply rewarded.

—*Author*
Kolkata (Calcutta), India

CHAPTER A

Background

A.1 INTRODUCTION

Information is now considered as a vital resource or input in almost every field of human endeavor. It is continuously being used by people in every walk of life, such as in education and research, in agriculture, in business and industry, in management and even in everyday life. Use of information, in turn, gives rise to new information, which are again used and the cycle goes on. Thus, the quantity of recorded information is increasing very fast. According to a recent estimate, the number of books being published every year in the world is more than 20 lakhs [1]. According to another estimate, there were about 25,400 active scholarly peer-reviewed journals in early 2009, collectively publishing about 1.5 million articles a year [2]. A well-known journal publisher, Elsevier, alone publishes more than 2,50,000 articles a year in around 2200 journals [3]. Besides, more than 75,000 patents and more than 5 lakh reports are also being published every year. Not only so, these figures are doubling in 12–15 years [4]. In other words, we are now living in the age of information explosion or information overload. To profitably utilize this huge quantity of information, it is necessary to organize all these information efficiently and to disseminate the pertinent information to the users as per their requirement.

A.2 CONCEPT OF IOD

The concept of information organization and dissemination (IOD) is not at all new. The library workers have been collecting, organizing, and disseminating books and journals, which are recorded sources of information, to their readers or users for a very long time. But the tools and techniques that they were using to do so were gradually found to be not matching with the changes in the mode and varieties of publication. Before 19th century the focus of research was mainly confined to humanities and science and books were mostly being used as sources of information, although periodicals had appeared in 17th century itself. In 19th century,

Elements of Information Organization and Dissemination
DOI: http://dx.doi.org/10.1016/B978-0-08-102025-8.00001-6
© 2017 Amitabha Chatterjee.
Published by Elsevier Ltd.

besides humanities, social sciences and science, importance of engineering, and technology came to the fore. From this time onwards the importance of articles in periodicals went on rising and need was felt for identifying relevant articles for researchers in various fields and reaching them to the right researchers speedily [4]. To do such work rapidly, newer techniques were evolved and such techniques were termed as documentation. These activities aim at efficient organization and dissemination of information.

A.3 NEED FOR IOD

In today's world the need and importance of documentation or IOD are certainly immense. The documents are now being produced not only in larger number, but also in varieties of forms. There is also a spurt in research activities not only for obtaining academic degrees, but for the all-round development of the mankind. The research has, as Prof. Guha points out, now become "more mission-oriented and time bound" [5]. Evidently, it is not possible for the specialists and research workers to wade through the vast mass of literature and find out the pertinent information by themselves. They have neither enough time at their disposal nor necessary training to do this work. The language barrier is another handicap for them. To meet this situation it is necessary to identify, collect, organize, and disseminate relevant information lying scattered and buried in various documents and make these readily available for effective use by the researchers and specialists. In the absence of such activities there will be national wastage either in the form of valuable research time of the specialists or duplication of research due to nonavailability of information on earlier research-findings resulting in delayed progress of the masses.

A.4 ROLE OF IOD

Mere availability of information or information sources cannot ensure availability of information to the users. IOD plays an important role in making information available to the users. The vital role of IOD may be depicted through this simple diagram:

It indicates that on the one hand there are sources containing information and on the other there are users who need information. IOD activities are undertaken to serve the users their needed information.

A.5 NOMENCLATURE

Paul Otlet, one of the founders of the International Institute of Bibliography in Brussels, was perhaps the first person to use the term "documentation" to "denote the specific activities of gathering, processing, storing, retrieving, and circulating documents" as early as in 1905 during a lecture [6]. Later in 1934, he brought out his *Traite de Documentation*, the first work in this new field. In 1937, the name of his institute was changed to International Federation of Documentation (FID). S.C. Bradford also chose this subject to write a treatise, titled *Documentation*, in 1948. The term gradually came to stay with some changes in the meaning and scope. It soon became an accepted term, especially in Europe. In United States too the term was accepted by many. Meanwhile, after World War II, UNESCO started a new division called Division of Documentation, Bibliotheques et Archives (DBA). The term "documentation" spreads in other countries of the world through the activities of this division. At the initiative of UNESCO, National Documentation Centres were developed in many countries. Centro de Documentacion Cientifica y Tecnica, Mexico; Jugoslovenski Centar za Tehnicku i Naucnu Dokumentaciju, Belgrade; Indian National Scientific Documentation Centre (now NISCAIR), New Delhi; Scientific and Technical Documentation Division of the National Research Centre of Egypt, Cairo; and Pakistan National Scientific Documentation Centre, Karachi (now PASTIC, Islamabad); are some of those documentation centers.

A.5.1 Other Names

In 1950s, when computers came into use in documentation work, a new term emerged for the concept of documentation, viz., information retrieval (IR). The term was first used by Calvin Mooers in a paper presented at a meeting of the Association for Computing Machinery at Rutgers University, USA, "to denote the activities pertaining to the term documentation" [7]. However, since retrieval of information depends on availability of a store of information, a new term tagging both the ideas—information storage and retrieval (ISR)—started to be used and subsequently both the terms remained in use as alternative terms. But "when the term Information Science was established in America to denote the documentation activities in general, the terms IR and ISR underwent some change in connotation. The terms 'Information Retrieval' and 'Information Storage and Retrieval' are now being used in more restricted sense of mechanized retrieval or the actual retrieval process only" [8]. It is now defined as "a field at the intersection of information science and computer science," which "concerns itself with the indexing and retrieval of information from heterogeneous and mostly textual information resources" [9]. The term Information Science was coined by Chris Hanson of ASLIB in 1956 [10], though the term "information scientist," was being used in the United Kingdom in the 1940s to describe scientists who specialized in helping their colleagues to find information [11]. American Documentation Institute adopted the term and rechristened itself as American Society for Information Science in 1968. Meanwhile, in mid-1960s another term to denote the same idea was evolved in Russia, viz., Informatics. The new term was proposed by A.I. Mikhailov, A.I. Chernyi, and R.S. Gilarevskii. Nevertheless, this term was not much used in other countries. Further, in mid-1980s another new term came in vogue, viz., Information Management to denote "means by which a center [i.e., library or information center] maximizes the efficiency with which it plans, collects, processes, controls, disseminates, and uses its information and through which it ensures that the value of that information is identified and exploited to the fullest extent" [12]. In a simple language, information management has been defined as "collection and management of information from one or more sources and distribution of that information to one or more audiences" [13].

A.6 DEFINITION OF DOCUMENTATION

By documentation Paul Otlet meant "a process by which are brought together, classified and distributed, all documents of all kinds of all the areas of human activity" [6], while according to R.R. Shaw, documentation is any process connected with "identification, recording, organization, storage, recall, conversion into more useful forms, synthesis and dissemination of intellectual content of print or any other recorded materials" [14]. In these definitions, the term documentation has been taken in a very broad sense. Almost all activities relating to all types of documents—collection, organization, and dissemination—are covered by documentation.

As a result, documentation and librarianship, which are connected with similar activities, look identical and it is difficult to differentiate them.

A.6.1 New Dimension

The term "documentation" acquired a new dimension when ASLIB adopted the following definition of "documentation" in 1945 for the *Journal of Documentation*: "recording, organization, and dissemination of specialized knowledge, or in other words, documentation means collecting, organizing and providing micro-thought to the scientist and research scholar." It clearly indicated that documentation dealt with specialized knowledge or micro-thought and was meant for specialists like scientists and research workers. ASLIB's contention was further strengthened by S.C. Bradford, who defined "documentation" as "the process by which… is…put before the creative specialist the existing literature bearing on his subject of investigation," [15] and by J.H. Shera who meant by "documentation," "the group of techniques necessary for the ordered presentation, organization, and communication of recorded specialized knowledge in order to give maximum accessibility and utility to the information contained" [16].

A.6.2 Clear Scope

Ranganathan clearly delineated the scope of documentation when he defined it as "pin-pointed, exhaustive and expeditious service of nascent micro-thought to specialists" [17]. Thus, according to him, documentation lays stress on (1) nascent thought, far more than on old thought; (2) micro-document, far more than on macro-document; and (3) specialist user, far more than on generalist user. He also emphasized the need for pin-pointed, exhaustive, and expeditious service as is required by the researchers and the specialists.

A.6.3 New Context

After the term Information Science came into existence, efforts were made to formulate a new definition of the subject, but the experts have not yet been able to arrive at an all accepted definition. To some experts, Information Science deals with automated IR, while to another expert it is a professional discipline relating to accumulation, storage, and transfer of recorded knowledge [8]. Again, according to another expert, it is a true discipline "that investigates the properties and behavior of information, and the means for processing information for accessibility and usability" [18]. Ranganathan, however, felt that there was no basic difference between documentation and information science. The new name was like changing of label on a bottle. Since main activities involved in all the above mentioned concepts relate to organization and dissemination of information, the term "Information Organization and Dissemination," has been used in this book.

A.7 MAIN FACETS

Before actually providing the required information to the specialists and research workers, it is necessary to undertake some preparatory work. It is something like preparing dishes and keeping them ready for serving dinner to a guest. Thus, there are some activities which are carried out behind the scene and some on the scene. Behind-the-scene activities in documentation are known as documentation work and on-the-scene activities as documentation service. Prof. Guha terms them as active documentation and passive documentation, respectively [5]. In the present context, however, we may call these activities as organization of information and provision of information service or dissemination of information, respectively.

A.7.1 Differences

Documentation work/information organization and documentation service/information service, therefore, refer to two different sets of activities. They may be differentiated in following ways [19]:

- Documentation work or information organization refers to preparatory activities, while documentation service/information service refers to final activities;
- Documentation work or information organization is done in anticipation of demand, while documentation service/information service is given in response to actual demand;
- While performing documentation work or organizing information documents are analyzed and their retrieval aids are prepared; in documentation service/information service documents/information are searched, located, and supplied;
- Documentation service/information service is provided by an individual center or library, but all documentation or information organization work necessary to give that service may not be done at the same center or library;

- Documentation work or organization of information is almost a continuous process, but documentation service/information service ends every time when a user gets his document or information.

A.8 IOD ACTIVITIES

The various types of activities involved in IOD may be grouped in the following way:

Information organization	Information service
Anticipation of users' demand	Precise enunciation of users' demands
Compilation of current awareness list/documentation list	Current awareness service
Preparation of document profiles and user profiles for SDI	Selective dissemination of information
Indexing	Serving index/indexing periodical to the users
Abstracting	Serving abstract/abstracting periodical to the users
Preparation of information consolidation products	Serving information consolidation products to the users
Bibliography/union catalog compilation	Bibliographic service
Translation index preparation	Compiling reading lists and providing those to users

However, in most cases, a user is not satisfied only by knowing the location of required information. He wants to get the information in usable form. Suppose a user gets information about a relevant article through current awareness service. He will certainly want to get the full article in original or at least a copy of it. If the article is in a language not known to him, he will like to get a translated version of the article in his known language. The services that may be required to meet such needs of the users are document delivery service and translation service respectively. Such services may be called backup services or supplementary services. Document delivery service is provided in various ways. If the desired document is available in the local library or information center, it may be directly supplied to the user. If it is not locally available, it may be procured from another library/information center having the document on inter-library loan and supplied to the user. If needed, a photocopy of the document may also be supplied. Later, help of fax and e-mail facilities are taken for providing such services [20]. Similarly, on getting requests from users, a translated version of the article may be procured from another organization having that version or from any translation pool, or, when it is not available, arrangement may be made for getting the required documents translated. Most of the above activities have been discussed in detail in the succeeding chapters.

REFERENCES

[1] Books published per country per year. <http://en.wikipedia.org/wiki/Books_published_per_country_per_year>.

[2] B.C. Bjork, et al., Scientific journal publishing: yearly volume and open access availability, Inform Res 14 (1) (2009) 391. <http://InformationR.net/ir/14-1/paper391. html >.

[3] Elsevier Website. <http://www.elsevier.com>.

[4] A.R. Chakraborty, Outline of Information Science [in Bengali], World Press, Calcutta, 1986, p. 11–12.

[5] B. Guha, Documentation and Information, second ed., World Press, Calcutta, 1983, p. 7–8.

[6] P. Otlet, As Quoted in: B. Guha. Documentation and Information, second ed., World Press, Calcutta, 1983, p. 2.

[7] C. Mooers, The theory of digital handling of non-numerical information and its implications to machine economics: Proceedings of the meeting of the Association for Computing Machinery, Rutgers University, New Brunswick, NJ, United States, 1950.

[8] H. Bose, Information Science: Principles and Practice, Sterling Publishers, Delhi, 1986.

[9] W. Hersh, Terms, models, resources, and evaluation, In: W. Hersh, Information Retrieval: A Health and Biomedical Perspective, third ed., Springer-Verlag, New York, 2009, 3–39.

[10] T. Wilson, Information science and research methods. <http://www.informationr.net/tdw/publ/papers/slovak02.html>.

[11] R.T. Bottle, Information science, In: J. Feather, P. Struges, (Eds.), International Encyclopedia of Information and Library Science, second ed., Routledge, London, 2009, pp. 295–297.

[12] I.K. Ravichandra Rao, Information management: scope, definition, challenges and issues, in: DRTC Workshop on Information Management, 1999. Paper – AA.

[13] Information Management. <http://sebokwiki.org/wiki/Information_Management>.

[14] R.R. Shaw, Documentation: complete cycle of information sources, Coll. Res. Libr. 18 (1957) 452.

[15] S.C. Bradford, Documentation, second ed., Crossby Lockwood, London, 1953, p. 11.

[16] J.H. Shera, Documentation and Organization of Knowledge, Crosby Lockwood, London, 1966,

[17] S.R. Ranganathan, Documentation and Its Facets, Asia, Bombay, 1963, Ch. B4.

[18] H. Borko, As quoted in: G.D. Bhargava. Information dissemination in academic libraries: a challenge, In: B. Guha (Ed.), In the Library and Information Science Horizon, Allied Publishers, New Delhi, 1986, pp. 118.

[19] A. Chatterjee, Elements of Documentation, The Author, Calcutta, 1983, p. 13.

[20] A. Chatterjee, Information: Organization and Service [in Bengali], West Bengal State Book Board, Kolkata, 2012, p. 8.

CHAPTER B

Information Sources

B.1 INTRODUCTION

Any object from which something can be obtained or found out may be called a source (e.g., river is the source of water or bank is the source of finance for industries). Thus, any object that provides information can be called an information source. On the other hand, when something is used to add value or create something new, it may be called a resource (e.g., when land is used for raising a crop or setting up an industry which creates some goods, it is considered as a resource). In case of a library or an information center, the information sources (IS) are essential resources, since these serve as the basis for all the services provided by it or products created by it. Evidently, the terms "sources" and "resources" are not synonymous and cannot be used interchangeably. It is only in the context of libraries and information centers that information sources and information resources refer to same thing.

B.2 GENESIS OF IS

The beginning of information sources may be traced back to man's earliest attempts to record thoughts, concepts, ideas, and events [1]. However, different sources have evolved at different times. For example, printed books mainly came into being after the discovery of movable types in 15th century by Gutenberg, while the first printed periodical was issued only in 17th century; patent emerged in mid-15th century, while trade catalog appeared in 18th century.

B.3 VARIETIES OF IS

Over centuries, several varieties of information sources have come up, the most widely known of them being books and periodicals. Information sources are now available both in tangible and intangible forms. Information sources in tangible form are mainly traditional print sources, while those in intangible form are digital sources. Thus, the information

Elements of Information Organization and Dissemination
DOI: http://dx.doi.org/10.1016/B978-0-08-102025-8.00002-8

sources, which are available in digital form—online as well as offline—can be called digital information sources or electronic information sources. Information sources can be broadly categorized as:

- Human Information Sources
- Institutional Information Sources
- Documentary Information Sources

B.3.1 Human Information Sources

There may be many experts and researchers in every subject field who themselves serve as sources of information. For example, David Baltimore (USA) is a human information source in the field of Medical Sciences, Stephen Hawking (UK) is so in the field of Physics, Amartya Sen (India) is so in the field of Economics, and so on. Valuable information may be available from them verbally through their lectures, and from their correspondence, diaries, notebooks, etc. There are also some other human information sources, who are specifically engaged in supply or transfer of information, such as technological gatekeepers, information brokers, or consultants.

- *Technological Gatekeeper:* A technological gatekeeper is "one who is integral in the diffusion of scientific and technical information from the environment into the R&D firm" [2]. A technological gatekeeper has more exposure to technological information through study of technical literature, participation in conferences/seminars in the concerned subject, and informal discussions with technologists. He also has expertise in internal and external communication, which helps in efficiently performing the task of information diffusion. The term "technological gatekeeper" was first used in a stream of research in the 1970s, headed by Thomas Allen of the Massachusetts Institute of Technology. The term was used to describe the role of a small number of key resources within R&D groups that acquired relevant information from the outside world, translated it so that it could be understood and used internally and then disseminated that information internally [3].
- *Information Broker:* An information broker (or independent information professional or information consultant) is a person who searches and collects information for his/her clients from offline and/or online information sources and provides the collected information to the respective clients for a fee. In other words, an information broker is

a freelance information supplier. An information broker presents the information "in the manner most appropriate for his/her client. This may mean summarizing the information or verifying the correctness of it. Many times raw information must be cleaned up" [4]. However, some people feel that the term "broker" is here a misnomer and "Information retrieval consultant" will be a more accurate term [5].

B.3.2 Institutional Information Sources

Similarly, in every country there are many organizations and institutions which serve as sources of information. For example, National Aeronautics and Space Administration (USA) is an institutional information source in the field of aerospace engineering, Royal Society of Chemistry (UK) is so in the field of chemistry, Bose Institute (India) is so in the field of biological sciences, and so on. The results of research conducted in these institutions can be obtained from them even before these are formally published in primary journals. Many unpublished information may also be available from them. Examples of such organizations and institutions are research establishments in government, industry, and private organizations; learned and professional societies; academic, scientific, and technological institutions; development associations financed by industry, which are concerned with the use and application of products like copper, aluminum, rubber, fertilizer, etc.; trade associations; export promotion councils; national productivity councils; consultation agencies, etc. [6]. Even government departments and agencies can be sources of valuable information. Besides, some institutions specifically serve as information intermediaries, such as libraries and information centers. These institutions collect, organize, and disseminate information to their clients.

B.3.3 Documentary Information Sources (DIS)

A documentary information source or document, according to dictionary meaning, is "something written which gives information or facts" [7]. It is, thus, "a recorded evidence of intellectual endeavor" or more precisely an "embodied thought" [8]. Earlier, the word "document" was used to refer only those records, which provided evidence for writing history or taking legal decisions. But in present denotation it covers all records of knowledge or information.

B.3.3.1 Definition

Ranganathan defined a document as "a record made on more or less flat surface or on surface admitting of being spread flat when required, made of paper or other material fit for easy handling, transport across space and preservation through time—of thought created by mind and expressed in language or symbols or in any other mode, and/or record of natural or social phenomena made directly by instrument without being passed through human mind and woven into thought created and expressed by it" [8]. In short, "a document is a graphic record of some idea or some phenomenon, made in words or in pictures" [9]. Hans P. Luhn used the term document "to designate a block of information confined physically in mediums, such as a letter, report, paper, or book" [10]. In view of the emergence of newer physical forms of documents in the present era, a document may be defined as "a record of a body of information created on paper or some paper like material manually by hand or by using a typewriter, or mechanically by using any technique of printing, copying, or duplicating; or a record created electronically by using analogue technology or digital technology on a suitable medium; or a virtual record stored in a computer hard disc or a server" [11].

B.3.3.2 Recording Media and Technology

In the beginning, human beings were creating records by hand or by using small tools or by using ink on clay tablets, stone, metal plate, animal skin, or palm-leaf. After the invention of paper, documents were created by writing using ink. In the next stage, typewriter or printing machine was used for creating documents. After the advent of computer, use of typewriter started declining and the process of printing saw enormous changes. In the 20th century besides printed documents, documents recorded in various visual media, audio media and audio–visual media and using analogue technology came into vogue, such as gramophone records, audio-tapes, video cassettes, microforms, films, and so on. After the advent of digital computers, documents recorded by using digital technology in such media as CD, VCD, DVD, etc. have come up. Besides, virtual documents are now available on the Internet.

B.3.3.3 Media of Presentation

From the point of view of medium of presentation, the documentary information sources can be broadly grouped under two categories—Printed and Nonprinted. Since the information sources recorded by analogue technology have now become almost obsolete, digital information sources are considered as the main nonprint information sources.

Advantages of IS in Print Medium

The traditional information sources in printed form have the following advantages:

- These are tangible in nature and hence can be consulted directly.
- These are not machine dependent for consultation.
- These can be physically preserved for future consultation by users.
- These can be consulted by both computer savvy and unsavvy users.

Advantages of IS in Digital Medium

The information sources in digital medium have some distinct advantages as compared to those in printed medium [12]:

- Access to information is instant.
- Effective searching is possible for a required information.
- Digital information sources can be easily networked.
- Digitized information can be made available to anyone, any time, and anywhere at minimal cost.
- The digital information source does not get damaged or exhausted by unlimited use.
- There is no need of re-shelving or no cases of missing, stealing, or willful damaging.
- Presentation of information through digital sources can be done within a reasonable time with speed and ease.
- Multiple access to digital sources simultaneously is possible.
- Downloading of the required information is very easy.
- It develops a distributed learning environment by which all the users can be benefited at a time.
- Remote access to information is possible.
- Large volume of data can be stored in the digital sources and made accessible to the users.
- Information transfer can be done with speed and accuracy.
- Addition of information in the digital sources is faster.
- Requirement of space for storage of digital sources is much less as compared to that of print sources.
- These sources do not require physical processing.
- Cataloging, editing, referring, indexing, etc. can be done with ease and speed.

- The quality of information service can be improved and maintained through digital sources.
- Education and training can be provided through digital sources effectively.
- Career planning and related information can be made accessible through digital sources effectively.

Besides, information sources in digital medium often have multimedia and hypermedia capabilities.

B.3.3.4 Categories of DIS

The documentary information sources can be categorized in various ways on the basis of physical characteristics, subject contents, levels of subject treatment, purposes to be served, etc. The views of some experts in this regard are summarized below.

Binary Division

C.W. Hanson has preferred a binary division. According to him, documents are of two types—*Primary* and *Secondary*. *Primary* documents contain original information and they exist of their own, while *Secondary* documents help easy access to the primary documents and therefore are dependent on them. His first group includes books, periodicals, reports, patents, theses, trade literature, and standards, while the second includes subject bibliographies, indexing journals, and abstracting journals, reviews, and surveys [13].

Trinary Division

Denis Grogan has distinguished three types of document, viz., *Primary*, which records new information for the first time; *Secondary*, which provides the same information in a reorganized form; and *Tertiary*, which does not provide any information as such but information about information. According to him, *Primary* documents include periodicals, research reports, theses, patents, standards, conference proceedings, and trade literature; *Secondary* documents include indexing and abstracting journals, reference books, reviews of progress, text books, treatises, monographs, etc.; and *Tertiary* documents include yearbooks and directories, guide to literature, research in progress, lists of books/periodicals/dissertations, etc. [14].

Quaternary Division

Ranganathan identified the following four kinds of document: *Conventional*—which is usually recorded on paper in a natural language by writing, typing, printing, or some near-printing process, e.g., books, periodicals, maps, atlases, etc.; *Neo-conventional* (or ultramicro)—a new class of micro-documents, such as standards, specifications, patents, newspaper clippings, and so on; *Non-conventional*—which is a record in non-conventional size, shape, or material, such as audio–visual materials; and *Meta document*—which is a record of a natural or social phenomenon made directly (by some instrument) unmediated by the human mind, such as a picture of a cyclonic storm or a photograph of the surface of mars. However, from the point of view of treatment of subject, he distinguished only two kinds of document—*Macro document*, dealing with a large expanse of subject, such as a treatise and *Micro document*, dealing with a subject of small extension but deep intension, such as an article in a periodical [8].

B.3.3.5 Characteristics of DIS

The categories of documentary sources, as suggested by Grogan, are now universally accepted categories. The basis of his categorization is the originality of information contained in such sources. Any information, especially scientific information, proceeds through an information flow chain. In the first stage, a new information is disseminated in an informal way through personal letters, e-mail messages, etc. In the second stage, such information is presented in any conference or seminar. Finally, it is published in a primary source. After publication it is included in any index and/or bibliographic database or discussed in any secondary source. A user comes to know about its existence through any secondary or tertiary source. Thus is created three categories of documentary information sources. The nature and characteristics of each of the categories are discussed below.

Primary Information Sources

As indicated earlier, primary information sources are those that contain original or newly generated information. These are the first and often the only published records of original research and/or accounts of application of the results of such research. "Primary sources also include new raw data or new interpretations of previously known facts or ideas. These unorganized and usually unrelated contributions appear almost exclusively in periodicals, separate research/technical reports, conference proceedings, standards, patents, theses and dissertations, government publications, and trade literature carrying specific information on particular products or processes. By its nature, the primary literature is widely scattered and it is difficult to locate the information contained in them which is as yet unassimilated into the body of scientific/technological knowledge" [6]. The main characteristics of such sources are [11]:

- Primary information sources contain some new idea; or information relating to new invention, new research, or new experiment; or new interpretation of known facts;
- In such sources new information are formally published for the first time;
- These sources bring out new information in its original form, i.e., without expanding, reducing, or critically evaluating the information;
- This type of information sources is brought out very soon after the generation of the new information;
- Information included in this type of sources can be used in research since such information are authentic and dependable.

Secondary Information Sources

Secondary information sources contain "materials derived from or referring to primary sources, organized and arranged according to a definite plan. Secondary sources deal with the results of the analytical processing of the information contained in the primary sources. By their very nature, they are more often widely available than the primary sources. By repackaging and reprocessing information from the primary literature, the secondary sources are not only repositories of digested data but also signposts of bibliographical key to the primary sources" [6]. The main characteristics of secondary information sources are [11]:

- Secondary information sources describe, explain, analyze, or evaluate the contents of primary information sources;
- These sources discuss or criticize the proof, justification, or reasons given in the primary information sources;
- These sources rearrange or repackage the contents of the primary sources according to the needs of the user.

Tertiary Information Sources

These sources are "usually compilations drawn from primary or secondary sources, organized and arranged according to a definite plan. Essentially these are [meant] to aid searchers in using the primary and secondary sources. A characteristic feature of these sources is that they do not carry any subject information at all" [6]. The main characteristics of the tertiary sources are [11]:

- Tertiary information sources list primary information sources and/or secondary information sources; or
- These sources show how the secondary information sources can be used or accessed efficiently; or
- These sources rearrange the contents of secondary sources in an easily usable manner.

Differences Between DIS

Every category of documentary information sources is different from other categories from the points of view of nature, contents, and arrangement of information. Nevertheless, it may be pointed out that the same source may be sometimes primary source and sometimes secondary source. Even same source can be sometimes secondary source and sometimes tertiary source. For example, when some information is included in an article published in a newspaper for the first time, it will be a primary source, but when an article in a newspaper reviews information published earlier, it will be a secondary source. Similarly, a bibliography is a secondary information source, but bibliography of bibliographies is a tertiary source. Moreover, a primary source may be created on the basis of secondary or tertiary sources, e.g., a research report on bibliographies. Therefore, a decision as to which source is primary, which is secondary, or which is tertiary has to be taken only on the basis of the nature of information contained in a particular source. The differences between categories of sources are shown below through examples:

Primary information source	Secondary information source	Tertiary information source
Book containing original information	Bibliography of such books	Bibliography of such bibliographies
Periodical	Index to periodicals	Directory of periodicals
Patent	Index of patents	Guidelines for using patents

B.3.3.6 Nature of Printed DIS

The nature and characteristics of each kind of information source are different from those of any other kind of information source. Even the characteristics of a specific information source of a particular kind may be different from that of other specific sources of that kind. The nature and characteristics of different kinds of documentary information sources are described below.

Book

A book is "a physical embodiment of an expression or an exposition of a subject" [9]. A book provides "cohesively organized information on a particular subject … .It is a kind of crystallized presentation of ideas helpful to readers about a subject" [15]. A book usually deals with a subject of great extension and less intension. It is a physically independent document complete in one volume or in a definite number of volumes. The pages of a book are stitched together with a cover fixed on them. According to UNESCO specification, a book should contain at least 49 pages, exclusive of the cover page [16]. The optimum height of a book should be between 22 and 32 cm and optimum thickness between 1.5 and 4 cm. From the point of view of treatment of subject and organization of contents, books are of following types.

- *Textbook:* A textbook deals with the basic principles of a subject in a language and a form that is suitable for the students. It usually contains no new theory propounded by the author. Example: *Elements of Information Analysis, Consolidation and Repackaging*, by Amitabha Chatterjee.
- *Treatise:* A treatise has been described as "a book or writing which treats of some particular subject, giving a systematic exposition or argument and containing a formal or methodical discussion of the facts and principles of the subject, reaching a conclusion" [17]. Example: *A Grammar of Politics*, by Harold Laski.
- *Monograph:* A monograph exhaustively deals with a small area of subject. It is a learned treatise on a limited subject area. Example: *Prolegomena to Library Classification*, by S. R. Ranganathan.
- *Reference Book:* A reference book (sometimes called reference tool) does not provide continuous exposition of any subject. It presents disjunctive pieces of information arranged in some convenient order. A reference book is consulted not for continuous reading, but for specific information. There are various types of reference books as mentioned below.
    - *Dictionary:* A dictionary is a list of words/terms along with their meaning usually arranged in alphabetical order. It may also include pronunciation, derivation, use, and other information regarding

the words/terms covered. Dictionaries may be monolingual, bilingual, or multilingual and the words/terms covered may belong to either a particular language or a particular subject area. A dictionary covering terms belonging to a specific field of knowledge and providing meaning or definitions is commonly known as glossary. Examples: *Oxford English Dictionary*, *The Science Dictionary*.

- *Encyclopedia:* An encyclopedia is a collection of articles/write-ups containing up-to-date information on topics belonging to the whole field of knowledge or a particular subject field usually arranged alphabetically. Examples: *Encyclopedia Britannica* (15th and last printed edition, 2010), *Encyclopedia of Library and Information Science*.

- *Gazetteer:* A gazetteer or a geographical dictionary is an alphabetically arranged list of geographical entities like cities, towns, rivers, mountains, etc., providing information, such as location, size, and so on. Example: *Columbia Lippincott Gazetteer of the World*.

- *Travel guide:* A travel guide provides all such information that may be useful to the travelers, e.g., location, route, communication, etc. Example: *Fodor's Guide to India*.

- *Map and atlas:* A map is a representation in a reduced scale of the shape of a geographical area on a flat surface. An atlas is a collection of maps in an easy-to-handle form. Maps and atlases may also be thematic, e.g., political, statistical, historical, ethnological, etc. Examples: *Times Atlas of the World*, *Tribal Map of India*.

- *Yearbook:* A yearbook is an annual publication providing brief but up-to-date information about a geographical area, an organization, a profession, a trade, etc. Examples: *The Statesman's Yearbook*, *International Court of Justice Yearbook*.

- *Almanac:* Originally, almanac was a book listing the days, weeks, and months of the year and providing information about festivals, holidays, astronomical phenomena, etc. In modern usage, it is an annual compendium of practical dates, facts, and statistics, current and/or retrospective, often arranged in tables to facilitate comparison. Almanac can be general or related to specific subject or academic discipline [18]. An astronomical almanac giving the daily positions of stars and other heavenly bodies is known as Ephemeris [19]. Example: *World Almanac and Book of Facts*, *Indian Ephemeris and Nautical Almanac*.

- *Directory*: A directory literally means a systematically arranged list (with necessary details) of persons or organizations. The term "directory" is also sometimes used in the sense of a yearbook. Example: *American Book Trade Directory*.
- *Handbook*: A handbook is a compact and handy volume containing factual information, data, tables, graphs, illustrations, formulae, etc. frequently required by a scientist, a technologist, or a practitioner of an art or profession. Example: *Handbook for Information Systems and Services*.
- *Manual*: A manual, according to original meaning, is a book providing instructions or directions for performing a job or pursuing an occupation, an art, or a study. But sometimes the term "manual" is also used as a synonym of handbook. Example: *Library Manual* by S. R. Ranganathan.
- *Data Book*: Data Book is a type of handbook containing numerical data or statistics, such as mathematical tables, statistical tables, tide tables, census tables, chemical tables (e.g., periodic table), critical tables, and so on. Example: *International Critical Tables of Numerical Data: Physics, Chemistry and Technology*, compiled by C. J. Jest and C. Hull (1933).
- *Bibliography*: A bibliography is a systematically arranged list of books and other documents, with the details of their authors, publishers, dates of publication, etc., on a subject, by an author, or a printer or a publisher. A bibliography may also list bibliographies. Examples: *World Shakespeare Bibliography*; *A World Bibliography of Bibliographies and of Bibliographical Catalogues, Calendars, Abstracts, Digests, Indexes and the Like*.
- *Books-in-Print*: Books-in-print is also a list of books providing bibliographical details, including price, of only those books which are available in the market. Example: *Books in Print*, published by Crossby Lockwood.
- *Biographical dictionary*: A biographical dictionary is a compilation of life-sketches of eminent persons arranged in an alphabetical or any other convenient order. Such a dictionary usually covers either a geographical area or an area of specialization. When a biographical dictionary contains life-sketches or only living persons, it is called "who's who," and when it covers those of dead persons only, it is called "who was who." Example: *Dictionary of National Biography*.

Periodical

A periodical is a publication which is brought out at regular intervals. According to Ranganathan, it has three main features, viz., periodicity, distinguishing number/date, and continuity [20]. According to UNESCO specification, a publication is considered to be a periodical "if it constitutes one issue in a continuous series under the same title, published at regular or irregular intervals, over an indefinite period, individual issues in the series being numbered consecutively or each issue being dated" [16]. There are different types of periodicals.

- *Subject Periodical:* Subject periodicals are important sources of research as they contain nascent micro thought. Subject periodicals can also be called primary, learned, scholarly, or research periodicals. "They push frontier of knowledge into further depths" [15]. A subject periodical is "one of the oft chosen forms of research communication" [15]. Example: *Knowledge Organization*, 1974–.

- *Indexing Periodical:* An indexing periodical is a periodically published list of current primary literature (micro-documents), such as periodical articles, conference papers, research papers, patents, standards, and so on. Thus, it brings together information regarding primary literature scattered in different journals and/or other micro-documents. An indexing periodical may have general coverage, i.e., covering all subjects and/or all types of documents, or may be restricted by a specific subject or subject group or a specific type of document or more than one type of document but not all types of document. An indexing periodical may cover a list of micro-documents published from all parts of the world or from a particular geographical area. Evidently, an indexing periodical does not provide any original information but only information about such information. Examples: *Readers' Guide to Periodical Literature*, 1900–; *Library Literature and Information Science*, 1936–.

- *Citation Index:* A citation index, brought out periodically, is an ordered list of cited documents, each of which is accompanied by a list of citing documents. The citing document is identified as a source, while the cited document is identified as a reference. The best example of citation index is *Science Citation Index*, 1964–.

- *Abstracting Periodical:* An abstracting periodical, like indexing periodical, is also a periodically published list of current primary literature, but each entry in it also contains an abstract of the micro-document referred to in the entry. An entry in such a periodical has two parts—bibliographical reference and summary or indication of the content. Its coverage and restrictions may be similar to those of indexing periodicals. Examples: *Library and Information Science Abstracts*, 1969–; *Indian Science Abstracts*, 1965–.

- *Digesting Periodical:* Digest is often a condensation of several documents together. Digesting periodical is thus a periodical containing digests. More specifically, it is "a periodical that collates the works of several authors and presents them in a heavily condensed form for quick yet varied reading" [21]. Example: *Keesing's Record of World Events*, 1931–.

- *Reviewing Periodical:* It is "a serial publication that surveys the most important works of original research and creative thought published in a specific discipline or sub-discipline" [22]. It cohesively integrates highly relevant information into a condensed text [15]. In other words, it provides a coherent view of the development or progress in a subject field. Example: *Annual Review of Information Science and Technology*, 1966–2012.

- *Newspaper and News Magazine:* These contain news relating to recent events, editorial articles, comments, and articles on recent events. Newspaper is published daily, while news magazine is published weekly, fortnightly, or monthly. Examples: *The Daily Telegraph*, 1855–; *Newsweek*, 1933–.

- *News Index:* A news index (also called newspaper index or press index) indexes news published in a single newspaper of a bunch of newspapers. Example: *New York Times Index*, 1913–.

- *News Clippings:* These are cuttings of news items from newspapers on different themes, such as environment, economy, natural disasters, sports, and so on, which are maintained in a library in a systematic manner.

- *Newsletter:* A newsletter is brought out by an organization. It contains reports relating to the events and progress of the organization, the significant activities of the members/employees of the organization and information required by them. A newsletter may also relate to a particular subject, a field of activity, or a project. Example: *WHO Pharmaceutical Newsletter.*

Report

A report is a document which records the results of, or the progress made in a research or development project. It is directly submitted to the person or organization, for whom the work had been carried out, and hence does not undergo any formal refereeing. Some reports are later made available to the public, while some continue to remain classified, i.e., allowed only restricted access. An important feature of reports is that most of these are usually issued in semi-published form. The quality of report literature varies a great deal. Some are progress reports and as such are produced more for administrative than for scientific reasons, while some others contain valuable scientific and technical information and are far more detailed. Reports emanate from different types of organizations, such as government departments, universities, industries, research organizations, and so on [23]. Since most of the reports are not available through normal trade channel, these are considered as gray literature (GL). The reports on scientific investigations have been separately discussed under research report, while the reports commissioned by industrial houses have been discussed under trade literature.

Pamphlet

A pamphlet has been defined by the Bookman's Glossary as "a booklet of few sheets of printed matter, usually within a paper cover" [24]. According to UNESCO specification, "a pamphlet is a non-periodic publication of at least five but not more than 48 pages, exclusive of the cover page". The uniqueness of a pamphlet is that it deals with an individual specialized topic. It is prepared by an expert in the topic concerned [15]. Example: *Alcohol and Substance Abuse: A Curse to the Society*—a pamphlet developed by Alcohol & Drug Information Centre-India, with the support of WHO.

Research Paper

Research papers provide information about research activities. They are of different types.

- *Research in Progress:* It is a directory providing brief description of research activities being carried out in a single organization or a group of organizations or in some specific subject area or in some specific geographical area. Example: *SodhGangotri: Repository of Indian Research in Progress Details (See also* Section G.8.5).
- *Research Report:* It is a record, brief or detailed, of the findings of any research project undertaken for a purpose other than obtaining academic degree. This is also sometimes known as technical report. Some technical reports may record research in progress. Such reports are issued either ad hoc or in series [15]. Example: *Scientific and Technical Aerospace Reports*, published by NASA.

- *Thesis/Dissertation:* It is also a type of research report, but it provides results of only such project which is carried out for obtaining an academic degree. Example: *The Influence of Ranganathan on Faceted Classification* (PhD thesis submitted by Geraldine Odessa to Case Western Reserve University, USA, 1980).

There may be also secondary information sources relating to thesis/dissertation, such as dissertations abstracts. Example: *Dissertations Abstracts International.*

Conference Paper

Valuable new information are generated in conferences, seminars, symposia, etc. as these are attended by specialists in the respective fields of discussion. The information so generated are found in papers and proceedings of such meetings. The papers and proceedings of a seminar/conference/symposium are sometimes published as a separate publication and sometimes accommodated in a subject periodical. When these are published separately and distributed only among the participants and are not available through normal trade channel, these are considered as GL. Example: *Proceedings of the 12th European Conference on Knowledge Management,* 2011.

Guide to Literature

It provides a detailed account of bibliographic apparatus and tools, basic literature, agencies, etc., through which it is possible to follow the development, status, and progress of a subject. There may be also guides to libraries and sources of information and guides to organizations. Example: *Guide to Information Sources in Engineering,* by Charles B. Lord.

Patent Literature

The word *patent* originated from the Latin *patere*, which means "to lay open" (i.e., to make available for public inspection). More specifically, it is a shortened version of the term *letters patent*, which was a royal decree granting exclusive rights to a person, predating the modern patent system [25]. In the modern sense, a patent is an exclusive right or monopoly granted by a government to a person or organization to make and/or sell a newly invented product for a specific period of time. Patents were systematically granted in Venice as of 1450. Later, the Republic of Venice issued a decree in 1474 by which new and inventive devices, once put to practice, had to be communicated to the Republic in order to obtain legal protection against potential infringers [26]. According to World Intellectual Property Organization (WIPO), "the patent literature is the general name for relevant data which contain the research and development and test results that have been applied or confirmed to be discovery, utility model, or industrial design as well as published or unpublished documents of materials which protect the right of the inventor and the patentee" [27]. Thus, patent literature contains details about the new inventions, new products/processes, or industrial designs that are granted patents. There are mainly three types of patents:

- *Utility patents*, which are granted for any new and useful process, machine, article of manufacture or composition of matter or any new and useful improvement thereof, e.g., patent for a new sewerage treatment system.
- *Design patents*, which are granted for any new, original, or ornamental design for an article of manufacture, e.g., patent for a new shape of car.
- *Plant patents*, which are granted for the discovery or invention and asexual reproduction of any new, distinct variety of plant, e.g., patent for a hybrid variety of plant.

Patent literature are well-structured sources of technical and other information. The information that can be obtained from patent documents or can be derived from analyzing patent filing statistics include [28]:

- *Technical information* from the description and drawings of the invention.
- *Legal information* from the patent claims defining the scope of the patent and from its legal status.
- *Business-relevant information* from reference data identifying the inventor, date of filing, country of origin, etc.
- *Public policy-relevant information* from an analysis of filing trends to be used by policymakers, e.g., in national industrial policy strategy.

Besides the original patent documents, which provide primary information, there are also secondary information sources relating to patents, such as list, index, or directory of patents and patent abstracts. There may be also tertiary sources on patents, such as a guidebook or a handbook on patents. Examples: *Patent Inventions of CSIR (India), 1940–1964*; *European Patent Handbook*, brought out by Chartered Institute of Patent Attorneys, London.

Standard

According to International Standards Organization (ISO), "standard is a document that provides requirements, specifications, guidelines, or characteristics that can be used consistently to ensure that materials, products, processes, and services are fit for their purpose" [29]. A standard can also be described as a document specifying the degree of excellence for a product or a uniform pattern of practice recommended by a competent body (standardizing body). In short, it is "a formal document that establishes uniform criteria, methods, processes, or practices" [30]. However, the term "standard" has been loosely applied to any agreed-upon way of doing things. From this point of view, standards may be of following types [31]:

- *Accredited standards*, which are developed and adopted as standards through an open consensus process, under the guidelines of national or international standards bodies.

- *Industry specifications*, which are formalized industry practices generally developed by a group within the industry, but often publicly available. There are no formal guidelines or procedures that ensure that the work is open to any interested party or open to review and comment during the development process.

- *De facto standards*, which are usually developed and owned by a single group or company, and gain credibility as the result of the use of a critical mass of people. These standards are subject to change, without notice, by the owner of the work. In some cases, the use of these standards requires payment of a licensing fee.

Nevertheless, from the point of view of application, standards can be of following types [23]:

- *Dimensional Standards*, which ensure interchangeability so that the same products, wherever and whenever they are made, are identical in size, e.g., Standard for library racks.

- *Standards for Performance or Quality*, which ensure that a product or practice is adequate for its intended purposes, e.g., Quality management system.

- *Standard Test Methods*, which prescribe method for testing constituents or properties of any material or substance, e.g., Standard for testing of paper for moisture content.

- *Standard Terminology*, which enables scientists, technologies, or other specialists communicate more precisely, e.g., Glossary of Classification Terms.

- *Code of Practices*, which ensures performance of any task in systematic and uniform manner, e.g., Codes for cataloging.

- *Physical and Scientific Standards*, which deal with physical quantities, etc., that form the basis of measurement, e.g., Metric system.

Besides texts of standards, which are primary sources of information, there may be also secondary information sources relating to standards, such as bibliography/catalog or directory of standards. Examples: *ISO/TR 11219:2012 Information and Documentation-Qualitative Conditions and Basic Statistics for Library Buildings-Space, Function and Design*; *ISO Standards Catalogue*.

Specification

ISO 9000:2005 defines specification as a document that states requirements. A specification can be related to activities (e.g., procedure document, process specification, and test specification) or products (e.g., product specification, performance specification, and drawing specification). In other words, it is an explicit set of requirements to be satisfied by a material, product, system, or service [32]. However, specification often refers to three different types of document, all of which serve as information sources:

- *Industry Specification*: A detailed description of the criteria for the constituents, construction, appearance, performance, etc. of a material, apparatus, product, etc. or of the standard of workmanship required in its manufacture [33]. It is usually prepared by technical or industry associations.
- *Patent Specification*: It is a description of nature, uses and other details of an invention, which accompanies an application for a patent for that invention.
- *Standard Specification*: A document that recommends or prescribes terminology; classification; attributes (such as dimensions, quality or performance) of materials, products, processes, or systems; or methods of measurement or testing. Such specifications are available to the public, developed with the approval of representatives of interested parties and approved by a recognized body [34]. Thus, standards are, in fact, recommended specifications.

Trade Literature

Trade literature are of various types, such as trade catalogs, house journals, technical reports, product guides, and so on. Some of these are only meant for publicity, but there are some which carry useful information, that may not be available elsewhere.

- *Trade Catalog*: A trade catalog is "a publication containing particulars of goods manufactured by, or sold by, a firm; frequently illustrated and containing prices" [19]. A trade catalog usually provides [35]: description of the products and information about their utility, availability, and method of procuring them. They may also include instructions in using the products and testimonials from satisfied customers. Trade catalog first appeared in 18th century. Today trade catalogs can be found in abundance. Example: *Amway Product Catalogue.*

- *Trade Directory*: Trade directory is "a directory which is concerned with one trade or a group of related trades" [19]. Such directories contain alphabetical lists of manufacturers/companies and/or dealers/suppliers, along with necessary details, such as names, addresses, contact details, and so on in a particular area. A trade directory is meant to serve the various trade purposes and is a handy tool in finding out manufacturers and/or suppliers of the required product all at one place. Example: *Anglo-American Trade Directory*.

- *House Journal*: Variously known as house organ, in-house magazine and house journal, it is a publication brought out by an organization, especially a commercial house, for its customers/clienteles and/or its employees. Thus, there are mainly two types of house journals—external house journals meant for customers or people outside the organization and internal house journals meant for the staff members of the organization. There may be also house journals meant for both customers and the staff members of an organization. The purpose of a house journal is to inform the targeted audience (i.e., customers/clienteles and/or employees) about an organization's performance and style of functioning and also to elicit their reactions, opinions, and suggestions about improving its performance and functioning. House journal was first published by the British Association of Industrial Editors in 1949. Today almost every big commercial house brings out its own house journal. Example: *Oil News: House Journal of Oil India Limited.*

- *Technical Journal:* It is a publication that is targeted to people in a very specific industry. Its main function is to report on new techniques within the industry concerned and monitor and report on new techniques developed outside the industry [23]. Technical journals carry many advertisements for new machinery or chemicals or processes, the details of which may not be available elsewhere. Example: *Bell Labs Technical Journal*

- *Trade Journal:* It is difficult to differentiate trade journals from technical journals as there is much overlap between them. Trade journals are more commercial than technical and more news oriented than subject oriented [23]. They cater important news relating to the industry, such as market news and company news, and general trade announcements. Example: *Electrical Review*, published by SJP Business Media Ltd., London.

- *Technical Report:* A technical report is "a formal report designed to convey technical information in a clear and easily accessible format. It is divided into sections which allow different readers to access different levels of information" [36]. In the field of trade and industry a technical report assists in decision making, e.g., in the purchase of an equipment, or finding solutions to technical problems. Example: *Technical Report on Waste Water Management in Chemical Industry*.

- *Forecast Report:* A forecast report gives an idea of future trend in a particular field. Such reports are based on careful analysis—sometimes statistical analysis—of the observations made during a considerable period of time. There may be various types of trade- and industry-related forecast report, such as trade forecast report, market forecast report, sales forecast report, and so on. Example: *Sales Forecast Report of Coca-Cola Company*.

- *Feasibility Report:* A feasibility report, or more precisely a techno-economic feasibility report, contains the result of feasibility study which is made to determine if a proposed new project or expansion/diversification plan/scheme of an existing enterprise will be a feasible one from the points of view of location, availability of finance, availability of raw material, availability of infrastructural facilities like power, technology, skilled labor, communication, installation cost, operational cost, etc. and easy marketability and whether invested capital will yield maximum return. Example: *Feasibility Study for a United Nations Technology Bank for the Least Developed Countries*.

Manuscript

The term manuscript is used to denote two types of material—written text of a book given to a printer for composing and printing, and ancient works written by hand on palm leaves, animal skins, etc. Thus, these are conventional documents but not exactly printed documents. Manuscripts of ancient works are unpublished sources, but lately many manuscripts are being published in the form of books.

Government Publication

International and inter-governmental organizations, like United Nations, World Bank, etc.; and governments at national, state, and local levels in different countries, bring out their own publications directly or through some authorized agencies. They are of various types, the chief among them being reports—administrative, research, and technical—and statistics, which provide the most authentic and official information. There may be also unpublished government records which are preserved in archives. Example: *Africa's Demographic Transition: Dividend or Disaster*, brought out by World Bank Group.

B.3.3.7 Nature of Non-printed DIS

As mentioned earlier, in 20th century, besides printed documents, documents recorded in various visual media, audio media, and audio–visual media and using analogue technology came into vogue, such as gramophone records, audio-tapes, video cassettes, films, and so on. These documents are mainly recorded non-textual materials. However, these have now almost been replaced by digital information sources. Digital technology is used for recording both textual and non-textual documents. Thus, today the term "non-printed" information source is mainly used to denote electronic or digital information source. Digital information sources may be broadly grouped as:

* Electronic publications;
* Databases, including institutional repositories;
* Internet or web resources.

While electronic publications and databases are available both offline and online, Internet or web resources are available only on the Internet.

Electronic Publications

Different types of conventional and neo-conventional information sources are now available in digital mode. These include books, journals, reference books, theses, conference papers, newspapers, patents, standards, technical reports, etc. These are known as e-books, e-journals, e–reference tools, e-theses, and so on. Sometimes, such sources are published simultaneously in print mode as well as digital mode, while some are published in digital mode only, especially online mode, e.g., *Britannica Online* (www.britannica.com).

Databases

Databases can be of various types depending on the mode used, the area of coverage, the information covered, etc. From the point of view of mode used, these can be of two types—online databases and offline databases.

Online databases are available through any network, especially on the Internet, while offline databases are available on CD or DVD. From the point of view of area of coverage, these can be local (e.g., library OPAC), national (e.g., OPAC of national library), and international (e.g., INIS database). From the point of view of type of information covered, there may be again different types of database, such as bibliographic database, full-text database, citation database, community information database, numeric database, institutional repositories, and so on.

- An *OPAC*, i.e., Online Public Access Catalog, contains bibliographic details of books and other documents available in a library. There can also be online union catalogs which show holdings of several libraries together with indication of the location of the documents. When an OPAC is available on the web, it is called Web OPAC. Examples: *University of Sydney Library OPAC* (https://opac.library.usyd.edu.au/), *National Union Catalogue of Scientific Serials* (India) (http://nucssi.niscair.res.in/default.aspx).
- A *bibliographic database* contains bibliographic information about documents, sometimes with abstracts. Example: *GEOBASE* (a bibliographic database for the earth, geographical, and ecological sciences).
- A *full-text database* contains complete texts of the documents. Example: *Patent Full-text Database* (of USA) (http://patft.uspto.gov/).
- A *citation database* contains information relating to cited and/or citing documents. Example: *Science Citation Index Database* of Web of Science.
- A *community information database* contains data needed by the residents of an area or a specific community. Example: *Database of Central Government Schemes for Tribal Students in India.*
- A *numerical database* contains numerical data. Example: *Database on Census of India.*
- An *expert database* includes information relating to experts in a subject field or several subject fields. Example: *Expert Database of Outstanding Female Scientists and Scholars*, developed by AcademiaNet (https://www.uni-erfurt.de/fileadmin/user-docs/Geschichte_der_Raeume/AcademiaNet_engl.pdf); *Vidwan* Expert Database, developed by INFLIBNET Centre, India (https://vidwan.inflibnet.ac.in/).
- An *institutional repository*, also known as e-print archive, is a database or "digital archive of the intellectual products created by the faculty, research staff, and students of an institution, with few, if any, barriers

to access" [37]. An IR may contain full-texts of published and unpublished research papers, book chapters, conference papers, theses/dissertations, technical reports, status reports, committee reports, and graphic and audio–visual materials brought out in course of any research project, etc. Some repositories also contain texts of original records of the institution. Many higher educational and research institutions have developed such repositories, which are available on the web. Example: *DSpace@MIT: Massachusetts Institute of Technology Institutional Repository* (http://dspace.mit.edu/), *NAL (India)'s Institutional Repository* (http://nal-ir.nal.res.in). More details about IR may be found in a later chapter.

- A *Digital Library* is a library in which collections are stored in digital format (as opposed to print, microform or other media) and accessible *via* computers. This concept has been discussed further in the next section. Example: *Librarian's Digital Library*, developed by DRTC, Bangalore, India (https://drtc.isibang.ac.in/).

Internet/Web Resources:

Internet owes its origin to ARPANET created by Advanced Research Projects Agency of USA, while Tim Barnes-Lee is considered to be the innovator of world wide web (www), which was superimposed on the Internet and incorporated its protocols [38]. Internet is now an important and possibly largest source of information. Obviously, Internet resources or web resources are always available online and that too on the Internet. Besides online electronic publications and online databases, there are various other types of web resource, such as websites, digital libraries, wiki, subject gateways, discussion groups/fora, FAQs, and so on. Major types of Internet sources are introduced below.

- *Website:* A website is a collection of related web pages, including a lead page known as home page, which is hosted on one or more web servers and accessible through Internet. Different types of organizations, such as libraries, museums, archives, research bodies, associations, learned bodies, industrial houses, and so on, as also individuals have created their websites, which can be accessed through Internet, e.g., *Website of the Food and Agriculture Organization of the United Nations* (http://www.fao.org/home/en/). Some websites have provision for interaction with the users, which are known as *Interactive websites*. Different types of interactive websites are blogs, social networking sites, wiki, etc. Such websites are characteristics of web 2.0.

- *Blog:* A Blog is a type of website or a part of website, which is developed or got developed by any individual or organization, maintained and regularly updated by adding and/or deleting information and has provision for posting views or comments by the users, e.g., *Library of Congress Blog* (http://blogs.loc.gov/loc/).
- *Social Networking Site:* The social networking websites provide facilities to the users to upload and update their own profiles, access the profiles of other users on the website, and communicate and exchange views, ideas, or information with them, e.g., *Facebook, Twitter,* etc.
- *Wiki:* Wiki is a kind of website which provides opportunity to create and update inter-related websites in required number. *Wikipedia* is the well-known such website. It is a multilingual encyclopedia, created by using this technology, covering 1.8 crore articles prepared by voluntary writers. Wikipedia is open for addition of new articles and revision of existing articles by the users.
- *Discussion Forum/Group:* Such groups consist of people having similar interests, who discuss and exchange views on topics of mutual interest through e-mail. The message e-mailed by a member to the forum automatically reaches other members of the forum. The various search engines are sponsors of this type of fora, e.g., *nmlis.yahoogroup* (New Millennium LIS Professionals' Group). It may be mentioned that in the beginning *electronic mailing lists* were started on the Internet which allowed wide distribution of information through e-mail. It is similar to a traditional mailing list maintained by an organization for sending its publications to its members or customers. An electronic mailing list has four main components—a list of e-mail addresses, subscribers who receive mail at those addresses, e-mail messages sent to those messages, and a *reflector,* which is a single e-mail address which receives a message and passes it on to all the other subscribers. There are two types of mailing lists—*announcement list,* or *newsletter,* which is used primarily as a one-way conduit for sending information, especially promotional information, to selected people and *discussion list,* which is used by a subscriber to send messages to all other subscribers, who may answer in similar fashion [39]. The term *Listserv* has been used to refer to a few early electronic mailing list software applications, allowing a sender to send one e-mail to the list, and then transparently sending it on to the addresses of the subscribers to the list [40].
- *Bulletin Board:* Other similar Internet resources are Bulletin Board and Newsgroup. Bulletin Board is an electronic communication system

that allows users to send or read electronic messages, files, and other data that are of general interest and addressed to no particular person. Bulletin boards were widely used before the Internet became popular, and many of their functions are now served by websites and newsgroups for specific topics or groups.

- *Newsgroup:* A Newsgroup is a discussion about a particular subject consisting of notes written to a central Internet site and redistributed through *Usenet*, a worldwide network of news discussion groups. Newsgroups are organized into subject hierarchies, with the first few letters of the newsgroup name indicating the major subject category and sub-categories represented by a subtopic name. Some major subject categories are: news, rec (recreation), soc (society), sci (science), comp (computers), and so forth (there are many more). Users can post to existing newsgroups, respond to previous posts, and create new newsgroups [41].

- *FAQ:* FAQ (Frequently Asked Questions) is a list of repeatedly asked questions on a specific topic, along with their answers, which can be accessed through Internet, e.g., *Wikipedia: FAQ* (http://en.wikipedia.org/org/wiki/wikipedia:FAQ).

- *Subject Gateway:* A Subject Gateway helps in accessing significant online sources in a subject field. Such gateways list the important sources identified and evaluated by subject experts, e.g., *AGRIGATE* (http://www.agrigate.edu.au/), *BIOGATE* (http://biogate.lub.lu.se/), etc. There are also gateways for accessing e-journals available across different networks and websites using different protocols, e.g., J-Gate (http://jgateplus.com/).

- *RSS Document:* RSS or Rich Site Summary (often called Really Simple Syndication) is a family of web feed formats used to publish frequently updated works—such as blog entries, news headlines, audio, and video—in a standardized format. An RSS document (which is called a "feed," "web feed," or "channel") includes full or summarized text, plus metadata, such as date of publication and author's name.

- *Web Directory*: A web directory is a directory on the World Wide Web. It provides links to other websites and categorizes those links. A web directory specializing on a subject is called subject directory. *The World Wide Web (WWW) Virtual Library* is the oldest subject directory of the web. *RSS directories* are similar to web directories, but contain collections of RSS feeds, instead of links to websites.

- *Web Portal*: A web portal is a website that brings information together from diverse sources in a uniform way. Usually, each information source gets its dedicated area on the page for displaying information (a portlet); often, the user can configure which ones to display. Apart from the standard search engine feature, web portals offer other services, such as e-mail, news, stock prices, information from databases, and even entertainment content [42]. For example, *india.gov.in* (https://india.gov.in/) is the national web portal of the Government of India.
- *WebOPAC*: The online public access catalog of a library is called OPAC. When such OPAC is available on the web, it is called WebOPAC. WebOPAC has been discussed in the previous section.
- *Institutional Repository*: Some institutional repositories can only be accessed locally, while some are available on the web and can be accessed remotely. The concept of institutional repository has been explained in the previous section as also in a later chapter.
- *Digital Library*: As mentioned earlier, a digital library is a library in which collections are stored in digital format. The digital content may be stored locally, or accessed remotely via computer networks. Many such digital libraries can be accessed through Internet, e.g., *Project Gutenberg* (www.gutenberg.org), which is the original free digital library of books that are no longer under copyright.
- *Online Database/Database Service*: As indicated earlier, some databases may be accessed locally, while some can be accessed remotely through Internet. Internet-based databases are known as online databases though technically an online database can be accessed locally on intranet, i.e., not through Internet. It may be mentioned that there are many popular online databases created by public institutions and also there are many commercially operated databases. Besides, there are also many database services which provide access to different databases often through a single search interface. Database services are like e-journal aggregators. Databases are mostly created by other organizations which are made available through one or more of these database services. All types of databases may be available from such database services, often including very specialized databases that are not available from other sources. Generally users of a database service are required to have their accounts with the service before they can do any search [43]. A few well-known databases/database services are briefly introduced below.

- *MEDLINE:* MEDLINE (Medical Literature Analysis and Retrieval System Online, or MEDLARS Online) is a bibliographic database created and maintained by National Library of Medicine (NLM) of USA. The MEDLINE database is the electronic counterpart of *Index Medicus, Index to Dental Literature,* and the *International Nursing Index.* The database is updated daily from Tuesday to Saturday, except in November and December when updating remains suspended for a few weeks. Engines designed to search MEDLINE (such as Entrez and PubMed) generally use a Boolean expression combining MeSH terms, words in abstract and title of the article, author name, date of publication, etc. Searching of the database is free of charge and does not require registration. PubMed (www.ncbi.nlm.nih.gov/pubmed/) is a free search engine released by NLM in 1996, while Entrez is the text-based search and retrieval system used at the National Center for Biotechnology Information (NCBI). MEDLINE also has a full-text database called "MEDLINE with Full-text," which covers full-texts of many of the most used journals in the MEDLINE index [44–46] (*See also* Section V.5.1.2).
- *Inspec:* Inspec is a value-added, high quality, multidisciplinary indexing database of scientific and technical literature, produced by the Institution of Engineering and Technology (IET, UK). Updated weekly, Inspec provides data from journals, conferences, and other sources including books, reports, dissertations, and videos. Inspec was initiated in 1967, based on the Science Abstracts service provided by the Institution of Engineering & Technology since 1898. In 2004, Science Abstracts from 1898 to 1968 were digitized and made available as a companion database called Inspec Archive. Inspec now contains over 15 million bibliographic records, and is growing at the rate of 500,000 records each year. Presently, Inspec can be accessed through *Inspec Direct* and various bibliographic services like ProQuest, Web of Science, etc. [47, 48].
- *ProQuest:* A subsidiary of Cambridge Information Group, ProQuest (www.proquest.com/) is a Michigan (USA) based global information content provider. It has a collection of multidisciplinary mostly full-text databases of journals, newspaper articles, e-books, conference papers, theses, and other publications. Its content holding encompasses 90,000 authoritative sources, 6 billion digital pages, and spans six centuries. It includes the world's largest collection

of dissertations and theses; 20 million pages and three centuries of global, national, regional, and speciality newspapers; more than 450,000 e-books; rich aggregated collections of the world's most important scholarly journals and periodicals; and unique vaults of digitized historical collections from great libraries and museums, as well as organizations as varied as the Royal Archives, the Associated Press and the National Association for the Advancement of Colored People. These can be accessed through a variety of web based interfaces [49,50].

- *Scopus:* Owned by Elsevier, Scopus (www.scopus.com/) is the largest abstract and citation database of scientific journals, books, and conference proceedings. It covers 21,500 journal titles from more than 5000 international publishers, more than 113,000 books; 7.2 million conference papers from 88,800 worldwide events; and 27 million patents from five patent offices, including WIPO [50]. Scopus also offers author profiles which cover affiliations, number of publications, and their bibliographic data, references, and details on the number of citations each published document has received. It has alerting features that allows registered users to track changes to a profile and a facility to calculate authors' h-index [51,52].

- *Web of Science:* Successor of Eugene Garfield's *Science Citation Index* and *Web of knowledge,* Web of Science, now maintained by Thomson Reuters, is an online citation indexing service that provides comprehensive citation search. As of September 3, 2014, Web of Science contained over 90 million records, including over a billion cited references. Updated weekly, this service indexes, on an average, around 65 million items per year. Web of Science now has indexing coverage from the year 1900 to the present. The multidisciplinary coverage of the Web of Science encompasses over 50,000 scholarly books, 12,000 journals, and 160,000 conference proceedings. The selection is made on the basis of impact evaluation, and comprises open-access journals, spanning multiple academic disciplines. The coverage includes the sciences, social sciences, arts, and humanities, and goes across disciplines. Web of Science consists of seven online databases [53,54]:

1. *Science Citation Index,* which covers more than 8,500 notable journals encompassing 150 disciplines starting from 1990 (author abstracts available from 1991 onwards).

2. *Social Science Citation Index*, which covers more than 3,000 journals in social science disciplines starting from 1956 (author abstracts available from 1992 onwards).

3. *Conference Proceedings Citation Index*, which covers more than 160,000 conference titles starting from 1900.

4. *Arts and Humanities Citation Index*, which covers more than 1,700 arts and humanities journals starting from 1975 (author abstracts available from 2000 onwards).

5. *Indus Chemicus*, which lists more than 2.6 million compounds, starting from 1993.

6. *Current Chemical Reactions*, which indexes over 1 million reactions starting from 1986 plus INPI Archives from 1840 to 1985.

7. *Book Citation Index*, which covers more than 60,000 editorially selected books starting from 2005.

• *LexisNexis:* LexisNexis (www.lexisnexis.com/) is the first commercial full-text legal information service started in 1973. The companion Nexis news and business information service was launched in 1979. Presently, a subsidiary of Reed Elsevier, LexisNexis is the world's largest database for legal and public-record related information hosting over 30 terabytes of contents. LexisNexis services are delivered through two websites. The two subject areas in which LexisNexis has extensive coverage of academic journals are law and medicine. The service includes the full-text of a large number of law review journals and medical journal article abstracts are available through a version of the MEDLINE database. Other subjects covered are news, business, finance, government, medicine, technology, etc. Dates of coverage for many of the publications in LexisNexis go back to the 1980s, with many of the legal documents dating back even earlier. Files are updated continuously [43,55,56].

• *Manupatra:* The name *Manupatra* (i.e., the letters of Manu, the ancient Indian saint) has been derived from Manu's classic Sanskrit work *Manusmriti* (i.e., Laws of Manu). This company was established in 2000 and in August 2001 it launched its flagship online legal database (www.manupatra.com), which is now possibly the largest and most comprehensive legal database in India. Manupatra covers full-text judgments of the Supreme Court and all high courts of India since inception. Manupatra also hosts an exhaustive repository of central and state statutes, notifications and circulars of the Government of India and other legislative, regulatory, and procedural material. Though started as an India-centric database, it now also covers case laws from United States, United Kingdom, Sri Lanka, Bangladesh, and Pakistan. In 2004, CD-ROM-based database was introduced for legal professionals not having access to Internet. Manupatra is currently engaged in all forms of publications which include, besides online legal database and CD-ROMs, books, journals, and mobile apps [57,58].

B.3.3.8 Gray Literature

GL is another type of important information source, which may be in printed or digital format. These are being treated here together. The term gray literature is often used to denote materials which are either unpublished or published but not available through normal book trade channel. However, in the present context when, besides printed and nonprinted documents, a good number of documents is available in electronic format, the 12th International Conference on Grey Literature, held in Prague in 2010, has adopted the following definition of GL: "Grey literature stands for manifold document types produced on all levels of government, academics, business, and industry in print and electronic formats that are protected by intellectual property rights, of sufficient quality to be collected and preserved by library holdings or institutional repositories, but not controlled by commercial publishers, i.e., where publishing is not the primary activity of the producing body" [59].

Characteristics of GL:

The main characteristics of GL are [60,61]:

- GL are not primarily produced as commercial publications.
- These provide such information which cannot be obtained elsewhere.
- Information contained in gray documents are often most up-to-date.
- These are ephemeral or transient in nature.
- These cannot be procured through normal publication or distribution channels.
- Often there is no bibliographic control of such literature.
- These may be of good quality, but are not peer reviewed.
- Gray documents do not have ISBN or ISSN.
- These are protected by intellectual property rights.

Types of GL:

Traditionally, the term "gray literature" encompassed such publications as reports, conference proceedings, and theses, which are mostly unpublished and not available through normal book trade channel. But today it includes various other types of materials. GreyNet International, a GL network service, located in Netherlands, has enumerated various types of gray documents as follows [62]:

Announcements
Annuals
Bibliographies
Blogs
Booklets
Brochures
Bulletin Boards
Bulletins
Call for Papers
Case Studies
Catalogs
Chronicles
Codebooks
Conference Papers
Conference Posters
Conference Proceedings
Country Profiles
Course Materials
Databases
Datasets
Datasheets
Deposited Papers
Directories
Discussion Papers
Dissertations
Doctoral Theses
E-prints
E-texts
Enhanced Publications

Essays
ETD (Electronic Theses and Dissertations)
Exchange Agreements
Fact Sheets
Feasibility Studies
Flyers
Folders
Glossaries
Government Documents
Green Papers
Guidebooks
Handbooks
House Journals
Image Directories
Inaugural Lectures
Indexes
Interactive Posters
Internet Reviews
Interviews
Journals
    Articles
    Gray Journals
    In-house Journals
    Noncommercial Journals
    Synopsis Journal
K-blogs
Leaflets
Lectures

Legal documents
Legislation
Manuals
Memoranda
Newsgroups
Newsletters
Notebooks
Off-prints
Orations
Pamphlets
Papers
    Call for Papers
    Conference Papers
    Deposited Papers
    Discussion Papers
    Green Papers
    White Papers
    Working Papers
Patents
Policy Documents
Policy Statements
Posters
Précis Articles
Preprints
Press Releases
Proceedings
Product Data
Programs
Projects
    Deliverables
    Information Documents
    (PID)
    Proposals
    Work Packages
    Work Programs
Questionnaires
Readers
Registers
Reports

Activity Reports
Annual Reports
Bank Reports
Business Reports
Committee Reports
Compliance Reports
Country Reports
Draft Reports
Feasibility Reports
Government Reports
Intelligence Reports
Internal Reports
Official Reports
Policy Reports
Progress Reports
Regulatory Reports
Site Reports
Stockbroker Reports
Technical Reports
Reprints
Research Memoranda
Research Notes
Research Proposals
Research Registers
Research Reports
Reviews
Risk Analyses
Satellite Data
Scientific Protocols
Scientific Visualizations
Show cards
Software
Specifications
Speeches
Standards
State of the Art
Statistical Surveys
Statistics
Supplements

Survey Results	Treatise
Syllabus	Website Reviews
Technical Documentation	Web Pages
Technical Notes	Websitess
Tenders	White Books
Theses	White Papers
Timelines	Working Documents
Trade Directories	Working Papers
Translations	Yearbook

Though the above list is quite exhaustive, some more documents may be added to this list, such as personal correspondence, diary, laboratory notebook, and so on. Nevertheless, when any of the above documents is published through normal publication channel, it cannot be treated as GL any more. Thus, only those documents which fulfill the main condition of not being commercially published/available/procured through normal publication channel can only be treated as GL. As indicated earlier, many gray documents are preserved in archives and lately in institutional repositories.

B.4 IMPORTANCE OF IS

All the three types of information sources—human, institutional, and documentary—are important for research and development. In documentary information sources only recorded information are available, but there may be many information which are either not recorded at all or recorded very late. Such information can be acquired from human and/or institutional sources. The results of new experiments and research are first recorded in primary documentary sources. New interpretations of the existing principles, theory, or results of earlier research are also recorded in such sources. Hence, primary documentary information sources are very helpful in research activities. But in the present era of information explosion, it is indeed difficult for a user or researcher to collect their needed information, which remain scattered in a huge number of sources. To help the users in collecting the needed information speedily and easily, new products are brought out by analyzing, consolidating, and repackaging the information available in primary sources. This process of increasing the utility of information is called value addition and the sources in which such value-added information are published are known as secondary documentary information sources. Thus, they serve as helpful aids to the users. Though, the tertiary documentary information sources do not contain any information as such, they help in identifying and locating the sources from which pertinent information can be collected.

REFERENCES

[1] I. K. Ravichandra Rao, Issues and challenges in information management in the context of fast emerging electronic sources, in: Proceedings of the National Conference on Information Management in E-libraries, Kharagpur, India, 2002, pp. 3–13.

[2] J. W. Brown, The technological gatekeeper: evidence in three industries, J Technol Transfer 3 (2, Spring) (1979), 23–36.

[3] M. O'Donnell, Digitizing the R&D social network: revisiting the technical gatekeeper, 2013. http://digitalbedouin.com/iscourse/forums/topic/digitizing-the-rd-social-network-revisiting-the-technological-gatekeeper/.

[4] K. Londrie, What is an Information Broker?http://www.4hb.com/0111infobroker. html.

[5] Information broker. Computer Desktop Encyclopedia. http://www.answers.com/topic/information-broker.

[6] T. N. Rajan, et al., Nature of information sources, in: Training Course in Documentation and Information Services: Course Material. INSDOC, New Delhi and DRTC, Bangalore, 1975. Paper-III.1.5.

[7] The Penguin Dictionary of English, Penguin Books, Baltimore, 1965, p. 217.

[8] S. R. Ranganathan (Ed.), Documentation and Its Facets, Asia Publishing House, Bombay, 1963, p. 29.

[9] S. R. Ranganathan, Documentation: Genesis and Development, Vikas, Delhi, 1973, p. 102.

[10] H. P. Luhn, As quoted in SENGUPTA (B) and CHATTERJEE (M). Documentation and information retrieval, World Press, Kolkata, 1977, p. 2.

[11] A. Chatterjee, Information: Organization and Service, West Bengal State Book Board, Kolkata, 2012, p. 13 [in Bengali].

[12] G. Krishan, Managing Digital Information Resources, NACLIN (2003), pp. 29–45.

[13] C. W. Hanson, Introduction to Science-Information Work, ASLIB, London, 1971, Pt. 3.

[14] D. Grogan, Science and Technology – An Introduction to Literature, second ed., Clive Bingley, London, 1973, Ch. 1.

[15] M. A. Gopinath, Current trends in information sources and communication. DRTC Refresher Seminar 25, 1984: Course material, DRTC, 1984.

[16] UNESCO. General Conference Meeting, 23rd Session, Sofia, October 8–November 9, 1985. Revised recommendation concerning the International Standardization of Statistics on the Production and Distribution of Books, Newspapers and Periodicals. http://portal.unesco.org/en/ev.php-URL_ID=13146&URL_DO=DO_TOPIC&URL_SECTION=201.html.

[17] A. K. Mukherjee, Reference Work and Its Tools, third ed., World Press, Kolkata, 1975, pp. 40–41.

[18] J. M. Reitz, Dictionary for Library & Information Science, Libraries Unlimited, Westport, Connecticut, 2004, p. 2.

[19] Harrod's Librarian's Glossary and Reference Book, Compiled by Ray Prytherch, ninth ed., Gower, Haunts, UK, 2000.

[20] S. R. Ranganathan, Classified Catalogue Code with Additional Rules for Dictionary Catalogue Code, fifth ed., SRELS, Bangalore, Reprint, 1991.
[21] http://www.businessdictionary.com/definition/digest.html#.
[22] Review Periodical. http://www.lrc.usuhs.mil/jargon_words.html.
[23] K. Ramaswami, et al., Information sources, in: Training Course in Documentation and Information Services: Course Material, INSDOC, New Delhi and DRTC, Bangalore, 1975, Paper-III.3.
[24] J. Peters (Ed.), The Bookman's Glossary, sixth ed., R R Bowker, New York, 1983.
[25] Patent, http://en.wikipedia.org/wiki/Patent.
[26] Wolfgang-Pfaller.d. Patentgesetz von Venedig [in German/Italian] as quoted in Patent, http://en.wikipedia.org/w/index.php?title=Patent&printable=yes#cite_ref-5.
[27] World Intellectual Property Organization, As quoted in Patent literature, http://www.aitrans.org/en/zlfy1.aspx?id=10.
[28] World Intellectual Property Organization, WIPO Guide to using patent information, http://www.wipo.int/export/sites/www/freepublications/en/patents/434/wipo_pub_l434_03.pdf.
[29] International Standards Organization, Standards, http://www.iso.org/iso/home/standards.htm.
[30] Standard vs. specification and guidance documents, http://asqasktheexperts.com/2012/04/12/standard-vs-specification/.
[31] Standard vs specification, http://www.npes.org/pdf/Standard-V-Specs.pdf.
[32] American Society for Testing and Materials International, Form and style for ASTM standards, http://www.astm.org/COMMIT/Blue_Book.pdf.
[33] Industry specification, http://www.thefreedictionary.com/specification.
[34] A. Cooper, Standard specification, in: J. Feather, P. Sturges, (Eds.), International Encyclopedia of Information and Library Science, second ed., Routledge, London, 2003.
[35] W. S. Buddington, Paradoxical trade catalogue, Special Libraries 46 (3) (1955) 113–179.
[36] H. Prance, Guide to technical report writing, 2004, http://joemoxley.org/sites/Joe_Moxley/Engineers/Resources%20for%20EngineersWriters/3-11-2.htm.
[37] R. Crow, The case for institutional repositories: a SPARC position paper, http://works.bepress.com/cgi/viewcontent.cgi?article=1006&context=ir_research&sei-redir=1&referer=http%3A%2F%2Fscholar.google.co.in%2Fscholar_url%3Fhl%3Den%26q%3Dhttp%3A%2F%2Fworks.bepress.com%2Fcgi%2Fviewcontent.cgi%253Farticle%253D1006%2526context%253Dir_research%26sa%3DX%26scisig%3DAAGBfm07J_03qBFVcu9kOEVzrzhzLTT1ew%26oi%3Dscholarr%26ei%3D_xOvU5StLdG9ugTYqoCQDg%26ved%3D0CBoQgAMoADAA#search=%22http%3A%2F%2Fworks.bepress.com%2Fcgi%2Fviewcontent.cgi%3Farticle%3D1006%26context%3Dir_research%22.
[38] R. Cohen-Almagor, Internet history, Int. J. Technoethics 2 (2) (2011) 45–64.
[39] Electronic mailing list, http://en.wikipedia.org/wiki/Electronic_mailing_list#Types.
[40] LISTSERV, http://en.wikipedia.org/wiki/LISTSERV.
[41] Definition: Newsgroup. http://searchexchange.techtarget.com/definition/newsgroup
[42] Web portal, http://en.wikipedia.org/wiki/Web_portal.
[43] What is Lexis-Nexis, http://www.smccd.net/accounts/brenner/lsci105/lexisdef.html.
[44] About Medline/PubMed, http://www.library.nhs.uk/help/resource/medlinefrompubmed.
[45] MEDLINE, http://en.wikipedia.org/wiki/MEDLINE.
[46] MEDLINE-1950 to date (MEZZ), http://www.library.nhs.uk/help/resource/medline.
[47] Inspect, http://en.wikipedia.org/wiki/Inspec.
[48] Inspec and Inspec Archive user guide, http://webs.um.es/isgil/Indizacion%20INSPEC%20IET%202006%20Gil%20Leiva.pdf.

[49] ProQuest, http://en.wikipedia.org/wiki/ProQuest.

[50] ProQuest, http://www.proquest.com/.

[51] Scopus Content. https://www.elsevier.com/solutions/scopus/content.

[52] Scopus, http://en.wikipedia.org/wiki/Scopus.

[53] Web of Science, http://en.wikipedia.org/wiki/Web_of_Science.

[54] Web of Science, Multidisciplinary resources, http://ip-science.thomsonreuters.com/m/pdfs/mgr/wok_multidisc_fs.pdf.

[55] M. Joshi, Secondary and tertiary electronic sources of information, in: DRTC Annual Seminar. Paper BE, 2000.

[56] LexisNexis, http://en.wikipedia.org/wiki/LexiaNexis.

[57] Manupatra, http://en.wikipedia.org/wiki/Manupatra.

[58] Manupatra, http://www.manupatrafast.com.

[59] Grey literature, http://en.wikipedia.org/wiki/Grey_literature.

[60] Finding grey literature, http://www.slideshare.net/Jolibrarianne/finding-grey-literature.

[61] E. Newbold, Grey literature – a hidden resource, http://www.slideshare.net/Rebecca/grey-literature-a-hidden-resource.

[62] GreyNet International, http://www.greynet.org/greysourceindex/documenttypes.html.

CHAPTER C

Information Users

C.1 INTRODUCTION

Users form one of the main pillars of a library or information center. It is for them that a library/information center exists and hence without users it will lose its relevance and possibly its existence. As such, library and information professionals should strive to achieve high degree of user satisfaction by providing effective and efficient services. For doing so, it is necessary to identify the precise needs of the users as also the way they seek information. Besides, users need to be empowered for making proper use of information.

C.2 USER

Any person who avails himself or herself of the services offered by a library or information center can be called a user. There are various other terms that are used to indicate the user of a library or information center, such as patron, client, reader, customer, and consumer. A user approaches a library/information center for one or more of the following purposes [1]:

- To browse through a collection of latest information resources procured by a library/information center;
- To seek a particular information resource for consultation or study in the library/information centre or borrow the same;
- To obtain current references on a specific topic or bibliography of references over a period;
- To obtain factual information on a topic, event, activity, etc. through reference/information sources;
- To obtain a photocopy of a journal article, a conference paper, a technical report, or any relevant document;
- To get the translated version of a research paper from other language to the language of his choice.

In the digital environment a user may also approach a library/information center to make online search on the topic of his/her interest.

Elements of Information Organization and Dissemination
DOI: http://dx.doi.org/10.1016/B978-0-08-102025-8.00003-X

C.2.1 User Community

Individuals and groups of persons visiting a library/information center for any of the above purposes are generally known as the community of users of the concerned library/information center. The community of users may be of diverse groups, comprising different categories of users such as:

- Students and teachers;
- Scientists and researchers;
- Professionals;
- Policy makers/planners;
- Entrepreneurs and business people;
- Managers/decision makers;
- Communicators/intermediaries;
- Community groups; and
- Common people.

Public libraries, including national libraries, usually serve a composite group of user communities, whereas special libraries or information centers orient their services to some specific category or categories of users.

C.2.2 Types of User

Whitetaker has categorized library users as [2]:

- *General users,* i.e., those who use the library with the main purpose of expanding their general knowledge or who read for pleasure; they do not have any specific subject in mind;
- *Specialist users,* i.e., those who use the library for the purpose of advancing knowledge in their subject area; they are usually interested in specific subject fields;
- *Handicapped users,* i.e., those who are handicapped in one form or the other; they are disabled either physically or intellectually;
- *Non-reading users,* i.e., those who make use of library services other than reading, such as borrowing/listening tapes, videocassettes, audiocassettes;
- *Non-literate users,* i.e., those who cannot read and write in any language, and those who are barely literate; they want to use a library to improve their literacy skills or even acquire literacy skills, such as farmers, artisans, and rural people.

Kunz has differentiated users in the following manner [3]:

- *On-site users,* i.e., those who personally visit the library/information center to collect the required information/information resource and

Remote users, i.e., those who collect the required information/information resources without being present in the library/information center. These two categories may also be called *Active users* and *Passive users.*

- *Actual users,* i.e., those who actually take information or information resources from a library/information center and *Potential users,* i.e., those who do not actually use information/information resources due to some reason, but they have the potentiality to become actual users. These categories can also be called *Users* and *Non-users.*
- *Regular users,* i.e., those who use information/information resources on regular basis and *Occasional users,* i.e., those who use information/information resources occasionally, i.e., as and when required.

In the digital environment, users can be categorized on the basis of their technological skills as below [4]:

- *Unskilled/Computer illiterate users:* The users of this category need help of third party to access information as they themselves do not have ICT skill to access digital information.
- *Semi-skilled/Semi-computer literate users:* Users of this category can use ICT to access information with or no support. But they can only use basic search facilities such as basic search engine; they cannot effectively use advanced search engine features.
- *Skilled/Computer literate users:* Users of this category can analyze their information needs, use basic and advanced search engines effectively and formulate queries and keywords effectively.
- *Ab-users:* These are unauthorized users who obtain illegitimate access to library resources/information resources online. They are often called hackers who use illegal software to carry out their illegal actions.

A library or information center needs to serve all these types of users, except of course the Ab-users. It may also have to take measures to convert non–users or potential users to actual users.

C.3 USER STUDY (US)

A user study may be defined as "a systematic study of information requirements of users in order to facilitate meaningful exchanges between information systems and users" [1]. In other words, it is a study of people's needs for, and use of, information. The term "user studies" is now preferred over "library surveys" because studies of information needs or information use behavior focus upon a wider range of information sources and channels rather than simply libraries [1].

C.3.1 Types and Scope of US

Guha has mentioned about three types of user studies quoting Prof. Herbert Menzel. They are [5]:

- *Behavior studies*, in which "the pattern of overall interaction of the users' community with the communication system, without reference to any specific information-retrieving event" has been studied;
- *Use studies*, in which the relative use of different information channels such as current awareness service, indexing and abstracting service, and cited references, have been found out;
- *Information flow studies*, which have been made from different viewpoints, the chief among them being the study of the flow of information from oral report stage to its publication in a primary document and ultimately its inclusion in a secondary document.

In fact, user studies, use studies, information need studies, information transfer studies, communication behavior studies, information dissemination and utilization studies, user research, etc., are all closely related and often not precisely defined. The terminology depends much on the approach and the angle from which one sees. There are several overlapping facets included in these studies. As such, scope of user studies is enormous. Broadly, all such research inquiries about users (including non-users as well as potential users) with a view to understand their characteristic features, needs, preferences, practices, opinions, attitudes, behavior, evaluations, etc., with respect to library and information services that are offered or likely to be or need to be offered, may be treated as user studies. The ultimate aim is to help designing, altering, evaluating and improving efficiency and effectiveness of library and information systems and their products/services in meeting their predetermined goals [6]. Two major aspects of user studies, viz., identification of information needs of users and information seeking behavior of the users, have been discussed here in some detail.

C.3.2 Need of US

User studies need to be conducted because of following reasons [1]:

- User attitudes are essential considerations in designing services of a library/information center;
- Users have ways of doing things and these should be accommodated in the design of services;
- Users have ways of doing things that should be changed.

C.3.3 Objectives of US

User studies are undertaken with one or more of the following objectives [1]:
- To identify actual strengths and weaknesses of resources and services of a library/information center;
- To identify levels and kinds of user needs;
- To identify the barriers or problems that discourage the use of a library/information center;
- To identify patterns of use of library/information center.

C.3.4 User Characteristics

No user-community of an information system is fully homogeneous. Though a majority of the users of a system would come together for a particular purpose and are comparable by one or two criteria, they are divided among themselves by many individual characteristics. Knowledge of the population being served by an information system is an essential requirement for providing useful services. Just like understanding the user is half the battle won in providing information services, knowing the structure and composition of the user community in terms of various characteristics by which they can be compared and contrasted is half the task done in understanding the users. The characteristics of users are innumerable and there are several ways of grouping them. User characteristics could be internal or external to the individual. They may also be classified as sociological, demographic, psychological, personality related (work related), organizational, professional, etc. Some specific characteristics of interest in user studies are age, experience, gender, educational level, performance, productivity, creativity, motivation, emotional stability, temperaments, interests, personal idiosyncrasies, productivity, communication, citation, and other activities, nature of work or function, various roles, responsibilities, and status of users. These have also to be understood in user studies [6].

C.3.5 Benefits of User Study

The aim of any library/information center is to provide right information to right user at right time. This aim can be better fulfilled if the concerned people in the library/information center have a fair knowledge about their users. User study helps in obtaining this knowledge. The main benefits of user studies are [1]:
- It helps in evaluating the information system, i.e., identifying the gaps or bottlenecks in information flow, if any, and taking steps to remove

the gaps/bottlenecks in order to improve the functioning of the system. It may also help in designing new services.

- It helps the users to perceive the information-related problems. Users often do not consider their problems as related to information. For example, an entrepreneur requiring supplementary finance considers it as a financial problem, but he/she may perceive it as an information-related problem, if he/she gets information about the agencies that provide finances.
- It motivates the users to seek required information from the library/information center. If the staff members of a library/information center understand a user's needs properly and provide him/her relevant information, he/she is motivated to seek information again, when required.

C.3.6 Guidelines for US

User study is a skilled task, requiring expert guidance. Unless such guidance is available, simple errors may creep in, which can invalidate the investigation. In view of this, UNESCO has brought out *UNISIST guidelines for the conduct of user studies* [7].

C.4 INFORMATION NEED

In day-to-day work, lack of self-sufficiency constitutes information needs. Information needs represent gaps in the current knowledge of the user. Apart from the expressed or articulated needs, there are unexpressed needs which the user is aware of, but does not like to express. The third category of need is the delitescent or dormant need which the user is unaware of. But the information service provider may be able to bring to light these needs [8]. A need is specific and generally time bound either immediate or deferred [9]. Deferred needs can be stored in a person's memory or addressed later; immediate needs are handled by the person with a sense of urgency. To meet an immediate need, the person is assumed to consciously select a source. Sources can be internal, coming from memory or direct observation, or sources can be external coming from direct (interpersonal) contacts or recorded (literature) sources [10]. Libraries and information centers are the main suppliers of recorded information sources.

C.4.1 Basis of Need

Derr has expressed the opinion that the primary conditions of information need are existence of a genuine or legitimate information purpose, and that the information, in question, contributes to the achievement of that information purpose [11]. The possible reasons that may create information need among the users, according to Crawford, are [12]:

- The activities or work in which the user is involved (work activity);
- The area or field of user's work (discipline);
- Availability of facilities to the user;
- User's hierarchical position in his/her place of work;
- Motivational factors;
- Decision making;
- Seeking new ideas;
- Validating correctness of something;
- Making professional contributions;
- Establishing priority for discovery, etc.

C.4.2 Affecting Factors

Information needs are affected by a variety of factors such as [13]:
- The range of information sources available;
- The uses to which the information will be put;
- The background, motivation, professional orientation, and other individual characteristics of the client;
- The social, political, economic, legal, and regulatory systems surrounding the client; and
- The consequences of information use.

C.4.3 Types of Need

Through user studies made by different experts it has been possible to find out various types of information needs and approaches. Some studies have categorized needs as "perceived" needs and "actual or idealized" needs, "immediate" needs and "deferred" needs, "continuous" needs and "discrete" needs, "regular" needs and "irregular" needs, needs for "known items" and "thematic" needs. Further, information needs could be unexpressed or expressed/articulated, felt or unfelt, dormant or delitescent. In addition, information needs of users can be expressed in terms of time (i.e., urgency), content and amount or quantity of information [6]. Information needs have been categorized by Childers as [14]:
- *Kinetic need*, which satisfies a special problem, diagnosed and immediate;
- *Potential need*, which satisfies unconscious hidden problem under layers of attitude, impulses, and values.

Again information needs have been categorized by Weight and others as [15]:
- Need for new information;
- Need to elucidate the information held; and
- Need to confirm information held.

Further, information needs have also been categorized as [16]:
- *Social or pragmatic information need*, i.e., need for information required to cope with day-to-day life;
- *Recreational information need*, i.e., need for information that satisfies the recreational and cultural interests of an individual;
- *Professional information need*, i.e., need for information required to operate competently within a business or professional environment;
- *Educational information need*, i.e., need for information required to satisfy academic requirements at an institution.

Guha has identified four types of need or approaches to information on the basis of analysis and studies made by Melvin Voigt and other workers in the field. These approaches are [5]:
- *Current approach*—for keeping oneself posted with the latest developments in a field of specialization and its allied fields;
- *Everyday approach*—for specific information required for day-to-day work;
- *Exhaustive approach*—for consultation of all relevant documents on a field of study or research; and
- *Catching-up or brushing-up approach*—for updating one's knowledge and information in an area.

It is to be noted that the first two approaches of the users have to be satisfied by a library or documentation/information center more frequently than the last two. By scanning some current journals and issues of indexing and abstracting journals the users may satisfy their current approach; a documentation/information center has to acquire and devise tools and techniques to satisfy other approaches.

C.4.4 Need Identification

For efficient organization of information sources in a library or information center as also for providing information sources which can precisely satisfy the need of a user, identification of the user's precise need is very important. But information need identification is not a simple process. There are various factors which make this process complex. Some such factors are [9]:
- Same information is perceived by different clients differently as their value systems differ due to their nature of work;

- Information is put to different uses (R&D personnel, application developers, and technicians all put information to different uses);
- Need is satisfied by having access to the identified information in a particular package and form, and at a suitable time;
- The flow of information and channels of communication are complex and add to the complexity; and
- Individual preferences and behavioral aspects add a further dimension.

Apart from the complexities mentioned above, there are problems due to individual behavior too [9]:

- A client may not like to reveal his need as he/she may like to show that he/she is above (any) requirements and that he/she knows his/her sources.
- To divert or mislead he/she may give pseudo information needs. Or, just because someone else is getting an information, he/she may give a pseudo need to receive the same information.
- A super-ordinate, to avoid a subordinate getting informed, may give it as a pseudo need and try to withhold the information received.

C.4.4.1 Objective of Identification

The objectives of identifying or studying information need may be [17]:

- Explanation of observed phenomena of information use or expressed need; or better yet
- The prediction of instances of information use; or better yet
- The control and thereby improvement of the utilization of information through manipulation of essential conditions.

C.4.4.2 Methods of Identification

Several methods have been proposed for identifying user need. These include the following:

- *Study of aims, objectives, and programs of the organization:* The users attached to an organization will always require materials that will help them carrying on their programs and ultimately fulfill the aims and objectives of the organization. As such, a study of the aims and objectives of the organization or organizations concerned and their programs may provide an insight into the nature of requirements of the users working there. As the programs may sometimes change or new programs may be taken up, a close watch on such developments should be maintained.
- *Familiarity with research projects:* A fair knowledge of the scopes of the research projects undertaken by individual research workers of groups

of workers jointly may also help in anticipating their possible needs. For obtaining such knowledge, the research workers may be contacted and/ or publications in which such scopes are reported, such as "research in progress," house journal, and information bulletin, may be consulted.

- *Meeting and discussion with users:* If the existing and potential users, for whom information are to be organized, are readily available at hand, they may be frequently contacted and their needs assessed through interview and/or discussion.

- *Analysis of records:* Some of the records maintained by a library or documentation/information center, such as record of reference and information services, record of micro-documents issued and record of all such demands which the library or the information center has not been able to satisfy, can provide an idea of the needs of the users and also reveal the existing gaps in the service rendered by the library or the center.

- *Analysis of response:* Some methods may be adopted for obtaining response or feed-back on the existing services from the users. Analysis of such response may also help in assessing the needs of the users. It may also bring out the shortcomings of the library or documentation/ information center.

- *Citation analysis:* Analysis of bibliographical references in journal articles and research papers of the users can give a picture of actual use of documents. Thus, it is possible to find out the periodicals and other publications which are frequently consulted, the language preference and other such useful information which can help in anticipating the demands of the users.

- *Users' survey:* The needs of each user usually differ from those of others. As such, it is not sufficient to know about the needs of one person out of a group, even if all of them may be working in the same field or in the same organization. For better assessment of the demands of the users, therefore, it may be helpful to conduct surveys which should cover at least all the cross-sections of the whole user community. Such surveys have already been conducted in several countries, especially in United States. The methods usually applied for such studies are questionnaire, interview, diary, and observation.

C.4.5 Conceptual Model

Devadason has observed that no single method will serve entirely. A careful selection and blending of several techniques depending on the client (i.e., user) whose need is being studied is necessary [18]. Devadason and

Pratap Lingam have proposed a formal procedure for studying information needs of the clients. According to them, besides gathering and recording the information needs, careful analysis is to be made to distill actual needs from the data gathered. To derive the advantages of a combination of "a priori" and "pragmatic" approaches, the proposed methodology involves the conceptual and empirical survey of client information needs [9]. The major steps in the process of identifying information needs, according to them, are [9]:

- *Study of subject(s) of interest to the organization/client(s):* The subjects (disciplines and sub-disciplines) of interest to the organization/system/clients are to be studies and the core, peripheral and supporting areas are to be identified. The methodology of studying a subject for information work and service developed by Bhattacharyya [19] may be used for the purpose.
- *Study of the organization and its environment:* The overall objectives, functions and the factors that affect the functions of the organization concerned are to be studied through the organizational chart, the functions/activities chart, annual reports, project reports, internal reports, and other publications of the organization.
- *Study of the immediate environment of the client(s):* For studying the specific environment of the client it may be necessary to delineate the category of users (say, supervisor and above) whose information needs are to be identified. It will also be necessary to be well acquainted with the department/unit to which the individual client is attached, before conducting any actual interview with the client for the identification of his/her information needs.
- *Study of the client(s):* For studying the clients, they are to be first categorized according to the nature of information use and the functions performed by them, etc. and each category of users may be studied through any direct method like questionnaire, observation, interview, etc. or any indirect method, like study of job description, information use record, job diary, etc. or through any combination of methods.
- *Formal interview:* Clients may now be formally interviewed for confirming their needs. Through such interview the work-roles the clients play, the type of information required, the form in which required, the frequency of requirement, etc. may be verified.
- *Identification and recording of information needs:* The information needs so identified are to be properly recorded in each case.
- *Analysis and refinement of the identified information needs:* The users may be contacted at intervals to ascertain the problems, if any, they are

facing and changes, if any, in their information needs for tuning the existing services to suit the changing needs.

They have also built up the following conceptual model incorporating the above steps [9]:

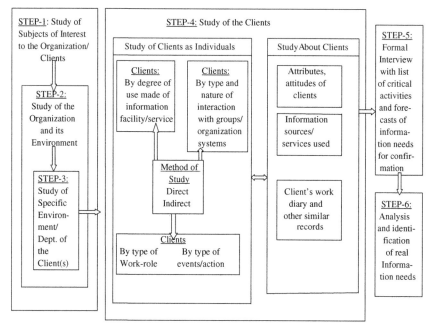

Annotation: *The first three steps constitute the "Study of the Clients" as part of the whole environment, which is different from the "Study of the Clients at Step 4."*

The "Study of specific Environment/Department of the Client"(Step 3) is within the "Organization and its Environment" (Step 2), which in turn is encircled by the "Study of Subjects of Interest to the Organization" (Step 1) under which both the Organization and the Clients operate.

A gradual progress is made in these three steps, telescopically, from gathering macro data, through broad organizational data to data relating to the specific environment (department/unit) of the clients.

Step 4 involves two different types of activities, viz., "Study of the Clients as Individuals" and "Study about the Clients."

A conceptual model of the process of identification of information needs. *From F.J. Devadason, P.P. Lingam, A methodology for the identification of information needs of users, IFLA J. 23 (1) (1997) 41–51.*

C.5 INFORMATION BEHAVIOR

The term "information behavior," is used "to describe the many ways in which human beings interact with information, in particular, the ways in which people seek and utilize information" [20]. Earlier, studies on information behavior were called "use studies," studies of "information seeking and gathering," or studies of "information needs and uses." Gradually, the term "information seeking research" was used to include all kinds of research on people's interaction with information. More recently, however, some researchers felt that "information seeking" suggested only explicit efforts to locate information, and did not include the many other ways people and information interacted. In the 1990s, the term "information behavior" came into wide use [20]. Evidently, information seeking is a major aspect of information behavior and the term information seeking behavior is still often used interchangeably with information behavior.

C.6 INFORMATION SEEKING

Information seeking is the process of searching or finding out required information from information sources. The way information is sought varies from user to user. The strategies adopted by different users for finding the relevant information may be termed as information seeking strategy or information seeking behavior. According to Wilson, information seeking behavior is purposive seeking of information as a consequence of a need to satisfy some goal [21], while according to Marchionini it connotes the process of acquiring knowledge; it is a problem-oriented approach and the solution may or may not be found [22]. More precisely, information seeking is a conscious effort to acquire information in response to a need or gap in one's knowledge [10]. According to Chen and Hernon, information seeking behavior represents an individual's reaction to the stimuli of information need, available sources, and the characteristics of the information seeker. Taken in combination, these elements will determine the nature of information seeking responses in a given context. Hence information seeking patterns of an individual are a determinant of that individual's information environment, which consists of [23]:

- Background and characteristics of the individual;
- The nature and type of information need with which he/she is confronted;
- The type and availability of information providers;
- Information provider's capability in responding to a request;
- Existence of barriers that serve to diminish or deter the effective linkage between the information provider and the information seeker; and
- The degree of satisfaction perceived by an individual with the ability of one or more information providers to respond to his/her information needs

C.6.1 Relation With Information Retrieval

Information seeking is related to, yet different from information retrieval (IR). While IR is more technology oriented, focusing on algorithms, and issues such as precision and recall, information seeking is a more human-oriented and open-ended process. In IR it is assumed that the information exists in the source and that a well-formed query will be able to retrieve it, but in information seeking, one does not know whether there exists an answer to one's query. The very process of information seeking may provide the learning required to satisfy the information need the user may have [24].

C.6.2 Affecting Factors

There are different factors which may affect the users' information seeking behavior [25]:
• Availability of information sources in the library/information center;
• Outdatedness of information sources;
• Lack of awareness about the available information sources;
• Search strategies/individual information seeking styles;
• Information scattering in too many sources;
• Lack of knowledge about information retrieving techniques;
• Non-supportive behavior of library/information center staff;
• Lack of infrastructure like computers, Internet connection, etc.;
• Negative outcome of information seeking process;
• Time available to conduct a search;
• The task or objective for which information is required.

Other difficulties or barriers being faced by the users in seeking needed information, which may also affect their information seeking behavior are [26]:
• Users do not know what information is available around them.
• They have difficulty in determining the quality, credibility, and accuracy of the information.
• The information they seek is too hard to find.
• They are unable to compare across information alternatives.
• They lack sufficient training.

C.6.3 Modes of Information Seeking

Bates has observed that "it is not unreasonable to guess that human beings absorb around 80% of all their knowledge through simply being aware, being conscious and sentient in their social context and physical environment." Basing on this contention, she has demonstrated different modes of information seeking through the following figure:

Modes of information seeking

Different modes of information seeking demonstrated by Bates. *From M.J. Bates, Toward an integrated model of information seeking and searching, in: M.J. Bates (Ed.), Information Users and Information System Design: Selected Works of Marcia J. Bares, vol III. (pp. 3–18), Ketchikan Press, Berkeley CA, 2016, p. 7.*

"Here 'Directed' and 'Undirected' refer, respectively, to whether an individual seeks particular information that can be specified to some degree, or is more or less randomly exposing themselves to information. 'Active' and 'Passive' refer, respectively, to whether the individual does anything actively to acquire information, or is passively available to absorb information, but does not seek it out. An enormous part of all we know and learn surely comes to us through passive undirected behavior, or simply being aware (cell 'D')" [27].

C.6.4 Information Seeking Models

A model may be described as a framework for thinking about a problem and may evolve into a statement of the relationships among theoretical propositions [28]. Models have been developed in some fields of library and information services too. In the field of information seeking by users several models have been developed, which have been found useful in the field of information literacy too. A few of such models are introduced below.

C.6.4.1 Self-Help Model

Robert Saxon Taylor has focused on the kind of formal information seeking activity that happens on the reference desk of a library. According to him, information seeking in a library can take two forms: (1) working through the human intermediary—the reference librarian—and (2) self-help, where the user interacts with the library and its components. In the self-help model, the user mills around unsure of what it is he/she is looking for, or uncertain of what tools are available to help him/her find the information he/she is seeking. Taylor says that the information seeker goes through several steps before coming to a library in search of information. First, the information seeker searches his/her own files. Then he/she may consult his/her colleagues. When he/she finally arrives at the library, the librarian serves as "an interlocutor between the inquirer and the system" [13]. Taylor has identified four levels of information seeking [13]:

- Identification of a *visceral need*, or a "vague sort of dissatisfaction" that is unexpressed;
- Formulation of a *conscious need* that is expressed as "an ambiguous rambling statement";
- Construction of *formalized need*, expressed as a "qualified and rational" statement of the need;
- Establishment of a *compromised need*, which is a query that is expressed in terms that fit the organization of the information system (such as library collection).

Taylor suggests that it is the librarian's job to help deal with the compromised question or answer the question with the resources available in the library and help the inquirer get back to answering formalized question through a fruitful search strategy. Information obtained from the interviews suggest that there are five filters that a question passes through from which a librarian can derive information to help formulate a search strategy. These filters are [13,25]:

- *Determination of subject:* This filter helps provide some delineation of the subject area.
- *Objective and motivation:* This filter helps the librarian to understand the point of view or the angle at which the question is being presented.
- *Personal characteristics of inquirer:* This filter determines what questions should and might be asked, because it is dependent on factors such as the inquirer's experience with the library, his/her background and his/her knowledge of the subject matter.
- *Relationship of inquiry description to organization:* Taylor is of the view that the inquirer is generally not familiar with the sources available to him.
- *Anticipated or acceptable answers:* Essentially the user comes to the library with a preconceived notion of an acceptable answer. Understanding what an acceptable answer is can be an important filter to comprehend.

C.6.4.2 Behavioral Model

Ellis's elaboration of the different behaviors involved in information seek-ing consists of a set of features (i.e., stages). Ellis makes no claim to the effect that the different behaviors constitute a single set of stages (He uses the term "features" rather than "stages."). The features identified by Ellis are [28,29]:

- *Starting*: the means employed by the user to begin seeking information, e.g., asking some knowledgeable colleague;
- *Chaining*: following footnotes and citations in known material or "for-ward" chaining from known items through citation indexes;
- *Browsing*: "semi-directed or semi-structured searching";
- *Differentiating*: using known differences in information sources as a way of filtering the amount of information obtained;
- *Monitoring*: keeping up-to-date or current awareness searching;
- *Extracting*: selectively identifying relevant material in an information source;
- *Verifying*: checking the accuracy of information;
- *Ending*: "tying up loose ends" through a final search.

The strength of Ellis's model is that it is based on empirical research and has been tested in subsequent studies [30]. According to Ellis, "the detailed interrelation or interaction of the features in any individual infor-mation seeking pattern will depend on the unique circumstances of the information seeking activities of the person concerned at that particular point in time" [29]. Wilson has diagrammatically shown how these features may relate to each other temporally, providing a partial order [30]:

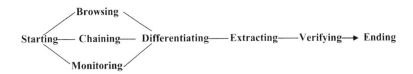

A process version of Ellis's behavioral framework.

One may *describe* any information seeking activity through Ellis's fea-tures. Indeed, they are general enough to fit a large number of empirical situations. However, if one is to *explain* information seeking behavior, say, in terms of the work tasks the subjects are engaged with, or their knowl-edge on the task, the features fall short because they are not explicitly related to such external possible causative factors [31].

C.6.4.3 Information Search Process Model

Kuhlthau developed in 1991 a model of the information search process from common patterns that emerged from her longitudinal investigation of high school students' information seeking behaviors. Her model encompasses the development of thoughts about a research topic, the feelings associated with the search process, and the actions of seeking and using sources. The model goes beyond the mere mechanics of information seeking; it incorporates three realms: the affective (feeling), the cognitive (thoughts), and the physical (actions and strategies) [32]. These realms are common to each stage of the search process, as described below [33].

- Stage 1—*Initiation*: This is the stage when a person first recognizes that information is needed to complete an assignment or solve a problem. It is similar to the information seeking behavior model previously discussed, where the user identifies a perceived information need in a given environment.
- Stage 2—*Selection*: The task in this stage is to identify and select a general topic to be investigated or the approach to be pursued.
- Stage 3—*Exploration*: The task in this stage is to investigate information on the general topic in order to expand one's personal understanding as well as to provide a focus for the topic. This stage involves gathering information which is general to the topic, rather than information which is specific or especially pertinent.
- Stage 4—*Formulation*: From the information gathered during the pre-focus exploration stage, the user now forms a focused perspective on the topic on the basis of the information found. A clear focus enables the user to move to the next stage. As the students' understanding of the topic grows, the information search can be more focused and direct.
- Stage 5—*Collection*: The user interacts with information systems (e.g., librarians, experts, friends, etc.) effectively and efficiently. Information specifically related to the defined focused topic is gathered. This stage comprises the major portion of the model.
- Stage 6—*Search closure* or *presentation*: The task is to complete the search and to prepare the written document. The search closure may be completed because all the necessary information has been located, or because the deadline for the paper is near. In the latter case, not all the information required may have been retrieved.

Kuhlthau's model is based on an intensive longitudinal study of a group of high school students. She determined that the model was valid across diverse user groups as well as appropriate for describing the search process longitudinally. The model is important as it suggests that the user is an active participant in the information search process. The student's knowledge grows as he/she interacts with the information. More importantly, cognitive processes are involved in information seeking. Throughout the process, the student engages in cognitive strategies such as brain storming, contemplating, predicting, consulting, reading, choosing, identifying, defining, and confirming. However, Kuhlthau's model does not seem to incorporate manipulation of the information; that is, analyzing, digesting, organizing, synthesizing, and evaluating the found information. Turning information and data into knowledge is not assumed in the model. The model, however, does highlight that affective feelings, such as apprehension, uncertainty, confusion, anxiety, anticipation, doubt, optimism, and confidence, interplay as the search for information proceeds. Kuhlthau stresses that students move through each stage sequentially. The stages of initiation, selection and exploration assist the student in exploring and identifying a topic of interest. The three stages lead the student from a general topic to a specific one. Kuhlthau's model focusses on the search process, the acts associated with finding information, rather than how to use, synthesize, and evaluate the found information [32].

C.6.4.4 Information Behavior Models

Wilson described information behavior as the totality of human behavior in relation to sources and channels of information, including both active and passive information-seeking, and information use. He described information seeking behavior as purposive seeking of information as a consequence of a need to satisfy some goal [2]. Conceived in 1981, Wilson's first model outlined the factors leading to information seeking, and the barriers inhibiting action. The model was based on two main propositions: (1) the information need is not a primary need, but a secondary need that arises out of needs of a more basic kind, viz., physiological, cognitive or affective and (2) that in the effort to discover information to satisfy a need, the inquirer is likely to meet with barriers of different kinds, viz., personal or individual barriers, social or role-related barriers or interpersonal barriers and environmental barriers. This model was based on an understanding of human information seeking behaviors that are best understood as three interwoven frameworks: the user, the information system, and the information resource. Wilson's model, depicted in the diagram below, suggests that information-seeking behavior results from the recognition of some need, perceived by the user.

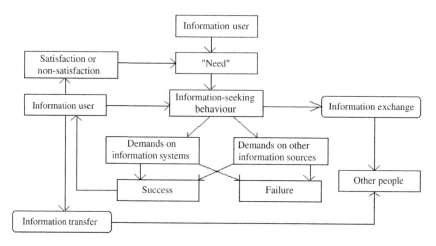

Wilson's model of information behavior, 1981.

That behavior may take several forms: e.g., the user may make demands upon formal systems that are customarily defined as information systems (such as libraries, online services, information centers), or upon systems which may perform information functions in addition to a primary, non-information function (such as estate agents' offices or car sales agencies, both of which are concerned with selling, but which may be used to obtain information on current prices, areas of "suitable" housing, or details of cars that hold their second-hand value) [34]. Alternatively, the user may seek information from other *people*, rather than from systems, and this is expressed in the diagram as involving "information exchange." The use of the word "exchange" is intended to draw attention to the element of reciprocity, recognized by sociologists and social psychologists as a fundamental aspect of human interaction [35]. In any of the above cases of information-seeking behavior, "failure" may be experienced: this is indicated in the diagram for the use of systems but, of course, it may also be experienced when seeking information from other people. Whatever the source of the information it will at some point be "used," if only in the sense of being evaluated to discover its relationship to the user's need. That "use" may satisfy or fail to satisfy the need and, in either event, may also be recognized as being of potential relevance to the need of another person and, consequently, may be "transferred" to such a person [34].

Upgradation of Wilson Model

Wilson has also periodically upgraded this model. One of his revised models incorporates the stages of information seeking identified by Ellis.

It also displays the physiological, affective, and cognitive needs that give rise to information seeking behavior. The model recognizes that an information need is not a need in and of itself, but rather one that stems from a previous psychological need. These needs are generated by the interplay of personal habits and political, economic, and technological factors in an individual's environment. The revised model is shown below [26]:

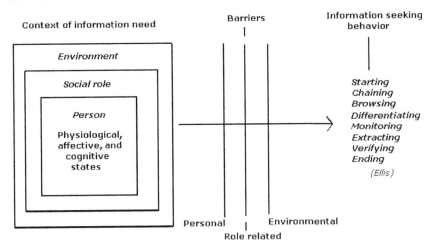

Wilson's model of information behavior, 1997.

C.6.5 Information Process Model

Marchionini's approach was a problem solving approach to understand information seeking process in the electronic environment. According to him information seeking behavior can have four levels [22]:

- At the coarsest level, people exhibit information seeking **patterns**, which are mostly unconscious sequences of behaviors.
- **Strategies** are the approaches that the information seeker takes to a problem, which may be broadly of two types, viz., analytical searching and browsing strategies.
- **Tactics** are discrete intellectual choices during an information seeking session, such as narrowing the search by selecting a date range.
- **Moves** are finely grained actions manifested as discrete behavioral actions, e.g., doing search, going to advanced search, downloading, etc. Marchionini's model involves eight processes [22]:
- Problem recognition;
- Problem definition;
- Selection of system/source;

- Problem articulation (query formulation);
- Search execution;
- Examination of results;
- Extraction of desired information; and
- Reflection, iteration, and stopping of search process.

C.6.5.1 Big Six Skills Model

Eisenberg and Berkowitz (1992) proposed the *Big Six Skills* for guiding the students in their research work. The model represents a general approach to information problem-solving, consisting of six logical steps or stages. The order of the stages changes with each search venture, but each stage is necessary in order to achieve a successful resolution of an information problem [36]. Eisenberg and Berkowitz's model closely resembles that of Kuhlthau [25]. With six major stages and two sub-stages under each, the Big6 covers the full range of information problem-solving actions. The Big6 Skills comprise a unified set of information and technology skills. Taken together, these skills form a process. The steps in Big Six Skills model are [36]:

1. *Task definition:* Eisenberg and Berkowitz maintain that most people spend very little time in defining their topics. They plunge right into the information seeking strategies (Step 2), rather than reflecting on the type of information that they need to find. By clearly defining and understanding the information problem, an information seeker can move more efficiently toward solutions. Therefore, the first step in information problem serving is to define the problem from an information seeker's point of view and identify the information needed.

2. *Information seeking strategies:* Once the information problem is defined clearly, an information seeker must determine all possible sources that may provide needed information and identify which among them are the most appropriate to solve the task. He/she also needs to consider various criteria when selecting the appropriate information source, including accuracy, reliability, ease of use, availability, comprehensibility, and authority.

3. *Location and access:* Location and access are the implementation of the information seeking strategy. These skills involve locating the selected sources through access tools (bibliographic databases and print indexes) and finding the needed information.

4. *Use of information:* Once the information seeker finds the needed information, he/she can employ skills to use the information. These skills

involve interacting, dialoguing, reading, listing, viewing, questioning, and reflecting on the information. The information seeker also needs to decide what is valuable and extract relevant information.

5. *Synthesis:* Synthesis is the application of all information to the defined task. Synthesis involves organizing, restructuring, and repackaging the information from multiple sources into a new and different form.

6. *Evaluation:* Evaluation is the examination and assessment of the information problem solving process. It determines the effectiveness and efficiency of the process. It also determines whether the information found met the defined task.

Eisenberg has emphasized that successful information problem solving does require completing each stage at some point in time, but the Big6 is not linear and prescriptive. It is not necessary to complete the stages in order; however all the stages must be completed for overall success [37].

C.6.6 Online Information Seeking

In the online environment, information seeking behavior of users may not be same as in traditional environment. A study of the Google Generation commissioned by JISC (Joint Information Systems Committee), a registered charity company of United Kingdom, and the British Library has found six different characteristics of online information seeking behavior [24]:

• Horizontal information seeking;
• Navigation;
• Viewing;
• Squirreling behavior;
• Checking information seekers; and
• Diverse information seekers.

Horizontal information seeking is the method sometimes referred to as "skimming." An information seeker who skims, views a couple of pages, then subsequently follows other links without necessarily returning to the initial sites. Navigators spend their time finding their way around. Wilson found that users of e-book or e-journal sites were most likely to spend, on an average, a mere 4–8 minutes viewing the said sites. Squirreling behavior relates to users who download lots of documents but might not necessarily end up reading them. Checking information seekers assess the host in order to ascertain trustworthiness. Diverse information seekers are users whose behavior differs from all the above [24].

REFERENCES

[1] P. S. Kwatra, Library User Studies, Jaico Publishing House, Bombay, 1992, 301 p.

[2] Whitetaker. *As quoted in*: Models of information users and behaviour. <http://macliagan. wordpress.com/tag/1992-eisenberg-and-berkowitz-1992-proposed-the-big-six-skills-which-represents-a-general-approach-to-information-problem-solving/>.

[3] W. Kunz, et al., Methods of Analysis and Evaluation of Information Needs: A Critical Review, Verlag Dokumentation; Munchen (1977), p. 16.

[4] I. E. Anvira, The Anatomy of library users in the 21st century, Lib. Philos. Pract. (2011). <http://unllib.unl.edu/LPP/>.

[5] B. Guha, Documentation and Information, second ed., World Press, Calcutta, 1983.

[6] M. S. Sridhar, Understanding the user – why, what and how? Lib. Sci. Slant. Doc. Inf. Stud. 32 (4) (1995) 151–164.

[7] UNESCO. UNISIST guidelines for the conduct of user studies, prepared by Geoffrey Ford et al. <http://unesdoc.unesco.org/images/0002/000299/029972EB.pdf>, (accessed 08.11.78).

[8] B. Cronin, Assessing information needs, Aslib. Proc. 33 (2) (1981) 40.

[9] F. J. Devadason, P. Pratap Lingam, Practical steps for identifying information needs of clients, In: Proc., 62nd IFLA General Conference, 1996.

[10] D. O. Case, Looking for Information: A Survey of Research on Information Seeking, Needs and Behavior, Academic Press, San Diego, 2007,

[11] R. L. Derr, A Conceptual analysis of information need, Inf. Process. Manage. 19 (5) (1983) 273–278.

[12] S. Crawford, Information needs and uses, Ann. Rev. Inf. Sci. Technol. 13 (1978) 61–81.

[13] R. S. Taylor, Question negotiation and information seeking in libraries, J. College Res. Lib. 29 (3) (1968) 178–194.

[14] T. Childers, Information Poor in America, Scarecrow Press, New York, 1975, pp. 36–37.

[15] W. Weigts, et al., Patients' information seeking actions and physicians' responses in gynecological consultations, Qual. Health Res. 3 (1993) 398–429.

[16] J. Tague, et al., The distribution of community information: the role of computer and computer based networks, ASLIB Proc. 28 (1976) 314–321.

[17] H. N. Prasad, Information needs and users. <http://lemi.uc3m.es/est/forinf@/index. php/Forinfa/article/viewFile/33/34>.

[18] F. J. Devadason, Identifying information needs: Discussion Paper at the Regional Consultation on Provision of Information Services to End Users, UN/ESCAP Fertilizer Advisory, Development and Information Network for Asia and the Pacific-Network of Fertiliser Information Systems (FADINAP/NFIS). Bangkok, November 20–24, 1989.

[19] G. Bhattacharyya, Project on study of subjects, Lib. Sci. Slant. Doc. 12 (1975). Paper G

[20] M. J. Bates, Information behaviour. <http://pages.gseis.ucla.edu/faculty/bates/articles/information-behavior.html>. 2010.

[21] T.D. Wilson, Human information behavior, Inf. Sci. 3 (2) (2000) 49–55.

[22] G. Marchionini, Information Seeking in Electronic Environments, Cambridge University Press, New York, 1995,

[23] C.-C. Chen, and P. Hernon, A regional investigation of citizens' information need in New England. US Department of Education, 1981.

[24] Information seeking behaviour. <http://en.wikipedia.org/wiki/Information_seeking_behavior>.

[25] Models of information users and behaviour. <http://macliagan.wordpress.com/tag/1992-eisenberg-and-berkowitz-1992-proposed-the-big-six-skills-which-represents-a-general-approach-to-information-problem-solving/>.

[26] T. D. Wilson, Information behaviour: an interdisciplinary perspective, Inf. Process. Manage. 33 (1997) 551–572.

[27] M. J. Bates, Towards an integrated model of information seeking and searching, In: M. J. Bates (Ed.), Information Users and Information System Design: Selected Works of Marcia J. Bates, vol. III, Ketchikan Press, Berkeley CA, 2016, pp. 3–18.

[28] T. D. Wilson, Models of information behaviour research, J. Doc 55 (1999) 249–270.

[29] D. Ellis, A behavioural approach to information retrieval system design, J. Doc. 45 (1989) 171–212.

[30] D. Ellis, M. Haugan, Modelling the information seeking patterns of engineers and research scientists in an industrial environment, J. Doc. 53 (1997) 384–403.

[31] K. Järvelin, T.D. Wilson, On conceptual models for information seeking and retrieval research, Inf. Res. 9 (1) (2003). Paper 163. <http://InformationR.net/ir/9-1/paper163.html>.

[32] B. Lakshminarayan, Towards developing an integrated model of information behavior. PhD dissertation submitted to Queensland University of Technology, Australia. 2010.

[33] C. C. Kuhlthau, A principle of uncertainty for information seeking, J. Doc. 49 (1993) 339–355.

[34] T. D. Wilson, On user studies and information needs, J. Doc. 37 (1981) 3–15.

[35] A. W. Gouldner, The norm of reciprocity. Am. Sociol. Rev. 25 (1960) 161–178. *As quoted in* T.D. Wilson. On user studies and information needs. J. Doc. 37 (1981) 3–15.

[36] M. Eisenberg, R. Berkowitz, Information Problem Serving: The Big Six Skills Approach to Library and Information Skills Instruction, Ablex, Norwood, NJ, 1990.

[37] M. Eisenberg, Information literacy: essential skills for the information age, DESIDOC J. Lib. Inf. Technol. 28 (2) (2008) 39–47.

CHAPTER D

User Empowerment (UEm)

D.1 INTRODUCTION

However rich a library or information center may be in its collection of information sources, it cannot be of any help to the users unless they are able to get the needed information speedily and make use of them for the purpose for which the information had been sought. So long the users have been depending upon the library personnel to help them in this work. This often caused delay in getting the information leading to frustration among the users. Unless this dependence of users on the library personnel is reduces possibly such frustration can never be avoided. Some libraries have, therefore, introduced user education programs in libraries to make the users more self-reliant. But this is not enough in the changing library scenario in the digital environment. The libraries need to take some more measures to enable the users to not only efficiently and speedily identify the pertinent information sources and find the needed information from those sources, but also to evaluate and utilize the information so obtained to their advantage. In other words, they need to adequately empower the users.

D.2 SCOPE OF UEm

According to dictionary meaning, "empowerment is the process of enabling or authorizing an individual to think, behave, take action, and control work and decision making in autonomous ways. It is the state of feeling self-empowered to take control of one's own destiny" [1]. Hewer, in the context of empowerment of students for efficient use of library resources, states: "Empowerment is providing our library users (students and teachers) with the necessary skills to find and use information they need for school, study and leisure. Empowerment is a step beyond the old library skills or user education programmes. Empowerment does not just provide users with the instructions on how to carry out certain library tasks, but equips them with transferable skills which they can use for all sorts of information retrieval and usage tasks enabling them to cope with

Elements of Information Organization and Dissemination
DOI: http://dx.doi.org/10.1016/B978-0-08-102025-8.00004-1

the Information Age. Empowerment requires commitment by both parties (information services/libraries and their users) and a supportive environment" [2]. The aim of user empowerment essentially is inculcating an
attitude and spirit of self-help among the users and reducing their dependence on library personnel.

D.3 METHODS OF UE~M~

As indicated, user empowerment involves all such activities that help in
developing the capability of searching and utilizing the resources of a
library efficiently and independently. Ideally in a digital environment it
may include [3]:

- *Maintenance of open access system in the library*: Open access provides the
  users opportunity to access any document of his/her choice without
  depending upon any assistance from the library personnel.
- *Providing computer facilities to the users:* The users need computer facilities
  for accessing library OPAC/Web OPAC and user interfaces; accessing
  digital information resources, like e-books and e-journals; accessing
  Internet resources and other e-enabled services, like e-reference service, e-CAS, e-SDI, etc. Libraries will have to provide such facilities in
  its premises.
- *Developing computer literacy among the users*: For handling computers
  to access various information resources and information services, the
  users need to develop necessary competency. They may develop this
  competency themselves by attending computer application courses.
  The library may also arrange training courses for the users for developing such competency.
- *Developing information literacy (IL) among the users*: IL does not merely
  mean the ability to use information. It includes the ability to know
  what information would help; the ability to know where to go to get
  information; the ability to retrieve information; the ability to interpret,
  evaluate, and organize information; and the ability to use and communicate information. It empowers people to benefit fully from the
  information age, in which we live now, and prepares them for lifelong
  learning. Hence, IL programs need to be organized for the users.
- *Arranging user education programs*: User education programs make the
  users familiar with various information resources available in the
  library, how they have been organized and how these can be searched
  and located.

- *Developing Online Public Access Catalog (OPAC) for easy location of needed resources*: OPAC enables the users to verify the availability of relevant information resources in the library and their location. Traditional catalogs also help in this direction, but OPAC brings speed and accuracy in search.
- *Developing library portals*: A library portal is an extension of the Web OPAC. As the use of electronic resources has grown, libraries have deployed portals or gateway systems online to provide some of the selection and organization services in the digital realm. Library portals enhance the value of electronic resources with functions such as resource description and discovery, combined searching of multiple resources, context-sensitive linking, and personalized services.
- *Developing user interface*: A library should not only develop effective and sophisticated retrieval mechanism, but also provide efficient interaction with the end-users. User interfaces are designed for this purpose.
- *Developing e-enabled services*: If the services provided by a library are turned into e-enabled services, i.e., made available online, the users can avail of these services even remotely without waiting for assistance of the library personnel.

Among these, some are indirect methods in which users are not directly involved, such as maintaining open access system or developing OPAC, user interface or library portal; while some are direct methods in which users' participation is necessary. Two such important direct methods are IL development and user education. Incidentally, some experts feel that user education is one of the facets of IL. These methods are described below.

D.4 INFORMATION LITERACY

As is known, information is that resource, the possession of which gives a person or an organization an edge over the one, who or which does not have it. Information-haves always remain better equipped than information-have-nots. But information-have-nots not necessarily always suffer for lack of information; they suffer mostly due to their inability to harness the available information efficiently at need. It is thus obvious that mere existence of information cannot bridge the gaps between the information-haves and information-have-nots. It is necessary that the users are empowered to identify, access, evaluate, and utilize relevant information. IL can play a vital role in this context. It may be pointed out that IL is important for not only users of a library or an LIS professional, it is important for every citizen. "Being information literate ultimately improves our quality of life as we make informed decisions when buying a house, choosing a school, hiring staff, making an investment, voting for our representatives, and so much more. Information literacy is, in fact, the basis of a sound democracy" [4]. Realization of this fact has given rise to IL movement.

D.4.1 Concept of IL

The term "Information Literacy" was first used by Paul G. Zurkowski, President of the Information Industry of USA, in a report to the National Commission on Libraries and Information Science of that country in 1974 [5]. The term is composed of two common words, "Information" and "Literacy." The word "Information," to most people, means something associated with news, useful facts or interpreted data, while the word "Literacy" is generally associated with the ability to read and sometimes more specifically associated with the ability to understand of interpret certain phenomenon. For example, visual literacy enables people to understand wordless no-smoking sign. In combination, however, the two words have a special meaning to the advocates of IL. They use the term information literacy to describe an assortment of abilities, which are essential survival and "thrival" abilities. Thus, IL is not merely the ability to use information; it has a much broader meaning. It is a holistic concept that includes knowing that information matters, knowing where and how to get information, and knowing how to use and communicate information [6]. In other words, information literacy is an expression that describes the range of skills required for effective handling of information. Those include the ability to locate, evaluate, manage, and use information from a range of sources for problem-solving, decision-making, and research. It empowers people to benefit fully from the information age, in which we live now, and prepares them for lifelong learning. In today's world, information literacy is no longer an optional competence. It is a survival skill [7]. According to Douglas, "information literacy is more than a library or education issue. It is crucial to issues of economic development, health, citizenship and quality of life" [8]. Incidentally, some synonyms of information literacy that are sometimes used are Information Fluency and Information Competency.

D.4.1.1 Definition of IL

Information literacy, according to Chartered Institute of Library and Information Professionals (UK), is "knowing when and why you need information, where to find it, and how to evaluate, use and communicate it in ethical manner" [9], while according to National Forum on Information Literacy of USA, it is "the ability to know when there is a need for information, to be able to identify, locate, evaluate, and effectively use that information for the issue or problem at hand" [10]. Alexandria Proclamation adopted by the High Level Colloquium on Information Literacy and Lifelong Learning in November 2005 defined information literacy as a means to "empower people in all walks of life to seek, evaluate, use and create information effectively to achieve their personal, social, occupational, and educational goals" [11].

D.4.1.2 Scope of IL

IL consists of an assortment of interconnected abilities having to do with the use of information [6]:

- The ability to know what information would help;
- The ability to know where to go to get information;
- The ability to retrieve information;
- The ability to interpret, evaluate, and organize information;
- The ability to use and communicate information.

According to Prague Declaration, "Information literacy encompasses knowledge of one's information concerns and needs, and the ability to identify, locate, evaluate, organize, and effectively create, use and communicate information to address issues or problems at hand; it is a prerequisite for participating effectively in the Information Society, and is part of the basic human right of lifelong learning" [12]. However, IL does not mean knowing how to read. It also does not mean knowing how to use the place where information is available. It is also not synonymous with either library instruction (i.e., user education) or computer literacy. But all these are important links in the chain of abilities that is information literacy [6]. An information literate person, having the aforesaid abilities, can [13–15]:

- Recognize that accurate and complete information is the basis for intelligent decision-making;
- Recognize the need for accurate and relevant information and formulate appropriate questions/search strategy based on that need;
- Identify potential sources of information;
- Develop successful search strategies;
- Access needed information/sources of information, including e-information sources, efficiently, ethically, and legally;
- Understand economic, social, and cultural issues in the use of information;

- Evaluate information/information sources effectively;
- Organize information for practical application;
- Use critical thinking skills to synthesize information, to integrate it into the existing body of knowledge, to apply it effectively in problem-solving, to make intelligent decisions, and to communicate more effectively;
- Use information effectively to accomplish a purpose.

In short, IL helps in developing abilities relating to four main areas, viz., Need, Location, Evaluation, and Use of information, which have been termed as four dimensions of IL [4]. According to ALA Presidential Committee on Information Literacy, IL makes the people "prepared for lifelong learning" [16].

D.4.2 Need for IL

The need for IL has been felt due to:

- Existence of required information/information sources is not known to majority of people;
- Method of accessing the required information from the known sources is also not known to many;
- Measures to verify the authenticity and reliability of the available information is not known to most of the people;
- Method of making proper use of information for decision-making, problem-solving or improving one's livelihood or avocation is also not known to many.

According to Association of College and Research Libraries of USA, IL is the solution to "Data Smog," a term coined by author David Shenk to refer to the idea that too much information can create barrier in our lives. This data smog is produced by the amount of information, the speed at which it comes to us from all directions, the need to make fast decisions, and the feeling of anxiety that we are making decisions without having all the information that is available or that we need. IL allows us to cope with this situation by giving us the skills to know when we need information and where to locate it effectively and efficiently. It includes the technological skills needed to use the modern library as a gateway to information. It enables us to analyze and evaluate the information we find, thus giving us confidence in using that information to make a decision or create a product [4].

D.4.3 Related Concepts

IL belongs to a family of "survival literacies" of the current era which also includes six more categories of literacies:

- *Basic literacy*, i.e., ability to read, write, speak, understand, and interpret the written messages;
- *Library literacy*, i.e., ability to search and utilize library resources efficiently;
- *Visual literacy*, i.e., ability to understand and use messages expressed through signs or images;
- *Media literacy*, i.e., ability to access, analyze, evaluate, and communicate messages in a wide variety of forms;
- *Computer/Digital literacy*, i.e., the ability to locate, organize, understand, and create information using computer/digital technology;
- *Network literacy*, i.e., ability to locate, access, and use information in networked environment.

These literacies are so closely related and mutually dependent that they are often considered as different aspects of IL.

D.4.4 Components of IL

Shapiro and Hughes have suggested seven important components of a holistic approach to IL [17]:

- *Tool literacy*, or the ability to understand and use the practical and conceptual tools of current information technology relevant to education and the areas of work and professional life that the individual expects to inhabit;
- *Resource literacy*, or the ability to understand the form, format, location, and accessing methods of information resources, especially daily expanding networked information resources;
- *Social-structural literacy*, or understanding how information is socially situated and produced;
- *Research literacy*, or the ability to understand and use the IT-based tools relevant to the work of today's researchers and scholars;
- *Publishing literacy*, or the ability to format and publish research and ideas electronically, in textual and multimedia forms … to introduce them into the electronic public realm and the electronic community of scholars;
- *Emerging technology literacy*, or the ability to continuously adapt to, understand, evaluate, and make use of the continually emerging

innovations in information technology so as not to be a prisoner of prior tools and resources, and to make intelligent decisions about the adoption of new ones;

- *Critical literacy*, or the ability to evaluate critically the intellectual, human and social strengths and weaknesses, potentials and limits, benefits and costs of information technologies.

D.4.5 Methods of IL

As indicated, IL does not only mean knowing about the availability of information sources, it is much more than that. Hence the user education programs run by libraries and information centers are not sufficient to make people fully information literate. Separate courses have been drafted and are being run for this purpose in different educational institutions, specially in USA. The different methods that can be followed for spreading IL are:

- Introduction of IL in the school and college curricula;
- Organization of specialized regular programs on IL at higher educational institutions;
- Conducting of workshops for those who have already passed out of educational institutions and have no opportunity to attend the regular programs;
- Supplementing literacy programs being conducted by government agencies and NGOs by incorporating essential elements of IL within the said programs.

Help of libraries and information centers will have to be taken in running any IL program due to availability of valuable information resource in these organizations and the expertise of the professional people manning such organization in handling these resources.

D.4.5.1 IL Models

A number of models is now being used for developing IL competency. These models have been developed to suit different groups of people. Some widely used models are:

- *The BIG6 (Mike Eisenberg and Bob Borkowitz, 1990):* This model developed for guiding the students in their research work, has six steps, viz., task definition, information seeking strategies, location and access, use of information, synthesis and evaluation. A modified version of this model for young learners is *Super3* involving only three steps—Plan, Do, and Review [18].

- *Information skills model (Ann Iriving, 1985):* This model includes nine steps: Formulating, Identifying, Tracing, Examining, Using, Recording, Interpreting, Shaping, and Evaluating [19].
- *Information search process (Kuhlthau, 1989):* This model, developed by Carol Kuhlthau, which shows how users approach the research process and how a user's confidence increases at each stage, comprises of seven stages—initiation, selection, exploration, formulation, collection, presentation, and assessment [20].
- *Pathways to knowledge model (Pappas and Tepe, 1995):* This model, with strategies, forms of expression, and method of teaching and learning embedded in it, includes the following stages: appreciation, pre-search, search, interpretation, communication, and evaluation [21].
- *The 8Ws model (Annette Lamb, 1990):* Developed in 1990 and updated in 1997 and 2001, this model comprises eight steps—all starting with the letter "W:" Watching (exploring), Wondering (questioning) Webbing (searching), Wiggling (evaluating), Weaving (Synthesizing), Wrapping (creating), Waving (communicating), and Wishing (Assessing) [22].
- *CILIP model:* This model contains eight competencies/understandings that a person requires to be information literate: a need for information; the resources available; how to find information; need to evaluate results; how to work with or exploit results; ethics and responsibility of use; how to communicate or share your finding; and how to manage your findings [23].
- *Seven pillars model (SCONUL, 1999):* Developed by the Society of College, National University Libraries of United Kingdom in 1999 and updated in 2004 and 2012, it was designed to be a practical working model that would help develop ideas amongst practitioners and generate discussion and includes ability to understand as well as carry out searches and is divided into a core model and different lenses [24].
- *Seven faces model (Christine, 1997):* This model aims at developing seven categories of conceptions: technology conception, information sources conception, information process conception, information control conception, knowledge construction conception, knowledge extension conception, and wisdom conception [25].
- *PLUS information skills model (Herring, 1996):* Developed by James Herring this model breaks information skills into four main parts (P =Purpose, L =Location, U =Use, S =Self-evaluation) and is well suited for use in schools [26].

- *SAUCE model (Trevor Bond):* It is a research and problem-solving process involving five steps—S (Set the scene)—A (Acquire)—U (Use)—C (Communicate), and E (Evaluate)—aimed to provide IL skills for learners to use in problem-solving and research [27].
- *DIALOGUE model (1998):* It involves the following processes: D (Define)—I (Initiate)—A (Assess)—L (Locate)—O (Organize)—G (Guide)—U (Use)—E (Evaluate) [28].
- *Noodle tools—Building bBlocks model (Debbie Abilock):* This model, which focuses on a set of core thinking and problem-solving meta-skills across disciplines, includes the following steps: Engaging—Defining—Initiating—Locating—Locating, Selecting, Comprehending, Assessing—Recording, Sorting, Organizing, Interpreting—Communicating, Synthesizing—Evaluating [29].
- *IFLA Empowering-8 model:* A by-product of two IFLA workshops held in Colombo (Sri Lanka) and Patiala (India), this is also a problem-solving model, which includes eight stages, viz., Identify—Explore—Select—Organize—Create—Present—Assess—Apply. This model has been specifically developed for the Asia and Pacific region [30].

Some of these models also serve as information seeking models and have been discussed in detail in the previous chapter.

D.4.6 IL Standards

Several organizations engaged in IL work have formulated IL standards, which serve as a framework for designing IL programs and also as a basis for assessment of the competency of the information literate person. Association of College and Research Libraries, a division of ALA, first brought out Information Literacy Competency Standards for Higher Education in 2000. Since then it has brought out IL standards for various sectors. These are [31]:

- Objectives for Information Literacy Instruction: A Model Statement for Academic Librarians (January 2001)
- Information Literacy Standards for Science and Technology (June 2006)
- Information Literacy Standards for Anthropology and Sociology Students (January 2008)
- Psychology Information Literacy Standards (June 2010)
- Information Literacy Standards for Teacher Education (May 2011)
- Information Literacy Competency Standards for Journalism Students and Professionals (October 2011)

- Characteristics of Programmes of Information Literacy that Illustrate Best Practices: A Guideline (January 2012)
- Information Literacy Competency Standards for Nursing (October 2013).

Standards/guidelines have also been framed by several other organizations at national and international levels.

D.4.7 IL Initiatives

Zurkowski had estimated in his report that only 1/6 of the US population really understood the emerging new information access routes and how these new routes would have a definitive impact on their economic and social lives. He observed that "people trained in the application of information resources to their work can be called information literates. They have learned techniques and skills for utilizing the wide range of information tools as well as primary sources in molding information solutions to their problems. The individuals in the remaining portion of the population, while literate in the sense that they can read and write, do not have a measure for the value of information, do not have an ability to mold information to their needs and realistically must be considered to be information illiterate" [5]. The call first given by Zurkowski in his report for the creation of a major national universal IL program by 1984 went unheeded. His vision for IL skill development was not library centric. He advocated for a universal approach in its delivery across all trades, occupations and professions. American Library Association formed a Presidential Committee on Information Literacy, which, in its report in 1989, again clearly recognized the importance of IL in a democratic society [16]. In 1990, the National Forum on Information Literacy was formed in USA with more than 85 organizational members who represented educational, business, labor, and social organizations, which had been working together to promote international and national awareness of the need of IL and to encourage activities leading to the acquisition of information skills. The forum supports, initiates, and monitors IL projects both in the United States and Abroad [10]. Association of College & Research Libraries has set up an Institute of Information Literacy, which "is dedicated to playing a leadership role in assisting individuals and institutions in integrating IL" [32]. Several universities in United States are now conducting IL programs regularly. Other countries of North America making significant progress in this direction are Canada and Mexico.

D.4.7.1 Initiatives in European Region

In United Kingdom the Standing Conference of National University Libraries created a task force in 1998 to prepare a statement on information skills for higher education. The Chartered Institute of Library and Information Professionals (CILIP) has also played an active role in promotion of IL. It created an Information Literacy Group, developed an IL website (http://www.informationliteracy.org.uk/) and started a *Journal of Information Literacy* in 2007 for this purpose. Since 2005 the Information Literacy Group, which is now a special interest group of CILIP, has been organizing a Librarians' Information Literacy Annual Conference (LILAC). Several universities are also taking active interest in imparting IL. An European Network on Information Literacy (EnIL) (http://enil.ceris.cnr.it/Basili/EnIL/) was started in 2001 for promoting interaction on IL activities at European level. In October 2013, the first European Conference on Information Literacy was held at Istanbul, which reviewed the progress of IL in different countries of Europe. Many other countries of the region such as Greece, Germany, and Sweden are also working for promotion of IL.

D.4.7.2 Initiatives in African Region

In Africa region, South Africa is in the forefront in IL movement. The country has started a noteworthy project, called INFOLIT, in 1995. It has helped the Western Cape librarians to develop curriculum integrated IL programs in academic institutions as well as schools and communities. In 2008, African Centre for Media and Literacy (AFRICMIL) was set up at Abuja in Nigeria following the resolution of the First Africa Media and Information Literacy Conference held earlier that year. It serves as a model reference point on media and IL on the continent and promotes media and IL as a key component in the education of young people in Africa. Besides, a Pan-African Alliance for Media and Information Literacy (PAMIL) has come up in 2013. PAMIL is expected to serve as an independent alliance of different organizations and individuals working on media and IL across the African Continent [33,34].

D.4.7.3 Initiatives in Asian Region

In Asia region, China has supported and encouraged the teaching of library and information skills in academic institutions since early 1980s. The Library of Chinese Academy of Sciences has also done impressive work on IL. Besides, several national conferences have been organized on the subject and also a national workshop on IL has been conducted.

In November 2004, an international workshop was held in Colombo, Sri Lanka, in collaboration with IFLA/ALP. In 2006, an International Conference on Information Literacy was organized by Universiti Teknologi, Kuala Lumpur, Malaysia, in association with Librarians Association of Malaysia. In Singapore, IL skills are taught at primary and secondary levels. In India, a good beginning toward promotion of IL was made in October 2005 with the holding of an international workshop to promote IL in south and south-east Asia by the Department of Library & Information Science, Punjabi University, Patiala, in collaboration with UNESCO and IFLA. Another Training of Trainers Workshop was also held in Patiala in 2008. The Indian Library Association (ILA) organized the 51st all India conference in December 2005 at Kurukshetra University, Kurukshetra, in which it deliberated on "Librarians, IL and lifelong learning." In this conference, ILA also recommended formation of a National Information Literacy Mission and a National Information Literacy Task Force in order to implement IL competency programs throughout the country and constitution of a high-power body to design and develop IL curricula at different levels of education [35]. At the International Conference on Knowledge Networking in ICT Era, which was organized by the Society for Advancement of Library and Information Science (SALIS) and B S Abdur Rahman Crescent Engineering College, in collaboration with UNESCO, in 2009 in Chennai, a special session was devoted on Information, Media and Digital Literacy. Several workshops have since been organized in different parts of the country in collaboration with UNESCO. Besides, a UNESCO-SALIS e-Learning Portal for Awareness Raising on Information Literacy (www.salisonline.org) has been launched. India has also joined International Alliance for Information Literacy. Networking Alliance for Voluntary Actions (http://www.navaindia.org) represents the country in the said alliance. Many LIS schools have also incorporated IL in their syllabi. But the recommendations of ILA are yet to be implemented and concerted efforts for developing IL among the masses are still not visible in the country.

D.4.7.4 Initiatives in Oceania Region

In Oceania region, academic librarians in Australia have taken a leading role in promoting IL. Council of Australian Librarians has framed Information Literacy Standards of Australia [36]. Griffith University has developed an information literacy blueprint, called Griffith Blueprint [37]. Besides, four national conferences have been organized by different university libraries. The Library and Information Association of New Zealand

(LIANZA) set up a task force on information literacy in 1998 which has taken up several initiatives [38]. Besides, information skills have been included in compulsory education in the country since 1993. Besides, Australian and New Zealand Institute for Information Literacy (ANZIIL) has also been set up, which has developed an information literacy framework that outlines what makes an information literate citizen [39].

D.4.7.5 International Initiatives

The international organizations like UNESCO and IFLA have also come forward and initiated very positive steps in promoting information literacy. The UNESCO supported an Information Literacy Meeting of Experts, organized by the US National Commission on Library and Information Science and the National Forum on Information Literacy, USA, in Prague, Czechoslovakia, in September 2003. The participants of the meeting representing 23 countries from all the seven major continents proposed a set of basic Information Literacy Principles, entitled "Towards an Information Literate Society," which came to be known as Prague Declaration, in which importance of IL in the information society was highlighted [12]. Another high-level colloquium organized by the National Forum on Information Literacy, USA, with the collaboration of UNESCO and IFLA at Bibliotheca Alexandria in November 2005, proclaimed that "information literacy and lifelong learning are the beacons of the Information Society, illuminating the courses to development, prosperity, and freedom" [11]. Under the framework of the United Nations Literacy decade (2003–12), UNESCO launched a new Information Literacy Programme during the 2004–5 biennium and again in its Strategic Plan for the "Information for All" Programme (2008–13) it identified IL as one of the priority areas and undertook a series of IL capacity-building events in different parts of the world during that period. Special mention may be made about conducting of Training the Trainers in Information Literacy Workshop, funded by IFAP, in different countries of the world such as Jamaica, Canada, Malaysia, Estonia, Turkey, South Africa, China, Spain, Egypt, Peru, and India. It cosponsored several international conferences on IL and also sponsored many projects on IL in different countries such as Nigeria, Kazakhstan, Ghana, Vietnam, Uganda, China, Congo, South Africa, and Egypt. UNESCO has also brought out several publications for promoting IL such as *Understanding information literary: a primer*, prepared by Forest Woody Horner, Jr. (2007) (http://unesdoc.unesco.org/images/0015/001570/157020E.pdf); *Guidelines for information literacy assessment*, prepared by Eileen Stec; *Towards information literacy indicators*, prepared by Ralph Catts and Jesus Lau (2008) (http://unesdoc.unesco. org/images/0015/ 001587/158723e.pdf); *Principles of Awareness-Raising for Information Literacy: A case study* (2006); *Teacher training curricula for media and information literacy: Background strategy* (2008); *Development of information literacy through school libraries in south-east Asian countries* (2006); and *information literacy competency and readership study of five specific localities in urban industrial and semi-industrial areas of Kolkata metropolitan city* (2008), etc. It has also floated a web portal on IL (http://portal.unesco.org/ci/en/ev.phpURL_ ID=15886&URL_DO=DO_TOPIC&URL_SECTION=201.html) [40]. IFLA widened the scope of its Round Table on User Education to create its "Information Literacy Section" in 2003 to foster international cooperation and leadership to promote IL efforts in all types of libraries. It has brought out *Guidelines on Information Literacy for Lifelong Learning*, prepared by Jesus Lau (2006) (http://www.ifla.org/files/assets/information-literacy/ publications/ifla-guidelines-en.pdf); and has also floated an online database *Information Literacy International Resources Directory* (http://www.infolit-global.info/directory/en/home) to record IL materials from different parts of the world, on behalf of UNESCO [41]. An International Alliance for Information Literacy (www.ceris.cur.it/Basili/Enlll/dailypage.html) has also been formed to facilitate the sharing of information and expertise on IL across regions and nations of the world.

D.5 USER EDUCATION (UED)

As early as in 1940, Ranganathan stressed on initiation of new readers of a library. He considered it to be the first phase of reference service and said "one of the first things to be done by the reference librarian is to relieve the bewilderment confronting a person coming to the library for the first time" [42]. In USA, another term came in use in 1960s, viz., Library Orientation conveying almost the same meaning. It was subsequently felt that the users not only needed such orientation when they first came to the library; they might require further training to enable them to search and make use of needed documents/information effectively. Thus a broader concept, viz., User Education came in vogue. "User education can be defined as the transfer to individual users of the techniques by which they can specify their needs and acquire, evaluate, organize and communicate information" [43]. Flemming has defined user education as "various programmes of instruction, education, and exploration provided by libraries to users to enable them to make more effective, efficient, and independent use of information sources and services to which these libraries provide access" [44]. For the purpose of a UNESCO programme, "user education and training has been defined in a generic way to include any effort or programme which will guide and instruct existing and potential users, individually or collectively, with the objective of facilitating: (a) the recognition of their own information needs; (b) the formulation of these needs; (c) the effective and efficient use of information services as well as (d) the assessment of these services" [45]. For planning an effective user education program study of information needs and information seeking behavior of the user community can be very useful. Thus, user study and user education are intimately related.

D.5.1 Need for UEd

The need for user education arises because [43,46]:
- The users are not often familiar with the library environment (i.e., collection, its arrangement, and search tools) and services, which create barriers in making efficient use of the library;
- The users are often not aware of how to search required information sources in an automated library;
- The users are not often familiar with various forms, types, and sources of information;
- The users are not always aware about existence of secondary information sources and their use to locate primary information;
- There is exponential rise in number of all kinds of information-bearing materials and it is difficult to search and identify required information from plethora of information sources;
- Several new methods of information transfer, such as the mechanized information retrieval systems, are being developed with which users are not familiar;
- Both educational and research topics are becoming increasingly multi-disciplinary in nature, thereby requiring collection of information from a wider range of sources.

D.5.2 Objectives of UEd

The main objective of conducting user education programs in a library, specially in an academic library, are [47,48]:
- Providing general orientation about facilities and resources available in the concerned library;
- Familiarizing with the organization of literature in various disciplines as well as basic reference tools in each discipline;

- Developing skills for independent information seeking and literature searching;
- Imparting training in handling information products in print and electronic forms effectively;
- Imparting training in use of information sources and services available through online, Internet, in-house database, etc.;
- Encouraging solicitation of assistance of library staff.

D.5.3 Prerequisites for UEd

For running user education programs effectively and successfully the essential prerequisites are:
- A well-thought out user education program structure;
- Availability of necessary infrastructure, including manpower and financial resources;
- Motivated and receptive users; and
- Patronage and support of the authorities of the library

D.5.4 Levels of UEd

Besides user education, several terms are in vogue denoting similar ideas, such as Library Orientation, Library Instruction, Bibliographic Instruction, User and Instruction. Though these terms are often used interchangeably by different experts, J. Rice, in his classic work *Teaching Library Use: A Guide for Library Instruction* (1981, Greenwood Press; London), has opined that Library Orientation, Library Instruction, and Bibliographic Instruction are three different levels of user education. In recent years, two more levels of user education have come into vogue, viz., User Awareness and Literature Search. Thus we can now think of five levels of user education. The nature and characteristics of these levels are briefly described below. It may be mentioned that the level or levels to be adopted in a library is to be decided on the basis of the type of library and the type of users to be served by that library.

- *User awareness:* User awareness aims "to increase user awareness of the library as a primary source of information and as an agency to which users may turn for assistance with their information needs" [49]. It is achieved through publicizing the library, with special reference to its resources and services available to the community. The methods often used for user awareness are distribution of printed guide to the library often titled "Know your library," exhibition of posters, inserting advertisement in the press, etc.

- *Library orientation*: "Library orientation provides an introduction for users to the physical library layout and selected resources and services. The more subtle objectives are to reduce user anxiety, motivate subsequent use, and promote the availability of helpful service" [50]. It is intended "(a) to familiarize users with the physical layout and the procedures for using the library units relevant to their needs, (b) to make users aware of the staff that is available to assist them and to make users comfortable seeking assistance, (c) to inform users about basic library holdings records such as card catalogue and serials list that can be used to locate materials within the system" [49]. Thus, in library orientation emphasis is given on the physical location of items and services in the library [51].
- *Library instruction:* Library instruction is more in-depth explanation of specific library materials. It includes techniques in using indexes, card catalogs, reference materials, and bibliographic tools. It often concentrates on specific subject areas to afford researchers opportunity to learn about library materials in their own fields. The aim of this stage is to provide guidance for understanding the features of specific information systems as well as information sources and tools [52].
- *Bibliographic instruction*: According to Rice, bibliographic instruction is concerned with formal courses in bibliography, while according to McAdoo, in bibliographic instruction emphasis is given on ideas and concepts typically associated with books such as card catalog, the history of books, and use/creation of bibliographies [53]. It also aims at providing assistance in understanding the subject coverage, limitation of a specific information source and in abstracting or repackaging work on retrieved information [52].
- *Literature search*: This level of user education is primarily meant for researchers. It aims at training the users in efficient searching of their relevant literature using secondary information sources. In the present context it may also include training in online literature searching.

D.5.5 Methods of UEd

In the traditional libraries, the methods that were often being used for imparting user education were lecture, guided tour including practical demonstration, distribution of printed library guide often titled "Know Your Library," individual assistance, etc. But in the new environment several new methods are being employed for the purpose, such as film/DVD show, slide show, PPT. presentation, computer-assisted instruction, conducting of work-shops, and web-based instruction. A single method may not be suitable for all users. As such, a combination of methods may be employed depending on the levels and capability of the users. Alternatively, an appropriate method may be selected for each homogenous group of users.

D.5.6 Designing UEd Program

A user education program needs to be designed carefully. The program will vary from library to library, and even user group to user group, depending upon the type and nature of the library, the type and nature of users, the type and nature of information resources available, the tools and techniques used in serving the users, the level or levels of user education to be imparted and availability of staff skilled in imparting such education. Obviously, the user education program for each level has to be designed separately. A general work-flow indicating the steps in designing and implementing a user education program may be depicted in the following diagram [52]:

D.5.7 Evaluation of UEd Program

Evaluation is the process of determining the quality of a user education program. There can be two types of evaluation: formative and summative. While formative evaluation aims at assessment of a progam's quality during the planning stage or during the instructional process, summative evaluation is done after the program is over so that future program can be planned in a better way [52]. Various methods and tools may be applied for evaluation of user education programs, such as using feedback form/questionnaire, conducting prestructured/exploratory interview, and observation.

D.5.8 Benefits of UEd

Educating users soon after they become members of a library has many benefits. Once the users are educated in a proper manner, the burden on the library staff is reduced to a great extent. The main benefits are:
- User education helps raise the information consciousness of the users;
- It enables the users to better perceive and express their information needs;
- It enables users to search and make the best use of the available information resources;

- It ensures proper handling of library resources thereby reducing the risk of their misuse and mishandling and consequent damage of the resources;
- It instills a sense of self-help among the users and saves the time of the library staff.

REFERENCES

[1] Empowerment. <http://humanresources.about.com/od/glossarye/a/empowerment_defatioand.htm>.
[2] S. Hewer, What is empowerment? School Lib. Bull. 5 (5) (1999). <http://www.qualityresearchinternational.com/glossary/empowerment.htm>.
[3] A. Chatterjee, Empowering library/information users: what, why and how. Keynote address delivered at UGC sponsored National Seminar on "User Empowerment through Information Technologies in College Libraries" organized by Ghatal Rabindra Satabarshiki Mahavidyalay Library, Paschim Medinipur, West Bengal, India. Nov. 22–23, 2011 (Unpublished).
[4] Association of College & Research Libraries (USA). Introduction to Information Literacy. <http://www.ala.org/acrl/issues/infolit/overview/intro-old>.
[5] P.G. Zurhowski, The information service environment relationships and priorities, National Commission on Libraries and Information Science (1974). <http://files.eric.ed.gov/fulltext/ED100391.pdf>.
[6] C. Curran, Information literacy and public librarian, in: A. Kent (Ed.), Encyclopaedia of Library and Information Science, V. 51, 1993, 15–172.
[7] International Alliance for Information Literacy and Lifelong Learning. <www.ceris.cur.it/Basili/EnlIl/dailypage.html>.
[8] J. Douglas, French military victories: keynote address (PPT. presentation) at LILAC, 2006. <http://www.cilip.org.uk/NR/rdonlyres/84438AF-5-E5A0-446F-BA69-CF6CC9188439/0/Douglas.ppt>.
[9] Chartered Institute of Library and Information Professionals (UK). CILIP Literacy Group. Information literacy. <http://www.informationliteracy.org.uk/definitions/il-models/>.
[10] National Forum on Information Literacy (USA). Paul G. Zurkowski. <http://infolit.org/paul-g-zurkowski/>.
[11] Bacon of Information Society: The Alexandria Proclamation on Information Literacy and Lifelong Learning. <http://archive.ifla.org/III/wsis/BeaconInfSoc.html>.
[12] The Prague Declaration: towards an information literate society. <http://www.unesco.org/new/fileadmin/MULTIMEDIA/HQ/CI/CI/pdf/PragueDeclaration.pdf>.
[13] Information Literacy in an Information Society, ERIC Digest. http://www.ericdigests.org/1995-1/information.htm.
[14] C.S. Doyle, Outcome measures for information literacy within the National Education Goals of 1990: Final report of National Forum on Information Literacy – Summary and Findings. Eric Document: ED 351033. 1992. p. 2.
[15] Information literacy. <www.wikipedia.org/wiki/Information_literacy>.
[16] American Library Association, Presidential Committee on Information Literacy. Final Report, 1989, The Association; Chicago, 1.
[17] J.S. Shapiro, S.K. Huges, Information literacy as a liberal art, Educ. Rev. 31 (2) (1996). https://net.educause.edu/apps/er/review/reviewarticles/31231.html.
[18] M. Eisenberg, R. Berkowitz, Information problem, the big six skill approach to library and information skills instruction, 1990, Ablex; Norwood, NJ.

[19] A. Irving, study and information skills across the curriculum, 1985, Heinemann Educational Books; London.

[20] C.C. Kuhlthau, Information search process: a summary of research and implications for school library media programs, *School Library Media Quarterly*, 18(1), 19–25.

[21] M.L. Pappas, A.E.Tepe, 1995, Pathways to Knowledge, Follett Software Company; Illinois. <http://www.intime.uni.edu/model/information/proc.html>.

[22] The 8Ws: Information literacy. <http://eduscapes.com/instruction/articles/topic-72model.pdf>.

[23] CILIP.Informationliteracyskills,<http://www.cilip.org.uk/cilip/advocacy-campaigns-awards/advocacy-campaigns/information-literacy/information-literacy>.

[24] SCONUL, 2011, The SCONUL 7 Pillars of Information Literacy, Core Model for Higher Education. <https://www.sconul.ac.uk/groups/information_literacy/publications/coremodel.pdf>.

[25] Website of Professor Christine Bruce. <http://www.christinebruce.com.au/informed-learning/seven-faces-of-information-literacy-in-higher-education/>.

[26] J.E. Herring,Teaching information skills in schools,The Library Association, London, 1996.

[27] SAUCE. <http://ictnz.com/SAUCE.htm>.

[28] DIALOGUE information literacy skills model. <http://www.infohio.org/about/id.htm>.

[29] NoodleTools. <http://www.noodletools.com/debbie/literacies/information/lover/infolit1.html>.

[30] IFLA Empowering 8 model of Information Literacy. <http://www.lisbdnet.com/ifla-empowering-8-model-of-information/>.

[31] Association of College & Research Libraries (USA). Information Literacy competency standards for higher education. <www.ala.org/acrl/standards>.

[32] Association of College & Research Libraries (USA). IIL Organization. <http://www.ala.org/acrl/issues/infolit/professactivity/iil/organization>.

[33] African Centre for Media and Information Literacy. <http://www.africmil.org/>.

[34] Chido Onumah. <https://en.wikipedia.org/wiki/Chido_Onumah>.

[35] Indian Library Association. All India Library Conference, 51st, Kurukshetra, 2005. Rapporteur General's report. <http://eprints.rclis.org/7340/1/ILA_Conference_RG_Report.pdf>.

[36] Council of Australian University Librarians. Information literacy standards of Australia, 2001. <http://www.caul.edu.au/caul-doc/InfoLitStandards2001.doc>.

[37] C.S. Bruce, Information literacy, a framework for higher education, Australian Library Journal 44 (3) (1995). http://www.tandfonline.com/doi/abs/10.1080/00049670.1995.10755718.

[38] Library and Information Association of New Zealand Aotearoa. <http://www.lianza.org.nz/>.

[39] A. Bundy (Ed.), Australian and New Zealand Information Literacy Framework, Principles, Standards and Practice, second edition, 2004.

[40] P. Godwin, UNESCO and Information Literacy, a Short Discussion, 2009. <http://www.sconul.ac.uk/sites/default/files/documents/unesco_godwin.pdf>.

[41] IFLA Information Literacy Section. <http://www.ifla.org/information-literacy>

[42] S.R. Ranganathan, Reference Service, second ed., Reprint. SaradaRanganathan Endowment, Bangalore, 1989. p. 81.

[43] P.S. Kwatra, Library User Studies, Jaico Publishing House, Bombay, 1992, 301.

[44] H. Fleming, User Education in Academic Libraries, Library Association Publishing Limited, London, 1990.

[45] J. Tocatlian, Training information users: programmes, problems, projects, UNESCO Bull. Lib. 32 (6) (1978) 355–362.

[46] K. Padmini, End user training in academic libraries vis-à-vis emerging technologies, in: Paper Presented at International CALIBER, 2nd, New Delhi, 2004. <http://ir.inflibnet.ac.in/bitstream/1944/321/1/04cali_14.pdf>.

[47] M. Kumbar, B.S. Birdar, User education in university libraries, in: Information Management in Academic and Research Libraries. CALIBER-98.

[48] J. Satyanarayana, et al., Library user education in digital era: a study of academic libraries, in: Libraray/information users in digital era: papers presented at All India IASLIC Conference, 27th, Bhubaneswar, India. 2009. pp. 425–432.

[49] University of Texas at Austin (USA). A comprehensive programme of user education for the general libraries, 1977.

[50] M.J. Du Mont, The evolution and reaffirmation of a library orientation programme in an academic research library, Ref. Serv. Rev. 23 (1) (1995) 85–92.

[51] National Forum on Information Literacy (USA). What is the NFIL. <http://infolit.org/about-the-nfil/what-is-the-nfil/>.

[52] T.K. Guha, Designing user education programme: a step-by-step approach, ILA Bull. 32 (3–4) (1997) 18–22.

[53] M.L. McAdoo, Fundamentals of Library Instruction, ALA, Chicago, 2012.

CHAPTER E

Organization of Information

E.1 INTRODUCTION

For providing effective information service, the information collected from the information sources need to be properly organized. Thus all those activities that help in providing effective and speedy information service are the work of information organization or documentation work. Evidently, the efficiency of information service greatly depends upon efficient organization of information. Information organization or documentation work is the foundation on which stands the edifice of documentation service or information service. Active documentation, as has been mentioned earlier, involves continuous analysis of new micro documents and preparation of aids to retrieve them. That is why Ranganathan has said that documentation work is the "work of preparing a documentation list" [1]. However, it is now felt that, besides compiling documentation lists, some more activities have to be carried out to facilitate rendering of information service.

E.2 TWO PHASES

The work of organizing information begins even before receipt of actual demands from the users. Therefore, the first phase of information organization is identification or anticipation of users' need or demand. It is indeed an important phase, as inaccurate anticipation or identification of users' need may lead to wastage of energy and money and inefficient service. On the basis of anticipated need or demand information retrieval aids are prepared or some user-friendly products are created. This is the second phase of information organization.

Elements of Information Organization and Dissemination
DOI: http://dx.doi.org/10.1016/B978-0-08-102025-8.00005-3

E.3 IDENTIFICATION OF NEED

The vital importance of this phase could not be fully realized till as late as 1950s. It is only since the beginning of 1960s that attention has been paid on conducting surveys to assess or identify the information needs of the users so that information organization work can be properly planned. Several such surveys have already been conducted yielding valuable results. When the information organization work is meant for service to a small audience, such as the staff members of a centralized research organization, it is rather easy to anticipate the need or demand through constant interaction with the users. But when it is meant for a larger audience, the job becomes very difficult. In the latter situation, only the trend may be determined or an approximate idea may be obtained; exact estimation may not be possible. The problems and methods of need identification have been discussed in an earlier chapter.

E.4 COMPILATION OF RETRIEVAL AIDS/IACR PRODUCTS

Document retrieval aids like classification and cataloging have been in existence for a long time, but these were mainly concerned with macro documents. With the emergence and onrush of micro documents, some new aids had to be evolved to cope with the situation. Even compilation of information consolidation products had to be taken up. The increased research activities also necessitated preparation of such aids which could retrieve documents or information in the shortest possible time. Computers were also pressed into service for this purpose.

E.4.1 Activities Involved

Compilation of retrieval aids/IACR products mainly proceeds in three stages:

- *Identification and location of relevant literature*: The literature which may be relevant to the users are first identified and located by searching through documents, mainly primary documents which contain nascent micro thought, like periodicals, conference papers, etc. The scanning of the primary documents should be regularly done preferably by an information worker having some basic knowledge in the subject concerned.
- *Analysis of relevant literature*: The contents of relevant documents are analyzed or bibliographical details are noted, depending upon the type of retrieval aids to be compiled.

- *Organization of analyzed information*: The analyzed information are processed and arranged in a format suitable for the target user group. The processing may also involve condensation, restructuring, or rewriting.

It may be mentioned that now-a-days many retrieval aids or information consolidation products are compiled and brought out by commercials publishers. The retrieval aids/information consolidation products which are compiled to speedily satisfy the information needs of the users are:

- Current awareness lists
- Document profile and user profile for SDI service
- Bibliographies
- Union catalogs
- Documentation lists
- Indexing periodicals
- Citation indexes
- Translation indexes
- Abstracting periodicals
- Digesting periodicals
- Review periodicals
- Trend reports
- State-of-the-art reports
- Review of progress
- Information sheets/files
- Databases, etc.

E.5 CHARACTERISTICS

It is evident from the foregoing discussion that information organization work has certain distinctive characteristics. These are [2]:

- Information organization or documentation work is done as a prelude to information service.
- It is based on anticipated or probable demands.
- It is a continuous process involving analysis and compilation of retrieval aids or IACR products.
- Organization of information may not be done at individual centers; even commercial organizations sometimes perform such work and make them available to whoever wants against payment.
- Organization of information involves some specialized techniques.

E.6 IMPORTANCE

The role of documentation/information service as an indispensable aid in research has been well described by Ranganathan on the analogy of Hindu Puranic story of churning of the milky ocean with the help of *Kurma Avatara*. Documentation, according to him, is a tool which helps churning the ocean of subjects steadily with research serving as the churn [3]. Documentation work or information organization is, then, creation or manufacturing of that vital tool and documentation service or information service is its proper application. Unless the tool is produced, there is, evidently no question of its use. Here lies the importance of information organization or documentation work.

REFERENCES

[1] S.R. Ranganathan, Documentation and its Facets, Asia Publishing House, Bombay, 1963, Ch. B3.
[2] A. Chatterjee, Elements of Documentation, The Author, Calcutta, 1983. p. 20.
[3] S.R. Ranganathan, Documentation: Genesis and Development, Vikas, New Delhi, 1973. p. 57.

CHAPTER F

Information Service

F.1 INTRODUCTION

The term "Information Service" may refer to any service which is "intended to provide information for a client or user, or assist a client or user in finding information" [1]. Thus, it may include any service rendered by a library or information center such as reference service and even document lending service. But in the context of specialist users, who require "nascent micro documents," or pin-pointed information, information service will mean documentation service or "passive documentation," i.e., actual provision of such documents or information to the users as distinct from active documentation or organization of information. Information service thus aims at dissemination of information to the users. According to Ranganathan, "documentation service" is "a new term used to denote reference service, when the emphasis is on service of micro documents—particularly of nascent micro documents—and on specialist readers" [2]. The efficiency of such service obviously depends upon the quality of retrieval aids/IACR products used to provide that service and of course on the efficiency of the documentalist or information worker.

F.2 FOUR PHASES

Information service is given in response to actual demands received from the users. Most of the users are not, however, able to express their demands in precise terms. Enunciation of exact demand is, therefore, the first phase of activities for providing information service. After ascertaining the clear scope of the information requirements, it is necessary to search through pertinent secondary and primary documentary information sources and identify the relevant literature. Thus, searching and identification of relevant literature are the activities of the second phase. The third phase of activities for providing information service involves collection of pertinent documents and/or processing and arranging of information in presentable form and the final phase is dissemination, i.e., transmission of information or information bearing documents to the users.

Elements of Information Organization and Dissemination
DOI: http://dx.doi.org/10.1016/B978-0-08-102025-8.00006-5
99

F.3 UNDERSTANDING USER NEEDS

Before embarking upon search of documents or information, it is necessary to have a clear idea about the exact nature and scope of the requirements of the users as "in most cases, correctly stating the problem to be
pursued is half the battle" [3]. It is more so because the information service is aimed at specialists whose requirements relate to nascent micro
documents. No specialist can be satisfied unless his/her exact area of interest is ascertained and information are supplied accordingly. If any user is
unable to express his/her demands in clear-cut terms, which is often the
case, he/she should be helped to do so by the information professional
through discussion and questioning. Ranganathan said that "the first step
in serving an actively participating specialist is to get the subject brought
up by him/her enunciated precisely. This is best done by judicious questions based on facet analysis" [3]. An alternative method may be showing the descriptors from a thesaurus on the relevant subject field to the
user and getting his/her queries expressed by him/her in terms of descriptors. Once the specialists become trained in placing the demands in exact
terms, the job of the information worker becomes easy.

F.4 SEARCHING

For efficient searching work, it may be helpful to formulate a search strategy at the outset. Formulation of search strategy involves fixing up the
sequence of the tools which are likely to be used in conducting the search.
For an experienced informational professional it is not a very difficult task.
In fact such a strategy takes shape in his/her mind as he/she proceeds on
enunciating the demands of a user in a precise manner. Literature or information search may be done using one or more of the following [4]:
* *Indexes and indexing periodicals*: Indexes list micro documents in a systematic manner. As such, a search through these may help identify the
  relevant documents easily and quickly. Indexes are perhaps the most
  used search tools of the information worker.
* *Abstracting periodicals*: As abstracts give an idea about the contents of
  documents, they are very useful for selection of pertinent documents.
  In areas where abstracting periodicals are available, they can be more
  profitably used for searching purpose. Sometimes an abstract itself may
  satisfy a user.
* *Digesting periodicals*: A digesting periodical also helps in identifying important documents in a field. A digesting periodical may itself

sometimes satisfy a user as a digest contains all the significant information contained in the original documents, though in a condensed
form.

- *Review periodicals*: As a review periodical surveys the most important
  works of original research, it can help in identifying the literature of
  high quality.

- *Citation indexes*: Citation indexes may be searched for finding out the
  documents which contain related ideas.

- *Translation indexes*: When the language of a relevant document is not
  intelligible to a user, translation indexes may have to be searched to
  locate translation of the document in required language.

- *Bibliographies*: Bibliographies, especially subject bibliographies, may have
  to be searched when a user's demand includes both macro and micro
  literature in a specified subject area.

- *Catalogs*: Catalogs—both local and union catalog—are searched for
  locating relevant documents. Searching in union catalogs is necessary
  for locating such documents which are not available locally.

- *Databases*: Databases—available in both offline and online mode—may
  be searched for collecting the relevant information.

- *Internet/www*: Since valuable information are now available on the
  web, necessary information may be searched on the Internet using any
  search engine.

- *Original documents*: Original documents may have to be scanned when
  a user wants some specific information and is not satisfied with whole
  documents.

It may be pointed out here that identification of relevant documents/
information goes on simultaneously with the search work.

F.5 MAKING PRESENTABLE

After searching and identification of relevant documents or information it
is necessary to collect the documents in original or in reproduced form or
arrange the information in an order that is convenient for consultation by
the user. As such, the activities involved in this phase may be as follows [3]:

- *Preparation of reading lists*: The bibliographical details of documents
  which are identified to be relevant for a user or a group of users are
  noted down, i.e., entries are prepared for these documents which are
  then arranged in any convenient manner in the form of a list. This is
  called a reading list. Any item of such a list may have to be procured, if
  asked for by the user concerned.

- *Procurement of original documents*: The relevant documents are procured for the users either from the local library or from any other library through interlibrary loan.
- *Arranging for translation*: The required translation may be located through translation indexes and procured from translation pools on loan or by payment, as the case may be. If translation of a document is not available, arrangement may have to be made to get it translated. Further discussion on this topic may be found in a later chapter.
- *Preparation of copies of documents*: When an original document is not available in a particular library, or when it is available but cannot be issued to a user due to it being rare and out-of-print or in heavy demand or in damaged condition, or when a user himself/herself wants a copy, arrangement has to be made to procure a copy of the document or get it copied.
- *Preparation of information sheets*: The items of information searched out and collected for a user are to be arranged and presented in a suitable manner for the convenience of the user. This work is done automatically if the whole system is computerized.

F.6 TRANSMISSION

Once the documents or information are ready for transmission, the users concerned are contacted and their required materials are handed over, their reactions are noted and further service is planned. It may be mentioned here that if the whole process is mechanized, and the items to be served are only information, the last three phases are gone through without any pause and the user is able to get his demand fulfilled in shortest possible time.

F.7 CHARACTERISTICS OF INFORMATION SERVICE

From the foregoing discussions we may find out the following distinctive characteristics of information service [4]:
- Information service is the ultimate goal of all information organization work.
- It is based on actual and expressed demands of the users.
- It is mainly concerned with searching, locating, and supply of documents or information.
- Information service is provided by individual centers or libraries.

F.8 INFORMATION SERVICE IN DIGITAL ENVIRONMENT

In traditional environment, searching is mainly carried out by the library staff, but in the digital environment searching may be mediated or non-mediated, i.e., the user may himself/herself search his/her required information/document from online of CD-ROM databases or the library may mediate between the user and the information sources. In the latter case a designated library staff performs search on behalf of the user and serves the retrieved information to him/her. Mediated search and non-mediated search can also be called delegated search and non-delegated search. The searching work in digital environment also proceeds in four main phases—understanding user needs, formulating search strategy, searching database, and disseminating retrieved information.

F.8.1 Understanding User Needs

The results of a search depend heavily upon the correct understanding of the users' precise needs [5]. This understanding can be developed through pre-search interview. This is crucial if the client is not to be present during the actual search. A pre-search interview is a conversation that takes place between a user and an information staff with a view to assess the actual information requirement of the user [6]. At this stage possible keywords to be employed in searching may be finalized in consultation with the user.

F.8.2 Search Strategy Formulation

Formulation of an effective search strategy is also very vital for the success of searching. Formulation of search strategy involves the following [7]:
- *Database selection*: Selection of a database depends upon the subject of the query and specialty of the database. It also depends upon depth and breadth of coverage of indexed resources in the database, coverage of indexed resources by regions and countries, and accessibility to database archive for retrospective searching and full-text searching.
- *Query formulation*: Query may be formulated for simple search or compound search depending upon the need of the user concerned. Besides, there can be also advanced search using various devices.
  - Simple query: In simple query, only keywords (or descriptors taken from a controlled vocabulary) are used. Sometimes, a phrase is also used in place of keywords. In such cases only records matching the phrase can be retrieved. If phrase is too long, chances of finding records matching the query is reduced. In case only keywords (i.e.,

without any operator) are used to express the query; the search output comprises records containing one or more keywords matching the query. Thus, the greater the number of keywords in the query the larger would be the size of the search output.

- Compound query: One of the strategies to keep the search output small is to construct a compound query using Boolean operators OR, AND, NOT. These can be used to group search terms to broaden or narrow the results of a search. Boolean searching is a method of combining search terms either to retrieve more documents (by using OR as the Boolean operator) or a smaller and more precise set of documents (by using AND or NOT as the Boolean operator). Most databases and search engines allow Boolean searching, but may also use special characters or commands. AND retrieves items in which both terms are found, e.g., adult AND community. OR retrieves items in which either term is found, e.g., adult OR community. NOT retrieves items in which the first term is present but the second term is not, e.g., information NOT knowledge. In other words, AND narrows a search, OR expands a search, and NOT excludes terms from the search.

- Advanced search: Simple or compound search can be further refined in the following ways:
  - Limiting the search: Many database search engines provide the facility to limit the search to any one or more fields, say, title, author, descriptors, language, publication year, and country of publication.
  - String search: Many database search engines allow searching data fields for character strings that are not in the index. For example, character string "adult education and learning" can be searched by employing string search technique. This facility is particularly useful in searching for specific characters.
  - Proximity search: Proximity operator between two terms is used to find records that contain both terms in the same field. For example, when searching for "adult WITH literacy," the word "adult" and the word "literacy" would both appear in the same search field. This operator can thus be used to make a search more precise than using the AND operator. Some search engines use the term "SAME" in place of "WITH" to represent proximity operator.

- Order of precedence: Parentheses override the order of precedence when using multiple Boolean and/or Proximity operators. The search statement "house★ and (finance$ or loan$)" retrieves documents that contain some variant of the word house and either one (or both) of the terms in the parenthesis.
- Truncation: Truncation can be used in a number of different ways: (a) at the end of the word to retrieve all mentions of the word, all forms of a root in cases of irregular plurals, and to retrieve more than one character (e.g., Lite★ will retrieve Literacy, Liter, Literature, Literate) and (b) internal truncation or wildcard characters to retrieve alternate spellings of words (e.g., Color$ will retrieve Color as well as Colour).

- *Search statement formulation*: Based on the decisions about type of search, a search statement is prepared which shows keywords used for expressing search query with or without operators.

F.8.3 Searching and Dissemination

Once search strategy is ready, the selected database is searched, and the search results, along with scanned images of relevant portions of identified documents, if necessary, are transmitted to the user concerned through intranet or as e-mail attachment, as the case may.

F.9 IMPORTANCE OF INFORMATION SERVICE

Ranganathan considered information service or documentation service as the hub of all library work. He felt that this service was not only inseparable from other items of library work, it held the focal position among them. Information service or documentation service, according to him, discloses [2]:

- the richness and the poverty of the library collection;
- the helpfulness or the unhelpfulness of the classification done;
- the inadequacies of added entries in the catalog—particularly the main reference entries;
- the helpfulness or otherwise of the sequence in which the main subjects are arranged; and
- groups of seldom-used documents obstructing a helpful continuous browsing of the documents in current use.

REFERENCES

[1] J. Koren, What is information service, 2007 version. <http://www.slideshare.net/joh5700/what-are-information-services2007-version>.

[2] S. R. Ranganathan, Documentation: Genesis and Development, Vikas, New Delhi, 1973. p. 30 Ch. Q.

[3] S. R. Ranganathan, Reference Service, Asia, Bombay, 1961. p. 219, 363.

[4] A. Chatterjee, Elements of Documentation, The Author, Calcutta, 1983.

[5] C. J. Armstrong, J. A. Large, Manual of Online Search Strategies, Gower, Aldershot, 1988.

[6] G. G. Chowdhury, Information Retrieval Systems, IASLIC, Calcutta, 1994. p. 74.

[7] S. M. Dhawan, Information dissemination services. <http://www.unesco.org/education/aladin/paldin/pdf/course02/unit_06.pdf>.

CHAPTER G

Current Awareness Service

G.1 INTRODUCTION

The clients of a library or documentation/information center do not have identical requirements. Their needs widely vary. While some are satisfied with a few bits of information, some want exhaustive materials on their areas of interest; some again come with an intention to update their knowledge or skill and some others want literature to keep themselves abreast of the latest developments in their fields of interest or work. Thus, their approaches to information also vary. As has already been mentioned earlier, there are four types of approaches of readers, viz., current approach, everyday approach, exhaustive approach, and catching-up or brushing-up approach. These approaches have vital impacts on the institutions providing information services as they have to find ways and means to satisfy these approaches.

G.2 CURRENT APPROACH

Current approach demands continuous provision of latest information on a broad subject field. In this approach no specific information is required and no specific question is to be answered. Often the users do not require original documents; they are satisfied by obtaining brief information only. Libraries had been satisfying this approach with the help of indexing and abstracting services and with original documents. But as the quantity of documents began to multiply speedily and the contents or coverage of documents became complex and complicated, gradually it became difficult to satisfy this approach with the existing tools. Users have no time to scan the large volume of current materials and the indexing and abstracting journals cannot handle the huge mass of literature in required speed to communicate the latest information quickly. As a result, the time gap between the actual birth of an information or micro document and its dissemination started increasing. Mainly to bridge this gap, new media of dissemination started emerging in 1950s. As these media are meant to

Elements of Information Organization and Dissemination
DOI: http://dx.doi.org/10.1016/B978-0-08-102025-8.00007-7

make the users aware of the current information, they have come to be known as current awareness services (CASs) [1].

G.3 DEFINITION OF CAS

CAS is then an information service aimed at providing current information to the users in shortest possible time. Strauss, Shreve, and Brown have described CAS as "a system for reviewing publications immediately upon receipt, selecting information pertinent to the programme of the organization served and noting individual items to be brought to the attention, by one means or other, of those persons to whose work they are related" [2]. In short, it is a method or technique of communicating current information to the users. Though Ranganathan did not use the term "current awareness service," he mentioned about a documentation periodical which lists "the documents appearing during the period covered, and without being selected to suit the requirements of a particular reader or of a specific topic under investigation". He further said that "this is of the nature of a general appetizer. It endeavors to keep the clientele informed promptly of all the nascent thought created in their fields of work and related fields" [3]. This list is nothing but a current awareness list (CAL).

G.3.1 Comprehensive View

The most appropriate and comprehensive definition of CAS has been provided by Guha, who says "a CAS is a device of the information system, through which the users of information can be informed promptly, as soon as possible after publication, but before absorption into the comprehensive secondary sources, of current literature on a broad subject field or on an area in which a group of persons are interested, and presented in a manner, volume and rhythm intended to facilitate or cultivate current approach to information" [4].

G.4 NEED FOR CAS

CAS is needed for [5]:
- Keeping the specialists and professionals better informed in their respective fields of interest
- Supporting and sustaining research, study, teaching, and business
- Helping the specialists/professionals in searching and retrieving relevant information, speedily, thus saving their time, input, and money
- Providing information in a preferred format for reuse.

G.5 CHARACTERISTICS OF CAS

CAS, as compared to other methods of documentation service, has certain distinct characteristics. They are as follows [6]:
- It is designed to meet the users' current approach to information.
- It gives a bird's eye-view of the latest development in any field and does not provide answer to any specific query.
- The subject covered is usually a broad one so that the users can not only know about developments in their own areas, but also about that in related subjects which may be relevant in their own fields of work.
- The most important aspect of CAS is speed or timeliness.
- As users have no search strategy, the items of information are so arranged that scanning can be done easily.
- It is for temporary use, i.e., for use before its contents are absorbed by indexing and abstracting journals.

G.6 PREREQUISITES OF CAS

There are four major prerequisites for an effective CAS [5]:
- Knowing what topics to cover
- Knowing who wants what
- Knowing the sources for obtaining the latest information
- Supplying the information regularly and reliably.

G.7 MEDIA OF CAS

There are various methods, sources or media through which current information can be obtained, some of them being informal and others formal. The informal methods are discussion with researchers working in the same field, exchange of off-prints and private letters and attending meetings, seminars, and conferences, while the formal methods are regular scanning of current issues of journals and reading book-reviews and advertisements relating to books and journals. As all the informal channels are not available to everybody, most people have to depend more on formal media.

G.8 NEW MEDIA OF CAS

With speedy rise in number of documents, it gradually became difficult to regularly scan the huge mass of literature even in one area of knowledge and keep track of the development in the area concerned. Such a rise also resulted in slowing down of the speed of the existing media. Consequently, some new media had to be developed so as to bridge the time gap between the generation of information and their communication through formal channels like indexing and abstracting journals. The new media thus developed were [1]:

- Current awareness list
- Current contents
- Routing of periodicals
- Selective dissemination of information
- Research-in-progress
- Forthcoming meetings
- Newspaper clippings.

G.8.1 Current Awareness List

Also known as "Title Announcement Service," Current Awareness List (CAL) is a type of documentation list which usually covers information about articles in current issues of periodicals, recently published research and technical reports and other macro documents on a broad subject field arranged in some convenient order for easy and quick scanning. A CAL manifests the recent developments in a subject field "through a judicious selection and featuring of the current literature in the field." Such lists are not, nevertheless, completely new. Even before the emergence of this distinct type of medium in 1950s some libraries had been bringing out periodical bulletins to make their clientele aware of the recent materials acquired by them. But in most cases the emphasis in these bulletins was not on micro documents.

G.8.1.1 Compiling Agencies

CALs are brought out at different levels. Individual libraries bring out local lists which are called local documentation lists or local CALs. Some organizations at the national level such as national libraries, national documentation/information centers, or national bibliography units also bring out CALs, which are circulated not only among its direct members but also among other libraries and documentation/information centers in the country. Similarly, some organizations at the international level or professional organizations or indexing/abstracting services also bring out such lists. CALs are also sometimes compiled and circulated on commercial basis, i.e., against some subscription or payment. However, a local CAL can provide more efficient service than other types. It is because the users, for whom it is prepared, are local, possibly working in the same organization, and as such the items may be selected keeping in view the exact nature of requirements of the users which can be easily assessed. Local lists can also be modified as and when required. But these advantages are not available with other CALs, as the community served by them remains at a long distance and their responses are not readily available. A few examples of different types of CALs are given below:

- *EQUATOR Oncology Project Quarterly Current Awareness Bulletin* (Enhancing the Quality and Transparency of Health Research)
- *NASA Spaceline* CAL (USA)
- *Current Awareness Bulletin* (International Maritime Organization, London)
- *Current Awareness Bulletin* (Centre for Women's Development Studies, New Delhi).

G.8.1.2 Arrangement of Contents

The contents of CALs are arranged in either of the following ways [1]:

- *Classified arrangement*: According to this method the entries are arranged by class numbers constructed on the basis of a recognized classification scheme. Such an arrangement, especially if it is based on a scheme which provides coextensive numbers and presents APUPA (Alien-Penumbral-Umbral-Penumbral-Alien) arrangement, is very helpful for easy scanning as class numbers bring together materials on a field scattered in different documents. But such arrangement is usually time consuming. Classified arrangement also necessitates preparation of an alphabetical index which further delays the process. Besides, classification of nascent micro thought may be sometimes difficult. As such this arrangement may not be favored for a CAL unless there is enough number of staff available to do the work speedily.
- *Broad subject grouping*: Another way of arranging entries in a CAL is under broad subject headings. It is especially useful when the CAL covers a group of subjects rather than a single subject. As the entries are not classified according to any classification scheme, compilation of the list does not take much time. It is also easy for the readers to consult as they do not have any definite search strategy. The only difficulty with this method is that sometimes it becomes difficult to place an entry under any specific subject heading. In such circumstances the items may be mentioned at one place with cross reference entries under other probable subject headings.

- *Division-wise grouping*: Entries in a CAL may also be grouped under names of divisions or projects of a particular organization. This method is very suitable for adoption in local lists. Although such an arrangement may be liked by the users, they may develop a tendency to look into specific items of their current interest and ignore those which may be of partial or of future interest. This arrangement has all the advantages of arrangement under broad subject headings, but it cannot be profitably employed in a list meant for users outside the organization. Besides, when there is any reorganization of divisions or restructuring of projects, the headings will have to be changed promptly.
- *Alphabetical arrangement*: When the number of items to be displayed is small, they may be arranged alphabetically by author or title. As the CAL caters information about nascent micro thought, the users are not expected to know the names of authors or titles of documents. Therefore, alphabetical arrangement will have no other function than to bring only some sort of order among the items. The users will have to scan through all the items as their relevant materials may remain scattered under various alphabets. This arrangement is sometimes preferred to do the job mechanically in shortest possible time.
- *Chronological arrangement*: Chronological arrangement is an arrangement according to date or time. This arrangement is employed when the information arranged are either news items (these may be more conveniently arranged under broad subject headings) or historical or biographical items.

G.8.2 Current Contents

Also known as "contents-by-journal," it is the most quick and easy process of providing CAS. The contents pages of all the current issues of journals received in the library are reproduced and stitched together and sent to the users at regular intervals. The work can be done almost mechanically as it requires very little intellectual activity. The contents pages may be arranged in any convenient order and these may be photocopied. Current contents has a distinct advantage of easy scanning facility, but it may psychologically prompt the users to look into contents pages of only those journals which they are accustomed to consult. *Current Contents*, published by the Institute for Scientific Information (now part of Thomson Reuters), USA; *Current Contents: Life* Sciences, published by Japan Society of Geoinformatics; *Current Contents in Management: Marketing*, brought out by National Information Centre on Management, Indian Institute of

Management, Ahmedabad, India, etc. are good examples of contents-by-journal. It may be mentioned here that some periodicals regularly publish contents pages of their own future issues or sometimes contents pages of other journals published on the same subject.

G.8.3 Routing of Periodicals

Another method of CAS, which is not a completely new one but widely used, is routing of periodicals, i.e., circulation of journal issues among the users in turn. For effective routing, it is necessary to predetermine which titles are to be circulated, among whom and in what order. The greatest limitation of this method is that all the users cannot get an issue simultaneously. As such, routing lists should be prepared in such a manner that a user can get priority for an issue according to the degree of its relevance to him. However, no user should be allowed to retain an issue beyond a specified period as otherwise the whole process will be delayed. Routing can be done more speedily if each user on the routing list passes on an issue to the one next in line and the last person returns it to the library. An issue of a periodical can, however, be taken for further study by any reader when it is released for loan. The process can be more useful and time-saving for a user if his relevant items are marked while sending an issue to him.

G.8.4 Selective Dissemination of Information

As has been mentioned earlier, SDI is organized to disseminate latest information in quickest possible time to each individual reader keeping in view his own specific area of interest. The next chapter provides a detailed discussion on this topic.

G.8.5 Research-in-progress

Research-in-progress provides information regarding the various research projects undertaken in one research organization or a group of such organizations. Its coverage may be sometimes limited by some specific area of knowledge. Each entry in such a publication may contain the following details: (a) title of the research project, (b) a brief account of the scope, (c) name(s) of research worker(s), (d) name of the sponsoring body, (e) target date for completion of the work, and (f) the source where the preliminary results have been reported or are expected to be reported. Research-in-progress, published either in the form of a directory or a periodical, helps (a) plan new research projects, (b) avoid research-in-parallel, and (c) anticipate birth of new information [6]. Thus, the consumers of information can remain alert and obtain new information speedily. *Progress Report on Brain Research*, published by Dana Foundation (USA) is a good example of this type of publication (*see also* "Research Paper" section in Chapter B).

G.8.6 Forthcoming Meetings

Considerable amount of new and useful information are generated in seminars conferences, meeting, etc. The consumers of information may directly collect such information by attending these events long before such information are covered by some journals or proceedings. Interested persons should be provided with prior information to enable them to attend such meetings. Although individual notices are issued for this purpose, it may not reach all the intending participants. As such a new channel was started by some national and international organizations for making advance notification about important meetings, e.g., *Scientific Meetings*, published quarterly by Special Libraries Association of USA, *World Meetings*, published quarterly by World Meeting Information Centre Inc., USA. Some newspapers, periodicals, and newsletters also bring out such notices. The following details are usually included in the meeting notices: topic for discussion, rules and deadline for submitting papers, speakers or important participants, venue, date, time, and rules, if any, for attending the meeting. Of late, directories listing forthcoming meetings are available on the Internet, e.g., *Conal: Conference Alert* (http://www.conferencealerts.com/), *All Conference Alert.Com* (http://www.allconferencealert.com/india.php), etc.

G.8.7 News Clipping Service

Clippings are the most current sources of information on any event. Till the news items are reshaped and included in digesting periodicals and yearbooks, there is no other substitute for these. To provide current materials quickly, it is necessary to make arrangement in a library for regular clipping and their maintenance in a suitable order. Usually paper clippings are stored in vertical file cabinets with subject headings on the folder tabs. Many organizations now provide this service, especially in online mode. Some examples of such newspaper clipping services are:

- *NewspaperClips.com* (http://www.newspaperclips.com/) of USA, which monitors both social media and traditional news media, combines it with comprehensive measurement and analysis tools, and delivers it online to the clients.

- *VIPRIS Clipset* brought out by VIgyan PRasar Information System (VIPRIS), a Government of India organization, which provides selected clippings of news items and feature articles on science, technology, and environment collected from more than 100 newspapers and news magazines and classified under seventeen subject areas [7].

G.9 IMPORTANCE OF CAS

CAS has, no doubt, come as a great boon to the users' community. The latest information and techniques developed in various fields can be brought to the notice of the users at the shortest possible time. This quickens the pace of research and development. As such, CAS is now considered as one of the important activities of documentation/information service. The main advantages of CAS are:

- It satisfies and/or helps in cultivating current approach to information
- It helps in keeping track of new developments or trends in a specific field of interest
- It supplements the user's own channels or media of obtaining information.

G.10 CURRENT TREND

It was H.P. Luhn, who, in 1958, proposed for the first time the use of computers for providing CAS. During 1960–1980, various computerize CASs and the use of CAS in specific business sectors were reported. Subsequently, several organizations started providing electronic CASs of different kinds such as electronic tables of contents, SDI services using CD-ROM databases, and e-mailing of search results [5]. Automation and networking of libraries also made it possible to provide CASs through organizational intranets and library networks. Emergence of Internet made it possible to start web based CAS. Modern procedures and techniques of CAS include individual notification of published information. Silverplatter, NISC, Ovid, Dialog, and Faxon allow the users to save profiles for this purpose. Some important websites which provide CAS are [8]:

- *Bibliotech review*—This site provides nascent information on global development of library automation industry. URL: http://www.gadget-server.com/bibliotech.

- *Current cites*—This is a monthly bibliography of some selected titles of books and electronic documents on information technology. URL: http://sunsite.berkeley.edu/currentcites/.
- *Oxford Journals' table of content service*—It provides contents of current journals published by Oxford University Press. URL: http://www3.oup.co.uk/jnls/tocmail/.
- *Scholarly article research alerting*—It provides table of contents of any of its 200 academic journals. URL: http://www.carfax.co.uk/sara.htm.

E-mail alerts, SMS alerts, and RSS feeds are also now being widely used for rendering CAS.

REFERENCES

[1] A. Chatterjee, Elements of Documentation, The Author, Calcutta, 1983.
[2] L. J. Strauss, et al., Scientific and Technical Libraries, second ed., Becker and Hayes, New York, 1972. p. 239.
[3] S. R. Ranganathan, Documentation and Its Facets, Asia, Bombay, 1963. Ch. B3.
[4] B. Guha, Documentation and Information, second ed., World Press, Calcutta, 1983. p. 46.
[5] A. Mishra, Current awareness service: a contemporary issue in digital era. <http://www.slideshare.net/anilmlis/current-awareness-service-a-contemporary-issue-in-digital-era-anil-mishra>.
[6] B. Guha, Current awareness service, In: Training course in documentation and information services (October 11–December 13, 1975): course material. 1976. INSDOC, New Delhi, Sec. IV. 4.4.
[7] Vigyan Prasar Science Portal. <http://www.vigyanprasar.gov.in/publication/vipris%20clipset.asp>.
[8] S. R. Hatua, Web based library and information services. A seminar presentation. ADIS, 1999–2001 session. DRTC, Bangalore, 2001. (Unpublished).

CHAPTER H

Selective Dissemination of Information

H.1 INTRODUCTION

A type of manual information service, in which librarians scanned new issues of journals and new books and notified the users of documents of probable relevance to their work had long been an established practice in libraries. But the term "Selective Dissemination of Information" (SDI) came into prominence in the literature of scientific communication only in late 1950s and 1960s. Hans Peter Luhn's paper, *A Business Intelligence System*, was probably the first published description of a system that used computer for the SDI. Luhn included SDI as a part of his design for a larger "Business Intelligence System," which also included information retrieval and a communication facility. The actual system proposed by Luhn was never implemented, but it served as a basis for planning a number of computerized SDI systems. A mechanized SDI system based on Luhn's design was first implemented in 1959 at the Advanced Systems Development Division of the IBM Corporation at New York, which came to be known as SDI-1 [1]. Subsequently, SDI-2, SDI-3, SDI-4, and SDI-5 have also been developed and experimented upon. SDI has now become an essential service in most of the special libraries and information centers.

H.2 DEFINITION OF SDI

An SDI service is a type of "alerting service" meant for individual users, mainly specialists, which is exclusively restricted to the area of interest of the user concerned. In other words, it is a user-oriented current awareness service. Strauss, Shreve, and Brown described it as "a refinement of the current awareness idea......that is designed to serve the individual scientist directly" [2], while Elhance explained it as "a type of personalized current awareness service which, under optimum conditions, involves screening of documents, selecting information exactly tailored to meet the specific research needs of each user or a group of users and supplying the

Elements of Information Organization and Dissemination
DOI: http://dx.doi.org/10.1016/B978-0-08-102025-8.00008-9
117

information directly to each individual or group so that the user can keep himself abreast of the latest developments in the area of his specialization" [3]. In short, SDI is "a personalized service, whereby individuals or groups of scientists are notified about the existence of current literature of potentially high utility to them" [4]. In the words of Luhn himself, it is "that service within an organization which concerns itself with the channeling of new items of information, from various sources to those points within the organization, where they can usefully serve someone's interest" [5].

H.3 NEED AND OBJECTIVES OF SDI

The information needs of any two users hardly tally with each other. They may be sometimes similar, but rarely identical. Their areas of interest also, as Luhn has pointed out, do not "conform with the conventional concepts of disciplines" [5]. As such, if a user wants to keep himself/herself posted with the new developments in his/her area of interest, he/she will have to scan through a large mass of literature that may be available not only on the "umbral" region of his/her subject of interest, but also on the "penumbral" region too. This is a huge task and perhaps physically impossible. The indexing and abstracting services and other CAS media may be of some help to him/her, but cannot satisfy him/her fully as even in those lists he/she will have to look through all the items for his/her required materials. Besides, by the time the indexing and abstracting journals cover the same information, their relevance may be reduced or lost. Because of all these reasons, SDI is now being adopted by more and more institutions. The main objectives of an SDI service, therefore, are:
- To keep a specialist personally informed of all the documents relevant to his/her interest;
- To save his/her time by "screening out irrelevant information, thus making the 'information explosion' a manageable problem" [4].

Thus SDI helps users to overcome the problem of information overload by effecting information filtering based on their needs.

H.4 CHARACTERISTICS OF SDI

It is evident from the foregoing discussions that SDI has four important characteristics. They are [6]:
- It is a personalized service meant for individual user or group of users with near identical areas of interest;

- It is a user-oriented service provided with clear understanding of the specific interests of the users;
- It is a speedy device, which provides information long before they are incorporated in indexing and abstracting periodicals;
- It has no provision of scanning as the service is pinpointed.

H.5 WORK-FLOW OF SDI

An SDI system is mainly based on two types of profiles—users' profiles and documents' profiles—which are matched to decide about the relevance of any new documents for an individual user. The workflow in an SDI system may be better explained through the following diagrammatic chart [6].

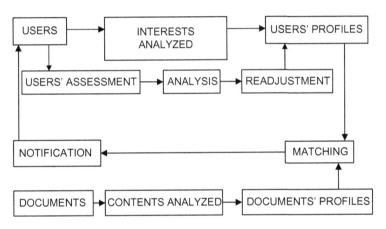

Workflow of SDI.

H.5.1 Users' Profiles

The first decision one has to take before starting an SDI service is about the group of users to whom this service is aimed at. The needs and interests of each user or a group having similar interests are ascertained and carefully analyzed. These are then expressed in terms of some keywords or code numbers. The usual practice is adoption of keywords from an accepted thesaurus. The individual profiles thus prepared are then filed together. This is called users' profile file. It may be pointed out here that making and maintenance of users' profile file are a vital part of the whole system, without which SDI will have no meaning at all. The work may be done by a user himself with the help of a manual supplied to him for this purpose, or by the SDI staff in collaboration with the user.

H.5.2 Documents' Profiles

As the documents come to the library, their contents are clearly analyzed and the unit concepts or facets are expressed in the same keywords, symbols, or code numbers which have been used in users' profiles, so that matching is possible. The individual profiles of documents so prepared are filed together. This is called documents' profile file. This work is done by the SDI staff.

H.5.3 Profile Matching

The above two profile files are matched at regular intervals. When positive results are obtained, that is, a close resemblance between a user's profile and a document's profile is found, the necessary details from both the profiles are recorded. For carrying out matching work effectively, it is necessary to determine beforehand a level of match for each user. Existence of what minimum number of concepts (keywords) and what combination of them in a document will make the document suitable for each user should be found out and noted on respective profiles for this purpose. Instructions provided by the users and analysis of responses received from them may help determine the best level of match.

H.5.4 Notification

Intimation is sent to a particular user, with whose profile the profile of a document matches closely. Thus he/she is alerted about the presence of a document in the library which may be of relevance to him/her. The notification may carry only minimum details necessary for identification of the document or abstract/keywords of the contents of the document along with the bibliographical details. Sometimes, a copy of the document or the document itself is also sent.

H.5.5 Feedback

There should be a mechanism in the SDI system for feedback from the side of the users. A printed card or sheet may be sent to each user along with the notification in which he/she has to indicate how far the reference supplied has been of use to him/her. The response of a user may also be assessed by observing whether mere bibliographical details were enough or he/she requested for an abstract or a copy of the document. The response may also sometimes take the form of referral response, when a user on getting an intimation, informs the SDI unit that the document referred to him may be of interest to another particular user. Although feedback is a very important aspect, which can improve the efficiency of an SDI system, it is often neglected. Through this mechanism, it is possible to detect slightest change in the interests of the users.

H.5.6 Readjustment

For improving the service of an SDI system, it is necessary to carefully analyze the views of the users obtained by above methods and modify the users' profiles, if necessary. Such modification is called readjustment, rejuvenation or updating. Continuous readjustment of the profiles certainly helps in raising the efficiency level of the system.

H.6 OPERATION OF SDI

Though when Luhn first spelt out his idea of SDI, he visualized the use of computer in SDI service, in practice, the operation of an SDI system can also be done manually. If the number of users is small and the area of coverage is not large, a manually operated SDI system can provide a fairly satisfactory service. In fact the idea of mechanized SDI system gained momentum when some computerized information systems and a few big indexing and abstracting services such as Institute of Scientific Information, Philadelphia, Chemical Abstracts Service, and MEDLARS began producing and making available files of large volume of documents in machine-readable forms, specially on magnetic tapes. These tapes, which were less expensive and had wider coverage as compared to an individual SDI system, could be conveniently used as documents' profiles. By compiling a users' profile file separately, any institution could easily start its own SDI service.

H.7 ADVANTAGES OF SDI

The SDI service has many distinct advantages as compared to other services provided by a library. These are [6]:

- It is possible to give a "tailor-made" service to individual users;
- The documents coming to the library are best utilized as they go to those persons to whom they will be most useful;
- The scanning time of the readers is reduced to nil;
- It requires no search strategy;

- The users need not remain alert themselves to keep track of the new literature coming in their fields as they are automatically alerted by the SDI system;
- The dissemination of any information through an SDI system is much quicker than dissemination of the same through any indexing or abstracting service;
- Because of the personalized nature of the service, SDI satisfies the users most.

H.8 DISADVANTAGES OF SDI

There are also a few disadvantages connected with the system, which are as follows [6]:
- It is sometimes difficult to pin-pointedly ascertain the interests and requirements of the users as they are often unable to express themselves in the manner required;
- It is difficult to satisfy a large number of users by a manual system and if any mechanical method is adopted, it may lose the personal touch which is a vital aspect;
- Many users are not alert enough to respond to all notifications, which affects the feedback mechanism and consequently the efficiency of the system;
- Properly trained staff in sufficient number are required for providing SDI service, which are usually not available in a small library.

H.9 SDI SERVICE PROVIDERS

An SDI service may be provided locally by an individual library or it may be provided by a national or international body. It may also be provided by a commercial agency. Though in majority of cases the SDI service is provided by individual libraries locally, some national abstracting services operate large-scale SDI services. But in such services there is always a chance of less interaction between the users and the SDI system due to distance between them. The insufficient feedback may affect the efficiency and pin-pointedness of the service.

H.10 SDI AS CAS

It is often questioned whether SDI can at all be considered a current awareness service. CAS, by its very nature, is not provided against any specific requirement and it covers a wide subject field. But the nature of SDI is not so. Nevertheless, it helps the users keep themselves abreast of the new developments in their own fields, which is also the main aim behind CAS. Besides, if a user wants to know about the new developments in the penumbral region also, along with those in the umbral region of his/her interest, he can do so by having, as Guha says, the level of match "kept in a comparatively diffused or lose form" [7]. SDI, therefore, is basically a current awareness service, though personalized in nature.

REFERENCES

[1] J.H. Conner, Selective dissemination of information: a review of the literature and the issues, Libr. Q 37 (4), (1967), 373–391.

[2] L.J. Strauss, et al., Scientific and Technical Libraries, second ed., Becker & Hayes, New York, 1972, p. 239.

[3] D. Elhence, Selective dissemination of information: Training Course in Documentation and Information Services (Oct. 18–Dec. 13, 1975): Course Material, INSDOC, New Delhi, 1976, Paper IV. 7.

[4] R. Satyanarayana, Computerized information services (SDI): Training Course in Documentation and Information Services (Oct. 18–Dec. 13, 1975): Course Material, INSDOC, New Delhi, 1975, Paper Vb20.

[5] H.P. Luhn, Selective dissemination of new scientific information with the aid of electronic processing equipment, Am. Doc. 12 (1961) 131.

[6] A. Chatterjee, Elements of Documentation, The Author, Calcutta, 1983,

[7] B. Guha, Documentation and Information, second ed., World Press, Calcutta, 1983, p. 103.

CHAPTER I

Index and Indexing

I.1 INTRODUCTION

Three groups of people are mainly concerned with documents and information. They are (1) the producers, i.e., authors, editors, publishers, etc.; (2) the middlemen, who organize the documents or information for serving them at need; and (3) the consumers or clients, i.e., readers, users, or information seekers [1]. Librarians and information workers, who play the important role of middlemen, have to devise and utilize some aids or tools which can help them to perform their function efficiently. Index is the most widely used such an aid.

I.2 EVOLUTION OF INDEX

It is queer that although printing came in vogue in 15th century, indexes appeared much later. It was perhaps due to, as Ranganathan and Neelameghan have pointed out, delay in spread of universal education [2]. Historically, the first significant work in this field came in 1737 in the form of *A Complete Concordance to the Bible*, compiled by Alexander Cruden, published from London. However, Knight has mentioned about a publication appearing much before Cruden's work which had some sort of an index, viz., Thomas North's translation of Plutarch's *Parallel Lives* (1595 edition) [3]. After the publication of Cruden's work, the practice of compiling indexes to individual works gradually developed. Subsequently, indexing of multi-volume works like *Encyclopedia Britannica* was started. In the next stage came the retrospective indexes to periodicals like *Poole's Index to Periodical Literature, 1802–1906*. Finally, in the beginning of the 20th century the present variety of indexing periodicals started appearing providing continuous indexing service. The pace was set in this direction by *Readers' Guide to Periodical Literature*, started by H. W. Wilson Co. of USA (now merged with EBESCO Publishing) in 1901.

I.3 NEED OF INDEX

Though appearance of index was delayed, its need was felt in 17th century itself, when some scholars described it as an essential implement and its

Elements of Information Organization and Dissemination
DOI: http://dx.doi.org/10.1016/B978-0-08-102025-8.00009-0

omission as a great sin. The famous critic, Dr. Samuel Jonson, said in 1750, that "when a reader recollects any incident, he may easily find it with the aid of an index." In 19th century, legal steps were suggested in some countries to prevent omission of indexes in books [2]. However, the index achieved its coveted position only in the 20th century and established itself as an essential adjunct to almost every work that was published. The main reasons for preparing indexes may be briefly stated as follows:

- Proliferation in production of literature, specially micro literature;
- Emergence of multi-faceted documents and documents dealing with interdisciplinary subjects;
- Rise in demand for quick retrieval of information;
- Repetitive use of documents containing information;
- Impracticability of scanning of literature beyond a limited number.

I.4 DEFINITION OF INDEX

The Latin word "indicare," from which has come the English word "index," means "he who or that which points the way" [3]. An index, therefore, indicates or refers to the location of an object or idea. It may thus be defined as "a systematic guide to (1) items contained in or (2) concepts derived from a collection (i.e., the materials indexed)" [1]. According to British Standards Institution, an index is "a systematic guide to the location of words, concepts or other items in books, periodicals or other publications. An index consists of a series of entries appearing, not in the order in which they appear in the publication, but in some other order (e.g., alphabetical) chosen to enable the user to find them quickly, together with references to show where each item is located" [4].

I.4.1 Characteristics of Index

The above definitions clearly reveal the following characteristics of an index:

- It is a guide to the items/concepts dealt with in a document;
- The items in an index are arranged generally in alphabetical order;
- There are references to show where these items are located in the document.

I.4.2 Difference from Bibliography

Although an index is also a list like a bibliography, it is basically different from the latter. While a bibliography lists documents, an index lists concepts or other items in a document. In other words, the unit for listing in a bibliography is a document, while that in an index is an item, concept or information. A catalogue also lists documents, but only those documents which are available in a library or a group of libraries.

I.4.3 Types of Index

Indexes can be grouped in various ways if we view them from different angles:
- Book index, periodical index, and news index
- Bibliographic index, analytical or subject index and annotated index
- Specific index and relative index
- Name index, place index, and word index
- Retrospective index, current index and cumulative index
- Comprehensive index and restricted index
- General index and special index
- International index, national index, and local index
- Citation index
- Literary index and review index
- Alphabetical index and classified index
- Author index and title index, etc.

In the digital environment, some new types of indexes have emerged, such as hypermedia index, multimedia index, and web index or Internet index.

I.4.4 Attributes of Index

The aim of index being quick access to relevant literature, the chief attributes of it are:
- It must be exhaustive and must be as specific as possible;
- It should be able to satisfy all possible approaches of the users;
- It should be simple and easy to handle.

I.5 INDEXING

If index is a conveniently arranged list of items or concepts, indexing is the art of preparing an index. It "refers to the process of identifying and assigning labels, descriptors, or subject headings to an item so that its subject contents are known and the index created can help in retrieving specific items of information" [5]. In short, indexing is systematic organization of information for their easy and quick retrieval.

I.5.1 Book Indexing

In early days, indexing was meant for the preparation of back-of-the-book indexes. The primary purpose of those indexes was to show as to where exactly in a book, a particular concept had been mentioned or discussed. Such indexes are appended to books even today. In the beginning, a book index used to cover broad topics and was of "one-concept-one-entry" type. In other words, such an index showed only a specific occurrence of a specific concept. This index is known as specific index. The main defect of this index is that it cannot show the various aspects of a concept and its relationship with other concepts. As such, a new type of index was evolved which could show along with each concept or subject, its related concepts, all angles, contexts and points of view from which it had been studied, etc. This index is known as relative index, the best example of which is the index of *Dewey Decimal Classification*. Ranganathan further developed the idea of relative index by introducing some abbreviations to indicate the various types of contexts, such as *irt* (in relation to), *rirt* (referred in relation to), *r by* (referred by), *def* (defined), and *desc* (described). He also introduced the devices of indention, punctuation, and inversion, etc.

I.5.2 Subject Indexing

Simultaneously with the emergence of Dewey's relative index, came Cutter's *Rules for a Printed Dictionary Catalog* (later came to be known as *Rules for a Dictionary Catalog*), which contained a generalized set of rules for alphabetical subject headings. The emergence of the present concept of subject indexing or information indexing can be traced to this idea of subject cataloguing developed around 140 years ago. A subject index, which is prepared by fully analyzing the contents of each document, helps locate the required concepts. An information worker or information service provider is more concerned with this type of index. As such, further discussion in the book will be confined mainly to subject indexing.

I.6 INDEXING IDEAS

As mentioned earlier, the ideas behind subject indexing originated from the ideas behind subject cataloguing. The purpose of subject cataloguing was to determine the "particular" subject of the book or document and represent it with a heading (i.e., subject heading) for the preparation of a subject catalogue. But it was soon realized that representing the "particular subject" of a document by a single phrase or heading was difficult in most of the cases. So full analysis of the subject of the document was made and the subject was represented from all angles. This was the stage when subject cataloguing gave way to subject indexing. Some important contributions which had significant impact in this process of development are briefly described below.

I.6.1 Cutter: Idea of Specific Subject

It was Charles Ammi Cutter who first gave, in 1876, the idea of "specific subject" in his *Rules for a Printed Dictionary Catalog*. He advocated cataloguing of a "work under its heading, [but] not under the heading of the class which includes that subject" [6]. Cutter envisaged a set of "stock subjects" under one of which every book had to be accommodated. But, evidently, there is a great difference between today's "specific" subject, and Cutter's "stock subject." It is rather impossible to compile a list of "stock subjects" to represent the subject of each and every document that is produced today. Cutter also laid down some rules for multi-word compound subject representations. He advocated cataloguing of "a compound subject name by its first word, inverting the phrase only where some other word is decidedly more significant or is often used alone with the same meaning as the whole name" [6]. But he failed to explain which one of the component parts of a compound heading would be "decidedly more significant." This depended solely on the flair of the cataloguer which brought uncertainly in its application.

I.6.2 Kaiser: Components of Compound Subject

In 1911, J. Kaiser, in his *Systematic Indexing,* laid down the rule for determining the relative significance of the different components of a compound subject. The rule said that all the subjects should be broken down into what he called a Concrete, followed by a Process. Kaiser categorized things, places, and abstract terms not signifying action or process as Concretes, while the terms signifying action or process as Processes. Process, according to him, also included the description or the mode of treatment of the subject by the author [7]. For example, if the subject of a document is "heat treatment of metals," this should be analyzed into "metals" as Concrete and "heat treatment" as Process. So the order of combination is Concrete followed by Process, i.e., METALS—Heat treatment (Concrete–Process). It can be easily said that by determining the order of significance of the components in a compound heading, Kaiser achieved what Cutter could not.

I.6.3 Coats: Significant Component

The most important work in the field of alphabetical subject heading is E.J. Coates's *Subject Catalogues: Headings and Structure*. In this book, he has found reasons for Kaiser's ideas of Concrete and Process, and put forward his own ideas of Thing, Material, and Action in that order. He said that "the most significant term in a compound is the one which is most readily available to the memory of the enquirer. This, in turn, is the word which evokes the clearest mental image." He further said that "in practice everyone makes an imaginative distinction between 'things' and 'actions'" [8]. For example, if we imagine "springing cats," it is the image of "cats" that comes to our mind first and then comes the image of "springing." Without the image of "cats," the concept of "springing" makes no clear meaning to us. Since the term "cats" produces a more definite image in our mind than "springing," the "cats" is the more significant word. So, the concept of "cats" belongs to Coates' Thing and the concept of "springing" belongs to Action and the order of significance is CATS, Springing (THING, Action). Etymologically, a "thing" is whatever one can think, that is to say, whatever can bring a static image. It includes not only the names of physical objects, but also systems and organizations of a mental kind. He further said that "a static image in mind is also produced by the names of materials out of which the things are made, and also the thing has a boundary while material has none. As a result, the name of a material is of lower significance than the name of a thing." Hence, the final order of significance among Thing, Material, and Action is Thing/Material/Action [8].

I.6.4 Ranganathan: Categories

Ranganathan developed from 1930 onwards his idea of categories or "facets" primarily as a basis for constructing his *Colon Classification* scheme. He successfully applied the idea of facet analysis in his *Dictionary Catalogue Code* as a basis for construction of compound subject headings for the dictionary catalogue. For this purpose, the order of significance was Energy, Matter, Personality, Space, and Time [9]. For example, the subject heading of "harvesting of grapes" will be HARVESTING, Grapes (ENERGY, Personality). There is little doubt that Ranganathan's idea of five fundamental categories was a marked improvement over Kaiser's Concrete and Process, but unfortunately, like Kaiser's Concrete, Ranganathan's Personality lacks a clear definition. In this respect Coates's Thing which is almost equivalent to Ranganathan's Personality is more clearly defined.

I.6.5 Farradane: Relational Operators

J.E.L. Farradane suggested in 1950 an alternative approach to compound subject headings, but not considering the component terms alone of the heading, as was done by both Kaiser and Ranganathan. He showed relationship between each pair of terms. Earlier, Kaiser and Ranganathan categorized the concepts basing on some superficial manifestations of modes of relationships between them, often conditioned by the "main class" under which they came and suggested a fixed order of precedence of those categories. For example, in the subject "harvesting of grapes" the categorization is GRAPES—Harvesting as CONCRETE—Process according to Kaiser and HARVESTING, Grapes as ENERGY, Personality, according to Ranganathan. Farradane, without considering the nature of concreteness or abstractness of the concepts, simply found out an "action" relationship between these two concepts in isolation and with the help of a relationship symbol or "operator" he formed the subject heading as follows: Grapes /- Harvesting. Here the symbol "/-" represents the "action" relationship between the two terms. Similarly, he has distinguished altogether nine kinds of relationships [10]. An important characteristics of Farradane's system is the indication of the relationship of concept terms by symbols or "operators" which easily reduces the importance of precedence order or significance of terms in a subject heading. Here, the components of the heading can be reversed according to necessity and the operators can be mentioned in reverse order.

I.6.6 Sharp: Selective Combination

Finding out the best combination order among the constituent elements of a composite subject heading is not an easy job, as one particular order may not suit all users. The solution of this problem may be preparation of multiple entries either by permutation or by cycling of the components. Complete permutation may result in a large number of entries (e.g., for five elements there can be 120 entries) and in rotation two concepts separated by other elements can never appear into juxtaposition (e.g., for four elements Homoeopathy—Treatment—Lungs—Cancer, the elements Treatment and Cancer cannot come together). J.R. Sharp found out a new solution to this problem in 1965. He felt that most of the users were unable to cite all the elements in a specific subject. As such, headings with full enumeration of all the elements might not be accessible to them. He, therefore, endeavored in his *SLIC Indexing* (Selective Listing in Combination) to find out only some selective combinations of elements contained in a document for using as index headings. According to Sharp, for four elements A, B, C, and D, there can be 24 entries by permutation, but all combinations can produce the following 15 entries: A, AB, B, ABC, BC, AC, C, BCD, ACD, CD, ABD, BD, AD, D and ABCD. But as the first seven combinations are covered by the last eight, the former combinations may be eliminated. Sharp has provided clear-cut formulae for calculating all combinations and the combinations to be retained for using as index headings [11].

I.7 INDEXING LANGUAGE

An index serves as an intermediary between the information contained in a document and their potential users. The language which serves as the medium of communication between the two is the indexing language [12]. In other words, the language used in expressing the concepts representing the contents of a document in an index is the indexing language. Indexing language is an artificial language, which uses the vocabulary of a natural language, but is different from that language in many ways. A detailed discussion on indexing language may be found in the next chapter.

I.8 INDEXING PROCESS

Basically, indexing proceeds in three stages: *Familiarization* —> *Analysis* —> *Conversion/Translation*. Here *familiarization* involves the indexer becoming conversant with the subject content of the document; analysis involves identification of concepts significant enough to be indexed; and *conversion* or *translation* involves representing those concepts by appropriate indexing language or terms. Different methods or techniques have been developed for indexing. Even classification and subject cataloguing are different methods of indexing. But these can be termed as traditional indexing methods. Of late, several newer indexing methods have come into vogue, which help in easy, speedy and effective retrieval of information, such as POPSI, PRECIS, and KWIC. These can be called modern indexing methods. The basic elements of indexing and different indexing systems or methods have been discussed in Chapter L.

I.9 EFFECTIVENESS OF INDEX

An index has two basic objectives to fulfill: it should be able to retrieve from a collection as many documents as are relevant to a query and the retrieved documents should be able to provide precise answer to the query.

As such, the efficiency of an index can be measured from these two angles by finding out "recall ratio" and "precision ratio". Recall ratio is the ratio between the number of relevant documents retrieved and total relevant document available in a collection and precision ratio is the ratio between the number of relevant documents retrieved and the total number of documents retrieved [13]. These can be shown through the following formulae:

$$\text{Recall Ratio} = \frac{\text{Number of relevant documents retrieved}}{\text{Number of relevant documents in the system}} \times 100\%$$

[For example, if only 40 documents are retrieved out of 100 relevant documents available in a system or file, in response to a query, the recall ratio will be $(40 \div 100) \times 100 = 40\%$.]

$$\text{Precision Ratio} = \frac{\text{Number of relevant document retrieved}}{\text{Total number of documents retrieved}} \times 100\%$$

[For example, if an index retrieves 60 documents in response to a query, out of which only 45 are relevant, the precision ratio will be $(45 \div 60) \times 100 = 75\%$.]

I.10 ADVANTAGES OF INDEX/INDEXING

The main advantages obtainable from indexes or indexing are as follows [14]:

- Indexing helps in effective organization of documents/information and their efficient retrieval;
- It minimizes search efforts and ensures optimum results;
- An index serves as a communication link between the sources of information and information searchers;
- It shows the trend of growth of a subject and its literature and manifests lacuna, if any;
- It displays the strengths and weaknesses of any collection of documents or store of information;
- It eliminates wastage of valuable research time.

REFERENCES

[1] P.B. Roy, Function of indexing and its historical role, in: S.B. Ghosh, J.N. Satpathi, (Eds.), Subject Indexing Systems: Concepts, Methods and Techniques, IASLIC, Calcutta, 1998, pp. 1–24.

[2] S.R. Ranganathan, A. Neelameghan, Physical Bibliography for Librarians, second ed., Asia, Bombay, 1974, Ch. PB.

[3] G.N. Knight, The Art of Indexing of Books and Periodicals, Allen & Unwin, London, 1979.

[4] British Standards Institution. Recommendation for the preparation of indexes for books, periodicals and other publications (B. S. 370:1954). London, 1964. p. 6.

[5] P. Atherton, Handbook of Information Systems and Services, UNESCO, Paris, 1977. pp. 130–139.

[6] C.A. Cutter, Rules for a Dictionary Catalogue, fourth ed., The Library Association, London, 1962.

[7] J. Kaiser, Systematic Indexing, Pitman, London, 1911.

[8] E.J. Coates, Subject Catalogues: Headings and Structures, The Library Association, London, 1960.

[9] S.R. Ranganathan, Classified Catalogue Code, with Additional Rules for Dictionary Catalogue, fifth ed., Asia Publishing House, Bombay, 1964.

[10] J.E.L. Farradane, A scientific theory of classification and indexing, J. Doc. 6 (1950) 83–99; (1952). 73–92.

[11] J.R. Sharp, Some Fundamentals of Information Retrieval, Deutsh, London, 1965.

[12] A. Chatterjee, Indexing languages and their attributes, in: IASLIC Short-term course on indexing: course material, 1993 (unpublished).

[13] T.N. Rajan, K. Ramaswami, Information storage and retrieval: indexing languages and indexing, in: Training Course in Documentation and Information Service: Course Material, Paper Va 6/10.

[14] A. Chatterjee, Elements of Documentation, The Author, Calcutta, 1983, p. 46.

CHAPTER J

Indexing Language

J.1 INTRODUCTION

Through indexing the contents of a document is so expressed that the information searcher gets precise indication about the relevant documents and their contents. In this sense, index is a means of communication. As is known, no communication is possible without the use of a set of symbols or a language. In fact the accuracy and speed of communication mainly depend on the qualities and the capabilities of the language used. This is true in case of indexing too. It may be mentioned here that as a system any language has three elements:

- Vocabulary, which comprises of some signs or combination of sounds (physical sounds or written marks), used to designate the physical objects or mental constructs they refer to (referents);
- Semantic relations which shows the relationships existing between the words; and
- Syntax i.e., meaningful sequence of words.

The semantic relationships are "fixed" by the structure of the language-system, whereas the syntactic ones are "selected" during the utterance of particular messages—the former are a priori, while the latter are a posteriori [1].

J.2 NATURAL LANGUAGE (NL)

A natural language is one which people use in their day-to-day communication—both spoken and written. It is possible, in indexing, to employ natural language simply as it is spoken or used in documents, without attempting to modify it. Such an index is often referred to as a natural index [2]. But such use of natural language creates several problems, specially in manual indexing. A natural language has a good vocabulary and has the flexibility of incorporating new terms. It also has a syntax to represent correct association of terms. These make it competent to express effectively. But its use in indexing may not be so effective.

Elements of Information Organization and Dissemination
DOI: http://dx.doi.org/10.1016/B978-0-08-102025-8.00010-7

The problems of using natural language in indexing are described below taking English language as an example [3].

- A concept may be represented by different terms, e.g., the concept "house" may be specified by not only the term *house*, but also *abode, dwelling*, etc. If all these terms are used in an index, the documents dealing with the concept will be scattered in the alphabetical file— This is the problem of synonym.

- There may be words with same spelling but different meanings, e.g., Game (*play*), Game (*trick*), Game (*hunted animal*). In natural language, the meaning becomes evident from the context, but when used alone, may not carry exact meaning—This is the problem of homograph.

- Different word-forms may be created by the use of suffixes, e.g., *Cool, Cooling, Cooler, Coolant*. They are related concepts, but will be scattered in alphabetical sequence due to difference in spelling—This is the problem of word-forms.

- With the change in the number of noun words, the spelling often also changes, e.g., *Calf, Calves* and consequently, these will be scattered in alphabetical order—This is the problem of number.

- With the change in gender of noun words, the spelling and even words change, e.g., *Dog, Bitch*. These will naturally get scattered in alphabetical order—This is the problem of gender.

- Even there may be different spellings of the same word, e.g., *Colour, Color; Connexion, Connection*, which, if used simultaneously, will scatter literature on the same subject in alphabetical order—This is the problem of spellings.

- Abbreviations, acronyms, etc. also create problem since some of them are well known, but some are not, or one abbreviation/acronym may indicated different entities, e.g., ILA is the abbreviation of International Literacy Association as well as International Leadership Association— This is the problem of contractions.

- Use of numerals along with words also creates problem, e.g., *3-dimension, three-dimension*—This is the problem of numerals.

- Many concepts require multiple or compound terms to convey the respective ideas. But the order of components cannot always be changed even if the latter component is more significant from the search point of view, as such change may give different connotations of the term, e.g., *School Library* and *Library School*—This is the problem of Compound Terms.

- Users may not be interested only in specific topics, but also in related topics. A natural language does not have any inherent capacity to manifest various types of relation—This is the problem of Related Subjects.
- The terms representing a specific subject need to be arranged in a searchable order. The arrangement by the syntax of the natural language may not often result in searchable order—This is the problem of Sequences.
- Finally, the vocabulary and syntax differ from language to language, which in itself makes an index language dependent—This is the problem of language dependency.

J.3 INDEXING LANGUAGE (IL)

The problems of natural language make it necessary to have a separate language for indexing which has the "power to control vocabulary, flexibility to show relation of different concepts and facility to build up a searchable file providing access to all possible access points of users" [4]. This is the indexing language, or more precisely subject indexing language (SIL). An indexing language is thus "an artificial language which is adapted to the requirements of indexing" [2]. It is "a language designed for a special purpose. Besides being a vehicle of communication of ideas, it has to perform some special functions" [4]. Indexing being the chief means of information retrieval, an indexing language is also called an information retrieval language. It may be mentioned that an SIL uses the vocabulary of a natural language, but effects necessary control over it.

J.3.1 Difference from NL

As both a natural language and an indexing language serve as media of communication, their basic components are same—vocabulary and syntax. But still they widely differ on several counts [5]:

- At the formal level, while in a natural language the written form is secondary to the verbal form and usually derived from it, in an indexing language it is the written form which is the basic means of communication.
- At the semantic level, an indexing language differs from a natural language in standardizing the vocabulary through control of *homonymity* and *synonymity* showing *hierarchical* and *related* structure of a subject;
- Whereas a natural language can function as its own meta language (i.e., a language used to talk about another language), an indexing language cannot;

- An indexing language being artificial, its governing rules are de jure (i.e., must to be followed) as opposed to de facto (i.e., may not be followed rigidly);
- An artificial language, such as an indexing language, is designed to fulfill a particular function, whereas a natural language does not have any specific purpose; it functions in many different contexts and many different purposes;

However, in the digital environment, the distinction is becoming blurred, since natural language terms are now being extracted directly from the text by computer for creating indexes.

J.4 TYPES OF SIL

Earlier, the work of indexing, using terms, and the work of classification, using notation, were thought to be different activities. But it has been later realized that the basic functions of both are same, viz., analysis and processing of the contents of documents for organization of a searchable file. Therefore, both are now taken to be variations of indexing language. Thus in the present context, the indexing languages can be of following types:

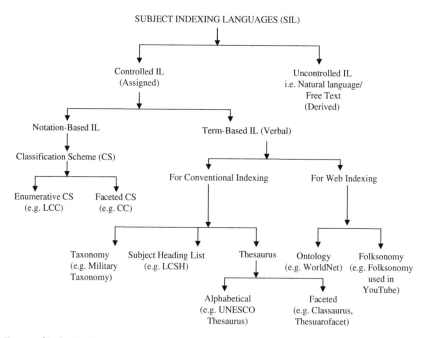

Types of Indexing Languages.

It is interesting to note that an alphabetical SIL is always dependent on a natural language since the main vocabulary of such language is borrowed from a natural language. Hence an SIL developed on the basis of a particular natural language cannot be used for an index to be consulted by persons not knowing that language. But a notational language is independent of any natural language. It may be mentioned that the notation-based indexing languages are mainly used for shelf arrangement and retrieval of macro documents and discussion on these languages may be found in any book on library classification. In this chapter, mainly term-based languages have been discussed.

J.5 ATTRIBUTES OF SIL

An SIL serves two purposes—representing contents of documents and organizing a searchable file. It is when the document description of an indexer and that of a searcher match, positive result is achieved. "This match is possible if the file is organized in a predetermined order and the users are aware of it. In successful organization of this file and subsequent matching of documents and requests, semantics and syntax of the indexing language have very important role to play" [4]. The main attributes of an indexing language are discussed below.

J.5.1 Vocabulary Control

The vocabulary of an SIL is controlled so that there is complete one-to-one relationship between the concepts and the terms representing them. This is done by strictly avoiding synonyms, near-synonyms, and homonyms. As indicated, in an SIL the basic vocabulary is often taken from an NL but the vocabulary, thus adopted, may differ from the vocabulary of the original language. In an indexing language where codes or symbols are used instead of terms, the difference in vocabulary is more apparent. Detailed discussion on vocabulary control may be found in the next chapter.

J.5.2 Concept Coordination

When a subject needs to be represented by more than one term, proper representation of the subject depends on correct coordination of terms. "In an indexing language, the syntax or order of words in subject formulation is much more important than in a natural language. In a natural language, apart from substantive words, a number of other auxiliaries like prepositions, conjunctions, etc. are used which help in bringing out the correct meaning of the construction as a whole. But, in an indexing language such auxiliaries are not available and the meaning of the subject or index heading has to be expressed largely through the order of the words" [4]. This problem is tackled by provision of some rules of syntax and these rules vary from one language to another. But in spite of such rules, sometimes it becomes difficult to show correct relationship among the terms. To solve this problem, some indexing languages have made provision for relational symbols which are known as *role operators*, *role indicators*, *indicator digits*, etc. It may be mentioned that coordination of terms is carried out at the input stage in pre-coordinate indexing and at output stage in post-coordinate indexing.

J.5.3 Multiple Accesses

When a subject representation is formulated with the help of rules of syntax, the concepts are arranged in a linear order which can provide only a single access in the searchable index file. To provide access from other terms, indexing languages provide some special rules of rotation of component terms. The rotation is done in such a way that each of the component terms is placed in the access position, which is followed by other terms showing its context so that the correct meaning of the subject is represented. "These rules of rotation are actually special rules of syntax in an indexing language" [6].

J.5.4 Syndetic Devices

Since indexing language is an artificial language, it requires some syndetic devices for the guidance and assistance of users. Apart from some sort of a manual, introduction or guide explaining the scope, structure and use of the language, the following devices are often used [3]:

- *Cross-references*: Cross-references such as *See* and *See also* or *Use* and *Used for* are used to link non-preferred and preferred terms and also, the terms related to the preferred term which are scattered in alphabetical order.
- *Glossaries*: The extension of the preferred term is sometimes limited or expanded to ensure definite coverage—this is indicated by scope notes, explanations, enumeration, etc. e.g., *CELL PHYSIOLOGY* (SN Structural property of cell).
- *Inverted headings*: The normal order of words in a heading is sometimes inverted to bring the potent word in the beginning, since users' approach is expected by that word, or to avoid scattering of related materials, e.g., BRIDGES, Concrete.

J.5.5 Relation Manifestation

Elementary terms of every language are related to each other paradigmatically (semantically) and syntagmatically (syntactically). This is true for indexing language also. "Paradigmatic relations are those which are known in advance before scanning any particular document, while syntagmatic relations are understood only after scanning a particular document" [4].

J.5.5.1 Paradigmatic Relation

In an indexing language, paradigmatic relations include broader-narrower relation and associative relation and these are often indicated by the arrangement of terms, etc., e.g.,

CHEMISTRY
    ORGANIC CHEMISTRY
    INORGANIC CHEMISTRY
      METALS.

This shows that Organic Chemistry and Inorganic Chemistry are parts of Chemistry; Organic Chemistry and Inorganic Chemistry are of same level and Metals is part of Inorganic Chemistry. These relations are known to users without any reference to a document. This relation is shown in different ways in different indexing languages.

J.5.5.2 Syntagmatic Relation

This relation is established between different concepts covered in the document only after analysis of the subject content, e.g., a document entitled "Law of inheritance and social status of women in rural India" has a combination of concepts from law, sociology, and geography, which is a special combination, not normally shown in any indexing language. They present syntagmatic relation in the context of a specific document. To manifest this relation, an indexing language has to devise some mechanism. A faceted classification, for example, provides separate schedules of isolates for different subjects and even for different facets under each subject, and the required combination of concepts is achieved by use of indicator digits.

J.5.6 Structural Presentation

Since an SIL aims at efficient retrieval of documents, it has to consider the characteristics of users' approaches. A user is normally interested in a particular subject, but in the event of non-availability of any document on the specific subject or his/her inability to decide about the exact extension of the subject of search or for collecting comprehensive literature on a topic, he/she may require materials on broader, narrower, and collateral subjects. An indexing language has to therefore structure and display the relationship in a systematic manner. This is done in different ways by different types of languages. For example, a classification scheme shows the broader-narrower relation by notation, whereas a thesaurus does so by prefixing abbreviations like BT, NT, etc. Thus indexing languages are structured languages.

J.6 THEORY OF SIL

The ideas of some of the pioneers in the field of subject indexing, which may be considered as early theories of SIL, have been discussed in the previous chapter. Through analysis of outstanding SILs developed by those pioneers, such as Cutter, Dewey, Kaiser, and Ranganathan, Bhattacharyya has developed a general theory of SIL, which is analogous to general theory of classification developed by Ranganathan. According to him, "the different SILs are not isolated and individual phenomena; but they are all developments within the general framework of a system of elements and relations which determines their structures" [7]. His "general theory of SIL is primarily concerned with the working concepts, postulates, principles, and rules of procedures that can form the basis for answering the 'why', 'what' and 'how' of different SILs; and at the same time that can serve as the basis for designing new SILs" [7].

J.6.1 SIL as Classificatory Language

The objective of any SIL is to create groups of sources of information to facilitate expeditious, exhaustive and pin-pointed retrieval of information from them. By implication, therefore, an SIL is a classificatory device, and in that sense, a classificatory language [8]. Bhattacharyya has shown that classification may be either organizing, or associative, or a combination of both. In organizing classification, the classes are grouped on the basis of their Coordinate—Super-ordinate—Sub-ordinate—Collateral (COSSCO) relationship; the result of which is always a hierarchy. In associative classification, a group is formed due to the presence of a mutual common factor among each of its members. To serve the purpose of exhaustive retrieval, an organizing classification must be complemented by an associative classification, or vice versa. An organizing classification can serve as the source for deriving an associative classification [7].

J.6.2 Features of SIL

The characteristic features of an SIL, as recognized by Bhattacharyya, are [7]:

* An SIL consists of elementary constituents and rules for formulation of admissible subject-propositions (i.e., names-of-subjects).
* It is used to summarize in indicative formulations what the contents of sources of information are all about.
* It is used to transform the structures of subject-propositions in a natural language for ready recognition of groups of subjects—both organizing and associative—on the basis of their transformed structures.
* The ultimate purpose of summarizing indicative formulations and structural transformations is to facilitate prompt retrieval of information about sources of information by providing necessary and sufficient access points.

J.6.3 Postulates and Working Concepts

A set of postulates and working concepts has been enunciated by Bhattacharyya for the General Theory of SIL based on the SILs developed by his predecessors. He felt that this set of postulates and working concepts was necessary to design a specific purpose-oriented SIL. The postulates and working concepts are briefly described below [7]:

* *Subject proposition:* A statement or any other formulation in a language—natural or artificial—denoting a subject is a subject proposition, e.g., Treatment of infectious diseases.
* *Elementary categories:* Each of the component ideas of a subject-proposition belongs to any one of the following elementary categories:
  * Discipline (D): An elementary category that includes conventional fields of study (such as Physics or History), or an aggregate of such field (such as Biological Sciences), or artificially created fields (such as Generalia).
  * Entity (E): An elementary category that includes manifestations having perpetual correlates, or only conceptual existence, as contrasted with their properties, and actions performed by them, e.g., Mineral or Heaven.
  * Action (A): An elementary category that includes manifestations denoting the concept of doing. Action may manifest as self-action (refers to internal processes and intransitive actions e.g., Migration) or External Action (capable of taking objects, i.e., transitive actions e.g., Treatment).

- Property (P): An elementary category that includes manifestations denoting the concept of attribute—qualitative (e.g., Virtue) or quantitative (e.g., Weight).
- Modifier (m): In relation to a manifestation of any one of the elementary categories, Modifier refers to an idea used or intended to be used to modify (qualify, differentiate) the manifestation concerned without disturbing its conceptual wholeness e.g., "Skilled" in "Skilled personnel." A Modifier (difference) generally creates a Species/Type of the modifyee (focus). Any manifestation of any Elementary Category may serve as the basis for deriving a Modifier. A Modifier can modify a single manifestation of any one of the Elementary Categories, as well as a combination of several manifestations of more than one Elementary Categories. Modifiers can be of two kinds: (1) common modifiers, having the potency of being used to modify manifestations of more than one elementary category, viz., Place (e.g., Indian), Time (e.g., 21st Century), Environment (e.g., Tropical) and Form (e.g., Periodical); and (2) Special Modifier, having the potency of being used to modify manifestations of one and only one elementary category (e.g., Infectious in Infectious Disease).

- *Simple subject:* A subject proposition consisting of one and only one manifestation (modified or unmodified), e.g., Agriculture (Discipline), or Harvesting (Action).
- *Compound subject:* A subject-proposition consisting of manifestations (modified or unmodified) of two or more elementary categories, e.g., Agriculture of Rice, or Rice Harvesting.
- *Complex subject:* When two subjects—simple and/or compound subjects combine with each other on the basis of some relationship—such as general, bias, comparison, difference, similarity, application, influence—the resulting subject is a Complex Subject.
- *Facet:* The term "Facet" refers to a manifestation of any one of the elementary categories, e.g., "Rice" manifests entity facet in "Agriculture" discipline.
- *Phase:* The term "Phase" refers to a subject component of a complex subject, e.g., in the complex subject "Mathematics for Engineers," each of the subject-components "Mathematics" and "Engineering" is a Phase.
- *Universe of subjects:* The term "Universe of Subjects" refers to any aggregate of different subjects under consideration for classification,

e.g., Physics, Chemistry, and Biology together constitute a Universe of Subjects and further Biology may also be considered as a Universe of Subjects, for, it consists of Botany and Zoology.

- *Attribute and characteristic:* Any property, quality, measure, etc. of a Universe of Subjects is its attribute and the difference in or the difference in degrees of an attribute on the basis of which a sub-universe of subjects can be distinguished from all other sub-divisions comprised by it, is a "Characteristic," e.g., if Man is considered as a universe of subjects, age, sex, height, etc. are its different attributes and "difference in sex" is a characteristic as it distinguishes males from females.

- *Extension of a universe of subjects:* The number of different subjects comprised by a universe of subjects is its extension, e.g., the number of states comprised by India is the extension of the universe of subjects India.

- *Intension of a universe of subjects:* The number of characteristics used to derive a universe of subjects from its source universe is its intension, e.g., if Howrah district in the state of West Bengal (India) is considered as a sub-universe, its derivation is based on characteristics "difference in state border" and "difference in district border" successively and hence the intension of Howrah district is 2.

- *Whole:* In relation to a Universe of Subjects, all the different subjects comprised by it, taken together, is a "Whole," e.g., "Human Bodies" viewed as comprising of "Male Human Bodies" and "Female Human Bodies" is a "Whole."

- *Type:* In relation to a universe of subjects deemed to be a whole (source universe), "Type" is one of its sub-universes, e.g., "male Human Bodies" and "Female Human Bodies" are types of its source universe "Human Bodies."

- *Part:* In relation to a Universe of Subjects deemed to be whole, a "Part" is one of its sub-divisions. A Part may be an "Organ" (e.g., wheel of a bicycle), a "Portion" (e.g., a district in relation to a state), a "Constituent" (e.g., protein in relation to milk), a "Step" of a process (e.g., analysis of subject matter of a document for indexing), or a particular "Facet" of a compound subject-proposition (e.g., India in History of India).

- *Multiple universe of subjects:* A Universe of Subjects amenable to division into types, e.g., the Universe of Subjects "Human Bodies" is amenable to more than one sub-universes formed by difference in sex (Male Human Bodies and Female Human Bodies), and by differences in age (Embryonic Bodies, Child Bodies, Adult Bodies, and Old Bodies).

- *Unitary universe of subjects:* A Universe of Subjects that is amenable to divisions into parts of successive orders, e.g.,

Respiratory System

> Nose

> Bronchi

> Lungs

>> Right Lung

>> Upper Lobe

(Note: Example does not show all the parts)

- *COSSCO relationships:* Two or more sub-universes derived from a universe on the basis of a single characteristic are "Coordinate" to each other, e.g., "Male Human Body" and "Female Human Body" derived from "Human Body." The source universe is "Superordinate" and each of the sub-universes is a "Sub-ordinate" and different coordinates are collateral to each other. The whole complex of these relationships may be described as COSSCO relationships.

- *Grouping through arrangement:* The purpose of subject indexing is grouping. Both organizing classification and associative classification result in creation of groups. The grouping of subjects in subject indexing is achieved through arrangement of subject-propositions.

- *Base:* In the context of constructing compound subject-propositions, when the purpose is to bring together all or major portion of information pertaining to (1) a manifestation, or (2) manifestations of a particular elementary category, the manifestation, or the elementary category, as the case may be, is the base. Thus "Discipline" will be the base when a document deals with any Discipline in general, but the Entity will be the base when a document deals specifically with manifestation of an Entity.

- *Core:* In the context of constructing compound subject-propositions, when the purpose is to bring together, within a recognized Base, all or major portion of information pertaining to manifestations of one or more elementary categories, the category or categories concerned may be deem to be the "Core" of the concerned Base, e.g., in DDC, Medicine is the Base, and "Anatomy", "Physiology" and "Disease" constitute the "Core" of the "Base."

- *Structure of compound subject-propositions:* The specific ideas used to formulate compound subject-propositions going with a recognized Base may be the manifestations of the elementary categories. A compound subject-proposition may consist of the Base and one or more manifestations of these categories.

J.6.4 Deep Structure of SIL

Bhattacharyya has recognized the following types of structure in a name of a subject for the purpose of designing an SIL [9]:

- *Semantic structure*: The structure in the dimension of denotation, based on "genus-species," "whole-part," "broader subject-narrower subject" relationships.
- *Elementary structure*: The structure in the dimension of different "categories" to which the different substantive constituents of subject-names belong; it is recognized on the basis of the semantic significance of the substantives and is artificially postulated.
- *Syntactical structure*: The structure originating from its rules of syntax which helps to preserve the meaning of the subject heading and to arrive at a consistent sequence of component elements.

The elementary and syntactic structures are closely related. Together they carry the responsibility of preserving the meaning of the name of a subject. They are rather peculiar to the SIL concerned and are postulated for the purpose of information retrieval. On the other hand, the semantic structure is more concerned with the denotation of the index terms belonging to the particular natural language concerned [8]. Bhattacharyya felt that "to be scientific in design work, it is essential to conceive a source-structure of SILs" [7]. As indicated above, through a logical abstraction of the results of analyses of the surface structures of the different outstanding SILs, he arrived at such a source-structure which he termed as deep structure of SIL. He, however, preferred to treat this as a postulate and further postulated that "a specific purpose-oriented SIL may be deemed to be a surface structure of the deep structure of SIL" [7].

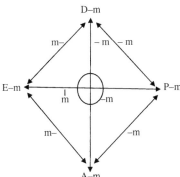

D = Discipline, E = Entity, A = Action, P = Property, m = Modifier

Schematic presentation of the deep structure of SIL. *G. Bhattacharyya, A general theory of subject indexing language. (Thesis submitted to Karnataka University, Dharwad, India, for Ph D degree), 1980. (Unpublished).*

Here, directions of the arrows indicate that any one of the ECs may be related to any one of another category, provided the product of their relation is meaningful.

J.6.4.1 Postulates of Deep Structure

Bhattacharyya has also enunciated a number of postulates with regard to deep structure of SIL, the major ones of which are briefly described below [7]:

- *Basic sequence*: The sequence D followed by E (modified or unmodified) appropriately interpolated or extrapolated by A and P (modified or unmodified) is the logical sequence of elements of a Basic Chain, manifested in a compound subject-proposition. Any A or P may have A and/or P related to it. Their positions are always after the A or P to which they are related.

- *Source organizing classification*: The basic sequence of manifestations, augmented by the interpolation and extrapolation of successive superordinates of each EC manifestation, whenever required, gives rise to a Basic Modulated Chain, which can generate a source organizing classification in alphabetical arrangement with the aid of suitable apparatus introduced for this purpose. The basic modulated chain can be manipulated to generate chains meant for different specific purpose-oriented organizing classification, which in turn may form the basis of different associative classifications.

- *Associative classification effect*: The simple cyclic permutation of each of the sought manifestation, in any style, with the indication of the structure of subject-proposition meant for organizing classification has every effect of an associative classification.

- *Systematic grouping*: Only the notational representation of modulated chains can ensure, in arrangement, the ideal systematic grouping by juxtaposition. Only the alphabetical arrangement of modulated chains with suitable apparatus (notation, punctuation, etc.) is the closest approximation to the purely notational grouping.

- *Controlling of synonyms*: Synonyms, quasi-synonyms, and antonyms can be controlled only by referencing or by some acceptable substitute for referencing.

- *Efficiency and effectiveness*: An SIL to be optimally efficient and effective should:
  - Make provision for all possible approach terms

- Ensure, as far as possible, organizing classification in general and also, under each approach term
- Ensure all possible associative classifications going with the different approach terms
- Make the structure of subject-propositions for organizing classification serve simultaneously the purpose of systematic grouping by juxtaposition, and creating organizing classification effect by referencing.

(*Note*: The basic sequence-based modulated chain complemented by cyclic permutation of sought components can endow an SIL with all these attributes.)

- *Sequence of components:* Each compound subject-proposition has a Base, which is the first facet. Core follows the Base. An Action follows the manifestation in relation to which it is an action. A Property follows the manifestation of which it is property. A modifier is to go with the manifestation modified.
- *Syntactic relationships:* There can be only following types of syntactic relationships between components of compound subject-propositions: Inter-facet Relationship, Modifyee-Modifier Relationship, Whole-Type (i.e., genus-species) Relationship, and Whole-Part Relationship.
- *Sequence of related subjects:* The sequence of related subjects in a complex subject-proposition is governed by the decision about the Base-subject.

J.6.5 Implications of General Theory of SIL

The set of postulates, principles, and working concepts constitute the general theory of SL. This theory furnishes the guidelines as to the recognition of Base and Core out of the Elementary Categories Discipline, Entity, Action, and Property. On the basis of the theory, a set of specific postulates and principles of sequence can be formulated to take care of a specific group of users. However, some of the general implications of the General Theory of SIL are [7]:

- On the basis of the set of general postulates, principles, working concepts, and methodologies, a "Classaurus"—that is, a faceted systematic scheme for classification having all the necessary features of a thesaurus—can be developed as the device for vocabulary control. (*See also Section K.4.5.3*)
- There may be several sets of specific postulates and principles of sequence formulated in conformity with the set of general postulates and principles of sequence.

- A coherent set of rules is to be formulated for the choice of terms-of-approach for generating associative classification and for rendering, recording, and arrangement of subject-propositions for organizing classifications and associative classifications.
- The deep structure of SIL may be regarded as the source structure to design a new SIL for implementing a specific policy or pattern of grouping. POPSI is an example of such a new design.

REFERENCES

[1] S.C. Biswas, Medium of communication of information: natural language vs. information language, Librarian 4 (1991), 59–65.

[2] M.J. Ramsden, An Introduction to Index Language Construction, Clive Bingley, London, 1974. Frame 1–2

[3] A. Chatterjee, Indexing languages: features and types, in: S.B. Ghosh, J.N. Satpathy, (Eds.), Subject Indexing Systems: Concepts, Methods and Techniques, IASLIC, Calcutta, 1998. pp. 27–40.

[4] A.R. Chakraborty, B. Chakrabarty, Indexing: Principles, Processes and Products, World Press, Calcutta, 1984. pp. 26–43.

[5] C.T. Meadows, The Analysis of Information Systems, John Wiley, New York, 1967. pp. 3–64.

[6] B. Guha, Problems of indexing terminology: natural language vis-à-vis controlled vocabulary, in: T.N. Rajan (Ed.), Indexing Systems: Concepts, Methods and Techniques, IASLIC, Kolkata, 1981. pp. 155–162.

[7] G. Bhattacharyya, A general theory of subject indexing language. Thesis submitted to Karnataka University, Dharwad, India, for Ph D degree. 1980. (Unpublished).

[8] S.C. Biswas, Subject heading by POPSI, in: S.B. Ghosh, J.N. Satpathi, (Eds.), Subject Indexing Systems: Concepts, Methods and Techniques, IASLIC, Calcutta, 1998. pp. 188–210.

[9] G. Bhattacharyya, POPSI: its fundamental and procedure based on a general theory of subject indexing languages, Lib. Sci. 16 (1979) 1–34.

CHAPTER K

Controlled Vocabulary (CV)

K.1 INTRODUCTION

Vocabulary is one of the main attributes of any language. In subject indexing, vocabulary plays a very important role since the subject matters of
the respective documents are represented by words or terms which are
constituents of the vocabulary of the language used in indexing. As indicated earlier, mainly two types of languages are used in indexing, viz.,
uncontrolled or natural language and controlled (artificial) language. The
difficulties faced while using natural language in indexing have been discussed in the previous chapter. The concept of Controlled Vocabulary has
emerged to obviate those difficulties.

K.2 DEFINITION OF CV

A controlled vocabulary is an authoritative list of terms to be used in indexing
(human or automated) [1]. More precisely, it is "an organized arrangement of
words and phrases used to index content and/or to retrieve content through
browsing or searching" [2]. A controlled vocabulary essentially includes
preferred terms and may or may not include variant terms for cross-reference.
A controlled vocabulary has "a defined scope or describes a specific domain"
[3]. The term "controlled" here signifies that only terms from the list (vocabulary) can be used for indicating the subject of a document while indexing.
It also signifies that "if it is used by more than one person, there is control over who adds terms or how terms can be added to the list. The list
could grow, but only under defined policies…..The objectives of a controlled
vocabulary are to ensure consistency in indexing, tagging or categorizing
and to guide the user to where the desired information is" [2].

K.3 CHARACTERISTICS OF CV

The characteristics of different types of controlled vocabulary may slightly
vary. But broadly the main characteristics of a controlled vocabulary are:
* It is based on any natural language vocabulary, but its size is always
  smaller than the vocabulary on which it is based;

Elements of Information Organization and Dissemination
DOI: http://dx.doi.org/10.1016/B978-0-08-102025-8.00011-9

- It allows only one term out of all synonyms and quasi-synonyms representing an idea for use in an index;
- It may allow use of variants of preferred terms for cross-referencing;
- It avoids use of homonyms, but in cases where it is at all not possible, qualifiers are added to indicate the context;
- The scope of the term is sometimes deliberately restricted to a selected meaning which is best suited for an indexing system;
- Spellings, number (singular/plural), and other word forms are standardized;
- A definite rule is followed for compound terms.

K.4 TYPES OF CV

Controlled vocabularies are structured to enable displaying the different types of relationships among the terms they contain. There are different types of controlled vocabulary, determined by their increasingly complex structure. The main types of controlled vocabulary fall in the following sequence of increasing complexity.

Authority List	Synonym Ring	Classification Scheme/ Taxonomy	Thesaurus	Ontology
		Increasing Complexity →		
Ambiguity control	Synonym control	Ambiguity control Synonym control Hierarchical relationships	Ambiguity control Synonym control Hierarchical relationships Associative relationships	Ambiguity control Synonym control Customized associations

ANSI/NISO Z39.19-2005 ISBN: 1-880124-65-3 Guidelines for the Construction, Format, and Management of Monolingual Controlled Vocabularies.

(*Note:* The figure is based on the one proposed by Redmond-Neal [1].) The different types of controlled vocabulary are introduced below. However, thesaurus being the most widely used controlled vocabulary in alphabetical subject indexing, it has been discussed in more detail.

K.4.1 Subject Authority List

The simplest form of controlled vocabulary is subject authority list or file. This is a bare list of subject headings consistently being used by an indexing system arranged primarily in alphabetical order. This is maintained to ensure avoidance of synonyms by the indexers doing indexing work simultaneously in an organization and also by the same indexer working at different times and different indexers working at different times. Such a list often does not indicate any type of relationship that might exist between the terms and as such is shorter in size.

K.4.2 Taxonomy

The word taxonomy means the science of classifying things, and traditionally the classification of plants and animals, as in the Linnaean classification. It has become a popular term now for any hierarchical classification or categorization system [2]. In the field of information retrieval it denotes "a kind of controlled vocabulary that has a hierarchy (broader term/narrower terms), but not necessarily the related-term relationships and other features of a standard thesaurus" [2]. Taxonomies are often displayed in a tree structure. Terms within a taxonomy are often called "nodes." A node may be repeated at more than one place within the taxonomy if it has multiple broader terms. This is referred to as a polyhierarchy. Another type of taxonomy, with a more limited hierarchy, comprises multiple sub-taxonomies or "facets," whereby the top-level node of each represents a different type of taxonomy, attribute, or context. This is used in post-coordinated searching, whereby the user chooses a combination of nodes, one from each facet. The use of equivalent synonyms or see references may or may not exist in a taxonomy. If a hierarchy is not too large and can be browsed, and especially if there are polyhierarchies, there is less of a need for non-preferred variants [4].

K.4.3 Subject Heading List

A subject heading list is "a standard list of terms to be used as subject headings, either for the whole field of knowledge or for a limited subject area, including references made to and from each term, notes explaining the scope and usage of certain headings, and occasionally corresponding class numbers" [5]. Such a list is normally arranged alphabetically. Both preferred and rejected terms are listed in the same sequence. The terms are linked by "See" and "See also" references. The most well known subject heading lists for the whole field of knowledge are *Library of Congress Subject Headings* and *Sears List of Subject Headings*, while Medical Subject Headings (MeSH) is an example of subject headings list on a limited subject area. However, most of the subject headings lists have now adopted thesaural structure. More discussions on subject headings lists may be found in any book on library cataloguing or resource description.

K.4.4 Classification Scheme

A classification scheme is a list of class terms with corresponding notation, accompanied by an alphabetical index. There are mainly two types of classification schemes: enumerative and faceted. An enumerative classification scheme consists of a single list or schedule of all class terms representing universe of subjects or a subject domain, while a faceted scheme consists of different schedules of class terms representing different facets of the concerned domain. A classification scheme contains a notational vocabulary, while its index represents an alphabetical vocabulary. More discussions on classification schemes may be found in any book on library classification or knowledge organization.

K.4.5 Thesaurus

As mentioned, thesaurus is the most widely used example of controlled vocabulary. The word "Thesaurus" is of Greek origin meaning "treasury or storehouse of knowledge" [6]. In modern usage, it denotes a list of terms arranged according to their relationships of ideas [7]. It was Peter Mark Roget who first conceived the idea of such a compilation and brought out in 1852 his *Thesaurus of English Words and Phrases* for the benefit of writers looking for appropriate words to express their ideas. Roget's thesaurus had nothing to do with information retrieval, but his novel idea was profitably utilized in compilation of modern IR thesauri. According to B.C. Vickery, Helen Brownson was the first person who used the term "Thesaurus" in the context of IR in her paper presented at Dorking Conference on Classification Research in 1957. Hans P. Luhn was possibly the first person to think about information retrieval thesaurus, who suggested the compilation, for indexing purposes, of "families of notions," and dictionary of "notional families," very similar to the principles of Roget [8]. The first thesaurus used in information retrieval was developed at the E I Dupont de Nemours Company in the United States around 1959 and since then a large number of IR thesauri have been brought out in different subject fields.

K.4.5.1 Definition of Thesaurus

An IR thesaurus, from the point of view of function, is "a terminological control device used in translating from the natural language of documents, by indexer or users into a more constrained 'system language' (i.e., documentation language, information language)." From the point of view of structure it is "a controlled and dynamic vocabulary of semantically and generically related terms which covers a specific domain of knowledge" [9]. According to Kent, it is "a compilation of terms of a given information system's vocabulary, arranged in some meaningful form and which provides information relating to each term that will enable a user of the information file to predict the relevance of responses to questions when this particular control mechanism is used" [10]. Briefly, it may be defined as a list of descriptors for use in information retrieval system arranged in a systematic order and manifesting various types of relationship existing between them [11].

K.4.5.2 Difference from S H List

Both thesauri and subject headings lists control the use and form of index terms and summarize the relationships between terms in an indexing language. But, thesauri and subject headings lists achieve these two objectives in different environments. Most of the main subject headings lists are geared to the alphabetical subject approach found in dictionary catalogues. The unique features that distinguish a thesaurus from a subject headings list are [12]:

- A thesaurus is likely to contain terms that are more specific than those found in a subject headings list;
- A thesaurus tends to avoid inverted terms (such as Art, French);
- Headings in a thesaurus are not subdivided, but this is common in traditional subject headings lists;
- The relationship display in a thesaurus is often more extensive than the relationship display in subject headings lists;
- Different types of relationships are shown in a thesaurus by the use of BT, NT, and RT, instead of *see also* which is frequently used to indicate all relationships, whatever their nature, in a subject headings list (Lately, however, many subject headings lists are also using BT, NT, and RT to show relationships);
- A thesaurus often has an additional explicit statement of the structure of the relationships between terms in the form of categorized lists or graphic display.

K.4.5.3 Similar Tools and Concepts

There are also some other concepts, viz., *Thesaurofacet* and *Classaurus*, which possess not only all the features of a thesaurus, but also some additional features. *Thesaurofacet* has been developed by Jean Aitchison and others for English Electric Company. It is basically a faceted classification scheme with an alphabetical index in the form of thesaurus. "The terms in the system appear once in the thesaurus and once in the schedules, the link between the two locations being the notation or class number" [13]. The *Classaurus* developed by G. Bhattacharyya of Documentation Research and Training Centre, Bangalore, has only one section consisting of separate schedules for different facets, but the schedules incorporate within themselves the features of both classification scheme and a thesaurus. The index of the classaurus is a usual alphabetical index.

K.4.5.4 Scope and Size of Thesaurus
No ideal scope or size can be prescribed for an IR thesaurus. These will vary depending upon:
* Scope and complexity of the subject to be covered;
* Kind of retrieval objects and data to be processed;
* Intended exhaustivity and specificity of indexing.
However, the scope of a thesaurus must be such that it can serve the specific needs, viewpoints and priorities of the users.

K.4.5.5 Need and Characteristics of Thesaurus
Any IR system, whether manual or mechanized, requires an articulate vocabulary free from homonyms and synonyms for its efficient functioning. An IR thesaurus fulfills this need. The main characteristics of an IR thesaurus are:
* It provides descriptors to be used in indexing and retrieval;
* It shows the intrinsic, semantic relationships existing between the terms.

K.4.5.6 Types of Thesaurus
From the point of view of terminological control, there are mainly two types of thesauri:
* Controlled thesauri—this type of thesauri allows only one term to denote a concept;
* Free language thesauri—this type of thesauri uses all terms found in relevant literature denoting a concept.
The use of free language thesauri in an IR system may create problems of matching at search stage and hence controlled thesauri are mainly used in information retrieval. In a controlled thesaurus, vocabulary control is effected by following ways [7]:

- Only one term out of all possible synonyms and quasi-synonyms is selected as a descriptor;
- The scope of the term is deliberately restricted to a selected meaning which is best suited for an indexing system. (The scope is clearly indicated in scope note wherever required);
- Spellings, number (singular/plural), and word-forms are standardized;
- A definite rule is followed for compound terms;
- Homographs (homonyms) are avoided as far as possible and differentiated by qualifiers, if at all used.

There can be another type of thesaurus known as Convertible Thesaurus or Source Thesaurus. This thesaurus serves as a "switching" or "reconciling thesaurus" for information interchange purposes.

K.4.5.7 Internal Structure of Thesaurus

The arrangement of different components of an entry and the arrangement of different entries in relation to one another constitute the structure of a thesaurus. Cross-references make explicit the ways in which entries relate to each other in a network of concepts [14]. An entry in a thesaurus consists of a bunch of terms led by a descriptor which is followed by the terms which are related in different ways. The different terms in an entry are displayed in the following format:

Descriptor
(with scope notes wherever needed)
Synonyms and quasi-synonyms
(displaying equivalent relationships)
Broader terms
(displaying hierarchical—super-ordinate relationships)
Narrower terms
(displaying hierarchical—subordinate relationships)
Related terms
(displaying associative relationships)
Top term
(displaying the broader class to which the descriptor belongs)

The *top term* is usually not repeated when all the descriptors belong to the same broad class. The meanings of the above concepts are described below.

- *Descriptors*: The notion of descriptor was first introduced by Calvin Mooers, an American pioneer in the field of coordinate indexing. The descriptors are the terms allowed by a thesaurus to be used in indexing. Descriptors are authorized and formalized terms or symbols used to represent unambiguously the concepts of documents and queries. Descriptors can be of two types:

- Terms denoting concepts and concept combinations, e.g., TELEVISION, SATELLITE TELEVISION
- Terms denoting individual entities (proper name identifiers), e.g., SAMSUNG TELEVISION.

The terms denoting individual entities are often excluded from a thesaurus in order to restrict the size and because these, if needed, can be supplied by the indexer without any fear of ambiguity.

- *Scope note*: A scope note clarifies or brings out the intended meaning or scope of the term. This is added to a descriptor whenever needed.
- *Non-preferred terms*: All the synonyms and quasi-synonyms displaying equivalence relationship with a descriptor, but not selected for indexing purposes are non-preferred terms. A cross-reference is made for each non-preferred term, e.g.,

    Microcopies

    USE MICROFORMS.

- *Broader/Narrower terms*: A term which is superordinate to a descriptor in a hierarchy is a broader term, while a term which is subordinate to a descriptor is a narrower term, e.g.,

    MICRO FORMS

    BT Data Media

    NT Micro Transparencies.

- *Related terms*: The terms which are neither non-preferred, nor broader, nor narrower, but are related to the descriptor conceptually are called related terms.

K.4.5.8 Relationships Between Terms

One of the most important functions of a thesaurus is to display how the concepts are related. The relationships that are shown in a thesaurus are broadly of two types, viz., *Hierarchical* and *Non-hierarchical*. Hierarchical relationship is easier to determine than non-hierarchical relationship.

- *Hierarchical relationship:* can be Hierarchical relationship shows the interrelationship between the concepts in a hierarchy. It expresses degrees or levels of superordination and subordination between concepts. This type of relationship is considered to be the basic relationship which differentiates a thesaurus from other controlled lists of terms. Hierarchical relationship can be of three types:
  - Genus–Species (Generic) relationship, e.g., SNAKES—COBRA

- Hierarchical Whole-Part relationship, e.g., HUMAN BODY—CHEST
- Instance relationship, e.g., CAMERA-NIKON

However, some experts do not consider Whole-Part relationship as hierarchical relationship, while instance relationship is often not shown to control the size of a thesaurus. Some terms may belong to more than one hierarchy and consequently may be related to more than one broader term and more than one set of narrower terms. Such relationship is called poly-hierarchical relationship, e.g.,

MAMALIA   MARINE ANIMALS

WHALE

- *Non-hierarchical relationship:* Non-hierarchical relationship can be of two types:
    - Equivalence (or preferential) relationship: Equivalence relationship is the relationship between preferred and non-preferred terms in an indexing language, in which each of two or more terms is regarded for indexing purposes, as referring to the same concept. In other words it is the relationship between synonyms and/or quasi-synonyms. Synonyms are the terms having the same meaning and are, therefore, interchangeable, while quasi-synonyms are those terms the meanings of which are not exactly same, but are regarded as same for the purpose of indexing. In case of equivalent terms, only one term is selected as descriptor, e.g., CYTOLOGY—Cell Biology

    It should be ensured that all documents associated with the equivalence category are retrieved whenever needed. Sometimes relationship between antonyms, i.e., terms with opposite meanings is also treated as equivalence relationship. Further, equivalence relationship is considered by some experts as a separate type of relationship and a not a kind of nonhierarchical relationship.
    - Associative (or affinitive) relationship: This type of relationship cannot be properly defined. It covers relationship between the terms in pairs of terms which are neither members of an equivalent set nor can they be organized in a hierarchy, yet they are semantically associated to such an extent that the link between them should be made explicit in a thesaurus. There may be associative relationship between two kinds of terms:
        - Terms of same category, e.g., SHIPS—BOATS
        - Terms of different categories, e.g., INDIANS—INDIA.

There are different ways in which two terms can be associated. Neelameghan has identified 29 types of such relationship. However, only those associative relationships need to be shown which are likely to be needed for retrieval in an information retrieval system [19].

It may be mentioned that whenever a relationship, whether hierarchical or non-hierarchical, is established between two terms, it is necessary to provide reciprocal entries for each term in the thesaurus. For example, if the term BROADCASTING and TRANSMITTER are considered related, the entry under BROADCASTING should display TRANSMITTER as a related term and the entry under TRANSMITTER should similarly display BROADCASTING as a related term.

K.4.5.9 Display of Relations

The relations between terms are displayed in a thesaurus in either of the following ways:
- By prefixing abbreviations
- By prefixing symbols
- By graphic method.

Display Using Abbreviations

UNISIST Guidelines have recommended the following abbreviations [16]:

BT (= Broader Term) to represent a concept of wider connotation

NT (= Narrower term) to represent a concept of more specific connotation

RT (= Related Term) to denote a term having associative relationship with the descriptor

SN (= Scope Note) to indicate the note attached to a descriptor restricting the meaning of the term

TT (= Top Term) to represent the broadest class

UF (= Use For) to indicate a nonpreferred term

USE to indicate a preferred term or descriptor

[*Note*: In some thesauri, the term SEE is used for USE and SEE FOR (SF) for USE FOR (UF).]

UNISIST Guidelines has also recommended that to distinguish generic relations from whole-part relations, the abbreviations may be modified as follows [15]:

BTG for Broader Term Generic

BTP for Broader Term Partitive

NTG for Narrower Term generic
NTP for Narrower term Partitive.

Display Using Symbols

A committee of the ISO has recommended the following symbols to indicate the various types of relationships [16]:

Hierarchical relationships

<   to precede a broader term

<P   to precede a broader term (partitive)

>   to precede a narrower term

>P   to precede a narrower term (partitive)

Equivalence relationship

=   to precede a preferred term (descriptor)

≠   to precede a nonpreferred term

Associative relationship

−   to precede a related term

Conjunction

&   to indicate that terms joined by the symbol should be used in combination to represent a compound concept.

Graphic Display

A number of graphic display devices are being used to show the relationships between the terms in a thesaurus, such as tree structure, arrow-graph, Euler circles, and circular display, of which the first two are more popular.

Tree Structure: In tree structure the terms are arranged in a tree showing the hierarchy such as shown below:

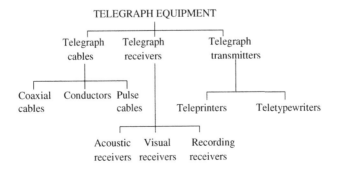

Arrowgraph: In an arrowgraph, the related terms are linked by arrows as shown below:

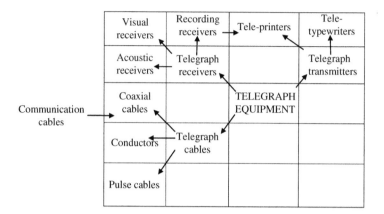

Euler Diagram: In this representation, each concept is defined by a polygonal domain or "circle." Synonymous terms, by definition, occupy the same domain and related subjects have overlapping domains. A subject which is perceived as being entirely contained within the bounds of another will have its "circle" totally within the boundaries of the domain of the broader subject [8], as shown below:

Circular Display: In this type of display, the central concept is shown as a central circle. Related topics are arranged in concentric circles around the central circle. Concepts which are only remotely related to the central concept will be positioned well away from the central circle [12].

Format of Display
An IR thesaurus may be arranged and presented in one or more of the following methods:
- Alphabetical—in which descriptors (along with their related terms) and cross-references are arranged in alphabetical order.

- Systematic or classified—in which the descriptors are arranged in their hierarchical order with levels of hierarchy represented by indentions, dashes, etc.
- Graphic—in which the hierarchy is shown by a tree or an arrowgraph.

K.4.5.10 Method of Compilation

Compilation of IR thesaurus is a specialized job requiring a fair knowledge of the subject to be covered as well as familiarity with the methodology of compilation. At the outset it is necessary to obtain fair knowledge of the subject to be covered by studying some standard and representative books and discussion with subject experts. For learning compilation methodology, guidelines brought out by ISO [9], BSI [17], and UNESCO [16], or the manual compiled by Aitchison and Gilchrist [18] may be consulted. The essential steps for compiling of a monolingual thesaurus are [11]:

- *Delineation of scope:* At first, the scope of the subject of the proposed thesaurus is to be clearly defined. The scope must be coextensive with the information retrieval system for which the thesaurus is being compiled. For a thesaurus meant for general use, the exact scope should be defined by demarcating boundaries of the subject field, and penumbral subjects should be identified.
- *Determination of characteristics:* A decision has to be taken regarding the following characteristics of the thesaurus:
  - The level of specificity;
  - The level of pre-coordination;
  - The extent of hierarchical and other relationships;
  - Auxiliary precision devices (e.g., links, roles) to be used;
  - Arrangement and layout of the main and auxiliary parts.
- *Division of subject field into facets:* The main areas or facets of the subject field may be identified with the help of representative books and subject specialists. This helps in term collection by ensuring inclusion of terms relating to all important areas of the subject field. Existing classification schemes and thesauri on related or broader subjects may be consulted for the purpose.
- *Identification of sources:* The sources from which terms are to be collected should be identified before starting term collection. Sources may include standard reference tools such as encyclopedias and, glossaries; representative books on the subject; available classification schemes and thesauri, primary and secondary periodicals, etc. It is advisable to prepare a main entry for all such sources in a standard format mentioning

all the bibliographical details of the document and including, if possible, an abstract. These entries should be arranged in a helpful order, or alphabetically, and numbered serially.

- *Collection and selection of terms:* Each of the sources may be scanned for collection of relevant terms. Where a concept is denoted by different terms, the term which will serve as the descriptor should be chosen keeping in view the frequency of use of the term in the literature, its present and possible use in retrieval queries as also its acceptability among the subject experts. The currency of the term and its ability to precisely express a particular concept should also be considered. Some definite rules should be followed for determining the form of the term. A term record should be prepared for each term selected in a specially designed term record card. At this stage it may not be possible to note down all the information required to be entered in the term record, e.g., the broader terms and narrower terms cannot normally be supplied until the hierarchy of the terms is established. In such circumstances gaps may be left which may be filled in at a later stage. Besides, full bibliographical details of the source need not be repeated in all term records; mentioning of serial number of the main entry may be sufficient.

- *Determination of relation:* Determination of interrelation between the terms is most significant task and should be done with caution. For determining the hierarchical relationship a hierarchical tree can be drawn covering all the descriptors. Help may be taken from the existing classification schedules and thesauri and the subject experts. Associative relationships should be established keeping in view the need of the information system and taking help of any guidelines. After determining all the relationships these should be noted down in appropriate places on the term records.

- *Preparation of entries:* An entry should now be prepared for each descriptor in previously determined format using necessary abbreviations or symbols as mentioned earlier. For each non-preferred term also, a cross-reference entry should be prepared in a predetermined format, e.g.,

     Microcopies USE MICROFORMS

The descriptors and nonpreferred terms may be differentiated typographically as above.

- *Arrangement of main part:* When the main part is alphabetical, the entries for the descriptors and non-preferred terms are all arranged in alphabetical order. In case of classified or systematic main part, the terms are arranged in a hierarchy displaying the order of the terms by indentions, dots, or dashes. Scope notes, synonyms, and related terms are added where necessary. For graphic display, a tree or arrowgraph is drawn showing the relationships of the terms.

- *Preparation of auxiliary part:* The auxiliary parts necessary to supplement the main part and to meet the needs of the indexing system should now be prepared.
- *Final editing:* The drafts of the main and auxiliary parts should be tested and checked on the following points:
  - Word forms and spellings;
  - Reciprocal entries;
  - Arrangement of entries;
  - Indentions, spacings, and layout;
  - Links between the main and auxiliary parts.

All mistakes discovered should be corrected and new relationships, if any found, should be added. An explanatory introduction explaining the scope, structure, features, and arrangement of the thesaurus and a "Guide to Users" should be prepared and prefixed. Finally necessary instructions should be added for printing.

- *Updating:* No thesaurus can be a static document. There should be a mechanism to update the thesaurus at regular intervals. Updating should be done keeping in view the developments in the subject-field covered and readers' queries. Updating may involve change in existing relationships and addition of new relationships.

K.4.5.11 Advantages of Thesaurus
Like any other vocabulary control tool, thesaurus too effects vocabulary control in the language being used in indexing and information retrieval and helps the indexer in selecting preferred terms. However, the advantages of using IR thesaurus in comparison to other such tools are:

- It provides more access points, in comparison to other vocabulary control devices;
- It enables the searcher to find out not only information on a specific topic, but also on related topics;
- By using indexing terms and search terms from the same thesaurus, the speed of retrieval can be increased.

K.4.5.12 Use of Thesaurus
According to Rowley, the early thesauri were constructed for use with card-based post-coordinate indexing systems and with early computerized information retrieval systems. These thesauri were typically printed (or typed) and were used alongside the index for which they were designed,

to assist with both indexing and searching of the database [12]. Even in the age of online databases thesaurus is important. It can be used in indexing the documents which are listed in databases as well as retrieving the needed information from the database. Many databases have their online thesauri. Thus a thesaurus can be used in [12]:

- The intellectual assignment of indexing terms to documents as their records enter the system;
- Searching of database through use of appropriate search terms selected by the users from the thesaurus.

K.4.5.13 Evaluation of Thesaurus

The efficiency of a thesaurus depends on its ability to index and retrieve information precisely and quickly. Evaluation of a thesaurus is, therefore, necessary so that lacuna, if any, can be found out and remedial measures can be taken. The factors to be considered for evaluation of a thesaurus are:

- Specificity of terms;
- Completeness of thesaurus;
- Extent of pre-coordination level;
- Word-forms, direct entry and other matters of consistency;
- Extent of linkage;
- Extent of synonyms.

Various quantitative measures have been developed for evaluation work.

K.4.6 Ontology

An ontology, like a thesaurus, is a kind of taxonomy with structure and specific types of relationships between terms belonging to a domain of knowledge and expressed in a format that is machine readable. In an ontology, the types of relationships are greater in number and variety and more specific in their function. Relationships can include, for example, *located in* to relate an organization to a place, *produces/is produced by* to relate a company and its product, and *employer/employed by* to relate a company and a person. Information, which, in a simple controlled vocabulary or taxonomy, is conveyed through indexing, is embedded into the ontology itself. Ontological relationships are used in more complex information systems, such as the Semantic Web [2,4]. Ontology has been discussed in detail in Chapter Y.

K.4.7 Synonym Ring List

A synonym ring is a set of terms that are considered equivalent for the purposes of retrieval. Synonym rings cannot be used during the indexing process. Rather, they are used only during retrieval. Thus although a synonym ring is considered to be a type of controlled vocabulary, it plays a somewhat different role than other controlled vocabularies. Use of synonym rings ensures that a concept that can be described by multiple synonymous or quasi-synonymous terms will be retrieved if any one of the terms is used in a search. A synonym ring allows users to access all content objects or database entries containing any one of the terms. Synonym rings are generally used in the interface in an electronic information system, and provide access to content that is represented in natural, uncontrolled language [18]. A synonym ring may be illustrated in the following way.

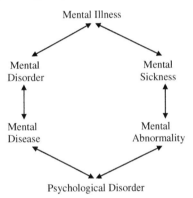

Adapted from ANSI/NISO Z39.19-2005 ISBN: 1-880124-65-3 Guidelines for the Construction, Format, and Management of Monolingual Controlled Vocabularies.

It may be pointed out that synonym rings are used specifically to broaden retrieval (this is often referred to as query expansion). Thus, synonym rings may, in fact, contain near-synonyms that have similar or related meanings, rather than restricting themselves to only terms with true synonymy [3].

K.4.8 Folksonomy

Folksonomy, is a user-generated classification system of web contents that allows users to tag their favorite web resources with their chosen words or phrases selected from natural language. These tags (also called concepts, categories, facets or entities) can be used to classify web resources and to express users' preferences. Folksonomy-based systems allow users to classify Web resources through tagging bookmarks, photos, or other Web resources and saving them to a public website. Thus, information about web resources and online articles can be shared in an easy way [20]. This concept has been discussed in more details in Chapter Y.

K.5 ADVANTAGES OF CV

So far as subject indexing is concerned, use of controlled vocabulary can be more advantageous than that of natural language vocabulary. The main advantages of controlled vocabulary are:

- It ensures consistent indexing;
- It helps the indexer in selecting preferred terms;
- It helps in achieving high precision in searching.

K.6 DISADVANTAGES OF CV

The disadvantages of using controlled vocabulary in subject indexing are:

- The use of controlled vocabulary is likely to be costly than that of natural language vocabulary;
- The user has to be familiar with the controlled vocabulary scheme to make best use of the system;
- Controlled vocabulary can be outdated quickly due to constant developments in the concerned domain.

REFERENCES

[1] A. Redmond-Neal, Building taxonomies (PPT presentation). 2006. <www.taxonomies-sig.org/presentations.htm>.
[2] H. Hedden, Taxonomies, thesauri, and controlled vocabularies. <http://www.hedden-information.com/taxonomies.htm>.
[3] What are controlled vocabularies? <http://www.getty.edu/research/publications/electronic_publications/intro_controlled_vocab/what.pdf>.
[4] American Society For Indexing. Taxonomy and Controlled Vocabularies SIG. About taxonomies and controlled vocabularies. <http://www.taxonomies-sig/about.htm#cv>.
[5] American Library Association, ALA Glossary of Library and Information Science, ALA, Chicago, 1983. p. 220.
[6] Shorter Oxford English Dictionary. V. 2. third ed., Clarendon Press, Oxford, 1975. p. 22.
[7] A. Chatterjee, Thesaurus – an aid to information retrieval, in: P. Dhyani (Ed.), Information Science and Libraries, Atlantic Publishers, New Delhi, 1990. pp. 43–65.
[8] P.M. Roget, Thesaurus of English Words and Phrases; Enlarged by John Lewis Roget, Grosset & Dunlop, New York, 1974.

[9] International Organization for Standardization. Guidelines for the establishment and development of monolingual thesauri (ISO 2788:1976, rev. in 1986).

[10] A. Kent, Information Analysis and Retrieval, third ed., Becker and Hayes, New York, 1971. p. 230.

[11] A. Chatterjee, Information retrieval thesaurus, its structure, function and construction, in: S.B. Ghosh, J.N. Satpathy, (Eds.), Subject Indexing Systems, Concepts Methods and Techniques, IASLIC, Calcutta, 1998, pp. 41–65.

[12] J. Rowley, Abstracting and Indexing, second ed., Clive Bingley, London, 1988.

[13] J. Aitchison, et al., Comp. Thesaurofacet, English Electric Company, Whetstone, 1969. p. XIV.

[14] A. Gilchrist, The Thesaurus in Retrieval, ASLIB, London, 1971. pp. 4–5.

[15] A. Neelameghan, Non-hierarchical associative relationships In: DRTC and INSDOC Seminar on Thesaurus in Information Systems: Papers, DRTC, Bangalore, 1975. pp. A1–A7.

[16] UNESCO-PGI, UNISIST, Guidelines for the Establishment and Development of Monolingual Thesauri, second ed., UNESCO, Paris, 1981.

[17] British Standards Institution, Guidelines for the Establishment and Development of Monolingual Thesauri (BS5723: 1979, BSI, London, 1979.

[18] J. Aitchison, A. Gilchrist, Thesaurus Construction: A Practical Manual, ASLIB, London, 1972. p. 48.

[19] Structure of controlled vocabularies. <http://marciazeng.slis.kent.edu/Z3919/3structure.htm>.

[20] A. Nouruzi, Folksonomies: (Un)Controlled vocabulary, Knowl. Org. 33 (4) (2006) 199–203.

CHAPTER L

Indexing Methods

L.1 INTRODUCTION

Indexing involves preparation of a retrieval aid for the users, through analysis of the contents of different documents, which can help them in identifying their relevant literature easily and speedily. The process or the method used for doing this work is often termed as indexing method, indexing system or indexing technique. An indexing technique is in itself an indexing language, as it shows semantic and syntactic relationships and also uses controlled or uncontrolled vocabulary. As indicated earlier, whatever technique may be adopted for indexing, it has to pass through three main stages, viz., [1] *Familiarization—>Analysis—> Conversion/ Translation* [1]. *Familiarization* involves the indexer becoming conversant with the subject content of the document. *Analysis* involves identification of the concepts significant enough to be indexed. *Conversion* or *Translation* involves representing those concepts in appropriate language.

L.2 ELEMENTS OF INDEXING

The different elements that are to be considered at the time of indexing are as follows [2]:
- Key terms or approach terms of an index entry;
- Principles of term order in compound concepts and in multifocal subjects;
- Controlled vocabulary and cross-references; and
- Arrangement of index entries.

These elements are required at various stages of indexing work.

L.2.1 Approach Terms

The unit of an index is an entry. Each entry has a heading consisting of a single word or combination of a few words representing a concept followed by a symbol or symbols indicating location of that concept within a

Elements of Information Organization and Dissemination
DOI: http://dx.doi.org/10.1016/B978-0-08-102025-8.00012-0

particular context. The following are the sample entries from an alphabetical subject index:

Current awareness service 6–7, 309

Data 63

Education of users 315

Here "Data" is a single word index entry, "Current awareness service" is a multiword but unifocal index entry, while "Education of users" is a multiword as also multifocal index entry. The numerals following the headings indicate the places where these concepts have occurred in the text. These terms are known as approach terms as through these terms the users approach a system (here index) to find their required information. They are also sometimes called key-terms, as they provide key to the user to locate the information in a document. Approach terms are selected by the indexer at the time of indexing.

L.2.2 Term Order

Next comes the act of framing a set of rules or principles for determining the priority of terms as approach terms in a multiword index entry. This is also concerned with the arrangement of words with a fixed relationship between them just like the arrangement and the relationship between the words of a sentence in a particular language as guided by its grammar. Sometimes this is referred to as the syntax of the system.

L.2.3 Controlled Vocabulary

At this stage of indexing, simply using the natural words or the words used by the author to represent some concepts as either approach terms or in any other part of the index entry leads to certain problems of inconsistency due to presence of synonyms and homonyms in a particular language. Therefore, it is necessary to use controlled vocabulary to bring consistency in their use. Different aspects of controlled vocabulary have been discussed in Chapter K. Once this is done, cross-references are necessary to guide a user from one concept to another or one term to another. Sometimes this is termed as the semantics of the system.

L.2.4 Arrangement of Entries

After finalizing the index entries, they are arranged in a suitable order, the most common order being the alphabetical order.

L.3 TYPES OF INDEXING

There are mainly two types of indexing methods, viz., *Assigned* and *Derived*. In assigned indexing, a specially created artificial indexing language is used instead of the language of the document. In derived indexing the terms that are used to denote the contents of a document are directly derived from the document itself and no help is taken of any guide or experience of the indexer. In case of the former, terms are assigned from outside to express the contents of the document, whereas in the latter, appropriate terms are taken from the title and/or text of the document to express the subject of the document. In assigned indexing, an indexer needs to take help of his or her own intellect and intelligence, but in derived indexing, there is no such scope. As such derived indexing is amenable to computerization.

L.3.1 Assigned Indexing

As indicated, in assigned indexing, the terms to represent the subject matter of a document are assigned by the indexer. Normally such terms are taken from any controlled vocabulary. In most cases, the contents or subject of a document cannot be expressed by a single term. Hence, more than one term are assigned for the purpose, but these terms need to be arranged or coordinated in a specific sequence to express the subject matter correctly. The coordination of the terms can be done at the time of indexing or at the time of searching. Thus, assigned indexing can be of two types—Pre-coordinate indexing and Post-coordinate indexing.

L.3.1.1 Pre-coordinate Indexing

The indexing systems in which coordination of terms representing the subject is done beforehand, i.e., at the indexing stage, are called pre-coordinate indexing systems. The main characteristics of these systems are:
- They are based on subject analysis of documents;
- They follow some specified citation order of terms; and
- The coordination is done at the input stage.

It is mainly due to the last characteristics that these types of indexing systems are called pre-coordinate indexing systems. In pre-coordinate indexing, some systems use terms to represent the subject matter, while some others use notation or symbols for the purpose. The indexing systems using terms are of two types—systems using limited number of terms to represent the subject matter, such as subject cataloguing using terms from subject heading lists; and systems using multiple (i.e., not limited) number of terms, such as Chain Indexing, POPSI, and PRECIS.

L.3.1.2 Post-coordinate Indexing

The indexing systems, in which coordination of terms are achieved only at the time of retrieval, are called post-coordinate indexing systems or simply coordinate indexing systems, such as Uniterm indexing system. The main characteristics of these systems are:
- They are also based on subject analysis;
- The heading of each entry consists of only one term;
- The coordination of terms or concepts is achieved at the output stage.

In case of post-coordinate indexing, two types of systems are in vogue. While one type of system uses Term Entries, such as Uniterm and Peek-a-boo; the other uses Item Entries, such as Edge-notched cards and Punched cards. However, the systems of the latter type have now become obsolete.

L.3.1.3 Difference

The main differences between pre-coordinate indexing and post-coordinate indexing are:
- In pre-coordinate indexing, mostly a heading consists of more than one term, but in post-coordinate indexing, a heading consists of only a single term;
- In pre-coordinate indexing, concept coordination is done at the input stage, i.e., at the time of indexing, while in post-coordinate indexing, it is done at the output stage, i.e., at the time of giving service to the users;
- In pre-coordinate indexing, the terms in the heading are arranged according to some fixed rule, but in post-coordinate indexing, no such rule is required to be followed.

L.3.2 Derived Indexing

As indicated earlier, in derived indexing, the terms needed to represent the subject matter of the document are derived directly from the title and/or text of the document. Since no controlled vocabulary is used in this type of indexing, it is also known as free language indexing. Two types of derived indexing are in vogue, viz., title based, such as KWIC and KWOC, and citation based, which is used in Science Citation Index.

L.4 GRAPHIC REPRESENTATION

All the above types of indexing systems may be graphically shown as below:

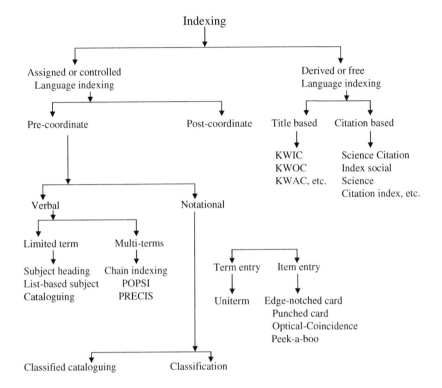

L.5 AUTOMATIC INDEXING

It may be pointed out that the advent of computer and its application in information retrieval work have given rise to some automated indexing systems. Automatic indexing or auto–indexing, as the term itself suggests, is indexing with the help of machine, i.e., without using human intellect. In other words, it is producing index using computer. In contrast, the index produce by humans using their intellect can be called human indexing. "Human indexers use their knowledge to find the 'aboutness' of the writing they are analyzing. They can find concepts within the writing and then use terms to help the searcher connect to that writing" [3]. In automatic indexing, "humans are involved with creating the programs for the computers and in setting the parameters, but the work is done by computers" [3].

L.5.1 Comparative Advantages/Disadvantages

The comparative advantages and disadvantages of human indexing and automatic indexing are [3]:

- Human indexing is more expensive because it is labor-intensive, but automatic indexing is less expensive per unit indexed;
- Human indexing involves more time per unit indexed, whereas a large amount of materials can be indexed in short period of time by automatic indexing;
- Human indexing is often based on abstract or summarization of text, while automatic indexing is based on complete text;
- Human indexing tends to be more selective, while automatic indexing considers most of the words in indexable material;
- Human indexing uses more generic terminology and smaller vocabulary, whereas automatic indexing uses more specific terminology and larger vocabulary;
- Human indexing uses multiterm context providing headings, while automatic indexing makes limited use of term combinations;
- Human indexing uses wide-range of syntactic patterns and can adapt quickly to include new terminology as well as older subject headings, whereas automatic indexing is becoming more sophisticated, and is selecting, combining, manipulating, and weighing terms (usually limited to keywords in, out of, or along-side context);
- Human indexing can cross-reference, link synonyms, or like terms, point to related terms easily; in case of automatic indexing, research is still going on in this matter;
- Surrogation is not often used in human indexing, but it is frequently used in automatic indexing—often as visual displays, such as icons or graphs.

Some other advantages of automatic indexing are [3]:

- It is predictable;
- It is good for materials that are similar (homogenous);
- It is able to extract terms as well as use clustering technique.

Some other disadvantages of auto-indexing are [3]:

- It is not flexible;
- It is not precise when looking at unique material;
- It is unable to do more than rough conceptualization;
- It cannot help searchers find the same information that they would have found with human indexing.

Different aspects of auto-indexing have been discussed in Chapter Y.

L.6 SELECTION

There is no readymade formula to decide which system should be selected for which library or information center. The selection has to be made keeping in view the following factors:

- The extension and intension of the subject to be covered in indexing;
- The specificity expected in the index;
- The types of documents to be indexed;
- The characteristics of the target user group;
- The characteristics of the indexing system;
- The indexer's knowledge and experience about the indexing system.

REFERENCES

[1] S. C. Biswas, Medium of communication of information: natural language vs. information language, Librarian, 4 (1991) 59–65.
[2] A. Chatterjee, Elements of Documentation, The Author, Calcutta, 1983,
[3] G. Shields, Automatic indexing assignment. 2005. <http://www.shieldsnetwork.com/LI842_Shields_Automatic_Indexing.pdf>.

CHAPTER M

Assigned Indexing

M.1 INTRODUCTION

It becomes obvious from the discussions in the previous chapter on assigned or controlled vocabulary based indexing systems that the main characteristics of such indexing are:

- In this type of indexing, a specially created artificial language is used;
- For the sake of expressing the subject matter of the document adequately, more than one term are used as per need;
- The terms used to represent the subject matter of a document are arranged in a special sequence;
- The coordination of terms is done either at the time of indexing or at the time of information search
- An indexer has to use his intellect in analysis of the subject, and selection and coordination of terms, etc.

Some well-known assigned indexing systems have been explained below with examples.

M.2 CHAIN INDEXING (CI)

Ranganathan's idea of Chain Procedure for deriving subject index entries for both alphabetical and classified catalogues is certainly one of the most important contributions in the field of subject indexing as well. The whole process of chain procedure or chain indexing (CI) is based on the classificatory process, or more precisely on the class numbers. Of course, the class number must be able to represent the contents of a document coextensively. For example, let us take up a document entitled *Treatment of heart diseases in India.* The class number of the document, according to Colon Classification (sixth edition) is L32:4:6.44 and according to Dewey Decimal Classification (19th edition) is 616.12060954.

Elements of Information Organization and Dissemination
DOI: http://dx.doi.org/10.1016/B978-0-08-102025-8.00013-2

M.2.1 Breaking of Class Number

The process of indexing begins with breaking of the whole class number at every digit and naming the digits according to the classification scheme adopted, as has been shown below for the above example:

For CC number		*For DDC number*	
L	Medicine (SL)	600	Applied Sciences (USL)
L3	Circulatory system (SL)	610	Medicine (SL)
L32	Heart (SL)	616	Diseases (SL)
L32:	(FL)		
L32:4	Disease (SL)	616.	(FL)
L32:4:	(FL)	616.1	Cardiovascular diseases (SL)
L32:4:6	Treatment (SL)	616.12	Heart diseases (SL)
L32:4:6.	(FL)	616.120	(FL)
L32:4:6.4	Asia (USL)	616.1206	Treatment (SL)
L32:4:6.44	India (SL)	616.12060	(FL)
		616.120609	(FL)
		616.1206095	Asia (USL)
		616.12060954	India (SL)

M.2.2 Indication of Links

The next step is to indicate the nature of each link. There are, according to Ranganathan, four types of links, viz.

- *Sought Link (SL)*—It represents a subject which is likely to be sought or looked up or enquired by the users and on which further documents can be anticipated.
- *Unsought Link (USL)*—It represents a subject which most likely may not be sought by the users and under a particular context there may not be documents under that subject.
- *False Link (FL)*—It does not represent a subject with a definite name, but a connecting symbol or a digit indicating any relation.
- *Missing Link (ML)*—If there is some lacuna in the classification scheme used to classify the document, some isolates may not appear in the chain. This gap in the chain is known as missing link. Such gaps are to be filled while analyzing the class number for CI.

The first three links have been shown in the above example in circular brackets.

M.2.3 Backward Rendering

Now for determining the specific subject of the document, a special method of backward rendering is followed. This process involves taking the last sought link first and moving upwards by picking up the "necessary and sufficient" sought links until the first one is reached. Accordingly, the specific subject of the above document will be as follows:

INDIA, TREATMENT, DISEASE, HEART, MEDICINE (according to CC)
INDIA, TREATMENT, HEART, DISEASE, MEDICINE (according to DDC).

M.2.4 Cross-References

From the above specific subject headings it can be easily visualized that the document which deals mainly with "heart disease" or at least "medicine" is indexed under a place "India." This is due to backward rendering process. Therefore, a very effective system of cross-references is necessary here to satisfy the users from all other angles of the subject. Ranganathan has suggested a series of cross-references from the first sought link to the last for this purpose. The following cross-references can be derived for the CC number.

1. MEDICINE
   See also
   INDIA, TREATMENT, DISEASE, HEART, MEDICINE
2. CIRCULATORY SYSTEM, MEDICINE
   See also
   INDIA, TREATMENT, DISEASE, HEART, MEDICINE
3. HEART, MEDICINE
   See also
   INDIA, TREATMENT, DISEASE, HEART, MEDICINE
4. DISEASE, HEART
   See also
   INDIA, TREATMENT, DISEASE, HEART, MEDICINE
5. TREATMENT, DISEASE, HEART
   See also
   INDIA, TREATMENT, DISEASE, HEART, MEDICINE.

The above cross-references are made from general to specific; therefore, "*see also*" cross-references are adopted. In the cross-references from no. 2 onward, the necessary qualifying terms are added to the headings to specify the particular context of the subject. The procedure for deriving cross-reference entries for DDC number will also be the same.

M.2.4.1 Coates's Modification

E. J. Coates modified the process of deriving the cross-reference entries and suggested that instead of always referring to the specific subject heading from each of the link, it would be better to refer to the next sought link [1]. The cross-reference entries, according to him, will be as follows:

1. MEDICINE
   See also
   CIRCULATORY SYSTEM, MEDICINE

2. CIRCULATORY SYSTEM, MEDICINE
   See also
   HEART, MEDICINE

3. HEART, MEDICINE
   See also
   DISEASE, HEART, MEDICINE

4. DISEASE, HEART, MEDICINE
   See also
   TREATMENT, DISEASE, HEART, MEDICINE

5. TREATMENT, DISEASE, HEART, MEDICINE
   See also
   INDIA, TREATMENT, DISEASE, HEART, MEDICINE.

The cross-reference entries, as modified by Coates, were found to be more useful and economical.

M.2.5 Filing

At the end all the cross-references and specific subject headings are arranged under alphabetical order in an alphabetical subject index.

M.2.6 Modified CI

Ranganathan later modified his own idea of deriving specific subject heading of a document. He suggested that instead of deriving the specific subject all through from the last sought link to the first sought link by backward rendering process it would be better to break at the point where a common isolate idea (if there was any) appeared and from that point onward to go higher up by backward rendering process and then to come to the common isolate. In the example described above, the necessary sought links are:

L	Medicine
L32	Heart
L32:4	Disease
L32:4:6	Treatment
	<—
L32:4:6.44	India

Out of these, the last link "India" is a common isolate. So a break can be made at the point between "Treatment" and "India." Now to derive the specific subject heading, one has to go higher up according to backward rendering process from first common isolate break point, i.e.,

TREATMENT, DISEASE, HEART, MEDICINE

and then has to come to the common isolate as

TREATMENT, DISEASE, HEART, MEDICINE, INDIA.

The above is then the specific subject heading of the document according to modified procedure, which is certainly a better one than the previously determined specific subject heading. If there is more than one common isolate, similar procedure can be repeated. The method of deriving cross-reference entries and arrangement of entries remain the same.

M.2.6.1 Job's Modification
M. M. Job proposed further modification of Ranganathan's modified chain indexing. According to him, Time isolate, wherever it may appear in the chain, should be treated as a necessary link, but should be placed only at the end of the chain. In no case any specific subject heading would start with time isolate, he stressed [2]. If in the above example time isolate is added, the specific subject heading will be:

TREATMENT, DISEASE, HEART, MEDICINE, INDIA, 1985.

M.2.7 Advantages of CI
The main advantages of CI are:
- Since it is based on class number of the document to be indexed, indexing can be done almost automatically, thus saving indexing time
- Indexing can be done by using any good classification scheme;

- The analysis of the subject matter of the document done for classifying also helps in indexing, thus again saving indexing time;
- With the help of this indexing it is possible for a user to get the required document by searching through any link;
- The references are so created that permutation of the components of the subject formulation is not required.

M.2.8 Disadvantages of CI

The disadvantages of CI are:
- Since it is based on class number, any lacuna in classification system may lead to lacuna in indexing;
- If there are shortcomings in the divisions and sub-divisions in the classification system, missing links, false links, and unsought links are created causing difficulties in indexing;
- Only one specific subject entry is created in this indexing and that entry can only answer a specific query formulation.

M.3 PRECIS

Preserved Context Indexing System (PRECIS) was developed by Derek Austin around the later part of 1960s as an alternative procedure for deriving the subject headings and subject index entries for the British National Bibliography (BNB). Almost since its very inception, BNB had been using Chain Procedure for the preparation of its alphabetical subject index, but when it got involved with MARC (Machine Readable Catalogue) project, some difficulties cropped up in generating the subject index entries directly from the machine readable records. So, an investigation was started for an alternative method for generating alphabetical subject index entries directly from the computer instead of through an indexer as was being done in Chain Procedure. PRECIS is, obviously, the result of that investigation. The objectives of the investigation were [3]:
- Computer, and not indexer, should produce all index entries. The indexer's responsibility would be only to prepare the input string and to give necessary instructions to the computer to generate indexes according to definite formats.
- Each of the sought terms should find an index entry and each entry should express the complete thought content/full context of the document unlike chain indexing where only one entry is fully coextensive with the subject and the others are cross-references describing only one aspect of the complete content of the document.

- Each of the entries should be expressive.
- The system should be based on a single set of logical rules to make it consistent.
- The system must have sufficient references for semantically related terms.

After trial application of the system in indexing some 95,000 documents in British National Bibliography from 1971 to 1973, the definitive version of the system was introduced in 1974, in which year the first volume of the PRECIS manual was also published. In light of the experience gained through the application of PRECIS in different countries of Europe as also in China, Austin brought out the second edition of the manual in 1984, in which some new codes were introduced and some existing codes were modified by making more generalized and simpler coding of the PRECIS input string [3,4].

M.3.1 Format and Structure

Format of an index entry means the size, form, or shape in which the components or parts of the entry are written, while the structure indicates the relationship existing between the components just as the relationship between component words in a sentence. For understanding the format and structure of PRECIS, let us take up the following example of a compound subject consisting of four terms cited by Austin himself [4].

Training of skilled personnel in the Indian textile industries

A close analysis of the above subject reveals that in India there are textile industries; and within textile industries there are skilled personnel and training is given to them. So the four components of the subject can easily be written as

India—Textile industries—Skilled personnel—Training

This arrangement of components of a compound subject is called a *string*.

M.3.1.1 Primary Notions

The string thus arrived at, manifests two special characteristics. They are:

- The component terms in a string are arranged in such a way that they are "context-dependent" to each other. That means, the meaning of each term in the string depends upon the meaning of its preceding term in the string, and taken together they all represent a single context. For example, the term "India" gives the geographical context, in which textile industries exist; and "Skilled personnel," being a part of "Textile industries," are being given "Training."
- The four components of the string have a one-to-one relationship to each other; that means each term is directly related to the next term is the string.

These two special characteristics, the first of which is called "Context, dependency" and the second "one-to-one relationship" are the primary notions on which the whole idea of PRECIS is based.

M.3.1.2 Approach Term

One of the most important characteristics of a good indexing system is its ability to retrieve the document from every point of approach. For this, each component term in a string must be able to work as an approach term for the user, and the entries derived out of an approach term must be able to specify the clear context of the document. In the above example, the first term "India" and the last term "Training" can easily be approach terms, such as

India–Textile industries–Skilled personnel–Training

or in the reverse way

Training–Skilled personnel–Textile industries–India

Both of these give the same context and preserve the one-to-one relationship of the component terms. But difficulty arises when the middle order terms "Textile industries" and "Skilled personnel" are made the approach terms. Definitely, bringing those terms to the beginning of the string as approach terms, as

Skilled personnel/India–Textile industries–Training

or

Textile industries/India–Skilled personnel–Training

does not give the clear context of the document, and the one-to-one relationship between the components of the string is also lost.

M.3.1.3 Three-Part Format

Therefore, in PRECIS a special two-line and three-part entry format is used to preserve this important characteristic. This is illustrated below:

Here the components of the entry format are named as:
- Lead: The term which acts as an approach term;
- Qualifier: The term/terms which qualifies/qualify the lead term or bring the lead term into its proper context; and
- Display: The remaining term/terms which also helps/help preserve the context.

Lead and Qualifier are together called Heading.

M.3.2 Generation of Entries

Adoption of this two-line three-part structure helps in generating a set of different index entries from a single string through simple mechanical process called "Shunting." For example, in the string "India–Textile industries–Skilled personnel–Training," the first term "India" is shunted out of the linear structure into the lead automatically by the computer giving us the following entry.

India
Textile industries. Skilled personnel. Training

As any term moves into the lead position, it is printed automatically in bold type. The rest of the terms are printed in normal form except in a few cases. At the next step, the term in the lead is shunted across into the qualifier, and the lead position if then occupied by the next term in the string. By this process we get the following entry:

Textile industries. India
Skilled personnel. Training

The lead and the qualifier form what is called the "heading." By repeating the same procedure we further get the following two entries:

Skilled personnel. Textile industries. India
Training
Training. Skilled personnel. Textile industries. India.

Thus all the four components become lead terms by turn keeping the context intact. However, the generation of lead terms is not entirely mechanized; it is under the control of the indexer who indicates his choice of leads. The generation of entries in the manner given above is called "Standard Format." There are two other formats known as "Inverted Format" and "Predicate Transformation," which will not, however, be discussed here.

M.3.3 Role Operators

Besides the principles of "context dependency" and "one-to-one relationship," which help in constructing the strings, PRECIS has also developed a "Schema of Role Operators" to regulate the writing of the strings. Each of the terms in an input string is prefixed by a role operator which indicates the role it plays in a particular context. Thus the role operators are "a set of notations which specifies the grammatical role or function of terms which follows the operators and which regulates the order of the terms in an input string" [3]. These operators also serve as computer instruction for determining the format, typography, and punctuations associated with each index entry. There are two kinds of Role Operators, viz.

- *Primary Operators:* Earlier known as Mainline Operators, these operators control the sequence of terms in the input string and also determine the format of entries in the printed index. Primary Operators consist of numbers in the range of 0–6 having built-in filing value. Certain conditions must be satisfied while writing the input string and these will be checked by the computer at the time of input. These conditions are:
  - Every string must begin with a concept coded with an operator in the range of (0) to (2).
  - Every string must contain a concept which is prefixed by the operator (1) and/or (2).
- *Secondary Operators:* Earlier known as Interposed Operators, these operators can be introduced into a string at any point to raise its level of exhaustivity, but these operators cannot be used to start a string. Any of the secondary operators is always to be preceded by a primary operator to which it relates.

The list of role operators is given below.

Primary Operators		
Environment of core concepts	0	Location
Core concepts	1	Key system
		Things when action not present.
		Things towards which an action is directed, e.g., object of transitive action, performer of intransitive action
	2	Action; Effect of action
	3	Performer of transitive action (agent, instrument); Intake; Factor
Extra-core concepts	4	Viewpoint-as-form
	5	Selected instance; study region, study example, sample population
	6	Form of document; Target user
Secondary Operators		
Co-ordinate concepts	f	"Bound" co-ordinate concept
	g	Standard co-ordinate concept
Dependent elements	p	Part; Property
	q	Member of quasi-generic group
	r	Assembly
Special classes of action	s	Role definer; Directional property
	t	Author attributed action
	u	Two-way interaction

Schema of Role Operators. *Derek William Austin, PRECIS: a manual of concept analysis and subject indexing, British Library, Bibliographic Services Division, 1984.* © *The British Library Board.*

M.3.4 Codes

The revised version of PRECIS has made provision of three types of Codes—Primary, Secondary and Typographic—for bringing expressiveness in the index entries. Besides, some more codes and techniques have also been provided for manipulation of string to derive index entries. The list of codes is given below.

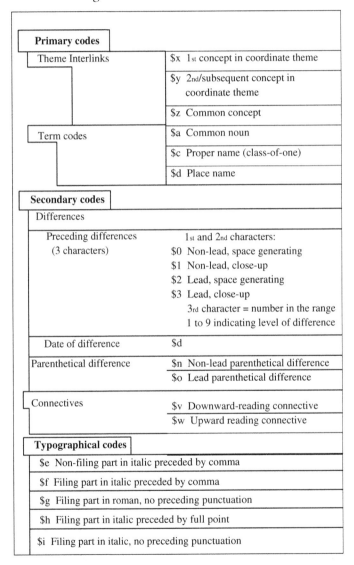

Primary codes		
Theme Interlinks	$x	1st concept in coordinate theme
	$y	2nd/subsequent concept in coordinate theme
	$z	Common concept
Term codes	$a	Common noun
	$c	Proper name (class-of-one)
	$d	Place name
Secondary codes		
Differences		
Preceding differences (3 characters)	1st and 2nd characters:	
	$0	Non-lead, space generating
	$1	Non-lead, close-up
	$2	Lead, space generating
	$3	Lead, close-up
	3rd character = number in the range 1 to 9 indicating level of difference	
Date of difference	$d	
Parenthetical difference	$n	Non-lead parenthetical difference
	$o	Lead parenthetical difference
Connectives	$v	Downward-reading connective
	$w	Upward reading connective
Typographical codes		
$e	Non-filing part in italic preceded by comma	
$f	Filing part in italic preceded by comma	
$g	Filing part in roman, no preceding punctuation	
$h	Filing part in italic preceded by full point	
$i	Filing part in italic, no preceding punctuation	

Three types of Codes – Primary, Secondary and Typographic. *Derek William Austin, PRECIS: a manual of concept analysis and subject indexing, British Library, Bibliographic Services Division, 1984. © The British Library Board.*

M.3.5 String Making

A fully expressive string is constructed in the following manner according to PRECIS:

- *Subject Analysis:* Like all other systems of indexing and classification, the first step in the preparation of a string is the analysis of the subject content of the document to be indexed. By analyzing the subject of the example referred above the following title like phrase may be formulated.

  Training of skilled personnel in the Indian textile industries

- *Search for "Action":* The next step is to find out whether a term denoting an action is present in the phrase or not. If present, the action will usually determine how the rest of the subject should be handled. Here the word "Training" denotes an action. This term should, therefore, be prefixed by the operator 2 in the following manner:

  (2) training

- *Kind of Action:* The next step is to find out the kind of action represented by the term, that is, whether the action is transitive or intransitive. If it is a transitive action, it will take an object according to the principles of grammar. In the present example "Training" is a transitive action. So it has taken an object "skilled personnel" who are being trained. The concept of "skilled personnel" therefore, is the key system which can be prefixed by the operator "1."

  Thus (1) skilled personnel
        (2) training

- *Part Concepts:* But a close examination of the term "Skilled personnel" shows that at least in the present context, it is a part of some other concept, viz., "Textile industries" and, therefore, the term "Textile industries" should be made the key system indicating "Skilled personnel" as a part of the key system by prefixing the interposed operator "p" which introduces a part or property to a concept. The revised string, thus, will be:

  (1) textile industries
  (2) skilled personnel
  (3) training

- *Environment:* The remaining concept in the subject, viz., "India" clearly functions as the environment in which the author has considered the whole subject. Therefore, this should be prefixed with the role operator "0." The final string now becomes:

(0) India
(1) textile industries
(p) skilled personnel
(2) training

- *Arrangement:* The arrangement of the component terms in the input string is guided by the following principles:
  - The numbered or primary operators are arranged according to their ordinal value;
  - All other operators are attached to the concept with which they are related;
  - Every string must begin with a primary operator in the range of 0–2; and
  - Every string must also contain a term which prefixed by the operator 1 and/or 2.

M.3.6 Final Entries

Now in the above input string, if it is assumed that each of these terms can come as the lead, then through the process of "shunting" the following entries can be generated:

India
    Textile industries. Skilled personnel. Training
Textile industries. India
    Skilled personnel. Training
Skilled personnel. Textile industries. India
    Training
Training. Skilled personnel. Textile industries. India

M.3.7 Advantages of PRECIS

The advantages of PRECIS are:
- As it is not dependent on class number, any deficiency in classification cannot influence indexing in any manner.
- Indexing is done by analyzing the subject content of the document and all aspects of the subject are included in the subject string; search through any aspect of the subject retrieves the required document.
- Since the subject string is formulated following some definite rules, subject string formulation will not change with change of personnel doing the indexing job.
- Shunting system ensures lead position to every component of the subject string and permutation of components is not required.

- This system can be used for deriving subject headings for documents covered in a bibliography or a catalogue.
- PRECIS indexing process can be easily mechanized.

M.3.8 Disadvantages of PRECIS

The disadvantages of PRECIS are:

- The shunting work can be mechanized, but the work of selecting appropriate role operator cannot be as it requires human intelligence.
- The sequence of different types of role operators has been fixed artificially.
- There are many exceptions to the rules of PRECIS, which often create dilemma in the minds of an indexer.

M.4 POPSI

Although Chain Procedure showed a new way for deriving specific subject headings, it was often criticized for being too much dependent on class numbers. Truly, Chain Procedure cannot index a document properly if the class number is constructed on the basis of a structurally defective classification scheme. As such, the associates of Ranganathan at DRTC, Bangalore, started thinking in 1960s on finding the ways to obviate the difficulties created by class number based indexing. In 1969 they came up with a system of formulating specific subject by analyzing the subject matter of a document through the first six steps of classification as propounded by Ranganathan [5]. Gradually a postulate-based full-fledged indexing system was developed which was named as Postulate-based Permuted Subject Indexing (POPSI) system. In the beginning the subjects were being analyzed on the basis of basic classes and facets of Colon Classification. Later, Bhattacharyya further developed and refined it. Devadason also introduced some changes in POPSI to make it suitable for computer application [6, 7]. The new system, as its name itself indicates, is based on some postulates and principles rather than class numbers. It is, in fact, a new improved version of Chain Procedure developed almost at the same time when PRECIS was developed by Austin.

M.4.1 Basis of POPSI

As mentioned in Chapter J, Bhattacharyya arrived at a Deep Structure of Subject Indexing Languages by logically abstracting the subject indexing languages of Cutter, Kaiser, Dewey, and Ranganathan and said that the structure of a specific SIL may be deemed to be a "surface structure" of the Deep Structure of Subject Indexing Languages. POPSI is based on the said Deep Structure of Subject Indexing Languages. It is specifically based on:

- A set of postulated Elementary Categories (ECs) fit to form components of subject propositions

- A set of syntax rules with reference to ECs
- A set of indicator digits (or notations) to denote the ECs and their subdivisions
- A vocabulary control tool, called Classaurus.

The postulates, principles and the working concepts of POPSI are the same as those of General Theory of Deep Structure of Subject Indexing Languages. The Deep Structure of Subject Indexing Languages postulates that the component ideas in the name of a subject can be deemed to fall in any one of the ECs—Discipline (D), Entity (E), Property (P), and Action (A) and a special component, called Modifier (m). (*See* Section 4 of Chapter J for understanding the functioning of POPSI.)

M.4.2 Different Versions

The Deep Structure of Subject Indexing Languages with its associated postulates suggests that it is possible to design a basic version of POPSI, which is readily amenable to conversion into specific versions (POPSI Specific) on the basis of certain rules and decisions of the indexer.

M.4.3 Subject-Proposition

POPSI as a process for preparing subject–propositions consists primarily of (a) analysis; (b) synthesis; (c) permutation. The tasks of analysis and synthesis are mainly guided by a table of notations as given below.

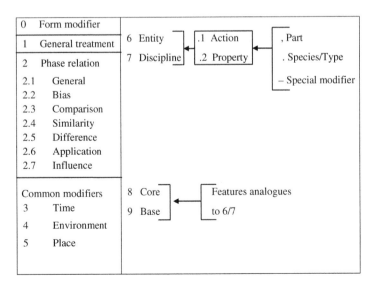

G. Bhattacharyya, A general theory of subject indexing language. (Thesis submitted to Karnataka University, Dharwad, India, for Ph D degree), 1980. (Unpublished)

The notations/indicators are used to indicate the manifestations of ECs and their relative position in the subject propositions. Manifestations of each of the ECs may admit subdivisions: Special modifier, Species/Type and Part. In POPSI Basic D is the BASE (B) and E is the Core (C). The notation for D is always omitted as it is understood to be the first digit in all subject statements. The same procedure is followed in case of any B. The different manifestations are arranged horizontally in the decreasing order of their ordinal values.

M.4.4 Syntactical Structure

As per Deep Structure of Subject Indexing Languages, POPSI follows the following syntactical structure in the subject-proposition [7]:

- DISCIPLINE followed by ENTITY, which is followed by PROPERTY and/or ACTION. PROPERTY and or ACTION may be further followed by COMMON MODIFIERS.
- The SPECIAL MODIFIERS and/or SPECIES/TYPES and/or PARTS, for each of the ECs follow immediately adjacent to the man-ifestation to which they are respectively SPECIAL MODIFIERS or SPECIES/TYPES or PARTS without the manifestation of any other EC intervening.

M.4.5 Indexing Steps

The indexing work is systematically performed in eight steps according to POPSI. How a simple title *Treatment of Heart Diseases in India* can be indexed by POPSI in those eight steps is demonstrated below:

- *Analysis of the Subject Indicative Expression:* Such expression may be the title of the book, article, etc. The analysis of the subject indicative expres-sion involves identification in the expression the facets in terms of ECs and modifiers. By such analysis of the above title we get the following:

  Medicine = Discipline (D)
  Treatment = Action (A)
  Heart   = Entity (E)
  Disease   = Property (P)
  India   = Space Common Modifier (Cm)

- *Formalization of the Subject-Proposition:* This involves writing down the component terms as a formalized expression in a context-dependent sequence following the rules of syntax of POPSI. This gives rise to the

Basic Chain. The formalized subject-proposition of the above book will be:

> Medicine (D), Heart (E), Diseases (P of E), Treatment (A on P), India (Cm)

- *Standardization of the Subject-Proposition:* This involves deciding the standard terms with the help of classaurus, specially for the terms having synonyms. In the present case the terms "Disease" and "Therapeutics" have been taken as standard terms for "Diseases" and "Treatment" respectively. Thus the standardized subject-proposition will be:

> Medicine (D), Heart (E), Disease (=Diseases) (P of E), Therapeutics (=Treatment), India (Cm)

- *Modulation of the Subject-Proposition:* This involves augmenting the standardized subject-proposition by interpolating and extrapolating, as the case may be, the successive superordinates of each manifestation by using standard terms with indication of their synonyms, if any. Help of classaurus may be taken in this work. This gives to Basic Modulated Chain. In the present case, after modulation the basic modulated Chain will be:

> Medicine (D), Circulatory System, Heart (E), Disease (P of E), Therapeutics (A), India (Cm)

- *Preparation of the Entry for Organizing Classification:* This involves inserting appropriate indicators or notation for ECs, their subdivisions and common modifier in the appropriate places with the help of POPSI table. All indications of synonyms are also removed. A set of modulated and standardized subject-propositions with appropriate notations, when just sorted alpha-numerically can produce an organizing classification effect, which will considerably reduce the need for *see also* type reference entries of both ascending and descending type. After this work the subject-proposition will take the following shape:

> 7 Medicine 6 Circulatory System, Heart 6.2 Disease 6.2.1 Therapeutics 5 India

- *Decision about Terms of Approach:* This involves deciding the terms of approach for generating associative classification or their effect and of controlling synonyms. For controlling synonyms, each standard term is to be referred to from each of its synonyms. Wherever warranted, it would be necessary to individualize the term-of-approach. In the above example all the terms may be taken as terms-of-approach. A reference entry may be made as:

Treatment
    See
Therapeutics

- *Preparation of Entries for Associative Classification:* This involves preparation of an entry under each term-of-approach by cyclic permutation of sought terms for generating associative classification effect in alphabetical arrangement in such a way that under each term a more or less systematic arrangement of the subject-proposition is found. In other words, in each entry under the term-of-approach, the whole subject proposition is mentioned as the context, e.g., for the above document, an entry for associative classification will be:

Circulatory System
    7 Medicine 6 Circulatory System, Heart
      6.2 Disease 6.2.1 Therapeutics 5 India

The same organizing classification will have to be repeated under each of the approach terms.

- *Arrangement of Entries in Alphabetical Sequence:* This involves arrangement of all the entries in alphabetical sequence according to a set of standardized rules being guided, wherever warranted, by the notations indicating the categories of manifestations.

M.4.6 Advantages of POPSI

The main advantages of POPSI are:
- It is also not dependent on class number and as such any deficiency in classification cannot influence indexing in any manner.
- This is also done through subject analysis of documents; not only the concepts discussed in the document being index are included in the subject-proposition, even the superordinate concepts of those concepts are also included and used as approach terms thus widening the scope of access by the users.
- The scope of access further widens due to provision of *see* references.
- The system can also be used for preparing subject headings in bibliographies and catalogues and also preparing back-of-the-book indexes.
- It can also be used in formulating search strategy for information retrieval.

M.4.7 Disadvantages of POPSI

The disadvantages of POPSI are:

- It requires use of a classaurus at different levels of work and hence before using the system a classaurus needs to be constructed in the subject concerned, if not available.
- Selection of terms-of-approach cannot be done mechanically; it depends on the views of the indexer.
- The notations attached to the terms in the subject proposition are not intelligible to the users and hence may not be liked by them.

M.5 UNITERM INDEXING

Uniterm indexing system is the best known coordinate indexing system based on term entry principle. It was Mortimer Taube who devised in 1953 this new system of indexing which depends on natural language and is free from the problem of a fixed citation order. Its main distinguishing feature is that coordination is done only at the output or service stage and not at the input or indexing stage.

M.5.1 Uniterms

The uniterms are single but significant words, just like keywords, selected directly from the document to be indexed. They represent the ideas or concepts discussed in the document. In other words, uniterms are units of information contained in a document. If a document contains more than one uniterm, it should be indexed under each uniterm. For example, a document discussing *Management of Libraries* contains two concepts—Management and Libraries. So, it should be indexed under both the terms.

M.5.2 Indexing Process

The process involved in indexing documents, according to a simple manual uniterm system, are as follows [8]:

- *Providing Identification Number:* A documents to be indexed is first accessioned or at least assigned a unique identification, e.g.,

    523 Management of Libraries
    718 Libraries and Society.

    The accession file is maintained as usual in numerical order.

- *Isolating Uniterms:* The subject content of each document is thoroughly and carefully analyzed and appropriate unit terms or concepts are isolated. In the above examples the unit terms will be:

  For document number 523
  > (1) Management and (2) Libraries
  For document number 718
  > (1) Libraries and (2) Society.

- *Entry Making:* For each uniterm a specially designed card of 5" × 8" size is prepared. The card has a space for heading where the uniterm is written in capital letters. The rest of the space is divided into ten columns from 0 to 9 for entering the document number.
- *Terminal Digit Posting:* The number of each document containing a particular uniterm is written in the card representing that uniterm. The "terminal" or final digit of the document number determines the column in which the number should be entered. In the above examples the document number 523 will be entered in column 3 and document number 718 will be entered in column 8, as digits 3 and 8 are terminal digits of the respective documents. As new documents are indexed, fresh cards are prepared for new concepts and if any document contains any of the concepts for which cards are already available, its number is entered in the appropriate existing cards and thus the process continues.

LIBRARIES

0	1	2	3	4	5	6	7	8	9
	411		523						99

MANAGEMENT

0	1	2	3	4	5	6	7	8	9
			523		705	66		718	

SOCIETY

0	1	2	3	4	5	6	7	8	9
100		212		514				718	

- *Filing:* All the cards are filed in simple alphabetical order.

M.5.3 Searching Process

When a request for documents on a topic is received, the documents are searched in the following manner:

- *Analysis of Request:* The subject of the documents sought is first analyzed and translated into appropriate uniterms.
- *Culling of Relevant Cards:* The cards representing those uniterms are then extracted from the alphabetical sequence.
- *Identifying Relevant Documents:* The relevant documents are then searched out by comparing the numbers in the culled out cards. Terminal digit posting helps in this work of number comparison. When a number is found common in these cards it is presumed that the document represented by that number discusses the concepts represented by the respective cards and is therefore likely to be relevant to the user. In the cards shown above document no. 523 appears in the first two cards and so it contains the two concepts Management and Libraries, while document no. 718 appears in the first card and the last card and therefore it contains the two concepts Libraries and Society.

M.5.4 Advantages of UNITERM

The following advantages may be obtained when UNITERM system is used [8]:

- The documents indexed by UNITERM may be arranged by their accession or serial numbers and no classification system is required for this purpose.
- The work at the input or indexing stage is very simple as coordination of concepts is done only at the output or dissemination stage.
- The system being very simple and using natural language, can be explained to the users easily.
- As many items can be included in a single card, the physical size of the index can be reduced.
- The reports and pamphlets indexed by this process can be conveniently stored in boxes as the new items are only added at the end and there is no question of insertion in between the existing sequence.

M.5.5 Disadvantages of UNITERM

The UNITERM system has some disadvantages too such as follows [8]:

- The uniterms used to index documents resemble the isolates of a faceted classification, but they are arranged in an artificial alphabetical order.

- The system uses only single terms as headings and coordination of the required terms is achieved only when a search is made.
- Coordination of terms may not always yield the required combination order, e.g., two entries under the headings "Management" and "Education" will enlist the identification numbers of all documents dealing with Management Education as also Management of Education and a user seeking documents on only Management Education will also get those on Management of Education.
- There may be also false coordination, e.g., a document entitled "Education in east Asia" covering two topics, viz., School Education in China and College Education in Japan, will be indexed under five uniterms, viz., School, College, Education, China and Japan, and a person seeking documents on College Education in China or School Education in Japan will get this document retrieved although these topics have not been discussed in the document.
- The terms by which a reader searches and the terms under which the documents have been indexed may not always tally; readers often search by generic terms, but generic relationships are not shown in the entries.
- Uncontrolled use of synonyms, homonyms, and singular and plural forms may affect the efficient functioning of the system.
- The system involves two-stage search—first, location of the required document number through card searching and second, finding out the document with the help of the number identified in the index cards.
- Only a limited number of documents can be entered on a single card; new cards can be prepared for the same heading but that increases difficulty in search work.

M.5.6 Solutions

Several suggestions have been put forth for solving some of the problems of UNITERM mentioned above. These include the following [8]:

- Use of a matrix film for automatic projection of the document, the number of which is identified as relevant for a user
- Use of role indicators where association of the same terms indicate two different meanings
- Use of a thesaurus for choosing terms to avoid the problem of synonyms and generic relations
- Use of fixed rules for choosing singular or plural forms

- Use of context in parentheses for the terms having more than one meaning
- Use of appropriate symbols to indicate the quantitative importance of a term in relation to the central idea, e.g., digit 3 attached to an index term may indicate that the term is most closely related to the central idea and digits 2 and 1 may indicate the closeness of the relation in decreasing order
- Use of links to avoid false coordination in multitopical documents, e.g., there will be no question of coordinating China with College, or School with Japan in the above example if links are attached with the terms as a form of interlocking device such as China (A), School (A), Japan (B), College (B).

It is, however, needless to stress that if role operators, links etc., as mentioned above, are employed, the main virtue of the system, i.e., simplicity will be lost to a great extent.

REFERENCES

[1] E.J. Coates, Subjects catalogues, headings and structure, Library Association, London, 1960.
[2] M.M. Job, Dictionary catalogue and chain procedure, Ann. Lib. Sci. Doc. 20 (1973) 58–62.
[3] J.K. Sarkhel, Subject indexing by PRECIS, in: S.B. Ghosh, J.N. Satpathi, (Eds.), Subject Indexing Systems, IASLIC, Kolkata, 1998, pp. 140–187.
[4] D. Austin, PRECIS, Lib. Sci. Slant. Doc. 12 (1975) 89–126.
[5] G. Bhattacharyya, A. Neelameghan, Postulate-based subject headings for dictionary catalogue system, DRTC Annual Semin. 7 (1969). Paper CA.
[6] F.J. Devdason, Computerization of deep structure bases indexes, Int. Class. 12 (1985) 87–94.
[7] F.J. Devdason, Computerized deep structure indexing system, 1986 (FID/CR Report No. 14). Indeks Verlag, Frankfurt.
[8] A. Chatterjee, Elements of Documentation, The Author, Kolkata, 1983,
[9] G. Bhattacharyya, A general theory of subject indexing language. Thesis submitted to Karnataka University, Dharwad, for PhD degree. 1980 (Unpublished).
[10] S.C. Biswas, Subject heading by POPSI, in: S.B. Ghosh, J.N. Satpathi, (Eds.), Subject Indexing Systems, IASLIC, Kolkata, 1998, pp. 188–210.

CHAPTER N

Derived Indexing

N.1 INTRODUCTION

From the discussions in the chapter on "Indexing Methods," it becomes clear that the characteristics of derived indexing are:
- No controlled or artificial language is used in this indexing;
- There is no need of content analysis of the document being indexed;
- The indexing work can be done mechanically;
- Indexing can be done easily and speedily;

Two widely used derived indexing methods are described below.

N.2 KWIC

Keyword in Context (KWIC) was originally introduced by Andrea Crestadoro as long back as in 1864, under the name Keyword in Titles, for a catalogue of Manchester public libraries. Nearly a century later, around 1958, it was developed by Hans P. Luhn of IBM for computer manipulation and applied to the American Chemical Society's current awareness publication *Chemical Titles*. The acronym KWIC was also coined by him [1]. As the name itself suggests, in this system, the keywords derived for indexing purposes are shown in a particular context. That means, they not only serve as approach terms to the users, but also specify the particular context of the document.

N.2.1 Indexing Process

Indexing of documents, according to KWIC, involves the following processes [2]:
- *Keyword selection*: The first important work is selection of significant terms or keywords. This is done from the title of the document and/or title like phrases. The selection may be done in two ways—either an editor may mark the significant terms or a "stop list" or "word exclusion list" may be fed into the computer beforehand so that the computer itself can exclude the insignificant words form the title.

Elements of Information Organization and Dissemination
DOI: http://dx.doi.org/10.1016/B978-0-08-102025-8.00014-4

Usually initial articles, prepositions, etc. are eliminated as insignificant terms. The keywords, thus selected, serve as approach terms. For a document entitled "*Treatment of heart diseases in India*" the significant terms or keywords will be (1) Treatment, (2) Heart, (3) Disease, and (4) India.

- *Entry generation*: Now index entries are generated with each keyword serving as an approach term. The title is so manipulated that the keyword comes in the beginning (or in the middle) followed by the rest of the title. Thus, in the above example, there will be four index entries for the four keywords, each of them coming in the beginning by rotation. The format of the entries has been described separately.
- *Filing*: The entries are filed alphabetically by keywords.

N.2.2 Format and Structure

Each entry, according to KWIC system, consists of the following three parts arranged in linear order:

- *Keyword*—This is written either in the beginning or in the middle, often in bold letters or capital letters or is underlined for easy filing and searching.
- *Context*—The rest of the title, besides the keyword, is used as the context. A stroke (/) separates the last word and first word of the title. The context helps in efficient retrieval.
- *Reference*—A code number or symbol identifying the document is added at the extreme right end.

Thus the index entries of the title mentioned above will be:

Treatment of heart diseases in India   −25
Heart diseases in India/Treatment of   −25
Diseases in India/Treatment of heart   −25
India/Treatment of heart diseases in   −25

If the keywords are brought in the middle, the entries will look like:

in India/   **Treatment** of heart diseases   −25
Treatment of   **Heart** diseases in India   −25
of heart   **Diseases** in India/Treatment   −25
diseases in   **India**/Treatment of heart   −25

The title written in the above manner is called wrap-around or recirculated title.

N.2.3 Advantages of KWIC

The main advantages of the KWIC system are [2,3]:

- It hardly requires any intellectual effort and hence the indexer is not required to be a subject specialist;
- Indexing can be done mechanically and speedily;
- The keywords are mainly selected from the titles of documents and hence it is not often necessary to go through the contents of the document to be indexed;
- The terminology used is always current as keywords represent actual terms used by specialist authors;
- It is based on natural language and hence no controlled vocabulary is required.

N.2.4 Disadvantages of KWIC

The technique also has some disadvantages such as follows [2,3]:

- Titles may not always be coextensive with the contents of the documents and when it is not so, it becomes necessary to formulate expressive title-like phrases;
- Since controlled vocabulary is not used, entries relating to same subject get scattered and consequently the searches yield low recall;
- The rendering of context with stroke (/) as a separator between the last word and the first word may not be liked by the users;
- The words used as keywords and the words used by the searcher may not always tally and in such cases it is necessary for a searcher to know the synonyms and the terms related to his subject of search;
- As related topics are scattered, a user needs to search by several keywords;
- It fails to meet the exhaustive approach to information from a large collection.

N.2.5 Variants of KWIC

Some variants of KWIC have also been developed with a view to overcome the shortcomings of the system. The main features of a few such important variants are described below.

- *KWOC*: According to Keyword out of Context (KWOC) system, the whole title of the document is used as context along with the keyword. The keyword and the context are written either in the same line or in two successive lines as shown below:

Treatment   Treatment of heart diseases in India   −25
Treatment
　　　　　Treatment of heart diseases in India   −25

- *KWAC*: In Keyword Augmented in Context or Keyword-and-Context (KWAC), the keywords are enriched with additional words taken from the contents or abstract of the document. Thus the dependence of the indexing system on titles is reduced.
- *KWWC*: Keyword with Context (KWWC) system prescribes use of only that part of the title as context which is relevant to a particular keyword.

N.3 CITATION INDEXING

An author usually mentions along with his work all those documents which he has consulted or referred to. This is called citing or referencing. Citations are thus the references made to other documents in the text of a work. A document to which a reference is made is called a cited document, while a document which makes reference to the cited document is called a citing document. A citation covers the essential bibliographical details of the cited document and those of the host document when the cited document forms a part of it. These information are arranged in some standard pattern. Evidently, when a document refers to some other documents, it can be assumed that there is some similarity or association of ideas between the citing document and the cited document. There can hardly be identical treatment of subject matter in both the documents; only some ideas or lines of the cited document may have been quoted by the author of the citing document either to explain or support his own contention or to discount those ideas by comparing them with his own findings. Thus the relationship existing between the cited document and the citing documents may be of varying degrees. "In general, a citation implies a relationship between a part or the whole of a cited paper and a part or whole of the citing paper" [4]. This relationship, in fact, forms the basis of citation indexing.

N.3.1 Underlying Principles

"The concept of citation indexing relies on three principles. Firstly, all knowledge from whatever discipline is always dependent on or related to tenets already accepted and established. Secondly, the core literature on a given subject is contained in only a selection of periodicals relevant to that subject and identification of these core periodicals will save research time. Thirdly, the product of research is knowledge, which is recorded and published, and a possible measure of its significance is the frequency of citation in subsequent research" [5]. Incidentally, when a document cites all or a few of the same documents cited by another document, it may also be assumed that the two citing documents are also related. Kessler has termed it as bibliographical coupling and suggested a method of measuring the coupling strength [6].

N.3.2 Genesis of Citation Index

Though the earliest known citation index was an index of biblical citations in rabbinic literature, the *Mafteah ha-Derashot*, attributed to Maimonides and probably dating to the 12th century, the first true citation index dates to the 1860 publication of Labatt's *Table of Cases.... California....*, followed in 1872 by Wait's *Table of Cases....New York....* But the most important and best-known citation index came with the 1873 publication of Shepard's Citations [7], which was an index to American legal cases linking the recent cases with the earlier cases of the same nature. Appreciating the usefulness of the system, Eugene Garfield stressed the need of adopting it in the field of science and technology in 1950s and the Institute of Scientific Information (ISI), Philadelphia, the institution of Garfield, started bringing out the *Science Citation Index (SCI)* on regular basis. *Social Science Citation Index* and *Arts and Humanities Citation Index* were also started later. The first automated citation indexing was done by CiteSeer in 1997. Other sources for citation data include Google Scholar and Elsevier's Scopus [7].

N.3.3 Definition of Citation Index

"A citation index is an ordered list of cited articles, each of which is accompanied by a list of citing articles. The citing article is identified as a source, while the cited article as a reference" [8]. In other words, it is "a structured list of all the citations in a given collection of documents. Such lists are usually so arranged that the cited document is followed by the citing documents" [9]. Becker and Hayes describe it as "a listing which collects in one place the bibliographical descendents of a given cited author" [10].

N.3.4 Characteristics of Citation Index

The chief characteristics of a citation index are [2]:
* It is an index of sets of documents, each set consisting of a cited document and its citing documents;

- It uses the citing document as a source and the cited document as a reference;
- It is arranged by cited documents and not under subject headings.

N.3.5 Difference from Other Indexes

Citation index is different from other types of indexes discussed earlier in the following ways [2]:

- Other indexes are based on either subject analysis or significant words taken from the titles or texts, while a citation index is based only on citations;
- Entries in other indexes are usually arranged alphabetically by their headings, while entries in a citation index are arranged alphabetically by cited authors;
- In other indexes either the full bibliographical details of a document indexed or a code number representing it are mentioned as a reference or as an aid for retrieval, while the details of cited documents are mentioned as reference in a citation index;
- In other indexes the documents representing the same subject area or same terms are collated and brought together, while in a citation index the documents having association of ideas are collated.

N.3.6 Indexing Process

Citation indexing is the technique of bringing together the documents which manifest association of ideas through mechanical sorting of citations. In other words, it is a process of finding out the relationship between documents through citations. A simple manual method of CI may involve the following steps [2]:

- *Deciding on the coverage:* At the outset a decision has to be taken about the subject and the period to be covered and the specific documents, the citations of which are to be indexed. Although periodicals are usually taken up for CI, other primary documents like conference proceedings, patents, standards, research papers, and even books may be covered, if required.
- *Scanning of source documents:* The selected source documents may now be scanned, relevant articles or sections identified and their citations checked. If any citation is found incomplete or doubtful, the cited document may be consulted and the citation concerned may be completed or rectified.

- *Preparation of entry*: An entry should be made for each citation on a standard-size card or slip. Each entry will consist of the essential details of the cited document and those of the citing document. An indication about the nature of the citing document, i.e., whether it is an article (review, abstract or original) or a standard or patent, etc., should also be given in the entry. Sometimes code numbers are used for indicating cited and citing documents.
- *Sorting of entries*: All the entries thus prepared are sorted out by cited documents or their code numbers. This yields a bunch of entries for each cited document.
- *Consolidation of entries*: Each bunch of entries are then consolidated so that the details of the citing documents are arranged in some order, usually in alphabetical order by their authors' names, and placed along with the details of the cited document, which is common to the bunch.
- *Arrangement*: The consolidated entries, each consisting of the details of a cited document and those of its citing documents, are now arranged in some convenient order, usually again alphabetically by the names of the cited authors.
- *Preparation of index*: For the convenience of the users, some indexes like index of the citing or source documents, index of the topics covered by the documents, the citations of which have been indexed, etc. may be compiled.
- *Press-copy making*: If the citation index is to be printed, the press copy should now be prepared by word processing or typing and affixing necessary instructions to the press.

N.3.7 Advantages of Citation Index

According to Garfield, "the citation index has the unique chronological ability to facilitate *prospective* as well as *retrospective* searches. As in traditional indexes, you can look backward to locate earlier papers. And you can go forward to determine who has cited an earlier work. By starting with a single paper or book, you can identify additional papers that have referred to it. And each retrieved paper, in turn, may provide a new list of references with which to continue the citation search. Thus, one may cycle backwards and forwards through several generations of related records" [11]. Besides this ability, the citation index has several direct and indirect advantages as mentioned below, most of which are not possessed by indexes prepared by other indexing techniques.

N.3.7.1 Direct Advantages

The direct advantages of citation index are [2]:

- A citation index helps in identifying relevant papers independent of language, title, author, or keywords.
- Unlike other indexes, a citation index is able to link up all recent papers on a subject with papers published earlier but with which the recent ones have association or ideas. This makes search of relevant materials easy.
- In indexes with subject arrangement, only those documents which belong to the same subject area are brought together, but in a citation index, documents which may not belong to exactly same subject area but are partially related are also brought together and, therefore, its coverage can be said to be multidisciplinary.
- In other types of indexes documents belonging to collateral or partially related subject areas are linked up by *see also* references, but it is not required in a citation index as such documents are automatically collected together.
- While all those indexes using subject headings or terms for indexing and arrangement have problems relating to terminology, a citation index does not have any such problem at all.
- The information retrieved through a citation index have a very high degree of relevancy, especially if the citations are carefully selected and checked before inclusion in the index.
- The searching of relevant materials can be done more easily and speedily in a citation index than in many conventional indexes.
- It is a self-upgrading index, as each new citation of an old paper are automatically listed making the list of citing documents up-to-date.
- As preparation of citation indexes needs no intellectual activity, it is amenable to mechanization.

N.3.7.2 Indirect Advantages

The indirect advantages of citation index are [2]:

- By analyzing the citation indexes, it is possible to find out the periodicals in which maximum number of original articles and articles of high standard are published (i.e., core periodicals). This helps in taking a decision about the periodicals to be procured in a library.
- The impact factor of journals can be measured with the help of citation index.
- An article can inspire other authors for a limited period of time, after which it becomes obsolete. Similarly, a volume of periodicals loses its

importance when its authors are no longer cited. These can be found out by analyzing citation indexes.

- How far a subject is related to or dependent upon other subjects may also be studied from citation indexes.
- The genesis of an inter-disciplinary or newly emerging subject can be found out with the help of citation indexes.
- The relative use of different types of documents like periodicals, books, standards, patents, thesis, etc. can be found out by looking into the extent of their citation.
- With the help of citation indexes an author of a cited document can know how far his ideas or research results have been appreciated, applied or criticized. This enables him to work further on his subject in proper line.
- It is also possible to know through citation indexes who are the main workers in a particular subject field.

N.3.8 Criticism of Citation Indexes

In spite of these advantages, citation indexes are not free from criticism. The main criticisms against these are [2]:

- It does not provide any logical or conventional subject arrangement to which the users are accustomed.
- At least one reference must be known to a user for starting the search in a citation index.
- Since the nature of relationship between the cited document and the citing documents is not clearly indicated, there is a possibility of retrieving documents not pertinent from the point of view of a particular user.
- While writing papers, some authors may miss some highly relevant documents—especially those in alien languages—and may not cite them. They are thus excluded from a citation index making it incomplete and incomprehensive.
- A citation index retrieves only related documents and not the contents of documents.
- Some critics also point out that a citation index, specially SCI, is not capable of meeting the exhaustive approach. But it must be kept in mind that a citation index is basically not meant to be used as an exhaustive subject index, it only shows the path into the literature of the subject.

N.3.9 Usefulness of Citation Index

Every indexing system perhaps suffers from some kind of shortcoming. Citation indexing is no exception. But many of the defects mentioned above arise out of such factors for which the system cannot be blamed. If the basic units of citation indexing, i.e., citations, are defective, the citation indexes are bound to be defective. In many cases the references are not properly selected and cited. Many citations are incomplete or inaccurate. Some cited documents do not have enough association of ideas with the citing documents to warrant citation. When such citations are indexed they may naturally lead to low precision in retrieval. Nevertheless, the very idea of indexing citations by treating the cited authors with their citing documents as almost quasi-classes, and collecting all items related to each of the cited documents is unique in itself and an index so prepared cannot be less helpful to the researchers than any conventional index. It is true that this type of index is not able to retrieve the contents of the documents directly, but, as it is claimed, "it is able to identify a specific work unambiguously and thereby the subject concepts discussed in it are also identified" [12]. Eugene Garfield, the chief advocate of this system, has pointed out that "if one considers the book as the macro unit of thought and the periodical as micro unit of thought, then the citation index in some respect deals in the sub-micro or molecular unit of thought... Thought indexes can be extremely useful if they are properly conceived and developed" [13].

N.4 SCIENCE CITATION INDEX (SCI)

SCI is the brain-child of Dr. Eugene Garfield, founder-director of the Institute of Scientific Information (ISI), Philadelphia, the publisher of the index, and is perhaps the best example of its kind. The first SCI in five volumes, brought out in 1963, covered the scientific literature published in 613 journals during the year 1961 and contained 1.4 million citations. SCI is now owned by Thomson Reuters and is a component of Web of Science (previously known as Web of Knowledge), which is an online subscription-based scientific citation indexing service that gives access to multiple databases, viz., Science Citation Index Expanded, Conference Proceeding Citation Index, Social Science Citation Index, Arts and Humanities Citation index, Index Chemicus, Current Chemical Reactions, and Book Citation Index. Incidentally, Thomson Reuters also markets several subsets of this database, termed Specialty Citation Indexes, such as the Neuroscience Citation Index and the Chemistry Citation Index [14].

N.4.1 Coverage of SCI

The SCI is based on citations made in the current literature in the field of science and technology. It started with the analysis of 700 periodicals. At present no significant periodical in science and technology is left out of its purview. SCI is now available in two versions—Science Citation Index and Science Citation Index Expanded (SCIE). While SCIE, which is available online, covers more than 860 major journals across 150 disciplines, SCI covers lesser number of journals and is available in CD/DVD format. All individual items in the selected periodicals with their citations are considered for inclusion in the index. The SCI not only includes articles but also short communications, letters, abstracts, reviews, corrections and errata, discussions, conference literature, editorials, tributes, obituaries, etc. Only advertisements, news notices and the items without citations are excluded. The book reviews, which were being covered earlier, are also now excluded. The journals covered in the SCI are known as source journals and the items they contain as source items.

N.4.2 Parts of SCI

Initially started with two parts, the SCI now consists of the following three parts.
- *Citation index*: A citation index entry consists of two types of information, viz. information about a cited item (reference) and information about citing items. The information mentioned about the cited item are the author's name (only first author's name when there are more than one author), year of publication, the title of the host document and its volume number, and the starting page of the item. The information included about a citing item are: author's name, the title of the host document, its year of publication, volume number, and the starting page of the citing item. The cited items are arranged alphabetically by the names of the first named authors. If there are more than one cited item of an author, they are arranged chronologically by their years of publication. The citing items are also arranged in the same manner immediately under each cited item. The citation index part also has two other sections on anonymous cited documents and

cited patents. The former is arranged alphabetically by titles and the latter, known as Patent Citation Index, numerically by patent numbers.

- *Source index*: The source index is an author index of the citing items. Each entry in this index covers the following information: the name of the first author, the names of co-authors (up to 10), the title of the host document, its volume number, issue number, starting page, year, code for the type of document (review, letter, correction, etc.), number of references in the bibliography of the citing item, accession number of the source periodical in ISI, and the full title of the article. These entries are also arranged alphabetically by the names of the first named authors. This part also has two other sections on anonymous items and the organizations where the researches reported in the source items have been carried out. Anonymous items are arranged alphabetically by their titles and are given in the beginning of the source index. In the other section, called Corporate Index, all the citing items are arranged alphabetically by the names of the authors under each organization. This part, being complete in itself, can also be used independently.

- *Permuterm subject index*: Keeping in view the difficulties of those users who are more accustomed to subject index, in consulting SCI, a Permuterm Subject Index was appended to it as a separate part in 1967. For preparing this index all the significant terms of the titles of the citing items are first selected. These terms are then permuted so that each of these terms serves as a primary term. All other terms, which are related to a primary term (i.e., co-terms), are listed alphabetically under the primary term as in the relative index of Dewey Decimal Classification. An author using the primary term as also one of the co-terms is mentioned against the co-term concerned, e.g.,

LIBRARY

CLASSIFICATION	ISAAC, F W
CATALOGUING	ORNER, J L

The names of the authors provide reference and help in finding out the details from the source index.

N.4.3 Examples from SCI

An example of a citation index entry and that of a source index entry (along with an entry of patent citation index), as provided by Garfield, is shown below [11].

CITATION INDEX ─────────────────────────────

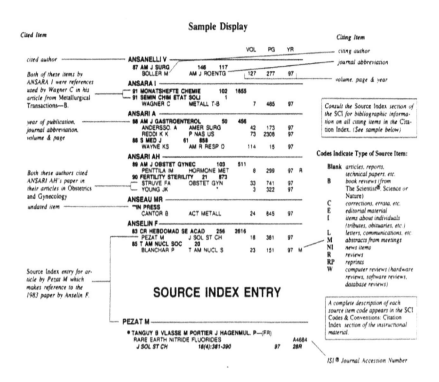

PATENT CITATION INDEX ──────────────────────

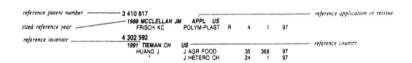

REFERENCES

[1] M. Riaz, Advanced Indexing and Abstracting Practices, Atlantic Publishers, New Delhi, 1989, p. 41.

[2] A. Chatterjee, Elements of Documentation, The Author, Kolkata, 1983,

[3] J.N. Satpathi, Keyword indexing systems, in: S.B. Ghosh, J.N. Satpathi, (Eds.), Subject Indexing Systems, IASLIC, Kolkata, 1998, pp. 263–276.

[4] B.P. Mookerjee, Citation indexing, in: S.B. Ghosh, J.N. Satpathi, (Eds.), Subject Indexing Systems, IASLIC, Kolkata, 1998, pp. 329–355.

[5] H.E. Chandler, V.de P. Roper, Citation indexing: uses and limitations, Indexer 17 (1991) 243–249.

[6] M.M. Kessler, Bibliographic coupling between scientific papers, Am. Doc. 14 (1953) 10–25.

[7] Citation index. <https://en.wikipedia.org/wiki/Citation_index>.

[8] E. Garfield, Science citation indexing; a new dimension in indexing, Science 144 (1964) 64.

[9] W. Melvin, Citation indexes, In: A. Kent, et al. (Eds.), Encyclopedia of Library and Information Science, V.5, Marcel Dekker, New York, 1971

[10] J. Becker, R.M. Hayes, Information Storage and Retrieval, Wiley, New York, 1964.

[11] E. Garfield, Concept of citation indexing. The Scientist, Philadelphia. <http://www.garfield.library.upenn.edu/papers/vladivostok.html>.

[12] K. Krishan, Reference Service, Vikas, New Delhi, 1978, p. 293.

[13] E. Garfield, Citation indexes for science, Science 122 (1955) 108–111.

[14] Science Citation Index. <https://en.wikipedia.org/wiki/Science_Citation_Index>.

CHAPTER O

Information Consolidation

O.1 INTRODUCTION

Information sought by a user may not always be readily available in a library or information center and, if at all available, may not be in the format preferred by him/her. Providing information service to the users in such cases will require identification, collection, processing and presentation of needed information in a manner that suits the target user or user group. This type of work is known as information consolidation or more precisely information analysis, consolidation, and repackaging (IACR). It is thus one of the important methods of organizing information for providing information service to the users. IACR work is carried out not only by individual libraries/information centers, but also by other agencies specially set up for this purpose and sometimes by private organizations which make the information consolidation products created by them available against payment.

O.2 MEANING AND SCOPE

"Information analysis, consolidation and repackaging" refers to a process, which culminates in creation of a user-friendly end-product in printed or non-printed form, which is commonly called Information Consolidation Product or IACR Product or simply Information Product. When such a product is brought out on a regular basis, it is often termed as a service, such as abstracting service, indexing service, and digesting service. The activities involved in this process include "selection, evaluation, analysis, interpretation, and synthesis of a body of information in a clearly defined specialized field with the intent of compiling, digesting, repackaging, or otherwise organizing and presenting pertinent information in a form most authoritative, timely, and useful to the differential requirements of the different categories of users" [1]. It is obvious that the work of consolidation cannot be done without first analyzing the information and that the new product emerging out of consolidation work invariably differs in structure/format and/or medium from the original. Thus, there are three main

Elements of Information Organization and Dissemination
DOI: http://dx.doi.org/10.1016/B978-0-08-102025-8.00015-6
217

facets of ICAR: information analysis, information consolidation and information repackaging.

O.2.1 Information Analysis

The term "Analysis" refers to a process of detailed or thorough examination or study of anything deemed to be a whole—either in the form of a compound or of a complex—in order to determine or separate its fundamental elements, or functional ingredients or component parts, for the purpose of understanding its nature, and describing it precisely, determining its essential features, elucidation, clarification, and explanation, in terms of its message, meaning, logical use, etc. [2]. In the context of information, the process of "analysis" is essentially an intellectual one; and the result of performing the operation does not, by itself, give rise to any new information [3]. It may, however, be pointed out that "information analysis" does not always mean the same thing. While in the context of indexing it denotes subject analysis, it is considered to mean "critical evaluation" when one refers to an information analysis center [4].

O.2.2 Information Consolidation

The term "Consolidation" refers to "a process of unifying firmly and coherently two or more loosely aggregated units in which the units of input undergo substantial changes to get converted into output" [2]. In the context of "information consolidation," it means bringing together the related information through analysis and arranging the aggregates of related information in a coherent sequence or logical structure, so that the user can get a unified view of the contents. This may involve merging, restructuring, and rewriting of information.

O.2.3 Information Repackaging

The term "Packaging" refers to the process of physically arranging some materials and providing a covering for easy handling. In the context of information packaging, it indicates "physical recording, arrangement and presentation of information in a given medium and a given form" [5]. Thus, two aspects to be considered in this context are *packaging medium*, i.e., the physical medium on which the information is recorded and displayed or presented to the users, such as print medium, audio medium, audio-visual medium, and digital medium; and *packaging format*, i.e., the arrangement, shape, and layout of information in a given product on a given medium [5]. Repackaging of information, therefore, means rearrangement or change of physical medium and/or the form in which the information has been presented. This is done to suit the requirement of a user or user group.

O.3 IACR PRODUCTS/SERVICES

IACR products have been described as publications—brought out in print, digital or any other suitable medium—carrying information collected from primary documentary sources and/or non-documentary sources in a condensed and/or restructured manner and/or arranged in user-friendly format or in a format that is different from the format in which the information were originally available. According to Seetharama, the IACR products may be demand-activated products, such as technical reports, critical reviews, state-of-the-art reports, and market reports, or purposive type products, such as newsletters, manuals, and handbooks. He has, however, pointed out that they are not exclusive categories as the same product may belong to either of the two groups depending upon the situation [6]. The major types of IACR products are [7]:

- *Trend related publications*, e.g., Reviews/Advances, State-of-the-Art Reports, Trend Reports;
- *Condensing publications*, e.g., Indexes/Indexing Periodicals, Abstracting Periodicals, Digests/Digesting Periodicals;
- *Ready reference publications*, e.g., Handbooks, Manuals, Directories, Yearbooks, Guide Books, Gazetteers;
- *Organizational publications*, e.g., House Journals, Newsletters;
- *Trade- and industry-related publications*, e.g., Forecast reports, Feasibility Reports, Technical Reports, Market Reports, Trade Directories, Trade Catalogues, etc.

Since IACR products serve as information sources, they have been introduced in the chapter on Information Sources (Chapter B). Their characteristics and methods of compiling them have been discussed in detail in a previous book on IACR by the present author [7]. It may be mentioned that compilation of all these products may not be necessary for providing information services to the users in every library. The librarian or information worker will select the product/products to be compiled basing on the need of the local user group and also the availability of ready-made products commercially. However, the most widely used information services in libraries are indexing and abstracting services. The process of indexing has been discussed in detail in earlier chapters and in the present chapter the process of abstracting is being discussed in detail, besides the general methodology of IACR. For further details, the book of the present author on IACR, as mentioned above, may be consulted.

O.4 METHODOLOGY OF IACR

Compilation of IACR products is certainly a skilled job. It has to be done systematically keeping in view the requirements of the target user group and following a suitable methodology. Obviously, the same methodology will not be suitable for all types of products. It will vary from product to product. A general framework of the methodology is described below. The steps discussed here may have to be suitably modified or adapted for compiling different types of products [7].

- *Initiation*: While undertaking compilation of any IACR product, some preliminary activities may be undertaken, which will help in pinpointing the need of the work to be undertaken as also raise the competency level of the compiler and thus help in efficient compiling of the product concerned. These involve:
  - *Identification of target user group*: The target user group should be identified at the outset to facilitate user study and for taking further measures in compilation of the product concerned. This may be done on the basis of demands placed by them for some specific types of information.
  - *Recognition/Assessment of user need*: The need for IACR work should be recognized/assessed before planning any IACR work through user study using some suitable method (See Section C.4.4).
  - *Identification of the subject area*: Basing on the needs of the target users, the subject area of the proposed IACR product is to be identified.
  - *Identification of appropriate type of product*: The type of IACR product that will suit the needs of a particular user or user group has to be identified while making the user study.
  - *Formation of working group*: Compilation of an IACR product can only be accomplished efficiently by the cooperation of several people with different specializations. A working group consisting of specialists in different fields should be formed, with a leader who will coordinate the work. The team leader will be adequately briefed, who can then initiate the work.

- *Study of subject*: If the person or persons responsible to undertake IACR work do not have at least working knowledge of the subject on which he/she/they will have to work, it will be difficult for him/her/them to do justice to his/her/their work. He/she/they may not even be able to ensure proper subject coverage of the planned product. Hence it is necessary for him/her/them to study the subject. Such study should give him/her/them a clear understanding of the highways and byways of the subject concerned. The method of studying a subject developed in DRTC (India) may be followed for this purpose [3].

- *Selection of model*: To have a better understanding of the characteristics and format of the type of product to be compiled, a detailed study may be undertaken at this stage of some well-known products of the type selected. This will provide an insight into different aspects of the product concerned. The study has to be done critically and the one found best should be taken as model for the planned product.

- *Identification of consultants*: Now a team of consultants may be identified who can be consulted at different stages of compilation work. This may include subject specialists, media specialists, language specialists, etc.

- **Determination of scope/product characteristics**: At this stage, some essential characteristics of the product have to be determined as mentioned below.

  - *Determination of subject scope*: Though the broad subject area has already been decided in the previous stage, it is necessary now to delineate the exact boundary of the subject concerned. "This involves the precise specification of a subject and would consist of recognizing each of the component ideas and the correct degree of interrelation among them, and expressing the totality of the subject coextensively and uniquely" [4]. This may also involve determination of depth of the component areas to be covered.

  - *Demarcation of geographical area of coverage*: Where IACR product relates to any geographical area (e.g., area profile), the exact boundary of the geographical area to be covered has to be decided. In case of other IACR products too, it has to be decided as to the sources from and/or relating to which geographical area or areas are to be covered in the proposed product.

  - *Fixing time limit/periodicity*: IACR products mostly cover current information. But on demand, retrospective information may also be covered. For products containing current information, it is necessary to decide the periodicity of the publication of the product. The decision regarding periodicity should be governed by the need of the users and the quantum of information available on the area of coverage.

- *Deciding packaging format and packaging medium*: The format and medium of packaging of the planned IACR product would vary from product to product. These should meet the requirements and comprehension level of the target users.

- **Planning and preparation**: Planning and preparation work may include the following:
  - *Deciding types of information sources to be consulted*: This involves decision regarding the types of information sources to be consulted for IACR work (e.g., journals, conference proceedings, etc. in case of an abstracting periodical) and also items, if any, in the selected sources that need to be excluded (e.g., book-reviews in newspapers while compiling a news digest).
  - *Phasing/distribution of work*: This involves deciding about different phases in which the compilation work has to be done and/or distribution of the tasks involved among the members of the working group.
  - *Fixing time schedule for completion of compilation work*: A time schedule may be prepared and the members of the working group may be asked to adhere to the schedule so that the product can be brought out in time as delay may reduce its utility.

- **Collection of information**: Now the work of selecting and/or collecting the appropriate information may be taken up. This will involve the following:
  - *Determination of method of collection*: At first, the method or methods to be adopted for collection of information (e.g., by examination of primary information sources, through direct questionnaire) need to be decided, which will depend upon the type of product to be compiled and the types of sources to be consulted.
  - *Identification of relevant information sources*: Now the exact information sources (e.g., titles of journals or the names of institutions or names of human sources) have to be identified keeping in view the need of the users. Secondary information sources may help in this work. Selection at this stage will only be a preliminary one. A competent person will check the relevancy of the information source in terms of subject coverage and utility for target users.

- *Collection of information*: The identified information sources may now be procured through direct purchase/subscription or on loan, if not available in the IACR center concerned. Each source may now be examined and relevant information collected and systematically recorded.
- *Evaluation of information*: The information so collected may need to be put through a process of appraisal or evaluation to mainly judge the relevancy or utility, quality or intrinsic merit, and authenticity or reliability of information. A designated person, with necessary expertise, may scan every item and take a final decision as to whether the item concerned should be retained for further processing.
- *Scope redefinition*: While evaluating the relevant information sources and their contents, it may be discovered that no new information are available in some sub-areas decided earlier and/or information are available on some other areas, not covered in the original scope, but falls within the broad subject area and likely to be relevant to the target users. This may happen due to obsolescence factor or new researches undertaken in a subject area. Similarly, a need may be felt about changing time coverage, resource coverage or geographical coverage. In such cases the scope/coverage of the proposed work may have to be redefined at this stage.

- **Processing and organization of information**: The collected information should now be processed and organized to give a concrete shape to the product being compiled. This will involve analysis of the contents of selected sources or set of sources, identification and extraction of relevant information, compression or condensation of information, synthesis and restructuring of information, etc.
  - *Arrangement of ideas/information*: At the time of synthesis and restructuring of information the question of arrangement or sequence will arise. It may be pointed out that one and the same set of ideas/ information can be arranged in several ways. The choice of the particular sequence should be based on its helpfulness to the users— intermediaries and/or end-users.
  - *Integration of information*: After arrangement of the analyzed information/ideas in a suitable sequence, these are to be integrated into an organized text. For this purpose, the target audience and their level, the intended use of the IACR product, the impact one desires of the product on the audience, and the peculiarities of the subject are some of the factors that need to be considered.

- *Undertaking complementary tasks:* The draft, so prepared, will, however, remain incomplete if some more tasks, as mentioned below, are not performed.
  - *Documenting and referencing:* Wherever required, proper documenting and referencing will have to be carried out.
  - *Illustrating:* For making the text more communicable, help of illustrations, such as tables, graphs, charts, pictures, may have to be taken.
  - *Preparation of supplemental aids:* Supplemental aids may include appendices, glossary, index, bibliography, etc. Wherever required such aids are to be prepared. All those materials which are relevant and useful to the users, but could not be included in full in the text, may be given in the appendices.
  - *Preparation of guide to users:* "Guide to Users" plays a very important role in enhancing the usability of a product. This has to be drafted cautiously with examples and illustrations so that it helps the users in consulting the product and locating the required information.
  - *Preparation of prelims:* The other preliminary components of the product, such as title page, contents page, informative abstract, list of illustrations, preface, as needed, may be prepared and added in the beginning of the draft text.
  - *Arrangement of component parts:* The main text, preliminaries and the supplemental aids may now be arranged in predetermined sequence. The final sequence or arrangement of the components or parts will vary from product to product. However, the general layout may be as follows: Title page—Contents—Informative Abstract (if required) —Guide to user or introduction—Main text (section wise or chapter wise as the case may be)—Indexes (where the main part is not alphabetical or where required)—Appendices (if necessary)—Bibliography/Bibliographical references—Glossary (if necessary). However, where found suitable, indexes may be brought after "guide to users" for the sake of convenience of searching by the users.
  - *Revision of draft:* The draft so prepared may now be checked with regard to language, expression, format and presentation, documenting and referencing, etc. and any errors found should be corrected. Subject specialists and/or consultants may help in this matter.
- *Consummation:* Once the whole draft of the product is complete, necessary measures, as described below, need to be taken so that the

product becomes ready for diffusion to the target users. However, actual dissemination will be done at the service stage, i.e., when the users will place the demand for the product or service.

- *Testing of draft*: The revised draft should be tested as to whether it is able to satisfy the users for whom it has been compiled. Some selected end-users may be asked to consult the product and give their reactions.
- *Finalization of draft*: The suggestions for modifications, omissions, additions, etc. received during the testing should now be incorporated in the draft to give it a final shape. The draft may also be subjected to editorial scrutiny in order to remove any linguistic error, inconsistency or lack of uniformity in presentation. The final text should be word-processed and copied, printed, or digitized and mounted on to the server, as the case may be, making it ready for diffusion.
- *Arranging feed-back*: A mechanism should be built up to obtain regular feed-back from the users, so that the product can be adapted to the changing needs of the users or replaced by a new product, if and when necessary. One suitable method may be attaching a feed-back form with the product for obtaining the views of the users.

0.5 ADVANTAGES OF IACR

IACR work helps in providing tailor-made information service, as information products/services are planned keeping in view the need of the users. A significant advantage of information consolidation is saving of the time of the users, as it usually results in a reduction factor. It has been estimated that information consolidation saves more than 80% of the time which specialists spend searching for information. In addition, information consolidation can be a substitute for large and expensive collection of primary literature [8].

0.6 ABSTRACTING

An abstract presents the contents of a document—usually a micro document—in a concise form. Thus "an abstract is a concise and accurate representation of the contents of a document, in a style similar to that of the original document" [9]. An abstract "condenses either the subject of the document or its objectives, scope and findings into a terse statement" [10].

More specifically, it is a "nonevaluative brief presentation usually in a natural or almost natural language, of selective essential contents of a document" [11]. Abstracting, then, is a technique of expressing the subject matter covered in the document in a precise but concise manner [12].

O.6.1 Types of Abstract

The contents of a document may be briefly expressed in two ways: (1) by giving indication about the contents, and (2) by providing all information contained in the document in a condensed form. Thus there are two main types of abstract, viz., Indicative and Informative. However, in practice there may be a hybrid type of abstract also, which may be termed as Informative–Indicative abstract [11].

O.6.1.1 Indicative Abstract

An indicative abstract "merely indicates that certain matters are dealt with in a document. It is a statement of the topic of the subject but does not attempt to summaries what is said about the subject" [10]. That means it gives hints about the contents, but does not provide the specific information contained in the document. Indicative abstract is often prepared for a descriptive and long text. It is, therefore, also known as descriptive abstract or abstract-summary. Here is an example of indicative abstract [12]:

> Keen (E. Mitchael). A retrieval comparison of six published indexes in the field of library and information science. UNESCO Bull. Lib. 30 (1) (1976) 26–36.
>
> The subject retrieval performances of five abstracting journals have been tested on the basis of seven different measurements. The subject approach of Library & Information Abstracts, Library Literature and Information Science Abstracts has been found preferable in nearly all measurements to Bulletin Signalitique, Referativnyi Zhurnal, and Computer & Control Abstracts. Some conclusions have been drawn, which may help design printed subject index in future.

Thus in an indicative abstract a user can get only some clues which merely help him to decide whether the document is relevant to him or her.

O.6.1.2 Informative Abstract

An informative abstract "contains in an abridged form all the significant ideas contained in the original document" [13]. In other words, an informative abstract reproduces the whole document in a very concise form. Since such an abstract provides all significant information contained in the document, it is also called comprehensive abstract or abstract-synopsis. Informative abstract is often prepared for an article, which reports some experiments or presents analysis of data obtained by application of any scientific or research method. The twin purposes that an informative abstract serves, according to Lewenz and others, are (1) as a source of information on new technical developments, and (2) as a source for retrospective searching [14], while those, according to Rowley are: (1) as an aid in the assessment of document relevance and selection or rejection and (2) as a substitute for the document when a superficial or outline knowledge of document content is satisfactory [9]. The contents of the above document are summarized below in the form of an informative abstract [12]:

Keen (E. Mitchael). A retrieval comparison of six published indexes in the field of library and information science. UNESCO Bull. Lib. 30 (1) (1976) 26–36.

The data collected through questionnaires filled up by six library science students, who had carried out literature search in five abstracting journals and one indexing journal, reveal that Library and Information Science Abstracts (LISA), Library Literature (LL) and Information Science Abstracts (ISA) as a group had a superior performance to Bulletin Signaletique (BS), Referativnyi Zhurnal (RZ) and Computer and Control Abstract (CCA) on recall ratio and perceived relevant selected measures. The selected precision ratio had similar values for all indexes, except LL, which carried no abstract. With a limit of 15 minutes, average search time showed only small differences. The measure of effort was made only for information searches, which indicated LL to be the best double-stage index. In nearly all measures the library science searches showed slightly better results than the information science ones. This was perhaps due to the searchers' greater familiarity with library science. The subject approach of LISA, LL, and ISA was found preferable to others in nearly all measures. The conclusions that emerged out of the test are: (1) provision of a subject index, rather than reliance on subject arrangement alone can give significant advantage in recall, time, and effort; (2) search time and effort marginally favour bare indexes and relevance predictability probably benefits from provision of abstracts; (3) there may not be large difference in recall, time, and effort result between broad subject-heading approach and specific entry approach; and (4) a full index string resembling a written sentence may lead to good relevance predictability and good precision performance.

O.6.1.3 Informative–Indicative Abstract

An informative–indicative is "partially informative and partially indicative in covering the essential contents of the original document" [10]. This is prepared normally when an article has both descriptive elements and scientific/research elements.

O.6.1.4 Difference

The indicative abstract and informative abstract differ in following ways [12]:

- An indicative abstract gives only an indication about the information contained in a document; an informative abstract provides all significant information in the abstract itself.

- An indicative abstract only alerts a user about the availability of a document; an informative abstract gives the essence of the contents of the document concerned.
- An indicative abstract necessitates consultation of original document for knowing the actual information contained in it; an informative abstract provides direct access to the information and, therefore, it may serve as a substitute of the original document to some extent.
- The size of an indicative abstract is always smaller than that of an informative abstract of the same document.

O.6.1.5 Other Types

Besides the main types of abstracts discussed above, there are some other types of abstracts too designed to suit the varying requirements. They differ mainly from the points of view of size, emphasis, expression, etc.

- By Size
  - *Titular abstract*: It is the author's title of a document expressing the content. This is the extreme case of an indicative abstract.
  - *Annotation*: A word that is sometimes used along with a title to amplify its meaning or to explain the nature and scope of a document is called an annotation.
  - *Micro abstract*: It is a highly condensed abstract indicating the contents of a document in a line or two. It is also called mini abstract or notation of content.
- By Emphasis
  - *Finding-oriented abstract*: It is an informative abstract giving stress on the findings, conclusions and recommendations mentioned in a paper.
  - *Mission-oriented abstract*. It is an abstract which is prepared for a mission-oriented abstracting service, or an abstracting service that has been charged to cater for the application of a specific branch of knowledge [9].
  - *User-oriented abstract*: This type of abstract begins with a "topic sentence" giving the essence of the contents, which is so displayed that the users can easily assess the relevance of the document for him or her. The bibliographical details are added only at the end of the abstract.
  - *Slanted abstract*: When the orientation or emphasis of the original document is changed in an abstract to suit a group of workers or a specific discipline, it is called a slanted abstract.

- *Critical abstract*: This type of abstract provides the essential information briefly and at the same time evaluates the level of treatment, presentation, new points and significance of the paper. It is also known as evaluative abstract.
- *Highlight abstract*: Sometimes the contents of a paper or an area of a paper are highlighted by some catchy words on the cover or the contents page of a journal. This may be called a highlight abstract.

- By Writer of Abstracts
  - *Author's abstract*: An abstract prepared by an author himself is called an author's abstract or synopsis. It is usually published along with the paper itself. Such an abstract is also called homotopic abstract.
  - *Specialist's abstract*: It is an abstract prepared by a subject specialist.
  - *Abstractor's abstract*: This type of abstract is prepared by a professional abstractor.

- By Document Abstracted
  - *Summary*: It is a brief statement of the main points of a book chapter or speech. A summary is usually added at the end of a book or chapter. It is also known as précis in the literary world.
  - *Article abstract*: When the contents of an article in a journal or a paper contributed to a conference is expressed in a condensed manner, it is called an article abstract or simply abstract.
  - *Patent abstract*: It provides the essential details of a patent in a brief form.
  - *Abstract of standard*: It gives the scope and essential elements of a standard.
  - *Abstract of bibliography*: This type of abstract describes the scope, coverage, arrangement, etc. of a bibliography.

- By Expression/Method of Preparation
  - *Abridgement*: An abridgement is usually taken to be a reduction of the original that necessarily omits a number of secondary points, and is, therefore, a relatively general term [9].
  - *Extract*: When some selected portions of a document are so arranged that they together can give a picture of the original contents in a miniature form, it is called an extract.
  - *Digest*: It is a combined summary of more than one document on the same topic providing a condensed but coherent view of the ideas contained in those documents.
  - *Graphic abstract*: In chemistry there are concise expressions to indicate substances and compounds which are known as formulae.

When these formulae are used to produce an abstract, the resultant abstract is called a graphic abstract.

- *Telegraphic abstract*: In this type of abstract the contents are indicated by using selected significant words from the document and some role indicators and punctuation symbols. This is also known as standardized or encoded abstract.

- *Numerical abstract*: This type of abstract presents data contained in a document in a tabular or numerical form. It is more suited for papers on topics relating to science and economics. This is also known as a statistical or data-type abstract.

- *Auto-abstract*: This abstract is based on analysis of frequency of occurrence of significant words in a document by a computer. The sentences containing the most frequently used words are found out and arranged in an order which can give a rough idea of the contents of the document concerned.

- *Term list*: The contents of documents being abstracted may be converted into keywords or terms and a list of such terms may be stored in a computer for future retrieval. The computer will tell a user, on request, which keywords in what order represent the contents of a particular document.

0.6.1.6 Modular Content Analyses

The requirement of abstracts usually varies from user to user and no abstract is expected to satisfy all types of users. As such, Lancaster and Herner have floated the idea of modular content analyses [15]. They have suggested preparation of a package of abstracts by subject specialists for each document. Such a package will consist of an indicative abstract, an informative abstract, a critical abstract and a set of modular index entries. "The package is so designed that, with a minimum amount of editorial effort, an abstracting service could process it to conform with its own unique requirements" [10].

0.6.1.7 Basis of Selection

The selection of the type of abstracts to be prepared should be based on the following factors [10]:

- The needs and preferences of the users;
- The purpose for which an abstract is being prepared;
- The scope and nature of the original;
- The degree of dynamism of the subject-field;
- The skill and the subject expertise of the abstractors;

- The number of abstractors and the time available for abstracting work;
- The budget for abstracting;
- The language of the original;
- The availability of the original;
- The intended immediate use of the abstracts;
- The subsequent use of the abstracts;
- The in-house standard for abstracting.

O.6.2 Qualities of Abstract

An abstract, if it has to properly serve the purpose for which it is prepared, must express maximum ideas contained in the original in minimum number of words. The main qualities of a good abstract are [11,12]:

- *Self-sufficiency*—An abstract should be self-sufficient or a self-contained unit, i.e., a complete report in miniature form.
- *Brevity*—An abstract should be as brief as possible, devoid of redundancy and repetition, but at the same time no essential information should be excluded.
- *Precision*—The contents of the original should be precisely enunciated in an abstract. No inaccuracy, unnecessary elaboration or vagueness should creep in.
- *Objectivity*—The ideas of the author should be depicted objectively in an abstract. It should be impersonal, although it is expressed in the abstractor's own language.
- *Intelligibility*—The language and expression of an abstract should be clear and unambiguous to enable the users (1) to identify the basic contents of the original document quickly and correctly; and (2) to determine its relevance to their interests; and (3) thus to decide whether they need to read the document in its entirety.
- *Recency*—The time-lag between the publication of the original and its abstract should be minimum for maintaining its utility.

O.6.3 Style, Content, and Length

Obviously, no one style, content or length can be appropriate for all abstracts. All the three must be tailored to the nature of the original document, the anticipated use of the abstract, and the resources available with the abstracting agency concerned. The important factors that should be considered in this regard are [9]:

- Length and scope of the original document;
- Subject of the original document;

- Language of the original document;
- Availability of original document;
- Author's style and emphasis.

O.6.3.1 Style of Abstract

A good abstract conveys the maximum quantity of information using the minimum number of words. The objective of writing an abstract is to summarize the main contribution made by the author of the original document, excluding any peripheral material. It may be pointed out that many devices that are accepted as good style in other types of writing, which indeed serve a useful function, are not suitable for writing an abstract and hence should be avoided [9]. Some guidelines which may help in maintaining good style in writing an abstract have been provided in a subsequent section.

O.6.3.2 Content of Abstract

An abstract should contain some elements to be useful to the readers. The following are considered to be essential elements of an abstract [12]:

- *Purpose*, i.e., the aims, objectives or goal of the work reported in the abstracted document;
- *Scope*, i.e., the exact boundary or extension of the subject dealt with in the document;
- *Method*, i.e., the methodology or technique adopted for the experiment or research work reported in the document;
- *Data*, i.e., the data or information collected during the experiment or research;
- *Results*, i.e., the findings of the experiment/research reported by the author;
- *Conclusions*, i.e., the conclusions drawn or interpretation of the findings;
- *Specialized information*, i.e., any special information that may be of importance in a particular field, e.g., the details of dose and sample in a medical experiment;
- *Collateral information*, i.e., the information, which are incidental to the main objective of the study but of importance to other fields, such as any new instrument designed or a new compound found;
- *Additional information*, i.e., information about tables, charts, diagrams, references, etc. included in the document.

O.6.3.3 Extent of Coverage

It may, however, be noted that all these elements may not be present in every abstract. The extent of coverage in an abstract will depend on the coverage of the original document. An informative abstract is expected to provide the significant details of each element, if available in the abstracted document, but an indicative abstract is not expected to do so. An indicative abstract usually begins with a statement of objectives and scope of the article, followed by a very brief statement of the results. The presence of other significant elements is only indicated at the end. Incidentally, the abstracts of articles relating to humanities and social science subjects may not follow the same pattern as above because the treatment of the subject in such articles often differs from the treatment of science subjects [12].

O.6.3.4 Exclusions

A document may contain various types of tables, charts, graphs, diagrams and other illustrations and appendices. They are given either to make the subject matter easily graspable, or to provide additional information or to explain a thesis. There is a controversy regarding their inclusion in an abstract. Russian abstracting services usually favor inclusion of important and relevant materials of these types. Some other leading abstracting journals like *Chemical Abstracts*, *Biological Abstracts*, and *Abstracts of World Medicine* also allow inclusion where necessary. However, the general tendency is to exclude these for the sake of brevity, but mention any vital information conveyed through such materials, in the body of the abstract. Mathematical and scientific formulae and symbols are also either excluded or represented in a generally understood language [12].

O.6.3.5 Length of Abstract

It may be pointed out here that though the abstract is expected to be as brief as possible, it is difficult to prescribe minimum or maximum length of an abstract. "Abstracts planned primarily as alerting devices may be shorter (typically 80–100 words) than those abstracts which are to be stored for permanent reference, where 400–500 words might, on occasions, be justified" [9]. In practice, the length of abstracts widely varies. While *Abstract of World Medicine* (UK) uses up to 500 words for an informative abstract, some other abstracting journals, like *Documentation Abstracts* (UK), do not go beyond 250 words. In case of indicative abstract, *Indian Science Abstracts* uses up to 50 words, while *Horticultural Abstracts* (UK) does not exceed 19 words [16]. *Biological Abstracts* prefers the length of an abstract to be 3% of the original, while some other abstracting journals prescribe 4–5%. Ranganathan felt that "it is not desirable to put in more words than can be taken with a comfortable sweep of the eyes" [17].

O.6.4 Format of Presentation

An abstract has two main parts: (1) citation or bibliographical details, and (2) abstract proper. Besides, an indication about the abstractor or abstractor's code is also often added at the end, especially when the abstract is not prepared by an author. An abstract entry consisting of all the three parts should be printed within an area specified by a standardizing agency, or by the abstracting periodical for which the abstract is prepared.

O.6.4.1 Citation

The full bibliographical details of the abstracted document and also those of host document, when the abstracted document forms part of it, should be provided in citation in such a manner that the abstracted document can be easily identified and located. The details to be mentioned are: name(s) of author(s); title of the abstracted document, including subtitle, if any; title of the host document, when the abstracted document forms part of a host document; bibliographical details of the host document, such as year, volume number, issue number, and the pages covered by the abstracted document. When the whole document is abstracted and there is no host document, the bibliographical details of the document concerned, such as place, publisher and date are mentioned instead of the details of the host document. Besides, the language of the document is also mentioned along with the title when the language of the abstract and that of the original document are different. Some abstracting periodicals also mention the name and address of the organization, with which the author or the first named author is attached or the e-mail address of the author, to enable the reader of the article to contact the author, if necessary. All these details are to be arranged, according to some standard pattern following an appropriate system of punctuation, capitalization, italicization, etc. It is needless to stress that "punctuation and capitalization contribute to the legibility and/or comprehension of the citation" [17]. While some abstracting journals have developed their own pattern of arrangement, punctuation and capitalization, etc., the standardizing agencies, like International Organization for Standardization (ISO), British Standards Institution (BSI), and Bureau of Indian Standards (BIS), have formulated rules for this purpose [12].

O.6.4.2 Abstract Proper

The abstract proper containing significant facts identified and organized in the manner stated in Section O.7.2 below follows the citation in a separate paragraph. Nowadays, the abstract is often followed by keywords or descriptors representing the subject matter of the document, which in fact is further condensation of the subject matter.

O.6.4.3 Abstractor's Code

The name of the abstractor, usually in short form or in the form of acronym or code symbol follows the abstract (normally on the right end of the next line). When the abstract, supplied by the author himself, is included in the abstracting journal, the term "Author" is usually mentioned in place of abstractor's code. Sometimes, the author's abstract is amended either to shorten it or to make it more communicable. In such cases, the term "Author-Amended" or any other suitable phrase is used in place of abstractor's code.

O.7 ABSTRACTING PROCESS

The abstracting work proceeds in three phases: identification of key ideas/facts—organization of ideas/facts—writing [16].

O.7.1 Identification

An abstract must contain all significant information or key facts contained in the document being abstracted. As such, it is necessary firstly to identify the key facts by analyzing the contents of the document. For doing so, the abstractor should begin with reading of the abstract or synopsis, if any, provided by the author or editor, which is likely to provide an idea about the information contained in the document. Next, he should go through the introduction, which is likely to indicate the purpose or objective of the work. Further, he should study the whole document, if it is a short one. Else, he can study the summary and conclusions usually given at the end of the document and also the section headings. Finally, he should scan the text for other information like the techniques used, data collected, etc. For convenience, the key information may be marked by pencil or noted down [12]. Before going to second phase, it may also be necessary to make an assessment of the utility of the information so identified keeping in view the need and requirements of the target user group.

O.7.2 Organization

In the second phase, the ideas, information or facts, which have been identified as essential or significant, are synthesized or organized in the sequence in which these have appeared in the original text, when that is found to be helpful; otherwise in a logical or developing sequence, such as the one in which the essential elements have been listed above, to enable the potential users have a better understanding of the contents of the document concerned. Obviously, there cannot be a completely standardized form or pattern because the contents, treatment and the style of presentation of documents widely vary. There will be occasions when the abstractor will have to apply his own judgment. The abstractor also has to take a decision in which case he will only provide indication about the presence of the key facts identified and in which case he will provide minimum details also.

0.7.3 Writing

Once the ideas are organized in a helpful sequence, the abstractor may now write down the abstract. While doing so he has to keep in mind the rules, if any, framed by the abstracting journal, for which it is being written. At first, a draft may be prepared, which may be subsequently checked and edited "to prune redundancy and improve quality" [11]. The aim of checking would be to find out inaccuracies and errors relating to format and/or language, if any, that might have crept into the draft, while that of editing would be to make the text free of all factual and linguistic errors and remove vagueness, if any, and improve expression for better communication.

0.8 GUIDELINES FOR ABSTRACTING

For preparing abstracts in an effective manner, some guidelines are available. Ranganathan provided some guidelines in his Classified Catalogue Code [18]. International Organization for Standardization brought out ISO 214: 1976 Documentation—Abstracts for Publication and Documentation in 1976, which provides guidelines for preparing abstracts. Similar standards have been formulated in several other countries. For example, Bureau of Indian Standards brought out IS 795:1976 Guide for Preparation of Abstracts in the same year. An American National Standard ANSI 239.14: Guidelines for Abstracts was first published in 1979, which has since been revised in 1987 and 1997. A set of guidelines framed on the basis of the existing guidelines is suggested here, which may be of help in practical abstracting work.

O.8.1 General Guidelines

The following are some general do's and don'ts for preparing abstracts [11,12]:

- The information, which can be readily inferred from the feature headings or subject heading under which the abstract is to be placed in an abstracting journal, need not be repeated.
- Information, which is readily conveyed by the title of the document, should not be repeated in the lead sentence or the text of the abstract.
- An abstract should include only facts and not conjectures.
- An abstract should give the most outstanding factual data, if they are not too many; otherwise it should give only the nature of the data provided in the document.
- Depending upon the needs of the users, if necessary, an abstract should be reoriented emphasizing the relevant facets of the information in the original.
- An abstract may mention any secondary advances, if necessary, but their importance should not be exaggerated, so that the user's attention is not diverted from the main theme.
- The opening sentence may be used as a topic sentence or lead sentence, as in a newspaper report, manifesting the main focus of the work concerned.
- General statements should be avoided and phrases like "the paper discusses," "in the present paper," "the paper concludes," "the author describes," etc. should not be used.
- Any statement, opinion or remarks of the author may be included, if needed, but should not be interpreted, except in case of critical abstracts.
- Size of the abstract should be restricted keeping in view the usual size adopted or recommended by the abstracting periodical concerned.
- Single paragraph should be preferred unless the size is not long enough to require more paragraphs.

O.8.2 Language Guidelines

Much of the quality and effectiveness of an abstract depend upon the language and expression used by the abstractor. The guidelines relating to these aspects are given below [11,12]:

- Simple and unambiguous language should be used so that the users can easily obtain the idea of the contents of the original.

- Simple sentences should be preferred to compound or complex sentences and verbs should be kept nearer to their subjects.
- Complete sentences should be normally used; incomplete sentences or telegraphic language may be used only when it is appropriate and economic, but never at the cost of clarity and precision.
- Wherever possible, phrases for clause and words for phrases should be used.
- Extra words, such as "however," "rather," "nevertheless," and interludes, such as "the author then goes on to show," "in the second part of the paper," should be avoided.
- Unrelated participles, unnecessary long words, avoidable articles, etc. should not be used.
- Standard terms should be preferred; technical terms and trade names may be used if that substantially saves space.
- Abbreviations, unless easily understood, colloquial or unused words, trade jargons, symbols, etc. should be avoided; if at all they are used, their meanings should be explained when they appear for the first time in the abstract.
- Use of passive voice and present tense may be preferred for indicative abstract, while active voice and past tense may be preferred in case of informative abstract; however, conclusions should be written in present tense.
- The expression should be concise and crisp, but the tone and emphasis of the original document should be maintained in the abstract, unless it is purposely slanted.

O.8.3 Uniformity and Consistency

Effort should always be made to maintain some uniformity and consistency in style of writing abstracts for a particular abstracting periodical. For this, some standard practices should be developed and rules framed. These standards and rules may include rules for format; rules for organization; standard abbreviations; standard symbols; standard phrases; nomenclature allowed; rules and illustrations of avoiding verbosity, redundancy, deletion, etc.; and rules for a standard order of components [11].

O.9 PRE-NATAL ABSTRACTING

Another method of reducing the time gap between the publication of a micro-document and the availability of its abstract is pre-natal abstracting.

The term "Pre-natal Abstracting" was coined by Ranganathan. It means abstracting before publication of the abstracted document. As such it is also known as pre-publication abstracting. In spite of its distinct advantages, this procedure is rarely adopted by the abstracting periodicals. CoDAS Condensed Matter Alerting Service, an electronic alerting service, provides pre-publication abstracts in the field of surface and coating technology and allied fields. Central Building Research Institute, Roorkee, India, has been bringing out *CBRI abstracts* containing pre-publication abstracts. Nevertheless, some journals in specialized fields have taken up pre-natal abstracting for the benefit of research workers and specialists. These journals provide abstracts in advance of papers to be published in future issues.

O.10 ABSTRACTOR

An abstractor is a person who prepares an abstract. Three types of persons may do the job of an abstractor, viz., an author, a specialist, and a professional library staff or information worker. There is no doubt that an author knows his subject best, but he may not be a successful abstractor because it is difficult for a person to be impartial to his own writing and to condense it beyond a certain extent. Similarly a subject specialist is also expected to understand well the contents of the papers pertaining to his area of specialization, but he may have his own opinion and own way of thinking about the subject, which will make it difficult for him to maintain impartiality and his language may also be too technical to be understood by the users of all levels. Besides, both an author and a specialist either may not know or may not like to follow the guidelines for abstracting. If, however, an author or a specialist can produce abstracts of required standard, there is no reason why those should not be acceptable. Nevertheless, an author or a specialist may be too engaged in their own pursuits to spare time for abstracting work. A professional librarian or information worker will, thus, be the natural choice for entrusting the job of abstracting. It is true that the subject knowledge will be of great advantage in abstracting work, but that knowledge need not be a specialist's knowledge. "The professional abstractor," as Foskett points out, "is more reliable in time, more consistent in style, and with proper training soon acquires familiarity with the subjects he writes about even though he may not have known much about them at the outset" [19]. Ranganathan also feels that in spite of his handicap in regard to newly emerging "specialized thought of great intension in a region already of narrow extension," a library expert is best qualified to do the abstracting work [18].

O.10.1 Pre-requisites

To be a successful abstractor a person is expected to possess the following qualities and qualifications [12]:

- He/she should have a fair idea about the specialization and needs of his/her audience.
- He/she should have at least some elementary knowledge about the subject of the documents to be abstracted.
- He/she should know the language of the documents and the language in which they are to be abstracted.
- He/she should have a thorough understanding of the guidelines to be followed.
- He/she should have the power of expressing any idea in a concise manner.

If a person has an inherent flair for abstracting work, much of the above requisites can be acquired by proper training and practical work.

O.11 ABSTRACTING SERVICE

An abstracting service, according to Shera, "is a process of regular production of abstracts in a given subject field or a group of fields. Such services may either be comprehensive or selective" [20]. Such a service, evidently, is provided by the abstracting periodicals. The first abstracting periodical "Pharmaceutisches Centralblatt" (later superseded by "Chemisches Zentralblatt") was started in 1830, and today several thousand abstracting and indexing journals are being published throughout the world. Some well-known abstracting journals are:

- Physics Abstracts
    Fortnightly. 1898 –
    Institution of Electrical Engineers, London
    (Presently it is part of Inspec, Section A—Physics database).
- Chemical Abstracts
    Weekly. 1907 –
    American Chemical Society, Washington
    (Presently it is known as Chemical Abstracts Service, which delivers the most current, complete, secured and interlinked digital information in the field of chemistry).

- Biological Abstracts
  Semi–Monthly.1926 –
  Bioscience Information Service of Biological Abstracts, Philadelphia (Presently produced by Thomson Reuters through its subsidiary BIOSIS).
- Indian Science Abstracts
  Monthly.1965 –
  NISCAIR, New Delhi
  (Presently available online).
- Library and Information Science Abstracts
  Bi–Monthly. 1950 –
  CILIP, London
  (Presently available through ProQuest).

O.12 ADVANTAGES OF ABSTRACTS

The emergence of abstracts has certainly proved to be a great boon to the researchers and the subject specialists. Their utility is unquestionable. The main advantages of abstracts and abstracting services are briefly stated below [12]:

- They help in identifying the required documents in a field of knowledge;
- They help in knowing the contents of the documents abstracted (even if the documents are in alien languages);
- They reduce the scanning time of the users;
- They help in surveying the retrospective literature rapidly;
- They provide a picture of the new developments in a subject field;
- A classified abstracting journal brings together abstracts of documents relating to same area of knowledge appearing in various journals.

REFERENCES

[1] S. Seetharama, Towards a methodology for information consolidation, paper presented at the meeting of UNISIST Working Group on Information Analysis and Consolidation, Kuala Lumpur, 1983.
[2] Webster's third new international dictionary of the English language. 1961.
[3] G. Bhattacharyya, Information analysis for consolidation: some basic considerations. DRTC Annual Seminar: Papers. DRTC, Bangalore, 1981, Paper-AA1.
[4] S. Seetharama, Information Consolidation and Repackaging: Format, Methodology, Planning, S S Publications, New Delhi, 1997.
[5] T. Saracevic, J.S. Wood, Consolidation of Information: A Handbook of Evaluation, Restructuring and Repackaging of Scientific and Technical Information, Pilot edition, UNESCO, Paris, 1981, (PGI-81/WS/16).

[6]   S. Seetharama, Guidelines for the Establishment of Information Consolidation Units (Draft), UNESCO, Paris, 1984, (PGI-84/WS/19).

[7]   A. Chatterjee, Elements of Information Analysis, Consolidation and Repackaging, Prova Prakashani, Calcutta, 2013.

[8]   UNESCO. Symposium on Information Analysis and Consolidation, Colombo, 1978. Final report.

[9]   J. Rowley, Abstracting and Indexing, second ed., Clive Bingley, London, 1988.

[10] W. Ashworth, Producing and using abstracts, in: W.E. Batten (Ed.), Hand Book of Special Librarianship and Information Work, fourth ed., ASLIB, London, 1975.

[11] G. Bhattacharyya, J.K. Sarkhel, Abstract and abstracting for secondary information work, Librarian 5 (1997) 26–43.

[12] A. Chatterjee, Elements of Documentation, The Author, Kolkata, 1983.

[13] B. Guha, Documentation and Information, second ed., World Press, Calcutta, 1983.

[14] India. Bureau of Indian Standards. Guide for preparation of abstracts (IS 795: 1976).

[15] F.W. Lancaster, S. Herner, Modular content analyses, Proc. Am. Doc. Inst. 1 (1964) 403–405.

[16] M.V. Ranga Rau, V.S. Padmanabhan, Guidelines for abstracting. DRTC Annual Seminar 6; 1996; Paper AA.

[17] S.R. Ranganathan (Ed.), Documentation and Its Facets, Asia, Mumbai, 1963. Chapter L5.

[18] S.R. Ranganathan, Classified Catalogue Code, with Additional Rules for Dictionary Catalogue code, fifth ed., Asia Publishing House, Bombay, 1964.

[19] D.J. Foskett, Information Service in Libraries, Crosby Lockwood, London, 1962.

[20] J.H. Shera, others, Documentation in Action, Rinehold, New York, 1956.

[21] G. Bhattacharyya, Methodology of studying subjects for information work and services. DRTC Annual Seminar-21. 1984, Paper-BA.

[22] G.F. Lewenz, others, Style and speed in publishing abstracts, J. Chem. Doc. 1 (2) (1961) 48–51.

[23] R.E. Maizell, et al., Abstracting Scientific and Technical Literature, Wiley-Interscience, New York, 1971, p. 1.

CHAPTER P

Documentation List

P.1 INTRODUCTION

As indicated earlier, organization of information or documentation work involves several activities, which ultimately leads to creation of a list of documents—bare or annotated—or a consolidation product, arranged in user-friendly order. Different aspects of information consolidation products have been discussed in the previous chapter. This chapter discusses about the other type of product, viz. documentation lists (DLs).

P.2 DEFINITION OF DL

A documentation list is obviously a list of documents prepared for providing documentation/information service. But as this service aims at catering nascent micro thought to the specialist users, a documentation list primarily contains information about micro documents and it is meant for those who are deeply engaged or interested in a specialized area of knowledge or calling. That is why Ranganathan explained the term "documentation list" as "the new name for bibliography with emphasis on the inclusion of micro documents and on the reader served being a specialist engaged in research, business, deliberation or administration" [1]. A documentation list can, then, be precisely defined as a systematically arranged list covering, wholly or mostly, the documents containing nascent micro thought, to serve mainly the specialist users.

P.2.1 Characteristics of DL

It is clear from the above that there are three main characteristics of a documentation list:

- It covers mainly micro documents, i.e., documents covering nascent micro thought and usually forming parts of their host documents such as books, periodicals, conference papers, etc.;
- The entries in a documentation list are arranged in an order which enables a user to scan it easily and find out their relevant literature;

Elements of Information Organization and Dissemination
DOI: http://dx.doi.org/10.1016/B978-0-08-102025-8.00016-8

243

- Such a list is consulted mainly by persons engaged in study and research or business or profession relating to the field covered by the list concerned.

P.2.2 Difference From Bibliography

A bibliography and a documentation list are similar in nature. Both of them are lists of documents. The main difference between them lies in emphasis. While in a bibliography the emphasis is on macro literature and the users to be served by it are of general type, in a documentation list the emphasis is on micro literature and the users to be served are mainly specialists. Ranganathan used another term "document bibliography" which he defined as "a list of embodied macro and/or micro ideas—i.e., of books and/or of articles of periodicals—on a specialized subject or on any number or on even all subjects" [2]. The term thus seems to be a generic term which covers both bibliography and documentation list.

P.3 NEED OF DL

The phenomenal rise in literature, specially micro literature, in the field of science and technology, and demand for information due to increased research activities in various fields necessitated development of some sort of efficient tools to effect bibliographical control over the huge mass of literature for quick dissemination of information. This resulted in the emergence of various kinds of documentation list. The main reasons for compiling documentation lists are the same as those mentioned in Section I.3.

P.4 HISTORY OF DL

It is not known exactly when the compilation of documentation lists began. Perhaps the first published documentation list was "Allgemeines Schregister uber die witchtigsten deutschen Zeitund Wochenschriften," an index of 11,000 periodical articles in German produced by J.H.C. Beutler and J.C.F. Gutsmuth in 1790. This was followed by "Pharmaceutisches Centralbiatt," an abstracting journal in German started in 1830 which is still being continued under the title "Chemisches Zentralblatt." The "Catalogue of Semantic Papers," a monumental project of listing all scientific papers produced in 19th century, was taken up by the Royal Society, London, in 1858. The catalogue was published in 19 volumes between 1867 and 1925. "Physics Abstracts" was started in 1898 and in 1900 H. W. Wilson Co. of United States, a well-known name in the field of documentation lists, started "Readers" Guide to Periodical Literature." "Chemical Abstracts" and "Biological Abstracts" were started in 1907 and 1926, respectively. The first published Indian documentation list "Indian Science Abstract" was started in 1935, which continued up to 1940 (this is different from the one published by NISCAIR under the same title). Since World War II, documentation lists have been compiled in larger numbers and today perhaps no area of knowledge remains uncovered by such lists.

P.5 ATTRIBUTES OF DL

A documentation list is meant for its users. As such it should be so compiled that it can satisfy their requirements. A good documentation list is expected to have the following attributes:

- *Comprehensiveness*: It is difficult to achieve full comprehensiveness in any documentation list. But efforts should be made to make it fairly comprehensive within the limitation of its scope and coverage. It must be assured that no significant document is left out.
- *Accuracy*: The information included in a list should be authentic and accurate. Otherwise, the precision ratio and the recall ratio of retrieval from the list will be hampered and it will not be able to serve the purpose for which it has been compiled.
- *Recency*: The aim of a documentation list is to provide information about nascent micro thought to the users. Hence, endeavor must be made to cut down the time gap between the publication of a document and its inclusion in a documentation list so that the list can cater the latest information speedily.
- *Easy accessibility*: A documentation list should be so arranged that a user can scan and identify his relevant items in the list easily. The list should be able to satisfy all possible approaches of the users. For this, necessary instructions for consultation of the list and additional approach facilities (indexes) should be appended wherever necessary.

P.6 TYPES OF DL

Various types of documentation lists form the point of view of their contents, coverage, standard, and services aimed at. But basically we can distinguish the following types of documentation lists.

P.6.1 Bare List

A bare documentation list is a list of documents, with stress on micro documents, providing only minimum bibliographical details of the documents listed and also of host documents when the listed documents from part of them. Bare documentation lists are of following types.

P.6.1.1 Library Bulletin

Library bulletin is perhaps the earliest known documentation list. A library bulletin may cover either the general information like those about the services and activities, or a list of recent additions or both. It may be mentioned that when a bulletin merely gives general information, it serves as the newsletter of the library concerned and when it lists recently acquired macro documents, it is called accessions list and merely serves as a bibliography. Only when it includes details of mainly micro documents, such as the contents of the latest issues of periodicals, it serves the purpose of a documentation list. Example: *Library Bulletin: Listing Selected Monographs, Reports and Journal Articles Recently Acquired by the ACIR Library*, published by the Library of Advisory Council for Inter-Government Relations of Australia.

P.6.1.2 Current Awareness List

A current awareness list usually includes recently published micro documents like articles in current issues of periodicals, papers presented at recent conferences, new research and technical reports, recently formulated standards, etc. (See Chapter G). Example: *NASA Spaceline Current Awareness List*.

P.6.1.3 Current Contents

Current contents is a bunch of reproduced pages of recent issues of periodicals (See Chapter G). Example: *Current Contents*, published by Institute for Scientific Information, Philadelphia (presently by Thomson Reuters).

P.6.1.4 Ad Hoc List

Sometimes ad hoc bare documentation lists are prepared for a particular occasion or to meet the requirement of a user or a group of users. Example: Women empowerment: a list of recent journal articles (published on the occasion of International Women's Day).

P.6.1.5 Index

Back-of-the book indexes are not documentation lists. But indexes to documents containing nascent micro thought may be called documentation lists. The three main types of such documentation list are:

- *Index to micro documents*: An index to micro documents may cover periodical articles, conference papers, dissertations, standards, patents, etc. A list may contain either any one type of these documents or all these types or a few of them. Example: *The Japanese Periodicals Index*, brought out by National Diet Library (http://www.ndl.go.jp/en/data/sakuin/sakuin_select.html).

- *Citation index*: this is a systematically arranged list of documents cited as references in periodical articles and other documents along with the documents which cite them (See Chapter N). Example: *Science Citation Index*.

- *News index:* This is a list of news items and other items related to news published in newspapers. Such an index is usually arranged under subject headings and contains details about the title of an item, the nature of the item (e.g., news, editorial, feature, letter), the name of the writer, if the item is signed, the title of the host document, its date of publication and location of the item in the host document. Example: *The Times Index*.

P.6.2 Enriched Lists

An enriched documentation list not only provides the bibliographical details of the documents listed, but also a brief description of the contents of each. Such lists are also of various types.

P.6.2.1 Annotated List

In an annotated documentation list, the bibliographical details of the listed documents are followed by, wherever necessary, brief statements of the scope, standard, and nature of the documents. A library bulletin may also take the form of an annotated list. Example: An annotated list of recent journal articles on social inclusion.

P.6.2.2 List With Abstracts

This is a list in which each entry consists of the bibliographical details of the document as also the essential elements of its contents in the form of an abstract. A library bulletin may also contain abstracts. Example: *Biological Abstracts*.

P.6.2.3 Review of Progress

This is a new type of documentation list in which the contents of the documents in a subject area are presented in a digested from so that it can give a concise but coherent view of the development or progress in the subject area as reflected in the documents. Such a review of progress is accompanied by the bibliographical details of the documents analyzed. (See also "Reviewing Periodical" in Section B.3.3.6.) Example: *Annual Review of Psychology*.

P.6.2.4 News Digest

Similarly, the news items and other writings pertaining to each incident or happening published in different newspapers are digested to give a brief and coherent view of the incident. The digested items, along with the details of the news items analyzed for making the digests, are listed in a news digest. Example: *Keesing's Record of World Events*.

P.6.2.5 Collectanea

This is another type of documentation list in which instead of providing only bibliographical details and/or a brief summary of each document, the exact information or the "complete original context" of the information are catered to the users. T.C. Hines produced a thesis on this subject at Rutgers University, USA, in 1961. According to him, collectanea is "a form of systematic subject bibliography, either selective or inclusive, which embodies significant or complete original context with most entries, and which contains duplicate of bibliographic units or sections of such units as required by the structure of the analysis system used. It is distinguished from other bibliographic forms, because it is primarily designed to supply the user with the information needed with each heading, rather than to direct him to another source, either within the file itself or outside it" [3]. The "morgue" or advance obituary files maintained by the newspaper libraries are examples of modern collectanea.

P.7 COVERAGE OF DL

Although theoretically we can think of an all-comprehensive documentation list or, as Ranganathan terms it, an "omnibus universal documentation list," covering all types of documents, published in all countries, in all languages and at all times, but practically it is not possible to compile such a list. Documentation lists, therefore, vary in their scope and coverage. According to Ranganathan, the documentation lists are restricted on the basis of one or more of the following characteristics [1]: (1) Area of origin, (2) Subject, (3) Period of publication, (4) Language, (5) Standard or level, and (6) Users to be served.

P.7.1 Area of Origin

Some documentation lists cover only those documents, the host documents of which have been published from a particular geographical area—a country, a region, or any bigger or smaller area. Example: *Eurasian Scientific Journal Index*.

P.7.2 Subject Coverage

A documentation list usually covers a particular area of knowledge since it is hardly possible to cover the whole universe of knowledge. A decision about the exact extension of the subject to be covered in a list, has to be taken keeping in view two main factors, viz., the resources available in a documentation center or organization, which will bring out the list, and the specializations of the users. A documentation list should include, besides the documents on the subject selected, documents dealing with related subject areas or those covering inter-disciplinary or multidisciplinary areas, if they seem pertinent to the users. Example: *Library Literature and Information Science.*

P.7.3 Period of Production

From the point of view of period of production of documents covered, there can be two types of documentation list—retrospective and current. Retrospective documentation lists are normally prepared on demand. The current documentation lists are usually produced periodically in anticipation of demands. The period to be covered in a current list depends on the periodicity of the list itself which in turn depends on the amount of micro literature produced in the selected subject area. In a current documentation list, produced periodically, the documents on a particular topic lie scattered in different issues of the list. Indexes and cumulated volumes try to solve this problem. Example: *Poole's Index to Periodicals (1802–1906)* published in 1948 (retrospective); *Library and Information Science Abstracts* (current).

P.7.4 Language Coverage

Documentation lists are sometimes restricted by the language of the documents as it is often difficult to cover documents produced in all languages of the world. It is often seen that the documents on a particular subject is produced in a particular language or languages, e.g. documents on a particular literature are produced mainly in the language of that literature or documents on nuclear science are mainly produced in English and some other European languages. In such cases, restriction in language comes in almost automatically. Sometimes, the language knowledge of the users and the documentalists i.e., compilers of the list, may also affect the decision about subject restriction. Example: *Index to Canadian Legal Literature* (bilingual index of English and French legal literature).

P.7.5 Level of Treatment

From the point of view of level of treatment of subject in documents listed, there can be three types of documentation list—elementary list, layman's list, and specialist's list. An elementary list covers documents providing elementary knowledge or those meant for the children. A layman's list covers documents written in a language and style which are easily understood by laymen. And a specialist's list covers documents meant for the specialists in a particular area. Although in documentation, we are mainly concerned with the last type, we should not neglect the other types, because, as Ranganathan pointed out, "the child of today is the adult of tomorrow" and "every venture of his amounts to his own tiny research" and "a specialist in one subject is a generalist in many others," but "he must have acquaintance with what is happening in other subject fields" [1]. Example: *Political Science Index*.

P.7.6 Users to Be Served

Documentation lists vary according to the users to be served. Accordingly, there can be following types of such list.

P.7.6.1 International List

An international documentation list aims at serving not only the specialists working in the country from where it is brought out, but also those working in other countries. Such a list is, therefore, expected to have an exhaustive international coverage. An international list invariably has some subject restriction as all subjects cannot be covered in one list. Example: *International Index to Music Periodicals.*

P.7.6.2 National List

A national documentation list is compiled to meet the exact requirements of the persons engaged in scientific and research activities, business, and administration in a country. Such a list usually covers the documents produced within the country and sometimes also those published abroad but related to the work going on in the country. A national documentation list can bring out the latest information more quickly than an international list. Example: *Hungarian Library and Information Science Abstracts.*

P.7.6.3 Local List

A local documentation list is a list brought out by an individual library or documentation center. The main characteristics of such a list are that it covers only those documents which are pertinent to the exact requirements of the users and almost all the documents listed are available in the library or center which compiles it. A local documentation list has some distinct advantages over other types of lists.

- It is able to provide any information much earlier than a national or international list, as the time lag between the receipt of a document and its inclusion in the list is minimum.
- The precision ratio and recall ratio of search from a local list are very high as the list is very selective covering only those documents which are most relevant to the users.
- Any modification in contents, coverage, or arrangement of the list, which may be necessary to suit the users, can be done quickly as constant interaction goes on between the compiling agency and the users.

P.7.6.4 Anticipatory List

This is a list prepared in anticipation of the demands of the users. The demands may be anticipated in various ways. The methods of anticipation have been described in Section C.4.4. A list of selected documents prepared by the House of Commons Library (UK) on an important topic to be discussed in the next session of the House may be an example of such a list.

P.7.6.5 List on Demand

This is a list prepared to fulfill the demands of a reader or group of readers. For preparing such a list, it is necessary to know the exact requirement of the reader concerned. The demand may be analyzed into its various facets and an idea may be formed about the coverage to be taken up for the list. Such a list is best produced by a local library. A list of documents compiled by the Bodleian Library of Oxford University on a specific topic of a research worker may be an example of such a list.

P.8 PERIODICITY OF DL

A documentation list may be either closed or open. A closed list is one that is compiled at one time; it is an independent volume having no scope for further addition. On the other hand, an open list is compiled at intervals; the later compilations supplement the earlier ones. An ad hoc documentation list compiled on some specific occasion or to meet the specific demand of a user is a closed list, while a documentation periodical is an open documentation list. A closed list does not have any periodicity, but an open one does have. The periodicity of a documentation periodical, i.e., an indexing periodical, an abstracting periodical or a digesting periodical, is decided on the basis of the amount of documents to be covered. If the amount is high, the list has to be brought out more frequently but if the amount is less, the list may be brought out at longer intervals. Another point that has to be kept in mind in this connection is the time lag between the publication of the documents and their inclusion in the list. Even when the materials published in an area are not much, we may have to opt for a quicker interval if it is found that the longer interval is likely to defeat the purpose of the list.

P.9 METHOD OF COMPILATION

Compilation of documentation lists is a skilled job requiring some initial training. The method may vary according to the kind of list to the prepared. The methods suitable for compiling different types of lists have been discussed in respective chapters. Here only those steps, which are common in all types of lists, have been mentioned [4].

P.9.1 Selection

Before starting compilation of a documentation list, a documentalist or information worker engaged in compilation of the list should select the type of list that may suit his users. For example, for a person engaged in active research and experiments, a current awareness list may be very helpful, while for a person specializing in a subject area, a list with abstracts may be suitable. The selection may also be affected by some practical considerations like availability of staff to work on the list or availability of duplicating facilities.

P.9.2 Scope and Coverage

The next task of the list compiler will be to take a decision on the following:

- *Subject coverage*: i.e., the exact subject to be covered, its various facets and the related areas to be included;
- *Period*: i.e., the period of the subject to be covered as in history or literature and/or the period of production of documents to be covered (See Section P.7.3);
- *Types of documents* i.e., what types of documents (e.g., periodical articles, conference papers, theses, research reports, pamphlets, standards, specifications, monographs) are to be included;
- *Language* i.e., the language or languages of the documents to be covered;
- *Level* i.e., the level of treatment of subject in the documents to be included;
- *Periodicity* i.e., whether the list will be an ad hoc one or an open one and if open, what should be its periodicity.

P.9.3 Scanning

On the basis of the decisions taken above, now the documents are to be scanned and the relevant materials which can be included in the list are to be identified. For this, not only the titles of the items are to be looked into, but also the authors' synopses or abstracts, if provided, or even the texts are to be consulted, if necessary. Listing of irrelevant materials only increases the bulk of the list and decreases the precision and recall ratios of information retrieval through that list.

P.9.4 Entry Making

In the next stage, the compiler of a list will have to prepare an entry for each item identified as relevant, preferably in a standard size card. The entry will contain all essential bibliographical details of the document, written in a standard pattern. It may also contain a brief description of the contents or scope of the document when the list is intended to be an enriched list. If the list is a bare list, the subject of the document may be noted down briefly for the purpose of arrangement under feature headings. The entries may differ according to the indexing technique followed (See Chapters L and N).

P.9.5 Arrangement

The entries thus prepared will now have to be arranged in some convenient order. Most of the indexing systems prefer alphabetical arrangement.

If no modern indexing system is followed, the entries may also be arranged in a classified order by assigning a class number to each entry according to some classification scheme or may be arranged under broad subject headings. Necessary feature headings (sub-headings or topic headings) may also be added, especially if the list is a longer one. In some cases, chronological arrangement may also be helpful (See also Section G.8.1.2). In fact, arrangement may vary according to the nature of the list and the service aimed at. For example, in a current awareness list, which is meant for speedy dissemination of current information, an alphabetical arrangement may be favored, while in an abstracting periodical any type of subject arrangement may be suitable.

P.9.6 Index Making

Keeping in view the fact that the approaches of the users are not always same, it may now be necessary to prepare indexes such as author index, title index, and subject index, so that any user can easily find out his material whatever may be his mode of approach. However, any index that may yield an order which is same as that of the list proper, need not be prepared. There may be even a combined index. The references in the indexes may be given by page numbers or preferably by entry numbers, if the entries are numbered.

P.9.7 Final Copy

The documentation list should now be neatly typed out or word-processed. An introduction may be added at the beginning explaining the scope, coverage and purpose of the list and providing hints to the users for finding out their relevant documents easily and quickly. "Guide to User" may also be given in a separate section. Views differ about placing of the indexes. Usually they are provided at the end, but they may be brought in the beginning, specially in a classified list, as they are in fact aids for quick and easy location of relevant documents. Thus the preferred format of a documentation list may be: (1) Introduction, (2) Guide to User, (3) Indexes, and (4) List proper. Necessary instructions to the printer may be affixed at appropriate places when the list is to be printed.

P.10 ADVANTAGES OF DL

The advantages of different types of documentation list have been discussed in respective chapters. The main advantages may be summarized below.

- They help the users to find out their relevant literature quickly;
- They minimize scanning time and search efforts of the users and the time thus saved are better utilized by them in study and research;
- They manifest the richness or lacuna, if any, in a store of documents or literature published in a field.

REFERENCES

[1] S.R. Ranganathan, Documentation and Its Facets, Asia, Bombay, 1963. (Chapter B3).

[2] S.R. Ranganathan, A. Neelameghan, Physical Bibliography for Librarians, second ed., Asia, Bombay, 1974. (Chapter AB).

[3] T.C. Hines, The collectanea as a bibliographic tool (Ph. D. thesis), Rotgers University, 1961. As quoted in: M.B. Hale, The Subject Bibliography of the Social Sciences and Humanities. Pergamon Press, New York, 1970, p. 17.

[4] A. Chatterjee, Elements of Documentation, The Author, Calcutta, 1983.

CHAPTER Q

Translation Service (TS)

Q.1 INTRODUCTION

Although organization and dissemination of information to the users are the main tasks of an information worker, he may also have to think of some other means to help his readers. Provision of translation service (TS) is one of those additional jobs to be undertaken by an information worker.

Q.2 MEANING OF TRANSLATION

Translation, according to literal meaning, is expression of the ideas or the sense of a sentence or passage into a language other than the original. In this process, the original idea contained in a document remain unchanged; only the language of expression is changed. Translation is different from transliteration, which means representation of the words of one language in the alphabets of another. In transliteration, pronunciation of the original words are kept intact; only they are rendered using a different species of alphabets. Micro-documents are usually translated for researchers, while transliteration is employed for preparing entries in a multilingual catalogue or a bibliography.

Q.3 NEED OF TS

Since World War II, the literature on science and technology has grown at enormous speed and at present there is virtually literature explosion in these fields. But all these materials are not published in one language. English has been the most used language in scientific literature, but today sizable amount of such literature is published in Russian, German, French, and even in Chinese. Evidently, it is not possible for a research worker to learn all these languages. Neither can he/she ignore them. The only other solution is, therefore, provision of translated versions of his/her required documents. Thus translation is required for (1) crossing over the language barrier and (2) saving the time of the researchers. It may be pointed out

Elements of Information Organization and Dissemination
DOI: http://dx.doi.org/10.1016/B978-0-08-102025-8.00017-X

that the need for translation arises when either the users belong to different language groups, or when resources of a library are in different languages, or when both the conditions prevail.

Q.4 DEMAND FOR TS

Translation work may be undertaken either on actual demand or on the basis of anticipated demand. When frequency of demand is less and there is no urgency in supplying the material, translation may be done or acquired on getting the actual demand. But when demand is received very frequently and they are to be met without loss of time, translation should be prepared or acquired in anticipation of the demand. For anticipating the demand, it is necessary to know about the nature of projects undertaken by researchers to be served. If necessary, a brief outline of each project may be obtained and studied and the researchers may be interviewed.

Q.5 KINDS OF TRANSLATION

Same passage or document may be translated by different persons in different ways. The quality of translation depends on the capacity of the translator to grasp the meaning of the original writing, his power of expression and vocabulary. Five kinds of translation are mainly noticed:

- *Literal translation:* This type of translation corresponds exactly to the original. Here words or terms are taken in their usual and obvious senses. The translator cannot employ any discretion or use any allegory or metaphor from his own side.
- *Free translation:* Here words or terms used in the original are not given any importance to. The general meaning or the ideas contained in a document are expressed in a suitable language by the translator. The translator has freedom of expression.
- *Adapted or tailored translation:* Here the translator keeps in mind the purpose for which the translation is required and molds the translation accordingly. Unnecessary elaboration of passages may be omitted by him and where necessary he may elaborate some points for the sake of clarity.
- *Technical translation:* In this type of translation technical jargon of the subject concerned are used instead of ordinary equivalents of words. Subject specialists prefer this type of translation.

- *Translation into/from code language:* Sometimes a passage or document is converted into a code language (e.g., shorthand) or a passage in code language is translated into a speaking or writing language.
- *Mechanical translation:* This type of translation is done by a machine and is often "approximate" rather than the exact version of the original.

Q.6 WHO'S JOB?

The translation work may be undertaken by various types of persons and agencies, such as (1) the reader of researcher himself, (2) the librarian himself, (3) a professional staff translator, (4) a professional freelance translator, (5) a translating agency, and (6) a translating machine. Neither the reader himself nor the librarian should be expected to take up the job and unnecessarily waste their time which can otherwise be better utilized in their respective spheres of work. Besides, they may also lack the competence of a professional translator. Therefore, the choice should be made from among the other alternatives.

Q.6.1 Professional Translator

A professional translator is one who has the requisite qualifications and competence to translate written material from one language to another and who has taken translation work as a profession either on full-time or on part-time basis. Such translators are often favored by many libraries. If the volume of translation work in a library is considerable and the flow of demand for translations is continuous, professional staff translators may be appointed. Otherwise, a list or panel of professional freelance translators may be maintained and they may be contacted whenever necessary. However, even where staff translators are appointed, the services of part-time translators may be requisitioned when the quantity or language of translation required is beyond the capacity of the former.

Q.6.1.1 Qualifications

Mere knowledge of a language is not sufficient to make a person a good translator. Translation work, specially of technical material, "is a highly specialized task which requires the combination of at least two skills: firstly, knowledge of the language in which it is to be translated (often called target language)," and secondly, "an adequate and competent knowledge of the subject" [1]. It is always preferable if a person translates only into his mother tongue or in a language in which he is as proficient as in his mother tongue. It must be stressed that the "knowledge of subject" does not mean only a general idea of a subject, but a thorough knowledge in the special field that the document to be translated deals with. The translator is also expected to know the technical jargon of the concerned subject area. The freelance professional translators should also possess the same qualifications.

Q.6.1.2 Translators' Register

Persons with a combination of language proficiency and subject knowledge are not found always. As such, it is necessary to maintain a register of persons with such combinations for reference at need. Such registers/ directories have been brought out in various countries. Even such registers are being maintained by some private organizations. In the digital age, many translation registers are being maintained online. Some examples of translators' registers are:

- Aslib Register of Specialist Translators.
- The Institute of Translation & Interpreting (ITI) Directory of Qualified Professional Translators and Interpreters (Great Britain).
- Professional Services Directory of the American Translators Association. 1976. Croton-on-Hudson, New York.
- Congrat-Butlar, Stefan. Translation and Translators: An International Directory & Guide. 1979. R R Bowker, New York.
- Indian Scientific Translators Association and NISSAT. Directory of foreign language scientific and technical translators in India. 1989.
- National Translation Mission (India). National Register of Translators (http://www.ntm.org.in/languages/english/nrtdb.aspx).
- Directory of Freelance Translators of TranslationDirectory.Com (http://www.translationdirectory.com/translator_directory.htm).
- Directory of Translators and Interpreters (http://www.proz.com/translator-directory/).
- American Translators Association. Online Directories of Translators and Interpreters (https://www.atanet.org/onlinedirectories/individuals_tabs.php).
- Directory of Qualified Professional Translators (http://www.directoryoftranslators.com/).

Q.6.2 Translation Agency

Translation agencies are in existence at different levels—local, national, and international. They employ translators and/or utilize the services of freelance translators and supply translations against payment like a business house. Some of these agencies maintain translation service primarily for their own groups of users and supply copies of translations available with them to others against payment. Since the work is done in a well-coordinated manner, the translations supplied by these agencies are revised and checked before dispatch and therefore these are generally of good standard. The following are some of the agencies which supply translations: National Translation Centre (Chicago), International Translation Centre (Delf, Holland), International Federation of Translators (Paris), NISCAIR (New Delhi), Malaysian National Institute of Translation, etc. It is interesting to note that in recent years many private players have also come up with translation services on commercial basis. Besides, there are also many websites through which translations can be obtained.

Q.7 MACHINE TRANSLATION

Research in machine translation i.e., translation with the help of computer has been going on since 1950s and many approaches have been developed for such work. The progress of machine translation has been described in Chapter Y.

Q.8 TRANSLATION POOL

The translation work is a costly and time-consuming job. If the translated version of a document is destroyed after meeting the specific demand, further money, and time may have to be spent if and when translation of the same document is demanded at a later date. As such, translations obtained by any information center may be filed for future use. Thus translation banks or translation pools are created. Such translation pools—maintained both at national and international levels—make available their holdings to each other through mutual cooperation.

Q.8.1 Important Pools

The following are some important translation pools operating at various levels:

- *National Translation Centre (NTC)*—Formerly known as SLA Translation Centre, NTC is located at the John Crerar Library, Chicago, USA. It maintains English translations of materials published throughout the world on natural sciences, physical sciences, medical sciences, and social sciences. Its present stock is around 20 million items.

- *International Translations Centre* (formerly European Translation Centre)—ITC is located at the Technological University of Delf, Netherlands. It is practically an international pool run by the support of 17 governments including those of Britain, France, and Canada. India, United States, Australia, and other governments and private organizations also cooperate with ETC.
- *British Library's Lending Division (BLL)*—Formerly known as National Lending Library, BLL at Boston Spa houses the largest translation pool in Britain. Its main collection consists of translations of Russian papers. Its present translation collection is around half-a-million items.
- *Transatom*—It is a specialized translation pool on atomic energy created jointly by European Atomic Energy Community (EURATOM) and the United States Atomic Energy Authority (USAEA). Transatom information office is located at Brussels.

Q.8.2 Translation Indexes

For easy and quick location of translations, the centers operating the translation pools maintain or bring out printed indexes. Union lists of translations are also brought out. Some important such indexes are briefly described below:

- *Aslib Index of Unpublished Translations*—Being maintained in card since 1951, it covered English translations from all languages of articles mainly in the field of science and technology (now ceased).
- *British Reports, Translations and Theses*—published since 1981 by the British Library's Lending Division, it succeeds *NLL Transactions Bulletin* and *BLL Announcement Bulletin* and provides a list of translations obtained in BLL. BLL also brings out quarterly *BLL Review* which covers book translations and cover-to-cover translations.
- *Commonwealth Index to Unpublished Scientific and Technical Translations*—Maintained by ASLIB on cards in three sections—journals, patents, and standards—since 1951, it covered English translations of articles in all languages and in various subjects, specially science and technology. Information was being collected from over 300 sources in Britain and other Commonwealth countries. In 1973, it provided location information for about 450,000 translations (now ceased).
- *Transatom Bulletin*—Published monthly by Transatom Information Centre since 1961, it indexes completed and under preparation translations of articles on nuclear science and also gives a list of journals translated cover-to-cover.

- *Bibliography of Russian Scientific and Technical Literature*—This is a retrospective bibliography covering the period 1954–56, published by NTC.
- *Consolidated Index to Translations into English*—This index was published by NTC in 1969.
- *Index Translationum*—Published annually by UNESCO since 1932, it covers translations of books only published throughout the world. Since 1979, it is available online.
- *Index Translationum Indicarum*—Compliled by the National Library, Kolkata, India, and published by UNESCO, it contained cumulated entries for India in *Index Translationum.*
- *World Translation Index*—It is a joint publication of International Translation Centre, Centre nationale de la researches scientific, France, and Commission of the European Communities (in cooperation with National Translation Centre at the John Crerar Library, University of Chicago, USA). Being published since 1987, it supersedes World Transindex and Translations Register Index.
- *World Index of Scientific Translations and List of Translations Notified to ETC*—Brought out monthly by International Translation Centre, it lists acquisition of the center arranged by journal titles in original language.
- *National Index of Translations*—Published quarterly by INSDOC (now NISCAIR), it provides information on all translations done in India by different organizations.
- *Bibliography of Translation*—Developed by National Translation Mission (India), this online bibliography lists translated titles belonging both to literary and nonliterary genres (http://www.ntm.org.in/languages/english/bibliography.aspx).

Incidentally, some of these indexes have now ceased publication.

Q.9 COVER-TO-COVER TRANSLATION

Cover-to-cover translation is an important development in the field of translation of micro documents. It is translation of whole periodical issue from front cover to back cover. It is "a special form of pre-fabricated translation......whose origin can be precisely determined from the date when the first Russian Sputnik was blasted into the sky" [1]. Following the Russian success, a crash program was taken up to translate the key writings in Russian to English, which resulted in the emergence of cover-to-cover translations. Such translation work obviously requires much time. According to an estimate, it takes about 18–24 months to prepare cover-to-cover translation of an issue. In spite of this disadvantage, several hundred journals are still translated in this manner [1]. Mainly Russian and Chinese (and some Japanese and Eastern European, other than Russian) primary research journals are translated into English on a cover-to-cover basis [2]. Cover-to-cover translations are covered in a list published along with *World Index of Scientific Translations and BLL Review.* The Special Libraries Association, USA, has also brought out *Guide to Scientific and Technical Journals in Translation*, compiled by C.E. Himmelsbach and G.E. Boyd which provides information regarding journals being translated cover-to-cover.

Q.10 LIBRARIAN'S ROLE

Should translation be considered as a task of librarians or information workers? is a debatable question. Some people still feel that librarian or information worker should have knowledge of many languages so that he can translate reading materials from one language to another for his users. Not long ago a foreign language was in the library science curriculum of some library schools. But it is now increasingly felt that the actual work of translation is not the function of the librarian or information worker, because, firstly, he/she cannot be expected to know all the languages and all the subjects in the world to be able to translate all types of materials and secondly, he/she has many other important jobs to perform. This is the reason why Ranganathan was of the opinion that translation was not a "documentation work" proper; it was, according to him, in the "fringe of our field of work." He said that the work of the librarian in this regard would be the liaison work [3]. That is, the librarian or information worker should work as a link between the user and the translator. He will receive demand for translation or anticipate the demand, get the translation done by a suitable translator or procure it form some agency or pool and then serve the translation to the user. In other words, the translation work will be done by the translator and the translation service will be provided by the librarian or information worker.

REFERENCES

[1] F. Liebesny, Handling of foreign language material and translation, in: W.E. Batten (Ed.), Handbook of Special Librarianship and Information Work, fourth ed., Aslib, London, 1975, pp. 350–356.
[2] M.H. Sable, Translation, in: A. Kent et al. (Eds.), Encyclopedia of Library and Information Science, vol. 31, Marcel Dekker, New York, 1981, pp. 123.
[3] S.R. Ranganathan, Documentation—Genesis and Development, Vikas, New Delhi, 1973, (Chapter G).

CHAPTER R

Document Delivery Service (DDS)

R.1 INTRODUCTION

As mentioned earlier, a librarian or information worker has to do some additional work besides compiling document lists, to satisfy his users. After consulting a documentation list, a user may want to see the texts of the original documents which he finds to be relevant. The original document may be supplied from own collection of the library or information center, if available, and if not, may be procured from some other library or information center on inter-library loan. But sometimes the original document cannot be supplied for some reason, such as rarity or brittleness of the document or lack of sufficient copies. Sometimes again the user may also want to obtain a copy of the document for consultation. In such cases, the librarian or information worker has to take help of some reprographic process for copying the document. Thus, provision of original documents or copies of documents is another additional job of the librarian or information worker.

R.2 DOCUMENT DELIVERY

The term "Document Delivery," literally means delivering the required document to a user. In that sense it is almost synonymous with circulation or lending of a document, either from its own collection, if available, or from the collection of some other library obtained through inter-library loan, by a particular library to a user, who has sought it. However, some people use the term in a narrower meaning i.e., "provision of material that may be retained by the user" [1]. In that sense inter-library loan cannot be called document delivery service (DDS), because the document so obtained has to be returned within a stipulated period. Due to technological developments in the fields of reprography and ICT it is now possible to provide the users their required documents in hard copy, prepared by using reprographic techniques, or soft copy by scanning the original text and recording the same in CD or DVD. The soft copy can also be transmitted online to the user through intranet or as e-mail attachment. Thus,

Elements of Information Organization and Dissemination
DOI: http://dx.doi.org/10.1016/B978-0-08-102025-8.00018-1

today the term "document delivery service" means "provision of published or unpublished document in hard copy, microform, or digital format, usually for a fixed fee upon request" [2]. Supply of faxed copy through telecommunication medium is also considered document delivery service. In short, document delivery "refers to the physical or electronic delivery of document from a library collection to the residence or place of business of a library user, upon request" [2]. The term "Document Supply Service (DSS)" is sometimes used as an alternative term of DDS.

R.2.1 Characteristics of DDS

The main characteristics of document delivery service, when taken in the broader sense, are:

- The document that is delivered to a user may be an original version, or a soft copy, a faxed copy, a scanned copy, or a photocopy of the original;
- Delivery of the document may be made physically within the library or at the residence or work-place of the user, or online through intranet, Internet, or any computer network;
- The document delivered to a user may be from the collection of the local library or from the collection of any other library obtained by the local library through resource sharing arrangement;
- Document delivery service is usually provided against a fixed fee and against request from a user.

R.2.2 Process of DDS

For providing document delivery service the following steps are to be followed:

- *Receipt and analysis of demand:* At this step, requisition for a document/ documents is received from the user by the document delivery section of the library. The bibliographical details, including the required pages, of the document/documents, provided by the user concerned are checked and any gap found is filled up by interviewing the user concerned before accepting the requisition.
- *Identification and location of document:* Now the required document is identified and located in the library's own collection, if available. If not, efforts are made to locate it in any other library by searching union catalogue/OPAC or through network.
- *Procurement of document:* The identified document is procured from the library stackroom, or from other library through inter-library loan, when it is not available in the library's own stock.

- *Copying the document:* If only a few pages are required, the required pages are photo-copied or scanned. Here, the library has to ensure that the fair use limit provided in the copyright law has not been violated.
- *Delivery of document:* The user concerned is now intimated about the availability of the document, and the document, in original, or photocopies of the required pages, as the case may be, are handed over to him/her and cost of acquiring/photocopying is realized, as per library rules. Document may be delivered through other modes also, as indicated below, such as by post/courier, through messenger, through intranet, as email attachment, through fax.
- *Feedback:* Feedback is obtained from time to time from the users availing of this service for improving the service.

R.2.3 Media of Delivery

A document may be delivered to a user in various ways:
- Delivering an original document or a photocopy of the document to the user from circulation desk within the library, or at the user's doorstep by messenger or by post/courier.
- Transmitting a document to the user through fax.
- Delivering a document recorded on CD or DVD to the user within the library, or at the user's doorstep by messenger or by post/courier.
- Transmitting a soft copy of the document to the user through intranet or a network, or through Internet as e-mail attachment.

However, mostly the whole document in hard copy is not required by the users and as such copies of required portions, prepared by using any reprographic technique, are delivered to the users. Thus, reprography plays an important role in document delivery service.

R.2.4 Prerequisites

The prerequisites for providing efficient document delivery service are:
- Availability of union catalogues or access to OPACs of libraries working in the same or related fields;
- Availability of adequate reprographic facilities;
- Availability of lists of foreign information centers working in the same field;
- Reciprocal arrangement with foreign information centers for supply of needed documents;
- Trained staff for manning the document delivery section, especially in handling reprographic equipment.

R.3 INTER-LIBRARY LENDING

Inter-library lending has been the earliest method used for document delivery. This system is still prevalent in many countries. As defined by the *Interlibrary Loan Code for the United States*, "Inter-library loan" is the process by which a library requests material from, or supplies material to, another library. The purpose of inter-library loan, as defined by this code, is "to obtain, upon request of a library user, material not available in the user's local library" [3]. The inter-library lending or loan system works in the following way: the user makes a request with their local library, which, acting as an intermediary, identifies owners of the desired item, places the request, receives the item, makes it available to the user, and arranges for its return. The lending library usually fixes the due date and overdue fees of the material borrowed. Although books and journal articles are the most frequently requested items, some libraries also lend audio recordings, video recordings, maps, sheet music, and microforms of all kinds. In many cases, nominal fees are charged for inter-library loan service [4]. Inter-library lending arrangements vary in type and practice. These include direct transactions between two libraries; loans organized between members of a co-operating group of libraries; and nationally-organized inter-library lending, operated either on a centralized (with material mainly being supplied from a single repository) or decentralized basis [1]. With the advent of library networks and consortia, inter-library loan has now become easier. Many countries have their own inter-library code for smooth running of this service. In the United States, the Inter-library Loan Committee of Reference and User Services Association (RUSA, a division of ALA) prepared *Inter-library Loan Code for the United States* in 1994, which has since been revised twice in 2001 and 2008. IFLA has also formulated a *Model Inter-Library Loan Code* (1983, Revised 2000), *International Lending and Document Delivery: Principles and Guideline for Procedure* (1954, Rev. 1978, Modified 1987 and Rev. 2001), and *Guidelines for Best Practices in Inter-Library Loan and Document Delivery* (latest revision 2007). IFLA has also introduced a Voucher Scheme for payments relating to inter-library transactions.

R.4 PHOTOCOPY SUPPLY

With the advent of various reprographic techniques, a new method of document delivery came into vogue. Popularly known as reprographic service, this involves supply of photocopies of required portions of documents to the users. This service is now provided in almost all big libraries.

R.4.1 Reprographic Techniques

The various reproduction techniques, processes or methods are usually grouped in two categories, viz., copying techniques and duplicating techniques. Copying techniques are meant for making limited number of copies, while duplicating techniques are meant for a large number of copies. However, in the context of document delivery service, the former techniques are mainly favored in libraries and information centers because of the following reasons:

- The number of copies of a document required is too less to need duplication;
- The readers require cheap copies in minimum time;
- No legal difficulty usually arises in supplying small number of copies.

Among the various copying methods again, mainly xerography is being used for preparing photocopies of documents for document delivery service. As such, only this method is briefly described below.

R.4.1.1 Xerography

The term "xerography" was coined by its inventor Chester Carlson of the United States by combining two Greek words "xerox" meaning dry and "graphein" meaning recording. Thus xerography means dry recording or dry printing. It is a convenient and simple but versatile process requiring less time. The following steps are involved in xerography [5]:

- *Charging*: A cylindrical drum is electrostatically charged by a high voltage wire called a corona wire or a charge roller. The drum has a coating of a photoconductive material.
- *Exposure*: A bright lamp illuminates the original document, and the white areas of the original document reflect the light onto the surface of the photoconductive drum. The areas of the drum that are exposed to light become conductive and therefore discharge to the ground. The area of the drum not exposed to light (those areas that correspond to black portions of the original document) remains negatively charged.
- *Developing*: The toner is positively charged. When it is applied to the drum to develop the image, it is attracted and sticks to the areas that are negatively charged (black areas), just as paper sticks to a balloon with a static charge.
- *Transfer*: The resulting toner image on the surface of the drum is transferred from the drum onto a piece of paper with a higher negative charge than the drum.

- *Fusing:* The toner is melted and bonded to the paper by heat and pressure rollers.

A negative photocopy inverts the colors of the document when creating a photocopy, resulting in letters that appear white on a black background instead of black on a white background. Negative photocopies of old or faded documents sometimes produce documents which have better focus and are easier to read and study. In modern Xerox machines, the whole process is completed automatically.

Digital Machines

Digital technology is now being widely used in Xerox machines replacing the earlier analog technology. Such machines effectively consist of an integrated scanner and laser printer and have several advantages, such as automatic image quality enhancement and the ability to "build jobs" (i.e., to scan page images independently of the process of printing them). Some digital machines can function as high-speed scanners. Such models typically offer the ability to send documents via email or to make them available on file servers. A great advantage of digital copier technology is "automatic digital collation." For example, when copying a set of 20 pages 20 times, a digital copier scans each page only once, then uses the stored information to produce 20 sets. In an analog copier, either each page is scanned 20 times (a total of 400 scans), making one set at a time, or 20 separate output trays are used for the 20 sets [5].

R.5 SOFT COPY SUPPLY

Availability of documents in digital format, development of scanners, and the advent of Internet and other library and information networks have opened up new opportunities in the sphere of document delivery. Soft copies of documents available in digital format can be directly transmitted by a library or information center to the respective users as email attachments through national and international networks/Internet. Even documents available in print format can be scanned and the scanned images can be similarly transmitted to the users.

R.6 LEGAL ASPECT

When a document is supplied through inter-library loan, no legal aspect is involved. But when a copy of any document or a portion of a document is supplied to the user it involves legal aspect since content of any document is the property of its author or his/her nominee who holds the copyright. Is then copying permissible under law? To get an answer to this question one has to look into the provisions of the existing copyright laws.

R.6.1 Right of Author

According to British copyright law, an author's right is protected from the date of publication of a work till 50 years after the death of the author, there being no need for formal registration of copyright. In the United States, the author or his nominee holds the right for 28 years and the period may be extended for another 28 years. Each copyrighted document should bear the information about the year for copyright and the name of the holder of copyright. Each copyrighted work also bears the following warning: "All right reserved. No part of this book may be reproduced or utilized in any form or by any means, electronic or mechanical, including xerography, photocopying, microfilming and recording or by any storage and retrieval system without permission in writing from the publisher." In Russia, the copyright is held by the holder till 15 years after the author's death. According to Indian copyright law, the author or his assignee has exclusive right to reproduce the author's work in any material form and he enjoys this right till 60 years after the author's death. There is provision for registration of both published and unpublished works with the Registrar of Copyrights. Thus, copying of any document without the prior permission of the copyright-holder is considered to be an infringement of copyright law is almost all countries.

R.6.2 International Convention

Under the Bern Convention (Bern, 1886), the right of an author belonging to any of the signatory countries is automatically protected in other signatory countries. Under the Universal Copyright Convention (Geneva, 1952), the right of an author belonging to the signatory country is protected in other signatory countries till 25 years after the death of the author, but each work should contain a statement showing that the work is copyrighted, the date of copyright, and the name of the holder of copyright.

R.6.3 Fair Use

It may, however, be noted that the aim of making copies of any portion of a document for the purpose of study and research is not to hamper the interest of the authors, but to promote proper use of their works. For this reason, the Royal Society of London called a conference of the British publishers of learned publications in 1948 to sign a "fair copy" declaration so that nonprofit-making organizations, including libraries, could make copies of articles from journals for the "genuine needs" of the scholars. Similarly, the Joint Committee on Fair Use in Photocopying (USA) recommended that the making of a single copy by libraries was a direct and natural extension of traditional library services, while the Committee of Experts on the Photographic Reproduction of Protected Works meeting in Paris pleaded in 1968 "to allow nonprofit-making libraries to provide one copy free of copyright for each user provided that such copy, in case of a periodical, shall not be more that a single article and, in the case of a book not more than a reasonable proportion of the said book" [6]. IFLA has also adopted the principle that "national copyright laws should aim for a balance between the rights of copyright owners to protect their interests through technical means and the rights of users to circumvent such measures for legitimate, non-infringing purposes" [7].

R.6.4 Legal Provisions

In the light of the above, many countries have made provision in their copyright laws to allow copying in a limited way for "fair use" by scholars and researchers. But provision varies from country to country. "On one extreme is the United States, which allows even the multiple copying of a copyright-protected work for classroom use as well as specific exceptions for libraries and archives, the other extreme is in the EU countries, which do not allow any free use of copyright-protected materials" [8]. However, the Copyright, Designs, and Patents Act, 1988 (CDPA) of the United Kingdom permits individuals to make a single copy of a "reasonable proportion" of literary, dramatic, musical, and artistic works for "research and private study" and "criticism, review, and news reporting" [9]. "Canada follows the golden mean where there is limited 'fair use' provision that generally does not permit multiple copying and some very limited exceptions for libraries and archives. Australia has provisions in the Act that allows reviewers and students to use copyrighted material without permission provided their use is fair. There are also special provisions for copying by libraries, educational institutions and government bodies. In some cases, certain procedures must be followed and in some cases fees must be paid. Japan copyright law very specifically iterates the exceptions wherein permission is not required to reproduce the work based upon the purpose and amount of reproduction required" [8]. The Indian copyright law does not consider "making of not more than three copies of a book (including a pamphlet, sheet of music, map, chart, or plan) by or under the direction of the person in charge of a public library for the use of the library, if such book is not available for sale in India" and "the reproduction for the purpose of research or private study" as infringement of the law [10]. Thus supplying of a copy of an article or a chapter of a book to a scholar or researcher is usually allowed provided the recipient declares that it is needed for his private study or research. Besides, to overcome the copyright problem, some systems have provision of payment of a fee to the copyright holder for making copies.

R.7 LIBRARIAN'S ROLE

As indicated earlier, document delivery service today involves supply of three types of documents—original documents procured from other libraries, supply of photocopies, and supply of soft copies of documents. A librarian has to play different types of roles for this purpose. For inter-library lending service, the librarian has to develop necessary links and reciprocal arrangement with different libraries specializing in the concerned subject field, procure union catalogues of such libraries, if available, or at least develop an understanding about where the books needed by his users will be available and delegate the responsibility of running this service to some appropriate section of the library, such as circulation section or reference section. Similar arrangement has to be made for procurement and supply of soft copies of required documents. The work of reprography is, however, a highly technical job requiring specialized training. The librarian is not expected to have ability to handle all the sophisticated reprographic instruments and it is not required too. A reprographer is essentially a technician. An information professional is not a reprographer; he is not expected to prepare a copy by himself. As Ranganathan said, "if you become a technician in reprography, you cease to be a documentalist (i.e., an information professional). You cannot find time or competence to do both the technician's work and the documentalist's work to full satisfaction." He was of the firm opinion that the work of reprography could not be called a documentation work proper. It was only in the "fringe of our field of work" like translation [11]. The roles to be played by a librarian or information professional with regard to reprography, then, are only the role of an organizer and the role of a middleman.

R.7.1 Organization

Although a librarian or information professional is not required to handle a reprographic equipment himself, he must have a fair knowledge about the various reprographic techniques and their relative merits and demerits for proper organization of a reprographic unit and maintenance of efficient service. For setting up a reprographic unit, a librarian/information worker has to first decide the nature of service to be provided keeping in view the nature of the organization of which the library is a part, the requirements of the readers and the availability of finance and trained personnel. He may also consider the availability of reprographic services in an organization nearby. Then he will select a suitable site for the unit and appoint properly trained and experienced technicians. He will now select and acquire the required equipment by surveying the market and comparing the relative efficiency of the various brands available. The technicians appointed for handling the equipment should help him in this work. The alternative method of organizing reprographic activities is out-sourcing the same i.e., giving this responsibility to some outside agency.

R.7.2 Liaison Work

Once the reprographic unit is set up, the service may be started. The librarian or informational professional receives the demands from the users, assesses which process will be suitable in which case and whether any legal aspect is involved and then passes on each requisition with necessary instructions to the technician concerned for processing. When the copies prepared in the reprographic unit come back to him, they are passed on to the users concerned after taking an undertaking from each that the copy supplied to him is meant for private study and it will not be sold or reproduced without the prior consent of the copyright holder. This liaison work may also be done by any library/information center staff appointed or delegated for this purpose. Even when no reprographic facilities are available in a library/information center, the librarian or in-charge of information center may have to supply copies of documents required by his users by procuring such copies from other libraries/information centers. For this, the librarian/information center in-charge must know from where necessary services can be obtained. It may be mentioned that if the library is a member of any network of consortium, it becomes easy to run the document delivery service without much hassle.

R.8 DDS PROVIDERS

Today inter-library loan service and photocopy supply service are being provided by many libraries at local level, national level, and international level. National library and every big library of almost every country provides such services to the users of the country and even to other libraries and individuals from outside the country based on their require-ments. Prominent among such libraries are the British Library of the United Kingdom, the Bibliotheque Nationale of France, VINITI of Russia, the Library of Congress and US National Library of Medicine, Canadian Institute of Scientific and Technical Information, National Library of China, National Diet Library of Japan, and National Library of Australia. In India, National Library, Kolkata (Calcutta); NISCAIR, New Delhi; and six univer-sity libraries identified by INFLIBNET provide document delivery service.

R.8.1 British Library Endeavor

Nevertheless, the most popular DDS provider is perhaps the British Library Document Supply Centre (BLDSC, earlier known as BLLD). With a stock of over 70,000 serials titles, it serves individuals and orga-nizations throughout the world. It is able to satisfy 90% of all requests from its own stock and delivers documents within 24–48 hours. As a first step, document delivery is being offered via ARIEL, which is a document delivery system run on the Internet. Since December 1997, *Inside*, a docu-ment delivery project of the British Library, has been launched. Initially called DISCovery this system had the objective of changing the way users accessed and received information from the British Library. Now, *Inside* allows end-users sitting at their personal computers to identify informa-tion of interest, order documents and have these delivered to their desk tops [12]. BLDSC has since been re-launched as "British Library on Demand." OCLC, a global library cooperative, runs the world's largest inter-library loan network, named WorldShare Inter-library Loan service. More than 10,000 libraries in about 50 countries use this service to bor-row and lend materials with each other. WorldShare ILL gets data for items in library collections from the more than 341 million items and 2 billion holdings included in WorldCat. For article data, the WorldCat knowledge base provides information about 13,903 content collections [13]. BLDSS and OCLC have now joined hands together to provide a new option for fast, flexible purchase from the British Library Document Supply Service that enables library staff to confirm the availability of required documents before placing an order, and provides a wide range of choices for deliv-ery and price. Rather than sending OCLC WorldShare Inter-library Loan requests without knowing whether the British Library can supply the required items, the new option makes clear whether an item is held in advance of ordering and also whether a digital delivery option is available that will reduce delivery times to as little as several minutes [14].

R.8.2　Private DDS Providers

As in the field of translation service, private players have also entered into the business of DDS, especially in digital mode. DocumentsDelivered.com (http://www.documentsdelivered.com/) is one such organization, which provides copies of copyright compliant documents—journal articles, book chapters, conference papers—needed by users. Inforetrieve (http://www.infotrieve.com/document-delivery-service), a part of US based Copyright Clearance Centre, is another such organization, which provides access to databases, research literature, corporate repositories, and even personal files. Some other similar DDS providers are Access Information (http://www.access-information.com/), Ingenta Connect (http://www.ingentaconnect.com/), Information Express (http://www.ieonline.com/), etc. Besides, several big publishing groups/houses like Elsevier (https://www.elsevier.com/), Emerald (http://www.emeraldgrouppublishing.com/), and Taylor & Francis (taylorand-francis.com/) also undertake DDS in partnership with other organizations.

REFERENCES

[1] P. Street, D. Norman, Document delivery, in: J. Feather, P. Sturges, (Eds.), International Encyclopedia of Information and Library Science, second ed., Routledge, London, 2003, pp. 145–147.

[2] J.M. Reitz, Dictionary of Library and Information Science, Libraries Unlimited, Westport, 2004, p. 229.

[3] American Library Association. Interlibrary loans: ALA Library Fact Sheet 8. <http://www.ala.org/tools/libfactsheets/alalibraryfactsheet08>.

[4] Interlibrary loan. <https://en.wikipedia.org/wiki/Interlibrary_loan>.

[5] Photocopier. <https://en.wikipedia.org/wiki/Photocopier>.

[6] Committee of Experts on the Photographic Reproduction of Protected Works, Recommendations, 1968, As quoted in: S.N. Sur, Management of reprographic services-II. Management of reprographic services: Course material of IASLIC Special Course, 1981. (Unpublished).

[7] IFLA position on copyright in the digital environment. <http://ifla.queenslibrary.org/V/press/copydig.htm>.

[8] N. Anilkumar, D. Surti, Copyright law in developed countries, IASLIC Bull. 50 (4) (2005) 249–253.

[9] The Copyright, Designs and Patents Act, 1988 (of UK).

[10] The Copyright Act, 1957 (of India).

[11] S.R. Ranganathan, Documentation—Genesis and Development, Vikas, Chicago, IL, 1973,

[12] Document delivery systems. <http://www.s-and-j.co.uk/college/What%20is%20document%20delivery.html#From1>.

[13] OCLC WorldSare Interlibrary Loan. <https://www.oclc.org/en-europe/worldshare-ill.html>.

[14] OCLC and the British Library offer new option for fast, flexible document delivery. <https://www.oclc.org/news/releases/2015/201501dublin.en.html>.

[15] JCCC@Digital Library Consortium. <http://www.inflibnet.ac.in/econ/jccc.php>.

CHAPTER S

Community Information Service (CIS)

S.1 INTRODUCTION

Community information service (CIS) is not an entirely new phenomenon. It is also not a service that is entirely in the realm of libraries. Since the dawn of human civilization and formation of larger societies, the human beings have been faced with community information (CI) needs and such information flowed to the needy through various channels, unmediated by librarians through informal networks [1]. The first attempts to improve access to information was noticed as early as in 18th century which involved establishing collections of books and printed materials, what was then called "community libraries" [2]. However, the modern day CIS was initiated in late 19th century and early 20th century by social welfare organizations. They did so to assist the members of the community in solving their day-to-day problems. Librarians came to the picture much later, but today CIS has become one of the important functions of the public libraries. Simultaneously, many NGOs, local governments, and sometimes even corporate houses now provide such services.

S.2 COMMUNITY INFORMATION (CI)

Community information is the information that people need or want in order to live their everyday lives. It enables individuals and groups to make informed decisions about themselves and the communities in which they live [3]. According to Donohue, considered to be one of the earliest creators of CIS, CI is the information needed to cope with crises in the lives of individuals and communities [4], while according to Kempson, it is the information for self-reliance and self-determination [5]. Edwards has defined CI as the information in the community for the community [6]. In a simple language, CI is that information which helps people to solve

Elements of Information Organization and Dissemination
DOI: http://dx.doi.org/10.1016/B978-0-08-102025-8.00019-3
279

the day-to-day problems related to their survival. According to Donohue, two types of information are needed by any community [4]:

- Survival information such as that related to health, housing, income, legal protection, economic opportunities, political rights, civil rights;
- Citizen action information, needed for effective participation as individuals or as members of a group in the social, political, legal, and economic process.

Durrance calls the former "information and referral" and the latter "public policy information." He mentions about a third component of CI called "local information," which according to him, is information appropriate and useful to the community, including a calendar of local events, courses and other educational opportunities, and basic information concerning government agencies, local organizations, fraternal groups, and clubs [7]. Another important and implied dimension is the neighborhood information or trans-local information, such as information about medical specialists, employment opportunities in the neighborhood [8].

S.3 COMMUNITY INFORMATION CENTER (CIC)

A community information center (CIC) is an organization that disseminates CI. The term Community Library is still being used in some countries to denote a center providing such information. However, community information center/service is now known by various other names in different countries and sometimes in the same country. Examples of such names are community based information center, community resource center, citizens' information bureau, citizens' information center, citizens' information service, community information support service, community information and referral service, community resource and information service, community information services and center, center for information and community services, citizens' information board, and so on. In USA, CIS is popularly known as information and referral service. Besides, there are also specialized information services/centers for different types of communities (such as senior citizens' information service, rural information center) and for different types of CI (such as health information service, educational information service). CICs sometimes serve as composite units providing other community services along with information needed by the community concerned.

S.3.1 Transformation of CIC

With the developments in ICT, the CICs have transformed into more dynamic centers from time to time. Initially, the focus of CICs was on acquiring, processing, storing, and disseminating the information that was needed by the community that they served. "During the 1980s, the nature of community information centers began to reflect the growing importance of information and communication technology in creating, storing, transmitting, and communicating information. 'Telecenters' and 'Community IT Centers' became the new buzz-words..... As the 1990s concluded, a new designation began to be used—Multipurpose Community Telecenters. It reflected the way that technological change, particularly the development of the Internet, had greatly extended the range of activities that could be undertaken by telecenters..... Since 2000, a further function has been added—community broadcasting" [9]. Consequently, these centers have become community multimedia centers. Nevertheless, the first generation CICs are still functioning in many countries.

S.4 CONCEPT OF CIS

Obviously, the information service through which community information is provided to the members of a community can be called community information service. The term community information service was first advocated by Durrance, who called it "an umbrella term which included provision of information for everyday participation in the democratic process" [7]. CISs, according to the Library Association (now CILIP)'s Working Party on CIS, are those services "which assist individual groups with daily problem solving and with participation in the democratic process. The services concentrate on the needs of those who do not have ready access to other sources of assistance on the most important problems that people have to face, problems to do with their homes, their jobs and their rights" [11]. It is different from other two similar concepts, viz., public information work, and local information service, in the following way [11]:

Public information work	Local information service	Community information service
A general information service, which makes no discrimination in favor of specific groups	An information service on purely local matters. It will involve building-up detailed local information and publishing directories and also acting as a sign-posting agency to other local services	A positive decision support system which concentrates on enabling people, particularly those in lower socio-economic groups, to act either individually or collectively on their problems in the fields of housing, employment, family, personal matters, consumer affairs, household finance, education, welfare rights, and civil rights

S.4.1 Need for CIS

The factors that call for provision of CIS, especially in rural areas, are [7,12]:

- *Disadvantaged users:* Right to information is the key to the progress of any society. Unfortunately, persisting inequalities in the society due to various factors such as social and economic status, physical and mental condition, literacy, and educational level, lack of fluency in language used by the dominant culture, all members of the society do not have equal opportunity to access all the information needed by them. CIS can be developed as an effective tool for providing equal opportunity to every member of the society to access his or her required information.
- *Information deprivation:* There is a close relationship between lack of access to information and deprivation. The success of various social welfare schemes depends to a great extent on the supply of information about how to utilize them to the target group. The restricted opportunity to get and use information is one of the major causes of deprivation. CIS is aimed to minimize this kind of deprivation for the person who requires such information urgently.
- *Scattering of government information:* Governments at all levels are the largest producers of information. But these are highly scattered information sources and difficult to acquire through normal publication channels. CIS must be developed to collect, organize, and disseminate this information for the target groups.
- *Social changes and democratic values:* Democracy needs informed citizenship. If people are to make informed decisions, they require accurate information at the time of need. CIS may help people to take part in the democratic process by organizing a maze of information sources.

S.4.2 Characteristics of CIS

According to Allan Bunch, who first attempted to synthesize definitions of CI, the two main characteristics of CIS are [13]:

- It provides information in the community to help people with daily problem solving or in raising the quality of their lives;
- It is concerned with a specific group of clientele, namely, those who belong to the lower socioeconomic groups or are disadvantaged through an inability to obtain, understand, or act on information that affects their lives.

Coleman has also identified four distinct characteristics of CIS. These are [14]:

- CIS offers materials that are different in both context and nature. The subject matter deals directly with the lives of people and the materials are often ephemeral, consisting of newspaper cuttings, pamphlets, and leaflets. There are virtually no established library procedures for either obtaining or organizing this type of material.

- In CIS, the degree of interaction needed to establish the user's problem is greater than that usually engaged in traditional public librarianship.
- CISs rely on close links with other agencies. It is part of an overall network of information and advising agencies. A CIS cannot operate in isolation. It will depend on other agencies/groups for information gathering and will need to refer the users to them.
- CISs are based on the principle that everyone has a right to equal access to information and to the nation's resources. In this sense, it is not a service but an aid to making democracy work. This point truly characterizes CIS.

S.4.3 Components of CIS

The components of CISs may be depicted through the following schematic representation [8]:

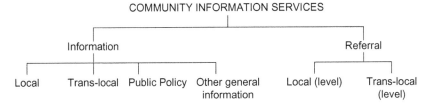

Reproduced from DESIDOC Bull. Inf. Technol. 19 (1) (1999) 5–14.

Local information	Defined as information appropriate and useful to the community, including a calendar of local events, courses and other educational and employment opportunities, and basic information such as those concerning government agencies local organizations, fraternal groups, and clubs
Trans-local information	Defined as information appropriate and useful to the community pertaining to the localities beyond the local area or community concerned (i.e., local information of neighborhood localities and/or trans-local areas)
Public policy information	Defined as information about the Government, and its operation, programmes, plans, schemes, activities, agencies, etc.
General information (i.e., conventional discipline-oriented information)	Defined as awareness generating information on important subject areas, such as health and hygiene, environment, conservation of energy and resources, agriculture, animal husbandry, useful arts and fine arts (i.e., vocational information), technology as well as political, and socio-economic awareness.

S.4.4 Thrust Areas of CIS

CIS should aim at satisfying the needs of the community to whom the service is to be provided. It may be helpful if a study of the area in which the target community lives and operates is undertaken and the needs of the community are identified before planning CIS for the concerned community. Nevertheless, in general the needs of any community relate to the following [16]:

- Agriculture, including weather, better farming techniques, seeds, insecticides, fertilizers, and financing and marketing of agricultural products, etc.
- Industry, including availability of raw materials, technical know-how, and finance and marketing facilities of industrial products, etc.
- Educational opportunities available locally as also nearby areas, availability of scholarships, educational loans, etc.
- Health, including first aid, immunization, health centers, and hospitals located nearby;
- Employment opportunities—local and outstation;
- Government welfare schemes and their implementing agencies;
- Savings, loan, and investment opportunities;
- Agencies maintaining law and order, such as police, civil defense;
- Emergency information such as ambulance, fire brigade;
- Agencies providing legal aid;
- Housing, including agencies providing house building loans;
- Local bodies and their activities;
- Local events and news;
- Recreational facilities;
- Transport facilities, including passenger transport and goods transport;
- NGOs and other social and social service organizations and their activities.

Obviously, the above areas should be the thrust areas of CIS.

S.5 ADVANTAGES OF CIS

Information is indispensible for the development of any community. CIS may help the members of a community, especially a deprived community, to obtain necessary information by reducing the barriers to information access (such as economic barrier, geographic barrier, technological barrier, psychological barrier, language barrier). CIS also helps to achieve the following goals [12]:

- Expanded social interaction;
- Decreased transaction cost;

- Employment and educational gains;
- Increased information exchange;
- Greater skill and confidence building;
- Increased knowledge of the community;
- Increased access to quality information;
- Ability to identify/share trusted information.

S.6 DIGITAL CIS

Internet has certainly broadened the concept of community. Consequently, the scope of CI has also been changing rapidly. The enhanced access opportunity in the present digital environment is facilitating CI flow. Digital CIS enables users to search CI from anywhere at any time. The major activities involved in providing such service are [12]:

- Designing of a working model of CIS;
- Providing access to CISs over the Internet through a seamless interactive Web interface; and
- Making searchable and browsable CI products on CDROM.

S.6.1 Organization of Digital CIS

The steps that may be followed for organizing an integrated system of digital CIS are:

- *Identification of thrust areas:* The thrust areas of the proposed CIS should be identified at the very outset. This will involve—
  - Study of existing local information systems and sources;
  - Survey of the needs of different groups of people belonging to the target community through questionnaire/interview;
  - Indirect analysis of need as reflected in the national, regional, and local newspapers and the demands placed by the members of the target community to existing information centers.
- *Determination of working procedures:* At this stage decision has to be taken regarding the methods to be followed in organizing and disseminating information. This will involve determining—
  - Information collection method (distributed/decentralized method is preferred);
  - Processing and controlling method (centralized method is preferred);
  - Method of disseminating information (decentralized dissemination at the point of utilization is preferred).

- *Identification and collection of sources for CI:* This will involve—
  - Identification of local and trans-local materials related to the thrust areas (including government and non-government materials, printed and non-printed materials);
  - Acquisition/collection of identified materials.
- *Collection of information at local and trans-local level:* This will involve—
  - Designing of information input sheet in a standard format (e.g., MARC 21);
  - Collection of information;
  - Recording of information on input sheet.
- *Organization of documents and information:* This will involve—
  - Organization of ephemeral documents;
  - Organization of information file for local use;
  - Repackaging of information based on local need;
  - Listing of referral centers;
  - Transmission of local information to the central node.
- *Linking of information dissemination centers:* An integrated community support system may be developed by linking various information dissemination centers, such as public libraries, community library and information centers (CLICs), local self-governments and other government departments, concerned NGOs, and voluntary and professional associations.
- *Dissemination of CI:* Dissemination of information will be done by the local nodes. This will involve—
  - Receiving demands from the members of the community;
  - Deciding the type CIS to be provided—direct information or referral;
  - Searching/noting/acquiring the required information;
  - Dissemination of information.
- *Obtaining feedback:* A mechanism should be devised for obtaining feedback from the user community.
- *Feedback analysis and system modification:* The feedback received from the users should be carefully analyzed and modification needed in the system for providing better CIS should be effected.

[Note: The above methodology has been formulated on the basis of the steps suggested in Ref. 12.]

S.7 CIS SCENARIO

Public libraries had long been a "Free Space" or a neutral place in the community, which welcomed people from different walks of life. Public libraries in many parts of the world have been oriented towards middle-class segment that tended to be from a relatively advantaged and educationally elite group in the society. Public libraries are best known for their support in recreational reading but a large section of the community that the public libraries are serving requires survival information [12]. Realization of this need prompted some countries to reorient their public library services, while in some countries to serve needed information to such section of the society a new genre of libraries/information centers/information service were started, which are known in different names in different countries as mentioned in Section S.3. A brief description of the CIS scenario in different parts of the world, based on available literature, is given below. If name of any country is not mentioned, it is because either there has not been much progress in providing CIS in that country or because no literature depicting such progress is readily available.

S.7.1 CIS in Americas

CIS first emerged in the United States and Canada in 1920s. Some welfare agencies took lead in this direction. During World War II, veteran's information centers were set up by the Department of Labour to deal with the crises presented by men returning from the front to their communities and in need of advice on such matters as rehabilitation and retraining. Over 3000 such centers were set up, but most of them were closed by 1949 [13]. Renewed activity was noticed during 1960s and 1970s as increasing affluence and a growth in publicly funded and volunteer services led to the creation of a new generation of CISs. According to Durrance, during this period CI resources and information retrieval services were developed in the United States by agencies, including public libraries, in response to community need evidenced by the frustrations of citizens attempting to obtain information to address daily life issues and exercise democratic rights [7,17]. Another important development in the United States with regard to CIS was launching of a neighborhood center project, called The Information Place (TIP), in Detroit Public Library in 1973. TIP is a free CI and referral service that helps people find answers to the problems of everyday living. Librarians link individuals to agencies and local non-profit organizations that offer services such as emergency food, health care, support groups, and parenting education. TIP was taken up as a model by other cities too [18,19]. In Canada, at least 35 CICs are now functioning throughout the country. The Association of Community Information Centers in Ontario has set up Online Ontario, a regional automated network of CISs [20]. In central American countries of Guatemala and Honduras, there are 65 community libraries, set up by Riecken Foundation, which render information services to the local communities [21]. In Brazil, in South America, a social network called The Rede Brasil de Bibliotecas Communitarias (The Brazil Network of Community Libraries) has been created for sharing community information. Besides, a project has been taken up to set up 3000 teleservice centers [22].

S.7.2 CIS in Europe

In UK, CISs started in 1930s through citizen advisory bureaux. These bureaux were set up to meet the community needs for information arising from the circumstances of economic depression and the imminent likelihood of World War II. They were established in 1939 by the National Council of Social Service, an umbrella body for voluntary social services. They were staffed by volunteers and received financial support from local councils. These bureaux helped to cope with the wartime problems like emergency regulations, missing relatives, evacuation, and separation of families. Gradually they increasingly started helping to solve family and personal problems not directly associated with war. While their number increased to over 1000 during the war years, funding decreased after the war and during the 1950s their number dwindled [13,17,23]. Interestingly, many municipal libraries were also called on to set up information offices during the war, and thus libraries performed a function similar to that of citizen advisory bureaux. But, afterwards, even where they remained under the control of the library service, these centers never assumed a wider role but generally limited themselves to the sign posting of local authority services, leisure activities and later to tourism [8]. However, 1960s and 1970s saw revival of CIS with the restoration of some funding and the emergence of library based CISs. The potential for public libraries to contribute as CI providers led to the development of a range of new services. It also brought about change in the attitude of the library profession regarding their involvement in CI provision as part of a public library service [13,17,23]. According to an estimate, there were nearly 2000 community information and advice services in Britain in 1986. Most offered a general service which included information and advice in any subject. Others specialized in a particular area of work [15]. Presently, Citizens Advice Bureau (now known as Citizens Advice) network consists of 316 independent charities throughout United Kingdom which provide free confidential information and advice to assist people with money, legal, consumer, and other problems [24]. Like Citizen's Advice, there is another charity organization, Neighborhood Advice Center, which was established in 1990 in Surrey to advice and provide information on various subjects, such as visa information, housing grant, welfare benefits, employments [25]. Neighborhood advice centers has since been set up in many areas of United Kingdom. Similarly, Family and Child Care Trust provides family information service at different places. Health and Social Care Information center provides information service relating to health and social care. Besides, local authorities and voluntary agencies in many areas are also running community libraries for providing CIS in their respective areas. The number of such libraries is not less than 400 [26]. Lately, many local authorities have been engaging voluntary agencies to run the community libraries set up and run by them earlier. Some local authorities have also resorted to rendering of web based CISs. Incidentally, it may also be pointed out that many public libraries in the country also provide CIS. In Spain, a citizen's advice bureau functions through its website http://citizensadvice.org.es/. Government of Gibraltar also runs a citizens' advice bureau for providing information and advice required by the citizens. In Russia, there are now about 36,000 rural libraries, but most of them are still being run in traditional manner. Only 16% of them have telephones and 9% have computers and four per cent have Internet access. But efforts are on to modernize and equip them for providing CIS to the rural community [27]. An organization, named Citizens Advice International, registered in Belgium, has been established in 2004. It is an umbrella organization that represents advice organizations throughout the world. It works at the European level with the European Citizen Advice Service, also a Belgium based organization which mainly works for empowering citizens to exercise their rights. Citizens Advice International aims to promote free advice services and provide support to Citizens Advice organizations throughout the world [28].

S.7.2.1 CIS in Nordic Countries

Thorhause has mentioned that CI supply is compulsory in Nordic public libraries and hence the public libraries collect, organize and disseminate official and non-official information needed by individuals, groups, and organizations [29]. Besides, Sweden, Denmark, Finland, and Norway established village based telecenters, known as telecottages, in the late 1980s to reverse a trend of outmigration from rural areas, and to increase IT awareness and capabilities. But while Sweden and Finland both still host a large number of such telecenters, the telecenters in Denmark and Norway have, with a few exceptions, all closed down [30].

S.7.3 CIS in Africa

The first examples of community based libraries as information centers were found in Africa in the 1960s. These were usually initiated and funded by development agencies, working in conjunction with national or public library systems [2]. Community libraries were set up in many countries as a strategy to meet the information needs of all sections of the society, as public library systems in most of the countries were unable to achieve full coverage of the population [31]. Nevertheless, CIS is still either absent or in a stage of infancy in many countries of the continent. Moreover, many of the existing community libraries provide only traditional library services and are yet to convert themselves into community based information centers. As indicated, many non-profit/non-government organizations from developed countries were instrumental in spreading the community library movement in Africa. Special mentioned may be made about Friends of African Village Libraries, which alone has set up 18 community libraries in different countries of Africa [32].

S.7.3.1 Northern Africa

In northern Africa, Egypt is possibly the only country, where community libraries have taken a shape. Fifty-two community libraries are functioning in that country and it has been planned to raise the number to 100 by 2020 [33]. Besides, 350 school libraries have been serving as community libraries since 1956 [34].

S.7.3.2 Southern Africa

In southern Africa, however, several countries have community libraries for providing CIS. In South Africa, there are around 1800 public and community libraries. Two important developments with regard to CISs in South Africa have been (1) introduction of LWAZI, a telephone based speech driven information system that allows South Africans to access government information and services in any of South Africa's eleven official languages using either landline telephone or mobile telephone, free of charge [35]; and (2) drafting of South African Community Library and Information Services Bill, 2010 [36], which, when enacted, will pave the way for improved CISs. In Botswana, four community libraries have been set up with the funding from Robert and Sarah Rothschild Family Foundation. Besides, there are also 69 village reading rooms, which are actually community initiated mini libraries [37]. In Namibia, a network of 64 community libraries are functioning across the country at present, most of which are publicly funded. Only one such library is funded by Evangelic Luther Church, one by a mining company and four by an NGO [38,39]. In Malawi, there are 244 rural CICs [40].

S.7.3.3 Eastern Africa

In this region many countries have been able to develop community libraries. In Kenya, the Kenya National Library Service Board adopted a community library development policy in 1990, following which the first community library was established at Karatina, in Nyeri district, on a pilot basis. The Board has so far established 21 community libraries countrywide to provide community library and information service [41]. In Tanzania, CIS to rural people is provided using a variety of approaches and channels such as through extension agents, individuals, farmer-to-farmer contact, print media, and electronic media [42]. According to Sturges and Neille, in 1989 Tanzania had over 3000 village libraries, located in schools, clinics, courthouses or the offices of local authorities providing library and information services to the rural community [43]. The country has also introduced a system of bare-foot librarians with the libraries owned and controlled by the communities served for providing such service [44]. Some NGOs have also come up to build community libraries in rural areas of the country. In Zimbabwe, several initiatives have been taken to provide books and information of the right type to the communities which are not served by the formal library services. One of such initiatives is establishment of small community libraries based mainly in primary schools in rural areas by the NGO Rural Libraries and Resources Development Programme. Twenty-three such centers have been set up by RLRDP [45]. The National Library and Documentation Services (NLDS), working with the National Free Library, has also facilitated the establishment of 41 school/community libraries [2]. The Zimbabwe Academic and Research Network (ZARnet), in partnership with some other government organizations, has also embarked upon setting up ICT based CICs in different parts of the country [46]. In Uganda, there are 36 community libraries. These have come up due to the efforts of concerned individuals, communities, and NGOs [47]. Among the NGOs, Under the Reading Tree has set up four community libraries, and Friends of the African Library has set up three [32,48]. In Malawi, a network of 200 community library centers has been developed by National Library Service of the country [31]. In Rwanda, Literacy, Language, Learning Initiative, funded by US Agency for International Development, has set up more than 60 community mobile libraries and plans to set up 85 such libraries by the end of the current year [10]. In Zambia, there are five community libraries supported by Zambia Library Service and three more are in the process of being established. Zambia Library Service is also in the process of introducing CIS at provincial libraries of the country, but the progress is very slow [49]. Besides, Lubuto Library Partners, a no-profit organization, has also set up five libraries which serve the communities residing nearby [50].

S.7.3.4 Western Africa

In Ghana, the Ministry of Education has undertaken a community library project to serve various communities. Six such libraries have been set up in the capital city of Accra [51]. Besides, four community libraries have been set up by Friends of African Village Libraries and another four by OSU Children's Fund in different parts of the country [48]. In Burkina Faso, Friends of African Village Libraries helped local communities establish and sustain operations in 14 community libraries during 2001–14. In January 2015, the organization has started work to establish 20 community libraries in northern region of the country [52]. In Nigeria, community-based library and information services are still very limited [53]. A report on public libraries in Africa has also found that "at present there is no appropriate structure for the implementation of community libraries" in Nigeria [54]. However, lately the State Library Board of Imo state in that country is developing a rural CI system consisting of eight rural CICs [55]. In Mali, there are one rural community library and 88 book deposits in rural areas, which provide CIS [56].

S.7.4 CIS in Oceania Region

In Australia, Citizens Advice Bureau, modeled on Citizens Advice of United Kingdom, were set up in several states in the late 1950s. The Citizens Advice Bureau now serving Western Australia has 10 branches and uses the same branding as the British charity [57]. Besides, a non-profit social enterprise, Community Information Support Service, works for providing improved access to high quality CI relating to health to those people belonging to different community groups who are vulnerable to disease and isolation within the community, such as people with mental and physical disabilities, senior citizens, young parents, aboriginals, and people suffering from chronic diseases. It has also developed the Australian Community Data Standards to facilitate access and exchange of information. It is also developing "My Community Directory" and "My Community Diary" websites for coordination of health and wellness activities in local communities [58]. New Zealand has over 83 Citizens Advice Bureaux sites situated in both North Island and South Island [59].

S.7.5 CIS in Asian Region

In China, the China Evergreen Rural Library Service (CERLS), which was set up in 2001, provides free access to information resources to China's rural communities through public school libraries. Today, CERLS has a network of eight public school libraries in the western provinces of Gansu, Shaanxi, and Qinghai, and in the northern province of Jiangsu. Recently, two elementary school libraries in Beijing have added to the network [60]. Food and Agricultural Organization, in collaboration with the Ministry of Agriculture of China, have made two studies in 2003 and 2009 about information service being rendered in rural areas, especially to farmers. These studies have identified the following four rural information service models [61]:

- *Service station*: The service station refers to an information service center operating in townships and villages where there is strong demand for information and that relies on the support of county agricultural agencies. The service station links government offices at the county, township and village levels and moves information both to and from farmers. As in 2008, there were 290 such service stations in Shucheng County, 152 service stations in Jinyun County, 97 service stations in Litong district, and 160 service stations in Fuyu County.

- *Farmers' home*: Organized by agricultural departments together with the departments of forestry, water conservancy, science and technology and education, the farmers' home is both a venue and a platform to serve farmers. It is a kind of one-stop shop in a central location for farmers to buy agricultural products, seek out technical information, and consult with experts (or a hotline service) on agricultural problems. Farmers' homes operate at city, county, town and township levels. Lately, such homes have been set up in some villages too.

- *Association-cooperative*: The association-cooperative consists of farmers in an area who are in need or interested in the same types of information. The association or cooperative provides members with information services before, during, and after the production of a certain type of agricultural product with the intent of improving their production and increasing their income. In addition to their own members, many associations provide useful information to non-member farmers too.

- *Government+company*: The government + company model is a business relationship designed to provide information directly to a large client base that includes farmers and other people involved in planting, breeding, processing or sale of agricultural products, agri-businesses and related organizations. It is essentially highly targeted professional information, with "public" information provided for free, and customized information delivered for a fee. Under this model, modernized communication networks, video equipment, telephone hotlines, mobile phone SMS, and video programmes facilities as well as printed information materials are provided.

In Japan there are 46 village libraries which provide information service to the village community. But these libraries are facing the challenge of providing information support in everyday problem solving [62]. In Indonesia, a movement of individuals, neighborhood and community organizations and NGOs starting and running their own libraries has emerged since 2001. Called Taman Bacaans—i.e., reading gardens—these simple libraries are often hosted in somebody's house or in a community building [63]. Though the exact number of reading gardens now functioning in the country is not known, it must be over 2000. Nevertheless, in India, CIS movement seems to have progressed more than many other countries of the region. Here not only the central government and the state governments in many states have come forward to set up CI kiosks, even corporate houses have shown interest in extending such facilities to the rural community. The developments are briefly described below.

S.7.5.1 CIS in India

The importance of dissemination of CI was felt in the country in ancient days itself. For instance, the edicts of Ashoka amply illustrate the method of dissemination of public policy information in ancient India. Information about the local events, penal sanctions, taxation, grants, local activities, and public/royal policies, etc. used to be disseminated among the masses through loud announcements by attracting their attention by beating tom-toms (drums). This system is still a very popular means of communication in rural India. The *gurukulas*, i.e., the ancient residential centers of education and learning were also centers of information and communication. In rural India, Gram Sabha venues or meeting places were the CICs of the respective villages. The village well also served as a center of information for the rural women folk. With the advances in the communication systems, the mass media, such as radio, television, and newspapers took up the responsibility of disseminating the CI in their own limited way but more efficiently and with a wider coverage [8]. Besides, the public libraries, especially those located in rural areas, have also been disseminating CI to the local residents. In the digital era, efforts are being made in different parts of the country towards developing suitable dissemination mechanism of CI utilizing information and communication technologies. Three types of agencies, viz., (1) government agencies (directly or indirectly)/semi-government/autonomous agencies; (2) non-government organizations (NGOs)/voluntary organizations/associations; and (3) corporate agencies i.e., industrial houses, are involved in this work. Even a few international agencies are also collaborating in some cases. A few important projects/schemes/initiatives aiming to provide e-governance and/or CIS facilities is described below.

Government/Semi-Government Initiatives

Some government/semi-government agency sponsored initiatives are [64]:

- *Akshay Kendras:* Altogether 1430 information kiosks, named Akshay Kendras (i.e., indestructible centers), first inaugurated in Mallapuram district, have been set up within a maximum of two kilometers from any household in all the 14 districts of Kerala, and networked, by the Government of Kerala. The villagers can make payment of electricity bills, get birth certificates, and contact police stations by e-mail, besides obtaining various other required information, such as information relating to agriculture, health, distance education, career, banking, insurance, police, through these kiosks [65].
- *CLI centers:* Community library—cum—information centers are being set up by the Government of West Bengal in villages not having government or government sponsored public libraries. To start with, such centers have been set up in 341 panchayat samity (i.e., rural intermediate level local government) areas. There are a total of 1640 gram panchayat areas having no such library. The centers, besides providing normal library services, specifically cater information relating to career and vocational opportunities, essential data needed for regional planning, and information pertaining to developmental activities being carried out by village panchayats [66].
- *CI centers:* The CIC Project has been implemented in North-Eastern states, including Sikkim, by the Ministry of Information Technology, Government of India. Under this project, CICs have been set up in all 487 blocks (i.e., district sub-divisions) of the region. Besides providing

e-mail and web access to the people of the area and other citizen-centric information and services, these centers provide access to several socio-economic databases [67].

- e-*Mitra kiosks*: Under UNDP-Government of India supported initiative, Jana Mitra (i.e., friend of the masses) kiosks were first set up in remote areas of Jhalwar district of Rajasthan for providing access to information pertaining to government services in 2002. Subsequently, the Government of Rajasthan opened such kiosks in Jaipur too and also took up Lok Mitra (i.e., friends of the people) project for setting up similar kiosks in the urban areas. These projects were later integrated into a single project called e-Mitra [68]. According to a report published in *Indian Express*, dated October 15, 2006, the state government had already set up 508 e-kiosks in 32 districts, including 59 in rural areas, and also planned to set up over 6700 such centers in rural areas under the Common Service Centers scheme of the Government of India and another 1000 in association with National Bank for Agriculture and Rural Development (NABARD). Besides providing e-governance services, these kiosks provide information about government schemes, agricultural information, mandi (i.e., large market) rates, etc.

- *Lok Mitra Soochna Kendras:* This NABARD funded project has been undertaken by Himachal Pradesh Government and first implemented in Hamirpur district under which Lok Mitra Soochana Kendras (i.e., friend of people information centers) have been set up in 25 panchayat areas of the district. The project, which is proposed to be extended to all districts of the state, aims at providing the general public, especially those living in distant rural areas of the state, easy access to government information, market rates, employment opportunities, local news, and the facilities of e-governance [69].

- *NATP Internet kiosks:* National Institute of Agricultural Extension and Management, Hyderabad, under its National Agricultural Technology Project (NATP), has taken initiative to set up these kiosks in 24 districts of seven states, viz., Andhra Pradesh, Bihar, Himachal Pradesh, Jharkhand, Maharashtra, Orissa, and Punjab. These kiosks provide facility of e-mailing and information relating to agriculture, weather, etc. [70].

- *NIRD public information kiosks:* The National Institute of Rural Development sponsored kiosks, with Internet connections, have been set up at Vikerabad in Ranga Reddy district of Telengana and Tenali in Guntur district of Andhra Pradesh. These kiosks, located in local public libraries, provide such information as examination results, directories, agricultural prices, governmental forms, land records, educational opportunities, etc. [71].

- *Raj Nidhi information kiosks:* These web-enabled kiosks, first inaugurated in the obscure hamlet of Nayala in Jaipur District in the year 2000, are being set up in all the 9184 panchayats (i.e., rural base level local government areas) of Rajasthan, which will be finally connected in a network. The *Raj Nidhi* (i.e., treasure of Rajasthan) kiosks provide wide range of information relating to health, employment, transportation, distance education, agriculture, civic facilities, tourism, fairs and festivals, investment, etc. [72].

- *Wired village project:* Fifty-four village information kiosks have been set up around Warananagar in Kolhapur district and Sangli District of Maharashtra by Warana group of sugarcane cooperatives with the help of National Informatics Centre. These kiosks provide a wide range of information and services relating to agriculture, health, employment, government schemes, educational opportunities, etc. to the residents of 70 villages around Warana in their local language [73].

NGO Sponsored Schemes

Some important NGO sponsored schemes are:

- *Drishtee's intranet:* Drishtee (i.e., eyesight) has been described as "a platform for rural networking and marketing services for enabling e-governance, education, and health services." It runs with the help of a state-of-the-art software that facilitates communication and information interchange within a localized intranet between villages and a district center. The services are provided through kiosks set up in villages. *Drishtee* first implemented *Gyandoot* scheme in Dhar (MP) in 1999 on behalf of Government of Madhya Pradesh. In 2000 it set up the first information kiosk in Haryana and since then has extended its services to several districts in six states, viz., Madhya Pradesh, Haryana, Punjab, Gujarat, Bihar, and Orissa. It has by now set up over 1000 such kiosks, the target being 50,000 kiosks throughout India [1,74,75].

- *Gyandoot scheme:* Under this scheme, information kiosks, known as *Soochanalayas* (i.e., houses of information), have been set up at gram panchayat buildings of 21 villages in five blocks in the tribal area of Dhar district in Madhya Pradesh and connected through an intranet, which has been named *Gyandoot* (i.e., messenger of knowledge). These *soochanalayas* not only serve the villages where they are located but also to surrounding 25–30 villages. The information relating to agriculture product auctions, commodity rates, government schemes, and announcements, etc. are available from these kiosks [76].

- *GRID center:* Tejas Samadhana Kendra (i.e., brilliant or bright solution center) or General Resources and Information Dissemination (GRID) center, designed and developed by the Indian Farmers and Industries Alliance (IFIA) and Federation of Farmers' Associations (FFA), started on July 13, 2004, at Gummadidala village of Medak District in Telengana. GRID is an information kiosk with a data bank, coordinating with government agencies and consultancies. It specializes in agricultural information [77].

- *Information village research project:* Under this project, initiated in 1998 by M S Swaminathan Research Foundation in a cluster of villages and hamlets near Pondicherry, with headquarters in Villianur, a market center, information village shops have been set up in 10 villages, which give access to over 100 databases containing updated information relating to crop prices, government schemes, weather, etc. [78].

- *SARI network:* The Sustainable Access in Rural India (SARI) project, sponsored by IIT-Madras; MIT Media Lab; Berkman Center for Internet and Society, Harvard University Law School; and the I-Gyan Foundation, is being implemented in three blocks of Madurai district of Tamil Nadu. Under this project, over 50 far flung villages have been wirelessly connected from a server in Melur in the pilot phase. A tele-kiosk set up in each village meets the need of e-governance and other information needs of the people of the concerned village [79].

- *TARAhaat centers:* Implemented by Development Alternatives, an NGO, and its rural marketing arm Technology and Action for Rural Advancement (TARA), in Bundelkhand, MP and Punjab, TARAhaat (haat means rural market) has a mother portal Tarahaat.com supported by franchised network of 150 village cybercafés, named *TARAkendras.* *TARAhaat* is now run by TARAhaat Information and Marketing Services. *TARAkendras* provide information relating to agriculture, water, law, government schemes, health, livelihood, railways, and e-governance [80].

- *DISK project:* At the initiatives of National Dairy Development Board (NDDB), around 2500 dairy cooperative societies in Gujarat have been using PC connected Automatic Milk Collection Systems (AMCS) for milk buying/selling transactions in an efficient manner. The Center for Electronic Governance of Indian Institute of Management, Ahmadabad, took up a project to develop a Dairy Information Services Kiosk (DISK) at each milk collection center utilizing the existing infrastructure and offer an extensive knowledge and service delivery mechanism through a Dairy Portal. The DISK software facilitates creation and maintenance of databases in the regional language of the society concerned. It stores and maintains the databases of cooperative society members, their cattle, artificial insemination, veterinary, cattle feed, and other service transactions in addition to the daily milk transactions. The Dairy Portal has textual as well as multimedia content useful to the farmers and others working in this field. The portal mainly offers services such as education, entertainment, discussion forum, frequently asked questions, data transfers, application forms for submission to various agencies, e-commerce, and e-banking [81,82].

Corporate Initiatives

Some important initiatives taken by corporate/business houses are:

*   *Hind Lever's iShakti:* iShakti (i.e., Internet power) is an Internet based rural information service, launched in Andhra Pradesh, by Hindustan Lever, in association with Andhra Pradesh Government's Rajiv Internet Village Programme. Under this project iShakti information kiosks have been set up in eight villages of the state. The vision is to have 3500 such kiosks delivering information service to over 10 million rural people across 7500 villages in future. The kiosks offer information chiefly in the form of audio–visuals in the areas of health and hygiene, e-governance, education, agriculture, animal husbandry, vocational training and employment, entertainment, legal services, and women empowerment. E-governance facilities are also provided by the state government through this channel [83].

*   *ITC's e-choupal:* The International Business Division of India Tobacco Company launched its *e-choupal* (choupal means village meeting place) project in June 2000 with setting up of six information kiosks *(e-choupals)*. By March 2010, *e-choupal* network reached out to over four million farmers growing a range of crops such as soybean, coffee, wheat, rice, and pulses in over 40,000 villages through 6500 kiosks across 10 states (Madhya Pradesh, Haryana, Uttarakhand, Uttar Pradesh, Rajasthan, Maharashtra, Kerala, Karnataka, Andhra Pradesh, and Tamil Nadu). These kiosks, managed by farmers—called *sanchalakas* (i.e., directors)—themselves, enable the agricultural community to access ready information in their local language on the weather and market

prices, disseminate knowledge on scientific farm practices and risk management, facilitate the sale of farm inputs and purchase farm produce from the farmers' doorsteps [84].

- *Ogilvy and Mather's Param: Param* (i.e., the best) is a rural electronic connectivity network, which was successfully field tested in Basti district of Uttar Pradesh by Ogilvy and Mather. The *Param* computer interacts with the operator in local language. The trial run has shown that even women and children use this facility to seek the needed information. The next phase of the project was scheduled to be launched in 2004 [85].
- *Indiagrainline:* EID Parry & Co. implemented this scheme in villages around Nellikuppam village in Cuddalore district of Tamil Nadu, where the factory of the company is located. Under this project, computers supplied by the company are located in the houses of villagers and connected into an intranet. The company's agricultural portal called indiagrainline.com places all its information on the intranet site for sharing among the villagers free of cost [86].

REFERENCES

[1] K. Toyama, et al., PC kiosk trends in rural India: Paper presented at the Seminar on Policy Options and Models for Bridging Digital Divides, Tampre, Finland, 2005. <http://research.microsoft.com/enus/um/india/projects/ruralkiosks/pc%20kiosk%20trends%20in%20rural%20india.doc>.
[2] S. Ndinde, W. Kododo, The role of community-based information centers in development: lessons for rural Zimbabwe, Int. J. Learn. Teach. Educ. Res. 2 (1) (2014) 44–53.
[3] C. Raven, G. Copitch, Community information, in: J. Feather, P. Sturges (Eds.), International Encyclopedia of Information and Library Science, second ed., Routledge, London, 2003, pp. 92–94.
[4] J.C. Donohue, Community information services—a proposed definition, in: M. Stock (Ed.), Community Information Politics: Proceedings of American Society for Information Science Annual Meeting, 39th, Washington, 1976.
[5] E. Kempson, Information for self reliance and self determination: the role of community information services, IFLA J. 12 (3) (1986) 182–191.
[6] M. Edwards, Cooperation in Community Information Provision: Practice and Potential, British Library Research and Development Department (1977), (Mimeographed).
[7] J.C. Durance, Community information services: an innovation at the beginning of its second decade, in: W. Simonton (Ed.), Advances in Librarianship, vol. 13, Academic Press, Orlando, 1986, pp. 99–128.
[8] V. Viswa Mohan, A.A.N. Raju, Community information concepts, DESIDOC Bull. Inf. Technol. 19 (1) (1999) 5–14.
[9] UNESCO, Communication and Information Unit, Bangkok. Community information and technology centres: focus on south-east Asia. <http://www.unesco.org/new/fileadmin/MULTIMEDIA/HQ/CI/CI/pdf/programme_doc_telecentre_study_en.pdf>.
[10] Literacy Language Learning. Community library initiative. <http://l3.edc.org/our-work/community-mobile-library-initiative>.

[11] The Library Association (London), Working Party on Community Information. Community Information: What Libraries Can Do? The Library Association, London, 1980.

[12] P.S. Mukhopadhyay, Community information services through web and CD-ROM: an open source framework for public libraries in India, in: Information support for rural development. Papers presented at the National Seminar of IASLIC, 21st, Kolkata, 2005, pp. 171–186.

[13] A. Bunch, Community Information Services: The Origin, Scope and Development, Clive Bingley, London, 1982.

[14] P. Coleman, Community information policy and provisions, ASLIB Proc. 38 (9) (1986) 305–316.

[15] D.C. Venner, S. Cotton, Information for a rural community: The South Molton community information project. (Library and information research Report 40) 1986. British Library, Boston Spa. *As quoted in* C. Steelwel, Community information services: a view of the theoretical foundations, DESIDOC Bull. Inf. Technol. 19 (1) (1999) 15–33.

[16] A. Chatterjee, Community information service in rural India, in: Librarianship in 21st Century: Festchrift in honour of Prof. A S Chandel (To be published).

[17] R. Day, Information connecting people with services: the information and referral role of community service organizations. <http://www.thefreelibrary.com/Information+connecting+people+with+services%3A+the+information+and...-a0169228024>.

[18] Detroit Public Library. TIP. <http://www.detroitpubliclibrary.org/specialservice/tip>.

[19] C. Stilwell, Community information services: a view of the theoretical foundations, DESIDOC Bull. Inf. Technol. 19 (1) (1999) 15–33.

[20] R.R.V. Lopes, A model and prototype for a community-related information retrieval system for public libraries in Brazil. Thesis submitted to City University, London for PhD degree in information science, 1995.

[21] Beyond Access. How public libraries contribute towards reaching the millennium development goals. <http://beyondaccess.net/wp-content/uploads/2013/07/Beyond-Access_MDG-Report_EN.pdf>.

[22] J. Ernberg, International perspective: empowering communities in the information society: Conference on Empowering Communities in the Information Society: Proceedings, CSIR, Pretoria, 1996.

[23] W. Martin, Community Librarianship: Changing the Face of Public Libraries, Clive Bingley, London, 1989.

[24] Citizens Advice. <https://en.wikipedia.org/wiki/Citizens_Advice>.

[25] Neighbourhood Advice Centre. <http://dnntech.com/nac/index.php>.

[26] Public Libraries News. List of UK volunteer libraries. <http://www.publiclibrariesnews.com/about-public-librariesnews/list-of-uk-volunteer-run-libraries>.

[27] Y.P. Melentyeva, Villages without access roads and libraries without telephones: rural libraries in Russia. *Kultura.* September 2008; 13–16. <http://www.kultura-rus.uni-bremen.de/kultura_dokumente/ausgaben/englisch/kultura_4_2008_EN.pdf>.

[28] Citizens Advice International. <https://en.wikipedia.org/wiki/Citizens_Advice_International>.

[29] J. Thorhause New trends in Scandinavian public libraries. 1988. The Danish Library Bureau Ltd., Ballerup, Denmark. *As quoted in* R.R.V. Lopes. A model and prototype for a community-related information retrieval system for public libraries in Brazil. Thesis submitted to City University, London for PhD degree in information science, 1995.

[30] M. Gurstein, Community Informatics: Enabling Communities with Information and Communication Technologies, Idea Group Publishing, Hershey, USA, 2000, pp. 301–309.

[31] K. Mchombu, N. Cadbury, Libraries, Literacy and Poverty Reduction: A Key to African Development, Book Aid International, London, 2006.

[32] Friends of African Village Libraries. <http://www.favl.org/>.
[33] T. Salma, Community libraries for adult education in Egypt. (PPT presentation). <http://www.unesco.org/education/aladin/pdfaladin/Community_Libraries_for_Adult_education_in_Upper_Egypt.pdf>.
[34] B. Bezirgan, Near east since 1920, in: W. Wiegand, D.G. Davis, (Eds.), Encyclopedia of Library History, Routledge, New York, 1994, pp. 461.
[35] LAWAZI. <http://www.meraka.org.za/lwazi/about/index.php>.
[36] South Africa. South African Community Library and Information Services Bill, 2010. Draft for stakeholder consultation (250110). <http://www.archivalplatform.org/images/resources/SACLIS_Bill_draft_for_stakeholder_consultation__02_02_2010_.pdf>.
[37] SESIGO: Botswana e-Public Libraries. <http://www.sesigo.org.bw/index.php?id=48>.
[38] Namibia Library and Archives Services. <http://nlas.info/>.
[39] R. Niksala, The need and use of community library services in Namibia (Master's thesis of University of Tampare, Namibia), 2008. <https://tampub.uta.fi/bitstream/handle/10024/79357/gradu02836.pdf?sequence=1>.
[40] A.S. Mwiyeriwa, Malawi, in: R. Wedgeworth (Ed.), World Encyclopedia of Library and Information Services, ALA, Chicago, 1993.
[41] Kenya National Library Service Board. Community library services. <http://www.knls.ac.ke/community-library-services>.
[42] W.P. Mtegal, B. Ronald, The state of rural information and communication services in Tanzania: a meta-analysis, Int. J. Inf. Commun. Technol. Res. 3 (2) (2013) 64–73.
[43] P. Sturges, R. Neille, The Quiet Struggle: Libraries and Information for Africa, Mansell, London, 1990.
[44] E. Banach, The role of the public library in a changing society, Artes Natales 7 (2) (1989) 5–11.
[45] L. Atherton, Community libraries in Zimbabwe, Inform. Dev. 9 (1/2) (1993) 36–43.
[46] ZARNET. <http://www.zarnet.ac.zw/>.
[47] R. Gomez, Libraries, Telecentres, Cybercafés and Public Access to ICT: International Comparisons: Information Reference, Hershey, USA, 2012, p. 482.
[48] African Village Libraries. <http://wikieducator.org/African_Village_Libraries>.
[49] Libraries in Zambia. <http://www.afran.info/modules/publisher/item.php?itemid=442>.
[50] Lubuto Library Partners. <http://www.lubuto.org/>.
[51] I.K. Bukenya, Africa: Public libraries, in: I. Abdullahi (Ed.), Global Library and Information Science: A Text Book for Students and Educators (IFLA Publications 136–137), K G Saur, Munchen, 2009, p. 31.
[52] M. Kevane, Partnership experience with community libraries in Burkina Faso, Paper presented at IFLA World Library and Information Congress, Cape Town, 2015.
[53] O.S. Agboola, A.H. Bolanle, Provision and use of community-based library and information services: a case study of Asa Local Government Area, Kwara State, Nigeria. Library Philosophy and Practice (e-journal). 2013; Paper 849. <http://digitalcommons.unl.edu/libphilprac/849>.
[54] A. Issak, Comp. Public Libraries in Africa: A Report and Annotated Bibliography, International Network for the Availability of Scientific Publications (INASP), Oxford, 2000.
[55] E.N.O. Adimorah, P. Ugoji, Rural community information system in Nigeria: Imo State Project Report, World Lib. 7 (2) (1997).
[56] M. Keita, The situation of community libraries in Mali. <http://www.libr.org/isc/issues/ISC24/A19-Keita.pdf>.
[57] Citizens Advice Bureau – Branches. <www.cabwa.com.au>.
[58] Community Information Support Services. <http://www.communityinfo.org.au/>.

[59] Citizens Advice Bureau, New Zealand. Annual report 2014. <http://www.cab.org.nz/aboutus/p/Documents/CABNZ%20Annual%20Report%202014.pdf>.
[60] G.Z. Liu, Evergreen: Bringing Information Resources to Rural China, Council of Library and Information Resources, Washington, 2005.
[61] Food and Agricultural Organization. Regional Office for Asia and the Pacific (Bangkok). Information services in rural China: an updated case study, 2012.
[62] H. Nagata, Public libraries in Japan: triggers for renovation models. Paper presented at the Comfenalco Antioquia Congreso Internacional de Biblioteca Publica: un Continetes, Medallion Colombia, 2007. <www.ke.tsukuba.ac.jp/div-comm/pdf/Library_in_Japan.pdf>.
[63] Community Libraries in Indonesia. <http://www.favl.org/blog/archives/2008/04/community-libraries-in-indonesis.htm>.
[64] A. Chatterjee, Information support for rural development in India. In Information support for rural development. Papers presented at the National Seminar of IASLIC, 21st, Kolkata, 2005. pp. 1–14.
[65] Akshaya. <http://www.akshaya.kerala.govt.in>.
[66] West Bengal. Directorate of Library Services. Annual report, 2005–2006 & 2006–2007.
[67] eGovernance in India. <https://egovindia.wordpress.com/2006/06/23/community-information-centre-cic-from-wikipedia-the-free-encyclopedia/>.
[68] eMITRA. <http://emitra.gov.in/>.
[69] Lokmitra: web enabled government-citizen interface of Himachal Pradesh Government. <www.himachal.nic.in/lokmitra.htm>.
[70] MANAGE (National Institute of Agricultural Extension Management). <http://www.manage.gov.in/publications/bulletin/Aug-Sep2k1.pdf>.
[71] P. Vyasamoorthy, Electronic libraries in rural India; some points for discussion, in: H.K. Kaul (Ed.), National Around Table on the Modernization & Networking of Libraries in India: Papers, DELNET, New Delhi, 2002.
[72] Rajasthan. <http://www.rajgovt.org/news/RajNidhiTrg.htm>.
[73] Maharashtra. Wired Village Project. <www.mah.nic.in/warana>.
[74] DRISHTEE. <http://www.drishtee.com>.
[75] Drishtee-the clock builder. <http://www.thealternative.in/business/drishtee-the-clock-buider/?print=pdf>.
[76] GYANDOOT. <www.gyandoot.nic.in>.
[77] Gummadidala. <http://en.wikipedia.org/wiki/Gummadidala>.
[78] M S Swaminathan Research Foundation. Information Village Research Project (IVRP). <http://siteresources.worldbank.org/INTEMPOWERMENT/Resources/14654_MSSRF-web.pdf>.
[79] SARI: Sustainable Access in Rural India. <http://edev.media.mit.edu/SARI/>.
[80] TAARAHAT. <http://www.tarahaat.com>.
[81] M. Raina, Empowering dairy farmers: a portal and dairy information and services kiosk: a case study. Paper presented at the International Conference on Achieving Connectivity for the Rural Poor in India, Baramati, India, May 31–June 3, 2001.
[82] T.P. Rama Rao, Dairy information services kiosk and dairy portal. <www.iimahd.ernet.in/egov/documents/disk-and-dairy-portal.pdf>.
[83] Hindustan Uniliver Ltd. <http://www.hul.co.in/mediacentre/news/2004/HLLLaunchesIShaktiRuralInfoServiceInAssociationWithAPGovt.aspx>.
[84] eCHOUPAL. <http://www.echoupal.com/frontcontroller.ech>.
[85] ITC. Narrowing digital divide. <http://www.itcportal.mobi/media-centre/press-reports-content.aspx?id=544&type=C&news=Narrowing-digital-divide>.
[86] EID Parry unveils corDECT revolution in a sleepy TN village. The Financial Express. April 24, 2001.

CHAPTER T

Evaluation of Information Service

T.1 INTRODUCTION

According to Wilson, "the idea of evaluation has come into the professional consciousness only in very recent years. True, in an earlier time, in the 1950s in the USA, the idea of the 'library survey' developed, and that had in it the seeds of evaluation (indeed, the library survey concept goes back at least to the 1920s in the United States). In more recent times, however, the impetus to evaluate has come from the need to justify budgets more explicitly than ever before. All service functions in all organizations are being reviewed in terms of their necessity for the aims of the organization and libraries and information systems are no exception" [1]. Obviously, any information service rendered by a library or information center also needs to be evaluated to justify the spending on this service and to assess the extent of benefit derived by the user community concerned.

T.2 CONCEPT OF EVALUATION

Evaluation is "the systematic investigation of the merit, worth, or significance of an object or effort" [2]. In a simple language, "evaluation consists of comparing 'what is' to 'what ought to be'" [3]. Evaluation aims at ascertaining the level of performance or value of something. Evaluation studies investigate the degree to which the stated goals or expectation have been achieved or the degree to which these can be achieved [4]. This is true for any product, service or system, information service being no exception. Evaluation practice has changed dramatically during the past three decades—new methods and approaches have been developed and it is now used for increasingly diverse projects and audiences [2]. Scanning of LIS literature shows that many evaluative studies have been made in different areas of library activities and services. Even some comprehensive books have been produced on this subject. Lancaster and his associates have made significant contributions in this field.

Elements of Information Organization and Dissemination
DOI: http://dx.doi.org/10.1016/B978-0-08-102025-8.00020-X
305

T.2.1 Types of Evaluation

There are many different types of evaluation depending upon the object being evaluated and the purpose of the evaluation. Perhaps the most important basic distinction in evaluation types is that between formative evaluation and summative evaluation [5]. Formative evaluation is conducted during the development/implementation of a program or service, the aim being improvement or raising the efficiency and effectiveness of the program or service, while summative evaluation is conducted after the program is completed or service is fully implemented, the aim being assessment of the impact or effectiveness of the program or service. Both types of evaluation are quite relevant for evaluation of an IS. An evaluation can use quantitative data or qualitative data, and often uses both for better results. According to Wilson, the two types of data are collected by the following methods [1]:

- Quantitative
  - Data collection by constant monitoring;
  - Data collection by ad hoc surveys of activities or costs;
  - Ad hoc surveys to solicit "hard" data from users.
- Qualitative
  - Ad hoc surveys to obtain information/opinion from users.

T.3 NEED FOR EVALUATION

An information service is introduced by a library or information center to meet the specific needs of some target user group. Once a particular service is started, it is necessary to ascertain whether it is able to meet those needs, as otherwise the whole endeavor will be wasted. Moreover, once started, it may not remain useful to the users forever as the needs and demands of the users keep on changing. Further, there is always a possibility that the service being rendered is not able to satisfy the needs of the users completely due to various reasons. It is, therefore, necessary to have a mechanism for evaluating the service concerned on regular basis.

T.4 OBJECTIVES OF EVALUATION

Evaluation of any information service aims at assessing how far the users have been benefited or satisfied by that service and if the service should be continued or withdrawn or replaced by a new service. More specifically it tries to find out [6]:

- Whether the service has been useful to the target user group, and if so to what extent?

- Whether the service is able to meet the changing needs of the users, and if so to what extent?
- How the quality and effectiveness of the service can be improved?
- What are the reasons for the success or failure of the service to meet the users' expectations?

T.5 LEVELS OF EVALUATION

With the adoption of ICT, more and more libraries and information centers have started providing automated or digital information service. In the context of digital libraries, Sarasevic has mentioned that evaluation can be made from a number of standpoints or levels [7]. This is possibly true for evaluation of any automated or digital information service too. Sarasevic has further mentioned that each of these levels can be translated into a goal for evaluation. He has pointed out that the big dilemma or difficulty in evaluation is the selection of the level of objectives to be addressed. He has divided the objectives, and thus evaluation of a technical computer-based system, into seven general classes or levels (of course they are not mutually exclusive) as below. The first three of the levels mentioned are more user-centered, while the last three more system-centered with an interface in between. He has also indicated the performance questions for each level [7].

- *Social level*: How well does a digital library (in the present context an automated/digital information service) support the needs and demands, roles, and practices of a society or community? This can be very hard to evaluate due to the diverse objectives of the society or community. Many complex variables are involved.
- *Institutional*: How well does a digital library (in the present context an automated/digital information service) support the institutional or organizational mission and objectives? How well does it integrate with other institutional resources? This is tied to institutional organizational objectives—also hard to evaluate for similar reasons.
- *Individual*: How well does a digital library (in the present context an automated/digital information service) support information needs, tasks, activities of people as individual users or groups of users with some strong commonalties? It turns out that most evaluations tend to be on that level, probably because it is most direct and easiest to evaluate, though differences in perceptions can prove troublesome, and it is not always easy to generalize to a larger population.
- *Interface*: How well does a given interface provide and support access, searching, navigation, browsing, and interaction with a digital library

(in the present context an automated/digital information service)? Questions can be asked in either the user or system direction or in both directions.

- *Engineering*: How well do hardware, networks, and related configurations perform? These questions yield more replicable measures and are more easily generalizable than many user-centered approaches.
- *Processing*: How well do procedures, techniques, algorithms, operations, and so on perform? These are also very systematic, though there may be variation due to differences in configuration, capacity, and other system variables.
- *Content*: How well the collection or information resources selected is represented, organized, structured, and managed? Although this is also fairly systematic, the related questions are how well, for whom, and for what purpose?

T.6 METHOD OF EVALUATION

Evaluation may be conducted from three points of view or perspectives—managerial, system, and user. Since an information service is designed to serve a particular user community, user-centered evaluation is obviously preferable. Of course evaluation from other perspectives also leads to better performance of the system which will be ultimately helpful to the users.

T.6.1 Pre-Evaluation Considerations

Before the evaluation is actually taken up, the evaluator/s should be clear about the following:

- What criteria will be used to judge the performance of the service, e.g., the number of users who are familiar with the service;
- What standards of performance on the criteria must be reached for the service to be considered successful, e.g., 80% of the users are familiar with the service;
- What evidence will indicate performance on the criteria relative to the standards, e.g., a random survey will demonstrate the users' awareness of the service and the changes in their lives brought by it; and
- What conclusions about performance of the service are justified based on the available evidence, e.g., the changes mentioned by the users are actually due to the service received or for any other reason.

(*Note*: The points mentioned above are based on the suggestions incorporated in Ref. [2].)

T.6.2 User-Oriented Criteria

According to Sarasevic and Wood, five general classes of criteria or dimensions which are found to be most often applied by users are [8]:

- Information or data quality, including:
  - Precision and accuracy of information
  - Credibility of the source(s)
  - Recency of information
- Scope, including:
  - Completeness of information
  - Comprehensiveness of subject or topic coverage
- Appropriateness, including:
  - Fitting with needs, requirements, request; degree to which information is personalized as requested
  - Degree of reaching or exceeding information overload or tolerance for processing information
  - Fitting with own capabilities: language, sophistication level
  - Degree of opinions, extraneous, irrelevant information
- Haggle and hassle factors, including:
  - Time lag in receiving information
  - Ease of usage of received information (e.g., format, additional steps required)
  - Ease of access to the service (e.g., minimum of red tape and paperwork, procedural delays, distances, channels)
  - Efforts required to get a response, support received in access and use
- Costs, including:
  - Direct cost of obtaining service
  - Indirect cost in accessing and using the service and in post-processing of information

However, Sarasevic and Wood feel that the ultimate evaluation by users should not be considered in terms of any of the aspects that deal directly with a given information product or service. "The ultimate evaluation is in terms of the benefits received: increased productivity; increased wellbeing; better life; more comprehensive understanding of a problem, action or consequence; more certainty in decision making; easier actions; promotion; healthier surroundings; etc." [8].

T.6.3 Other Criteria

Various criteria have been proposed by different experts for evaluation of an information retrieval system [9–12], many of which may be found relevant for evaluation of any information service too since the users retrieve their required information through such service. The following criteria may be identified from among the above proposals which may be helpful in evaluation of an information service [6]:

- Comprehensiveness in coverage of relevant information;
- Precision of information provided vis-à-vis users' need;
- Value of information obtained from the service in terms of authenticity, reliability, accuracy, currency, etc.;
- Presentation of information in terms of format and layout;
- Searchability of information in terms of ease and speed;
- The intellectual and physical efforts needed on the part of the user to retrieve the needed information;
- Cost of generating and maintaining an information service vis-à-vis its value to users.

Besides, the five criteria proposed by Wilson [1] for evaluation of library and information systems, viz., success, efficiency, effectiveness, benefits and cost can also be used profitably for evaluation of an information service. In the context of information service these may be interpreted as below:

- *Success:* The success will have to be measured against the objectives of the service;
- *Efficiency:* The efficiency has to be measured according to consumption of the resources—manpower, money, and other resources;
- *Effectiveness:* Effectiveness must be measured in terms of how well the service satisfies the demand placed upon by its users [13];
- *Benefits:* The benefits of the service must relate to the community it serves;
- *Cost:* Cost may be evaluated independently or in association with any of the above.

T.6.4 Steps in Evaluation

Lancaster [14] has identified five major steps that are involved in the evaluation of an information retrieval system. These are quite relevant for evaluation of any information service. These steps, with necessary modification in the context of evaluation of an information service, are discussed below.

T.6.4.1 Defining the Scope of Evaluation

This step involves:

- Formulation of a set of objectives that the evaluation study is going to meet;
- Setting purpose and scope of the whole evaluation program;

- Deciding the environment in which the evaluation study will be conducted, i.e., in a controlled setup or real life situation;
- Deciding the level of evaluation, i.e., macro-evaluation or micro-evaluation;
- Identification of constraints in terms of cost, staff time, etc.

On the basis of the above, a detailed plan will have to be chalked out which will form the basis of the rest of the program.

T.6.4.2 Designing of Evaluation Program

This step involves:
- Identification of the points on which data are to be collected;
- Determination of the parameters on which data are to be collected;
- Deciding about the methodology of data collection;
- Planning the methodology of manipulation of data to arrive at a conclusion.

It is also necessary to prepare a detailed plan of action. It may be pointed out here that while conducting an evaluation program, the designer of the evaluation program may need to control some of the parameters. It is, therefore, necessary that, while preparing the detailed plan of action, the designer indicates which parameters are to be held constant during the study and how this is to be done. Besides, the designer should also indicate the major caution points where more care is needed to avoid faults.

T.6.4.3 Execution of the Evaluation

Execution of the evaluation program is obviously the most time-consuming step in evaluation study. The designated personnel collects data in the way prescribed at the design stage. In most cases, repeated number of observations is required to avoid sampling error and bias. Although the evaluator at this stage has to follow the plan of action thoroughly, he/she may find some interesting features of the system (here information service) that were not mentioned at the design stage. It is thus important that there should be a communication between the evaluator and the designer at this stage in order to share any interesting observations that may call for redesigning of the evaluation program [4].

T.6.4.4 Analysis and Interpretation of Results

The whole fate of the evaluation program rests upon interpretation of results and its accuracy. On the one hand the evaluator has a set of objectives of the evaluation program and on the other the observations, i.e., data collected on different parameters. Although the methodology for manipulation of data is determined at design stage, the evaluator might need to make some changes so as to arrive at a better conclusion. Once the data have been manipulated in a suitable way, the evaluator gets a set of results that is to be interpreted in the light of the set of objectives. The evaluator might need to conduct failure analysis so as to justify the results and also to suggest improvements [4].

T.6.4.5 Modification/Replacement of Service

Finally, the system or service (here information service) is modified, if necessary, in the light of the evaluation results. However, in case of an information service, modification may not always be sufficient; it may be necessary to discontinue the service or replace the same by a new one.

T.7 INVOLVEMENT OF USERS

As an information service is meant for the users, the users should be actively involved in the evaluation work and the evaluation program should be cautiously designed. For collection of data, a mechanism for regular feedback from the users may be introduced by way of supplying feedback forms while providing the service and the users should be encouraged to return the forms with their views. The data so collected may be analyzed and interpreted to arrive at a decision for continuation, discontinuation, or improvement of the service concerned. Another method that may be followed is seeking opinion of a cross-section (sample group) of users (instead of all users) if that can yield reliable data.

REFERENCES

[1] T. Wilson, Evaluation strategies for library/information systems. <http://www.informationr.net/tdw/publ/papers/evaluation85.html>.
[2] B. Milstein, et al., A framework featuring steps and standards for programme evaluation, Health Promot. Pract. 1 (3) (2000) 221–228. An adapted version of this paper "Recommended framework for program evaluation in public health practice" is available at http://ctb.ku.edu/en/table-of-contents/evaluate/evaluation/framework-for-evaluation/main.
[3] N. Van House, et al., Measuring Academic Performance: A Practical Approach, ALA, Chicago, 1990.
[4] G.G. Chowdhury, Introduction to Modern Information Retrieval, second ed., Facet Publishing, London, 2003.
[5] Introduction to evaluation. <http://www.socialresearchmethods.net/kb/intreval.php>.

[6] A. Chatterjee, Elements of Information Analysis, Consolidation and Repackaging, Prova Prakashani, Calcutta, 2013, (Chapter L).

[7] T. Sarasevic, Digital library evaluation: towards an evolution of concepts, Lib. Trends. 49 (3) (2000) 350–369.

[8] T. Saracevic, J.S. Wood, Consolidation of Information: A Handbook of Evaluation, Restructuring and Repackaging of Scientific and Technical Information, UNESCO, Paris, 1981,

[9] C.W. Cleverdon, User evaluation of information retrieval systems, in: D.W. King (Ed.), Key Papers in Design and Evaluation of Retrieval Systems, Knowledge Industry, New York, 1978, pp. 58–74.

[10] F.W. Lancaster, The cost effectiveness analysis of information retrieval and dissemination systems, J. Am. Soc. Inf. Sci. 22 (1971) 12–27.

[11] G. Salton, M.J. McGill, Introduction to Modern Information Retrieval, McGraw Hill, New York, 1983,

[12] B.C. Vickery, Techniques of Information Retrieval, Butterworth, London, 1970,

[13] F.W. Lancaster, The Measurement and Evaluation of Library Services, Information Resource Press, Washington, 1977.

[14] F.W. Lancaster, Information Retrieval Systems: Characteristics, Testing and Evaluation, John Wiley, New York, 1979.

Information Centers

U.1 INTRODUCTION

For a long time, libraries have been performing the duties of collecting, storing, and disseminating various kinds of documents. As the number and the speed in which documents were being produced were not very high, the need for documentation and information services of the present kind was not felt until World War II. But after the war, the situation gradually changed as generation of information went up in quantum leaps and documents started coming up in greater quantity and speed and in increasingly complex varieties. The librarian's traditional tools and techniques were rendered incapable of satisfying the users. They wanted some devices by which they could select the pertinent documents, especially micro documents, more easily, and quickly. This required analysis of the contents of such documents. The emphasis thus started changing from documents to information contained therein. To meet the new challenge, all big libraries, especially the special libraries, started setting up separate documentation sections, and gradually a new kind of organizations with the primary objective of providing documentation or information service came up. These came to be known as documentation centers and later as information centers (ICs).

U.2 DEFINITION OF IC

In a simple language, an information center is an organization from where information users can collect their needed information. More specifically, it is an organization which has the responsibility of collecting, analyzing, and organizing information in a specific area, on the one hand, and on the other, speedy retrieval, and dissemination of required information to the users. Though in a broad sense, information center and documentation center may mean one and the same thing, some people feel that "information centers ought to undertake information analysis and supply evaluated data and information, whereas documentation centers may be satisfied with the function of contents analysis of documentary sources towards

Elements of Information Organization and Dissemination
DOI: http://dx.doi.org/10.1016/B978-0-08-102025-8.00021-1

pointing out to the existence or raw information" [1]. There are of course some other centers which are also basically ICs, but the information handled by them and/or their functions are slightly of different kind, such as data centers, data banks, information analysis centers, referral centers, and information clearing houses.

U.3 NEED FOR IC

The need for establishing documentation centers/information centers was felt because of the following reasons:
- Enormous rise in information output;
- Increase in specialist clientele;
- Increase in research activities; and
- Inability of the libraries to provide documentation service/information service speedily and to the complete satisfaction of the specialist users.

U.4 TYPES OF IC

There are various types of documentation centers/information centers which may be categorized under three groups on the basis of their ownership, specialization, and level [1]. However, the same center may fall in different groups.

U.4.1 By Ownership

From the point of view of ownership, there may be following three types of documentation center/information center.
- *Public/Government owned:* Public documentation centers/information centers are set up and run by public funds. They serve not only the public in general, but also private organizations. They are either attached to some specialized organizations or they function as government agencies or as autonomous or semi-autonomous bodies under the aegis of the government. They may or may not specialize in any field of knowledge. Thai National Documentation Center is an example of this type.
- *Semi-government:* These centers are attached to learned, professional, research, government, or voluntary organizations. They mainly serve the members of the respective parent bodies, but sometimes outsiders are also allowed to enjoy the facilities. They usually specialize in the

fields of specialization of the organizations to which they are attached. SENDOC of India is an example of this type.

- *Private:* Such centers are attached to private business or commercial houses. They specialize in the areas of interest of the respective houses and serve the officials and employees of the concerned houses only. The Media Documentation Center of Air France is an example of this type.

U.4.2 By Specialization

There may be four types of documentation center/information center from the point of view of specialization.

- *Specialization by subject:* Some centers specialize in some specific or broad subject fields such as science, social sciences, agriculture, and medicine. UNESCO Social and Human Sciences Documentation Center (Paris) is an example of this type.
- *Specialization by type of documents:* Some centers specialize in some special types of documents, such as standards, patents, and drawings. A good example of this type is INPADOC—International Patent Documentation Center, Vienna.
- *Specialization by kind of information:* Some centers specialize in only a specific kind of information such as statistical information, biographical information, and industrial information. For example, KADOC—Kenya Agricultural Documentation Center specializes in information relating to agriculture.
- *Specialization by the place of origin of information:* Some centers specialize in information that has originated in a specific geographical area. The Russian Information Center of NISCAIR, New Delhi, is a very good example of this kind.

U.4.3 By Level

From the point of view of level, there may be following five types of center.

- *International centers:* International centers are established by either international agencies like UNESCO, FAO or by several countries together by collaboration. World Agriculture Information Centre (WAICENT) is an example of such a centre. There are also some centers set up by national agencies but they function at the international level.
- *National centers:* National centers are usually public documentation centers/information centers set up by the national governments. They

serve the people and the organizations of the countries concerned. NISCAIR, PASTIC, BANSDOC, etc. are some examples of this type.

- *Regional centers:* Regional centers are established to serve a region. The region may cover some countries of the world or some areas of a country. It may be an independent body or a unit of a central body. Southern African Research and Documentation Center, Harare, Zimbabwe, is an example of this type.

- *Branch:* Branch centers are "devoted to specific discipline or mission." They are "built around the nucleus of an individual information center which has already developed a strong base; but services are available on a national scale for those engaged in the discipline or mission" [1]. Such centers have been established in India under the erstwhile NISSAT.

- *Local centers:* Local centers are set up in individual organizations and they meet the specific needs of the organizations concerned and their staff. The documentation center of European Trade Union Institute, Brussels, is of such type.

U.4.4 Variants of IC

As indicated above, there are also some more types of ICs which also either directly serve information to the users or help users find their needed information, but they are not considered as ICs or documentation centers in the traditional sense because of peculiarities in the type of information handled by them or the peculiarities of their function. These centers can also be categorized according to ownership, specialization, and level. Such centers are introduced below.

- *Data center:* "A data center is a centralized repository, either physical or virtual, for the storage, management, and dissemination of data and information organized around a particular body of knowledge or pertaining to a particular business" [2]. Data centers have been set up at international, regional, national, and even local levels for different types of data. A well-known data center at international level is World Data Center System set up by International Council for Science, which has since been renamed as ICSU World Data System. At regional level there are several European data centers on pollution, biodiversity, climate change, land use, and water. In USA, some well-known data centers at national level are National Oceanographic Data Center, Silver Spring, Maryland; National Climatic Data Center, Asheville, North Carolina; National Snow and Ice Data Center at

University of Colorado, Boulder; and Atmospheric Data Center of NASA. In the United Kingdom, some important data centers at national level are British Oceanographic Data Centre, Liverpool; Polar Data Centre, Cambridge; and National Biodiversity Data Centre Waterford, Ireland. In India, some well-known data centers at national level are Indian Space Science Data Centre, Bangalore; National Oceanographic Data Centre-India, Hyderabad; National Data Centre of India Meteorological Centre, Pune, etc. Incidentally, the term data center is used in a different sense in IT environment. In that context, a data center is a repository that houses computing facilities like servers, routers, switches, and firewalls, as well as supporting components like backup equipment, fire suppression facilities, and air conditioning.

- *Data bank:* Data banks are similar to data centers, except that whereas data centers handle both data and documents containing data, data banks handles data only. According to Science Dictionary, a data bank is "a large repository of data organized in large files, accessible to many users" [3]. In today's digital environment, a data bank actually refers to a large database on one or more subjects accessible online. Such data banks are functioning at both international and national levels. Some examples of data banks at international level are NEA Data Bank of Nuclear Energy Agency, Paris; and Worldwide Protein Data Bank (http://www.wwpdb.org/). At national level, examples of data banks are National Practitioner Data Bank of USA, First Data Bank (on healthcare) of United Kingdom and Export Import Data Bank of Ministry of Commerce and Industry, Government of India.

- *Information analysis center:* An information analysis center is a center "which indexes, abstracts, translates, reviews, synthesizes, and evaluates information and/or data in a clearly defined specialized field or pertaining to a specific mission, to provide definite user groups with digested, repackaged or otherwise, organized pertinent information or data" [4]. Information analysis center is also known as Information consolidation center; and information analysis, consolidation, and repackaging center. Such specialized centers have been set up in many countries, some examples of which are Ergonomics Information Analysis Centre of University of Birmingham, United Kingdom and Defense Systems Information Analysis Center of the Department of Defense, USA. However, in India such centers are possibly nonexistent though many ICs undertake information analysis, consolidation, and repackaging work as one of their activities.

- *Information referral center:* A "referral centre is an organization for direct-ing researchers for information and data to appropriate source, such as libraries, information evaluation centres, documents and documenta-tion centres and individuals" [5]. It is thus an agency, which does not directly provide information sought by a user, but suggests or refers to sources (organizations or individuals), which may satisfy his/her need. Such a center maintains lists or inventory of various kinds of informa-tion sources which help in referral work. A referral center often forms a part or unit of an IC and it is rare to find a center exclusively doing referral work. A good example of a referral center is National Referral Centre: Science and Technology (of the Library of Congress).

- *Information clearing house:* In the context of information dissemination, an information clearing house "is a depository of documents with the additional mission of serving as a central agency for collection, classifica-tion, and distribution of information" [4]. A clearing house may collect information about documents, especially non-conventional documents, originating from a number of sources from different places and in differ-ent languages; sort them according to the requirements of participating libraries/ICs; and pass on the relevant information to respective librar-ies/ICs. It may also procure the documents requisitioned by partici-pating libraries/ICs, may or may not process them and then pass these documents on to the respective libraries/ICs. A clearing house may be organized either on a cooperative basis or by an international or national agency. However, several clearing houses have now come up which directly caters information to the users. Some examples of informa-tion clearing house are Tribal Energy and Environmental Information Clearing House (USA); National Injury Information Clearing House (USA), Veterans Health Information Clearing House (USA), and Canadian Pollution Prevention Information Clearing House.

U.5 FUNCTIONS OF IC

The main aim of a documentation center/information center is to satisfy the information requirements of its clientele. "In general, a documentation center brings to the attention of the specialist users current and recent literature of value to them; sieves through the information sources and indicates pin-pointedly or with high precision the right kind of informa-tion; makes an exhaustive search of literature resources so as not to miss worthwhile information; and provides documentation and information services on demand and in anticipation" [1]. Thus, the main functions of an IC are organization and dissemination of information, "which include (1) collection, registration, and classification of documents, (2) extraction and processing of information in the required form, and (3) storage and supply of information to the users" [6]. However, it may be noted that the functions or activities may slightly differ from center to center depending upon the resources, facilities, and clientele of each center.

U.6 INTERNATIONAL ICs

The importance of information services in research and development has been felt throughout the world, which is manifested by the fact that almost all big libraries, especially the special and research libraries, have introduced documentation/information services. However, many advanced countries and even some developing nations have established national documentation centers/information centers specifically for rendering such service. Besides, some international organizations are also playing an important role in promoting information services. The activities of some important international centers are briefly described below.

U.6.1 WAICENT

The World Food Summit Plan of Action (FAO, Rome, November 1996) highlighted information as one of the priority areas in achieving food security. In direct relation to this undertaking, FAO established WAICENT as its strategic program on agricultural information management and dissemination. WAICENT program provides the information systems platform for accessing FAO's information resources, and makes the accumulated knowledge of FAO on all fields of food security and agricultural development available to everyone [7]. Thus, WAICENT serves as a virtual IC through its web portal http://www.fao.org/waicent/.

U.6.1.1 Objectives of WAICENT
The principal objectives behind the creation of WAICENT were [9]:
- To increase the extent of information coverage handled by FAO;
- To improve and streamline in-house data management;
- To strengthen and simplify the flow of information to and from the member countries;

- To reduce processing costs in all phases of receiving, treating, and disseminating information; and
- To reach FAO's target audiences more effectively and at less cost.

U.6.1.2 Scope of WAICENT

The scope of the WAICENT's information program is very broad, covering all aspects of food and agriculture: nutrition, fisheries, animal husbandry, forestry, and sustainable development.

U.6.1.3 Components of WAICENT

WAISCENT plays the "umbrella" role in FAO's information dissemination activities. It is made up of three interactive and complementary components [9]:

- *FAOSTAT:* This system contains a collection of time-series data on demography, agriculture, fisheries, and forestry covering 210 countries and territories to date, merged into one statistical database service. There are data on trade flows, food aid, development assistance, and the results of the World Agricultural Census on household budget and food consumption surveys.
- *FAOINFO:* The intent of FAOINFO is to develop the infrastructure and procedures to prepare, organize, store, and disseminate textual and hypermedia information. Like FAOSTAT, a key activity of FAOINFO is to manage the change in the way the information is prepared and handled by FAO. There are at present several on-going projects under FAOINFO: the public information text and multimedia service; a Virtual Library project to make library and other information resources available on the staff's computers; and the full-text document storage and retrieval system project. AGRIS is part of the Virtual Library project, along with the FAODOC database and the online catalog of David Lubin Memorial Library, the main library of FAO. Current Agricultural Research Information System (CARIS) has also been incorporated into WAICENT.
- *FAOSIS:* Like FAOSTAT and FAOINFO, it brings together information under its own discipline-heading. For FAOSTAT interactive web service, special software was developed allowing users to select and organize the statistical information into tables and charts that meet their individual requirements. FAOSTAT provides a regularly updated table of hits/database downloads for each calendar month. At present, there are four major information systems accessible under FAOSIS [7,9]:

- *Global Information and Early Warning System on Food and Agriculture (GIEWS):* It is an information system for compiling and exchanging information that is essential for providing regular bulletins on food crop production and markets at the global level, and situation reports on a regional and country-by-country basis. (URL: http://www.fao.org/WAICENT/faoinfo/economic/giews/english/giewse.htm).
- *World Information and Early Warning System on Plant Genetic Resources (WIEWS):* The World Information and Early Warning System (WIEWS) on Plant Genetic Resources for Food and Agriculture (PGRFA), has been established by FAO, as a world-wide dynamic mechanism to foster information exchange among member countries and as an instrument for the periodic assessment of the state of the world's PGRFA. (URL: http://apps3.fao.org/wiews/wiews.jsp).
- *Domestic Animal Diversity Information System (DAD-IS):* It is the key decentralized information tool for the Global Programme for the Management of Farm Animal Genetic Resources (AnGR); it provides extensive searchable databases, tools, guidelines, references, and contacts. (URL: http://www.fao.org/ag/againfo/resources/en/gis/05-DAD-IS.pdf).
- *Emergency Prevention System for Transboundary Animal and Plant Pests and Diseases (EMPRES):* The information system in support of FAO's Emergency Prevention System for transboundary animal and plant pests and diseases has two components: Livestock Diseases, and Desert Locust Management. (URL: http://www.fao.org/ag/againfo/programmes/en/empres.html).

U.6.1.4 Functions of WAICENT

WAICENT plays the following three key roles in FAO [8]:

- Acts as a clearing-house for information by establishing norms and methodologies for quality, developing standard categorization schemes, and implementing metadata for efficient and effective storage, dissemination, search, and retrieval of information;
- Provides outreach to members by discerning the information needs of FAO stakeholders and the international community associated with agricultural development, food security, and capacity building through the transfer of WAICENT "best practices" in information management systems and tools development to national and international information providers; and

- Acts as an intergovernmental forum for members through the Consultation on Agricultural Information Management (COAIM) to discuss issues and decide policies on information management, thereby reinforcing FAO normative and operational programs, and the participatory efforts of members in working toward WFS goals.

U.6.1.5 Resources of WAICENT

Besides providing access to the specialized information systems mentioned above, WAICENT provides access to its open archive and a large number of databases and informative websites [7,9]:

Open Archive

FAO created an online catalog, known as FAODOC, which contained bibliographic metadata of electronic and printed documents produced by FAO since 1945. In 1998, it also launched a Corporate Document Repository (CDR) of FAO documents and publications, as well as selected non-FAO publications, in electronic format. This repository has also served as a platform for publication of all its electronic documents. In 2012, FAODOC and CDR were merged to form FAO Open Archive (FAO OA)—a digital open repository—to collect, manage, maintain, and disseminate all material published by FAO. As in 2012, the archive contained more than 58,400 records, of which 40,100 were full-text documents. The open archive enables users to easily access the accumulated knowledge and information produced by FAO directly on the Internet.

Databases

The important databases maintained by FAO are [7]:
- *FAO statistical database:* It contains a complete data set on all relevant agricultural domains from around the world. The database, which can be queried free on the Internet, provides statistics for more than 210 countries and territories and 3000 items in the areas of Agriculture, Fisheries, Forestry and Nutrition. (URL: http://apps.fao.org).
- *FAO events calendar:* It is an interactive calendar of events, major meetings, and conferences. The Conference, Council, and Committee meeting announcements also provide links to meeting documents, whenever available (URL: http://www.fao.org/events/default.htm).
- *FAO publications catalog:* The catalog provides up-to-date information both on new publications and electronic products produced by FAO (URL: (http://www.fao.org/CATALOG/GIPHOME.HTM).

- *FAO documentation catalog:* The complete catalog of FAO documentation is searchable directly on the Internet, with links to full text where available (URL: http://faowfsh01.fao.org/library/ils_home1.html).

Websites

The main web page of FAO Governing Bodies is http://www.fao.org/unfao/bodies/. Since its first appearance online in 1996, the FAO website has grown exponentially to more than half a million pages of technical materials and information systems. The website gives a description of the structure of the main governing bodies of FAO and links to any documentation available on the meetings in Arabic, Chinese, English, French, and Spanish. As part of efforts to expand access to WAICENT, especially in member countries where the Internet is not yet widely available, a portable set of WAICENT CD-ROMs has been developed, which includes, among others, FAOSTAT, AGRIS, and CARIS, Gender and Food Security, and Combating Desertification [7,9]. Other important websites created under WAICENT for imparting specialized information are [7]:

- *Gender and food security website:* The gender and food security website displays a single entry point for a wealth of statistics, information and knowledge on the numerous and varied topics covered by FAO's mandate. (URL: http://www.fao.org/gender/gender-home/en/).
- *Agricultural trade website:* The agricultural trade website reflects a well-structured framework for accessing all the available information, documents and expertise from the FAO pertinent to the negotiations on Uruguay Round Trade Agreements on food and agriculture. (URL: http://www.fao.org/trade/en/).
- *INPhO website:* The Information Network on Post-harvest Operations (INPhO) website offers information systems support to the network of international and national organizations participating in this important program worldwide. The information and knowledge systems on the site are also available on CD-ROM, using the same Internet technologies. (URL: http://www.fao.org/in-action/inpho/home/en/).

WAICENT has developed a search-engine named WAICENT Information Finder, which is a system offering users an improved thematic access (searching by major topics) to the many pages of the FAO website. The Information Finder uses Internet technologies allowing the authors of the web pages (in the different departments and programs of FAO), to catalog their own pages. The cataloged information is stored in a database made available to users via this search-engine [7].

U.6.1.6 Other Activities of WAICENT

The other important activities of WAICENT are:

- *Information management systems:* WAICENT makes available information management systems for use by institutions in member nations. For instance, the Electronic Information Management System (EIMS) collects metadata on web pages, documents and other material and disseminates information on the Internet; the News and Events Management System (NEMS) publishes information that changes frequently, such as events calendars and news items [10].

- *Outreach program:* WAICENT has an outreach program for the developing countries of Asia and Pacific region, the aim of which is to enhance the ability of individuals and communities in member countries to improve the efficiency, quality, and relevance of information and knowledge exchange among the various stakeholder groups involved in agricultural development and food security, with focus on the most vulnerable and deprived groups. This program includes technical assistance to national and regional ICs, and cooperation with countries in Asia and the Pacific through the decentralized Information Management Specialist based in the Regional Office in Bangkok [8].

U.6.2 UN Documentation Center on Water

Developed by the UN-Water Decade Programme on Advocacy and Communication (UNW-DPAC) with the support of the Municipality of Zaragoza, Spain, the UN Documentation Center on Water and Sanitation (UNDCWS) acts as a clearing house on water and sanitation-related information materials produced by the United Nations system (programs, agencies, etc.). The UNDCWS facilitates search, increases dissemination, and improves visibility of UN information materials on water and sanitation by facilitating online and offline access to these materials. In order to do so, the UNDCWS project builds on three main components: a network of twin libraries and documentation centers, where you can find these publications in hardcopy; an online repository, and a UN information working group [11].

U.6.3 European Documentation Centers

A European Documentation Center (EDC) is a body designated by the European Commission to collect and disseminate publications of the

European Union (EU) for the purposes of research and education. There are 400 such centers in all member states of the EU [12] and even in some countries outside EU. The mandate of an EDC is to receive all official EU publications, documents, contracts, and electronic databases and make them available to researchers, educators, students, and interested members of the general public. The centers are also legal depositories of Acquis communautaire (EU law) [13]. Although EDC is primarily academic in nature, anyone can visit an EDC to consult official EU publications. EDCs were founded in 1963 by the European Commission. They are predominantly located at universities, university libraries, affiliated academic institutions, and non-university research institutes, both public and private. EU policy is that at least one EDC should be located in each region of a European Union member state. Candidate states and other countries can also have a designated EDC, supported jointly with local university libraries and the European Commission [14,15]. The EDCs collect documents and publications that they receive from the various official institutions of the European Union. They also provide training and advice on the organization and use of electronic information generated by EU institutions. Some of the important databases which are made available by EDCs are: CORDIS: The EU Research Information Service; Curia: EU Jurisprudence; EUR-Lex: EU legislation; Eurostat: European statistics; and SCADplus: EU Legislation [16].

U.7 NATIONAL ICS

The activities of some well-known national documentation centers/information centers (NICs) are described below.

U.7.1 NIC of Russia (VINITI)

The Institute of Scientific Information, which was established in 1952 in Moscow as an affiliated organization of the USSR Academy of Sciences, started functioning in 1953. The institute was reorganized and renamed as All-Union Institute for Scientific and Technical Information (in Russian Vserossiisky Institut Nauchnoi i Tekhnicheskoi Informatsii or in short VINITI) in 1955. The institute subsequently came to be known as All-Russian Institute of Scientific and Technical Information [17]. VINITI's library collection has over two million documents [18]:

U.7.1.1 Objectives of VINITI

The main goal of VINITI is to supply scientific and technical information about the achievements in fundamental, natural, and applied sciences to the national and world community [18]. The specific objectives of VINITI are [19]:

- To collect, process, store, and disseminate scientific and technical information to the user;
- To produce the information products in print and electronic forms;
- To conduct research on informatics and scientific information activities; and
- To train researchers in informatics and to conduct training for improvement of the qualifications of information specialists in organizations connected with VINITI.

U.7.1.2 Activities of VINITI

The main task of VINITI is to produce information products and services on the basis of world and Russian scientific and technical publications [18]. Currently, VINITI processes literature on various fields of science and technology, published in 70 countries in 40 languages, selected from books, journals, conference proceedings, invention descriptions and patents, and deposited scientific papers. They review about a million publications annually, two-thirds of which are taken from foreign sources. This comprehensive information flow forms the largest database in Russia on natural, applied, and technical sciences. The database, with files dating back to 1981, contains about 30 million records, and about 80,000–1,00,000 new records are added monthly. The database consists of numerous subfields covering a vast variety of scientific disciplines and technologies, economic issues and medicine. There are separate databases for 19 subject divisions. The database is accessible online. It allows a quick access to bibliographic descriptions, abstracts, full texts, multimedia, and other information. VINITI receives approximately one thousand search requests a day [18]. The other activities of VINITI are [18–20]:

- *Primary journal publication:* VINITI publishes a monthly peer-reviewed journal *Scientific and Technical Information* (Nauchno-Tekhnicheskaya Informatsiya).
- *Abstracting service:* Since 1953, VINITI has been bringing out a monthly abstracting journal named *Referativnyi Zhurnal*, containing abstracts, summaries, and bibliographic descriptions of publications in all fields of natural, applied and technical sciences, economics, and medicine.

The Journal consists of nineteen cumulative volumes, each focusing on a specific field of science, with a total of 286 issues (sub-fields of science). It annually abstracts about 1 million documents, published in 40 languages from 70 countries. Of the documents abstracted 70% are foreign and 30% Russian. Since 1995, it is issued both in print and electronic versions.

- *Meeting alert:* VINITI brings out *Bulletin of International Scientific Congresses, Conferences, Meetings, and Exhibitions*, which covers systematized information on forthcoming and current events.
- *Prepublication manuscript collection:* VINITI became the state repository for deposited manuscripts by a Government law in 1967. A deposited manuscript is a paper submitted to a peer-reviewed journal, accepted by its editorial board, and deposited in VINITI at the authors' discretion. The abstract of the paper is published in *Referativnyi Zhurnal* and indexed in *Index of Deposited Manuscripts (IDM)*, after which it gets the status of published document. The total collection of prepublication manuscripts till the end of 2011 was around 2,20,000. The annual collection amounts to about 1000 manuscripts.
- *Factual database creation:* VINITI has created two special factual databases, viz., the Structural Database of Chemistry and the Database on Macrocyclic Compounds and their Complexes.
- *Delivery service:* On the basis of VINITI's science and technology collections, the Center of Scientific Information Services (CSIS VINITI) processes requests of organizations or individuals for the following information services: copying (on paper, microfilms or electronic copies in PDF format) of primary sources processed for VINITI products and databases; current awareness on a specified subject through weekly *Express Information*; and compiling of retrospective bibliographies and documentation lists.
- *Review service:* Reviews in different fields are brought out under *Advances in Science* series. In Russian language this series is known as "Itogi."
- *Glossary compilation:* Regular research is conducted at VINITI on scientific terminology and glossaries and dictionaries are published in different scientific subject areas, such as *English-Russian and Russian-English Dictionary on Physics and Engineering.*
- *Development of information system:* VINITI has developed a computerized information system in the field of science and technology known as ASSISTANT, through which users can avail direct and speedy information service.

- *Translation service:* To meet the users' demands as also for inclusion in its own publications, translations are prepared in VINITI in sizable quantity and these are indexed on regular basis.
- *UDC Russian version:* VINITI has been a member of the Executive Committee of the UDC consortium since 2000. The Institute has exclusive rights to publish and disseminate print and electronic versions of UDC editions in Russian. It renewed regular publication of Extensions and Corrections to the UDC and complete edition of UDC Tables on Russian language and State "Rubricator" (Classification) of Scientific and Technical Information.
- *Continuing education:* VINITI arranges various workshops on science evaluation for information professionals and librarians. It also conducts annual seminars on classification system (UDC).
- *Cooperation and collaboration:* VINITI cooperates with around 600 organizations throughout the world, including UNESCO and UNIDO. VINITI has also long been in collaboration with Thomson Reuters, providing access to Web of Science, Elsevier, Springer, EBESCO, Kluwer, Blackwell, OUP, and other partners.

U.7.2 NIC of Canada (NSL)

The Canada Institute for Scientific and Technical Information (CISTI), located in Ottawa, started in 1924 as the library of the National Research Council of Canada (NRC). It took on the role national science library unofficially in 1957 and became so officially in 1967. Further, the name changed to CIST in 1974 to reflect its new role in developing electronic information products and service for the science and technology community [21]. The name of CIST has since been changed again to National Science Library (NSL). The main objective of NSL is to provide information services to NRC and Canada's research community to accelerate discovery, innovation, and commercialization [22]. The library has branches at eleven cities across the country. The library attached to the headquarters houses one of the world's most comprehensive collections on science, technology, engineering, and medicine. Access to this collection is provided by Infotrieve Canada Inc. (a Copyright Clearance Center Company) on behalf of NRC [23].

U.7.2.1 Activities of NSL

The various activities of National Science Library are [21–23]:
- *Shared library service*: NSL provides services to four federal departments/agencies and technical support services to Health Canada as part of a partnership since 2010.

- *Federal science library*: A partnership of seven Government of Canada science departments/agencies implementing a common platform and processes to deliver information discovery and access services to clients, with NCL serving as the project's technical lead.
- *Digital repository*: In December 2013, NSL has implemented a Digital Repository that holds a number of collections, including NRC Archives photograph collection of over 12,000 photographs dating back to 1916.
- *DataCite Canada*: It is a data registration service that provides Canadian data centers and libraries with a mechanism to register research data and assigning digital object identifiers (DOIs) to them so that the data can be searchable, citable, and accessible for replication and further use.
- *Docline in Canada:* It is an online interlibrary loan routing system for health sciences information, which encourages resource sharing among libraries having collections on health sciences.
- *PubMed Central Canada*: It is a free online archive of published, peer-reviewed health, and life sciences research that allows users to quickly and easily search and download the latest research papers in the field of health sciences.
- *Document delivery service*: NSL is one of the largest document providers in the world in the fields of science, technology, and medicine. At present document delivery service is provided in partnership with Infotrieve.
- *Scientific article discovery*: NSL has launched a mobile website, which provides location and search services to popular mobile devices, including Android, Blackberry, and iPhone. The website provides facility for federated searching across several science and technology information sources.
- *International cooperation/Partnership*: NSL is a founding member of DataCite, the worldwide consortium for allocating DOIs to datasets, and Research Data Canada, the organization which works for improving the management of research data in Canada. It is also a member of Worldwide Science Alliance, International DataCite Federation, International Council for Scientific and Technical Information, etc.

U.7.3 NIC of Belgium (NCSATD)

The National Center of Scientific and Technical Documentation (NCSATD) was created in 1964 in Brussels, in close association with Royal Library of Belgium, to provide the scientists and researchers facility to access literature relating to medicine, physics, chemistry, engineering, and information science. Its main functions are [24,25] :

- Maintaining a permanent inventory of Belgian scientific publications;
- Publication of the Belgium and Luxembourg Union Catalogue of Foreign Periodicals;
- Publication of the Directory of Belgian Research centers;
- Provision of translation service;
- Provision of consultancy services to special libraries and documentation centers;
- Provision of referral service;
- Representing Belgium in the international scientific and technical information community;
- Conducting research on information science problems (such as automation of libraries and ICs);
- Provision of SDI and online retrospective retrieval services.

U.7.4 NIC of Greece (EKT)

EKT, the National Documentation Center of Greece, operates at the National Hellenix Research Foundation, Athens. Its various activities are [26]:

- Development of Digital S&T Library, providing cohesive and efficient access to organized sources of information and knowledge (Greek S&T databases, National Archive of PhD Theses, international databases and electronic journals);
- Digitization of Greek S&T content;
- Operation of Electronic Reading Room;
- Provision of information retrieval and document ordering services;
- Cooperation with relevant institutions (libraries, archives, universities, museums, etc.) and development of common actions for the establishment of a knowledge-based institutions network;
- Development and provision of software for the automation of the Greek libraries' operations (ABEKT) and development of bibliographical tools, such as Greek edition of the Dewey Decimal Classification System, and Greek Thesaurus;
- Development of library networks (National Network of Science and Technology Libraries, consortium of research centers and academic libraries);

- Operation of inter-library loan system and provision of union catalogue of journals;
- Supporting activities toward public and private libraries for the automation of their operations, the online provision of catalogs and the training of personnel;
- Provision of Greek CORDIS web service for information on research and innovation issues (www.cordis.lu/greece), in cooperation with CORDIS (Community Research and Development Information Service).

EKT also serves as the National Contact Point for the European Framework Programmes and the programs "eContent," "ASIA IT&C," and "Security Research". It is the coordinator/partner of the EU projects IDEAL-IST, EuroMEDANet and EuroMEDANet2, ERA-WestBalkan, ASBIMED, SMEs go LifeSciences, FISH, and EASIER. It publishes bimonthly magazine *Innovation, Research & Technology*, biweekly eNewsletter *Research and Innovation* and eNewsletter for the public libraries [26].

U.7.5 NIC of Hungary (BME OMIKK)

The National Technical Information Center and Library at the Budapest University of Technology and Economics (BME OMIKK), Hungary, is the successor of two organizations, viz., the Library of the Budapest University of Technology and Economics and the National Technical Information Centre and Library. The primary task of BME OMIKK is to support the high quality education, scientific training, research, development and innovation in the fields of engineering, technology, natural sciences, business, and social sciences. Besides providing lending, reference and readers services, it performs the following functions [27]:

- Photocopying and scanning service;
- National and international interlibrary loan service;
- eServices to provide access to electronic journals and databases;
- Quick access service, i.e., speedy cataloging of books demanded by users;
- Publishing scientific monographs and serials, including Journal of Library and Information Science;
- Providing information on copyright regulations;
- Providing Internet access;
- Translation service; and
- User training.

U.7.6 NIC of China (ISTIC)

The Institute of Scientific and Technical Information of China (ISTIC) was established in 1956 as a national research and service institute under the Ministry of Science and Technology to provide decision making support to the government agencies that take care of science and technology activities in the country, in addition to providing comprehensive information services to industry, universities, research institutes, and research personnel. The core operations of ISTIC are [28]:

- Information research and service;
- National science and technology reports system;
- IT applications and services;
- Information collection and service;
- Scientific and technical papers analysis and journal evaluation;
- Creation and maintenance of national databases for science and technology.

U.7.6.1 Activities of ISTIC

ISTIC has developed National Engineering and Technology Digital Library, which provides a range of customized services, such as document search, full-text delivery, resources navigation, knowledge service, and scientific evaluation. ISTIC maintains the following databases: Foreign Journals Abstracts; Foreign Proceedings Abstracts; Foreign Science and Technology Reports Abstracts; Foreign Dissertation Abstracts; Chinese Journals Abstracts; Chinese Proceedings Abstracts; Chinese Thesis and Dissertations Abstracts; Foreign Journals Citation; Chinese Journals Citation; Chinese Patent Abstracts. ISTIC serves as member/focal point of several international organizations like UNESCO Information for All Programme, International Council of Scientific Unions/International Council for Scientific and Technical Information (ICSU/ICSTI) and Asia Pacific Information Network (APIN). It has also set up ISTIC-Thomson Reuters Laboratory for Scientometrics, in collaboration with Thomson Reuters, and ISTIC-MI Research Centre, in collaboration with Millennium Institute of USA [28].

U.7.7 NIC of Japan (JST)

Japan Information Center of Science and Technology (JICST) was set up in August 1957, with funding from the Government of Japan and private industry, for collecting, processing, storing and retrieving national and international scientific information for Japanese scientists and researchers.

The main work of JICST was preparation of Current Bibliography on Science and Technology (CBST), a comprehensive abstracting journal. Besides it also provided photocopy supply service, current contents service, translation service, and literature search service [29]. In 1996, JICST and the Research and Development Corporation of Japan, which had been founded in July 1961, were merged to form Japan Science and Technology Corporation (JST). In October 2003, the JST was reorganized as an independent administrative institution, Japan Science and Technology Agency (abbreviation still continues to be JST).

U.7.7.1 Activities of JST

One of the major functions of this agency is dissemination of scientific and technical information, which it does through the following [30]:

- *J-Global*: It is comprehensive gateway linking multiple scientific and technological databases of research papers, patents, researchers, and chemical substances. It provides a one-stop search service covering a broad array of science sources—both internal and external of JST—and links based on various correlations, such as coauthorship of papers and patents.
- *J-Global foresight*: It is a project to connect an array of information, including information on research papers and patents, to analyze and visualize such information, and to provide knowledge to help the national government and private companies determine policies and strategies. It applies evidence-based evaluation methods, bibliometric analysis, and cluster analysis on JST information assets linked with third-party assets.
- *J-Global knowledge*: J-Global knowledge is capable of performing SPARQL search for science and technology information in different sources such as research papers, patents, and researchers that are described in the format of the RDF (Resource Description Framework). J-Global knowledge has published chemical substances data in the RDF format (Nikkaji RDF data) contained in J-Global knowledge with creative commons license.
- *Researchmap*: Researchmap is a multifunction research information platform covering information of over 230,000 researchers. The platform offers registered researchers a tool to easily gather information, including research papers and other works. It also helps researchers create their own personal web pages where their CV and research achievements can be stored and tailored for possible funding

applications. Further, it also serves as an online research community to exchange views and ideas for future collaboration. Users can search registered researchers by name, institution, keyword, and research area.

- *J-Stage*: It is Japan's largest electronic journal platform for academic societies J-Stage provides access to both current and archived peer-reviewed articles from approximately 1700 journals published by academic societies in Japan. Full-text search and forward and backward citation links via various databases are also available.
- *Gakkai Meikan database*: This website stores data on academic societies within Japan in the fields of Humanities and Social Sciences, Life Sciences, Physical Sciences, and Engineering (mainly the Associate Societies of the Science Council of Japan). The database contains the details of around 2100 academic societies.
- *Japan Link Centre*: Japan Link Center (JaLC), the joint project of Japan's information-related institutions, including JST, assigns DOIs and provides sustainable access to Japanese electronic scholarly content. The International DOI Foundation has appointed JaLC as an official DOI registration agency.
- *Joho Kanri Web*: This site provides latest information and trends and news items related to the contents of the *Journal of Information Processing and Management* (founded 1958), published monthly by JST.
- *JDream III*: Japan's largest scientific, technological, and medical database JDream III is a comprehensive scientific, technological, and medical bibliographic database containing over 60 million records from sources in Japan and worldwide, including journals, conference proceedings, and technical papers. The database records are abstracted and indexed in Japanese with original thesaurus support.
- *Chinese-Language Research Database (JST China)*: It is a free service offering Japanese-language searches of major science and technology-related research published within China.
- *National Bioscience Database Center (NBDC)*: It promotes the integrated use of life science database resources and provides a database portal website, with an aim to maximize the value of research data.

U.7.8 NIC of Thailand (TNDC)

The Thai National Documentation Center (TNDC) was established by the Government of Thailand, with technical assistance from UNESCO in 1961. The center is a part of the Applied Scientific Research Corporation of Thailand located in Bangkok. Besides its other activities, TNDC collects the scientific and technological documents published in Thailand or abroad on Thailand and on the basis of its acquisition publishes two periodicals, viz., *Thai Abstracts* and *List of Scientific and Technical Literature relating to Thailand*. It also publishes various specialized monographs such as Water Hyacinth and Water Resources in Thailand. The center has developed TNDC Thesaurus for use in *Thai Abstracts* [31]. The center has also developed a Union List of Scientific Serials in Thai Libraries.

U.7.9 NIC of Pakistan (PASTIC)

Pakistan National Scientific and Technical Documentation Center (PANSDOC) was set up by the Government of Pakistan, with the technical assistance of UNESCO in 1957 at Karachi under the Pakistan Council of Scientific & Industrial Research (PCSIR). In 1974, an expanded project namely Pakistan Scientific and Technological Information Center (PASTIC) was built around the nucleus of PANSDOC and was transferred from PCSIR to Pakistan Science Foundation, an autonomous organization under the Ministry of Science and Technology. After transfer, its scopes and facilities were expanded. The PASTIC National Center (Headquarter) is located at Islamabad and housed in its own building situated in the Quaid-i-Azam University Campus, Islamabad. It has six sub centers located at Karachi, Lahore, Faisalabad, Peshawar, Muzaffarabad, and Quetta. PASTIC has set up a Science Reference Library at the National Center having a collection of more than 6000 books; 900 titles of journals, out of which 300 are regular; around 300,000 patents, 1340 NTIS reports and 4000 miscellaneous documents [32].

U.7.9.1 Objectives of PASTIC

The main objectives of PASTIC are [32]:

- To acquire, process and disseminate scientific and technological information to the R&D community;
- To provide bibliographic information and document supply service;
- To develop interlibrary cooperation, resource sharing at national level;
- To develop and strengthen the National Science Reference Library;
- To publish an abstracting journal entitled *Pakistan Science Abstracts* covering ten science and technology disciplines;
- To compile Directory of S&T Periodicals of Pakistan, Union Catalogue of S&T Serials and other information tools;
- To train information personnel in contemporary techniques and methods of information handling;
- To interact with regional and international information agencies/networks.

U.7.9.2 Activities of PASTIC

Besides providing traditional references and referral services through the National Science Reference Library, PASTIC provides the following services: document supply service; bibliographic service; abstracting and indexing service; access to online resources, such as *Pakistan Science Abstracts*, INIS database, and union catalog of scientific periodicals. PASTIC undertakes screening and survey of scientific and technological libraries of the country to collect information about their serial holdings. The information received from the libraries is standardized and computerized and published in the form of a union catalog. PASTIC serves as the National Focal Point of WHO/CEHANET: Environmental Health Regional Information Network of the World Health Organization (Eastern Mediterranean Region) and SAARC Documentation Center, New Delhi; and as distributor of WINISIS database management software of UNESCO. It also conducts short-term training programs on library management, WINISIS and GEN/ISIS. It also brings out the following publications: *Pakistan Science Abstracts*; *Directory of Scientific and Technological Periodicals of Pakistan*; *Union Catalogue of Serial Holdings of S&T Libraries of Pakistan*; *Technology Roundup* (e-Bulletin bimonthly) [32].

U.7.10 NIC of Bangladesh (BANSDOC)

A regional office of PANSDOC was established in 1963 in the then East Regional Laboratories of Pakistan Council of Scientific & Industrial Research in Dhaka. It was functioning in order to help researchers, academicians, industrialists, technicians and, in general, all those who were active in the field of science and technology. After creation of Bangladesh, this regional office was renamed as Bangladesh National Scientific Documentation Center (BANSDOC). BANSDOC houses the National Science Library (BANSDOC Library) that acts as a major information resource center in the country in the field of science and ICT [33].

U.7.10.1 Objectives of BANSDOC

The main objectives of BANSDOC are [33]:

- To procure, process, preserve, edit, and disseminate information in all fields of scientific research and experimental development in the area of natural science, agriculture, medical science, engineering, industry, and technology;

- To provide information as per needs of researchers working in research organizations, academic institutions, nationalized industries, or any other sectors; and
- To manage information for researcher, policy maker, planner, and manager.

U.7.10.2 Activities of BANSDOC

Besides providing traditional library services, BANSDOC provides the following services: document procurement and supply service; delivery of science and technology-related bibliographical references; scientific contact service, i.e., supply of scientific contacts to scientists/researchers in the similar fields of interest; bibliographic service; abstracting service; and translation service. BANSDOC has developed a well-equipped cyber center, with a comfortable environment, where users can access online and offline digital resources. The center serves as the national focal point for SAARC Documentation Centre. BANSDOC has brought out the several important publications such as *Directory of Scientists and Technologists of Bangladesh*; *Directory of Scientists and Technologists of Bangladesh Living Abroad*; *Directory of Bangladesh R&D Organizations and their Current Scientific and Technological Research Projects*; *Current Scientific and Technological Research Projects of Bangladesh*; *Current Contents on various fields of science*; *Bangladesh Science and Technology Abstracts*; *National Union Catalogue of Scientific and Technological Periodicals in Bangladesh*; and *Survey Report on Research and Development (R&D) Activities in Bangladesh* [33].

U.7.11 NICs in India

India is possibly the only country where several national level documentation centers/information centers pertaining to different subject areas have been set up. The activities of a few well-known such centers are described below.

U.7.11.1 NISCAIR

The Government of India established the Indian National Scientific Documentation Center (INSDOC) in Delhi in 1952, with the initial technical and financial assistance of the UNESCO. It started functioning as an ancillary unit of the National Physical Laboratory under the Council for Scientific and Industrial Research (CSIR). In 1963, INSDOC became an independent unit under the CSIR. On September 30, 2002 INSDOC and another organization under the CSIR, viz., National

Institute of Science Communication (NISCOM), merged together to form a new organization under the name National Institute of Science Communication and Information Resources (NISCAIR). The mission of the new organization is "to become the prime custodian of all information resources on current and traditional knowledge systems in science and technology in the country, and to promote communication in science to diverse constituents at all levels, using the most appropriate technologies" [34].

Objectives of NISCAIR

The objectives of NISCAIR are [34]:

- To provide formal linkages of communication among the scientific community in the form of research journals in different areas of S&T;
- To disseminate S&T information to general public, particularly school students, to inculcate interest in science among them;
- To collect, collate and disseminate information on plant, animal and mineral wealth of the country;
- To harness information technology applications in information management, with particular reference to science communication and modernizing libraries;
- To act as a facilitator in furthering the economic, social, industrial, scientific, and commercial development by providing timely access to relevant and accurate information;
- To develop human resources in science communication, library, documentation, and information science and S&T information management systems and services;
- To collaborate with international institutions and organizations having objectives and goals similar to those of NISCAIR;
- To perform any other activity in consonance with the mission statement of NISCAIR.

Activities of NISCAIR

To implement the above objectives NISCAIR undertakes [34]:

- Publication of 17 primary and two secondary scientific journals of international repute to cater to the needs of scientific community, which includes *Journal of Scientific and Industrial Research* (JSIR, monthly), *Annals of Library and Information Studies* (ALIS, quarterly), *Medicinal and Aromatic Plants Abstracts* (MAPA, bimonthly);

- Publication of encyclopedic volumes on natural raw material resources "The Wealth of India' in English and "Bharat ki Sampada" in Hindi;
- Publication of three popular science magazines *Science Reporter* in English, *Vigyan Pragati* (i.e., progress of science) in Hindi and *Science ki Duniya* (i.e., world of science) in Urdu to meet the science information needs of the masses;
- Publication of two newsletters, entitled *CSIR News* (in English) and *CSIR Samachar* (in Hindi) that bring out the news and significant contributions of CSIR and its constituents;
- Publication of monographic and popular science books, besides a series of popular science books on IT;
- Development and maintenance of specialized databases on *Indian Science Abstracts (ISA)*; *National Union Catalogue of Scientific Serials in India (NUCSSI)*; *Medicinal and Aromatic Plants Abstracts (MAPA)*, and *Natural Raw Material Resources*;
- Development of *NISCAIR Online Periodicals Repository (NOPR)*, which provides full-text access to all the research journals and popular magazines published by it.
- Provision of different types of information services as also services relating to communication of scientific information;
- Conducting of training programs in library and information science, science communication, and herbarium techniques with an objective of human resource development.

Services of NISCAIR

The services provided by NISCAIR are [34]:

- *Medicinal and Aromatic Plants Information Services (MAPIS):* The users are supplied required information relating to above subjects on the basis of "Wealth of India" and MAPA databases;
- *Contents, Abstracts and Photocopy Service (CAPS):* In this highly personalized service, the contents information, abstracts, and photocopies of articles from journals selected by an individual user from 7000 core journals are supplied on a regular basis;
- *Literature search service:* The users are provided access to over 6000 international databases;
- *Science and technology translation service:* English translations of science and technology related articles in major foreign languages such as Japanese, German, French, Spanish, Chinese, and Russian are supplied to the users;

- *Bibliometric services:* Bibliometric services are carried out for studying growth, development and spread of any area of research, and also for identifying centers of excellence, influential authors, etc.;
- *Patent information service:* In this service, searching of traditional indigenous art and culture and preparation of patent documents are undertaken and information relating to patents are supplied; the full name of this service is National Prior Art Search, Patent Drafting, and Patent Information Service Facility (NPASF);
- *Document copy supply service:* The users are supplied copies of required micro documents;
- *Interlibrary loan service:* Documents not available with NISCAIR are procured from other libraries on interlibrary loan for the users;
- *E-journal access service:* The users are given opportunity to access over 5000 e-journals subscribed through the National Knowledge Resource Consortium (previously known as CSIR e-journal consortium) and over 2500 open access journals;
- *Walk-in user facility:* The National Science Library, located at NISCAIR, provides walk-in user facility to researchers, scholars, scientists, etc. irrespective of their affiliation, for online access to over 7000 full-text e-journals of international nature free of charge for scholarly work;
- *Editing, designing, printing and production service:* NISCAIR takes up editing, composing, designing and printing jobs for its clients, preferably in digitized form;
- *Consultancy services:* Consultancy services are provided in automation, modernization, and reorganization of libraries and ICs and in design and development of specialized databases for organizations on turnkey basis.

Special Responsibilities

NISCAIR has the following four special responsibilities:

- *National Science Library:* The idea to set up a National Science Library (NSL) was conceived by CSIR in 1963 and accordingly it started functioning as a part of the then INSDOC. The NSL has over 2,51,000 printed collection of S&T documents which includes monographs, bound volumes of journals, reports, theses/dissertations, standards, and patents etc. The NSL's collection policy is to build resources with an emphasis on high end R&D reference sources, Indian S&T publications, foreign language dictionaries, library and information science, information and communication technology, computer science, conference proceedings, technical reports, and other sources relevant to S&T community of the country [34].

- *International standard serial number:* NISCAIR serves as the national center of ISSN International Center, Paris, in India for assigning ISSN numbers to serial publications from the country [34].

- *National Science Digital Library:* National Science Digital Library (NSDL) aims at providing comprehensive S&T information to students of science, engineering, and technology in the country. NSDL is the only one of its kind that provides curriculum based content to address the information needs of the undergraduate students of science. The content creation and development for NSDL has gone through rigorous procedures to make available quality content for the students. A discussion forum has also been started for interaction amongst NSDL users [34].

- *Traditional Knowledge Digital Library:* NISCAIR is the implementing agency for TKDL, a Government of India initiative to establish "prior-art" of Indian medical knowledge system by documenting classical herbal formulations and their therapeutic uses in a computerized form that can be searched by patent offices world-wide in order to evaluate (and reject) patent claims based on prior-art belonging to Indian systems of medicine [34]. As in June 2011, TKDL database contains 34 million pages of formatted information on 2,260,000 medicinal formulations in multiple languages. This database has enabled the cancellation or withdrawal of a large number of applications claiming patent on use of various Indian medicinal plants in foreign countries [35].

Important Projects

NISCAIR is implementing the following three important projects [34]:

- *National Knowledge Resource Consortium:* Established in 2009, the National Knowledge Resource Consortium (NKRC) is a network of knowledge resource centers (libraries and ICs) of 39 CSIR and 24 DST (Department of Science and Technology, Government of India) institutes. NKRC's origin goes back to the year 2001, when the CSIR set up the Electronic Journals Consortium to provide access to 1200 odd journals of Elsevier Science to all its users. At present NKRC provides access to more than 5000 e-journals of all major publishers, patents, standards, citation, and bibliographic databases and also a large number of open access resources.

- *Directory of S&T Awards in India (DSTAI) updation:* The Directory of S&T Awards in India (DSTAI), which was brought out by the erstwhile INSDOC in 1998, is being updated by NISCAIR under the sponsorship of National Science and Technology Management Information System (NSTMIS), Department of Science and Technology, Government of India.
- *Database of Intra-mural R&D Projects updation:* This database was also developed by erstwhile INSDOC under the sponsorship of National Science and Technology Management Information System (NSTMIS). The database, available on CD-ROM, provides information on nearly 8000 R&D projects in S&T institutions of central and state governments, private and public sector undertakings and academic institutions covering disciplines ranging from pure sciences to applied sciences. NISCAIR has taken the responsibility of updation of this database.
- *CSIR-Knowgate:* CSIR Knowledge Gateway and Open Source Private Cloud Infrastructure (KNOWGATE) is a Network Project, which is being implemented in a network mode by CSIR-NISCAIR as nodal laboratory. Under this project, so far data of 26 knowledge resource centers (KRCs) of CSIR laboratories have been migrated to Koha successfully; OPAC of 23 KRCs have been uploaded on Internet; and data of 26 KRCs have been harvested to CSIR Virtual Union Catalogue, which now contains more than eight lakh records.

U.7.11.2 NASSDOC

Indian Council of Social Science Research, which was established in May 1969, is responsible for organizing, sponsoring, promoting, coordinating, publishing, and utilizing research in social sciences in the country. One of the important programs taken up by the council to fulfill its objectives was development of a documentation center for providing high quality information service to the social scientists. The work of this center was initiated in April 1970, with the beginning of work on compilation of *Union Catalogue of Social Science Serials.* The documentation center was named as Social Science Documentation (SSDC), and was rechristened as National Social Science Documentation Center (NASSDOC) in 1985 [36].

Objectives of NASSDOC

The main objectives of NASSDOC are [36]:
- To provide full range of information services to the social scientists of India;

- To retain all social science periodicals and reference materials which may be of use in the country; and
- To provide photocopying and other reprographic facilities to the social scientists of the country.

Activities of NASSDOC

NASSDOC undertakes different activities to help the social scientists [37]:

- *Library and Information Services:* The library of NASSDOC has different types important documents, besides books relating to social sciences, such as unpublished theses, research project reports, and Indian and foreign journals on social sciences. It maintains a bibliographic database of all the documents available in the library. The library provides information and reference services, literature search service, documentation list compilation service, document delivery service, etc. Besides, it provides access to social science related information resources available on the Internet through cyber café.
- *Information product compilation:* NASSDOC itself, as also with the cooperation of some selected institutions, compiles databases, union catalogs, bibliographies, indexes, etc. An important database compiled by this center is *Indian Social Science Periodical Literature*, which contains bibliographical information regarding 97,491 articles published in 119 Indian social science periodicals till 1970.
- *Continuing education:* NASSDOC conducts short-term training programs/workshops for researchers, social scientists, librarians, and IT professionals.
- *Consultancy:* NASSDOC provides consultancy to different organizations in the matter of organization of libraries and documentation services/information services.
- *Financial assistance:* NASSDOC provides financial assistance for documentation work, for publication and to libraries and ICs for their own activities. Many bibliographies and indexes have been compiled and published through such assistance.
- *International and regional cooperation:* At international level NASSDOC cooperates with International Committee for Social Science Information and Documentation, Paris; International Bulletin of Bibliography on Education; International Geographical Bibliography, Paris; and supplies information generated in India to DARE data bank of UNESCO. At regional level it serves as the national contact center of UNESCO's Asia Pacific Information Network in Social Sciences (APINESS).

U.7.11.3 DESIDOC

The Defence Research and Development Organization (DRD) came into being in 1958 as a wing of the Ministry of Defence and along with that a Scientific Information Bureau (SIB) was also set up as a division of the Defence Science Laboratory (DSL) (now called the Defence Science Center) for providing better information service. The DRDO library became a division of SIB in 1959. In 1967, SIB was expanded and renamed DESIDOC, which was declared as a DRDO laboratory on July 29, 1970. The Defence Science Library now serves as the central library of DESIDOC [38].

Objectives of DESIDOC

The objectives, with which DESIDOC started, were revised in 1981 to meet the changing environment and needs of defense scientists. The revised objectives are [36]:

- To function as the central resource center for providing information/documentation/library services, reprographic service and translation service to DRDO headquarters/laboratories/establishments and to coordinate DRDO's scientific programs;
- To develop a data bank on scientific information for DRDO and an information system for defense science and technology, and to interface with other national/international agencies in the field of scientific information;
- To conduct training and user education programs for DRDO and all defense users and carry out R & D work in the field of scientific information/documentation;
- To provide consultancy and referral services to Technical Information Centers (TICS) libraries of DRDO and other defense organizations; and
- To publish scientific and technical journals, books, and monographs of the DRDO.

Activities of DESIDOC

The main responsibility of DESIDOC is collection, analysis, organization, and dissemination of required information to the scientists of DRDO. Its various activities are briefly described below [38].

- *Library services:* Defence Science Library, the central library of DESIDOC, has the largest and best collection of documents related to defense science and technology in the country. Its collection consists of more than 262,000 documents including books, reports, patents, bound volumes of journals. Besides, it subscribes to around 900 current journals. It also has an important collection of reports of NASA and RAND of USA. The services provided by the library are CD-ROM search service, interlibrary loan service, document delivery service, e-journal access service, access to the database of different types of documents available in the library, etc.

- *Information services:* Besides above services, the DESIDOC also provides information services of various kinds, such as current awareness service to DRDO scientists through *Current Contents in Military Science and Technology* and *IEE/IEEE Contents,* SDI service based on about 10 CD-ROM databases, newspaper clipping service, and translation service, compilation of information products.

- *Database creation:* DESIDOC regularly collects data on the acquisitions made by all the DRDO libraries and maintains a database. This database presently covers holdings of books and periodicals. Other types of holdings will also be covered in future. Besides, it has also created several other databases, such as database of SPIE/IEE/IEEE conference proceedings and database of journal articles in the field of defense science and technology.

- *Digitization:* DESIDOC has taken up an initiative of digitizing complete research papers of DRDO scientists.

- *Information research:* DESIDOC has set up an Information Research and Review Cell for assessing the information needs in the field of defense science and technology, review and analysis of developments in the field of defense in different countries and make the organizations working in the field of defense research and development in the country aware of the results of such analysis.

- *Network formation:* Steps have been taken to set up a defense information network to provide better information services to those organizations in the country which are engaged in defense research and development.

- *Software development:* A library management software, named *Suchika,* has been developed, which is being successfully used for automation of the DESIDOC central library as also libraries attached to other DRDO establishments.

- *Publications:* DESIDOC functions as the publication wing of DRDO. It brings out specialized publications, monographs, technical bulletins, online journals and popular science publications. The periodicals published include *Defence Science Journal* (bimonthly, *DRDO Newsletter* (monthly), *DRDO Samachar* (Hindi monthly), and *DESIDOC Bulletin of Informational Technology* (bimonthly).

- *Continuing education:* DESIDOC organizes short-term training in the areas of library automation, database development, online searching, e-mail and internet use, technical communication, multimedia development, and other relevant aspects of information technology.
- *Other activities:* Other important activities of DESIDOC include providing secure e-mail and Internet connectivity to DRDO labs through the networks of ERNET (of Department of Electronics) and NICNET (of Planning Commission), designing and printing of DRDO publications and preparation of high quality presentation materials for DRDO scientists.

U.7.11.4 SENDOC

The Small Enterprises National Documentation Center (SENDOC) was set up in 1970 at Small Industries Extension Training Institute (now known as National Institute of Micro, Small and Medium Enterprises), Hyderabad, to revitalize the micro, small and medium enterprises in India and developing countries by providing their required information. Gradually it has developed as a one-stop global and IT powered IC for a wide spectrum of micro, small and medium enterprises and academia, students, research institutions, industry associations, and entrepreneurs [39].

Objectives of SENDOC

The main objectives of SENDOC are [36]:

- To collect, collate and store information, data and documents useful for the technological and managerial advancement of micro, small, and medium industries;
- To disseminate information to the persons or organizations engaged in activities related to micro, small, and medium industries development; and
- To be the national center for coordinating and collaborating with the information activities of other national institutions and maintaining liaison with similar centers in other countries.

Activities of SENDOC

The main functions of SENDOC are collection and dissemination of information relating to organization, technology, machineries, government and other institutional programs and policies, statistics, etc. needed by persons connected with micro, small, and medium industries for the development of their respective enterprises. More specifically, the activities of SENDOC are [39,40]:

- *Library services:* The library of the center has over 50,000 books, 10,000 back volumes of journals, 13,500 reports, 65,000 journal abstracts, 5448 product profiles, and subscribes to 600 national and international periodicals. It has also a collection that provides information on statistics, economics, production, finance, marketing, technology, machinery and equipment, raw materials, consultants, government policies and programs, exports and imports, investment, trade and area literature, licensing, etc. Experts working in the center scan and arrange information systematically for quick retrieval. The services available in the library include, besides lending, interlibrary loan of documents; reference service, including preparation of bibliographies and literature search; newspaper clipping service; and technical inquiry service. Certain information is also accessible through the center's website.
- *Consultancy services:* SENDOC provides the following consultancy services: answering technical enquiries; conducting pre-investment studies; preparing product profiles; and SDI service to small entrepreneurs;
- *Photocopying service:* SENDOC provides photocopying service to small entrepreneurs;
- *Publications:* SENDOC publishes some journals which are important for micro, small and medium entrepreneurs: *SEDME Journal* (quarterly); *SME Technology* (bimonthly); *SME Policy* (bimonthly); *MSME Clusters News* (quarterly); and *ni-msme Bulletin* (monthly).
- *Continuing education:* SENDOC organizes short-time training courses/workshops on different aspects of rendering information services, especially indexing and abstracting.
- *Cooperation:* SENDOC also cooperates with national and international organizations working in the field of micro, small, and medium industries and also serves as a clearing house for information related to such industries.

REFERENCES

[1] T.S. Rajagopalan, Documentation centres, in: Training Course in Documentation and Information Services (1975): Course Material, INSDOC, New Delhi, 1976.
[2] M. Rouse, Data center. <http://searchdatacenter.techtarget.com/definition/data-center>.
[3] What is data bank? <http://thesciencedictionary.org/data-bank/>.

[4] S.I. Islam, Information analysis and referral centres, in: Training Course in Documentation and Information Services (1975): Course Material, INSDOC, New Delhi, 1976.

[5] Harrod's Librarians Glossary and reference book, compiled by Ray Prytherch. tenth ed., 2005. Ashgate, Fernham, Surrey, UK.

[6] O. Frank (Ed.), Modern Documentation and Information Practices, FID, The Hague, 1961.

[7] A. Mangstl, F. Perez-Trejo, WAICENT – The World Agricultural Centre of FAO. <http://www.cnshb.ru/aw/iaald_news_cee/4_2000art3.htm>.

[8] Food and Agricultural Organization. Regional Conference for Asia and the Pacific, 26th, Kathmandu, Information on World Agricultural Information Centre (WAICENT), 2002. <http://www.fao.org/docrep/MEETING/007/Y6210E.HTM>.

[9] A. Mangstl, et al., The World Agricultural Information Centre (WAICENT): FAO's information gateway. <http://eprints.rclis.org/15749/1/WAICENT%2C%20World%20Agricultural%20Information%20Centre-FAO%27s%20information%20gateway.pdf>.

[10] World Agricultural Information Centre (WAICENT)—Global. <http://www.com-minit.com/natural-resource/node/119675>.

[11] UN Documentation Centre on Water and Sanitation. <http://www.zaragoza.es/ciudad/medioambiente/onu/en/>.

[12] European Documentation Centres at the European Union. *As quoted in*: European Documentation Centre. <https://en.wikipedia.org/wiki/European_Documentation_Centre>.

[13] EuroVoc: Community acquis. *As quoted in* European Documentation Centre. <https://en.wikipedia.org/wiki/European_Documentation_Centre>.

[14] European Documentation Centre, Chulalongkorn University, Bangkok. <http://www.car.chula.ac.th/iic/html/edc.htm>.

[15] European Documentation Centre, Hong Kong Baptist University, Hong Kong. <http://europe.hkbu.edu.hk/edc/edc.html>.

[16] European Documentation Centre. <https://en.wikipedia.org/wiki/European_Documentation_Centre>.

[17] VINITI Database RAS. <http://en.wikipedia.org/wiki/VINITI-Database-RAS>.

[18] S. Yashukova, All-Russian Institute of Scientific and technical information. <www.viniti.ru/download/engl>.

[19] V.V. Bonder, All Union Institute for Scientific and Technical Information for USSR, INICAE (1985), pp. 46–49.

[20] V. Markusova, All-Russian Institute for Scientific and technical information (VINITI) of the Russial Academy of Sciences, Acta Informa Med 20 (2) (2012) 113–117.

[21] Canada Institute for Scientific and Technical Information. <http://www.world-library.org/ARTICLES/CANADA_INSTITUTE_FOR_SCIENTIFIC_AND_TECHNICAL_INFORMATION>.

[22] National Research Council of Canada National Science Library. <https://en.wikipedia.org/wiki/National_Research_Council_Canada_National_Science_Library>.

[23] National Research Council of Canada. National Science Library. <http://nsl-bsn.nrc-cnrc.gc.ca/eng/home/>.

[24] C.-C. Chen, Scientific and technical libraries, in: A. Kent, et al.(Ed.), Encyclopedia of Library and Information Science, vol. 27, Marcel Dekker, New York, 1979, pp. 1–86.

[25] A. Cockx, The National Center of Scientific and Technical Documentation. Library Bulletin of France. 1966. <http://bbf.enssib.fr/consulter/bbf-1966-01-0009-003>.

[26] National Documentation Centre (of Greece). <http://www.eie.gr/ekt-en.html>.

[27] National Technical Information Cerntre and Library. Budapest University of Technology and Economics. <http://www.omikk.bme.hu/>.

[28] Institute of Scientific and Technical Information of China (ISTIC). <http://www.istic.ac.cn/English>.
[29] T. Fukudome, The Japan information center of science and technology (JICST): Its organization and function, Am. Doc. 18 (3) (1967) 146–152.
[30] Japan Science and Technology Agency. <http://www.jst.go.jp/EN/about/history.html>.
[31] J.Valls, Pilot Project on Mechanization of Documentation Services in Asia, UNESCO, Paris, 1975.
[32] Pakistan Scientific and Technological Information Centre. <http://pastic.gov.pk/ > .
[33] BANSDOC. <http://old.bansdoc.gov.bd/>.
[34] About NISCAIR. <www.niscair.res.in>.
[35] V.K. Gupta, Protecting India's traditional knowledge. WIPO Magazine. June 2011. <http://www.wipo.int/wipo_magazine/en/2011/03/article_0002.html>.
[36] P. Kaushik, Documentation services in India, in: P. Dhyani (Ed.), Information Science and Libraries, Atlantic Publishers, New Delhi, 1990, pp. 231–232.
[37] National Social Science Documentation Centre (of India). <http://www.icssr.org/doc_intro.htm>.
[38] Defence Scientific Information and Documentation Centre. <http://drdo.govt.in/drdo/English/index.jsp?pg=homebody-jsp>.
[39] SENDOC. <http://www.nimsme.org/files/sendoc.php>.
[40] S. Dutta, Information services for small industries, J. Lib. Inform. Sci 2 (1) (1977) 37–50.

CHAPTER V

Information Systems and Networks

V.1 INTRODUCTION

A system is "a set of interacting components each of which is designed to serve a specific function for a specific purpose and all these components are interrelated to achieve a goal" [1]. In the context of information service, this goal is retrieval of required information. Thus, a system, the aim of which is information retrieval, can be called an information retrieval system or in short information system. From the point of view of functions, an information system may be defined as a well-coordinated system of collection, processing, storage, and retrieval of information. In the digital environment, an information system is "an integrated set of components for collecting, storing, and processing data and for delivering information, knowledge, and digital products" [2]. In above sense, every information centre itself is an information system.

V.2 WORK-FLOW

Any information system has three main components—Input unit, Processor, and Output unit. How information is retrieved with the help of these is shown below with the help of a diagram.

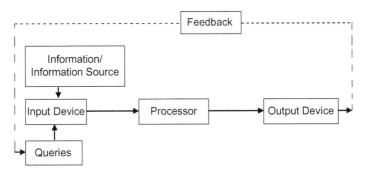

It is evident from the above diagram that on the one hand the information or the details of the information sources and on the other hand the

Elements of Information Organization and Dissemination
DOI: http://dx.doi.org/10.1016/B978-0-08-102025-8.00022-3

queries are entered into the processor through input device; the processor analyses and organizes the information and against each query retrieves the required information. Such information or details of information source containing that information are retrieved through the output device.

V.3 TYPES OF INFORMATION SYSTEM

An information system may not always be bibliographic or textual. There can also be non-bibliographic or non-textual information systems, such as a travel related information system or a share market related information system. Similarly, all bibliographic or textual information systems may not always be sponsored or maintained by libraries or information centres. They may be created and maintained by other organizations, especially by commercial organizations, e.g., Chemical Abstracts or Engineering Index. Here only different aspects of information systems created and maintained by libraries or information centres have been discussed. Different types of bibliographic/textual information systems have been shown below diagrammatically.

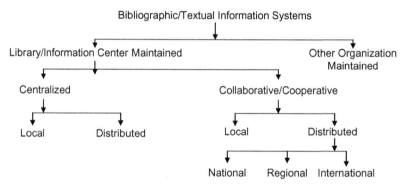

It may be mentioned that any of the above systems may be run with or without the help of computer. Now most of the information systems are automated systems. Due to application of computer, it has now become possible to develop full-text retrieval systems. Nevertheless, in the present chapter only library/information systems have been described.

V.4 ORIENTATION OF SYSTEM

An information system/network may be either subject-oriented or mission oriented. In a subject-oriented system, the orientation may be either toward science and technology covering physical sciences, life science, technology, and interdisciplinary areas or toward socioeconomic field covering behavioral sciences and interdisciplinary areas; while in a mission-oriented network the orientation may be toward public services, resources, production, or management [3]. In the era of information overload, it is not possible to have one single system for all types of information. As such, such orientation is quite natural.

V.5 CENTRALIZED SYSTEMS

Centralized or one-center-based information system is developed basing on the resources of a single library or information center and the users of that library or information center mainly retrieve their required information through that system, such as the information system of a large business house. Sometimes, branches of an organization are located at different places. The central library/information center of that organization and the libraries/information centers of different branches may jointly develop an information system. Again a system developed on the basis of the resources of one library/information center may serve at national or international level. MEDLARS and OCLC are such centers though now they also get inputs from other libraries and/or agencies set up for the purpose. The activities of these systems are described below.

V.5.1 MEDLARS

MEDLARS (Medical Literature Analysis and Retrieval System) is a computerized biomedical bibliographic retrieval system, which was formally launched by the National Library of Medicine, USA, in 1964, mainly to improve the quality and speedy publication of *Index Medicus*, the well-known indexing periodical in the field of medicine, being compiled by it, as the manual system of indexing and publication of the periodical in time had become difficult due to enormous rise in publication of micro documents in the field. It made possible, for the first time, to provide large-scale computer-based retrospective search service to the medical fraternity [4,5].

V.5.1.1 Phases of Development

MEDLARS was developed by the General Electric Company in three phases beginning August 1961. The first phase covered detailed exploration of the parameters of the system, refinement of notions as to capabilities required and their underlying machine analogs, and preliminary design of the system, with an outline of the required machine configuration. The second phase, which began in February 1962, covered the detailed design of the system, including stabilization of system concepts, detailed programming of the computer operations, and the writing of specifications for special equipment and initiation of its procurement. The final phase, beginning February 1963, covered implementation of the system. The operation of the system began in February 1964. As certain problems arose in the operation of MEDLARS, its expansion, and up-gradation were planned. Accordingly, MEDLARS II was developed during August 1967–June 1971. In 1979, NLM began development of MEDLARS III as a part of its continuing efforts to improve access, transfer, and use of information contained in the world's biomedical literature. The compilation of MEDLARS database was being done earlier on the basis of the literature available in NML, but now MEDLARS centers have been set up in different countries, which do the indexing work of the local literature for inclusion in the MEDLARS database [6].

V.5.1.2 MEDLINE

With the advent of on-line technology, NLM also introduced MEDLINE i.e., MEDLARS On-line in October 1971. MEDLINE is the largest database in the field of medical science. The majority of the publications covered in MEDLINE are scholarly journals; a small number of newspapers, magazines, and newsletters considered useful to user community are also included. In compiling this database help is taken of Medical Subject Headings (MeSH), the controlled vocabulary of NML. As of July 2015, MEDLINE indexes 5111 titles covered by Index Medicus and 495 additional titles—current publications in 39 languages and older publications in 60 languages—covering biomedicine and health. The total number of citations covered in MEDLINE database till 2010 was 18,340,055 from 1950 to the present, with some older materials. The number of citations added in the database in 2014 was 765,850. About three percent of MEDLINE indexing is performed by indexers at the International MEDLARS Centers in Sweden, China, and Brazil. PubMed provides free access to MEDLINE and links to full-text articles when possible. Document delivery is provided by partner libraries in Antigua and Barbuda, Australia, Austria, Brazil, Canada, Chile, China, Croatia, Czech Republic, Denmark, Estonia, Finland, France, Germany, Hong Kong, Iceland, India, Israel, Italy, Japan, Korea, Latvia, Lithuania, New Zealand, Norway, Poland, Russia, Slovakia, Slovenia, South Africa,

Spain, Sweden, Switzerland, and the United Kingdom [4,7,8]. The indexes that are brought out on the basis of MEDLINE database are *Index Medicus, International Nursing Index,* and *Index to Dental Literature.* Since 1984, MEDLINE is being made available on CD-ROM too (*see also* Section-B.3.3.7).

V.5.2 OCLC

On-line Computer Library Centre (OCLC) is a non-profit organization located at Dublin, OH, USA. Originally named the Ohio College Library Center, OCLC began in 1967 through a collaboration of Ohio university presidents, vice-presidents, and library directors who wanted to create a cooperative, computerized network for Ohio libraries [9]. Computerized services of OCLC began in 1970 and the next year on-line remote access facility was introduced which resulted in expansion of its services. Though OCLC started as one library based information system, gradually many libraries joined the system. In view of change in its character, its sponsoring organization was renamed as On-Line Computer Centre Inc. in 1981. More than 4000 computer terminals located in the member libraries throughout the world are directly connected with the main computer of OCLC. Those member libraries, where such facility is not available, connect their systems with the OCLC system through dial-up connection. More than 2500 libraries of the United States and Canada are connected with OCLC. Besides, many libraries in other parts of the world, especially in European countries, are also connected with this system. OCLC's database contains records in MAchine Readable Cataloging (MARC) format contributed by library catalogers worldwide who use OCLC as a cataloging tool. These MARC format records are then downloaded into the libraries' local catalog systems. This allows libraries to find and download records for materials to add to their local catalog without the lengthy process of cataloguing each item individually [9,10].

V.5.2.1 Objectives of OCLC
The objectives of OCLC are [11]:
- To establish, maintain, and operate a computerized library network to be accessible worldwide;
- To promote the evolution of library use, of libraries themselves, and of librarianship;
- To provide processes and products for the benefit of library users and libraries;

- To increase availability of library resources to individual library patrons;
- To reduce the rate-of-rise of library per–unit costs; and
- To provide easy access to and use of the ever-expanding body of worldwide scientific, literary, and educational knowledge and information.

V.5.2.2 Products and Services

OCLC provides bibliographic, abstract, and full-text information to anyone. It has developed many products and services for its members, of which the important ones are described below [9,10]

- *OCLC WorldCat:* This on-line union catalog is the biggest database of its kind in the world. It is cooperatively produced and maintained by OCLC and its member libraries. WorldCat connects library users to hundreds of millions of electronic resources, including e-books, licensed databases, online periodicals, and collections of digital items. In October 2005, the OCLC technical staff began a wiki project allowing readers to add commentary and structured-field information associated with any WorldCat record.
- *OCLC WorldShare:* It is the new inter-library loan service, which has replaced the earlier WorldCat Resource Sharing service. More than 9000 libraries participate in this global resource sharing network.
- *OCLC WebJunction:* Since its launch in 2003, WebJunction has helped more than 50,000 library staff build the job skills they need to meet the challenges of today's libraries. The training facility is available to that library and information professionals free of cost.
- *DDC revision:* DDC is owned by OCLC since 1988. The four-volume print edition of DDC 23 was published in May 2011. It provides many new and updated numbers and topics, as well as tools to enhance classifier efficiency. The first electronic version *Web Dewey*, based on DDC23, was also made available at the same time.
- *OCLC WorldShare metadata:* WorldShare Metadata provides a complete metadata management solution for physical, licensed, and digital resources across multiple formats. This set of new applications and services will be made available in phases over the next few years.
- *Electronic collection management:* OCLC provides libraries with the tools to manage and maximize the use of their electronic collections. To complement the e-books, e-resources and digital items already indexed in WorldCat, OCLC is working with libraries and partners to build

a comprehensive knowledge base of the e-collections licensed by all member libraries.

- *Digital content management:* OCLC has developed CONTENTdm Digital Collection Management Software which can make everything in a digital collection available to online researchers, everywhere.
- *QuestionPoint:* This reference management service provides libraries with tools to communicate with users. This round-the-clock reference service is provided by a cooperative of participating global libraries.
- *Consultancy services:* OCLC offers a range of solutions to support the digital life cycle, including managing, sharing, and preserving primary source materials. It also has a full range of management services that can improve the entire library system.

V.6 COLLABORATIVE SYSTEMS

This type of system is developed by collaboration or cooperation of many libraries/information centers. Such systems are often known as library/information networks. Nevertheless, a system connecting a library/information center and its branches can also be called information network. When the libraries/information centers connected with the network exist in a small area, this is known as local area network (LAN) in computer parlance, such as Health Sciences Library Network of Kansas City (USA) or ADINET (Ahmadabad Library Network, India). But when such libraries/information centers are located in a bigger area, it is called wide area network, such as International Nuclear Library Network or INFLIBNET (India). The latter type of network can be formed at the national, regional, or international level. In recent decades, a type of collaborative loosely-knit library and information networks are coming up which are known as consortia. A consortium in the context of library and information services is a "community (a cooperative) of two or more information agencies which have formally agreed to coordinate, cooperate in, or consolidate certain functions to achieve mutual objectives" [12]. More specifically, it is "a group of libraries that agree to pool their resources by allowing the users of each institution some type of access to the resources of all other institutions, either through inter-library loan or borrowing privileges" [13]. A few well-known collaborative library/information systems, both conceptual and existing, at the international level and national level, are described below.

V.6.1 International Information Systems

Before application of computer began in the sphere of library and information services, no effort to set up an information system at the international level in the area of science and technology could bear results. In the context of successful deployment of ITC in library/information activities in 1960s, efforts began again to set up such library/information systems and gradually several international library/information systems have come into existence. It is needless to stress that an international library/ information system can develop only in a decentralized manner. Hence the national systems have to be strong for the success of the international system. A few well-known international library/information systems, both conceptual and existing, are described below.

V.6.1.1 UNISIST

Realizing the need for increased worldwide flow of scientific information UNESCO and International Council of Scientific Unions (ICSU) jointly formed a committee in January 1967 to carry out a feasibility study for a world science information system, the report of which was published in 1970. The recommendations and the program proposed in the report were discussed in an inter-governmental conference held in Paris in October 1971. At the 17th session of UNESCO's General Conference, held in Paris in 1972, a long-term intergovernmental program named UNISIST (United Nations International Scientific Information System) was launched with a view to facilitating transfer of scientific and technical information for the economic and social development of nations [14]. A steering committee was also formed for implementing the program. A second intergovernmental conference on scientific and technical information for development was held in Paris in 1979 to review development since the launching of UNISIST. This came to be known as UNISIST –II. According to a study report on the project, UNISIST was "planned as a continuing, flexible programme to coordinate existing trend towards cooperation and to act as a catalyst for the necessary development in scientific information. The ultimate goal is the establishment of a flexible and loosely connected network of information services based on voluntary cooperation" [15]. Thus, UNISIST was not conceived as a "world system" in the sense of a pre-planned, integrated formal system, but as a flexible international network of co-operating information services, linked, and coordinated through common standards.

Importance of UNISIST

UNISIST was "an international effort to synthesize a diversity of philosophies, programmes, and policies that relate to the free flow of scientific and technical information." It was "an unprecedented attempt to stabilize and coordinate existing trends towards international cooperation in the communication of scientific information." It was described as "a philosophy, a movement, and an organization" [16]. Wikipedia has termed it as a model of information dissemination [17].

Organization of UNISIST

UNISIST was not conceived as "a rigid, pre-designed super-structure," which would provide the world scientific community with all available information in science and technology. The report of the feasibility study did not even contain a system analysis of the existing state and relationship of scientific information systems in the world. A more pragmatic approach was adopted by considering the feasibility of the system from a technical, as well as from the political and economic point of view [16]. As per recommendations in the report of the feasibility study, UNISIST had the following three interrelated managerial bodies [16]:

- An intergovernmental conference which was responsible for approving the programs of the UNISIST and reporting on the progress of those programs;
- An international scientific advisory committee having strong representation from the International Council of Scientific Unions and its affiliated unions, as well as information experts and services, which was responsible for assessing the progress in communication practices and changes in user requirements, as a basis for, and as a result of UNISIST program;
- An executive office, serving as the permanent secretariat of UNISIST, which was responsible for preparing and administering programs and budgets.

It was also proposed that each country should establish a governmental agency at the national level to guide, stimulate, and conduct the development of information resources. Consequently many governments set up their respective national agencies or focal points. The NISSAT advisory committee functioned as the national committee of UNISIST in India.

Objectives and Scope of UNISISIT

UNISIST aimed at "unimpeded exchange of published scientific information and data among scientists of the world; hospitality to diversity of disciplines and fields of science and technology; promotion of compatibility, cooperative agreements and interchange of published information among the system; cooperative development and maintenance of technical standards to facilitate the interchange; development of trained manpower and information resources in all countries; increased participation of the present and coming generation of scientists in the development and use of information systems; reduction of administrative and legal barriers of the flow of scientific information in the world; and assistance to countries which seek access to present and future information services in the sciences" [16]. Initially UNISIST program was to be concerned with the sciences, applied sciences, engineering, and technology. However, at the 18th session of UNESCO General Conference held in Paris in 1974 a decision was taken to extend the program to the field of social sciences as well.

Functions of UNISIST
Broadly, UNISIST had two main functions, viz., "(1a) a catalytic function by which UNISIST is to stimulate international cooperative agreements among autonomous information systems, and (2) an initiating function by which UNISIST will encourage new projects designed to improve the world information tools and resources" [16]. The following were the program objectives as mentioned in the first issue of *UNISIST Newsletter*, which started in 1973:

- Improvement of tools of systems interconnections;
- Strengthening the role of institutional components of the information transfer chain;
- Development of specialized manpower;
- Development of scientific information policies and structures; and
- Assistance to developing countries in the development of scientific and technical information infrastructure.

These obviously indicated the main functions involved in UNISIST program.

Achievements of UNISIST
The important achievements of UNISIST were:

- An International Information Centre for Terminology (INFOTERM) was set up in 1971 under the framework of UNISIST. Affiliated to the Austrian Standards Institute, INFOTERM aimed at "coordinating terminological activities carried out throughout the world for the development of a network of terminological agencies."

- A UNISIST International Centre for Bibliographic Description (UNIBID) was created by the British Library within the conceptual and operational framework of UNISIST for working toward standardization of bibliographic descriptions.
- An International Serials Data System (ISDS) was developed with the objective of setting up a computerized index file of world serial publications.
- An International Symposium on Information Systems and Services in Ongoing Research in Science was organized in Pairs in October 1975.
- A Broad System of Ordering (BSO) was developed to link different individual classification schemes and thesauri in the process of information transfer.
- NATIS concept was discussed at an intergovernmental conference in 1974.
- Several important publications were brought out which included *Reference Manual for Machine-Readable Bibliographic Description* (1974), *Guidelines on the Conduct of a National Inventory of Current Research and Development Projects* (1975), *Education and Training of Users of Scientific and Technological Information: UNISIST Guide for Teachers* (1978), *Guidelines on Referral Centres* (1979), *Information Services on Research in Progress: A World-wide Inventory*, and *UNISIST Guide to Standards for Information Handling* (1980).
- The quarterly UNISIST Newsletter was being published since 1973.
- Working groups were set up on Bibliographic Data Interchange, Education and Training Policy and Programmes, Information Analysis Centres, and Technology of Systems Interconnection.
- A Science and Technology Policies Information Exchange System (SPINES) was launched under the conceptual framework of UNISIST.

Present Status of UNISIST
The UNISIST program was closed in 2003.

V.6.1.2 INIS

International Nuclear Information System (INIS) is perhaps the first computer-based international information storage and retrieval network. Sponsored by the International Atomic Energy Agency (IAEA), Vienna, it started operation in January 1970 "to foster the exchange of scientific and technical information on peaceful uses of atomic energy" [18]. As of February 2016, there are 168 member countries of IAEA which voluntarily cooperate in its activities "for mutual benefit of efforts in controlling the world's scientific literature in the field of nuclear science and technology with the object of achieving maximum economy in time, money and efforts and to avoid duplication at various levels." In every member country there is an INIS Center, having the responsibility to perform necessary functions relating to INIS. In India, Bhaba Atomic Research Centre is the designated INIS center.

Mission and Objectives of INIS

The mission of INIS has been "to produce and disseminate in a decentralized manner a computer-based bibliographic database containing records and abstracts of the literature produced throughout the world on the peaceful applications of nuclear science and technology and to collect and make available the full text of those items not readily available through normal commercial channels" [19]. In view of the above mission the specific objectives of INIS are:

- To create a reservoir of nuclear information for current and future generations;
- To provide quality nuclear information services to member states; and
- To assist with the development of a culture of information and knowledge sharing.

Characteristics of INIS

The main characteristics of INIS are:

- Information collection and dissemination are completely decentralized to national INIS centers in member states; only information processing and database compilation are centralized at the INIS headquarters at Vienna;
- It is not only an information retrieval system, but also a document retrieval system;
- It is a dynamic and flexible system which incorporates change and adjustments as and when warranted;
- It has a system of communicating with the participants through "INIS Technical Notes," "INIS Newsletter," conferences, seminars, etc.

Structure of INIS

INIS consists of a network of members contributing scientific and technical information on the peaceful use of nuclear energy through an INIS

Secretariat. The INIS Secretariat function is vested in the International Atomic Energy Agency (IAEA) and located at the IAEA's Headquarters in Vienna. INIS activities are implemented through a regular program of IAEA and by work done in Member States. As INIS Secretariat, the IAEA is responsible for the management and co-ordination of INIS, including, among other things, the processing of input and distribution of products to members. The IAEA also contributes scientific nuclear information to INIS, and is responsible for the contributions from other international organizations. In carrying out its functions INIS Secretariat is assisted by: (1) an Advisory Committee, reporting directly to the Director General of IAEA; (2) the INIS Liaison Officers Assembly; (3) the INIS Technical Committee, ad hoc advisory and technical committees and other mechanisms [19].

Workflow of INIS

The national INIS centers identify and select documents pertaining to the field of coverage, published within their respective geographical areas (or organizational confines if an international body), and carry out the preparatory work such as description, categorization, indexing, abstracting, and submit the same to the INIS office in Vienna in accordance with prescribed rules, procedures, formats, and guidelines and provides the full text of each item of nonconventional literature, either as originally published or in a form jointly determined prepared to a standard specification, provided there is no legal prohibition or limitation. The INIS Secretariat integrates the inputs from INIS members into the INIS file (database) after necessary editing. The secretariat regularly distributes INIS output in electronic form to INIS members. The INIS centers of the respective member countries/organizations provide information services and maintain contact with, to the extent practicable, the users of INIS information products and services within the applicable boundaries/confines [20].

INIS Products

Besides the main database containing data relating to 3.7 million items (as at the end of 2014), INIS has brought out around 30 reference products such as guides, manuals, rules/instructions and dictionaries/thesauri, etc., a few important of which are: INIS: Guide to Bibliographic Description; INIS: Samples for Bibliographic Description; INIS/ETDE Manual for Subject Analysis; INIS: Transliteration Rules for Selected non-Roman Characters; INIS: Thesaurus; INIS: Database Manual [18,19].

Strong Points of INIS

The strong points of INIS are:

- It achieves widest coverage of national nuclear-related literature;
- It overcomes cultural and language barriers; and
- It gives every INIS member the right to access nuclear information of all other INIS members.

V.6.1.3 AGRIS

To overcome the problem of scientific communication within the field of agricultural sciences Food and Agricultural Organization of the United Nations initiated in 1970s steps to develop an International System for Agricultural Science and Technology (AGRIS) in two levels. Level-I aimed at bibliographical listing of documents, while Level-II aimed at content analysis. The Level-I was envisaged to be universal in scope and complete in coverage and was expected to provide current awareness service. Level-II was envisaged to be specific in scope and selective in coverage and was expected to provide SDI and retrospective retrieval service [20].

AGRINDEX

As a first step toward implementing Level-I, an experimental issue of the bibliography, named *AGRIDEX*, was generated in 1973 from a master computer tape prepared with data inputs from nine institutions in different countries. It contained 7000 entries relating to a worldwide sample of current conventional and nonconventional literature, but it did not contain any abstract. In 1979 abstracts started to be provided, when available from the national or regional input centers. AGRIS became fully operational in 1975 and since then AGRIS has accumulated a database of more than seven million bibliographic references. At present 159 national and 31 international and intergovernmental centers participate and submit about 14,000 items per month to AGRIS database. However, publication of *AGRINDEX*, the monthly printed bibliography of AGRIS was stopped by the end of 1995 [21].

Scope and Coverage of AGRIS

AGRIS database covers world literature published in all types of documents, such as journal articles, monographs (books), conferences papers, reports, theses and dissertations, drawings, maps and atlases, patents, literature reviews, bibliographies, multimedia (films/videos, sound recordings, photos, slides, computer media, etc.), and other miscellaneous and nonconventional ("grey literature" not available through normal distribution channels) dealing with all aspects of agriculture (including forestry, fisheries, human nutrition and environment). The composition of AGRIS database is: 75% journal articles, 18% monographs, 6% conferences papers, 1% others, and 16% refer to nonconventional literature (not commercially available). About 21% of the entries include abstracts. Of the documents included in the database 58% are in English, 8% French, 7% German, 7% Spanish, 4% Japanese, 3% Italian, 3% Russian, 2% Portuguese, and 8% are in other languages [22].

Work-Flow of AGRIS

AGRIS is a cooperative system in which participating countries input references to the literature/documents produced within their boundaries and, in return, draw on the information provided by the other participants. The bibliographic references forwarded by participating countries are collected and processed in the AGRIS Processing Unit, Vienna, which is hosted by the Division of Scientific and Technical Information of the IAEA. AGRIS is managed centrally by the WAICENT/FAOINFO Dissemination Management Branch of the Library and Documentation Systems Division (GIL) of FAO. A thesaurus, named AGROVOC, has been developed for processing of bibliographic references [22,23].

CD-ROM Products

AGRIS database in now available on CD-ROM as well as on-line. The CD-ROM products are [22]:

- *AGRIS CD-ROMs*: all collected information, stored on archival CD-ROMs and one current CD-ROM, which contains the last collected information (quarterly updated);
- *AGRIS FHN CD-ROM*: contains information in the domains of Food and Human Nutrition extracted from all AGRIS CD-ROMs (semi-annually updated); and
- *AGRIS FORESTRY CD-ROM*: contains information in the domains of forestry and primary forest products extracted from all AGRIS CD-ROMs.

On-line access to the global AGRIS database is provided by [22]:

- AGRIS DATABASE ON-LINE (FAO/WAICENT, FAO Web Server)
- DIALOG (Palo Alto, USA): nonUSA portion only
- DIMDI (Cologne, Germany)

Besides, the AGRIS processing Unit also brings out AGRIS Reference Series.

Other Products/Services

AGRIS Processing Unit provides on request the following products/services (in printed form or on magnetic media as required) [22]:

- *Retrospective searches* through the entire data base;
- *Selective dissemination of information (SDI)* service, by which users can request the AGRIS Processing Unit, to keep them informed of any new AGRIS entries on specific subjects of concern to them.
- *National bibliographies*, containing all entries generated in a country and those concerning that country published outside. Master copies can be prepared on a high resolution laser printer in AGRINDEX format, ready for reproduction by offset or photocopy.
- *Subject bibliographies* are also prepared upon request from specialized cooperating centers.

Besides, the AGRIS Processing Unit also develops and distributes *AGROVOC Thesaurus, AGRIS Working Methodologies, Software for AGRIS Input Data*, and *training materials*. The multilingual AGROVOC Thesaurus is available in the five FAO official languages which are English, French, Spanish, Chinese, and Arabic. It is also available in Czech, Portuguese, and Thai. It is being translated into some other languages such as Italian, Korean, Japanese, Hungarian, and Slovak, The main role of AGROVOC is to standardize the indexing process in order to make searching simpler and more efficient, and to provide the user with the most relevant resources. Currently, it is downloaded regularly [23].

New Developments

AGRIS adopted a new vision in 2000. In 2009, AGRIS adhered to Coherence in Information for Agricultural Research for Development (CIARD), a global initiative committed to working for increasing the public benefits deriving from investment in agricultural research and innovation for development. The underlying principle shared by CIARD partners, which FAO is contributing to with its AGRIS portal, is that, information is to be made publicly "available," "accessible," and "applicable." On December 5, 2013, AGRIS 2.0 was released. Access to the AGRIS Repository is now provided through the AGRIS Search Engine. AGRIS data have been converted to RDF and the resulting linked dataset has created some 200 million triples. AGRIS is also now registered in the Data Hub at http://thedatahub.org/dataset/agris [23].

V.6.1.4 DEVSIS

Development Science Information System (DEVSIS) is a global decentralized and mission-oriented information system in the field of economic and social development, co-sponsored by International Development Research Centre (IDRC), the International Labour Office (ILO), the Organization for Economic Co-operation and Development (OECD), the United Nations Department of Economic and Social Affairs (UN/ESA), the United Nations Development Programme (UNDP), and the United Nations Educational, Scientific and Cultural Organization (UNESCO). Basically, it was created for meeting the information needs of policy-makers, planners, and project administrators in developing nations. This information system was conceived for providing information about socioeconomic developmental activities throughout the world. It covers information generated in other areas but which is relevant for the developmental studies. This includes data and information from different sectors [24,25].

Objectives of DEVSIS

The objectives with which DEVSIS was planned are [26]:

- To improve access to economic and social development information to individual and institutions, particularly in developing countries of the world, and to foster the building and utilization of national and international resources to meet this goal;
- To improve coordination between the existing information facilities, including libraries;
- To provide information services to users working in the development field at national, international, governmental, and nongovernmental levels;
- To be responsive to the expressed needs of its users and, following reviews and evaluation, to adjust to effective needs;
- To encourage all the nations of the world to give consideration to development information as an important component in the formulation of both their national development polices as well as their information policies.

Coverage of DEVSIS

It was planned to cover five categories information materials in DEVSIS [27]:

- *Basic economic and social information data:* These include statistical and other factual information, descriptions of economic and social situations, reports on trends in economic and social conditions, papers on socioeconomic models, econometric models, development indicators, and techniques for computing and forecasting.
- *Theories, models, and methodologies:* These include papers on socioeconomic models, econometric models, development indicators, tools, and techniques helpful in forecasting, planning, and other developmental studies, theoretician and similar studies and evaluation of such studies.
- *Development policy statements and plans:* These include theoretical studies on economic and social development, official statements of development policy, official plans and official and nonofficials commentaries, reviews and evaluations of plans, and programs.
- *Studies on and for development tactics:* These include pre-investment studies and tools for such studies, development resources, and operational experiences.
- *Studies of consequences of development efforts and activities:* These include information relating to economic impact, social impact, and evaluatory reports on specific development strategies, programs, and projects.

Structure and Function

DEVSIS is a global, decentralized, and mission-oriented system. According to the original plan, at the basis of the system would be the acceptance by each country participating in DEVSIS of the responsibility to contribute standardized records of the relevant documents generated within its territory. The DEVSIS central unit would convert these records to machine readable form, merge them with the contributions of other national units, and produce a monthly index publication, called Devindex. In addition, the central unit would make the same collection of data available on machine readable form which could be searched in a computer. The national DEVSIS centers, both in developing and developed countries, would be thus the foundation of the network. They would identify and report to the central unit development information generated in member countries. More importantly, they would identify their own needs for development information, and provide their own experts with tailor-made services from the stores of information received from the central unit. The pattern, in other words, would be similar to that of INIS and AGRIS [24].

Services of DEVSIS

DEVSIS is to provide the following services [28]:

- *Devindex*: Devindex will be the principal published product of the DEVSIS system. It will be an index to all the items of information reported by the participating countries and merged at the central unit. It will have supporting indexes by subject, geographic location, author, and by report number. The DEVSIS central unit will prepare and distribute magnetic tapes bearing, in machine-readable form, the same information from which Devindex is compiled. The format of such information will correspond to internationally agreed standards for the exchange of bibliographic information, to facilitate merging with other machine-readable information files.

- *Retrospective search*: It will be possible to search the DEVSIS file retrospectively by subject, author, and geographic and language fields, and even for specific statistical and investment data. For purposes of subject indexing, a specially designed standardized vocabulary will be used, and the same vocabulary will be used in computer searches to obtain a selection relevant to the user's needs.

- *SDI and current awareness services*: These services will be made available to users wishing to monitor, over a period of time, developments in a highly specific field. Where the need is more generalized, this service can be expanded to match the interest of a group of subscribers: thus, if groups such as transportation planners, rural development specialists, or investment decision-makers are interested in the experience of all countries in the fields of their special interests, a "recurring bibliography" can be developed for their use.

- *Special purpose file creation:* The files of machine-readable information received from the central unit, at the option of the receiving country, can be modified in many different ways. Thus, for example, it may be possible to merge a selection of references received from DEVSIS with a selection of references received from, say, AGRIS to create a specialized database dealing with rural development.

- *Referral service*: The basic bibliographic services and products of DEVSIS will be derived from the information in "File One," namely the bibliographic records of government and international documents, books, periodical articles, reports, unpublished studies, etc. The DEVSIS central unit will also prepare a "File Two," on which the national centers may build their referral services. "File Two" will contain descriptive information about sources of development information throughout the world, such as statistical services, information services in particular sectors, registers of ongoing research and development, indexes of equipment manufacturers, specialized magazines, and bulletins. The central unit will publish periodic compendia of "File Two" information under the title Devprofile, and at the same time will make the information available on magnetic tape to be searched by the national participants.

- *Document availability*: It is most frustrating to hear of a report that would be essential to a project but that is not available locally and whose supplier is unknown. In anticipation of a need to make the full texts of documents available to the user, the DEVSIS Steering Committee has proposed a microfiche back-up service to provide the full texts for some 60,000 nonconventional reports annually. The central unit will make these microfiches, or if desired paper copies derived from them, available to the national DEVSIS centers at cost.

Progress of DEVSIS

Though DEVSIS as a global system could not be fully implemented, yet a number of regional and sub-regional development information systems have emerged during the last few decades which are funded by various funding agencies such as INFOPLAN, i.e., Latin American Planning Information Network; CARISPLAN, i.e., Caribbean Information System for Economic and Social Planning; and PADIS, i.e., Pan African Documentation and Information System. In addition, ESCAP and IDNAC, i.e., International Database for Information for NonAligned Countries have also been in existence for a long time [25].

DEVINSA

In the South-Asian region, the DEVINSA, i.e., Development Information Network for South Asia, was started in 1986 with financial support from IDRC, Canada. The main objective of this network is to organize a computerized database on socioeconomic development in South Asia containing data primarily about nonconventional material like research project reports, doctoral theses, working papers, etc., and share this development information between academia, policymakers, etc., so as to contribute to the socioeconomic development of the region. DEVINSA is coordinated at the Marga Institute, Sri Lanka, and the other members of this network are Bangladesh, India, Male, Nepal, and Pakistan [25].

V.6.1.5 INFOTERRA

The Stockholm Conference on the Human Environment, convened by the United Nations in 1972 to consider the condition of the environment, called for an international mechanism for the exchange of environmental information. As a follow-up action, an International Referral System (IRS) was set up in 1975 under the United Nations Environment Programme (UNEP). The system was later renamed as International Environmental Information Network (INFOTERRA). The main goal of INFOTERRA, which began its operation in 1977, was to develop a mechanism to "facilitate the exchange of environmental information within and among nations." Together with International Register of Potentially Toxic Chemicals (IRPTC), the Global Environmental Monitoring System (GEMS) and the Global Resource Information Database (GRID), INFOTERRA is a complement of UNEP's Earthwatch Programme and thereby "plays an important part in fulfilling UNEP's global mandate of monitoring, assessment and dissemination of information on the environment, catalyzing and spurring others to action at international, regional and national levels" [29].

Structure of INFOTERRA

INFOTERRA is a decentralized information system operating through a worldwide network of national environmental institutions designated and supported by their governments as national focal points (NFP) and coordinated by a Programme Activity Centre at UNEP Headquarters in Nairobi. INFOTERRA started with a dozen partner countries. At present the system consists of 170 NFP, 11 regional service centers, and 34 special sectoral sources [29].

Activities of INFOTERRA

In the early years INFOTERRA operated only as a referral system. However, in 1981 INFOTERRA expanded its services to include substantive information and document delivery services. The NFP of INFOTERRA are usually located in the information and documentation sections of environment ministries, and national environmental protection agencies which are often also the focal points for national information networks. They act as the primary access points through which queries from users are routed to INFOTERRA and through which users receive their replies. Each national focal point compiles a "who's who" of environmental expertise in their country, and selects the best sources for inclusion in

INFOTERRA's main publication the International Directory of Sources, which is compiled by the Programme Activity Centre in Nairobi. As a component part of a United Nations program, the INFOTERRA network has access to specialized databases and information sources on environment related subjects located in UNEP such as IRPTC; other UN agencies especially UNESCO, FAO, WHO, ILO, UNIDO; and major international organizations including International Union for Conservation of Nature (IUCN), World Wide Fund for Nature (WWF) and Centre for Agricultural Bioscience International (CABI). Many of these organizations are also special sectoral sources contracted to provide information to the INFOTERRA network. The INFOTERRA network as a whole handles more than 30,000 queries per year on every aspect of the human and physical environment, including the control of lead pollution or acid rain to sustainable management of national parks and conservation of fragile ecosystems. Over 85% of enquiries are responded to with substantive information, sometimes in the form of existing publications or research data, and sometimes tailor-made to a specific enquiry in a specialized area of concern [29].

Products of INFOTERRA

The main product of INFOTERRA is the above directory, which is constantly monitored and updated, and new sources added. The directory is available both as a printed "hardcopy" and as a computerized database. It contains more than 7000 sources of information on over 1000 environmental subjects. The sources are located in government ministries and documentation centers, research institutes, universities, nongovernmental and international organizations, United Nations agencies, and private consultancies. The Programme Activity Centre also periodically publishes specialized directories and sourcebooks and quarterly *INFOTERRA Bulletin*. The center has also published *Thesaurus of Environmental Terms*; *Operations Manual*; and publications under "Exchange of Environmental Experiences Series," besides promotional materials [29].

V.6.1.6 Other International Systems

There are several other information systems functioning in different parts of the worlds, a few well-known such systems are described below.

AgNIC

The Agricultural Network Information Centre (AgNIC) was started in 1995 as a voluntary alliance of four land-grant university libraries and

National Agricultural Library (NAL) of USA with the objective of providing access to quality agricultural information in electronic format available over the world wide web (www) via the Internet. The alliance has grown over the years and today it has more than 60 partner institutions spread over the United States, Canada, Latin America, and Europe, besides three international organizations, viz., SIDALC (Agricultural Information and Documentation System for America); Canadian Agriculture Library; and the International Rice Research Institute (Philippines). AgNIC has developed a web gateway providing immediate access to a cross-section of evaluated agricultural, food, and environmental information resources, and a distributed network of over 80 subject and information experts. The alliance uses "centres-of-excellence" approach whereby each partnering institution takes responsibility for developing reliable and useful contents on topic(s) in which it has expertise and specialized resources and providing access to the same through its website. The AgNIC home page links to these websites and offers both keyword searching and individual site browsing functions [30–33]. The main characteristics of the alliance are [34]:

- Consensus decision making (whenever possible);
- Cooperation and collaboration (not competition);
- Minimal overhead or central bureaucracy; and
- Dynamic structure, with most work accomplished by committees.

Some of the important databases and services available through AgNIC are [30]:

- AgDB: A database directory of quality agriculture-related databases, datasets and information systems which describes and links to 1000 + web based agriculture information resources;
- AGRICOLA: A bibliographic database of more than three million records created by NAL and its collaborators;
- AGRICOLA Subject category codes: An electronic version of the codes used to create AGRICOLA database records (Agric CC);
- AgCal: A calendar of agricultural conferences, meetings and seminars containing information about more than 600 agriculture-related meetings and also provides links to 100 calendars maintained by other institutions;
- CB Pest: Database of the Occurrence and Distribution of Pesticides in Chesaeake Bay;
- DirAg IR: Directories of Agriculture-Related Internet Information Sources;

- AgExp: Directories of Experts in Agriculture which provide links to about 40 directories of experts in agriculture-related disciplines that are on the Internet;
- On Ref: Online Reference Services and Collection of Resources by AgNIC participants;
- PDA: A searchable archive of emerging plant disease announcements posted to the ProMED-mail (an Internet-based reporting system dedicated to rapid global dissemination of information on outbreaks of infectious diseases) mailing list.

The alliance has since been renamed as Agricultural Network Information Collaborative and NAL serves as its secretariat.

APINMAP

The Asian Pacific Information Network on Medicinal and Aromatic Plants (APINMAP) was launched in 1987 by UNESCO. It is a voluntary flexible decentralized network presently with 14 member countries in Asian and Pacific region (Australia, People's Republic of China, India, Indonesia, Republic of Korea, Malaysia, Nepal, Pakistan, Papua New Guinea, the Philippines, Sri Lanka, Thailand, Turkey, and Vietnam). The national node in each participating country is responsible for data input and for serving their national users. The Network Centre, located at the Agricultural Information Bank for Asia (AIBA), Philippines, is responsible for technical coordination and the merging of national inputs into integrated databases and redistribution of data to the member countries, while the Secretariat, located in Bangkok, is responsible for the promotion and for the overall administration of the network. The objectives APINMAP are [34]:

- Provide access to information from regional and international sources, including scientific research results.
- Develop and improve specialized information services for member states.
- Assist in the development of information product and services for the targeted end-user communities.
- Establish linkages to regional and international networks or services in the fields of medicinal or aromatic plants and natural product chemistry.

APINMAP is developing a factual database, which will contain actual research data. Data is stored and maintained using micro CDS/ISIS software. A separate retrieval software program was written to provide easy data access [34].

ARKISYST

The World Information System for Architecture and Urban Planning (ARKISYST) aims at optimizing information services already available in the field of architecture and urban planning and maximizing their use and identifying necessary service developments and means by which they can be achieved through integrated international action. According to the final feasibility report for the proposed system, sponsored by the UNESCO, the Government of Spain, UN Centre for Human Settlements and International Union of Architects, ARKISYST will have NFP (designated by the respective governments) which will identify all potential resources of information in their respective areas and refer information seekers to these resources. They will also serve as nodes of an international center, which will maintain an integrated information resource file and sponsor international referral activities [35].

ASFIS

The Food and Agriculture Organization of United Nations and the Inter-governmental Oceanographic Commission (IOC) of the UNESCO joined hands to set up the Aquatic Sciences and Fisheries Information System (ASFIS) in 1975. It is run by the Fisheries Resources and Environment Division of the FAO. The system aims at collecting and disseminating information relating to the entire science and technology of marine and fresh water environments, including pisciculture, ocean and fresh water environments, biology and ecology of aquatic organisms, pollution, etc. The system maintains the following registers [36]:

- Register of Experts in Aquatic Sciences and Fisheries;
- Register of Aquatic Sciences and Fisheries Institutions;
- Register of Aquatic Sciences and Fisheries Meetings;
- Register of Aquatic Research Equipment; and
- World List of Aquatic Sciences Serials Titles.

The system makes available computer tapes of information collected and brings out several useful publications including monthly *Aquatic Sciences and Fisheries Abstracts*, monthly *Marine Sciences Contents Tables*, *World List of Periodicals in Marine and Fresh Water Sciences,* and *Register of Experts and Institutions in Aquatic Sciences.*

ASTINFO

ASTINFO is a co-operative program which aims to promote the exchange of information and experience in science and technology among countries in the Asia/Pacific region. It was initiated in 1984. ASTINFO comprises coordinating units in 18 Member States; and some 82 national/regional institutions now hold the status of ASTINFO Associated Centres and Networks. A quarterly Newsletter is published [37] UNESCO maintains a Secretariat for ASTINFO in its Regional Office in Bangkok, Thailand. ASTINFO aims at promoting exchange of information, data, and experience in information field. Its specific objectives are [38]:

- To strengthen bibliographic control of the participating countries' own scientific and technological output and establish computer-based bibliographic databases in subject areas of interest to the region, supported by document clearing-houses;
- To stimulate and promote the creation of nonbibliographic databases in science, technology, and socioeconomic fields of importance to development in the region;
- To develop and promote the technical and organizational structures and capabilities for cross-border exchange of data and for the sharing of processing facilities;
- To develop specialized information networks in high-priority subject areas and strengthen existing networks;
- To improve the national information infrastructure to meet the needs of the regional network so as to ensure that all those in the country who should benefit from the regional network have access to it;
- To introduce improved or new information services, in particular by utilizing databases available in or outside the region and by improving information support, including consolidated and repackaged information for development;
- To train information specialists;
- To promote awareness and use of existing systems and services, in particular those established by United Nations agencies, and to encourage user training programs.

Although ASTINFO is actually a regional information program rather than an operational system, one of its major goals is the promotion of operational information networks in priority areas for the region. In this context one of UNESCO's major activities in Asia and the Pacific, within the overall framework of ASTINFO, has been the establishment of a regional information network in the area of medicinal and aromatic plants, called APINMAP [38]. This network has been described above. India has made significant contributions to ASTINFO activities by way of execution of projects on subjects of specific interest and strength of India, such as the project on chemical reaction database at National Chemical Laboratory, Pune, as a part of the international program on Chemical Information Network and provision of resource persons at ASTINFO supported workshops and seminars.

CARIS

Current Agricultural Research Information System (CARIS) was created by FAO in 1975 to identify and to facilitate the exchange of information about current research projects on all aspects of agriculture, including forestry, fisheries, human nutrition, and environment, being carried out in, or on behalf of, developing countries. It is a cooperative system in which participating countries input references to the research conducted within their boundaries and, in return, draw on the information provided by the other participants. The references forwarded by participating countries are collected and processed in the WAICENT/FAOINFO Dissemination Management Branch of the Library and Documentation Systems Division (GIL) at FAO Headquarters. Altogether 132 national and 19 international and intergovernmental centers participate in CARIS. These centers have submitted exhaustive information on roughly 30,000 currently active projects. In addition, two regional centers submit input on behalf of six countries in their respective regions. CARIS maintains an on-line active database to which information relating to new projects are added and from which information relating to completed projects are deleted. The database is also available on CD-ROM. CARIS now aims at decentralized data processing using ICT and capacity building for enhancing autonomous management of national agricultural information [39].

COMNET

International Network of Centres for Documentation on Communication Research Policies (COMNET) was created in 1970 to improve and accelerate international and regional exchanges of information and documentation in the field of communication research, policy, and practice, to contribute significantly to scientific development in the field of communication in all regions of the world. Its specific objectives are [40]:
- To consolidate the COMNET network and expand its range and representation at international, regional, and national levels.

- To automate, in a gradual and phased manner, the COMNET documentation network.
- To set and apply standards and provide maintenance, and training support for indexing, retrieval and exchange of information in the fields covered by the network.
- To increase the range and quality of activities, products, and services provided within the COMNET framework.

COMNET is currently organized in eight regional networks in Africa, the Arab States, Asia, the Pacific, the Caribbean, Latin America, North America and Europe, consisting of the member institutions in each of the regions, and a global COMNET Coordinating Committee (COMNET COC), consisting of one representative from each of the regional networks. The tasks of the COMNET COC are [40]:

- To formulate policies and provide the instruments necessary for the implementation, of COMNET activities, in accordance with the overall objectives of the network;
- To monitor compliance with the rules of membership among its member institutions, and provide a mechanism for negotiation and appeal in case of conflict;
- To encourage and facilitate inter-regional co-operation on matters of common concern to member institutions;
- To co-operate with other international organizations on matters directly concerned with the improvement of scientific communication and information exchange in the field of communication research, policy and practice; and
- To represent and further the interest of COMNET in relation to the international community at large.

In conformity with the general principles articulated by the COMNET COC, each regional network organizes its own membership and activities, according to the specific needs of the respective regions [40].

GINC

The Global Information Network on Chemicals (GINC) is a project to build a global information network that will link international, national, and other organizations working for the safe management of chemicals in order to exchange information and improve communications. WHO, ILO UNEP, and OECD, within the framework of the Inter-Organization Programme for the Sound Management of Chemicals (IOMC), with the support of the National Institute of Health Sciences

(NIHS Japan), initiated the project. The purpose of the GINC project is to foster generation and circulation of chemical-related information among all countries and international organizations for the promotion of chemical safety. The base system (http://www.nihs.go.jp/GINC/index.html) has been developed and maintained solely by the National Institute of Health Sciences (NIHS) of Japan, under the support of the Ministry of Health and Welfare (MHW), Japan. Asia, particularly East Asia and the Pacific region, was chosen as the feasibility study region for this project. GINC aims at promoting the collection of relevant locally generated information required for sound management of chemicals in countries. The GINC project is designed to link different individual projects carried out at international and national levels, to facilitate dialogue and exchange between them, thus promoting a global information network for sound chemical management. It also aims at enhancing the capacity of developing countries in establishing and operating their own chemical information systems and networking among themselves. GINC has three major elements:

- An institutional network with national, regional, and international components to sustain and exploit the system;
- A computerized network based on a distributed client/server architecture and making use of Internet platform, ensuring efficient information management and exchange; and
- At the center of the system will be chemical information of various types (e.g., chemical identification, hazard identification, physical/chemical properties, hazard and risk assessment, risk management, emergency response, emergency response, regulatory information) and from various sources, including international and national institutions as well as private sources.

In its initial phase, the project will not create new international information sources, but will make the best use of existing ones for the benefit of all users. The implementation will be at national, regional, and global levels, thus allowing direct feedback from the users regarding their needs and views. In the pilot phase undertaken in 1995, efforts were made to provide access to selected sources of chemical information using Internet and e-mail. Each of the international organizations is to set up its own homepage on Internet, providing information on the information sources they develop. At the regional level, work has been initiated among selected countries of the Asia and Pacific with a view to establishing facilities for information exchange [41,42].

HeLLIS

Health Literature Library and Information Services (HeLLIS), is a network system among the 10 member countries of WHO South-East Asia Region, viz., Bangladesh, Bhutan, DPR Korea, India, Indonesia, Maldives, Myanmar, Nepal, Sri Lanka, and Thailand. HeLLIS network was initiated in August 1979 by World Health Organization, with a vision to provide health literature to its member countries for upgrading their health services [43]. The HeLLIS network was organized into national networks with NFP coordinating activities at the national level and a regional network (served by SEARO) linking the national, regional, and international focal points and establishing liaison with other international organizations. To strengthen medical libraries, regional training programs for health science librarians were carried out. Following an evaluation of the network in 1984, it was agreed that further strengthening of its activities was needed, including links to other developing networks in this region. One of the main products of HeLLIS is Index Medicus for the South-East Asia Region (IMSEAR), a database of full-text scientific journal articles published in the region, currently with over 1,00,000 articles, made available through library contributions within SERO [44].

ISONET

ISONET is a global information network on standards sponsored by the International Organization for Standardization (ISO), Geneva. Launched in 1977, it is designed to promote the flow of information on standards, technical regulations, and related documents. It also aims at assistance in transfer of technology, reducing technical barriers to trade, and encouraging coordination on standards. ISONET is a decentralized information system. Each national member of ISONET is responsible for information about all documents valid within its territory which fall within the scope of ISONET. The ISO/IEC Information Centre in Geneva has a similar function for international documents. ISONET has 91 national members, seven international members and three associate members. Electronic links between information systems of ISONET members are provided via WSSN (World Standards Services Network), which is a network of publicly accessible World Wide Web servers of standards organizations around the world (URL: www.wssn.net). The objective of WSSN is to simplify access to international, regional, and national standards information available through the Web. WSSN aims to link the websites of members of WSSN and beyond, through links provided on the sites of WSSN members, into a comprehensive global network through which users can obtain the information they need about standards and related activities; provide a harmonized environment for users to navigate through. ISONET publishes a biannual newsletter entitles *ISONET Communique.* It has also brought out several important publications, such as ISONET Principles and procedures, ISONET Directory, ISONET Guide, ISONET Manual, and Directory of international standardizing bodies [45,46].

ISORID

The International Information System on Research in Documentation (ISORID) was set up by the Department of Documentation, Libraries and Archives of UNESCO in cooperation with FID in 1972 to collect, organize, analyze, and disseminate information research activities in the field of documentation, libraries, and archives for the use of research workers, documentalists, librarians, and archivists. As per UNESCO guidelines, ISORID covers [47]:

- Research projects and reports in the field of documentation, including doctoral dissertations and research reports in closely related fields applied to documentation, such as information system analysis and design, data banks, machine translation, etc.
- Reports of other selected activities of interest to research and development, which are not generally covered by abstracting and indexing services, such as state-of-the-art surveys, feasibility studies, and user studies.

The information on research projects and the reports of such projects are collected and sent to UNESCO secretariat in Paris by the institutions designated as National Information Transfer Centres (NITCs) by the respective governments. The Information are fed into the central ISORID information files and reports are filed in a depository. The NITCs are expected to maintain national information files on research projects and research reports and a national collection of research reports corresponding to those maintained centrally. Based on the central ISRID information files the ISORID office at UNESCO secretariat provides current awareness service, annual cumulative indexes, and computer-based information retrieval services and supplies copies of research reports.

POPIN

The Population Information Network (POPIN) is a joint project of the Population Division of the Department of International Economic and Social Affairs of the United Nations and the UN Fund for Population Activities (UNFPA). The network project, which was initiated in 1979, is a decentralized community of population institutions organized into global, regional, and national networks. The coordinating unit for the network is located in the UN Population Division at the UN headquarters, New York. POPIN strives to make international, regional, and national population information, particularly information available from United Nations sources, easily available to the international community. The following regional population networks have been set up so far by different regional organizations, under POPIN [48]:

- POPIN Africa-POPIA (Economic Commission for Africa);
- Asia-Pacific POPIN (Economic and Social Commission for Asia and the Pacific);
- IPALCA (Economic Commission for Latin America and the Caribbean);
- POPIN Europe (Economic Commission for Europe);
- POPIN Western Asia (Economic and Social Commission for Western Asia); and
- Northern American POPIN (Association for Population/Family Planning Libraries and Information Centers-International for Northern America).

POPIN hosts a dedicated website http://www.un.org/popin/home/about.html. The following bibliographic databases are maintained by the global and regional POPIN networks [48]:

- DOCPAL bibliographic database of citations to Latin American population literature. Produced by the Latin American Demographic Centre (CELADE) of the United Nations Economic Commission for Latin America and the Caribbean (ECLAC/CEPAL). It is also available in CD-ROM format from CELADE.
- EBIS POPFILE bibliographic database of citations to Asia-Pacific population literature. Produced by the Economic and Social Commission for Asia and the Pacific (ESCAP). It is also available on diskette from ESCAP.
- PADIS bibliographic database of citations to African population literature. Produced by the Economic Commission for Africa (ECA). It is also available on diskette from the ECA.

The following publications provide updates on POPIN activities [48]:

- *Population newsletter:* "POPIN Update" column includes information about Global POPIN activities at the United Nations Population Division. Published biannually by the Population Division/DESA;
- *Asia-Pacific POPIN bulletin:* Includes information and articles about POPIN activities in the Asia–Pacific region;
- *PADIS newsletter:* Includes information about POPIN and development activities in Africa and other regions. Published four times a year in English and French by the Pan African Development Information System (PADIS) of the United Nations ECA;
- *Boletin del PROLAP:* Includes information about POPIN activities in Latin America and the Caribbean. Published four times a year in Spanish by the Programa Latinoamericano de Actividades en Población, Buenos Aires, Argentina;
- *APLIC-international communicator:* Published periodically, it includes information about the activities of the Association for Population/Family Planning Libraries and Information Centers-International (APLIC-I), which serves as the Northern American POPIN.

RLIN

The Research Libraries Group consisting of major US research institutions, formed in 1974, operated a computerized bibliographic and technical processing network called the Research Libraries Information Network (RLIN). Its objectives were [11]:

- To work with and for its member organizations;
- To enhance members ability to provide research resources;
- To design and to deliver innovative information discovery services;
- To organize collaborative programs; and
- To take an active role in creating and promoting relevant standards and practices.

The RLG/RLIN had a number of web-accessible databases. The databases hold bibliographic information of traditional library materials, including books, journals, music, and maps. RLG/RLIN also provided access to indexes to archival collections, art and rare book auction catalogs, and digital images of works of art and cultural artifacts though its RLG Union Catalog. The *RLG Union Catalog* was the online database of RLG/RLIN contributed by many types of libraries and other institutions, like, national libraries, archives, museums, historical societies, book clubs, and international book vendors. This online database was the major source of bibliographic descriptions for use in research collections management. This database had records for about 130 million items contributed by 600 institutions, reflecting combined holdings of members of the Research Libraries Group, Inc. (RLG) and other RLIN users. It was a multidimensional database that covered many subjects, many types of material and as many as 400 languages. This collaborative database of research collections was being shared among member libraries to pool and share their holdings. In 1993, RLG developed Eureka as a user-friendly interface for use of the database by nonlibrarians. The multitude of this union catalog expedited the research and academic activities of participating institutions. However, in June 2006, RLG merged with OCLC. Its catalog became part of OCLC's WorldCat. Its current programs joined with OCLC Research to become OCLC Programmes and Research [12,49].

WLN

Western Library Network (WLN) was a successful bibliographic utility network started in early 1970s by the state of Washington (USA) as state-library-sponsored automation system "Washington Library Network" [50]. The WLN online system was introduced in 1975 and became fully operational in 1977. The WLN initially served 10 Washington libraries. It originally operated as a division of Washington State Library. It was renamed as "Western Library Network" in 1985. In 1988, WLN was converted to a private not-for-profit corporation. Throughout the late 1980s and early 1990s, WLN was a regional bibliographic utility network serving only western region of North America, particularly, the Pacific Northwest. Later it expanded to other states of the United States and Canada. In January 1999, it merged with Online Computer Library Center (OCLC) and became a part of *OCLC Western Service Center* [51]. Its union catalog records were added to OCLC's WorldCat. At that time WLN had 550 member libraries in the Pacific Northwest region of the United States and Canada [11].

V.6.2 National Information Systems

"A national information system is basically a network of existing information resources together with new services for identified gaps, so coordinated as to reinforce and enhance the activities of the individual units and thus enable specific categories of users to receive the information relevant to their needs and abilities" [3]. A national information system, obviously, has the responsibility of storing and disseminating the entire information output of a country. A few well-known national library/information systems, both conceptual and existing, are described below.

V.6.2.1 NATIS

The concept of National Information System (NATIS) was developed by UNESCO to encourage the creation in individual countries of a clear and coherent program and policy for recognizing the important elements in the nation's information systems and assigning priorities for their development [52]. The Inter-Governmental Conference on the Planning of National Documentation, Library, and Archive Infrastructure held in Paris in 1974 accepted the general concept of NATIS. The concept was approved at the eighteenth session of UNESCO General Conference held in Paris later that year, following which the program was launched. According to the objectives of NATIS, as adopted at the above Inter-Governmental Conference, "building up a national information system (NATIS) involves meeting basic requirements and establishing its foundation and planning the various phases of its implementation. Its action should be planned in an international context and based on principles of compatibility and standardization. The precise form and character of the national information system (NATIS), composed of a number of subsystems, will vary in different countries, but coordination of all its elements must be the goal. The elements that should constitute NATIS are all services involved in the provision of information for all sectors of the community and for all categories of users. The task of NATIS was to ensure that all engaged in political, economic scientific, educational, social, and cultural activities received the necessary information enabling them to render their fullest contribution to the whole community" [53,54]. The NATIS plan for any country should be developed keeping in view the objectives of its own national policy, specially information policy, the information needs of the country and the available resources and facilities and it should be implemented "taking into account the priorities of national over-all and sectoral planning" [53].

Characteristics of NATIS

There were four distinctive characteristics of the NATIS program [55]:

- NATIS embraced all fields and all disciplines at all levels and was applicable in all countries. Through the national component it had international applicability.

- NATIS recognized that the various processes and institutions involved in the transmission of knowledge and ideas were functionally interdependent, and that networks existed in formal and informal ways.
- NATIS was flexible. It took account of variations in national, political, social, economic, and cultural development and conditions, and was, therefore, applicable to developing, and industrialized countries alike.
- NATIS made possible the integrated planning of documentation, library, and archives services with the other elements in the national plan or policy, however articulated, such as national or area community development programs.

Structure of NATIS

A national information system usually has a multilevel structure and it functions through several units. The main links in a national network should be [3]:

- State authorities for planning and cooperation of the system of services in a country;
- A national center (or centers) for data, documentation, and referral;
- A network of specialized (subject or mission) information and data services;
- A national network of information collections; and
- Service centers to handle specialized materials and primary publication services.

Functions of NATIS

A national information system was expected to perform the following basic functions [3]:

- Collection and processing of primary information obtained through conventional and nonconventional channels;
- Collection, processing, and storage of primary documents (i.e., creation of stocks of reference materials);
- Dissemination of information to users on demand and in anticipation; and
- Smooth management and operation of the system.

In order that all the components of the sub-systems of a national information system can function in perfect harmony, it is necessary that they have "a common organizational structure, a single information retrieval language, suitable hardware (including interfaces), uniformity of software, a uniform method of selecting and processing ... information, uniformity of documentation and a standard method of coding" [56].

Current Status

Unfortunately, "the theoretical basis for NATIS had hardly been set out and the process of recognizing focal points had hardly been started, when yet another international information programme emerged—UNESCO's GIP, which replaced NATIS" [57]. Nevertheless, the GIP (General Information Programme) has since been again replaced by IFA (Information for All) Programme.

V.6.2.2 NISSAT

To meet the situation created by generation of information in a greater quantity and also big rise in demand for new information, several documentation, and information centers like INSDOC (now NISCAIR), DESIDOC, SENDOC, etc. came into existence in India after independence. These documentation centers have been providing documentation services in their respective fields and to limited groups of people. Their levels and standards of services differed and they worked in isolation without any relation or cooperation among them. This caused duplication of some work on the one hand and on the other some subject areas as well as a considerable portion of information-seekers remained uncovered. It was, therefore, felt that there should be a system through which everyone can access information.

Genesis of NISSAT

The National Committee on Science and Technology (NCST) first took up the initiative in this regard. An outline for a national information system was prepared by Dr. Peter Lazar, a UNESCO expert, at the request of the Council of Scientific and Industrial Research (CSIR). The final NISSAT plan, formulated on the basis of Dr. Lazar's outline was included in the Science and Technology Plan under the Fifth Five-Year Plan. NISSAT was finally launched in 1977. "In tune with the changing global scenario and in pursuance of the national efforts in liberalization and globalization of the economy, NISSAT reoriented its programme activities continually in order to be useful to a wider base of clientele in diverse subjects" [58].

Objectives of NISSAT

The broad objectives of NISSAT were [55]:
- Development of national information services;
- Promotion of existing information systems and services;
- Introduction of modern information handling tools and techniques;
- Promotion of international cooperation in information;
- Development of indigenous products and services;

- Organization of skill development programs; and
- Promotion of R&D in Information Science and Technology.

It was also envisaged in the NISSAT plan that the system would provide particular attention to the development of the following [58]:

- A national science information policy;
- Techno-economic information facilities for management and decision making and on the application of modern computer and reprography technology to information work;
- Information services in new areas, capable of supporting economic, and social development;
- Coordinated policy for the information system of all sectors of national activity;
- National plans for important types of information services, especially mechanical services;
- Information services at all levels (local, branch, regional, and national); and
- A national network of mission-oriented centers of information.

Organizational Features

According to the original plan, the components of NISSAT would be some existing information centers as well as some new ones to be created to fill up the lacuna in some areas. These units would function under various types of ownership and would be run and developed by their respective parent bodies. But all of them would work in close cooperation with each other under a coordinating body toward a common goal. The organizational structure envisaged for NISSAT was as follows:

NISSAT
↓
National Information Centers (NCs)
(such as INSDOC, National Science Library, National Medical Library, SENDOC, DESIDOC)
↓
Branch or Sectoral Information Centers (BCs)
(to be set up in various fields like food, leather, transport, fertilizer, aeronautics, etc.)
↓
Local Information Units (LIUs)
(i.e. centers in individual organizations like Hindustan Aeronautics, Thumba Equatorial Rocket Launching Station, etc.)

Besides, some regional information centers could be set up by any National Information Center.

Main Functions

The main functions of NISSAT, as envisaged in the original plan, had to be changed to some extent in the context of changing situation. The latest activities of NISSAT were [59]:

- Strengthening of information services through information centers in science and technology, value added patent information services, national access centers to international database services, CDROM database facilities etc.;
- Development of an Indian S&T Web server Vigyan (i.e., science) covering a variety of Indian S&T information and establishment of an Internet School;
- Development of Indian websites on specific sectors like Tea, Ocean Data, Food and Technology, IPR Law, IPR on Biotechnology etc.;
- Promotion of information resource sharing in Science and Technology through city-based library and information networks with emphasis on web-based information content development;
- Development of skills in entire gamut of library and information activities and promotion of indigenous database development activities;
- Implementation of a National Plan of action on Scientometrics/ Bibliometrics and conducting of a series of R&D studies;
- Distribution and technical backup services on internationally developed software CDS/ISIS, MINISIS and IDAMS and development and promotion of CDS/ISIS-based products like SANJAY;
- Coordination of international activities in collaboration with UNESCO and ASTINFO;
- Development of information market—marketing of information, revenue generation, industry-user interaction etc.—and publication of the NISSAT Newsletter "Information Today and Tomorrow."

Progress of Work

The work done by NISSAT till the financial year 2002–03 were [59]:

- *National information centers:* NISSAT established 14 national information centers in specific sectors like Leather Technology, Drugs and Pharmaceuticals, Food Technology, Machine Tools Production and Engineering, Textiles and Allied Subjects, Chemicals and Allied Industries, Advanced Ceramics, Crystallography, Bibliometrics, etc. The information centers were usually built around the existing information resources and facilities.

- *Virtual information center:* A virtual Information Center at ICICI Knowledge Park, Hyderabad, was set up under a three-year project for providing a gateway to existing information centers and fast and reliable access to information and interaction among industry, academia and public research institutions in the area of Science and Technology.
- *Knowledge network:* NISSAT initiated a project for a Knowledge Network using local language electronic database. The objective of the project was to collect, document and digitize innovations and examples of outstanding traditional knowledge mainly from rural areas, organize these in a multimedia database, translate the information in local languages and establish a mechanism for dissemination and sharing of information on innovations.
- *National Access Centres to International Database Services (NACID):* NISSAT established 11 NACID facilities in Ahmadabad, Bangalore, Kolkata, Chennai, Delhi, Hyderabad, Mumbai, Pune, Thiruvananthapuram, Guwahati, and Bhopal for providing online facility to access international database services such as Dialog and STN databases.
- *National server on factual science and technology information:* The aim of this project was to collect and collate factual information from diverse sources, and host these on a server christened VIGYAN (http://www. vigyan.org.in) for national and international access. Indian Institute of Science, Bangalore, set up the server and managed the operations.
- *National websites on S&T subjects:* NISSAT initiated creation of several national websites for national and international access, such as websites on Intellectual Property Rights (http://www.iprlawindia.org), Knowledge Management (http://www.kmindia.org), Indian Traditional Textile Design (http://www.indiantextiledesign.com), Food Science and Technology (http://www.mylibnet.org), etc.
- *Vidyanidhi database:* Vidyanidhi was an information infrastructure, a digital library, a portal of resources, tools and facilities for doctoral research in India. Vidyanidhi was envisioned to evolve as a national repository and a consortium for e-theses through participation and partnership with universities, academic institutions and other stake holders. Vidyanidhi was created at Mysore University with the support of NISSAT.
- *E-publishing of scholarly journals:* With the help of NISSAT, Indian National Science Academy started converting the back volumes of its journal in e-format and established a mechanism to publish the current

journals also in e-format. INSA was expected to help other organizations in this matter in future.

- *Database development activities:* NISSAT completed 11 database development projects such as Biographical database of Indian Scientists, Directory of Libraries and Information Centres in Gujarat, databases on Virus and Virology, Directory of S&T institutions in India, S.R. Ranganathan's works and letters, Database on Folk Wisdom, etc.

- *Information resource sharing:* NISSAT took initiatives in setting up library networks in Kolkata, Delhi, Mumbai, Pune, Ahmadabad and Mysore for promoting resource-sharing activities to ensure better utilization of S&T information resources, minimization of functional load of information centers and encouragement of motivational factors to a large extent.

- *I T applications:* NISSAT acquired proven software packages like CDS/ISIS for bibliographic information processing and retrieval and IDAMS for statistical data processing and obtained the official rights for distribution of the two packages in India from UNESCO. Around 2000 libraries installed CDDS/ISIS, while around 100 organizations installed IDAMS. NISSAT also developed an integrated library management package "Sanjay" to help the libraries and information centers in India, which was adopted by 65 institutions.

- *Skill development:* NISSAT encouraged and supported a variety of manpower development programs which covered topics such as CDS/ISIS, WINISIS, Internet and Web Designing, TQM in Library Services, Patent Information for R&D and Industry, and ISO 9000 Quality Management System.

- *Post-graduate course on information and knowledge management:* A post-graduate course on information and knowledge management was designed in collaboration with National Centre for Science Information (NCSI) and Indian Institute of Science, Bangalore, to evolve a model that could fill in the gap in professional manpower demand and supply and could be replicated elsewhere.

- *Model for web-driven distance education:* NISSAT, in collaboration with Indira Gandhi National Open University, New Delhi, initiated a project to evolve a model that would include online lectures, chat, discussions with experts, online submission, and evaluation of exercises, etc.

- *National mapping of science:* In consultation with and active participation of subject specialists, NISSAT formulated a plan of action for scientometric and informetric studies in India. As a first step in the implementation of a program of coordinated research, ten projects on National Mapping of Science using CAB, Compendex, Inspec, Science Citation Index, MEDLINE Plus, BIOSIS, EMBASE, Georef, CAB, Agricola, and Indian Science Abstracts were taken up.

- *Other studies:* NISSAT also promoted and supported research and development and survey studies. NISSAT completed a study on "Assessment of Information Needs of Small and Medium Enterprises in MP and setting up of information centres for fulfilling those needs." Two other studies on "Food Informatics and Training Opportunities in Food Technology Networking (FITOFTN) and Digital library of Natural History of Collections were also taken up."
- *Publications:* NISSAT had been bringing out its *NISSAT Newsletter*—a quarterly newsletter, since the beginning of the program. It was later renamed as *Information Today & Tomorrow (ITI)* and its contents were augmented in changing information scenario. The newsletter was being distributed free to 5000 individuals and institutions. The last issue of the newsletter was published in 2002.

Closure of Project

Unfortunately, the NISSAT Project was not included as a component of the Tenth Five-Year Plan by the Planning Commission. Consequently, the project was closed by the end of financial year 2002–03. Though, it has not been possible to provide financial assistance to many of the schemes under NISSAT, some have continued by obtaining funds from other sources.

V.6.2.3 ENVIS

Environmental information plays a vital role not only in formulating environmental management policies but also in the decision-making process aiming at environmental protection and improvement of environment for sustaining good quality of life for the living beings. Realizing this importance of environmental information, the Government of India, in December 1982, established an Environmental Information System (ENVIS) as a plan program. The focus of ENVIS since inception has been on providing environmental information to decision makers, policy planners, scientists and engineers, research workers, etc. all over the country [60].

Objectives of ENVIS

ENVIS has some long-term as well as some short-term objectives. These objectives are [61]:

Long-term objectives:

- To build up a repository and dissemination center in Environmental Science and Engineering;
- To enable application of modern technologies of acquisition, processing, storage, retrieval, and dissemination of information of environmental nature; and
- To support and promote research, development, and innovation in environmental information technology.

Short-term objectives:

- To provide national environmental information service relevant to present needs and capable of development to meet the future needs of the users, originators, processors, and disseminators of information;
- To build up storage, retrieval, and dissemination capabilities with the ultimate objectives of disseminating information speedily to the users;
- To promote national and international cooperation and liaison for exchange of environment-related information;
- To promote, support, and assist education and personnel training programs designed to enhance environmental information processing and utilization capabilities; and
- To promote exchange of information amongst developing countries.

Structure of ENVIS

Since environment is a broad-ranging, multidisciplinary subject, a comprehensive information system on environment would necessarily involve effective participation of concerned institutions/organizations in the country that are actively engaged in work relating to different subject areas of environment. ENVIS is, therefore, being developed as a decentralized system with a distributed network of such participating institutions/organizations serving as nodes, ensuring integration of national efforts in environmental information collection, collation, storage, retrieval, and dissemination to all concerned. The Focal Point of the network is located in the Ministry of Environment and Forests, Government of India. ENVIS has already established 81 partner nodes, known as ENVIS centres, out of proposed 85 nodes, which include 30 government departments, 36 institutions, and 15 NGOs. These centers have been set up in the areas of pollution control, toxic chemicals, central and offshore ecology, environmentally sound and appropriate technology, bio-degradation of wastes and environment management, etc. [60].

Functions of ENVIS

Both the Focal Point as well as the ENVIS centers have been assigned various responsibilities for achieving the objectives of ENVIS. The broad responsibilities of the Focal Point and ENVIS centers are [60]:

Focal point: The focal point ensures integration of national efforts in environmental information collection, collation, storage, and retrieval. Its specific responsibilities are:

- Overall coordination of ENVIS network;
- Identification of ENVIS centers in specialized areas, their location in selected institutes/organizations and their linkage with the Focal Point;
- Farming guidelines and uniform designing procedures for ENVIS centers;
- Collection, storage, retrieval, and dissemination of information on areas in which ENVIS centers have not been established and in some general areas of environment like environmental research, environmental policy and management, environmental legislation, environmental impact assessment, etc.; responding to user queries directly or through the ENVIS centers;
- Establishment of Data Bank containing data on some selected parameters, and computerization in important application areas of environment;
- Identification of data gaps and knowledge gaps in specified subject areas and action to fill these gaps;
- Liaison with relevant international information systems and other national information systems;
- Publication of a quarterly abstracting journal *Paryavaran Abstracts* (i.e., Environment Abstracts);
- Bringing out various on current awareness publications;
- Organizing training and seminars;
- Monitoring and reviewing of ENVIS; and
- Assisting the Scientific Advisory Committee of ENVIS with inputs and rendering other secretarial help.

ENVIS centers: ENVIS centers serve as interface for the users on the assigned subject. Their specific responsibilities are [60]:

- Building up a good collection of books, reports and journals in the particular subject area of environment;
- Establishment of linkages with all information sources in the particular subject area of environment;
- Responding to user queries;
- Establishment of a data bank on some selected parameters relating to the subject area;

- Coordination with the Focal Point for supplying relevant, adequate, and timely information to the users;
- Helping the Focal Point in gradually building up an inventory of information material available at the center; identification of information gaps in the specified subject areas and action to fill these gaps; and
- Bringing out newsletters/publications in their subject area for wide dissemination.

Special Tasks

ENVIS, due to its comprehensive network, has been designated as the National Focal Point (NFP) for INFOTERRA, a global environmental information network of the United Nations Environment Programme (UNEP). In order to strengthen the information activities of the NFP, ENVIS was designated as the Regional Service Centre (RSC) of INFOTERRA of UNEP in 1985 for the South Asia Sub-Region countries. ENVIS has also started implementing the World Bank assisted Environment Management Capacity Building Technical Assistance Project (EMCBTAP) since January 2002, which aims at structuring the ENVIS scheme by extending its reach through involvement of institutions/organizations in State Governments, academia sector, corporate sector, NGO sector, etc. The project also aims at broadening the ambit of ENVIS to include varying subject areas, themes, local conditions, issues, information/data needs of the country pertaining to environment and planned to be achieved through enlargement of participatory organizations/institutions, called EMCB-Nodes in various sectors and through introduction of ICT [60].

V.6.2.4 BTISnet

India is the first country in the world to establish a national bioinformatics network. This network, known as Biotechnology Information System Network (BTISnet), was launched during 1986–87, by the Department of Biotechnology, Government of India. BTISnet is a distributed network covering 168 bioinformatics centers spread across the country. The BTISnet is also the first network which established BioGrid India of large bandwidth and high speed network connectivity among various institutions in the country and also setting of high performance national computing facility.

Objectives of BTISnet

The broad objectives of Biotechnology Information System Network program are [62]:

- To provide a national bio-information network designed to bridge the interdisciplinary gaps on biotechnology information and establish link among scientists in organizations involved in R&D and manufacturing activities in the country.
- To build information resources, to prepare databases on biotechnology, and to develop relevant information handling tools and techniques.
- To continuously assess information requirements, to create and improve necessary infrastructure, and to provide informatics based support and services to the national community of users working in biotechnology and allied areas.
- To coordinate efforts to access Biotechnology information worldwide including establishing linkages with some of the international resources of Biotechnology information (e.g., databanks on genetic materials, published literature, patents, and other information of scientific and commercial value).
- To undertake research into advanced methods of computer-based information processing for analyzing the structure and function of biologically important molecules.
- To evolve and implement programs on education of users and training of information scientists responsible for handling of biotechnology information and its applications to biotechnology research and development.
- To establish regional and international cooperation for exchange of scientific information and expertise in biotechnology through the development of appropriate network arrangements.
- To build networking capabilities of BTISnet in terms of speed and capacity of the network to make fast Internet access feasible at all nodes of the network.

Structure of BTISnet

BTISnet has its apex BTIS center in New Delhi, with network centers at various levels as shown below [62]:

Biotechnology Information Center (Apex Network Center)
↓
Centers of Excellence
↓
Bioinformatics Centers (Distributed Information Centers)
↓
Bioinformatics Centers (Distributed Information Sub-centers)
↓
Bioinformatics Infrastructure Facilities

These centers have been established on modern lines with computer facilities to provide bibliographic, SDI, and current awareness services, in addition to providing several research tools such as nucleic acid and protein sequence databases. The centers have been networked through satellite and terrestrial links provided by NICNET. The entire network has emerged as a very sophisticated scientific infrastructure for bioinformatics involving state-of-the-art computational and communication facilities.

- *Apex network center:* The Biotechnology Information Centre (BTIC), the apex network center located at the Department of Biotechnology, Government of India, in New Delhi, coordinates the activities of the network. The center hosts a home page on the activities of the Department of Biotechnology and its major programs, as well as maintains several directories and databases on the research projects funded by this department. A Biotechnology Patent Facilitating Cell has recently been established which uses the facilities of the BTIC to provide full scale patent search services.

- *Centres of Excellence (CoE):* Six Centres of Excellence (CoE) in Bioinformatics and Computational Biology have been established as part of BTISnet. These centers are well equipped with state-of-the-art Bioinformatics infrastructure to support research within the Institute as well as neighboring institutions. The focus of these centers is high-quality research education and services. These centers are located at Bose Institute, Kolkata; Indian Institute of Science, Bangalore; Jawaharlal Nehru University, New Delhi; Madurai Kamaraj University, Madurai; University of Pune, Pune; and Centre for Cellular and Molecular Biology, Hyderabad.

- *Distributed Information Centres (DIC):* Eleven Distributed Information Centres (DICs) in Bioinformatics and Computational Biology have been established with the task of providing discipline-oriented information to all institutions belonging to the branch as well as other institutions and individual users interested in particular subject related to Biotechnology. The focus of these centers, like that of CoEs, is high-quality research, education, and services. These centers are located at IARI, New Delhi; Kerala Agricultural University, Thrissur; National Institute of Immunology, New Delhi; University of Calcutta, Kolkata; Anna University, Chennai; Institute of Microbial Technology, Chandigarh; M. S. University of Baroda, Baroda; National Brain Research Centre, Manesar, Gurgaon; North Eastern Hill University, Shillong; Pondicherry University, Puducherry; and Centre for Cellular & Molecular Biology, Hyderabad.

- *Sub-Distributed Information Center (DISCs):* Fifty sub-DICs have been established at various institutions/universities. These centers were mainly established with the aim to provide service to the research community. However, these centers are now also imparting training in bioinformatics through workshops. Many centers have now ventured in bioinformatics related R&D activities and have also developed information resources in the form of Databases.
- *Bioinformatics Infrastructure Facilities (BIFs):* The aim of these centers is biology and biotechnology teaching through bioinformatics. The scheme is designed to expose teachers, scientists, and students to the use of bioinformatics in solving hard core biological problems. The centers use lecture materials, video clippings, demonstrations, tutorials, and online facilities for teaching. Hundred and one educational institutions have so far been supported under this scheme and some more are in pipeline.

Activities of BTISnet

The BTISnet permits remote login, file transfer, e-mail, etc. as well as connecting to various international networks which are providing up-to-date information support on all aspects in biotechnology ranging from bibliographic information to sequence analysis and management information. Besides providing bibliographic, SDI, and current awareness services, through its website and information centers at different levels, BTISnet also promotes education and research in the field of biotechnology and bioinformatics. Its different activities are [62]:

- *BTISnet website:* The BTISnet through its website with URL *http://*www.btisnet.gov.in provides a central resource to all the bioinformatics centers in respect of the work done by each one of them in the area of bioinformatics. Through this site, the BTIC provides all information such as budget release, status of submission of accounts and progress report by the BTISnet centers. The site provides a list of open access journals, details of the fellowships provided through the bioinformatics division like BINC, studentship and traineeship, access to online lecture portals and their links, announcements of the national bioinformatics coordinators meetings and its proceedings, bioinformatics publications from India and the bioinformatics resources like software and databases. Several home pages have been hosted on the Internet to give details of the services being provided to the scientific community.

- *Facilities for molecular modeling:* Six national facilities have been set up for interactive graphics-based molecular modeling and other bio-computational needs. Four long-term courses at the level of post M.Sc. Diploma in Bioinformatics, at Pune University, Jawaharlal Nehru University, Calcutta University, and Madurai Kamaraj University, are fulfilling the long outstanding need for trained human resources in this interdisciplinary area.

- *Database searching:* More than 100 databases dealing with different aspects and of relevance to R&D efforts in biotechnology are now available on the network. A national node of EMBnet (European Molecular Biology Network) has been established at the Centre of DNA Fingerprinting and Diagnostics (CDFD), Hyderabad.

- *Mirror sites:* Four mirror sites for mirroring important biological databases are being established at IISc, JNU, Pune University, and IMTECH to promote and support R&D activities in Genomics and Proteomics, the two emerging fields of biotechnology requiring critical support of genomic databases.

- *Bio-computing facilities:* Six bio-computing facilities under the umbrella of "National Facilities on Interactive Graphics and Molecular Modeling" have been established with the task of providing discipline wise facilities to the scientists working in the area of molecular structure modeling, 3D structures, active site modeling, crystal structures, conformational analysis, protein and DNA structures and interactions, homology studies, and like.

- *Supercomputing facility*: A high-end data center with supercomputing facility has been established at IIT, Delhi. This facility is accessed by student and scientists all over the country.

- *Human resource development:* Madurai Kamaraj University, Madurai, Pondicherry University, Puducherry, and Anna University, Chennai have initiated a network program on higher education in "M.Sc. Computational Biology" on consortium basis. The classes are being conducted through video conferencing and virtual class room approaches. Besides, basic understanding and hands on experience in the area of Bioinformatics is provided to the researchers and students, by each of the BTISnet center by conducting one or more short-term training programs each year.

- *Open access newsletter:* An open access newsletter BIOBYTES of BTISnet has been started in 2006. The newsletter is compiled by COE/MKU Madurai. BIOBYTES is meant to serve as a medium of continuous update of ideas and information. It will also provide news, views, and information regarding the current scenario in the areas related to bioinformatics and biotechnology both at the national and international level. The BIOBYTES is accessible through URL http://biobytes.bicmku.in

- *Other publications:* BRSnet has also brought out a *Compendium of Bioinformatics and Computational Biology Publications from India*, compiled by Prof. M. Vijayan and other important publications relating to its area of work.

NEBInet

Under the special drive to strengthen the North Eastern States of the country a North-Eastern Bioinformatics Network (NEBInet) consisting of 29 Bioinformatics centers was established across eight states. NEBInet has 1 DIC (at North-Eastern Hill University, Shillong), 2 DISCs (at the Institute of Bioresources and Sustainable Development, Imphal, and Sikkim State Council of Science and Technology, Gangtok), and 26 BIFs (at various universities, colleges, and institutions) [62].

V.6.2.5 INFLIBNET

Information and Library Network (INFLIBNET) Centre is an autonomous Inter-University Centre of the University Grants Commission (UGC) of India. INFLIBNET is a major National Programme initiated by the UGC in 1991 with its headquarters at Gujarat University Campus, Ahmadabad. Initially started as a project under the Inter-University Centre for Astronomy and Astrophysics, (IUCAA), Pune, it became an independent Inter-University Centre in 1996. INFLIBNET is involved in modernizing university libraries in India and connecting them as well as other information centers in the country through a nation-wide high-speed data network using the state-of-the-art technologies for the optimum utilization of information [64,65].

Objectives of INFLIBNET

The primary objectives of INFLIBNET as envisaged in Memorandum of Association are [65]:

- To promote and establish communication facilities to improve capability in information transfer and access, that provide support to scholarship, learning, research, and academic pursuit through cooperation and involvement of agencies concerned.

- To establish INFLIBNET: Information and Library Network a computer communication network for linking libraries and information centers in universities, deemed to be universities, colleges, UGC information centers, institutions of national importance, R&D institutions, etc. avoiding duplication of efforts to:
    - Promote and implement computerization of operations and services in the libraries and information centers of the country, following a uniform standard;
    - Evolve standards and uniform guidelines in techniques, methods, procedures, computer hardware and software, services and promote their adoption in actual practice by all libraries, in order to facilitate pooling, sharing and exchange of information toward optimal use of resources and facilities;
    - Evolve a national network interconnecting various libraries and information centers in the country and to improve capability in information handling and service;
    - Provide reliable access to document collection of libraries by creating on-line union catalog of serials, theses/dissertations, books, monographs and nonbook materials (manuscripts, audio–visuals, computer data, multimedia, etc.) in various libraries in India;
    - Provide access to bibliographic information sources with citations, abstracts, etc. Through indigenously created databases of the sectoral information centers of NISSAT, UGC information centers, city networks, and such others and by establishing gateways for on-line accessing of national and international databases held by national and international information networks and centers, respectively;
    - Develop new methods and techniques for archival of valuable information available as manuscripts and information documents in difference Indian languages, in the form of digital images using high density storage media;
    - Optimize information resource utilization through shared cataloguing, inter-library loan service, catalog production, collection development and thus avoiding duplication in acquisition to the extent possible;
    - Enable the users dispersed all over the country, irrespective of location and distance, to have access to information regarding serials, theses/dissertation, books, monographic and nonbook materials by locating the sources wherefrom available and to obtain it through the facilities of INFLIBNET and union catalog of documents;

- Create databases of projects, institutions, specialists, etc. for providing on-line information service;
- Encourage co-operation among libraries, documentation centers and information centers in the country, so that the resources can be poled for the benefit of helping the weaker resource centers by stronger ones; and
- Train and develop human resources in the field of computerized library operations and networking to establish, manage, and sustain INFLIBNET.

- To facilitate academic communication amongst scientist, engineers, social scientists, academics, faculties, researchers, and students through electronic mail, file transfer, computer/audio/video conferencing, etc.;
- To undertake system design and studies in the field of communications, computer networking, information handling, and data management;
- To establish appropriate control and monitoring system for the communication network and organize maintenance;
- To collaborate with institutions, libraries, information centers, and other organizations in India and abroad in the field relevant to the objectives of the center;
- To promote R&D and develop necessary facilities and create technical positions for realizing the objectives of the center;
- To generate revenue by providing consultancies and information services; and
- To do all other such things as may be necessary, incidental, or conducive to the attainment of all or any of the above objectives.

Mission and Vision of INFLIBNE

The mission and vision of INFLIBNET are [65]:

- Leveraging on the latest technology, create a virtual network of people and resources in academic institutions with an aim to provide effective and efficient access to knowledge through perseverance, innovation, and collaboration;
- Provide seamless, reliable, and ubiquitous access to scholarly, peer-reviewed electronic resources to the academic community in all educational institutions with a focus on services and tools, processes and practices that support its effective use and increase value of this information;

- Build and strengthen ICT infrastructure in educational institutions with value-added services;
- Develop tools, techniques, and procedures for secure and convenient access management enabling users to access information in electronic format from anywhere, anytime;
- Develop resource selection guides and online tutorials for effective delivery and usage of e-resources;
- Facilitate creation of open-access digital repository in every educational institution for hosting educational and research contents created by that institution.

Goals of INFLIBNET

The goals of INFLIBNET are [65]:

- Achieve complete automation of libraries in educational institutions;
- Create union catalogs of documents available in libraries in online and real-time environment;
- Provide seamless and ubiquitous access to scholarly, peer-reviewed electronic resources to the universities;
- Promote digitization of legacy documents and creation of content in e-format (including electronic theses and dissertations, electronic version of research articles, working papers, technical reports, concept papers, technical reports, annual reports, statistical data, etc.) in universities;
- Promote setting up of open access digital repositories in universities for hosting content created in the process mentioned above;
- Develop expertise in:
  - Digital content creation;
  - Process of digitization; and
  - Managing digital depositories.
- Impart training in applications on various aspects of new technology to achieve goals mentioned above.

Functions of INFLIBNET

In order to achieve the above goals INFLIBNET undertakes the following functions [65]:

- Promote and implement computerization of operations and services in the libraries and information centers of the country, following a uniform standard;

- Evolve standards and uniform guidelines in techniques, methods, procedures, computer hardware and software, services and promote their adoption in actual practice by all libraries, in order to facilitate pooling, sharing and exchange of information toward optimal use of resources and facilities;
- Evolve a national network interconnecting various libraries and information centers in the country and to improve capability in information handling and service;
- Provide reliable access to document collection of libraries by creating on-line union catalog of serials, theses/dissertations, books, monographs, and nonbook materials (manuscripts, audio-visuals, computer data, multimedia, etc.) in various libraries in India;
- Provide access to bibliographic information sources with citations, abstracts etc. through indigenously created databases of the Sectoral Information Centres of NISSAT, UGC Information Centres, City Networks, and such others and by establishing gateways for on-line accessing of national and international databases held by national and international information networks and centers, respectively;
- Develop new methods and techniques for archival of valuable information available as manuscripts and information documents in different Indian Languages, in the form of digital images using high density storage media;
- Optimize information resource utilization through shared cataloguing, inter-library loan service, catalog production, collection development, and thus avoiding duplication in acquisition to the extent possible;
- Enable the users dispersed all over the country, irrespective of location and distance, to have access to information regarding serials, theses/dissertations, books, monographs, and nonbook materials by locating the sources wherefrom available and to obtain it through the facilities of INFLIBNET and union catalog of documents;
- Create databases of projects, institutions, specialists, etc. for providing on-line information service;
- Encourage co-operation among libraries, documentation centers, and information centers in the country, so that the resources can be pooled for the benefit of helping the weaker resource centers by stronger ones;
- Train and develop human resources in the field of computerized library operations and networking to establish, manage, and sustain INFLIBNET;

- Facilitate academic communication amongst scientists, engineers, social scientists, academics, faculties, researchers, and students through electronic mail, file transfer, computer/audio/video conferencing, etc.;
- Undertake system design and studies in the field of communications, computer networking, information handling, and data management;
- Establish appropriate control and monitoring system for the communication network and organize maintenance;
- Collaborate with institutions, libraries, information centers and other organizations in India and abroad in the field relevant to the objectives of the center;
- Create and promote R&D and other facilities and technical positions for realizing the objectives of the center.
- Generate revenue by providing consultancies and information services;
- Do all other such things as may be necessary, incidental or conducive to the attainment of all or any of the above objectives.

Activities of INFLIBNET

The activities of INFLIBNET are [65]:

- *Document delivery service:* INLIBNET has initiated inter-library loans and document delivery services from the comprehensive collection of subscribed journals under JCCC@UGC- INFONET. INFLIBNET has designated 22 libraries as document delivery centers to fulfill inter-library loan (ILL) requests from the users, affiliated to 149 universities covered under UGC. The ILL libraries together subscribe for 2000 plus journals that is not available through consortia. Universities can request for articles from the journal holdings of those libraries wherever they find useful articles in JCCC search, that are not available in that library.
- *Databases creation:* Creation of databases is one of the major activities of INFLIBNET. This activity has been initiated since inception of the program. Currently there are eight databases under development. These are grouped under following two categories: Bibliographic Databases—Serials Holdings, Current Serials, Secondary Serials Catalogue, Theses, Books; Nonbibliographic Databases—Research Projects, *Vidwan*: Expert Database. The bibliographic databases represent the holdings of university libraries, for which the data is contributed by participating libraries. These databases provide an access to large pool of information available besides, serving as tool for resource sharing. Nonbibliographic databases are created to promote the communication among the scholars.

- *Infonet connectivity program*: The UGC-Infonet Connectivity Programme, was inaugurated in December 2002 for maintaining high standards in university education with aim to bring qualitative changes in the academic infrastructure for delivering the e-resources subscribed through the UGC-Infonet Digital Library Consortium to the academic community on the campuses. Under this initiative, each university was provided Internet bandwidth with dedicated IP addresses through a national level ISP. The network was switched to BSNL backbone w.e.f. 1st April 2010 and renamed as UGC Infonet 2.0. The scheme was closed on 31st March 2012 and all universities were migrated to NKN National Knowledge Network (NKN)/National Mission on Education through Information and Communication Technology (NME-ICT) project. About 200 universities were connected to the network till December 2011.
- *Infonet digital library consortium:* The UGC-Infonet Digital Library Consortium provides current as well as archival access to more than 7500 core and peer-reviewed journals and 11 bibliographic databases from 25 publishers including commercial publishers, scholarly societies, university presses, and aggregators in different disciplines. At present 209 universities are being provided differential access to subscribed e-resources covering almost all subjects.
- *Service to walk-in users:* The center has 15 Internet-enabled PCs dedicated for the use of students and researchers for accessing electronic resources subscribed under the UGC-Infonet Digital Library Consortium. All the e-resources signed under license agreements with the publishers of UGC-Infonet Digital Library Consortium provide access to walk-in users.
- *Library services:* The INFLIBNET Centre has a small, specialized library consisting of 2000 documents on computer, communication, information and library science. The library is fully computerized using SOUL integrated library management software. The collection of the library is available online through the web OPAC facility of the SOUL. Its services include reference service, document delivery service, current awareness service, electronic information service, and CD-ROM base search service.
- *Institutional repository:* INFLIBNET has set up an institutional repository named IR@INFLIBNET using DSpace open source software to host full-text research publications in the field of LIS. It provides a platform for researchers in LIS to deposit, reuse and share their

research publications. All the articles published in the proceedings of CALIBERs and PLANNERs as also full-text of research articles of technical staff and other publications of the center are available in the repository. The repository also has the ability to capture, index, store, disseminate, and preserve digital materials created in the center.

- *E-Journal archival library (print version):* Besides receiving access to e-resources on complementary basis under the UGC-INFONET Digital Library Consortium, the center maintains a separate Archival Library consisting of print journals received as a part of the agree-ment with the participating publishers of the UGC-INFONET Digital Library Consortium. Under the agreement, the publishers are requested to submit a copy of all the issues of the journals. This archi-val library is open to all users interested in using these print resources for their study or research.

- *Software development:* INFLIBNET has designed and developed the *Software for University Libraries (SOUL)*, a state-of-the-art integrated library management software, suitable for college and university librar-ies. The software has been installed in about 1700 libraries in the coun-try. The center has established region-wise SOUL Support Services by deploying SOUL Coordinators. A dedicated team of scientists at INFLIBNET is also working on a middleware open source tech-nology, called *Shibboleth*—a standard-based open source middleware software that provides web single sign-on (SSO) access to subscribed e-resources across or within organizational boundaries. It allows web-sites to make informed authorization decisions for individual access to protected online resources maintaining the privacy.

- *Theses repository:* INFLIBNET has developed a PhD theses repository *Sodhganga*, to make those available to the scholarly community in open access. The repository has the ability to capture, index, store, dissemi-nate and preserve ETDs submitted by the researchers. Over 7000 the-ses accepted for PhD degree in more than 115 universities have so far been uploaded.

- *Open journal access system:* INFLIBNET took an initiative, named "OJS@INFLIBNET" (now changed to OJAS), to encourage universi-ties and institutions that are publishing journals in print format to use OJAS for hosting electronic version of their journals free-of-cost on servers at the INFLIBNET Centre. The Open Journal System (OJS), an open source solution developed by the Public Knowledge Project, facilitates hosting of electronic version of journals into open access mode with all processes of submission, peer-reviewing, editing, layout designing, and publishing built into it. The initiative also encourages faculty in universities to start their own open access journals using the platform. Journals hosted on OJAS are freely accessible. At present nine primary journals and all parts of *ICSSR Indian Psychological Abstracts and Reviews* can be accessed.

- *N-LIST project:* Project entitled "National Library and Information Services Infrastructure for Scholarly Content" (N-LIST), being jointly executed by the UGC-Infonet Digital Library Consortium, INFLIBNET Centre, and the INDEST-AICTE Consortium, IIT Delhi, provides for access to scholarly content to colleges, universities, as well as to centrally funded technical institutions. N-LIST has registered a total number of 1799 colleges.
- *Subject gateway for Indian E-resources:* The INFLIBNET Centre promotes open access to Indian scholarly content through the InfoPort: A subject gateway for Indian Electronic-Resources. The gateway open-ups the Indian scholarly content scattered over the Internet through an integrated interface that support search, browse and multiple listing. The center intends to collaborate with librarians and scholars in college and universities in the process of identification and selection of resources.
- *Conventions on automation:* INFLIBNET, in collaboration with different universities, regularly organizes two conventions—Convention on Automation of Libraries in Education and Research Institutions (CALIBER) and Promotion of Library Automation and Networking in North-Eastern Region (PLANNER).
- *Publications:* The INFLIBNET Centre regularly publishes *Current Report: The* annual report of the center; quarterly *INFLIBNET Newsletter*, Proceedings of Annual Conventions PLANNER and CALIBER; and *INFLIBNET Directory*, which includes information about the UGC funded universities and Inter-University Centres with year planner. Besides, it has published several other useful documents, such as *Guidelines for Data Capturing: a manual, SOUL Guidelines for Data Capturing: a user manual*, and *MARC21 Code List for Field Identification*.

V.6.2.6 DELNET

The erstwhile NISSAT initiated setting up of several city-based information networks, such as CALIBNET, DELNET, MALIBNET, ADINET, of which DELNET has been most active. Delhi Library Network, as it was known earlier, started functioning in 1988, but it was registered in 1992 as a society. As indicated, it was initially supported by NISSAT and later by the National Informatics Centre and the Ministry of Culture, Government of India. Its geographical limitation was subsequently removed and its name changed to Developing Library Network. As in April 2013, DELNET had 4627 member organizations, including 23 from outside India [66].

Objectives of DELNET

The main objectives of DELNET are [66]:

- To promote sharing of resources among the libraries by developing a network of libraries, by collecting, storing, and disseminating information and by offering computerized services to the users;
- To undertake scientific research in the area of Information Science and Technology, create new systems in the field, apply the results of research and publish them;
- To offer technical guidance to the member-libraries on collecting, storing, sharing, and disseminating information;
- To coordinate efforts for suitable collection development and reduce unnecessary duplication wherever possible;
- To establish/facilitate the establishment of referral and/or research centers, and maintain a central online union catalog of books, serials, and nonbook materials of all the participating libraries;
- To facilitate and promote delivery of documents manually or mechanically;
- To develop specialized bibliographic database of books, serials, and nonbook materials;
- To develop databases of projects, specialists, and institutions;
- To possess and maintain electronic and mechanical equipment for speedy communication of information and delivery of electronic mail;
- To coordinate with other regional, national, and international networks and libraries for exchange of information and documents.

Activities of DELNET

The important activities of DELNET are [66]:

- *Union catalog databases:* DELNET has been actively engaged with the compilation of various Union Catalogues of the resources available in member-libraries. These databases can be accessed by the member libraries of DELNET. The databases so far compiled and the number of records available in them as in April 2013 are:

- *Union catalog of books:* This union catalog contains around 1,63,000 records. The information can be retrieved by author, title, subject, conference, series, etc.

- *Union List of Current Periodicals:* DELNET has created union lists of current periodicals in science and technology, social sciences and humanities. This database is available online to DELNET users. It covers around 36,000 periodicals and is regularly updated and new titles are added annually. It is a major resource for Document Delivery Services.

- *Union catalog of periodicals:* DELNET maintains a union catalog of periodicals, which contains full holdings data of the libraries. The database contains more than 20,000 records.

- *Database of periodical articles:* The database has details of articles which can be searched under the title, author, compiler, name of the periodical, and subject. The database is being extensively utilized by the researchers and scholars. The database contains more than 900,000 records.

- *CD-ROM database:* A bibliographic database of CD-ROMs available with the member-libraries is being compiled. It has more than 22,000 records.

- *Union list of video recordings:* This is a database of video cassettes available in DELNET member-libraries and has about 6000 listings.

- *Union list of sound recordings:* This union list consists of audio cassette records available in member-libraries. This database has more than 1000 records.

- *Database of theses and dissertations:* Creation of a database of theses and dissertations submitted to Indian Universities has been started, which covers various subjects. The database has more than 70,000 records.

- *Union list of newspapers:* The database has 70 records and contains information about the newspapers including title, name of the editor, published from, e-mail address, and also the web address of the INTERNET edition if available on the WWW.

- *Database of E-books:* It has over 1600 records.

- *Profile of member-libraries:* A directory of member-libraries is available and contains necessary information about them.

- *Access to other databases:* DELNET also provides access to:
  - Cambridge Dictionaries online
  - Networked Digital Library of Theses and Dissertations
  - ODLIS : Online Dictionary of Library and Information Science
  - GISTNIC Databases
  - MEDLINE and other databases of NLM
  - U.S. Patents: Full Text
  - Full-Text Medical Journals
  - Open Access Journals
  - Engineering and Technology E-Journals: Table of Contents
  - Full-Text Medical Books
  - Full-Text Engineering and Technology E-journals
  - Learning Resources for LIS Professionals
  - Digital Libraries of the World
- *Document delivery service:* DELNET provides inter-library loan and document delivery services to its member libraries. DELNET has prepared Inter-Library Loan Guidelines for use by the member-libraries.
- *Reference service:* DELNET maintains a referral center which provides reference facilities to participating libraries. This center also looks after the access to central database and provides prompt replies.
- *Retro conversion:* DELNET undertakes retro-conversion projects selectively.
- *Software development:* DELNET has developed DELSIS, a library networking software and a 10-module Del-Plus library management software suitable for small and medium size libraries, following internationally recommended standards, which is also bar code enabled. It has also developed a customized version of Koha open source library management software.
- *Consultancy and support service:* DELNET provides consultancy to libraries in adopting new technologies. It also offers technical support to member institutions in the selection of hardware, software and communication links; database creation; and in solving technical problems faced by member-libraries from time to time.
- *Continuing education:* DELNET arranges tutorials, workshops, lectures, and training programs, besides organizing the National Convention on Knowledge, Library and Information Networking (NACLIN) every year.
- *Publications:* DELNET brings out half-yearly *DELNET Newsletter* and *Proceeding of NACLIN.*

Important Projects

DELNET has embarked upon implementation of two important projects [66]:

- *Knowledge centers:* The first project envisages up setting up of a National Knowledge Center at its own premises and in public libraries and centers of learning in different states with the support of the Government of India and the respective state governments. The National Knowledge Centre would make knowledge accessible through the Knowledge Gateway www.knowledgegateway.org. It will also promote the creation of suitable content at the knowledge centers and make it available to the public in the country. It will add link to every existing useful information and make all knowledge available to the public, including researchers, students, and teachers. The main objectives in promoting knowledge centers are:
  - Coordinate with Knowledge Centers in different states in the country;
  - Serve the National Knowledge Centre;
  - Develop collections on important subjects;
  - Create databases, develop an Intranet and maintain information on important knowledge repositories;
  - Develop catalogs and indexes in machine readable form using international standards of physical and electronic resources;
  - Give integrated access to information available with DELNET on the subjects and collect relevant information on the subjects from other sources. (DELNET offers more than 70 lakh, i.e., 7 million records of books, etc. today, and promotes sharing of information available with more than 1100 libraries in India and 6 other countries.)
  - Connect each component of knowledge with a set of experts and develop an active database of such experts;
  - Develop links with resources both physical such as institutions and individuals, and, electronic such as electronic resources available through the Internet,
  - Capture knowledge from projects, assignments, gray literature, case studies, experts etc. on given subjects and makes them accessible in database form;
  - Give as much information to the users as the users need to complete their assignments,

- Make each Knowledge Centers as a one-stop center for accessing knowledge on different subjects or topics of interest to users in the public libraries; and
- Train every user in accessing information and guide the users to appropriate resource.

Knowledge Centers will have to cull out knowledge from a variety of sources including printed sources such as newspapers, books, journals, gray literature; digital resources including CD's, Internet, databases, metadata etc. and adopt research methodologies to collect information on the issues of particular interest to each Knowledge Center. Eventually a full-text library on topics in digital form will get developed with links and in-house resources all ready for use of the users 24 hours.

- *National bibliographic database:* DELNET undertook the compilation of the National Bibliographic Database with the support of the Department of Culture, Government of India in 1998 as a Pilot Project. Fifty thousand records of books: 20,000 in English, 15,000 in Tamil, and 15,000 in Punjabi were created at the Punjabi University, Patiala, and International Institute of Tamil Studies, Chennai. At Andhra University Library, Visakhapatnam, 15,000 records in English and 10,000 records in Telugu were also created. Similarly 25,000 records each were created at the Asiatic Society, Mumbai, and the Asiatic Society, Kolkata.

V.6.2.7 ARISNET

Indian Council of Agricultural Research embarked upon a project called Agricultural Research Information System with the financial aid from World Bank during Eighth Five Year Plan so that agricultural scientists could carry out research more effectively by having systematic access to research information available in India as well as in other countries. Subsequently it started implementation of Agricultural Research Information System Network (ARISNET) with the help of ICT. ARISNET has four modules, viz., Agricultural Research Personnel Information System (ARPIS), Agricultural Research Financial Information System (ARFIS), Agricultural Research Library Information System (ARLIS), and Agricultural Research Management Information System (ARMIS).

V.6.2.8 City-Based Networks

As mentioned earlier, several city-based library and information networks have been developed, or being developed in different cities of the countries.

Some of these were initiated by NISSAT, while some others were voluntarily set up by some libraries of those cities. However, all of them are not fully integrated systems. A few city-based networks are briefly described below.

ADINET

ADINET is a Network of Libraries and Information Centers situated around Ahmadabad. It was established in 1994 with an initial grant for a few years from National Information System for Science and Technology (NISSAT), It provides access to over 2000 libraries of all types—academic, institutional libraries, and even public libraries—through the network. The main vision of ADINET is to link existing libraries, to enable them to achieve what cannot be done by one library alone. This will enable these libraries to harness their limited resources and collective strengths.

The specific objectives of ADINET are [67]:

- To bring about cooperative mode of working amongst the libraries and information centers in and around Ahmadabad;
- To integrate the economic, scientific, and technical information systems into an effective network in and around Ahmadabad;
- To facilitate and promote sharing of resources amongst the libraries and information centers in and around Ahmadabad by developing and maintaining a central online union catalog containing bibliographic information on books, serials, and nonbook materials of all the participating libraries;
- To coordinate with other regional, national and international networks, libraries information and documentation centers for exchange of information and documents;
- To offer technical guidance to member libraries on selecting, storing, sharing, and disseminating information;
- To coordinate efforts for suitable collection development and reduce unnecessary duplication wherever possible
- To develop database projects, specialists, and institutions in and around Ahmadabad;
- To create awareness amongst all use groups and to educate them in utilization of information;
- To develop resources and to propagate in ways appropriate to the needs of users in and around Ahmadabad; and
- To help the users of libraries and information centers and also individuals who practice different professions in getting specialized information of their interest.

A centralized union catalog database of periodicals, books and nonbook materials available in the libraries of Ahmadabad and adjoining areas has been created. At present this database includes only the present/current holdings of libraries. Retrospective conversion will be taken up in due course. ADINET has also planned to procure some databases on special subjects and mount them on to the host computer. ADINET maintains a website which provides links to its own databases and many open access resources and hosts an electronic discussion forum. The main services provided by ADINET are [68]:

- *Online search:* Information can be searched by the participating libraries accessing the Union Catalogue. Presently, the database of periodicals covering over 5500 periodicals can be searched online. This facility will gradually be extended to other databases also.
- *Current awareness service:* Librarians of the member institutes and library professional members are regularly supplied photocopies of the contents pages of library and information science journals. Current awareness service can also be provided on demand using commercial databases that are available in machine-readable form in some libraries.
- *Inter-library loan:* ADINET enables a user to locate a periodical/book/ report of his interest. Once located the document including the audio-visual material can be borrowed on inter-library loan basis.
- *Photocopying service:* The users can get full text of the selected articles. For meeting the photocopy requests the relevant journal is procured from other libraries in and around Ahmadabad, the required article is photocopied and sent to the customer on payment basis.
- *Internet service:* Individuals can come to ADINET and access Internet with e-mail, downloading, and printout facilities against payment.
- *Consultancy service:* ADINET provides consultancy services to libraries and information centers in the matter of creation of websites and institutional repositories, completion of backlog in processing work of documents, digitization, etc.

The other activities of ADINET are [68]:

- *Continuing education:* ADINET conducts monthly study circle meetings, quarterly seminars on current trends in libraries and computer training programs for library and information professionals.
- *Publications:* Besides bringing out quarterly *ADINET Newsletter*, it has published many other important documents such as *Union List of Current Journals* and *Directory of Institutions in Ahmadabad and Gandhinagar.*

BONET

The Bombay Library Network (BONET) was set up at the National Centre for Software Technology (NCST), Bombay (now Mumbai), in 1992 at the initiative of NISSAT. The aim of BONET is to make information available to researchers at low cost using ICT. The focus of BONET is on inter-library cooperation, rather than on computerizing individual libraries, which will computerize their own operations and are likely to share their experiences with each other. BONET offers training related to library computerization and networking to speed up computerization of libraries in Bombay. Under BONET the following databases have been created [69,70]:

- 25,000 items in a bibliographic database on computers and software technology;
- Union catalog of journals and other periodicals in libraries in the region;
- Tables of contents of 250 Indian periodicals created by the national center for information;
- A number of CDROM databases mounted on a Novell Server for use to members.

The services offered through BONET include the following [71]:

- Access to an online catalog of periodicals in member libraries named UNICAT;
- Access to online information on books available in member libraries. Currently, NCST catalog is available on the network and other libraries are being encouraged to put their catalogs on the network;
- Inter-library lending service for books and periodicals;
- Photo-copying service;
- Access to an online information retrieval system in the fields of computer science and software technology;
- Online access to foreign library catalogs; and
- Online access to commercial databases, such as DIALOG.

Besides, arrangements are also being made for procuring photocopies of requested materials not available in India from overseas sources.

CALIBNET

Calcutta Library Network (CALIBNET) was the first city-based library network visualized and initiated by NISSAT in 1993. It is now managed by a registered society named CALIBNET Society. CALIBNET was established to institute systematic inter-library cooperation and document delivery amongst the libraries of Calcutta (now Kolkata). Its dual objectives were [72,73]:

- Launching its library network programs, facilitating remote online access to the holding data of Calcutta libraries and other specialized databases as well—a significant step toward bibliographic resource sharing amongst Calcutta libraries; and
- Providing electronic access to globally available information, imbibing its information center approach.

The Centralized Database (CDB) of CALIBNET, which its bedrock, holds around 30,000 records covering [72,73]:

- Conference documents held by libraries in and around Calcutta;
- Social sciences documents, predominantly journals, held by management libraries in South Asia, libraries of Indian Statistical Institute and Indian Institute of Management, Calcutta; and
- Index to contents of serials published by Asiatic Society in previous two centuries.

The other achievements of CALIBNET are [72,73]:

- *Software development:* Initially an application software *Maitreyee*, was developed through Computer Maintenance Corporation (CMC) with the financial assistance of NISSAT, the use of which was, however, limited. Later, it developed a multi-user storage and retrieval software *Sanjukta* to support CDB and to provide online access to its from remote locations and a conversion software package *Parapar* to support interchange of bibliographic data between USMARC, UNIMARC, and CCF files and also from non-standard formats to standard ones.
- *UNIMARC guidelines:* CALIBNET has brought out *Guidelines for Implementation of UNIMARC*, based on *UNIMARC Manual* (1987) under a project sponsored by NISSAT, which has taken care of special requirements of Indian libraries. It is a helpful tool for developing and upgrading databases to international standard.
- CALIBNET has initiated a program for development of Indian resources databases of historical value covering manuscripts and rare books and personal collections and databases of intellectual assets of West Bengal.

The services provided by CALIBNET are [72,73]:

- *Web based services:* Besides providing access to its CDB, the website of CALIBNET provides active links to various other resources, such as Indian library and network resources, overseas library resources on India, including rare documents—printed and manuscripts, worldwide library catalogs, national libraries of the world, newspapers and journals, electronic reference tools, factual information sources, and book-trade databases; and

- *On demand information service:* CALIBNET's *ConFile* service reaches at one's desk contents of any journal of one's choice out of over 20,000 high-impact journals, while its *RetroFile* offers latest status and trend of research on any specific topic. Through its *ConAlert service* CALIBNET delivers current and tailored bibliographic information at user's desk.
- *Access to CD-ROM databases:* CALIBNET provides access to in-house CD-ROM databases.
- *Document delivery service:* CALIBNET's on demand, *CalibOrder* offers the requisite back-up service by way of delivery of full-text of any article, and even patents.
- *Institutional resources development services:* Some of the key institutional resources development services offered are: (1) retrospective conversion of existing card catalog in libraries into computerized local databases via electronic mode by downloading from international databases; (2) consultative services on LIS automation; and (3) manpower development for operating and manning automated LIS environment through a wide range of graded training programs, and customized courses for individuals or groups at client's site.
- *E-mail connectivity:* A special feature of CALIBNET is the CalibLink, an email connectivity (from its ERNET hub). This has been installed in four institutions.

MALIBNET

Madras Library Network (MALIBNET) was registered as a society in 1993 in Madras (now Chennai). Nearly 83 libraries contribute actively to the MALIBNET. Thirty-seven major educational/research institutions have joined as member institutions of MALIBNET.

The main objectives of MALIBNET are [74]:

- To encourage co-operation among libraries, documentation centers and information centers in Chennai so that the resources can be pooled for the benefit of helping the weaker resource centers by the stronger ones;
- To evolve a network, interconnecting various libraries and information centers to improve capability in information handling and services;

- To provide reliable access to document collection of libraries by creating a union catalog of library holdings and housing it in a centralized host system of the network;
- To provide better access to bibliographic information through access to national and international databases;
- To optimize information resource utilization through shared cataloguing, and inter library loan services and avoiding duplication in acquisition to the extent possible;
- To centrally acquire information, specially the contents and abstracts from all the journals and then disseminate information as and when required, thus avoiding duplication in journal acquisition and reducing the expenditure of individual libraries;
- To organize conferences, lectures, workshops, and seminars; and
- To undertake scientific research in the field of library and documentation.

The services provided by MALIBNET are [74,75]:

- *Contents search service:* This allows a search on the contents database existing at MALIBNET covering nearly 7750 journals. This database is searchable through journal title, year, volume, and issue.
- *Literature search service:* MALIBNET provides keyword based literature search service from four databases—contents database, Autobst (database on automotive industries), patent database, and polymer science database.
- *Database search service:* MALIBNet also provides access to NUCSSI (National Union Catalogue of Scientific Serials) and MAPA (Medicinal and Aromatic Plants Abstracts) databases of NISCAIR and extends search on international databases through DIALOG, DATASTAR and STN International to its users. It provides current and constantly updated information. These databases include bibliographic, commercial, statistical, full text, patents, and variety of other databases.
- *Internet search service:* MALIBNet also provides search on Internet for users requesting information found at various sites on the net. This service provides Directory List, Patents Abstract Search, Literature/Bibliographic search, Library Catalogues, File transfer, Data and Software Archives, Information about Companies, Organizations and Associations, etc.
- *Database creation:* MALIBNET undertakes the work of specialized database compilation at user's request.

- *CAPS service:* MALIBNET provides CAPS (Contents, Abstracts, and Photocopy) Service from about 1200 journals through NISCAIR.
- *Abstracting service:* MALIBNET provides standing order/demand- based journal article abstracting service.
- *Document delivery service:* MALIBNET provides copies of full texts of articles from science and technology journals.

Other activities of MALIBNET are [74,75]:

- Publications: Besides publishing a half-yearly newsletter, MALIBNET Newsletter, has brought out four important directories, viz., Directory of Current Serials in Engineering Science Institutions in Madras (1998), Directory of Current Serials in Basic Sciences Institutions in Madras (1998), Directory of Current Serials in Medical Sciences in Madras (1998), and Directory of Current Serials in Social Science Institutions in Madras (1998). These are available in hard copy as well as soft copy.
- Library automation: MALIBNET undertakes library automation projects.
- Continuing education: MALIBNET organizes short-term training courses on topics relating to library automation and networking.

MYLIBNET

Mysore Library Network (MYLIBNET) was established at Mysore city in the year 1995 with the financial assistance of NISSAT. Central Food Technological Research Institute (CFTRI), Mysore, is hosting this net-work in its premises. MYLIBNET has established its web server www.mylibnet.org to provide services globally. A radio link with the local earth station of Software Technology Parks of INDIA (STPI) has been established. The union catalog of periodicals available in the libraries of Mysore, compiled by it in 1996, has been ported on this web server for easy access over network. Information related to food patents and the publications of National Information Centre for Food Science and Technology (NICFOS) attached to CFTRI are available on this website. A portal on Mysore city covering information relating to tourist attractions and cultural activities of Mysore has been created and made available on the web. An on-line directory of manufactur-ers, consultants, professionals, doctors, associations, various service providers, etc. in Mysore city can be accessed on-line through the Web. MYLIBNET regularly organizes short-term courses for LIS pro-fessionals [71,76].

PUNE-NET

PUNE-NET (Pune Libraries Networking Project) is a joint program of the University of Pune, the Centre for Development of Advanced Computing (C-DAC) and the National Chemical Laboratory (NCL). It was initially funded by NISSAT. It is hosted in the Bioinformatics Centre. It maintains centralized databases of information resources available in the participating libraries and is accessible over the Internet at http://punenet.ernet.in or at http://202.41.70.50/index.html. A user can search books and periodicals database online from this site and know the location of the desired information source in the participating libraries. Data from participating libraries are collected and stored at the PUNE-NET server. Each participating library uses different library management software. As such standardized data input is vital. PUNE-NET is following its own standard, based on the international standard for information exchange-ISO 2709 [77].

The major activities of PUNE-NET are [77]:

- *Database search service:* PUNE-NET hosts several databases, such as Database of Books, Union Catalogue of Periodicals, Booksellers Database, LIS Professionals Database, PUNE-NET Libraries Database. These databases can be accessed by the users online using the PUNE-NET website.

- *Direct access to libraries:* Access to C-DAC and Jayakar Library has been provided on-line through HTML interface. Using this facility the user can directly access these libraries, and get more information regarding the lending status of a particular book (issued, on shelf, etc.). It gives not only access to the books recorded in these databases of these libraries, but also the holdings of the libraries including CD-ROM databases, microfiche, video cassettes, etc.

- *E-mail and Internet connectivity:* PUNE-NET not only provides e-mail facility to participating libraries but also acts as a gateway to the Internet. In all, 36 libraries are using e-mail and Internet facilities.

- *CD-ROM database services:* PUNE-NET subscribes to a few bibliographic databases on CD-ROM, such as Inside Science Plus and Inside Humanities and Social Sciences by BLDSC.

- *Table of contents service:* It provides table of contents (TOC) service based on over 10,000 high-impact current serials.

- *Online search service:* As the PUNE-NET project is hosted in Bioinformatics Centre the bibliographic databases subscribed by the center are also being used to serve the needs of PUNE-NET users. These databases are *Wealth of Asia*, *Medline,* and *Biotechnology Citation*

Index. Besides, PUNE–Net also subscribes to STN and Bioline database services. STN provides access to several databases covering almost all subject areas. Bioline provides access to 40 full-text journals in life sciences. It has full-text access to three Indian journals as well.

REFERENCES

[1] G.G. Chowdhury, Information Retrieval System, IASLIC, Calcutta, 1994, p. 7.

[2] Information System. <http://www.britannica.com/topic/information-system>.

[3] UNESCO, Handbook for Information Systems and Services, prepared by Paulin Atherton, Paris, 1977, p. 17.

[4] MEDLINE. <http://en.wikipedia.org/wiki/MEDLINE>.

[5] USA National Library of Medicine. <http://www.nlm.nih.govt/>.

[6] R.P. Dixit, Information systems—AGRIS, MEDLAR and UNISIST, in: P. Dhyani (Ed.), Information Science and Libraries, Atlantic Publishers, New Delhi, 1990, pp. 133–186.

[7] MEDLINE-1950 to date (MEZZ). <http://www.library.nhs.uk/help/resource/medline>.

[8] MEDLINE on PubMed. <http://www.nlm.nih.gov/bsd/num_titles.html>.

[9] OCLC. <http://en.wikipedia.org/wiki/OCLC>.

[10] OCLC. <http://www.oclc.org/>.

[11] A.K. Das, B. Dutta, Bibliographic utility networks. <http://eprints.rclis.org/7209/1/DAS_DUTTA_Bibliographic_Utilities.pdf>.

[12] G.N. Narasimhan, Resource sharing focus on history ILL and document delivery, cooperative collection development – assumptions, problems, solutions, in: V.K.J. Jeevan, S. Parthan, (Eds.), Proceedings of the National Conference on Information Management in E-libraries, Kharagpur, India, Allied Publishers, New Delhi, 2002, pp. 556–564.

[13] T.A.V. Murthy, Resource sharing and consortia for India. Information management in e-libraries, in: V.K.J. Jeevan, S. Parthan, (Eds.), Proceedings of the National Conference on Information Management in E-libraries, Kharagpur, India, Allied Publishers, New Delhi, 2002, pp. 14–15.

[14] P. Dhyani, International organizations in pursuit of information services, in: P. Dhyani (Ed.), Information Science and Libraries, Atlantic Publishers, New Delhi, 1990, pp. 187–227.

[15] UNESCO and ICSU, UNISIST – study report on the feasibility of a world science information system by the United Nations Educational, Scientific and Cultural Organization and the International Council of Scientific Unions, Paris, 1971.

[16] A.A. Wysocki, World science information system – necessary and feasible, UNESCO Bull. Lib 25 (1971) 62–66.

[17] UNISIST Model. <https://en.wikipedia.org/wiki/UNISIST_model>.

[18] International Nuclear Information System. <https://www.iaea.org/inis/>.

[19] C. Todeschini, The International Nuclear Information System (INIS): The First Forty Years (1970–2010), IAAE, Vienna, 2010,

[20] H. Buntrock, Problems and issues in agricultural classification and indexing systems, in: A. Neelameghan (Ed.), Ordering Systems for Global Information Networks: Proceedings of the Third International Study Conference on Classification Research (Bombay, 6–11 June 1975), FID/CR and Sarada Ranganathan Endowment for Library Science, Bangalore, 1977, pp. 346.

[21] AGRIS Categorization Scheme. <http://www.fao.org/docrep/003/u1808e/U1808E. htm>.

[22] What is AGRIS? <http://hdl.handle.net/10068/697974>.

[23] AGRIS. <http://www.fao.org/agris>.

[24] International Development Research Centre, Sharing experience – DEVSIS: an information service for decision makers, 1977. <http://idl-bnc.idrc.ca/dspace/bitstream/10625/2019/1/IDL-2019.pdf>.

[25] K.G.Tyagi, Information support for development, DESIDOC Bull. Inf.Technol. 18 (4) (1998) 9–19.

[26] DEVSIS Steering Committee. First session: final Report, 1974.

[27] DEVSIS Steering Committee. Second session. Subject scope of DEVSIS, 1975.

[28] S.Adams, DEVSIS:An Information Resource for National Development, International Development Research Centre (IDRC), Ottawa, 1976,

[29] About INFOTERRA Mailing List. <http://www.cedar.at/sitemap.htm?page=/ unep/infoterra/>.

[30] Agriculture Network Information Centre. <http://www.cni.org/wpcontent/ uploads/2013/06/Agriculture-Network-Information-Center.pdf>.

[31] AgNIC, The Agriculture Network Information Centre Initiative: using technology and partnerships to link people to the information they need. <http://usain.org/ library_extensioncollab/AgNICmarketing2.pdf>.

[32] AgNIC, Agricultural Network Information Collaborative: a knowledge discovery system for agriculture. <http://www.agnic.org/>.

[33] M. Gardner, Making the most of what we do best – Agriculture Network Information Centre, 2009 [PPT presentation]. <https://www.google.co.in/?gfe_rd=cr&ei=Vu9M VJKTK8Wh8wfQrIHoCg&gws_rd=ssl#q=Making+the+Most+of+What+We+do +Best+-+%0BAgriculture+Network+Information+Center+-+AgNIC>.

[34] McCarthy, APINMAP – an Asian medicinal plant database, Probe 2 (3) (1992). <http://www.nal.usda.gov/pgdic/Probe/v2n3/apinmap.html>.

[35] UNESCO, ARKISYST Feasibility Study: Final Report, UNESCO, Paris, 1981,

[36] V.S. Bhatt, Aquatic sciences and fisheries information system, Mahasagar 8 (3–4) (1975) 213–217.

[37] ASTINFO. <http://www.unesco.org/webworld/regoff/astinfo.htm>.

[38] J.B. Rose, The UNESCO General Information Programme and its role in the development of regional cooperative networks, IATUL Q 4 (4) (1989) 231–245.

[39] What is CARIS? <http://www.icpa.ro/AgroWeb/AIC/RACC/Caris.htm>.

[40] COMNET. <http://hdl.handle.net/10220/2538>.

[41] Global Information Network on Chemicals. <http://www.chem.unep.ch/irptc/ irptc/canbginc.html>.

[42] T. Kaminuma, K. Nakata, Global information network on chemicals and its Asian component. <http://www.ncbi.nlm.nih.gov/pubmed/12909401>.

[43] About HELLIS. <http://www.nheicc.gov.np/about_hellis/about_hellis.htm>.

[44] K. Lee, J. Fang, Historical Dictionary of the World Health Organization, second ed., Scarecrow Press, Lanham, MD, 2013,

[45] ISONET, ISONET: ISO Information Network, ISO, Geneva, 2001,

[46] ISONET, ISONET Manual, second ed., 1998. <http://www.iso.org/iso/prodsservices/otherpubs/pdf/isonetmanual_1998-en.pdf>.

[47] UNESCO, Guidelines for National Information Transfer Centres on theestablishment of the International Information System on Research in Documentation (ISORID). <http://unesdoc.unesco.org/images/0000/000014/001479EB.pdf>.

[48] United Nations Population Information Network. <http://www.un.org/popin/>.

[49] Research Libraries Group. <http://en.wikipedia.org/wiki/Research_Libraries_Group>.

[50] W. Saffady, The bibliographic utilities in 1993: a survey of cataloging support and other services, Lib. Technol. Rep. 29 (1) (1993) 9–34.

[51] J. Jordon, Merger of WLN and OCLC provides synergy, new opportunities, OCLC Newsl 237 (1999) 3–4.

[52] D. Davinson, , second ed. Bibliographic Control, 72, Clive Bingley, London, 1981,

[53] NATIS News, UNESCO Bull. Lib 29 (1975) 114.

[54] UNESCO, NATIS: National Information Systems, 1975. <http://unesdoc.unesco.org/images/0000/000097/009793EB.pdf>.

[55] S. Green, NATIS: the theme for the 1970s, UNESCO Bull. Lib 29 (3) (1975) 117–122.

[56] N.B. Arutjunov, The requirements to be met by national scientific and technical information systems, UNESCO Bull. Lib 27 (1973) 246–249.

[57] G. Chandler, International and National Library and Information Services: A Review, Elsevier, Kidlington, 2014, p. 19.

[58] India. Department of Science and Technology, Science and Technology Plan for India (1974–79), 2 vols., 1973.

[59] India. Department of Scientific and Industrial Research, Annual Report 2002–2003.

[60] About ENVIS. <http://envis.tropmet.res.in/AboutEnvis.aspx>.

[61] Environmental Information System. <http://envis.nic.in/>.

[62] Biotechnology Information System Network. <http://www.btisnet.nic.in/>.

[63] Biotechnology Information System Network, North-Eastern Bioinformatics Network. <http://btisnet.gov.in/nesbif.asp>.

[64] R. Chandrakar, J. Aurora, Initiative of the INFLIBNET Centre for delivering information to the Indian academic community, in: Paper Presented at World Library and Information Congress: IFLA General Conference and Assembly, 77th, Puerto Rico, 2011.

[65] INFLIBNET Centre. <www.inflibnet.ac.in>.

[66] DELNET: Developing Library Network. <http://delnet.nic.in/>.

[67] NISSAT Networks, Ahmedabad library network, Inf. Today Tomorrow 20 (3) (2001) 14–15 <http://itt.nissat.tripod.com/itt0103/adinet.htm>.

[68] Ahmedabad Library Network. <http://www.alibnet.org/>.

[69] D. Kar, P. Bhattacharya, S. Deb, Library networking in India for resource sharing: present status and prospects, World Lib 9 (1) (1999).

[70] Library Dot Com. <http://librarydotcom.webs.com/apps/blog/>.

[71] R.S. Aswal, Information Networks in India, Ess Ess Publications, New Delhi, 2003,

[72] CALIBNET. <http://www.calibnet.org/>.

[73] CALIBNET: An Overview. <http://itt.nissat.tripod.com/itt9904/calibnet.htm>.

[74] P.K. Jha, Library networks and network based information services in India (AIS dissertation, 1991–2001), INSDOC, New Delhi (Chapter 4). <http://pawankumarjha.tripod.com/dissertation/chapter4.html#MALIBNET>.

[75] MALIBNET. <http://www.malibnetonline.com/>.

[76] S.N. Krishna Rao, Mysore Library Network: MYLIBNET (network with a difference), Inf. Today Tomorrow 21(1) (2002) 13–14, 30. <http://itt.nissat.tripod.com/itt0201/mylibnet.htm>.

[77] S. Nagarkar, Pune-Net: current status, Inf. Today Tomorrow 19 (3) (2000) 16–18. <http://www.dsir.gov.in/pubs/itt/itt20003/punenet.htm>.

CHAPTER W

Promotion of IOD Activities

W.1 INTRODUCTION

With the realization of the importance of information in national development and the development of the human beings at large, several international organizations have come forward to bridge the gap between the information-rich and the information-poor through international cooperation and assistance, so that everybody can benefit from the information being generated throughout the world. Their main focus have been the third world countries (TWC), as they suffer most for want of vital information. "The role of international and regional organizations and of international co-operation and assistance in bridging the gap is two-fold: facilitating information flow in science, technology and related fields from developed countries to TWCs, so that the latter may obtain information at affordable cost; and enhancing national capacity and strengthening the infrastructure of TWCs, enabling them to negotiate, choose from and integrate external information with that generated internally for effective application and exchange" [1]. Along with the international organizations, several national organizations in different countries are also playing important role in the promotion of IOD activities. It may be mentioned that some of the organizations promote IOD activities by taking direct measures, while some others do so indirectly by providing funds, or training required manpower or evolving tools and standards, and some others take both direct and indirect measures for doing so. Role of some prominent international and national organizations are described below.

W.2 ROLE OF UN AGENCIES

The United Nations and, more particularly, some of its specialized agencies such as the Food and Agriculture Organization (FAO), UNESCO, the United Nations Development Programme (UNDP), the United Nations Industrial Development Organization (UNIDO), and the World Health Organization (WHO), have been assisting, directly or indirectly, in the development of libraries, information systems, archives, and

Elements of Information Organization and Dissemination
DOI: http://dx.doi.org/10.1016/B978-0-08-102025-8.00023-5

resource-sharing, as well as the development of international co-operative information systems. United Nations Regional Commissions have been similarly involved. Further, they have set up information systems to aid planning and management of their own programmers, projects, field missions, etc., mostly in TWC [1].

W.2.1 UNESCO

"The United Nations Educational, Scientific, and Cultural Organization (UNESCO) has been concerned with information matters since its founding in 1946, and in fact occupies a unique position among the specialized agencies of the United Nations insofar as it has specific and sizable programmes devoted to information *per se*, ranging from libraries and archives to information and data systems, and covering methods of information and data handling as well as application areas, covers a wide range of the knowledge spectrum—education, science and technology, the social sciences, culture, and communication—and organizes information exchange among peoples of the world in order to promote international understanding in accordance with its charter", which says that it shall "maintain, increase, and diffuse knowledge ... by encouraging cooperation among the nations in all branches of intellectual activity ... the exchange of publications ... and other materials of information; and by initiating methods of international co-operation calculated to give the people of all countries access to the printed and published materials produced by any of them" [2].

W.2.1.1 UNISIST Programme

"Over the years, particular attention has been given to issues related to the flow of scientific and technical information, beginning especially in the mid-1960s, when the international scientific community became aware of the shortcomings of the existing information services for mission-oriented, inter-disciplinary research and development. In 1967, UNESCO joined forces with the International Council of Scientific Unions to carry out a feasibility study on the establishment of a world science information system, UNISIST" [2]. Subsequently, UNISIST Programme was initiated in 1972. The details of this programme have been discussed in the previous chapter.

W.2.1.2 NATIS Programme

As mentioned earlier, the concept of National Information System (NATIS) was developed by UNESCO to encourage the creation in individual countries of a clear and coherent program and policy for recognizing the important elements in the nation's information systems and assigning priorities for their development [3]. The program was initiated in 1974. Several countries made efforts to implement the program. In India launching of NISST program was an effort toward implementation of the concept of NATIS. The details of this program have also been discussed in the previous chapter.

W.2.1.3 General Information Programme

The General Information Programme (PGI) was created by the merger of two existing UNESCO programs—NATIS and UNISIST—to respond to the problems involved in the development and promotion of scientific and technological information systems and services, as well as the development of national information infrastructures [4,5]. An intergovernmental council composed of 30 Member States replaced the former UNISIST steering committee and has guided the planning and implementation of PGI [2]. PGI/UNISIST activities are essentially designed to enhance the capacity of Member States to handle, transfer, and share information and information resources, and to effectively utilize information and data in development activities. Such information and data may be generated either within the country or abroad. UNESCO's action involves assisting Member States in formulating national information policies; developing library, archives, and information system infrastructures; training information personnel; and making users increasingly aware of the value of information. The PGI/UNISIST program has provided a framework within which Member States and international organizations can collaborate by sharing resources, developing compatible international information systems, and taking part in program activities [2].

W.2.1.4 Information for All Programme

In 2000, the PGI program and Inter-governmental informatics program of UNESCO were replaced by intergovernmental Information for All Programme (IFAP). Through IFAP, governments of the world have pledged to harness the new opportunities of the information age to create equitable societies through better access to information. The Information for All Programme is closely integrated with UNESCO's regular program, especially in the area of communication and information. IFAP works closely with other intergovernmental organizations and international NGOs, particularly those with expertise in information management and preservation, for example the International Federation of

Library Associations and Institutions (IFLA) and the International Council on Archives (ICA). The Programme is guided in its planning and implementation by an Inter-governmental Council comprising 26 UNESCO Member States that are elected by UNESCO's General Conference. There are IFAP National Committees in different countries to interpret and mobilize the IFAP vision for local communities [6]. As a transverse UNESCO program, the Information for All Programme provides a framework for international cooperation and international and regional partnerships. In order to implement the above-mentioned policies, the program shall support the development of common strategies, methods, and tools for building a just and free information society. In particular, the Information for All Programme aims to [7]:

- Promote and widen access through the organization, digitization, and preservation of information;
- Support the production of local content and foster the availability of indigenous knowledge through basic literacy and ICT literacy training;
- Promote international reflection and debate on the ethical, legal, and societal challenges of the information society;
- Support training, continuing education, and lifelong learning in the fields of communication, information and informatics;
- Promote the use of international standards and best practices in communication, information and informatics in UNESCO's fields of competence; and
- Promote information and knowledge networking at local, national, regional, and international levels.

The Information for All Programme covers five areas [7]:

- Development of international, regional, and national information policies
- Development of human resources and capabilities for the information age
- Strengthening institutions as gateways for information access
- Development of information processing and management tools and systems
- Information technology for education, science, culture, and communication.

W.2.1.5 Information Exchange

UNESCO played an important role in promoting regional cooperation in the field of information exchange. Its actions in this regard aimed at strengthening national capabilities for information exchange and creating the necessary mechanisms for sharing experience and resources and for coordinating regional activities. UNESCO acted as a catalyst for regional cooperation, providing the necessary stimulus, technical back-up, organizational methodologies, standards, and tools, as well as limited financial support. Two distinct and complementary types of regional co-operation are being promoted within UNESCO's program: broad co-operative schemes, and specialized operational information networks [2].

Broad Schemes

Several regional schemes for co-operation in the information field have been encouraged and supported by UNESCO, with the general aims of promoting resource sharing and harmonization of national information policies, development of standardized information-handling tools, elaboration of co-operative projects on information manpower training and information system development, and more effective use of limited international assistance [2]. ASTINFO is one such important project, the details of which have been given in the previous chapter. Another regional co-operation scheme along the same lines as ASTINFO is the Sub-Regional Network for the Exchange of Information and Experience in Science and Technology for Development in the Caribbean Region (CARSTIN), which was initiated in 1984. Twelve countries have designated National CARSTIN Coordinating Units (CCUs), and a number of Associated Centres are also affiliated to the Network, which is supervised by a Management Committee of representatives of the CCUs. By 1988, five sub-regional pilot projects had been initiated [2]. Other such projects are Arab League Documentation Centre (ALDOC), which was set up in 1981, and its Arab Regional Information System Network (ARIS-NET), and Information Society Programme for Co-operation for Latin American and the Caribbean (INFOLAC).

Specialized Networks

UNESCO has also been promoting the development of operational co-operative information systems in fields of priority interest to its Member States. For example, UNESCO has supported the development of the Asian Pacific Information Network on Medicinal and Aromatic Plants (APINMAP), the general objective of which is to provide a framework for co-operation among Member States, through jointly developed information tools and related user services, so that the user communities in the region have access to information they need in the field of medicinal and aromatic plants [2]. The activities of APINMAP have been described in the previous chapter. Another specialized regional network in which UNESCO has been actively involved is the Pan African Network for a

Geological Information System (PANGIS), which was launched in 1986 at the initiative of the International Centre for Training and Exchanges in the Geosciences (CIFEG) in Paris. The objective of PANGIS is to facilitate the collection and dissemination of information on the earth sciences that African countries urgently need for their development [2].

W.2.1.6 Information Service
For dissemination of information relating to UNESCO's fields of competence, viz. education, natural sciences, culture, social and human sciences, information and communication, it has set up a library at its headquarters in Paris as also in its other offices and institutions in different countries, which provides reference service and SDI service and database searching, Internet searching, and reading room facilities.

W.2.2 FAO

Food and Agricultural Organization (FAO) is a specialized United Nation agency that leads international efforts to defeat hunger. It acts as a neutral forum where all nations meet as equals to negotiate agreements and debate policy. It is also a source of knowledge and information. Article-1 of the FAO Constitution says "The Organization shall collect, analyze, interpret, and disseminate information relating to nutrition, food, and agriculture." The new focus of FAO, as approved by FAO Council, is "facilitating access to the scientific and technical literature in agriculture in developing countries" [8]. According to an independent external evaluation, 'FAO's principle task is to work to ensure that the world's knowledge of food and agriculture is available to those who need it when they need it and in a form which they can access and use" [8]. One of the corporate strategies of FAO, according to the strategic framework for FAO, 2000–15, is to improve decision-making through the provision of information and assessments and fostering of knowledge management for food and agriculture [9]. FAO has adopted several measures to fulfill its goal and the tasks assigned to it, which are discussed below.

W.2.2.1 Setting Up of WAICENT
For implementing the provisions of the aforesaid strategy, FAO reinforced the World Agricultural Information Centre (WAICENT) as a corporate framework for agricultural information management and dissemination. WAICENT plays the "umbrella" role in FAO's information dissemination activities. The activities of WAICENT have been discussed in Chapter-U.

W.2.2.2 Setting Up of Information Systems

FAO has set up a few information systems in agriculture and related areas, such as AGRIS, CARIS, and ASFIS, the details of which have been provided in Chapter-V.

W.2.2.3 Creation of Open Archive

FAO created an online catalogue, known as FAODOC, which contained bibliographic metadata of electronic and printed documents produced by FAO since 1945. In 1998, it also launched a Corporate Document Repository (CDR) of FAO documents and publications, as well as selected non-FAO publications, in electronic format. This repository also served as a platform for publication of all its electronic documents. In 2012, FAODOC and CDR were merged to form FAO Open Archive (FAO OA), a digital open repository to collect, manage, maintain, and disseminate all material published by FAO. As in 2012 the archive contained more than 58,400 records, of which 40,100 were full-text documents. The open archive enables users to easily access the accumulated knowledge and information produced by FAO directly on the Internet.

W.2.2.4 Creation of FAO Website

The FAO website provides access to information on agriculture, forestry, fisheries, sustainable rural development, economics, food, and nutrition. It is a comprehensive source of agricultural information, having more than half a million web pages, over 100 databases, and thousands of documents. With over 2 million visits per month, the website gives access to the accumulated knowledge and expertise of FAO [9]. The details of the important websites have been provided in Chapter-U.

W.2.2.5 AGORA Programme

Access to Global Online Research in Agriculture (AGORA) is a program to provide free or low cost access to major scientific journals in agriculture and related biological, environmental and social sciences to public institutions in developing countries. Launched in October 2003, AGORA provides access to more than 3000 journals from the world's leading academic publishers. The goal of this program, initiated by FAO, is to improve the quality and effectiveness of agricultural research, education, and training in low-income countries, and in turn, to improve food security. Through AGORA, researchers, policy-makers, educators, students, technical workers, and extension specialists have access to high-quality, relevant and timely agricultural information via the Internet. Currently 82 publishers contribute journal content to AGORA [10].

W.2.2.6 Development of Standards/Methodologies/Tools

For over 20 years, FAO has been setting standards in information management in agricultural development and food security. FAO works with Member Nations and other partners to develop and disseminate global standards and procedures for agricultural information management and exchange. Three important initiatives taken by FAO in this regard are [9]:

- *AGROVOC:* A multilingual controlled vocabulary AGROVAC has been developed to standardize the indexing process in order to make searching simpler and more efficient. AGROVOC covers all areas of interest to FAO, including food, nutrition, agriculture, fisheries, forestry, environment, etc. At present AGROVOC contains over 32,000 concepts in a hierarchy, each concept may have labels in up to 22 languages [9,11].
- *Agricultural Metadata Standards Initiative* (AgMES), launched in November 2000, is an attempt to promote the use of metadata through use of standardized agricultural metadata terms for the purpose of facilitating resource discovery and interoperability between richly described agricultural resources (http://www.fao.org/agris/agmes/). One of the first AGMES applications was the AGRIS application profile, which is a format that allows sharing of information across dispersed bibliographic systems.
- *Agricultural Ontology Service (AOS)*, which by making use of knowledge contained in vocabulary systems and thesauri such as AGROVOC, is committed to developing specialized domain-specific terminologies and concepts that will better support information management for the web environment (http://www.fao.org/agris/aos/).

W.2.2.7 Facilitation of Information Access

FAO works closely with stakeholders in Member Nations and fosters international partnerships under the WAICENT framework to develop facilities and networks for access to and sharing of agricultural information. Some areas of collaboration include improving efficiency, quality, and relevance of knowledge exchange in agriculture, and using electronic media to enhance communication for rural development. Special mention may be made about following two activities in this regard [9]:

- *Capacity building activities:* Advice and technical assistance for governments, institutions, and rural communities to strengthen capacities in agricultural information management and the effective use of information and communication technologies. Several national level agricultural information networks have been set up with active involvement of AGRIS under capacity building initiative, such as AGRORED (Peru) and KAINet (Kenya).

- *Information management resource kit:* A partnership-based e-learning initiative comprising a comprehensive suite of distance learning resources covering concepts, approaches, and tools for agricultural information management.

W.2.2.8 Clearing House for Standards

Efforts are being made to establish an Information Management Clearinghouse (IM Clearinghouse) to bring together information on methodologies, standards, and tools. Its specific goals would be [9]:

- To establish a network of partners who adhere and agree to the primary goal of the initiative "to provide unified and free access to information management approaches and tools";
- To bring together information about currently available standards (such as thesauri, classification schemes, metadata sets, ontologies, controlled vocabularies) used in management of Agricultural Information;
- To encourage the re-use of these standards to facilitate interoperability between information systems;
- To increase awareness of these freely available resources and promote sharing of good practice examples; and
- To provide channels for communication between different actors in the community.

W.2.3 Other UN Agencies

Several other United Nations agencies have initiated measures for improving information dissemination activities in their respective fields of work, some of which are briefly described below.

- *UNIDO:* United Nations Industrial Development Organization (UNIDO) has set up a technology-transfer information system (BITS) to respond to queries. It has also assisted TWC to develop a national register of technology agreements, information centers, and services for small industries, as well as playing a role in training industrial information personnel [1]. It has also brought out a *World Directory of Industrial Information Sources* in 2001.
- *UNEP:* United Nations Environment Programme (UNEP), through its INFOTERRA program, has developed large databases on the

environment through the co-operation of centers around the world. Databases in specialized areas such as desertification are provided free of charge to the centers concerned. Technical assistance and training are also provided. The related HABITAT program on human settlements provides similar facilities and makes available the UNDMS (Urban Data Management) software [1]. The details of INFOTERRA may be found in Chapter-V.

- *ESCAP:* ESCAP set up Asian and Pacific Centre for Transfer of Technology in 1977 in Bangalore, India, with the objective of facilitating technology transfer in the Asia-Pacific region. The center moved to New Delhi in 1993. One of the major objectives of this center is dissemination of information and good practices to small and medium-scale entrepreneurs of the region. For this purpose, APCTT has developed a state-of-the-art Information Center to provide technology information services, with internet access. The Information Center provides the following services [12]:
    - Access to the Internet under expert supervision;
    - Access to the APCTT technology database and other relevant national and international databases available on-line;
    - Assistance in identifying national and international information services;
    - Reference services;
    - Referral services; and
    - Information packages for members.
- *WHO:* WHO contributes to improved health information through its activities in the following three areas: maintaining the *Global Health Observatory*, the common gateway to the wealth of WHO data and statistics, analysis and reports on key health themes; formulating standards, tools, and methods for data collection, compilation, analysis, and dissemination and country measurement and evaluation; and collaborating with countries on data collection, analysis and approaches to address priority data gaps and strengthen country health information systems. It has developed a Country Health Intelligence Portal and, in December 2013, launched an online database MiNDbank containing information relating to mental health [13]. WHO has also initiated Health Literature and Information Services (HeLLIS) network in South-East Asia region with a view to provide health literature/information support to health team and researchers in the region [14]. The details of HeLLIS may be found in the previous chapter.

W.3 ROLE OF OTHER INTERNATIONAL AGENCIES

Several other intergovernmental and international agencies also play important role in dissemination of vital information. Role of a few some important agencies are described below.

W.3.1 World Bank

Usually the World Bank provides assistance for information system development as part of a larger project. For example, in Indonesia as part of the project for improving higher education facilities that begun in 1988, libraries in some 45 universities and higher education centers received substantial financial support. The bank's InFodev program, which brings together private and public funding, supports projects, related to telecommunication reforms, information infrastructure, and information systems [1]. According to Independent Evaluation Group of World Bank, the Bank is currently involved in nearly 85 global and 35 regional programs and another dozen are under development. Almost half of the programs, in which the Bank is involved, relate to knowledge, advocacy, and standard-setting networks that are generating and disseminating knowledge about developments in their respective sectors [15].

W.3.2 European Commission

The EC has assisted the development of selected libraries and information facilities in the least developed countries of Africa, the Pacific and the Caribbean region (ACP countries) within the framework of the Lomé Agreement. In particular, through the Technical Centre for Agricultural and Rural Cooperation (CTA), it has supported the development of agricultural information services through meetings and training sessions. It has also supported formation of Agence de Coopération Culturelle et Technique (ACCT), in 1970 in Niamey (Niger), which is mandated to develop the necessary programs and activities as well as coordination mechanism for harmonization and the complementarity of programs relating to documentation and information dissemination [1].

W.3.3 IDRC

Among the NGOs, IDRC is one that has had for a long time a separate division with budgeted programs for the development of information systems and services. IDRC's mission is "empowerment through knowledge" for coping with the complex challenges facing TWC. IDRC has provided direct financial and technical assistance to a number of information-related projects in many developing countries and regions of the world, and has supported some others in co-operation with inter-governmental organizations, regional organizations, and NGOs, in setting up international co-operative development information systems and networks. AGRIS is one of the early international cooperative information systems which received IDRC support. At the regional level, AGRIASIA, for example, received financial and technical support for its establishment and operations. In the mid-1970s, IDRC initiated DEVSIS (Development Science Information System) at the national, regional, and global levels, and supported the national/regional collection, bibliographic control, and dissemination of development literature. IDRC began supporting, often in association with other agencies such as UNESCO, the development of information science schools such as Regional Centre for Information Science (ARCIS) at the University of Ibadan in Nigeria and School of Information Studies for Africa (SISA) at the University of Addis Ababa, Ethiopia [1]. The latter has been renamed as Department of Information Science in 2002.

W.4 ROLE OF INTERNATIONAL PROFESSIONAL BODIES

Professional bodies in the field of LIS also play vital role in the promotion of IOD activities. The role played by a few such professional bodies is described below.

W.4.1 FID

An international organization named Institut International de Bibliographie (IIB) was set up in Brussels, the capital city Belgium, at the initiative of Henri la Fontaine and Paul Otlet and with the cooperation of the Belgium Government in 1895, with the aim of compiling a comprehensive universal bibliography. The work on this bibliography continued till the First World War when the number of entries in the bibliography stood at around 1.5 crores. The work of this organization stopped during the war and it faced financial crisis. After the war in 1924 its constitution changed making it a federal international organization. In 1931, it was rechristened as Institut International de Documentation (IID). The name of the organization was again changed in 1937 to Federation Internationale de Documentation (FID) and its headquarters shifted to The Hague in the Netherlands. In 1988, its name changed yet again to Fédération Internationale d'Information et de Documentation (International Federation for Information and Documentation), but its acronym continued to be FID.

W.4.1.1 Organizational Structure of FID

FID was functioning as a coordinating agency in the field of information services. Its principal organ was General Assembly, which had full plenary powers for effective and smooth functioning of FID. Besides, it had a Council, a Bureau, and a Secretariat. The Council had the power to appoint the Secretary General and was responsible for carrying out all plans and programs. It performed all executive functions, but its decisions were subject to ratification by General Assembly. Its main functionaries were president and secretary general [16]. In 1986–87, the membership strength of FID was 270 from 69 countries, the most of them being national members [17]. The expenses were being met from voluntary donations, membership fees, and sale of publications.

W.4.1.2 Objectives of FID

With changing time and need, the objectives of FID changed several times. The latest objectives were [18]:

- To promote, through international cooperation, research in the development of documentation, which includes *inter alia* the organization, storage, retrieval, dissemination, and evaluation of information, however recorded in the fields of science, technology, social sciences, arts, and humanities;
- Coordinate at international level the efforts of organizations and individuals interested in documentation, providing an international forum;
- Contribute to international network of information systems;
- Promote and coordinate research and training in documentation;
- Promote reprographic and computerized techniques; and
- Encourage establishment of information analysis centers.

W.4.1.3 Functions of FID

FID was mandated to perform two types of functions, viz., scientific and methodological functions and applied (or field tasks) functions. The scientific and methodological functions were [18]:

- To study formalized and non-formalized, conventional, and non-conventional methods and means of communication and make recommendations for their improvement;

- To contribute to the elaboration of new methods and means in communication based on the newer technological advances such as modern computer, photo-type-setting, and reprography;
- To study the information needs of users of information, and develop programs for better means of both meeting these needs and testing to validate the improved methods;
- To define the criteria and techniques for evaluation of the effectiveness of documentation work of all kinds;
- To further improve the UDC and develop other retrieval languages designed for documentation search;
- To study and elaborate principles of data compilation, processing, storage, search, retrieval, and transmission
- To elaborate better methods for the preparation of analytical (synthetic) information reviews;
- To elaborate the theoretical and methodological bases for documentation and define its principal terminology; and
- To identify the main research trends in documentation and promote them and their coordination at the international level.

The applied (or field tasks) functions of FID were [18]:

- To help in setting up information activities and establishing documentation centers in countries where they do not exist, and assisting in the development existing centers;
- To encourage the establishment of information analysis centers, specially in the presently more rapidly progressing fields of science and technology;
- To promote the training of documentalists at all levels of accomplishment, especially in developing countries;
- To promote the education of document users in the efficient utilization of documentation services;
- To publish and promote the publication of manuals, textbooks, and other materials for general and specialized training of documentalists and users of documentation;
- To organize on a regular basis, international conferences on the most important problems of documentation; and
- To seek better cooperation with other international organizations in the field of documentation.

To fulfill its objectives FID took up several plans and proposals. It may be specially mentioned here that it was FID which initiated the development of Universal Decimal Classification, which is now widely used in special libraries and information centers throughout the world. Another important creation of FID was Broad System of Ordering, which was compiled under UNISIST project and serves as a switching language between the classification schemes and thesauri for the purpose of information transfer.

W.4.1.4 Commissions and Committees

FID created a few regional commissions for working in different regions of the world. These were:
- FID/CLA: Regional Commission for Latin American Countries
- FID/CAO: Regional Commission for Asia and Oceania
- FID/CAR: Regional Commission for African Region

Similarly, it created some study committees for working in different fields. These were:
- FID/CCC: Central Classification Committee
- FID/CR: Classification Research Committee
- FID/ET: Education and Training Committee
- FID/DT: Committee on Terminology of Information and Documentation
- FID/II: Committee for Information for Industry
- FID/IM: Committee on Informatics
- FID/LD: Committee on Linguistics in Documentation
- FID/RI: Committee on Research on the Theoretical Basis of the Information Science
- FID/PD: Committee on Patent Information and Documentation
- FID/SD: Committee on Social Science Documentation

Besides, it also created ad hoc committees and sub-committees as per need.

W.4.1.5 Publications of FID

FID published many valuable books and journals in the field of documentation and information services, which includes *A Guide to World's Training Facilities in Documentation*, *World List of Library and Documentation Journals*, *FID News Bulletin*, *International Forum on Information and Documentation*, etc.

W.4.1.6 Cooperation With Other Bodies

FID maintained close cooperation with many international organizations, such as UNESCO, Economic and Social Council of the United Nations (ECOSOC), Food and Agricultural Organization (FAO), International

Atomic Energy Agency (IAEA), United Nations Industrial Development Organization (UNIDO), International Telecommunications Union (ITU), World Intellectual Property Organization (WIPO), International Federation of Library Associations and Institutions (IFLA), International Organization for Standardization (ISO).

W.4.1.7 Discontinuation of FID

Unfortunately, a deepening financial crisis gradually brought FID to a point at which the Secretariat had to be closed down and its office furniture auctioned off in 2002. The existing Council's terms of office expired at the end of 2001 and no elections were held to replace them. Although FID was not dissolved as a legal entity at this time, it effectively ceased to exist. Its archive continues to be held by the Royal Library at the Hague, Netherlands, and will be safeguarded by the UDC Consortium [19]. The closure of this important organization is certainly a great loss in the field of documentation and information services.

W.4.2 IFLA

The International Federation of Library Associations and Institutions (IFLA) is an independent, international, non-governmental, not-for-profit organization representing the interests of library and information services and their users. It came into existence in 1927 in the form of a committee, when a resolution for the establishment of an International Library and Bibliographical Committee was adopted at the 50th anniversary conference of the British Library Association (now CILIP). In the second meeting of the committee held in Rome in 1929, the statute of the organization was approved and the name of the committee was changed to International Federation of Library Associations (IFLA). In 1976, a new statute was approved and it was recommended that the word "Institutions" be added to the name, but the acronym be retained as IFLA. In 2004, the Governing Board of IFLA decided to endorse a new model for IFLA's operations, consisting of three pillars, which are supported by the infrastructure offered by the Federation's governance structures, its website, and its headquarters (HQ) in The Hague. The three pillars are [20]:

- *The Society Pillar*, which focuses on the role and impact of libraries and information services in society and the contextual issues that condition and constrain the environment in which they operate across the world. Those issues are addressed currently through the Committee on Freedom of Access to Information and Freedom of Expression

(FAIFE), Committee on Copyright and other Legal Matters (CLM), International Committee on Blue Shield ICBS), and IFLA's advocacy in the World Summit on the Information Society (WSIS) and other arenas.

- *The Profession Pillar*, which focuses on the issues covered by the long established Core Activities—Action for Development through Libraries Programme (ALP), IFLA—CDNL Alliance for Digital Strategies (ICADS), Preservation and Conservation (PAC), UNIMARC—and the Sections and Divisions. They lie at the core of IFLA's professional practice and help libraries and information services to fulfill their purposes and to shape responses to the needs of clients in a rapidly changing global environment.

- *The Members Pillar* is of course central to IFLA. It includes the services IFLA offers to members, management of their membership of IFLA, conferences, and publications.

W.4.2.1 Objectives of IFLA

Initially, the aim of IFLA was "to promote cooperation in the field of librarianship and bibliography, and particularly to carry out investigations and make propositions concerning international relations between libraries, library associations, bibliographers, and other organized groups" [21]. With the changing time and expansion of its activities, its objectives have also changed. Currently, its objectives are [21]:

- Promote high standards of provision and delivery of library and information services;
- Encourage widespread understanding of the value of good library and information services;
- Represent the interests of our members throughout the world.

W.4.2.2 Core Values of IFLA

In pursuing these aims IFLA embraces the following core values [21]:

- The endorsement of the principles of freedom of access to information, ideas and works of imagination and freedom of expression embodied in Article 19 of the Universal Declaration of Human Rights;
- The belief that people, communities, and organizations need universal and equitable access to information, ideas and works of imagination for their social, educational, cultural, democratic, and economic well-being;
- The conviction that delivery of high-quality library and information services helps guarantee that access; and

- The commitment to enable all Members of the Federation to engage in, and benefit from, its activities without regard to citizenship, disability, ethnic origin, gender, geographical location, language, political philosophy, race, or religion.

W.4.2.3 Structure of IFLA

IFLA is a federation of 154 associations, 935 institutional members and affiliates, 180 personal affiliates, and 15 bodies with consultative status in 135 countries. IFLA has consultative status with UNESCO, associate status with the International Council of Scientific Unions, and observer status with the World Intellectual Property Organization (WIPO) and the International Organization for Standardization (ISO) [1]. According to the new governing structure adopted in 2008, the General Assembly of Members is the supreme governing body, consisting of delegates of voting Members. It normally meets every year during the annual conference. It elects the President and members of the Governing Board. It also considers general and professional resolutions which, if approved, are usually passed to the Executive Committee and the Professional Committee for action as appropriate. The Governing Board is responsible for the managerial and professional direction of IFLA within the guidelines approved by the Assembly. The Executive Committee has executive responsibility delegated by the Governing Board to oversee the direction of IFLA between meetings of this Board within the policies established by the Board. It is the duty of the Professional Committee to ensure coordination of the work of all the IFLA units responsible for professional activities, policies and programs [21]. IFLA works through five divisions, and 47 sections and roundtables. IFLA has three regional sections (Africa, Asia and Oceania, and Latin America and the Caribbean), which are concerned with all aspects of library and information services in the respective regions. They promote IFLA activities and work closely with the IFLA Regional Offices, located in Pretoria, South Africa; Singapore; and Rio de Janeiro, Brazil.

W.4.2.4 Core Activities of IFLA

IFLA has been playing its leadership role through a number of core programs: Universal Bibliographic Control (UBC), Universal Availability of Publications (UAP), Preservation and Conservation (PAC), the Advancement of Librarianship in the Third World Programme (ALP), and Universal Dataflow and Telecommunications (UDT). The core programs, most of which were hosted and supported by national libraries, provided professional leadership and coordination of international work in strategic areas of the profession. During the 1990s the core programs were re-conceptualized and renamed core activities [22]. New core activities were taken up, while some of the older ones were renamed or modified (ALP, ICABS, and UBCIM) or were phased out (UAP, UBC, and UDT). The earlier core programs were:

- *Universal Bibliographic Control and International MARC:* In 1973 the IFLA General Conference in Grenoble made Universal Bibliographic Control (UBC) a core program. It was initially hosted by the British Library. The search for guidelines for machine-readable cataloguing which started in the 1970s led in 1983 to the establishment of a universal MARC format and its inclusion in the UBC Core Programme. In 1988, the title of the Programme changed to Universal Bibliographic Control and International MARC (UBCIM) and the headquarters moved to the Deutsche Bibliothek in Frankfurt, Germany [4]. The UBCIM Programme achieved a great deal over the thirty years of its existence. It has been responsible for the creation of the ISBDs as well as UNIMARC, and for maintaining a full publishing and seminar program. It was *closed on March 1, 2003* [23].

- *Universal availability of publications:* The Core Programme for the Universal Availability of Publications was started in the late 1970s. The objective of UAP was the widest possible availability of published material (that is, recorded knowledge issued for public use) to intending users, wherever and whenever they needed it and in the format required. Published materials included not only printed materials, including so-called "gray literature," but audio-visual materials and publications recorded in electronic (digital or analogue) form. To work toward this objective, the program aimed to improve availability at all levels, from the local to the international, and at all stages, from the publication of new material to the retention of last copies, both by positive action and by the removal of barriers. UAP aimed to ensure that improved access to information on publications was matched by improved access to the publications themselves. Under this project several valuable seminars and workshops were organized in different countries and a good number of publications were brought out, including a Model National Inter-library Loan Code. The program was closed on March 31, 2003, and the coordination of bibliographic standardization was moved to the IFLA—CDNL Alliance for Bibliographic Standards (ICABS), which was later, changed to IFLA—CDNL Alliance for Digital Strategies (ICADS). In 2011, it was decided to discontinue ICADS [23–25].

- *Universal dataflow and telecommunications:* A Core Programme under the title Transborder Dataflow was hosted by the National Library of Canada, Ottawa in 1986. In 1988, it became Universal Dataflow and Telecommunications (UDT) [4]. UDT has been working toward the establishment of an electronic information infrastructure for IFLA that would permit enhanced communications and information exchange. UDT's well-regarded web service, which provides information about IFLA and about trends and issues of concern to the library community as a whole, was the starting point for this effort. When IFLANET was first proposed by the UDT Core Programme in 1993, one of the possibilities was to distribute electronic newsletters and electronic journals, which has now become a reality. IFLANET used a combination of networking and communications technologies to provide IFLA with an unprecedented opportunity to deliver information services to members and non-members alike. The UDT Core Programme initiated a series of electronic Occasional Papers to address current technological developments. It created LIBJOBS, a new mailing list that provides a moderated employment listing service for library and information professionals around the world [26]. However, the program was closed in 2003 and some functions were taken over by ICABS [27].
- *IFLA—CDNL Alliance for Digital Strategies (ICADS):* ICADS was a joint alliance of IFLA and the Conference of Directors of National Libraries (CDNL) that was established in 2008 as a successor to ICABS (IFLA CDNL Alliance for Bibliographic Standards) which had been established as a national libraries initiative in 2003. The focus of the ICADS alliance is strategic and state-of-the-art digital library developments at national libraries. Through a web directory of project that resides within the framework of PADI (Preserving Access to Digital Information), the alliance provides the international library community with current information, documentation, and links to a wide variety of information about innovative digital projects in which partners are involved. There were three broad themes within the ICADS focus:
  - Creating and building digital collections;
  - Managing digital collections; and
  - Accessing digital collections.
- ICADS, and its predecessor ICABS, made a significant contribution to promoting and embedding digital awareness within the IFLA community. However, in December 2011 the ICADS Advisory Board decided to close ICADS and cease its activities [28].

The present core activities of IFLA are [21]:

- *Action for Development through Libraries Programme* (ALP): The IFLA Action for Development through Libraries Programme (IFLA ALP), launched in 1984, works in collaboration with libraries, library associations, partner organizations and library professionals in developing and emerging countries to deliver relevant, sustainable activities for equitable access to information and better library communities. IFLA ALP delivers community-led change through its training programs, online learning activities, and other opportunities, and access to IFLA's international network. IFLA ALP is based on a platform of policies and standards developed and endorsed by IFLA at the international level, and local priorities at the grassroots level. IFLA ALP's two main programs are the Building Strong Library Associations program, and IFLA ALP Small Projects. The centerpiece of ALP is the Building Strong Library Associations program. This is a comprehensive program offering a strategic and coordinated approach to capacity building and sustainability of library associations.

- *Preservation and Conservation (PAC)*: The IFLA Strategic Programme on Preservation and Conservation (PAC) was officially created during the IFLA annual conference in Nairobi in 1984 to focus efforts on issues of preservation and initiate worldwide cooperation for the preservation of library materials. The PAC program was effectively launched in Vienna during the 1986 Conference on the Preservation of Library Materials co-organized by the Conference of the Directors of National Libraries, IFLA, and UNESCO. PAC has one major goal : to ensure that library and archive materials, published and unpublished, in all formats, will be preserved in accessible form for as long as possible according to the following principles [29]:
  - Preservation is essential to the survival and development of culture and scholarship;
  - International cooperation is a key principle; and
  - Each country must accept responsibility for the preservation of its own publications.

The activities undertaken under PAC program are [29]:
  - Raising awareness among library professionals, the public and the authorities, of the urgent need to preserve our endangered documentary heritage;
  - Publishing and translating preservation literature in order to make it accessible to a larger professional audience around the world;

- Disseminating information through printed and online publications;
- Organizing training courses, workshops, seminars, etc.;
- Promoting research on best preservation practices; and
- Fund raising.

- *IFLA UNIMARC:* As a successor to the IFLA UBCIM Core Activity, the IFLA UNIMARC Core Activity (UCA) was started in 2003 with the responsibility for the maintenance and development of the Universal MARC format (UNIMARC), originally created by IFLA to facilitate the international exchange of bibliographic data. The purpose of UCA is to coordinate activities aimed at the development, maintenance and promotion of the UNIMARC format, now a set of four formats-Bibliographic, Authorities, Classification and Holdings, and related documentation, through the Permanent UNIMARC Committee (PUC). By agreement with IFLA, the UCA has been hosted by the National Library of Portugal since 2003 [30].

- *Copyright and other Legal Matters (CLM):* It is the only IFLA core activity which currently does not have a permanent office or staff, but relies entirely on voluntary efforts for its extensive and very successful work of international advocacy on intellectual property and related matters. This involves current awareness, policy analysis, awareness rising in the profession, and representation and interventions at international meetings of bodies such as the World Intellectual Property Organization (WIPO) and UNESCO. An important element of its success is partnerships with other bodies such as the European Bureau of Library, Information and Documentation Associations (EBLIDA) and Electronic Information for Libraries (eIFL) [22].

- *Free Access to Information and Freedom of Expression (FAIFE):* The overall objective of IFLA/FAIFE is to raise awareness of the essential correlation between the library concept and the values of intellectual freedom. To reach this goal IFLA/FAIFE collects and disseminates documentation and aims to stimulate a dialog both within and outside the library world. FAIFE works to protect intellectual freedom and freedom of expression. This work includes [31]:
  - Publishing reports, participating in national and international conferences and organize workshops;
  - Monitoring the state of intellectual freedom within the library community world-wide and publish newsletters and online news;

- Responding to violations of free access to information and freedom of expression and make press releases; and
- Supporting IFLA policy development and cooperating with other international human rights organizations.
- FAIFE supports and co-operates with relevant international bodies, organizations or campaigns such as UNESCO, PEN International, Amnesty International.

W.4.2.5 Other Activities of IFLA

IFLA undertakes various activities for improved information dissemination throughout the world.

- *World Library and Information Congress:* IFLA organizes World Library and Information Congress in different parts of the world. The IFLA World Library and Information Congress is the international flagship professional and trade event for the library and information services sector. It brings together over 3,500 participants from more than 120 countries. It sets the international agenda for the profession and offers opportunities for networking and professional development to all delegates [32].
- *IFLA guidelines:* IFLA has brought out a large number of important guidelines under different names, such as policies, plans, codes, statements, and manifestos, which provide valuable directions to the LIS professionals. The important manifestos brought out by it are:
  - Alexandria Manifesto on Libraries, the Information Society in Action;
  - IFLA Manifesto on Transparency, Good Governance, and Freedom from Corruption;
  - The IFLA Internet Manifesto;
  - The IFLA Multicultural Library Manifesto;
  - IFLA/UNESCO Public Library Manifesto;
  - IFLA/UNESCO School Library Manifesto.
- *IFLA websites:* IFLA maintains a number of websites for online dissemination of information relating to IFLA and its activities in different fields. These include:
  - www.ifla.org (The main IFLA website);
  - www.conference.ifla.org (About IFLA conferences);
  - www.express.ifla.org (Serves as the ongoing news providing site during the IFLA's annual World Library and Information Congress);

- www.learning.ifla.org (IFLA's online learning platform, accessible to registered users only);
- www.codex.ifla.org (Closed web space with manuals and tutorials for web editors, translators, and others who do work for IFLA);
- www.blogs.ifla.org (Blogs of IFLA sections and people);
- www.archive.ifla.org (The old, "frozen" websites);
- www.ifla-world-report.org (IFLA's online report on the state of the world in terms of library facts, freedom of access to information, freedom of expression and related issues);
- www.iflastandards.info (IFLA's official namespace);
- IFLA Mailing Lists (IFLA maintains a series of mailing lists for discussions through email. Various IFLA groups set up lists, either open or closed); and
- Success Stories Database (Stories of libraries and library departments all over the world).

- *IFLA publications:* The results of the programs developed by IFLA's professional groups are recorded and disseminated through its publications [33]:
  - *IFLA Journal* is published four times a year. Each issue covers news of current IFLA activities and articles, selected to reflect the variety of the international information profession, ranging from freedom of information, preservation, services to the visually impaired and intellectual property.
  - The *Annual Report* records IFLA's achievements during the previous years.
  - The *IFLA publications series*, published by IFLA's publisher, De Gruyter Saur in Berlin, Germany, includes such titles as: *Digital Library Futures: User perspectives and institutional strategies, Strategies for Regenerating the Library and Information Profession*, and *The World Guide to Library, Archive and Information Science Associations*.
  - The *IFLA Global Studies in Libraries and Information:* This is an English language monograph series published by IFLA's publisher, De Gruyter Saur in Berlin, Germany, the first volume of which entitled "E-Government: Implementation, Adoption and Synthesis in Developing Countries, Volume 1, has been published in 2014.
  - The *IFLA Professional Reports* series feature reports of professional meetings and guidelines to best practice. Recent reports include: *Using research to promote literacy and reading in libraries: Guidelines for*

librarians, Mobile Library Guidelines, International Resource Book for Libraries Serving Disadvantaged Persons: 2001–08.

- *Continuing Education Programmes:* IFLA regularly sponsors continuing education programs like seminars, workshops, etc. for the LIS professionals in different parts of the world.

W.5 ROLE OF NATIONAL AGENCIES

Many government and nongovernment agencies/organizations in different countries, including national library associations, have also played important role in promotion of IOD activities. The role of a few such well-known agencies/organizations is described below.

W.5.1 CILIP

Chartered Institute of Library and Information Professionals (CILIP), was formed in 2002 by the merger of two well-known professional bodies of UK, viz. The Library Association (founded in 1877) and Institute of Information Scientists (founded in 1958). CILIP is a founder member of IFLA. CILIP's work is governed by its Council, set up under the Royal Charter. The President and Councilors of CILIP are elected by the members. There are several local branches across the United Kingdom, 28 special interest groups and over 20 organizations in liaison including such bodies as the African Caribbean Library Association, the Librarians' Christian Fellowship and the Society of Indexers. As of May 2014, CILIP had about 13,470 members [34]. "CILIP is committed to promoting a society where intellectual activity and creativity, freedom of expression and debate, and access to information are encouraged and nurtured as vital elements underpinning individual and community fulfillment in all aspects of human life" [35]. CILIP has adopted a Policy Statement for Information and Library Research and prepared a strategy document to fulfill that policy. The Policy statement outlines CILIP's position on a range of aspects of research and development (R&D) as they affect theory and practice in the management of information and library services and their associated disciplines. According to this policy statement, CILIP claims a role in, among other areas, disseminating information regarding R & D activities and ensuring the free flow of information that stimulates R & D [36]. CILIP also endorses the Council of Europe Guidelines on "Public Access to and Freedom of Expression in Networked Information."

W.5.1.1 Objectives of CILIP

CILIP seeks to work for the public good to promote the highest standards of professional practice and service delivery in the library and information domain. The objectives of CILIP are [35]:

- To position the library and information profession at the heart of the information society;
- To develop and enhance the roles and skills of all its Members, enabling them to achieve and maintain the highest professional standards, both for the professional and the public good;
- To present and champion those skills, including the new skills which will be acquired through continuing professional development;
- To set, maintain, monitor, and promote standards of excellence in the creation, management, exploitation, and sharing of information and knowledge resources; and
- To support the principle of equality of access to information, ideas, and works of the imagination which it affirms is fundamental to a thriving economy, democracy, culture, and civilization.

W.5.1.2 Activities of CILIP

The main activities of CILIP are [34,35]:

- The Library Association (later CILIP) has been bringing out the well-known abstracting journal in the field of LIS, *Library and Information Science Abstracts* (previously known as *Library Science Abstracts*) since 1950. *LISA* provides abstracts of articles from over 500 periodicals published in 68 countries in more than 20 different languages, as well as papers from major English-language conference proceedings. It is now available online through ProQuest.
- CILIP has been serving as the accrediting body for LIS education programs in the United Kingdom.
- It publishes a monthly magazine, *CILIP Update*, including listings of job vacancies.
- It brings valuable textbooks and monographs in the field of LIS through its publishing wing Facet Publishing, the number of title published so far being more than 200.
- It hosts a conference every two years called "Umbrella" (containing "LA" the acronym of the Library Association) to discuss various professional issues.
- It has a Chartership program, the completion of which is considered to be the recognition of the highest standard for information professionals.

- The Information Literacy Group of CILIP aims to provide a forum across all sectors of the profession, which encourages debate and allows the exchange of knowledge in all aspects of Information Literacy.
- The Special Library and Information Service Group brings out an electronic journal *REFER* and a supporting website called *REFERplus*.
- The Special Library and Information Service Group has also brought out a document exemplifying key aspects of current good practices in information and library services.
- The Cataloguing and Indexing Group publishes a quarterly journal *Catalogue and Index*.
- CILIP brings out an Annual Buyers' Guide, which is a directory of over 400 Library suppliers.
- There are many CILIP discussion lists to help members who are working in isolation from professional colleagues.

W.5.2 ASLIB

The Association of Special Libraries and Information Bureaux (ASLIB), was established in 1924 in London at the initiative of Prof. Hutton and financial support of Carnegi United Kingdom Trust. The British Society for International Bibliography merged with the ASLIB in 1948. ASLIB has played a significant role in the field of information management throughout its history. "During World War II ASLIB used information management expertise and innovation to provide leadership and monitor overseas newspapers. ASLIB fed relevant information to Government departments. It also stepped in to provide professional education and training when the only university course in existence (in Britain) at the time had to close down. ASLIB continues to play a strong role in professional development through its training courses and publishing programme". ASLIB also played a key role in the development of BOPCAS (British Official Publications Current Awareness Service) in partnership with the University of Southampton [37]. ASLIB later came to be known as ASLIB: The Association for Information Management.

W.5.2.1 Objectives of ASLIB

The various objectives of ASLIB were:
- To facilitate the co-ordination and systemic use of sources of knowledge and information in all public affair and in industry and commerce and in all the arts and sciences;

- To increase the contribution of information to the economy, social, and cultural life of community management;
- To serve information professionals and librarians across all sectors;
- To supports members to enhance their own performance through the provision of comprehensive resources; and
- To provide expertise in information governance and management and the development of procedures and skills to steer organizations successfully in these areas.

W.5.2.2 Activities of ASLIB

The core areas of ASLIB's activities were governance and regulatory compliance issues such as Copyright, Data Protection and Freedom of Information. The specific activities of ASLIB were:

- ASLIB organized annual conferences to discuss various issues confronting the LIS profession;
- It provided training and development for busy information professionals in key aspects of information work; it offered public courses and workshops, as well as on-site and individual development programs by distance;
- It was bringing out membership magazine *Managing Information* ten times a year;
- It was bringing out very well-known journal, *Journal of Documentation*, and several other important journals, such as monthly *ASLIB Proceedings*, monthly *ASLIB Booklist*, quarterly *Privacy and Data Protection*, online database *ASLIB Current Awareness Abstract*, covering all major topics in library and information management, and other professional and bibliographic literature;
- It was bringing out *ASLIB Membership Directory and Yearbook*;
- It was providing microfilming and other duplicating services;
- It was maintaining a location index to unpublished translation of foreign scientific articles and a register of specialist translations;
- It was catering direct and indirect information service; and
- It was providing consultancy service in library management and employment.

W.5.2.3 Transformation of ASLIB

At the beginning of 20th century ASLIB encountered difficult times. It sold its journals to Emerald and its book publishing business to Taylor and Francis in 2002, and went into voluntary liquidation in 2004, following which it was reconstituted as a limited liability company providing membership services to library and information professionals. In 2010, ASLIB was acquired by MCB Group, the holding company for Emerald Group Publishing Limited. Emerald and ASLIB have been working closely together since 2001, when ASLIB's collection of research journals, including *Journal of Documentation* and *ASLIB Proceedings*, were acquired by Emerald. It was stressed from the side of Emerald that after the acquisition ASLIB's services to members would continue and grow, and the operating name and identity of ASLIB would be preserved. It was also declared that ASLIB would be run independently, but would draw on services from Emerald, as well as other publishers [38].

W.5.3 ALA

Established on October 6, 1876, and chartered in 1879, the American Library Association (ALA) is the oldest and largest library association in the world. The mission of ALA is "to provide leadership for the development, promotion, and improvement of library and information services and the profession of librarianship in order to enhance learning and ensure access to information for all" and its motto is "*the best reading, for the largest number, at the least cost*" [39]. ALA maintains that "libraries are major sources of information for society and they serve as guardians of the public's access to information more generally. The advent of the digital world has revolutionized how the public obtains its information and how libraries provide it. Libraries help ensure that Americans can access the information they need—regardless of age, education, ethnicity, language, income, physical limitations or geographic barriers—as the digital world continues to evolve. Core values of the library community such as equal access to information, intellectual freedom, and the objective stewardship and provision of information must be preserved and strengthened in the evolving digital world." ALA Council is the governing body of ALA. Council determines all policies of the Association and ALA Executive Board acts for Council in the administration of established policies and programs [39].

W.5.3.1 Action Areas of ALA

The key action areas of ALA are [39]:

- *Advocacy for libraries and the profession:* The association actively works to increase public awareness of the crucial value of libraries and librarians, to promote state and national legislation beneficial to libraries and library users, and to supply the resources, training, and support networks needed by local advocates seeking to increase support for libraries of all types.

- *Diversity:* Diversity is a fundamental value of the association and its members, and is reflected in its commitment to recruiting people of color and people with disabilities to the profession and to the promotion and development of library collections and services for all people.
- *Education and lifelong learning:* The association provides opportunities for the professional development and education of all library staff members and trustees; it promotes continuous, lifelong learning for all people through library and information services of every type.
- *Equitable access to information and library services:* The Association advocates funding and policies that support libraries as great democratic institutions, serving people of every age, income level, location, ethnicity, or physical ability, and providing the full range of information resources needed to live, learn, govern, and work.
- *Intellectual freedom:* Intellectual freedom is a basic right in a democratic society and a core value of the library profession. The American Library Association actively defends the right of library users to read, seek information, and speak freely as guaranteed by the First Amendment.
- *Literacy:* The American Library Association assists and promotes libraries in helping children and adults develop the skills they need-the ability to read and use computers-understanding that the ability to seek and effectively utilize information resources is essential in a global information society.
- *Organizational excellence:* The association is inclusive, effective, and responsive to the needs of ALA members.
- *Transforming libraries:* ALA provides leadership in the transformation of libraries and library services in a dynamic and increasingly global digital information environment.

W.5.3.2 Activities of ALA

ALA has eleven divisions, each with a type-of-library or type-of-library-function specialization. ALA divisions publish journals, books, newsletters, and other materials; provide continuing education in a variety of venues and formats; offer awards and scholarships; sponsor institutes and conferences; and maintain networks of affiliates, chapters, and other collaborative relationships. Some of its important activities are [39,40]:

- ALA has formulated three important instruments which express its intellectual freedom principles, viz., *Freedom to Read Statement*, which asserts the public interest in the preservation of the freedom to read;

the *Library Bill of Rights*, which urges libraries to "challenge censorship in the fulfillment of their responsibility to provide information and enlightenment"; and the *ALA Code of Ethics*, which calls on librarians to "uphold the principles of intellectual freedom and resist all efforts to censor library resources."

- The ALA maintains an Office for Intellectual Freedom responsible for implementing ALA policies relating to intellectual freedom, which is defined by ALA as "the right of every individual to both seek and receive information from all points of view without restriction. It provides for free access to all expressions of ideas through which any and all sides of a question, cause or movement may be explored."
- ALA serves as an accrediting body for master degree programs in library and information science and also runs on-line continuing education programs for the benefit of library and information professionals;
- It organizes annual conferences to discuss vital issues confronting library and professionals, which draws more than 25,000 participants;
- It has joined the Information Access Alliance to promote open access to research;
- The Copyright Advisory Network of ALA's Office for Information Technology Policy provides copyright resources to libraries and the communities they serve;
- It works for bringing balance in copyright law ensuring fair use of copyrighted materials;
- The Publishing Department of ALA provides all librarians a comprehensive, one-stop resource for print and digital materials dedicated to professional development, improving library services, and the promotion of libraries, literacy, and reading;
- It brings out two journals—bi-monthly *American Libraries*, which keeps library and information science and technology workers in touch with the profession's most current concerns, and *Booklist*, a book review journal, which is considered as an essential collection development and readers' advisory tool by thousands of librarians for more than 100 years.
- The Information Technology and Telecommunications Services Department of ALA provides advice, support and maintenance service in the areas of web services, network services, telecommunication services, project management, database administration, and technical training.

W.5.4 SLA

The Special Libraries Association (SLA) was established in 1909 in New York at the initiative of some government departments, commercial organizations and research institutes. It is an international professional association for library and information professionals working in business, government, law, finance, nonprofit, and academic organizations and institutions. It is now an international organization with over 15,000 members in over 75 countries [41]. SLA functions in a decentralized manner through 32 chapters and 16 divisions. The mission of SLA is "to advance the leadership role of SLA members in putting knowledge to work for the benefit of decision makers in corporations, government, the professions, and society as well as to shape the destiny of our information and knowledge based global society" and its motto is "Putting Knowledge to Work" [42]. SLA plays vital role in supporting professional knowledge workers in their work as they provide practical and utilitarian information, knowledge, and strategic learning to their identified knowledge customers and clients [43]. The association has 58 regional chapters located throughout the world. SLA celebrated its centenary in 2009.

W.5.4.1 Activities of SLA

The main activities of SLA are [41–43]:

- It organizes annual convention of librarians and information professionals for discussion on common problems;
- It publishes *Information Outlook* (formerly *Special Libraries*) (eight issues per year), *Technical Book Review Index* (ten issues per year), and other professional literature;
- It runs a translation center which collects and supplies translations;
- It provides reprographic services;
- It offers scholarships and loans to library science students and also placement service to its members and consultancy service in the field of special library management; and
- It hosts a website containing a wealth of information on its events and conferences, networking and professional development opportunities, and other resources on the information industry and special librarians and information professionals.

W.5.5 ASIS&T

The Association for Information Science and Technology (ASIS&T) was established in March 1937, as the American Documentation Institute

(ADI), an organization made up of individuals nominated by and representing affiliated scientific and professional societies, foundations and government agencies. Its initial interest was in the development of microfilm as an aid to information dissemination. ADI had an impressive record of achievement in its early years: development of microfilm readers, cameras and services; fostering negotiations and research, which resulted in the so-called "gentleman's agreement" covering the photo duplication of copyrighted materials; establishment of programs for the storage and reproduction of auxiliary publications in support of journal editors; operation of an Oriental scientific literature service during World War II; support of interlingua, an early rival of Esperanto, to foster international science communications; and co-sponsoring of the 1958 International Conference on Scientific Information. In 1952, it started admitting individual as well as institutional members. In January 1968 ADI was renamed American Society for Information Science (ASIS) "reflecting change in its total range of activities, as well as emergence of information science as an identifiable configuration of disciplines." In 2000, the society changed its name to American Society for Information Science & Technology (ASIS&T), reflecting the range of its members and again in 2013 the name was again changed to Association for Information Science and Technology, reflecting its growing international membership [44].

W.5.5.1 Mission and Vision of ASIS&T

The mission of ASIS&T is "to advance the information sciences and related applications of information technology by providing focus, opportunity, and support to information professionals and organizations," while its vision is to "establish a new information professionalism in a world where information is of central importance to personal, social, political, and economic progress by: advancing knowledge about information, its creation, properties, and use; Providing analysis of ideas, practices, and technologies; Valuing theory, research, applications, and service; Nurturing new perspectives, interests, and ideas; Increasing public awareness of the information sciences and technologies and their benefits to society" [44]. ASIS&T has regional chapters as well as a students' chapter. It also has special interest groups.

W.5.5.2 Activities of ASIS&T

To achieve its goals ASIS&T performs the following functions [44]:
- It sponsors research in the fields of mechanization in literature search, use of television for communication, machine translation, etc.;

- It sponsors research in classification and information science;
- It conducts training in documentation techniques;
- It edits, publishes, and disseminates publications concerning research and development;
- It convenes annual meeting for providing a forum for presentation of papers, discussions, and major policy statements; and
- It hosts Information Architecture Summit annually and smaller chapter and special interest group meetings as well as symposia on specific topics.

W.5.5.3 Publications of ASIS&T

ASIS&T has a few valuable publications. It has been publishing a refereed scholarly journal, entitled *American Documentation* (quarterly) since 1950, which in 1970, was renamed as *Journal of American Society of Information Science & Technology (JASIST)*. The current name of the journal is *Journal of ASIS&T* (i.e., *JASIST*). It also used to publish *Annual Review of Information Science and Technology*, which comprehensively reviewed and synthesized yearly trends in the different branches of information science, but it ceased publication in 2012. Other important publications of ASIS&T are:

- *Bulletin of the Association for Information Science and Technology*, which is the bi-monthly newsletter covering the developments and issues affecting the field, pragmatic management reports, opinion pieces, and news of people and events in the information science community.
- *Proceedings* of the ASIST Annual Meetings, being brought out continuously since 1963, contains the contributed papers presented at the annual meetings.

W.5.6 NCLIS

US President Lyndon B. Johnson appointed a National Advisory Commission on Libraries in 1966 to "make a comprehensive study and appraisal of the role of libraries as resources for scholarly pursuits, as centers for the dissemination of knowledge, and as components of the evolving national information systems." On the basis of recommendations of the Advisory Commission, a law was enacted for setting up a National Commission on Libraries and Information Science (NCLIS). The commission came into being in 1970 as a permanent, independent agency of the Federal government of the United States. However, in 2008 the activities of the National Commission of Libraries and Information Science were consolidated under Institute of Museum and Library Services [45].

W.5.6.1 Activities of NCLIS

NCLIS Reported directly to the White House and the Congress on the implementation of national policy and played important role in promotion of library and information activities during its tenure. The major tasks performed by the commission were [46]:

- Conducted studies, surveys, and analyses of the nation's library and information needs;
- Promoted research and development activities;
- Conducted hearings and issued publications as appropriate;
- Developed overall plans for meeting national library and informational needs and for the coordination of activities at the federal, state, and local levels.

Between 1973 and 2000, NCLIS published at least 10 reports dealing with public libraries. These reports dealt with funding, providing Internet access to the public, and establishing community information and referral services and organized a conference on information literacy held in Prague in 2003, and two White House Conferences on library and information services in 1979 and 1991 [45].

W.5.7 CLIR

The Council on Library and Information Resources (CLIR) was created in 1997 through the merger of the Council on Library Resources and the Commission on Preservation and Access. The Council on Library Resources (CLR) was formed in 1956, during a decade marked by explosive library growth and the emergence of new technologies, while the Commission on Preservation and Access was established as a permanent body in 1986, which working closely with the National Endowment for the Humanities (NEH), developed a national strategy to undertake massive microfilming projects in major research libraries and initiated formation of the Digital Library Federation. The CLIR aims "to transform the information landscape to support the advancement of knowledge." CLIR has published more than 160 reports on topics relating to preservation, digital libraries, economics of information, trends in information use, international developments, and the changing role of the library [47,48].

W.5.8 Gates Foundation

Bill & Melinda Gates Foundation, established by Bill Gates and Melinda Gates in 2000, is the largest private foundation in the world. Besides its other philanthropic activities, it aims "to improve the lives of one billion 'information poor' people by 2030 while positioning the world's 320,000 public libraries as critical community assets and providers of information through relevant technologies." In a document entitled "Global Libraries: Strategic Overview," the foundation has stressed that "with their existing infrastructure, dedicated staff, and mission to connect individuals to information, libraries are uniquely suited to offering public Internet access and training to people who would otherwise be left behind in the digital world." It expressed the hope that "if libraries can reinvent themselves and embrace their role as online information centers, the impact on individuals and communities will be significant" [49]. It has, therefore, taken a strategy to extend Internet access facilities to the people through public libraries not only in the United States but in the world at large. The main areas of focus of the foundation with regard to library and information services are [49]:

- *Research and innovation*: It funds projects and research on public access to information and the Internet, trends that affect how libraries serve their communities, and ways to foster innovation in libraries.
- *Training and leadership*: It supports efforts to identify strong library leaders and equip them to create high-impact libraries.
- *Delivery*: It supports efforts to create library programs and services that can be replicated on broad scale and customized for different settings. It supports technology access in public libraries on a national scale, particularly in developing countries and emerging economies.
- *Impact, advocacy, and policy*: It works to ensure adequate resources and public policy support for libraries, and helps public libraries, library staff, and library field measure the impact of public access in libraries and strengthen their advocacy skills.

In addition to its work in the United States, the foundation has supported large-scale efforts in Chile, Mexico, Botswana, Lithuania, Latvia, Romania, Ukraine, Poland, Bulgaria, Vietnam, Colombia, Indonesia, Moldova, Jamaica, South Africa, and Turkey. It has also worked in a smaller-scale, through intermediaries, in Nepal, Bhutan, India, Guatemala, and Honduras.

W.5.9 UGC (India)

University Grants Commission (UGC) was on December 28, 1953, but was formally established as a statutory body in 1956 by an Act of Parliament for "the coordination, determination and maintenance of standards of university education in India" [50]. The UGC has been functioning as an autonomous advisory organization since its inception.

It performs much wider functions than what is suggested by its name. Realizing the importance of library and information services in higher education, UGC from the very beginning made efforts to strengthen the libraries of the higher educational institutions in order to improve dissemination of information required by the faculty, researchers, and students. It has taken several important measures during the last six decades for the improvement of library and information services in the higher educational institutions of the country. The significant steps taken by UGC in this regard are briefly described below.

W.5.9.1 Appointment of Committees

One of the first steps that UGC took for the development of libraries in higher educational institutions was to appoint a Library Committee in 1957 under the chairmanship of Ranganathan "to advise the commission on matters relating to the proper functioning and management of libraries." The Committee systematically surveyed the academic libraries and was very much disappointed to find poor facilities, services, and budget of the university libraries. The Committee submitted its report, entitled "University and College Libraries", in 1959 making very comprehensive and concrete recommendations on several aspects viz. utilization of library grant, collection development, cultivation of reading habits, weeding out and loss of books, reference and documentation services, building of microfilm collection, open access system, preparation of union catalogue of books and serials to facilitate co-operation among libraries, library personnel, library building and furniture, etc. On the recommendation of this committee a Review Committee on Library Science was set up in 1961, again under the chairmanship of Ranganathan for reviewing the LIS education system in the country and recommend measures for its improvement, since the quality of library and information services depends on the quality of staff, which in turn greatly depends on the quality of training they receive. The committee in its report, entitled "Library Science in Indian Universities" reviewed the existing LIS education scenario in the country and made recommendations relating to admission, examination, course duration, qualifications, and training of teachers, staff requirement, physical facilities, research, etc. It also set up Curriculum Development Committees in LIS in 1990 under the chairmanship of Prof. P.N. Kaula (Report, 1965) and in 1997 with Dr. C.R. Karisidappa as convener (Report, 2001), which prepared model syllabi for LIS courses to meet the changing manpower requirements in libraries and information centers.

W.5.9.2 Financial Assistance

The UGC accepted most of the recommendations of the above committees as well as other committees and commissions set by the Government of India for the development of higher education. It played an extraordinary developmental role by providing financial assistance to university and college libraries for collection development, purchase of furniture and equipment, construction/expansion/renovation of library building, and so on [51].

W.5.9.3 Wheat Loan Programme

The Wheat Loan Educational Exchange Programme came into existence in 1951 when the American Congress passed the Public Law 480 (P.L.480). Under this Act, a loan of $190,000,000 was provided to India for the purchase of wheat from America to relieve acute food shortage in India after Independence. The Act further specified that a sum of $5,000,000 of the interest accruing from the loan should be used for promoting higher education by purchasing books and journals, scientific equipment, and also for the exchange of educationists and academicians between India and United States of America. Wheat Loan Funds were also used to establish and equip three extension libraries in Ludhiana, Madurai, and Udaipur. The Wheat Loan grant also helped 33 librarians from university and research libraries to travel and study in the United States. Some American librarians also visited India to establish a useful professional relationship between two countries. Thus, the Wheat Loan grant and exchange program promoted libraries of the universities and research institutes to render effective services to users [51].

W.5.9.4 Book Banks

In 1963–64, the UGC introduced a new scheme of "Book Bank" and provided grants to acquire multiple copies of costly textbooks, recommended in all the disciplines. The objective of this scheme was to provide textbooks to poor, needy and deserving students for home study on long term basis charging nominal deposits. This proved to be a boon to the students. However, the UGC Review Committee in 1981 felt that there were gaps in implementation of book bank scheme and it had not made a uniform impact in all the universities and colleges. Consequently, the scheme was discontinued.

W.5.9.5 National Information Centres

UGC has set up three information centers covering different disciplines—the National Centre for Science Information (NCSI) at Indian Institute of Science Bangalore, National Humanities Information Centre at SNDT Women's University Mumbai, and National Social Science Information Centre at M.S. University at Baroda, to provide information services, including document delivery service, to students, teachers, and researchers.

National Centre for Science Information

National Information Centre for Science Information (NCSI), was set up in 1983 as a UGC Inter-University Centre at Indian Institute of Science (IISc), Bangalore. It covered science disciplines such as physical sciences, biological sciences, chemistry, mathematics, earth sciences, and engineering. Over the years NCSI pioneered information services based on information technology for research scholars all over India. In disseminated the know-how gained to library professionals across India through its highly effective training programs. Over years NCSI had had many firsts to its credit, which included [52,53]:

- Provision of national level current awareness services to researchers in Indian universities during 1984–2002;
- Provision of computerized selective dissemination of information (SDI) and document delivery Services 1980s and 1990s;
- Initiating India's first interoperable, open access institutional repository, ePrints@IISc (http://eprints.iisc.ernet.in), in 2002;
- Starting of Electronic Theses and Dissertations (ETD) repository of IISc (http://etd.iisc.ernet.in) in 2005;
- Conducting workshops at the national level to train people in Internet Technologies, including creation of Digital Libraries and setting up and maintaining inter-operable open access institutional repositories.

Nevertheless, UGC has since stopped its funding and it has now become a part of Indian Institute of Science. At present the vision of the center is to bring world class electronic information services to the IISc academic community. The specific objectives of the center are [52]:

- To provide seamless, network access to worldwide scholarly information resources of relevance to the IISc academic community, facilitating improved learning, teaching, research, collaboration, and information sharing;

- To provide orientation and training to the IISc academic community in making effective use of electronic information sources, tools, and services;
- To participate in the e-publishing and e-dissemination of Institute's intellectual contributions; and
- To conduct teaching, research, and training in Library and Information Management, with focus on setup, operation, and management of digital information facilities and services.

The center provides variety of electronic information services [54]:

- Intranet and Internet access to world's leading bibliographic databases;
- Gateway services for electronic journals and open access resources on the Internet;
- Customized web access through *MySciGate* portal;
- Document delivery services;
- ePrints@IISc (Open Access Repository of IISc Research Publications);
- etd@IISc (Electronic Theses and Dissertations of IISc); and
- e-JIS (Electronic Journal Information Service).

All the services provided by NCSI are integrated via the *Scigate: The IISc Science Information Portal*. *SciGate* is a science information portal and gateway website developed for the use of students, staff and faculty of IISc. SciGate provides single point access to a variety of locally hosted and Internet-based science, engineering, medicine, and management information resources. Portion of content on *SciGate* (open sources, InfoWatch, IISc Publications) and E-JIS (free e-journals) are freely accessible on the Internet. NCSI also publishes a monthly electronic newsletter *InfoWatch* reporting new Internet resources of relevance to Science and Technology researchers [54].

National Humanities Information Centre

The National Humanities Information Centre (NHIC) was set up by the UGC in SNDT Women's University, Mumbai, in 1986. The center covers the subject fields like sociology, Gujarati, Women's Studies, home science, library science, and special education. It provides current awareness service, reference service, and document delivery service to students, teachers, and researchers. The university library now manages the center [55,56].

National Social Sciences Information Centre

National Social Sciences Information Centre (NSSIC) was set by UGC at MS University of Baroda, Vadodra. It covers subjects like economics, political science, education, and psychology. The center provides current awareness service and reference service to the academic community. Resources available in university library and other local libraries are optimally utilized and services developed on a computational database built up by scanning hundreds of Indian and foreign journals [56]. It also organizes seminars and workshops in the field of social sciences.

W.5.9.6 INFLIBNET Programme

An Inter-University Centre of UGC, the INFLIBNET serves toward modernization of Libraries, serves as Information Centre for transfer and access of information, supporting scholarships, and learning and academic pursuits through a National Network of Libraries in around 264 universities, colleges, and R&D institutions across the country [57]. INFLIBNET has introduced several measures for improved access to information to the academic community of the country, the details of which may be found in the previous chapter.

W.5.10 NKC (India)

The National Knowledge Commission (NKC) was constituted on June 13, 2005, with a time-frame of three years, from October 2, 2005, to October 2, 2008, which was extended up to March 31, 2009. As a high-level advisory body to the Prime Minister of India, the National Knowledge Commission was given a mandate to guide policy and direct reforms, focusing on certain key areas such as education, science and technology, agriculture, industry, e-governance. Easy access to knowledge, creation and preservation of knowledge systems, dissemination of knowledge, and better knowledge services were the core concerns of the commission [58]. The focus of the NKC was mainly on the following with action oriented sub-themes [59]:

- Building excellence in the educational system to meet the knowledge challenges of the 21st century and increase India's competitive advantage in fields of knowledge.
- Promoting creation of knowledge in S&T, social sciences, and other academic institutions.
- Improving the management of institutions engaged in intellectual property rights.
- Promoting innovation and entrepreneurship, and knowledge applications in agriculture, industry, and healthcare.

- Promoting the use of knowledge capabilities in making government an effective, transparent, and accountable service provider to the citizen and promote widespread sharing of knowledge to maximize public benefit.
- Promoting the utilization of traditional knowledge.

W.5.10.1 Working Group on Libraries

It was felt that "to realize this dream which is also being called 'Mission Impossible,' one major all pervading area which needs immediate and sustained attention is the Library and Information Services (LIS) sector. The stakeholders of each focus area will need well organized and systematic Library and Information Services to support these activities." NKC, therefore, set up a Working Group on Libraries with the following broad Terms of Reference [60]:

- Redefine the objectives of the country's Library and Information Services (LIS) sector.
- Identify constraints, problems, and challenges relating to the LIS sector.
- Recommend changes and reforms to address the problems and challenges relating to the LIS sector, to ensure a holistic development of information services in all areas of national activity.
- Take necessary steps to mobilize and upgrade the existing Library and Information Systems and Services, taking advantage of the latest advances in Information Communication Technology (ICT).

The working group created four committees to deal with different issues and after a lot of deliberations and consultations with the experts in the field of LIS, the working group came out with a comprehensive report.

Working Group Report

The preamble of the report stated: "In today's context, libraries have to play two distinct roles–to serve as a local center of information and knowledge, and be a local gateway to national and global knowledge. Keeping in view the above, the Mission Statement of the LIS sector should be: The library and information sector is committed to support the creation of a knowledge society by providing equitable, high quality, cost effective access to information and knowledge resources and services to meet the informational, educational, recreational and cultural needs of the community through a range of national, institutional and public libraries." The working group recognized the following as the objectives of all libraries [60]:

- To disseminate knowledge as widely as possible;
- To serve as a major vehicle to facilitate creation of new knowledge;

- To facilitate optimal use of knowledge by all sectors, such as government, industry, rural sector, and civil society; and
- To ensure that people from all sectors and all parts of the country have easy access to knowledge relevant to their needs, in their own language.

W.5.10.2 NKC Recommendations

The National Knowledge Commission has given a good number of recommendations for development of library and information service as we as other areas which aim at improving dissemination of information to the masses.

On Libraries

Keeping the aforesaid objectives of libraries in view, the NKC Working Group on Libraries gave 29 recommendations, grouped under the headings LIS policy, finance, library management, access and networking, private collections, digitization and open access, staffing pattern, and public–private partnership. NKC, after extensive consultations with the working group members and diverse stake-holders, finally recommended the following for formulating strategies in the LIS sector [59]:

- A permanent, independent, and financially autonomous National Commission on Libraries should be set up by the Central Government as a statutory body to address the information and learning needs of the citizens of India. To launch the process in a mission mode, a National Mission on Libraries should be set up immediately, for a period of three years.
- A national census of all libraries should be prepared by undertaking a nation-wide survey.
- The proposed Mission/Commission on Libraries must assess as soon as possible the manpower requirements of the country in the area of LIS management, and take necessary steps to meet the country's requirement through LIS education and training.
- In the changed context, it is necessary to assess the manpower requirements for different types of libraries and departments of library and information science, keeping in mind job descriptions, qualifications, designations, pay scale, career advancement, and service conditions.
- A specified percentage of the Central and State education budgets must be ear-marked for libraries. In addition, a Central Library Fund should be instituted for upgrading existing libraries over a period of 3–5 years.

- Libraries should be so organized and the staff so trained that they become relevant to user communities (including special groups) in every respect. Also, to optimize resources, efforts should be made to synergize the strengths of different types of libraries through innovative collaboration. NKC proposed the creation of a model Library Charter, a list of services to be performed by libraries, a Library Network, and a National Repository for Bibliographic Records.
- It is necessary to involve different stakeholders and user groups in the managerial decision-making process for libraries. Libraries should integrate with all other knowledge-based activities in the local area to develop a community-based information system.
- The catalogues of all libraries should be put on local, state and national websites with necessary linkages. This will enable networking of different types of libraries and setting up of a National Repository of Bibliographic Records and a centralized collaborative virtual enquiry-handling system using the latest ICT. To enable equitable and universal access to knowledge resources, libraries should be encouraged to create more digital resources by digitizing relevant reading materials in different languages, which can be shared at all levels. Peer-reviewed research papers resulting from publicly funded research should also be made available through open access channels.
- There are numerous rich private and personal collections in India which need to be identified, documented, and preserved for posterity.
- Philanthropic organizations, industrial houses, and other private agencies should be encouraged through fiscal incentives to support existing libraries or set up new libraries.

The NKC also said that in order to facilitate the coordinated development of libraries across different sectors and to provide the legislative framework, required legal support and financial backing to the library sector, the Government could, in course of time, consider including libraries in the Concurrent List of the Constitution of India.

On Information Systems and Services

NKC also gave valuable recommendations relating to translation, knowledge network, health information network, and portals, which will further improve facilities for information access. The major recommendations in above areas are mentioned below [59].

On Translation

- Impetus should be provided for developing translation as an industry.
- A store-house of information on all aspects of translation involving Indian languages should be established, and make this available by creating, maintaining and constantly updating information on translations published, training programs, translation tools/instruments and new initiatives, and facilities such as a "National Register for Translators."
- Printed as well as virtual publication of works on translation studies should be promoted; and a clearing house should be created for all translation activities, both in theoretical and applied subjects, in as many Indian languages as possible.
- Various tools for translation, including digital tools like Thesauri, Bilingual Dictionaries, and software for translation should be created and maintained. In addition, machine translation should be promoted.
- Quality training and education should be provided for translators.
- A national web portal on translation as a one-stop shop should be set up for all information on translation and to provide a forum for dialogue by creating a bulletin board for people to post questions and answers.

On National Knowledge Network

NKC strongly felt that "to optimally utilize the potential of institutions engaged in generation and dissemination of knowledge in various areas, such as research laboratories, universities and other institutions of higher learning, including professional institutions, it is important to connect them through a high-speed broadband network" [59]. As such it recommended building of a national knowledge network with gigabit capabilities to connect all universities, libraries, laboratories, hospitals, and agricultural institutions to share data and resources across the country.

On Health Information Network

NKC also felt the need of a health information network for promoting delivery of efficient health care in the country. Hence it recommended, among others, initiation of development of an Indian Health Information Network, creation of a common electronic health record and create appropriate policy framework to protect health data of citizens [59].

On Web Portals

NKC also recommended that "National web-based portals should be set up on certain key sectors such as Water, Energy, Environment, Education, Food, Health, Agriculture, Employment, Citizens' Rights. These would serve as a single point of access for consolidated information, applications and resources on the sector and will cater to a wide spectrum of users from citizens, entrepreneurs, small-scale industries, students, professionals, researchers, local practitioners etc." It also recommended that "All government departments should easily make available data sets they have, in a digital format to the portal consortium. Data from different sectors needs to be analyzed holistically so that planning becomes more data-driven and reflects the ground situation. This means that data that is traditionally collected and managed separately, unrelated to each other, should now be seen together" [59].

W.5.10.3 Implementation of NKC Recommendations

The Government of India has already taken some positive steps toward implementation of the NKC recommendations. The steps taken so far are described below.

On Libraries

As a first step toward implementation of the recommendations relating to libraries, the Government of India set up the National Mission on Libraries (NML) in May 2012, with Raja Rammohun Roy Library Foundation as the nodal agency. In the first meeting of the NML held on May 18, 2012, some decisions were taken for improvement in the library sector. These include conducting of a national census of libraries, content creation and setting up of community information centers, up-gradation of the existing public libraries, school and college libraries and use of school libraries as community libraries, and improvement in library and information science education training and research facilities. The NML also set up four groups on up-gradation of existing public libraries; LIS education, training and research facilities; creation of national virtual library; and national census of libraries, content creation, and community information centers [61]. According to a report, quoting former Prime Minister Dr. Manmohan Singh, published in *Outlook* on March 22, 2012, nearly 9000 libraries across the country will be digitally linked under NML to enable the readers easily access books and information needed by them.

National Virtual Library

The NML has also submitted to the Ministry of Culture, Government of India, a Concept Note on National Virtual Library (NVL), according to which, NVL will be the focal point of varied activities of the NML and will provide "a platform for users from all sectors to seek information through well-researched services implemented in user-friendly interfaces" [62]. According to the note, the vision of the NVL will be "to empower people with right information in order to create a knowledge society and ensure preservation of digital content for the posterity," while the objectives will be [62]:

- To provide access to information for everyone in an Open Access Environment;
- To undertake content development—all existing digital resources to be identified and sourced;
- To organize information resource base using standard tools and techniques;
- To plan, design, and implement digital information services and searching;
- To facilitate Multilingual Information Resource collection;
- To Implement robust and secure computing infrastructure;
- To provide usage and impact indicators through user, resources, and service use statistics; and
- To incorporate procedures for feedback and up-gradation of the system.

The note has also described the phases of its implementation, the methods of content organization and development, the standards to be followed, research and development activities to be undertaken for the purpose and the services that the NVL will render [62].

On Information Systems and Services

The Government of India has taken steps for linking 15,000 colleges and universities to create the National Knowledge Network through a 15 gigabit broadband connectivity. It has also set up a National Translation Mission, with Central Institute of Indian Languages, Mysore, as the nodal agency. Two national web portals on Water and Energy have also been launched in January 2007. The Water portal (India Water Portal) has been developed by the public charitable Arghyam Trust, Bangalore (URL: http://www.indiawaterportal.org/), and the Energy portal (India Energy Portal) by The Energy and Research Institute (TERI), New Delhi. (URL: http://www.indiaenergyportal.org/) [63,64]. India Health Portal

(URL: http://www.nhp.gov.in/) has also been launched by the Ministry of Health and Family Welfare. It may be mentioned that the recommendations of the NKC and NML, when fully implemented, will not only enhance the accessibility of information, but also make the libraries and information centers better equipped for information dissemination.

W.5.11 DRTC

Documentation Research and Training Centre (DRTC) was established in 1962 at the initiative of Dr. S.R. Ranganathan and Prof. P.C. Mahalanobis as a unit of the Indian Statistical Institute, Bangalore Centre. With the efforts of Ranganathan, who served as an Honorary Professor till his death, and his colleagues, like Prof. A. Neelameghan, Prof. Ganesh Bhattacharyya and others, it gradually developed into the country's foremost research and training center in the field of documentation and information science. DRTC has made very significant contribution in developing suitable manpower for documentation and information work. It has celebrated its golden jubilee in 2012.

W.5.11.1 Objectives of DRTC

The main objectives of DRTC, as envisaged by Ranganathan, are [65]:
- To do research in documentation techniques, continuously refining and sharpening them;
- To train students for advanced documentation work and service;
- To give refresher courses on the subjects to the practicing documentalists;
- To train students and other documentalists in the preparation of the depth version of Colon Classification; and
- To train students and other documentalists in doing research in the techniques of documentation work.

However, with the changing time and need of the LIS profession a new set of objectives have been set for DRTC, which are [66]:
- Organizing world class training and workshops;
- Strengthening information industry and mobilizing resources and support for libraries and information infrastructure development;
- Improving the existing infrastructure through advocacy, policymaking, and goodwill;
- Preparing for the digital economy by research; and
- Developing human resources for the career as industry-ready and place students as trained professionals.

W.5.11.2 Activities of DRTC

The various activities of DRTC are [66]:

- *Education:* DRTC has been running an Associateship in Documentation course since its inception, which was later renamed as Associateship in Documentation and Information Science. From 2008 to 2010 session the course has been converted into Master of Science in Library and Information Science (MS-LIS). Intense training is provided in this course in documentation and information work with emphasis on computer application in such work.
- *Research:* Research in different fields of LIS, specially in documentation and knowledge organization was started in DRTC by Ranganathan and his associates. The tradition still continues, but the focus has been changed to natural language processing, development of ontologies and taxonomies, digital libraries, and web-based information services. It has a very strong research program and a PhD collaboration with the University of Trento, Italy.
- *Projects:* The faculty members of DRC are involved in several national and international projects, the most significant of them being Living Knowledge Project, funded by European Commission, which aims at studying the effect of diversity and time on opinions and bias as reflected on the web, which may lead to evolving search and navigation tools that will automatically classify and organize opinions and bias resulting in more insightful, better organized, easier-to-understand output.
- *Continuing education:* Initially, DRTC used to conduct two seminars—one annual seminar and one refresher seminar—every year for the benefit of the students and working professionals. At present one seminar and a number of short-term training programs/workshops on latest trends and development in the field of LIS are being conducted at DRTC.
- *Librarian's digital library:* DRTC has created a digital repository for library professionals, named Librarian's Digital Library, using DSpace software, where any digital resource related to Library and Information Science domain can be archived and accessed by anybody across the world.
- *Ranganathan archive:* DRTC has taken up a project to build up an archive-cum-museum on Ranganathan, the work for which has already been started.
- *Publications:* DRTC publishes the proceedings and course materials for the seminars and workshops being conducted by it.

W.5.12 RRRLF

Established in 1972, Raja Rammohun Roy Library Foundation (RRRLF) is a central autonomous organization established and fully financed by the Ministry of Culture, Government of India. It is the nodal agency of the Government of India to support public library services and systems and promote public library movement in the country. The supreme policy-making body of RRRLF is called the Foundation. Director General is the executive head and ex-officio Member-Secretary of the Foundation. The Foundation functions in each State/U.T. through a machinery called State Library Planning Committee (SLPC) or State Library Committee (SLC).

W.5.12.1 Objectives of RRRLF

RRRLF functions as a promotional agency, an advisory and consultancy organization and a funding body for public library development in India. Some important objectives of RRLF are [67]:

* To promote library movement in the country;
* To enunciate national library policy and to help build up a national library system;
* To provide financial and technical assistance to libraries;
* To provide financial assistance to organizations, regional or national engaged in the promotion of library development;
* To publish appropriate literature and to act as a clearing house of ideas and information on library development in India and abroad;
* To promote research in problems of library development; and
* To advise the government on all matters pertaining to the library development in the country.

W.5.12.2 Activities of RRRLF

The various activities of RRLF which help in improving dissemination of information to the public are [67]:

* RRRLF promotes public library services rendering book and financial assistance to the public libraries under different schemes of assistance in collaboration with Library Department or Department in charge of Public Library Services.
* It has undertaken several promotional activities for qualitative improve-ment of library services. Besides organization of many seminars and conferences, it has played a major role in the preparation of National Policy on Library and Information System.
* It has also issued guidelines on public library systems and services.

- Since 2005–06 the Foundation has also taken up the initiative to develop the District Youth Resource Centre (DYRC) in collaboration with Nehru Yuvak Kendra Sangathana, an autonomous organization under the Ministry of Sports and Youth Affairs.
- Besides carrying on Research Projects on public library or allied subjects, the Research Cell of RRLF renders advisory and consultancy services whenever required.
- To disseminate innovative and new concepts and ideas for the development of Public Library Services and system in the country through research oriented activities, the Foundation has introduced Annual Raja Rammohun Roy Award to the best contributor of an article covering the area of development of Public Library Systems and Services or suggesting measures for promotion of reading habit.
- The Foundation has also undertaken a program of giving seven awards annually—one for the best State Central Library and six for the best District Libraries of six regions in the country. Since 2005 the Foundation has also instituted RRRLF Best Rural Library Awards-one for each state.
- RRRLF also organizes Raja Rammohun Roy Memorial Lecture by a scholar of eminence every year.
- It publishes a bi-annual journal entitled, *Granthana, Indian Journal of Library Studies* and a bi-monthly newsletter *RRRLF Newsletter*. It has also brought out some other important publications, including *Directory of Indian Public Libraries.*

W.5.13 ILA

Indian Library Association (ILA), which was formed in 1933 at the first all-India library conference held in Calcutta (now Kolkata), is the national professional organization of library and information workers now located in Delhi. It aims at developing high standards of librarianship and library and information services.

W.5.13.1 Objectives of ILA

According to the constitution of ILA, the specific objectives of the association are [68]:

- Promotion of library movement and improvement in library services in all its aspects in India;
- Promotion of library science education and the improvement in the training of libraries in India;

- Promotion of bibliographical study and research in library science;
- Improvement in the status and conditions of services of librarians;
- Affiliation of the state and other library association with Indian Library Association and co-operation with international organization with same objectives;
- Publication of bulletins, periodicals, books, etc. which will help in the realization of the objectives of the association;
- Establishment of libraries, documentation, and information centers and assistance in their establishment and working;
- Promotion of appropriate library legislation in India;
- Providing a common forum to all persons engaged or interested in library and information work by holding conferences and meetings for discussion of professional, technical, and organizational issues;
- Accreditation of institutions imparting library and information science education and training;
- Promotion as well as formulation of standards, norms, guidelines, etc. for management of library and information systems and services; and
- Carrying out all such other things that are incidental or conducive to the attainment of the above mentioned objectives.

W.5.13.2 Activities of ILA

ILA has been providing a wide variety of services to its members and others in the library community since its formation. Some of its important activities are [68]:

- It conducts annual conferences to discuss topics of current interest;
- It organized an International Conference on "Relevance of Ranganathan's Contributions to Library Science," in 1985 and IFLA Conference in 1992 to commemorate the birth centenary of Ranganathan;
- It regularly brings out *Journal of the Indian Library Association*, *ILA Newsletter*, and *proceedings* of all-India conferences organized by it;
- It has developed its own website as well as an LIS Gateway for providing access to all types of literature on LIS.

W.5.14 IASLIC

Indian Association of Special Libraries and Information Centres (IASLIC) is basically a voluntary non-profit making national organization of librarians, documentalists and information scientists and not a documentation center as such. But it performs various types of documentation work and renders documentation services. IASLIC was established in 1955 in Calcutta mainly to act as a center of research in special librarianship and documentation techniques and as a center of information in scientific, technical and other fields. With a membership of over 1500, IASLIC now functions through six divisions. It is a member of IFLA [69].

W.5.14.1 Objectives of IASLIC
The objectives of IASLIC are [69]:
- To promote the quality of Library and Information Services;
- To coordinate the activities, and foster mutual cooperation and assistance among the special libraries, scientific, technological and research institutions, learned societies, commercial organizations, industrial research establishments as well as centers of studies in social sciences and humanities;
- To improve the technical efficiency of the professionals;
- To act as a center of research and studies in special librarianship and documentation techniques;
- To act as a center of information in scientific, technical, and other related fields of LIS in pursuance of the aforesaid objectives.

W.5.14.2 Activities of IASLIC
The main activities of IASLIC are [69]:
- It organizes annual seminars/conferences;
- It provides document delivery services, specially photocopies, and microfilm copies;
- It provides translation service (English translation of foreign technical literature);
- It organizes short-term courses and workshops on different areas of library and information science, such as indexing, information consolidation, thesaurus construction, computer application;
- It conducted foreign language courses for some time;
- It has formulated a code for inter-library loan;
- It brings out quarterly *IASLIC Bulletin*, quarterly *Indian Library Science Abstracts*, and monthly *IASLIC Newsletter*;
- It brings out special publications containing proceedings of national seminars and conferences organized by it;
- It brings out monographs, technical pamphlets, and manuals on various aspects of library and information science;
- It has brought out a directory of special libraries in India; and
- It has sponsored a Study Circle which regularly discusses problems and issues relating to library science and documentation (over 300 study circle meetings have been organized).

REFERENCES

[1] A. Neelameghan, International cooperation and assistance, in: UNESCO. World Information Report, 1997–98 (Chapter 27). <http://www.unesco.org/webworld/wirerpt/wirenglish/chap27.pdf>.

[2] J.B. Rose, The UNESCO General Information Programme and its role in the development of regional cooperative networks, IATUL Q. 4 (4) (1989) 231–245.

[3] D. Davinson, Bibliographic Control, second ed., Clive Bingley, London, 1981, p. 72.

[4] H.C. Campbell, IFLA: library universality in a divided world, IFLA J. 28 (2002) 118–135.

[5] K.H. Roberts, The Thrust of UNESCO'S General Information Programme: Paper Presented at the Annual Conference of the American Library Association, San Francisco, CA, 1981.

[6] UNESCO. Information for All Programme. <http://www.unesco.org/new/en/communication-and-information/intergovernmental-programmes/information-for-all-programme-ifap/about-ifap/>.

[7] UNESCO. Information for All Programme. <http://www.ifap.ru/ofdocs/unesco/programe.pdf>.

[8] S. Katz, FAO's role in facilitating access to the scientific and technical literature in Agriculture in developing countries. (PowerPoint presentation), in: Berlin 5 Open Access: From practice to impact: Consequences of Knowledge dissemination, Padova (Italy), 2007. <http://eprints.rclis.org/10862/>.

[9] G. Salokhe, et al., FAO's Role in information management and dissemination—challenges, innovation, success: Lessons learned. <http://www.fao.org/docrep/008/af238e/af238e00.htm>.

[10] AGORA. <http://www.aginternetwork.org/en/about_agora/>.

[11] Food and Agricultural Organization. Agricultural Information Management Standards. AGROVAC Multilingual agricultural thesaurus. <http://aims.fao.org/standards/agrovoc/about>.

[12] Asian and Pacific Centre for Transfer of Technology. <www.apctt.org/>.

[13] World Health Organization. <https://en.wikipedia.org/wiki/World_Health_Organization#Data_handling_and_publications>.

[14] About HELLIS. <http://www.nheicc.gov.np/about_hellis>.

[15] World Bank Group—Independent Evaluation Group. <http://ieg.worldbankgroup.org/content/ieg/en/home/reports/grpp_eval.html>.

[16] F.A. Siridov, Role and activities of International Federation for Documentation, UNESCO Bull. Lib. 21 (1967) 196–197.

[17] Europa Year Book—A World Survey. Europa Publications, London, 1986, p. 266.

[18] H. Arntz, in: A. Kent, et al. (Eds.), International Federation for Documentation, vol. 12, Marcel Dekker, New York, 1974, pp. 377–402.

[19] S. Keenan, FID, in: J. Feather, P. Sturges (Eds.), International Encyclopedia of Information and Library Science, second ed., Routledge, New York, 2003.

[20] IFLA. IFLA's Three Pillars. <http://www.ifla.org/three-pillars>.

[21] IFLA. More about IFLA. <http://www.ifla.org/about/more>.

[22] P.J. Lore, The role and functioning of IFLA. Paper of International Congress on Professional Associations, Madrid, October 2007.

[23] IFLA. Universal Bibliographic Control. <http://archive.ifla.org/VI/3/ubcim.htm> (closed web page).

[24] IFLA. Professional Statement on Universal Bibliographic Control. <http://www.ifla.org/files/assets/bibliography/Documents/IFLA%20Professional%20Statement%20on%20UBC.pdf>.

[25] IFLA. Universal Availability of Publication. <http://archive.ifla.org/VI/2/uap-archive.htm> (closed web page).

[26] IFLA. UDT Newsletter. <http://archive.ifla.org/VI/5/nd1/udtnwann.htm>.

[27] R. Prytherch (Ed.), Harrod's Librarians' Glossary, tenth ed., Ashgate, Farnham, UK, 2005.

[28] IFLA-CDNL Alliance for Digital Strategies (ICADS). <http://www.ifla.org/icad>.

[29] IFLA. About the Preservation and Conservation Programme. <http://www.ifla.org/about-pac>.

[30] IFLA. About the UNIMARC Strategic Programme. <http://www.ifla.org/about-unimarc>.

[31] IFLA. Committee on Freedom of Access to Information and Freedom of Expression. <http://www.ifla.org/faife>.

[32] IFLA. World Library and Information Congress. <http://conference.ifla.org/>.

[33] IFLA. IFLA Publications. <http://www.ifla.org/ifla-publications>.

[34] Chartered Institute of Library and Information Professionals. <https://en.wikipedia.org/wiki/Chartered_Institute_of_Library_and_Information_Professionals>.

[35] Chartered Institute of Library and Information Professionals. <http://www.cilip.org.uk/>.

[36] R.R. Powel, et al., Library and information science research and information science practitioners, Lib. Inform. Sci. Res. 24 (2002) 49–72.

[37] Association for Information Management (ASLIB), Library & Information Science Gateway, <http://www.lisgateway.com/index.php?option=com_content&view=category&layout=blog&id=10&Itemid=6>.

[38] Emerald Group Publishing. Emerald News. <http://www.emeraldinsight.com/about/news/story.htm?id=2257>.

[39] American Library Association. About ALA. <http://www.ala.org/aboutala/>.

[40] American Library Association. <http://en.wikipedia.org/wiki/American_Library_Association>.

[41] Special Libraries Association. <http://en.wikipedia.org/wiki/Special_Libraries_Association>.

[42] R.F. Casey, The Special Libraries Association (SLA)—putting knowledge to work, INSPEL 32 (1997) 119–123.

[43] G.S. Clair, et al., Special Libraries Association (SLA): Encyclopedia of Library and Information Sciences, third ed, Taylor & Francis, Abingdon, Oxford, 2009.

[44] ASSIS&T. <http://www.asis.org/>.

[45] National Commission on Libraries and Information Science. <https://en.wikipedia.org/wiki/National_Commission_on_Libraries_and_Information_Science>.

[46] National Commission on Libraries and Information Science. <http://liswiki.org/wiki/National_Commission_on_Libraries_and_Information_Science>.

[47] Council on Library and Information Resources. <https://en.wikipedia.org/wiki/Council_on_Library_and_Information_Resources>.

[48] Council on Library and Information Resources. <https://www.clir.org/>.

[49] Bill and Milinda Gates Foundation. Global libraries: strategy overview. <http://www.gatesfoundation.org/What-We-Do/Global-Development/Global-Libraries>.

[50] University Grants Commission (India). Genesis. <http://www.ugc.ac.in/page/Genesis.aspx>.

[51] Librarian's Diary. <http://librariandiary.blogspot.in/2012/03/ugc-and-library-committe.html> (relevant web page deleted).

[52] National Centre for Science Information. <http://www.ncsi.iisc.ernet.in/> (closed web page).

[53] National Centre for Science Information. <http://ncsinet.org/ncsi>.

[54] National Centre for Science Information. <http://en.wikipedia.org/wiki/National_Centre_for_Science_Information>.

[55] National Humanities Information Centre. <http://www.webpages.uidaho>.

[56] S.S. Pawar, University Grants Commission (UGC) and Development of Libraries, Deep and Deep Publications, New Delhi, 1998.

[57] University Grants Commission (India). Inter-University centre: Information and Library Network Centre. <http://www.ugc.ac.in/page/INFLIBNET.aspx>.

[58] National Knowledge Commission (India). <http://knowledgecommission.gov.in> (closed web page).

[59] National Knowledge Commission (India). Report to the nation, 2006–2009.NKC, New Delhi, 2009.

[60] National Knowledge Commission (India). Working Group on Libraries. Libraries: Gateways to Knowledge. NKC, New Delhi, 2007.

[61] National Mission on Libraries (India). <http://www.indiaculture.nic.in/nml/index. html>.

[62] National Mission on Libraries (India). National Virtual Library: a concept note. <http://www.nmlindia.nic.in/nml_adm/webroot/writereaddata/upload/download/ NVL_Concept_Note-Annnex_V.pdf>.

[63] National Knowledge Commission (India). NKC Impact – Follow-up on NKC Recommendations. <http://knowledgecommission.gov.in/impact/nkc_recomm. asp> (closed web page).

[64] Press Information Bureau (India). Prime Minister launches first two knowledge portals. <http://pib.nic.in/newsite/erelease.aspx?relid=24026>.

[65] S.R. Ranganathan, Documentation: Genesis and Development, Vikas, Delhi, 1973, p. 167.

[66] Documentation Research and Training Centre. <http://drtc.isibang.ac.in/DRTC/>.

[67] Raja Rammohun Roy Library Foundation. <http://rrrlf.nic.in/>.

[68] Indian Library Association. <http://www.ilaindia.net/>.

[69] Indian Association of Special Libraries and Information Centres. <http://www. iaslic1955.org.in/Default.aspx?PageID=120>.

CHAPTER X

Standards for IOD Activities

X.1 INTRODUCTION

A standard is a minimum degree of excellence for a product or a uniform pattern of practice/process voluntarily accepted and maintained by the concerned people or recommended by a competent body (standardizing body) for adoption by the concerned people. A standard thus ensures either a minimum quality of a man-made or machine-made material or uniformity in any procedure or practice. The importance of standardization was felt in the field of library and information services quite early. The worldwide use of standard catalogue cards of $12.7\,cm \times 7.6\,cm$ size for a long time bears testimony to this fact.

X.2 STANDARDIZING AGENCY

Every country is expected to have an organization to formulate national standards suited to its own conditions. British Standards Institution (also known as BSI Group) is the world's first national standardizing body, which was set up in 1901 [1]. Many countries have since set up such organizations. ISO website lists 163 national member organizations [2]. The standardizing body of the United States is known as American National Standards Institute (ANSI), which was set up in 1918. Interestingly, in the United States there is also a specialized agency that formulates standards relating to information, viz., the National Information Standards Organizations (NISO). NISO, which is a non-profit association accredited by ANSI, identifies, develops, maintains, and publishes technical standards to manage information in our changing ever-more digital environment. NISO standards apply to both traditional and new technologies to the full range of information-related needs, including retrieval, repurposing, storage, metadata, and preservation [3]. The Indian Standards Institution as also its Documentation Sectional Committee was set up in 1947. The first Documentation Sectional Committee was headed by Dr. S.R. Ranganathan. At present, this section is known as Documentation and

Elements of Information Organization and Dissemination
DOI: http://dx.doi.org/10.1016/B978-0-08-102025-8.00024-7

Information Sectional Committee (MSD-5). Indian Standards Institution has since been renamed Bureau of Indian Standards (BIS). Besides the national organizations, there are also several regional standardizing bodies, such as the European Committee for Standardization (CEN), the European Committee for Electrotechnical Standardization (CENELEC), the European Telecommunications Standards Institute (ETSI), the Institute for Reference Materials and Measurements (IRMM) in Europe, the Pacific Area Standards Congress (PASC), the Pan American Standards Commission (COPANT), the African Organization for Standardization (ARSO), the Arabic Industrial Development and Mining Organization (AIDMO) [1]. Furthermore, there is also an international standardizing body known as International Organization for Standardization (ISO) (formerly International Standardization Association), which was set up in 1947. Its three technical committees, ISO/TC 37 (on terminology), ISO/TC 46 (on documentation), and ISO/TC 97 (on computer and information processing), formulate standards relating to documentation and information work.

X.3 NEED FOR STANDARDS

Standards are required in the field of information organization and dissemination (IOD) because of the following reasons [4]:
- To maintain a minimum standard or quality of information service;
- To bring uniformity in sizes and quality of materials used in organization of information;
- To bring uniformity in procedures and practices followed in the field of IOD;
- To facilitate application of computer in transfer/exchange of computer processed information; and
- To expand the scope of services through national and international cooperation.

X.4 AREAS OF STANDARDIZATION

There seems to be no scope for standardizing the actual information organization work, except those done mechanically, like auto-indexing, auto-abstracting, or auto-translation, since the manual organization work involves intellectual effort. But some guidelines may be framed for manual/intellectual organization, including information consolidation work, and standards may be formulated for materials used in organization work such as stationary and accessories. The information/documents are usually disseminated in the form of documentation lists, copies made by reprographic processes, or information consolidation products. Uniform practices may be developed for arranging the various items in an entry and arranging the entries themselves in documentation lists, and information consolidation products. Thus, the format, the layout, and the arrangement of documentation lists, information consolidation products, etc. may be standardized. Similarly, the size and the quality of reprographic equipment and their accessories and the prints to be obtained may be standardized. Besides, standardization is also required in related fields like terminology, transliteration, abbreviation, proof reading, etc. However, though computers and related accessories are now widely used in IOD activities, the standards relating to these are not handled by the section of the standardizing body that formulates standards relating to documentation and information activities.

X.5 STANDARDS FOR IOD

National and international standards have already been formulated in various areas relating to IOD. The relevant standards are being briefly introduced below.

X.5.1 Information Retrieval

Today information retrieval (IR) is carried out manually as well as by using computer. Standards have been formulated for both.

X.5.1.1 Indexing

BSI formulated the standard BS 1749 *Alphabetical Arrangement* in 1951, which was thoroughly revised and the new version *Specification for Alphabetical Arrangement and the Filing Order of Numerals and Symbols* was published in 1969. BSI also published BS 3700 *Recommendations for Preparing Indexes to Books, Periodicals and other Publications* in 1964, which was revised twice in 1976 and 1988. In 1959 American Standards Association (predecessor of ANSI) formulated the standard Z39.4 *Basic Criteria for Indexes* which was revised in 1968 and 1984. In 1993 ANSI/NISO drafted a revised version entitled *Proposed American National Standard*

Guidelines for indexes and Related Information Retrieval Devices (ANSI/ NISO Z39.4-199X) for replacing the existing standard, but it could not finally be approved. ISO formulated ISO 999 *Guidelines for the Content, Organization and Presentation of Indexes* in 1975, which was revised in 1996. Much of the provisions of BS 3700 were incorporated in this standard. The revised standard provides guidelines for the content, arrangement, and presentation of indexes to books, periodicals, reports, patent documents, maps, and other written documents and also non–print materials, such as electronic documents, films, sound and video recordings, and even three-dimensional objects. It covers the choice and form of headings and subheadings used in index entries once the subjects to be indexed have been determined [5]. BSI formulated a complementary standard BS 6529 *Recommendations for Examining Documents, Determining their Subjects and Selecting Indexing Terms* in 1984, following which ISO also formulated its standard ISO 5693 *Methods for Examining Documents, Determining their Subjects, and Selecting Index Terms*, in 1985, which covers the selection of subjects primarily for databases and other indexes. These standards have been adopted by many countries. Besides, BSI also formulated BS 1749 *British Standard Alphabetical Arrangements* in 1951, which was revised in 1969 as *Alphabetical Arrangement and the Filing Order of Numerals and Symbols* and again in 1985 as *Recommendations for Alphabetical Arrangement and the Filing Order of Numbers and Symbols*. In India, no standard has yet been formulated covering the field of indexing comprehensively. However, there are two Indian standards that are related to index and indexing: IS: 382: 2003 *Practice for Alphabetical Arrangement* (First Revision, Reaffirmed December 2012) (*Note*: This standard was first published in 1952); IS: 1275: 1976 *Rules for Making Alphabetical Indexes* (Reaffirmed February 2011) (*Note:* This standard was first published in 1958, revised in 1976, and reaffirmed in 2011).

X.5.1.2 Vocabulary Control

Importance of controlled vocabulary in IR is well known. The most used controlled vocabulary is thesaurus, which may be monolingual or multilingual. The first international standard for thesauri construction was ISO 2788 *Guidelines for the Establishment and Development of Monolingual Thesauri*, originally published in 1974 and updated in 1986. In 1985, a complementary standard ISO 5964 *Guidelines for the Establishment and Development of Multilingual Thesauri* was brought out. Over the years, these two standards have been adopted as national standards in several countries, such as Canada, France, and the United Kingdom. In the United Kingdom, they were numbered as BS 5723 and BS 6723, respectively. The British standards have since been revised to meet the networking needs of the new millennium [6]. The revised British comprehensive standard BS 8723 *Structured Vocabularies for Information Retrieval* has been brought out in following five parts during 2005–08:

Part 1: Definitions, symbols, and abbreviations

Part 2: Thesauri

Part 3: Vocabularies other than thesauri

Part 4: Interoperability between vocabularies

Part 5: Exchange formats and protocols for interoperability

ISO has since revised ISO 5964 as ISO 25964 *Thesauri and Interoperability with Other Vocabularies* (in two parts)—Part 1: *Thesauri for Information Retrieval* (published in August 2011) and Part 2: *Interoperability with Other Vocabularies* (published in March 2013). This standard intends to support IR and specifically to guide the choice of terms used in indexing, tagging, and search queries. ISO 25964 has been adopted by the national standardizing bodies in a number of countries. For example, The British Standards Institution (BSI) has adopted it and brought it out as BS ISO 25964-1. Similar consideration is underway for Part 2. The American standard ANSI/NISO Z39.19: 2005 (R2010)—*Guidelines for the Construction, Format, and Management of Monolingual Controlled Vocabularies* covers some of the same ground as ISO 25964-1. It deals with monolingual lists, synonym rings, and taxonomies as well as thesauri but does not provide a data model nor addresses multilingual vocabularies or other aspects of interoperability, such as mapping between knowledge organization systems [6]. BIS adopted ISO 2788 in 1999 and brought it out as IS 14720: 1999/ISO 2788: 1986 *Guidelines for the Establishment and Development of Monolingual Thesauri.*

X.5.1.3 Computerized IR

Keeping pace with the digital age requirements, ISO brought out a series of standards relating to computerized information processing, retrieval, and exchange. Many of these standards have been adopted in several countries, such as the United Kingdom, China, Australia, New Zealand, Singapore, India. Some of these standards adopted in India (with corresponding ISO numbers) are mentioned below:

- IS 7900:2007/ISO 8601:2004 Data Elements and Interchange Formats—Information Interchange—Representation of Dates and Times (Third Revision, Reaffirmed Dec 2012) *Note*: This standard, originally published in 1976, was based on ISO 2014:1976. In the first revision of this standard in 1999, ISO 8601: 1988 was adopted. In the second revision in 2001, ISO 8601: 2000 was adopted.

- IS 14873:2012/ISO 2709:2008 Format for Information Exchange (First Revision) *Note*: This standard was first published in 2000 which was based on ISO 2709: 1996.
- IS 15389:2003/ISO 17933:2000 GEDI—Generic Electronic Document Interchange (Reaffirmed December 2012).
- IS 15390:2003/ISO 23950:1998 Information Retrieval (Z39.50)— Application, Service Definition and Protocol Specification (Reaffirmed December 2012).
- IS 15991:2012/ISO 8459:2009 Bibliographic Data Element Directory for Use in Data Exchange and Enquiry.
- IS 15992:2012/ISO 15836:2009 The Dublin Core Metadata Element Set.
- IS 15993:2012/ISO 20775:2009 Schema for Holdings Information.
- IS 15995:2012/ISO 25577:2008 MarcXchange.

BIS has also issued IS 11370:2008 *Guide for Data Elements and Record Format for Computer based Bibliographical Databases for Bibliographic Description of Different Kinds of Documents* (First Revision, Reaffirmed March 2014) and a standard relevant for information exchange, viz., IS 13194: 1991 *Indian Script Code for Information Interchange—ISCII*.

X.5.2 Information Consolidation

Every library has to undertake some kind of information consolidation work. This work is also being done by private organizations. Standards are required on various aspects of this work. Condensation or abstracting is the most popular mode of information consolidation. ISO formulated ISO 214 *Abstracts for Publications and Documentation* in 1976 (last reviewed in 2010), which provides guidelines for preparing abstracts by authors and also for abstractors for secondary publications. American standard ANSI/NISO Z.14-1997 (Revised 2009) *Guidelines for Abstracts* also provides similar guidance. The Indian standards formulated for abstract and abstracting are IS 795 (Second revision): 2013 *Guide for Preparation of Abstracts* (*Note*: This standard was first published in 1966 under the title "Canons for making abstracts." It was first revised in 1976 and published under the present title. The standard was reaffirmed in 2003 and again revised in 2013); IS: 7150: 1974 *Library catalogue and abstract card* (Reaffirmed February 2011); and IS 10455: 1983/ISO 5122: 1979 *Guidelines for Presentation of Abstract Sheets in Serial Publications* (Reaffirmed December 2012).

X.5.2.1 Consolidation Products

At the international level, ISO formulated standard ISO 5966: 1982 *Presentation of Scientific and technical reports*, which provides guidance on preparation and presentation of scientific and technical reports. Earlier, BSI brought out BS 4811 *Presentation of Research and Development Reports* in 1972, which also provides similar guidance. American standard, ANSI/NISO Z39.18-2005 (Revised 2010) *Scientific and Technical Reports—Preparation, Presentation, and Preservation* outlines the elements, organization, and design of scientific and technical reports. BIS has brought out guidelines for technical report in three parts: IS 8010: 1976 (Part 1) *Guidelines for Preparation of Technical Reports: Part 1 Research and Development Reports* (Reaffirmed 2003, December 2012); IS 8010:1982 (Part 2) *Guidelines for Preparation of Technical Reports: Part 2 Feasibility Reports* (Reaffirmed December 2012); IS 8010:1987 (Part 3) *Guidelines for Preparation of Technical Reports: Part 3 Industrial Potential Survey Reports* (Reaffirmed December 2012). Besides, it has also formulated two more related standards: IS 9400:1980 *Guidelines for Preparation of Bibliographic Description Sheets for Technical Reports* (Reaffirmed 2003, December 2012); IS 9637:1980 *Guidelines for Presentation of Information in Technical Manuals* (Reaffirmed 2003, 2012). Another information consolidation product, trade catalogue, has attracted the attention of standardizing bodies of some countries. BSI brought out BS 1311 *Manufacturers' Trade and Technical Literature* in 1955, which covers trade catalogues, while American Standards Association (predecessor of American National Standards Institute) brought out ASA Z39.6 *American Standard for Trade Catalogs* in 1966. BIS brought out a similar standard IS 11956 *Guidelines for Preparation of Trade Catalogue* in 1987 (Reaffirmed 2003). For yet another information consolidation product, directory of periodicals, BIS has formulated the standard IS 15282: 2003 *Entries in a Directory of Periodicals*, which has been reaffirmed in December 2012. There seems to be no parallel standard on this product formulated by ISO, ANSI, or BSI. There seems to be no standard for other varieties of information consolidation product.

X.5.3 Documentation List

A documentation list is a list of documents, specially micro documents. It can be a bare list or a list augmented with abstracts of documents. Since there can be different varieties of documentation lists, there cannot be a comprehensive standard covering all such lists. ISO brought out the standard ISO 18: 1981 *Documentation—Contents List of Periodicals*, which provides rules for the presentation and the position of contents list of periodicals. BIS has formulated two standards that specifically relate to compilation of documentation lists: IS 11957: 1987 *Guidelines for Contents List of Periodicals* (Reaffirmed 2003); and IS 15283: 2003 *Layout of an Entry in a Union Catalogue of Periodical Publication* (Reaffirmed December 2012). Besides, several other standards can be helpful in the compilation of documentation lists, such as those related to alphabetical arrangement. BSI formulated BS 1749: 1951 (revised 1985, confirmed 2003) *British Standard Recommendations for Alphabetical Arrangement and the Filing Order of Numbers and Symbols*, while NISO brought out a technical report NISO TR03-1999: *Guidelines for Alphabetical Arrangement of Letters and Sorting of Numerals and Other Symbols*. BIS has brought out IS: 382:2003 *Practice for Alphabetical Arrangement*, and IS: 1275 (1976): *Rules for Making Alphabetical Indexes.*

X.5.4 Bibliographical References

An important area in which the need for standardization has been felt for a long time is bibliographic references as insufficient information in references often makes it difficult to identify and find out the referred documents, if required. The items of information to be included and their sequence in a bibliographic reference may not be the same in every case. The items required in a reference given by an author at the end of his writing and the items required in a citation in any indexing/abstracting journal may be different though some essential items will be common. Any standard formulated in this field must take care of both the situations. The Indian standard IS: 2381 *Recommendations for Bibliographic References: Essential and Supplementary Elements* (first published in 1963 and first revised in 1978) had two sets of recommendations for the two types of citations mentioned above. In 2009 it has been further revised on the basis of ISO standard 690. The latest revised version is in two parts— *Bibliographic References: Part 1 Content, Form and Structure* [IS 2381 (Part 1): 2009/ISO 690-1: 1987] and *Bibliographic References: Part 2 Electronic Documents or Parts thereof* [IS 2381(Part 2): 2009/ISO 690-2: 1997]. Thus, it now also includes references to be given in case of electronic publications. In a latest development, a revised version of Part 1 of this standard, retitled as *Guidelines for Bibliographic References and Citations to Information Resources*, has since been circulated for eliciting opinion. The first standard in this field was, however, formulated by the BSI in 1950 (BS 1629: *Bibliographic References*), which was amended several times and was finally replaced by BS/ISO 690: 2010. The original British Standard did not have separate provisions for two types of citations. Incidentally, ISO first brought out its recommendation ISO/R77 *Bibliographic References: Essential Elements* in 1958, which was revised in 1968 as ISO/R690 *Bibliographic References: Essential and Supplementary Elements* [7].

X.5.5 Reprography

ISO has formulated a large number of standards in this field since 1980s, and many of these standards have been adopted in several countries. However, the first Indian standard in the field of reprography IS 3130: 1965 *Code of Practice for Storage and Use of Microfilms of Permanent Value* was formulated long before ISO standards were brought out. This standard was first revised in 1972 to include microfiche and also to cover some of the important aspects, namely, care in handling to check physical damage and packing methods for transmitting the microcopies, and accordingly the title of the standard was changed to *Code of Practice for Handling and Storage of Microtransparencies (microfilm and microfiche) (silver halide)*. The second revision of this standard was brought out in 1985, and the same was reaffirmed in December 2012. This revision was done in the light of ISO 5466 *Practice for the Storage of Processed Safety Photographic Films* [8]. Other standards brought out by BIS in this field are:

- IS 3083: 1966 Code of Practice for the Processing of Microfilms (silver halide) (Note: This was revised in 1985 as Code of Practice for the Processing of Microtransparencies (microfilms and microfiche) (silver halide) (First Revision) (Reaffirmed February 2011)).
- IS 6299: 1971 Guide for Handling, Testing, and Storage of Monochrome Photographic Prints (Reaffirmed December 2012).
- IS 9450:1980 Guidelines for Placement of Images in Roll Microfilm (Reaffirmed February 2011).
- IS 10456: 2003 Density of Silver-Gelatin Type Microforms—Specification (First Revision), (Reaffirmed December 2012) (Note: This standard was originally published in 1983. It is not technically equivalent to corresponding international standard ISO 6200: 1999) [9].

X.5.6 Terminology

With the growth of any subject field, new terms automatically come in use. This has happened in case of IOD too. As the same term may have different meanings in different contexts and different subject fields, it is necessary to standardize the terms used in a subject by clearly defining them. This has already been done in various areas relating to IOD, such as classification, reprography. BSI formulated BS: 5405 *Glossary of Documentation Terms in 1976*. Between 1983 and 1998 ISO has brought out ISO 5127 *Information and Documentation—Vocabulary* in 12 parts. BIS adopted Parts 1–6 of this standard and issued them in parts during 1992–94 under the same title. Subsequently, in 2001, ISO replaced the standards earlier issued in parts with a comprehensive standard bearing the same title. The standard was issued to "facilitate International communication in the field of information and documentation" [10]. BIS again adopted this standard and issued it as IS 13550: 2003 (First Revision, Reaffirmed December 2012). Standards have also been formulated on vocabularies of different fields of IOD. For example, in the field of reprography, ISO first formulated ISO: 260 *Terms Relating to Microcopies and their Bases* in 1962. Subsequently, it brought out a comprehensive standard ISO 6196 *Micrographics—Vocabulary* in 10 parts during 2001–03. This standard has been adopted in many countries like Poland, China, Japan, Singapore, India, etc. The Indian standard is numbered as IS 15027. BIS has also produced IS: 2550: 1963 (Reaffirmed December 2012) *Glossary of Classification Terms* and IS: 796: 1966 (First Revision February 2011) *Glossary of Cataloguing Terms*, which are somewhat related to IOD.

X.6 STANDARDS IN RELATED FIELDS

Many standards have been formulated both at international level and national level, which are not related to main activities of IOD but certainly have some bearing with such activities, such as ISBN, ISSN, ISBD, ISMN. A few standards that are often needed to be consulted in IOD work are only introduced below.

X.6.1 Translation Service

The most well-known standard relating to translation service is EN 15038: 2006 *European Quality Standard for Translation Services*, which was developed by European Committee for Standardization, especially for translation service providers. The most outstanding features of this standard are firstly, it defines the translation process where quality is guaranteed not by the translation which is just one phase in the process but by the fact of the translation being reviewed by a person other than the translator and secondly, it specifies the professional competences of each of the participants in the translation process, mainly translators, reviewers, revisers, and proofreaders [11–13]. Thus, it ensures the consistent quality of service. It requires regular audits by the certification body, and if any discrepancy is found, the certification is revoked. ISO developed its own translation service management standard ISO 17100:2015 mainly based on the European standard with some key differences. It gives more emphasis on the use of appropriate style and terminology and is more customer oriented [13]. Earlier, ISO had also formulated ISO 2384 *Guidelines for Presentation of Translations*, which has since been adopted as Indian standard (IS 10454: 1983, Reaffirmed 2012).

X.6.2 Transliteration

Transliteration means representation of words and phrases of one language by the alphabets of another keeping their pronunciation intact. Transliteration is required in documentation when the documents being processed and listed are in different languages. The problem of transliteration is quite serious in India where documents are produced in 15 languages and several dialects. Unless a standard pattern of transliteration is followed, there is always a chance of misplacement and hiding of entries. ISO was the first organization to bring out a standard in this field in 1955, viz., ISO/R-9 *International System for the Transliteration of Cyrillic Characters*, which was revised in 1968. It has so far brought out 16 standards for transliteration of different types of characters, including ISO 15919: 2001 *Transliteration of Devanagari and Related Indian Scripts into Latin Characters*. A British standard on the subject, BS 2978, was formulated in 1958. BIS has formulated IS 15341 *Transliteration of the Indian Scripts to the Roman Script* in 2003.

X.6.3 Abbreviations

Two types of standards for abbreviations have been formulated— abbreviations of periodical titles and codes for countries. ISO brought out ISO 4: *1997 Rules for the Abbreviation of Title Words and Titles of Publications*. ANSI formulated Z39.5: *1963 American national standard for the abbreviation of titles of periodicals*, which was revised in 1969. The Indian standard on abbreviation of periodical titles was first published as IS 18: 1949 *Abbreviations for Titles of Periodicals*. It was first revised after more than 20 years and retitled as *Guide to Abbreviations of Words in Titles of Periodicals Using Roman Alphabet* [IS 18 (First Revision): 1970]. It was further revised and its scope widened in 1988 [IS 18 (Second Revision): 1988 *Rules for the Abbreviations of Title Words and Titles of Publications*]. It was again revised in 1999 in the light of ISO 4: 1997 as IS 18: 1999/ ISO 4: 1997 *Rules for the Abbreviations of Title Words and Titles of Publications* (Third Revision, Reaffirmed September 2009). For abbreviations of country names, ISO formulated ISO 3166: 1974 *Country Codes*. It was revised in 1981, 1988, and 1993, and in 1999 it was further revised and published in three parts. Except for the numeric codes, ISO 3166 codes were adopted in the United States as FIPS 10-4. However, on September 2, 2008, FIPS 10-4 was withdrawn by the National Institute of Standards and Technology (NIST) of the US Deprtment of Commerce as a federal information processing standard. It was replaced by the *Geopolitical Entities, Names, and Codes (GENC)*, which is based on ISO 3166 [14]. BIS formulated IS 14836 *Codes for the Representation of Names of Countries and their Subdivisions—Part 1: Country Codes* in 2000. In 2009 it was revised in the light of ISO 3166-1: 2006 (IS 14836 (Part 1): 2009/ISO 3166-1: 2006 *Codes for the Representation of Names of Countries and their Subdivisions: Part 1 Country codes (First Revision)*). Again a revised version of this standard has been drafted and circulated for eliciting opinions of experts [15].

X.6.4 Proof Correction

BSI brought out BS 5261: 1958 *British Standard Recommendations for Proof Correction and Copy Preparation*, which has been revised in 2005. A similar standard was issued by NISO (of the United States) viz., Z39.22: 1989 *Proof Corrections: American National Standard for Proof Correction* and also by BIS viz., IS 1250:1958 *Proof correction for Printers and Authors* (Reaffirmed 2003).

REFERENCES

[1] Standards Organization. <https://en.wikipedia.org/wiki/Standards_organization>.
[2] International Standards Organization. <http://www.iso.org/>.
[3] National Information Standards Organization. <http://www.niso.org/about/>.
[4] A. Chatterjee, Elements of Documentation, The Author, Calcutta, 1983.
[5] ISO 999. <https://en.wikipedia.org/wiki/ISO_999> Standards Organization. https://en.wikipedia.org/wiki/Standards_organization.
[6] ISO 25964. <https://en.wikipedia.org/wiki/ISO_25964>.
[7] B. Guha, Documentation and Information, second ed., World Press, Calcutta, 1983.
[8] Bureau of Indian Standards. Code of Practice for Handling and Storage of Micro-transparencies (microfilm and microfiche) (silver halide) (*Second Revision*) (IS 3130: 1985). <https://archive.org/stream/gov.in.is.3130.1985/is.3130.1985#page/n3/mode/2up>.
[9] Bureau of Indian Standards. Density of Silver-Gelatin Type Microforms—Specification (*First Revision*) (IS 10456: 2003).

[10] International Standards Organization. ISO 5127: 2001(en). <https://www.iso.org/obp/ui/#iso:std:iso:5127:ed-1:v1:en>.

[11] EN 15038. <https://en.wikipedia.org/wiki/EN_15038>.

[12] European Committee for Standardization. BS EN15038 European quality standard. <http://qualitystandard.bs.en-15038.com/>.

[13] International Standards Organization. ISO 17100—The New Translation Services Standard. <http://www.isoqsltd.com/general/iso-17100-new-translation-services-standard/>.

[14] List of FIP codes. <https://en.wikipedia.org/wiki/List_of_FIPS_country_codes>.

[15] Bureau of Indian Standards. Management and Systems Department. Programme of Work (as on April 1, 2014).

CHAPTER Y

Automated Information Organization

Y.1 INTRODUCTION

As is known, information and communication technologies have now touched every sphere of human activity. It is now being increasingly employed in libraries and information centers for improving organization and dissemination of information. Many of the activities, which were earlier being done manually, have now been automated. Besides, a sizable amount of information sources are now available in electronic or digital format, and Internet has become an important source of information. These developments have made it imperative for libraries and information centers to reorient their activities. Not only the existing libraries and their services are now being automated, libraries of new varieties, such as digital libraries and virtual libraries are also coming up. Some important developments in the fields of information organization in the digital world are described below.

Y.2 AUTO-INDEXING

Auto-indexing or automatic indexing, as the term itself suggests, is indexing with the help of a machine or computer, i.e., without using human intellect. In other words, "it is the process of assigning and arranging index terms for natural language without human intervention" [1]. Nevertheless, the term computerized indexing or automatic indexing embraces techniques ranging from manual indexing with a minimum assistance of computer to a minimum of human efforts and maximum of computer assistance [2].

Y.2.1 Approaches to Auto-Indexing

In general, automated indexing can use four approaches [3]:
- *Statistical:* This is based on counts of words, statistical associations, and collation techniques that assign weights and cluster similar words;
- *Syntactical:* This stresses on grammar and parts of speech, identifying concepts found in designated grammatical combinations, such as noun phrases;

Elements of Information Organization and Dissemination
DOI: http://dx.doi.org/10.1016/B978-0-08-102025-8.00025-9
497

- *Semantic Systems:* These systems are concerned with the context sensitivity of words in texts. What does cat means in terms of its context? House cats? Big game hunting? Heavy earthmoving equipment?
- *Knowledge-Based:* These systems go beyond thesaurus or equivalent relationships to *knowing* the relationships between words, e.g., tibia is a part of a leg, thus we know to index the document under leg injuries.

Y.2.2 Method of Auto-Indexing

The simplest method of auto-indexing is to prepare a negative dictionary or stop words list, i.e., list of oft-occurring words, which have no retrieval value, such as articles, adverbs, pronouns, prepositions, conjunctions, and then feed the same to the computer. The computer scans the title, abstract, and/or text (either full-text or on parts of the text), ignoring these stop words. The remaining words serve as possible index terms. An algorithm is now used to stem words. This allows a given search term to match with different forms of a word at the searching stage. After stemming, there is a count of the frequency of occurrence. The most important words are considered to be those that occur most often. This process can involve statistical weights to refine the previous frequency count. Automatic indexing moves up the scale in complexity by introducing the idea of proximity. The premise is that if particular words keep appearing in the text in the near neighborhood of each other, then this has some sort of significance. For example, if missiles, ground, and air are close together, it indicates the topic air-to-ground missiles [3].

Y.2.3 Auto-Indexing Systems

The earliest and most primitive forms of automatic indexing were the derived indexing systems Keyword in Context and its variants, which were based on simple, mechanical manipulations of terms derived from document titles. Related forms were the Permuterm Subject Index and the KeyWord Plus known from Institute of Scientific Information's citation indexes (the last system is based on assigning terms from cited titles) [4]. Several attempts were also made to create entries by following assigned indexing methods with the help of computer. For example, *British Technology Index* developed and employed in 1968, a computer-assisted indexing system using chain indexing. In this system, the computer was programmed so that it was to take semantically organized strings of terms given as subject heading, reverse them, progressively truncating the string in the manner first thought of by Ranganathan, at the same time preserving intelligibility [5]. In 1996, an automatic indexing system, *Prometheus* was developed, which was based on POPSI [6]. PRECIS indexing, which had been adopted by BNB in 1974, replacing chain indexing, for generation of index entries in BNB, was dropped in 1991 for a more simplified computer-aided system of subject indexing, known as Computer Aided Subject System (COMPASS). In this system the index string is organized by the PRECIS principles of context dependency and role operators. In order to minimize the complexity of PRECIS role operators, primary role operators (O), (4), (5), and (6) are not used. Besides, dates as difference (coded with $d) are not used in all cases. The initial step of subject analysis is done only once while preparing the COMPASS input string for a document, and this input string is taken as the basis for all latter decisions relating to the document and their incorporation in the relevant fields of the worksheet. The methods associated with the generation of COMPASS index entries are same as that of PRECIS index entries [7].

Y.2.4 Auto-Indexing of Digital Documents

However, in recent years, especially after the advent of documents in digital formats and Internet, an "automatic indexing" system is primarily thought to be as a system used for organizing and accessing digital and Internet resources. In this sense, an automated index is an index produced using algorithms, which work on databases containing document representations (full text representations, bibliographical records, or partial text representations and in principle also value-added databases) and also on non-text databases such as images or music. In text databases the algorithm may perform string searching but is mostly based on searching the words in the single document representation as well as in the total database (via inverted files). The use of words is mostly based on stemming. Algorithms may count co-occurrences of words (or references); they may consider levels of proximity between words, and so on [4].

Y.2.5 Indexing Software

Several indexing software are now available for performing indexing work, either fully or partially, e.g., Cindex (for DOS, Windows, and Macintosh),

HTML Indexer (for Windows), HyperIndex. Cleveland and Cleveland have identified four general classes of indexing software [3]:

- *Embedding Software:* Such a software puts indexing codes into the electronic text and allows updating of locators as the text is changed. While working with a file, the indexers tag terms that should be indexed on that particular page. If there is a change in the document, the tag clings to the terms wherever they go in the text. It should be pointed out that some types of software packages (e.g., word processors) come with embedded indexing capabilities.
- *Stand-alone Software:* This type of software allows the indexer to work independently of the published material and is generally used for back-of-the-book indexing, but the evolving features of such software often make it adaptable to other types of indexing.
- *Automated Indexing Software:* This type of software searches for words in the text and builds a list of words. This is useful as an aid, but to produce a true index, humans need to turn the list into a true index.
- *Computer-Assisted Indexing:* As differentiated from automatic indexing, this is the use of computers to do mundane work, while a human still does the intellectual task of indexing.

Y.3 AUTO-ABSTRACTING

Auto-abstracting, i.e., automatic abstracting is the process of abstracting with the help of a computer or machine. A machine-produced abstract consists of some words, sentences, or quotations selected from the abstracted document. Such an abstract, therefore, provides only an approximate idea of the contents and is more like an extract than a man-made abstract. Because of the nature of its contents, it is also sometimes called "auto-quotation." Since the 1950s many experiments have been conducted on auto-abstracting, most of which depend on significant terms or phrases used in the original text. The two basic processes involved in auto-abstracting are:

- *Finding out the significant sentences or phrases:* This is done by a computer on the basis of the frequency of the use of significant (uncommon) words in the text of the document being abstracted. A word-exclusion list fed into the computer beforehand may be of help in this work. Sometimes, the choice of the significant sentences is indicated by the computer operator.
- *Arranging the significant sentences:* The selected significant sentences are joined together in an order that can represent the main ideas contained

in the text. Experiments have been carried out to arrange the sentences by machine on the basis of semantical and syntactical relationships, but a fully satisfactory system has not yet been found. It may, therefore, be necessary to edit a machine-made abstract to make it more intelligible and readable.

Y.3.1 Luhn's Approach

Hans P. Luhn was a pioneer in this field. "The original method of Luhn assigned weight to each sentence of the document according to statistical criteria, in fact, a simple function of the number of high frequency word occurring in the sentence. Common words, such as "the," "and," "at" and "are" were disregarded because of their very high frequency alone, and the remaining words were assigned frequency weights that provided sentence weights for measuring sentence significance" [8]. According to Lancaster, the procedure suggested by Luhn was as follows [9]:

- A stop-list eliminates all the non-substantive terms from further processing.
- Occurrences of all remaining words are counted and the words ranked by frequency of occurrence.
- All words occurring more than x times are defined as "high frequency" or "significant" words.
- Sentences containing concentrations of these high-frequency words are located. Two words are considered related within a sentence if there are no more than four intervening words.
- A "significance factor" for each sentence is calculated as follows:
  - The number of "clusters" in the sentence is determined (a cluster is the longest group of words bounded by significant words in which the significant words are not separated by more than four intervening words).
  - The number of significant words in the cluster is determined and the square of the number is divided by the total number of words within the cluster.
  - The significance factor for the sentence can be defined either as the value of the highest cluster or the sum of the values of all the clusters in the sentence.

According to this procedure, the sentences having the highest significance factors are selected and are printed out in the sequence in which they occur in the text to form the abstract. Most of the studies that followed, except those based on natural language processing (NLP) techniques, are some kind of modifications or improvements of Luhn's work [10]. Thus, all early efforts towards automatic indexing centered round automatic extracting.

Y.3.2 Basic Approaches

According to Edmundson, the automatic extracting system was based on assigning to text sentences numerical weights that were functions of weights assigned to certain machine-recognizable characteristics or clues. For computational simplicity, the sentence weights were taken as sums of the weights of these characteristics [8]. He distinguished two types of world lists, viz., *Dictionary*, which was regarded as a list of words with numerical weights that formed a fixed input to the automatic extracting system and was independent of the words in the particular document being extracted and *Glossary*, which was regarded as a list of words with numerical weights that formed a variable input to the automatic extracting system and was composed of words selected from the document being extracted. The four basic methods used for automatic extraction as identified by Edmundson are [8]:

- *Cue Method:* It is based on some cue words that determine the significance of a given sentence within a text. This method uses a pre-stored "cue dictionary" which includes a list of words that receive a positive weight, a list of words with a negative weight, and a list of null words that are irrelevant. The final cue weight for each sentence is the sum of the cue weights of its constituent words.
- *Key Method:* The principle of this method is similar to that of Luhn. In this method a key glossary is compiled for each document, ideally consisting of topic words statistically selected from the body of that document. The words comprising a key glossary are selected by listing all words not in the cue dictionary in order of decreasing frequency of occurrence in the document. The frequencies are cumulated, from the highest downward to a given percent of the total number of word occurrences. Non-cue words with frequencies above this threshold are designated key words and are assigned positive weight equal to their frequency of occurrence in the document. The final key weight of the sentence is the sum of the key weights of its constituent words. Initially, key words were defined as non-cue words of the highest cue-weighted sentences, but in the final system, key words were chosen from a given percent of the total number of words in the document

and their key weights were taken to be their frequency of occurrence over all words in the document.

- *Title Method:* In this method it is assumed that the words occurring in titles and subheads are good indicators of the contents of the document. Sentences are given a significance value based on the number of words appearing in the title and subheads they contain.
- *Location Method:* In this method weight is given to a sentence on the basis of where it appears in the document. Sentences appearing in certain sections of the text, such as the first or last paragraph or the first and last sentences of a paragraph, are assumed to be more significant and given weight accordingly.

Y.3.3 New Approach

The extracting approach to abstracting has been termed by Goldstein as shallow approach. Experiments have been started with approaches that are deeper in nature. Such approaches, according to Shao-Fen Liang et al, "usually involve natural language generation from the semantic or discourse level representation" [11].

Y.3.4 Some Experiments

Several experiments have been made using one or more of the above methods in combination for automatic abstracting. A few important among them are briefly described below.

Y.3.4.1 Contextual Inference

A method developed by Rush, Salvador, and Zamora has provision for both sentence selection and sentence rejection based on contextual inference. Explaining the term "contextual inference," they said "given a data element (word or word string) within a sentence and some surrounding context, it is generally possible to infer whether a sentence should be rejected or selected for inclusion in an abstract. Contextual inference may be made based on either the physical arrangement of the linguistic elements of a document or on word strings which comprise these linguistic elements" [12]. "The extracting method they described is based on the matching of text against a Word Control List (WCL), which includes a list of expressions that, if present in a sentence, would cause it to be rejected and a much smaller list of expressions that would cause it to be selected" [9].

Y.3.4.2 Sentence Rejection

Pollock and Zamora reported in 1999 about the development of an automatic abstracting program, known as Automatic Document Abstracting Method (ADAM), at Chemical Abstracts Service. Like other automatic abstractive methods, "it does create an extract, editing is performed on the original sentences to produce somewhat different sentences. However, ADAM does not create new sentences, either *de novo* or by conjoining original sentences, as human abstracts do" [13]. They said that ADAM differed from most automatic abstracting methods in two important aspects: while others relied heavily on statistical criteria as a basis for sentence selection and rejection and they were designed to select sentences for abstracts, ADAM used statistical data only peripherally and was designed for sentence rejection rather than selection. According to them, in ADAM, sentence rejection and selection are based mainly on the use of cue words, relevance of sentence to title, and frequency criteria. The last two are important conceptually as they allow the algorithm to adapt itself, to some extent, to each individual document. Coherence criteria are also used in sentence rejection and selection and in increasing readability of the Abstracts. ADAM was designed to produce indicative abstracts, i.e., abstracts that enable the reader to judge whether he needs to read the original document [13]. ADAM abstracts have the following characteristics [13]:

- Their size is typically 10%–20% of that of original documents (but no arbitrary cutoff is used);
- They use the terminology of the original document;
- They consist of character strings from the body of the text. No equations, footnotes, tables, graphs, figures, etc., are given;
- Preliminary remarks, negative results (unless these are the only results), methodologies of data gathering, explanations, examples, and opinions are excluded; and
- Objectives, results, and conclusions are given.

Y.4 INFORMATION ORGANIZATION TOOLS

Several types of tools have been designed for organization of information, which represent the semantic relationships among disciplines and their constituent concepts, such as classification schemes, subject heading lists, thesauri. Information resources are mapped against such tools in order to process their semantic content to facilitate better organization and access. Although such tools have been successfully used for a long time, they have some inherent limitations that make them unsuitable for use in the digital environment. As such, efforts have been made to adapt a few such tools to meet the requirements of the new era as also "to devise several sophisticated tools that allow computers to process and organize information based on the meaning of their constituent parts" [14].

Y.4.1 Thesaurus

Summarizing the work done in the field of designing and managing thesaurus to make this tool suitable for working in digital environment, as reported by different experts, Silvia Arano has mentioned the following [15]:

- The first element to be considered is the enriching of the thesaurus structure functionality based on hypertexting. This leads to the establishing of hyperlinks among all the structural elements (descriptors, non-descriptors, scope notes, etc.) and also among the different parts of the thesaurus.
- The second element is the reduction of updating and maintenance costs. Due to the growing digitalization of thesaurus-construction processes and the gradual abandoning of paper formats in publishing these tools, cost-reduction is perfectly viable.
- The third element is user-integration into the process of creating, managing, and optimizing thesauruses, through usability tests, the use of user-modeling techniques, etc. This makes it possible to create tools that take user requirements into account and rules out their creation as simple theoretical structures.
- The fourth element is the possibility of applying methods of reuse and interoperability at the time of planning and creating the thesauruses. This makes it possible to use and make the most of the conceptual and linguistic information already generated for other artifacts.

Y.4.2 Ontology

Ontology is one of the new tools that help in organization of web resources. The term "ontology" has originated from philosophy, where it is used to denote that branch of metaphysics which is concerned with, simply speaking, the kinds of things that exist and how to describe them. The origin of the term "ontology" can be traced back to 1721 as an abstract philosophical notion. Over the past few years the term has gained a new meaning and is used in several fields of study, including knowledge engineering, knowledge management, information retrieval (IR), and, of

course, the World Wide Web [10]. Vickery was one of the first information scientists to draw attention to the term "Ontology," who reviewed
some important ontologies of the time in a paper published in *Journal of
Information Science* in 1997 [16].

Y.4.2.1 Concept of Ontology

Many experts have defined ontology, but the most widely used definition
of ontology in the context of information and knowledge management
appears to be the one proposed by T R Gruber: "An ontology is a formal,
explicit specification of a shared conceptualization" [17]. This definition
highlights certain characteristics of ontology, viz. *Formal, Explicit, Shared,*
and *Conceptualization.* The word *Formal* suggests that an ontology should be
based on formal logic in order to be machine-readable; the word *Explicit*
indicates that the type of concepts used and the constraints on their use
are explicitly defined; the word *Shared* reflects the notion that an ontology captures consensual knowledge, that is, it is not private to some individual but accepted by a group; and the word *Conceptualization* refers to
"an abstract model of phenomenon in the world by having identified the
relevant concepts of those phenomenon" [18]. In the context of information science, "ontology formally represents knowledge as a set of concepts
within a domain using a shared vocabulary to denote the types, properties,
and interrelationships of those concepts" [19]. An ontology thus consists of
a finite list of terms, representing concepts or classes of objects and their
relationships (specially the hierarchical relationships), and providing other
information such as properties, value restrictions, disjointness statements,
and specification of logical relationships between concepts [20]. More specifically, it is a set of classes arranged in a hierarchy or taxonomy, where
real-world concepts are modeled as classes, their characteristics as attributes,
and inter-object relationships as relationships, properties, or axioms [21]. In
the context of web, ontologies provide a shared understanding of a domain
that is necessary to understand differences in the connotations of terms and
thus to facilitate interoperability and data processing by computers [14].

Y.4.2.2 Types of Ontology

Based on their formality and complexity, ontologies have been categorized
as [22]:
- *Highly Informal:* Ontologies that are expressed loosely in natural
  language;
- *Semi-Informal:* Ontologies that are expressed in a restricted and structured form of natural language;

- *Semi-Formal:* Ontologies that are expressed in artificially formally defined language; and
- *Rigidly Formal:* Ontologies that are expressed in clearly defined terms with semantics, theorems, and proofs.

Ontologies may also be categorized in the following way [23]:
- By the level of detail
  - *Reference (offline) ontologies;*
  - *Shareable (online) ontologies.*
- By the level of dependence of a particular task or point of view
  - *Top-level ontologies:* These ontologies describe general concepts like time, space, matter, and event that are independent of domain or a particular problem;
  - *Domain ontologies:* These ontologies pertain to specific domains;
  - *Task ontologies:* These ontologies pertain to specific tasks;
  - *Application ontologies:* These ontologies describe concepts that depend upon both a domain and a particular task, usually being specializations of both ontologies.
- Representation ontologies.

Y.4.2.3 Components of Ontology

The common components of ontologies are [19]:
- *Individuals:* instances or objects (the basic or "ground level" objects);
- *Classes:* sets, collections, concepts, classes in programming, types of objects, or kinds of things;
- *Attributes:* aspects, properties, features, characteristics, or parameters that objects (and classes) can have;
- *Relations:* ways in which classes and individuals can be related to one another;
- *Function terms:* complex structures formed from certain relations that can be used in place of an individual term in a statement;
- *Restrictions:* formally stated descriptions of what must be true in order for some assertion to be accepted as input;
- *Rules:* statements in the form of an if-then (antecedent-consequent) sentence that describe the logical inferences that can be drawn from an assertion in a particular form;
- *Axioms:* assertions (including rules) in a logical form that together comprise the overall theory that the ontology describes in its domain of application; as used here, "axioms" also include the theory derived from axiomatic statements;
- *Events:* the changing of attributes or relations.

Y.4.2.4 Uses of Ontology

The different uses of ontologies, according to McGuinness, are [24]:

- Provides controlled vocabulary that can be used by users, authors, and databases for accessing and managing information;
- Supports site organizations and navigation;
- Supports expectation setting, i.e., users may have realistic expectation from a site by looking at the ontology;
- Serves as umbrella structure which may be extended for individual application;
- Supports browsing;
- Supports searching;
- Supports sense disambiguation, i.e., if the same term appears in multiple places the respective hierarchies help a user to distinguish between the different contexts of the term.

More sophisticated ontologies, according to McGuinness, may have some additional uses [24]:

- May use simple kinds of consistency checking by using the properties of classes and value restrictions on the properties;
- May be used for completion, i.e., to augment the information obtained by a user from corresponding classes/subclasses/properties in the ontology;
- Provides support for interoperability among systems; and
- May be used to support validation and verification testing of data.

Y.4.2.5 Ontology Design Principles

According to Gruber, the criteria for design of formal ontologies are [17]:

- *Clarity*: Ontology should be able to effectively communicate its intended meaning to its users;
- *Coherence*: Ontology should support inferences that are consistent with its definitions;
- *Extendibility*: Ontology should be designed to anticipate the uses of shared vocabulary; one should be able to define new terms based on the existing definitions;
- *Minimal encoding bias:* The conceptualization should be specified at the knowledge level without depending upon any symbol or language encoding;
- *Minimal ontological commitment:* Ontology should not restrict the domain being modeled, allowing the users the freedom to specialize and instantiate the ontology as required.

Y.4.2.6 Ontology Engineering

Ontology engineering deals with ontology development process, ontology life-cycle, and the methods and methodologies for building ontologies. An ontology can be built from scratch, from an existing global or local ontology, from a corpus of information sources only, or from a combination of latter two approaches [25]. A simple methodology known as Skeletal Method, as suggested by Uschold and Gruinger, consists of the following phases [26]:

- *Identification of purpose*: At the outset it is important to be clear about why the ontology is being built and what its intended uses are.
- *Ontology building*: This involves three activities:
  - Capture: Ontology capture involves identification of key concepts and relationships in the domain of interest, production of precise unambiguous text definitions for such concepts and relationships and identification of terms to refer to such concepts and relationships, and finally, agreeing on all of the above.
  - Coding: Coding means explicit representation of the conceptualization captured in the previous stage in some formal language, which will involve committing to the basic terms that will be used to specify the ontology, choosing a representational language and writing the code.
- *Integrating existing ontologies*: During capture and/or coding processes, a question may arise as to how and whether to use wholly or partly ontologies that already exist. Effort should be made to bring agreement on ontologies that can be shared among multiple user communities.
- *Evaluation:* This will involve judging the newly created ontology technically.
- *Documentation:* It may be desirable to have established guidelines for documenting ontologies, possibly differing according to type and purpose of the ontology.

Another simple ontology building methodology suggested by Noy and McGuinness consists of following steps [27]: Determining the domain and scope of ontology, considering if reuse of existing ontologies is possible, enumerating important terms to be included in the proposed ontology, defining the general concepts in the domain and specialized concepts coming under each general concept and developing a class hierarchy, defining the properties of classes (termed as slots), defining facets of the slots, and creating individual instances of classes in the hierarchy. According to Denny, "an ontology building process may span problem specification, domain knowledge acquisition and analysis, conceptual design and commitment to community ontologies, iterative construction and testing, publishing the ontology as a terminology, and possibly populating a conforming knowledge base with ontology individuals. While the process may be strictly a manual exercise, there are tools available that can automate portions of it" [28]. Several more sophisticated and elaborate ontology engineering methods have been suggested by different experts.

Y.4.2.7 Ontology Language

The language used for building an ontology is called ontology language. An ontology language is a formal language that allows the encoding of knowledge about specific domains and often includes reasoning rules that support the processing of that knowledge. Ontology languages are usually declarative languages and are commonly based on either first-order logic or on description logic [19]. An ontology language should have [20]:

- a well-defined syntax—necessary for machine processing of information;
- a formal semantics—a prerequisite for reasoning support;
- convenience of expression;
- efficient reasoning support; and
- sufficient expressive power.

Several specialized languages have been developed to support ontology building, the most well-known being DAML + OIL and OWL. DAML + OIL has been developed as an ontology language that describes the structure of the domain. The structure is described in terms of classes (concepts) and properties (roles). Ontology in DAML + OIL consists of set of axioms (e.g., asserting class subsumption/equivalence). Classes can be names or expressions and various constructors provided for building class expressions [29]. DAML + OIL has since been superseded by Web Ontology Language (OWL). The OWL is a family of knowledge representation languages or ontology languages for authoring ontologies or knowledge bases. The languages are characterized by formal semantics and RDF/XML-based serializations for the Semantic Web. OWL is endorsed by the World Wide Web Consortium (W3C) [19]. Some other ontology languages are DOGMA, IDEF5, OBO, etc.

Y.4.2.8 Ontology Building Tools

Many tools or ontology editors are now available to facilitate ontology building. A widely used such tool is Protégé (http://protege.standford.edu/) developed by Standford Medical Informatics. Some other well-known tools are WebOnto, developed by KMi Technologies; HOZO developed in Osaka University; Java Ontology Editor; OBO-Edit developed by Gene Ontology Consortium; OWLGrEd, a graphical ontology editor, etc. For selection of appropriate tool the following factors need to be considered [28]:

- It should be ensured that expressivity is not lost and consistency is not compromised when moving between tools;
- When editors do not natively support OWL import and export, specific translator tools should be identified to seamlessly bridge between the editor's native language(s) and OWL.
- Ontology tools may differ markedly in their level of use and maturity. Some tools have very active development and user communities that increase the likelihood that the tool will continue to be available and kept up to date.
- The level of technical support and training available from the software provider is also important.
- Editors with a software architecture that allows easy extension with addition of functionality and integration with other tools is advantageous.
- Product factors like licensing terms, purchase price, documentation, update policy, and upgrade path are also to be considered.

Y.4.3 Folksonomy

Another tool for organizing web resources that has emerged in recent years is Folksnomy. The term "Folksonomy" has been coined by Thomas Vander Wall. It is a portmanteau of two terms "folks" and "taxonomy" [30]. Folksonomy is an Internet-based IR methodology. It is a type of collaborative tagging system in which the classification of data is done by users. Folksonomies consist of three basic entities: users, tags, and resource. Users create tags to mark resources, such as web pages, photos, videos, and podcasts. These tags are used to manage, categorize, and summarize online content. This collaborative tagging system also uses these tags as a way to index information, facilitate searches, and navigate resources. Folksonomy also includes a set of URLs that are used to identify resources that have been referred by users of different websites. These systems also include category schemes that have the ability to organize tags at different levels of granularity [31]. Collaborative tagging is also known as social classification, social indexing, and social tagging, while the user given tags are also called concepts, categories, facets, or entities. Folksonomy tags are *index terms* from the point of view of the user. *Index term* is the representation of a concept, preferably in the form of a noun or noun phrase derived from natural language. Nouns are chosen because they are the most concrete part of speech. An index term can consist of more than one word [32]. It may be pointed out here that the term folksonomy has little to do with taxonomy since folksonomy establishes categories (each tag is a category) that are theoretically equal to each other, i.e., there is no hierarchical relation between them, whereas taxonomy mainly depicts a hierarchy.

Y.4.3.1 Types of Folksonomy

Vander Wall has distinguished two types of folksonomy, viz., broad folksonomy and narrow folksnomy. A broad folksonomy is the one in which multiple users tag particular content with a variety of terms from a variety of vocabularies, thus creating a greater amount of metadata for that content. A narrow folksonomy, however, occurs when a few users, primarily the content creators, tag an object with a limited number of terms. While both broad and narrow folksonomies enable the searchability of content by adding textual description—or access points—to an object, a narrow folksonomy does not have the same benefits as a broad folksonomy, which allows for the tracking of emerging trends in tag usage and developing vocabularies [33].

Y.4.3.2 Comparison With Ontology

Togia has compared ontology with folksonomy in the following way [34]:

Ontology	Folksonomy
Designed by knowledge engineers	Collaboratively created by users
Laborious	Quick and easy
Requires expertise	No expertise needed
Hard to implement on a large scale	Used on large-scale document collections
Controlled vocabulary	No vocabulary control
Formal specification of knowledge domains	Informal metadata on documents
Structured	Unstructured (but structure emerges)
Not necessarily web based	Typically web based
Essential for the semantic web	Important in web 2.0 (social web)
High expressive power	Low expressive power
Explicit meaning	Ambiguity
Synonyms, homonyms, etc., can be clearly stated	Synonyms separated; homonyms conflated

Y.4.3.3 Application of Folksonomy

Folksonomies gained popularity after sites like *Flickr* and Del.icio.us started using them. They work by aggregating the tags that users attach to items in the system. In *Flickr*, users tag photographs. In Del.icio.us, users tag bookmarked web pages. By aggregating the tags, the system can illuminate trends that are not apparent otherwise [35] According to Nouruzi, the most popular, widely used folksonomy-based systems are [32]:

1. Del.icio.us: www.del.icio.us
2. Flickr: www.flickr.com
3. YouTube: www.youtube.com
4. CiteULike: www.citeulike.org
5. Connotea: www.connotea.org
6. Technorati: www.technorati.com
7. Furl: www.furl.net
8. TagCloud: www.tagcloud.com
9. Yahoo's MyWeb:http://myweb.yahoo.com
10. Simpy: www.simpy.com
11. Unalog: www.unalog.com
12. Shadows: www.shadows.com
13. Spurl: www.spurl.net
14. Scuttle: www.scuttle.org
15. Tagzania: www.tagzania.com
16. Dabble: www.dabble.com
17. LibraryThing: www.librarything.com
18. Wink: www.wink.com

Incidentally, some experts have expressed the hope that Folksonomy may hold the key to developing a Semantic Web, in which every web page contains machine-readable metadata that describes its content. Such metadata would dramatically improve the precision (the percentage of relevant documents) in search engine retrieval lists. Besides, some libraries are adding tagging features into their OPACs, in addition to the use of standardized subject headings, in order to encourage a more participatory nature to the catalog [36].

Y.4.3.4 FolksOntology

One of the shortcomings of folksonomies is that these are unsupervised vocabularies which frequently suffer from inconsistencies and redundancies. However, there is insufficient involvement of users in construction of ontologies. Celine Van Damme and her associates have expressed the view that the social interaction manifested in folksonomies should be exploited for building and maintaining ontologies. They have proposed a method of deriving domain ontologies from folksonomies by integrating multiple resources and techniques. They have named this approach as FolksOntology [37].

Y.5 MACHINE TRANSLATION

Translation service has been one of the important information services sought by scientists and researchers as this helps in overcoming language barrier. Many libraries and information centers were taking help of professional translators for getting the required materials translated for their users. Machine translation (MT), which is also known as auto-translation, computer translation, and mechanical translation, was first conceived by Warren Weaver, Director of the Natural Sciences Division of the Rockefeller Foundation, United States. He first mentioned the possibility of using the computer in translation in March 1947 in a letter to the cyberneticist Norbert Wiener and in a conversation with Andrew Booth, a British scientist. He elaborated his idea in a memorandum, entitled simply "Translation," which he wrote in July 1949 [38]. Subsequently, experiments started in various learned institutions such as Cambridge University, Massachusetts Institute of Technology, Soviet Academy of Sciences, etc. The first automatic translator (very basic) was developed in 1954 by a group of researchers from Georgetown University, in collaboration with IBM, which translated more than 60 Russian sentences into English. Research has continued in this field since then [39]. Today there are even websites that provide instant MT facilities such as Google Translate (http://translate.google.co.in/) and Yahoo's BabelFish (http://in.babelfish.com/).

Y.5.1 Basic Requirements

Basically every translation system requires programs for translation and automated dictionaries and grammars to support translation. The translation quality of the MT systems can be improved by pre-editing the input. Pre-editing means adjusting the input by marking prefixes, suffixes, clause boundaries, etc. Translation quality can also be improved by controlling the vocabulary. The output of the MT should be post-edited to make it perfect [40].

Y.5.2 Types of MT

There are mainly two types of MT systems. The systems that produce translations between only two specific languages are called bilingual systems and those that produce translations for any given pair of languages are called multilingual systems. Multilingual systems may be either unidirectional or bidirectional. Multilingual systems are preferred to be bidirectional and bilingual as they have ability to translate from any given language to any other given language and vice versa [40].

Y.5.3 Approaches to MT

The process of MT can be broadly classified into the following approaches: direct MT, rule-based MT, corpus-based MT [41].

Y.5.3.1 Direct MT

Direct MT is one of the simplest MT approach. In direct MT, a direct word by word translation of the input source is carried out with the help of a bilingual dictionary and after which some syntactical rearrangement are made. In direct MT, the language in which input is given is called the source language and the language in which output is obtained is called the target language. Typically, the approach is unidirectional and only takes one language pair into consideration at a time [41]. This method is also known as dictionary-based MT. The first generation of MT (late 1940s to mid- 1960s) was entirely based on machine readable or electronic dictionaries. To some extent, this approach is still helpful in translation of phrases but not sentences [42].

Y.5.3.2 Rule-Based MT

The rule-based MT system takes into account semantic, morphological, and syntactic information from a bilingual dictionary and grammar and based on these rules generate the output in target language from the input in source language by producing an intermediate representation. Rule-based system is further classified as transfer-based MT and interlingua-based MT depending on the intermediate representation [41]:

- *Transfer-Based Translation:* The transfer-based approach became the centerpiece of second-generation MT (mid-1960s to 1980s). The transfer-based approach uses translation rules to translate any matter in input language to that in output language in three phases: analysis, transfer, and synthesis. Firstly, the source language representation is converted into intermediate representation that is subsequently converted into target language representation. A source language dictionary, a target language dictionary, and a bilingual dictionary are used for this purpose [41,42].

• *Interlingua-Based Translation*: The interlingua approach converts words into an intermediate language (IL), which is typically a universal language created for the system to use it as an intermediate for translation into more than one target language. The interlingua approach has an analyzer that produces the intermediate representation of the source language. The synthesizer takes over from the analyzer and produces target sentences given by the analyzer [41]. Interlingua approach has been one of the highlights of the third-generation MT systems, which began in late 1970s and focused on semantics and pragmatics rather than syntax [42].

Y.5.3.3 Corpus-Based MT

In this approach, a training corpus of already translated texts—a parallel corpus—guides the translation process. A parallel corpus consists of two collections of documents: a source language collection and a target language collection. Each document in the source language collection has an identical counterpart in the target language collection [43]. The corpus-based approach is mainly used in the statistical MT and the example-based MT system.

• *Statistical MT:* In statistical MT, a bilingual corpus is trained and statistical parameters are derived in order to reach the most likely translation. Statistical MT takes place in three phases, namely language modeling, translation modeling, and decoding. The language model determines the probability of the target language that helps in achieving the fluency in the target language and choosing the right word in the translated language. The translation model, however, helps to compute the conditional probability of the target language. Finally, in the decoding phase, the maximum probability of product of both the language model and the translation model is computed, which gives the statistically most likely probable sentence in the target language [41]. There are three different statistical approaches in MT: wordbased, phrase based, and hierarchical phrase based. In the word-based model, the words in an input sentence are translated word by word individually, and these words finally are arranged in a specific way to get the target sentence. In phrase-based model, each source and target sentence is divided into separate phrases instead of words before translation. Hierarchical phrase-based model is a more sophisticated model that provides more accuracy, as hierarchical phrases have recursive structures instead of simple phrases [44].

- *Context-Based MT:* It is being developed as a corpus-based method that requires neither rules nor parallel corpora. Instead it requires an extensive monolingual target text corpus, a full-form bilingual dictionary, and optionally (to further improve translation quality) a smaller monolingual source-text corpus to run its algorithm [45].
- *Example-Based MT:* This system usually uses previous translation examples to translate from source to target language. The basic idea of this system is to retrieve examples of existing translation in its example base and provide the new translation based on that example. Example-based MT generally takes place in three phases: matching, alignment, and recombination. In the matching phase, the system searches examples from the example base that are similar to the input. In the alignment phase, the part of the example that is to be used is identified and aligned comparing with other examples. In the final phase, the reusable parts identified during the alignment phase are put together and produce the translation in target language [41].

Y.5.3.4 Other Approaches

Lately, researchers have used some new approaches in MT. These are briefly introduced below [44]:

- *Knowledge-Based Approach:* Knowledge-based MT (KBMT) is characterized by a heavy emphasis on functionally complete understanding of the source text prior to the translation into the target text. KBMT does not require total understanding but assumes that an interpretation engine can achieve successful translation into several languages. KBMT is implemented on the Interlingua architecture; it differs from other inter-lingual techniques by the depth with which it analyzes the sought link and its reliance on explicit knowledge of the world.
- *Principle-Based Approach:* Principle-based MT systems employ parsing methods based on the Principles & Parameters Theory of Chomsky's Generative Grammar. The parser generates a detailed syntactic structure that contains lexical, phrasal, grammatical, and thematic information. It also focuses on robustness, language-neutral representations, and deep linguistic analyses.

- *Online Interactive Approach:* In this interactive translation system, the user is allowed to suggest the correct translation to the translator online. This approach is very useful in a situation where the context of a word is unclear, and there exists many possible meanings for a particular word. In such cases, the structural ambiguity can be solved with the interpretation of the user.
- *Image-Based Approach:* This is a new approach introduced in 2010 by Samir Kumar Borogohain and Sivashankar Nair using Pictorially Grounded Language (PGL). In this approach, symbols of both the source and the target languages are grounded on a common set of images and animation. PGL is a graphic language and acts as a conventional IL representation. The translation system is implemented in such a way that images and objects are tagged with both the source and target language equivalents, which makes the reverse translation much easier.
- *Lexical Functional Grammar–Based Approach:* This is a very different approach to MT that is intended for dissemination of information to the deaf people in India and was proposed by Tirthankar Dasgupta, Sandipan Dandpat, and Anupam Basu. At present, a prototype version of English to Indian Sign Language has been developed, and the ISL (i.e. Interactive Systems Laboratories) syntax is represented based on Lexical Functional Grammar formalism.
- *Adaptable Frame-Based Approach:* In this approach, karaka relations for sentence comprehension are used in the frame-based translation system for Dravidian languages. Two pattern-directed application-oriented experiments were conducted, and the same meaning representation technique was used in both cases. In the first experiment, translation was done from a free word order language to fixed word order one, where both the source and destination were natural languages. In the second experiment, however, the TL was an artificial language with a rigid syntax. Even though there is a difference in the generation of the target sentence, the results obtained in both experiments were encouraging.

Y.5.4 Problems of MT

Several problems have been identified in MT such as [46,47]:
- *Lack of equivalent terms:* Not all the words in one language have equivalent terms in another language, e.g., in some cases a word in one language can be expressed only by group of words in another language [47].
- *Syntactical difference:* Two given languages may have completely different syntactical structures, e.g., a language may follow subject–verb–object structure, while another may follow subject–object–verb structure.

- *Differences in parts of speech*: Sometimes there is lack of one-to-one correspondence of parts of speech, e.g., a word may be noun in one language, but its equivalent in another language may be adjective [47].
- *Homonymity*: Words can have more than one meaning, and sometimes group of words or whole sentence may have more than one meaning in a language. This problem is often called as ambiguity [47].
- *Stylistic difference*: There may be stylistic differences in expressing the same idea in different languages and sometime in the same language itself, e.g., "Advances in technology created new opportunities (English)" and "Because technology has advanced, opportunities have been created (Japanese)" [46].

Nevertheless, Sylvia has rightly pointed out that "the main problem with MT is that machine is only machine. It matches components and follows rules. *It doesn't actually know what it's talking about*" [48].

Y.5.4.1 Problems in Multilingual Countries

In a multilingual country like India, the problem has a different dimension. Here the scientists and researchers need translations of research materials not only from foreign languages but also from different indigenous languages. Today MT facilities for many European languages to English are available. Several institutions and researchers have taken up initiatives for developing MT systems for materials in different Indian languages to English and vice versa and also from one Indian language to another. Among the MT initiatives in India, Sampark project is very well known. Sampark is a multipart MT system developed with the combined efforts of 11 institutions (IIIT Hyderabad, University of Hyderabad, CDAC (Noida, Pune), Anna University—KBC Research Centre, Chennai, IIT Kharagpur, IIT Bombay, IISc-Banglore, Tamil University, IIIT Allahabad, Jadavpur University) under the umbrella of consortium project "Indian Language to India Language Machine Translation" (ILMT) funded by TDIL program of Department of IT, Government of India. ILMT project has developed language technology for 9 Indian languages resulting in MT for 18 language pairs. These are 14 bidirectional between Hindi and Urdu/Punjabi/Telugu/Bengali/Tamil/Marathi/Kannada and 4 bidirectional between Tamil and Malayalam/Telugu. The Sampark system is based on analyze-transfer-generate paradigm. First, analysis of the source language is done, then a transfer of vocabulary and structure to target language is carried out and finally the target language is generated [49]. There are more than 40 other initiatives implemented or being implemented in different institutions across the country.

Y.6 NATURAL LANGUAGE PROCESSING

NLP is the computerized approach to analyzing text that is based on both a set of theories and a set of technologies. And, being a very active area of research and development, it has no single all-agreed definition. The goal of NLP is "to accomplish human-like language processing" [50]. NLP began in the 1950s as the intersection of artificial intelligence and linguistics. NLP was originally distinct from text IR, which employs highly scalable statistics-based techniques to index and search large volumes of text efficiently. With time, however, NLP and IR have converged somewhat. Currently, NLP borrows from several, very diverse fields, requiring today's NLP researchers and developers to broaden their mental knowledge base significantly [51]. Key among the contributors to the discipline and practice of NLP are: Linguistics, which focuses on formal, structural models of language, and the discovery of language universals—in fact the field of NLP was originally referred to as Computational Linguistics; Computer Science, which is concerned with developing internal representations of data and efficient processing of these structures, and Cognitive Psychology, which looks at language usage as a window into human cognitive processes, and has the goal of modeling the use of language in a psychologically plausible way [50].

Y.6.1 Focuses of NLP

While the entire field is referred to as NLP, there are in fact two distinct focuses—language processing and language generation. The first of these refers to the analysis of language for the purpose of producing a meaningful representation, while the latter refers to the production of language from a representation. The task of NLP is equivalent to the role of reader/listener, while the task of Natural Language Generation is that of the writer/speaker [50].

Y.6.2 Natural Language Understanding

NLP was originally referred to as Natural Language Understanding (NLU) in the early days of artificial intelligence. NLU is still the main aim of NLP. There are more practical goals for NLP, many related to the particular application for which it is being utilized. For example, an NLP-based IR system has the goal of providing more precise, complete information in response to a user's real information need. The goal of the NLP system here is to represent the true meaning and intent of the user's query, which can be expressed as naturally in everyday language as if they were speaking to a reference librarian. Also, the contents of the documents that are being searched will be represented at all their levels of meaning so that a true match between need and response can be found, no matter how either are expressed in their surface form. NLU requires the knowledge of how the words are formed and how the words in turn form clauses and sentences. In addition, to successfully understand a set of sentences in a given context, one should have higher levels of linguistic knowledge [50].

Y.6.3 Levels of NLP

The most explanatory method for presenting what actually happens within an NLP system is by means of the "levels of language" approach. This is also referred to as the synchronic model of language and is distinguished from the earlier sequential model, which hypothesizes that the levels of human language processing follow one another in a strictly sequential manner. Psycholinguistic research suggests that language processing is much more dynamic, as the levels can interact in a variety of orders [50]. The various levels of work involved in MT are [50,52] as follows:

- *Morphological:* This level deals with the morphological structure of words, like word root, prefix, suffix, and infixes. The basic unit in a written word is a morpheme. Thus, this level gives knowledge of word formation.
- *Lexical:* At this level, humans, as well as NLP systems, interpret the meaning of individual words. Thus, this level deals with thesaurus lookup, spelling variations, acronyms, abbreviations, etc.
- *Syntactic:* This level focuses on analyzing the words in a sentence so as to uncover the grammatical structure of the sentence. This requires both a grammar and a parser. The output of this level of processing is a (possibly delinearized) representation of the sentence that reveals the structural dependency relationships between the words.
- *Semantic:* Semantic processing determines the possible meanings of a sentence by focusing on the interactions among word-level meanings in the sentence. This level of processing can include the semantic disambiguation of words with multiple senses.
- *Discourse:* While syntax and semantics work with sentence-length units, the discourse level of NLP works with units of text longer than a sentence. Discourse focuses on the properties of the text as a whole that convey meaning by making connections between component sentences.

- *Pragmatic Level:* This level is concerned with the purposeful use of language in situations and utilizes context over and above the contents of the text for understanding. The goal is to explain how extra meaning is read into texts without actually being encoded in them. This requires much world knowledge, including the understanding of intentions, plans, and goals.

Besides, there is also phonological level that deals with interpretation of speech sounds within and across words, and thus it falls in the area of voice/speech recognition system.

Y.6.4 Approaches to NLP

Broadly there are four types of approaches to NLP [50]:

- *Symbolic Approach:* Symbolic approaches perform deep analysis of linguistic phenomena and are based on explicit representation of facts about language through well-understood knowledge representation schemes and associated algorithms. Logic or rule-based systems and semantic networks are good examples of such approach.
- *Statistical Approach:* Statistical approaches employ various mathematical techniques and often use large text corpora to develop approximate generalized models of linguistic phenomena based on actual examples of these phenomena provided by the text corpora without adding significant linguistic or world knowledge.
- *Connectionist Approach:* Connectionist approaches also develop generalized models from examples of linguistic phenomena. What separates connectionism from other statistical methods is that connectionist models combine statistical learning with various theories of representation.

Y.6.5 Applications of NLP

Researches are being conducted on application of NLP in various fields. The applications that are mainly related to information dissemination are briefly described below.

- *IR:* NLP techniques are often used both for facilitating descriptions of document content and for presenting the user's query, all with the aim of comparing both descriptions and presenting the user the documents that best satisfy their information needs [53]. There is also possibility of applying NLP for retrieving multilanguage information, i.e., retrieving information when the questions and/or documents are in different languages. In such cases, automatic translators can be used on the documents and/or questions, or interlingua mechanisms can be used to interpret documents [54].

- *Information Extraction (IE):* IE involves extraction of entities, events, and existing relationships between elements in a text or group of texts. This is one way of efficiently accessing large documents since it extracts parts of the document shown in its content [55]. These extractions can then be utilized for a range of applications including question answering, visualization, and data mining [50].

- *Question Answering:* Question answering aims to give a specific response to the formulated query. The information needs must be well-defined: dates, places, etc. Here the processing of natural language attempts to identify the type of response to be provided by disambiguating the question, analyzing the set restrictions, and the use of IE techniques. These systems are considered to be the potential successors to the current IR systems. START natural language system is an example of one of these systems [21].

- *Automatic Indexing:* In automatic indexing, NLP can be applied to tackle the problems of compound words and that of plurals and irregular plurals [52].

- *Summarization:* The higher levels of NLP, particularly the discourse level, can empower an implementation that reduces a larger text into a shorter, yet richly constituted abbreviated narrative representation of the original document [50].

- *MT:* Perhaps the oldest of all NLP applications, various levels of NLP have been utilized in MT systems, ranging from the "word-based" approach to applications that include higher levels of analysis [50].

REFERENCES

[1] M. Tulic, Automatic indexing. <http://automatic-analysis-gido.blogspot.in/2007/02/automatic-indexing_15.html> 2005.

[2] P.K. Panigrahi, Computerized indexing and clustering techniques, in: S.B. Ghosh, J.N. Satpathi, (Eds.), Subject Indexing Systems: Concepts, Methods and Techniques, IASLIC, Kolkata, 1998, pp. 277–307.

[3] D.B. Cleveland, A.D. Cleveland, Introduction to Indexing and Abstracting, third ed., Libraries Unlimited, Colorado, 2001,

[4] B. Hjorland, Automatic indexing. <http://www.iva.dk/bh/lifeboat_ko/CONCEPTS/automatic_indexing.htm>.

[5] H.F. Fangmeyer, Semi-automatic Indexing: State of the Art, AGARD, NATO, Neuilly-sur-Seine, France, 1974, http://ftp.rta.nato.int/public//PubFullText/AGARD/AG/AGARD-AG-179///AGARD-AG-179.pdf.

[6] A.R.D. Prasad, PROMETHEUS: an automatic indexing system. Knowledge organization and change, in: R. Green, (Ed)., Proceedings of the Fourth International ISKO Conference, 15–18 July 1996, Washington, DC, Frankfurt/Main: Indeks Verlag, (Advances in Knowledge Organization, 5, 1996, pp. 329–335).

[7] S. Haider, Information Access Through the Subject: An Annotated Bibliography, MLIS dissertation submitted to Aligarh Muslim University (2002), http://www.geocities.ws/salman_mlisc/dissertation.

[8] H.P. Edmundson, New methods in automatic extracting, J. ACM 16 (2) (1969) 264–285.

[9] F.W. Lancaster, Indexing and Abstracting in Theory and Practice, University of Illinois, Campaign, 1991.

[10] G.G. Chowdhury, Introduction to Modern Information Retrieval, Library Association Publishing, London, 1999.

[11] S-F. Liang, et al., Can automatic abstracting improve on current extracting techniques in aiding users to judge the relevance of pages in search engine results? 7th Computational Linguistics UK, 2004, 54-59.

[12] J.E. Rush, et al., Production of indicative abstracts by application of contextual inference and syntactic coherence criteria, JASIS, (1971) 260–274.

[13] J.J. Pollock, A. Zamora, Automatic abstracting research at Chemical Abstracts Service, in: I. Mani, M.T. Maybury, (Eds.), Advances in Automatic Text Summarization, Massachusetts Institute of Technology (1999).

[14] G.G. Chowdhury, S. Chowdhury, Organizing Information From Shelf to the Web. Facet Publishing (2007).

[15] S. Arano, Thesauruses and ontologies. <http://www.upf.edu/hipertextnet/en/nume­ro-3/tesauros.html>.

[16] B.C. Vickery, Ontologies, J. Inf. Sci. 23 (4) (1997) 277–286.

[17] T.R. Gruber, Towards principles for the design of ontologies used for knowledge sharing, Int. J. Hum. Comput. Stud. 43 (5/6) (1995) 907–928.

[18] R. Studer, et al., Knowledge engineering: principles and methods, Data Knowl. Eng. (1998) 161–197.

[19] Ontology. <http://en.wikipedia.org/wiki/Ontology_(information_science)>.

[20] G. Antoniou, F. Van Harmelen, A Semantic Web Primer, MIT Press, Cambridge, MA, 2004.

[21] V. Kabilan, Ontology for information systems (04IS) design methodology (Doctor of Technology Thesis). Royal Institute of Technology, Stockholm, 2007.

[22] M. Uschold, M. King, Towards a methodology for building ontologies, Workshop on Basic Ontological Issues in Knowledge Sharing (IJCAI-95). (1995). *As quoted in* V. Kabilan. Ontology for information systems (04IS) design methodology (Doctor of Technology Thesis). Royal Institute of Technology, Stockholm, (2007).

[23] N. Guarino, Formal ontology and information systems, in: Proceedings of Formal Ontology and Information Systems (FOIS), 1998. *As quoted in* V. Kabilan. Ontology for Information Systems (04IS) Design Methodology (Doctor of Technology Thesis). Royal Institute of Technology, Stockholm, (2007).

[24] D.L. McGuinness, Ontologies come of age, in: D.F. Fensel, et al. (Eds.), Spinning the Semantic Web: Bringing the World Wide Web to its Full Potential, MIT Press, Cambridge, MA, 2003.

[25] M. Uschold, Creating, integrating and maintaining local and global ontologies. <http://citeseerx.ist.psu.edu/viewdoc/download?doi=10.1.1.28.7554&rep=rep1&type=pdf>.

[26] M. Uschold, M. Gruninger, Ontologies: principles, methods and applications, Knowl. Eng. Rev. 11 (2) (1996) 93–136.

[27] N.F. Noy, D.L. McGuinness, Ontology development 101, a guide to creating your first ontology. <http://protege.stanford.edu/publications/ontology_development/ontology101.pdf>.

[28] M. Denny, Ontology tools survey, revisited. <http://www.xml.com/pub/a/2004/07/14/onto.html>.

[29] J. Cai, et al., Semantic web and ontologies. <http://www.mpi-inf.mpg.de/departments/d5/teaching/ss03/xml-seminar/talks/CaiEskeWang.pdf>.

[30] T. Vander Wal, Folksonomy coinage and definition, 2007. <http://vanderwal.net/folksonomy.html>.

[31] B. Berlin, Ethnobiological Classification, Princeton University Press, Princeton, 1992. *As quoted in* Folksonomy. http://en.wikipedia.org/wiki/Folksonomy.

[32] A. Nouruzi, Folksonomies: (un)controlled vocabulary? Knowledge Organization 33 (4) (2006) 199–203.

[33] T. Vander Wal, Explaining and showing broad and narrow folksonomies. <http://www.vanderwal.net/random/entrysel.php?blog=1635>. *As quoted in* Foksonomy. <http://en.wikipedia.org/wiki/Folksonomy>.

[34] T. Togia, Ontology vs. folksonomy. <http://www.cl.cam.ac.uk/~aac10/R207/ontology_vs_folksonomy.pdf>.

[35] J. Porter, Real world uses of folksonomy. <https://www.uie.com/brainsparks/2005/09/28/real-world-uses-of-folksonomies/>.

[36] Folksonomy. <http://www.gutenberg.us/articles/folksonomies#cite_note-21>.

[37] C. Van Damme, et al., Folks Ontology: an integrated approach for turning folksonomies into ontologies, in: Paper Presented at International Workshop on Bridging the Gap between Semantic Web and Web 2.0, Innsbruck, Austria, 2007. <http://www.kde.cs.uni-kassel.de/ws/eswc2007/proc/FolksOntology.pdf>.

[38] Warren Weaver Memorandum, July 1949. MT News International, no. 22; July 1999; 5–6, 15. <http://www.hutchinsweb.me.uk/MTNI-22-1999.pdf>.

[39] M.A. Chéragui, Theoretical overview of machine translation, in: Proceedings of the 4th International Conference on Web and Information Technologies (ICWIT), Sidi Bel-Abbes, Algeria, (2012). 160–169. <http://ceur-ws.org/Vol-867/ProcIcwit2012.pdf>.

[40] Robin, Machine translation—overview. <http://language.worldofcomputing.net/machine-translation/machine-translation-overview.html>, 2009.

[41] S. Sanyal, R. Borgohain, Machine translation systems in India. <http://arxiv.org/ftp/arxiv/papers/1304/1304.7728.pdf>.

[42] V. Shou-Chuan Yang, Electronic dictionaries in machine translation, in: A. Kent et al., (Eds.), Encyclopedia of Library and Information Science, 48. Suppl. 11. (1991). Mercel Decker, New York. 74–92.

[43] A. Ramanathan, Statistical machine translation (PhD seminar report). <http://202.141.152.9/clir/papers/statistical_mt.pdf>.

[44] P.J. Antony, Machine translation approaches and survey for Indian languages, Comput. Linguistics Chin. Lang. Process. 18 (1) (2013), 47–78.

[45] Carbonell, et al., Context-based machine translation. in: Proceedings of the 7th Conference of the Association for Machine Translation in the Americas, 2006, 19–28.

[46] J. Hutchins, Machine translation: problems and issues. <http://www.hutchinsweb.me.uk/SUSU-2007-2-ppt.pdf>, 2007.

[47] Robin, Challenges in machine translation. <http://language.worldofcomputing.net/machine-translation/challenges-in-machine-translation.html>, 2009.

[48] SYLVIA, The problem with machine translation. <http://foundintranslation.berkeley.edu/?p=6329>.

[49] Sampark system: automated translation among Indian languages. <http://sampark.iiit.ac.in/sampark/web/index.php/registration/validuser>.

[50] E.D. Liddy, Natural language processing, in: M. Decker (Ed.), Encyclopedia of Library and Information Science, second ed., New York. <http://surface.syr.edu/cgi/viewcontent.cgi?article=1043&context=istpub>.

[51] P.M. Nadkarni, et al., Natural language processing: an introduction, J. Am. Med. Inform. Assoc. 18 (2011) 544–551.

[52] A.R.D. Prasad, Natural language processing, in: S.B. Ghosh, J.N. Satpathy, (Eds.), Subject Indexing Systems, IASLIC, Kolkata, 1998, pp. 308–325.

[53] J. Allan, Natural language processing for information retrieval. <http://citeseer.ist.psu.edu/308641.html>.

[54] M.D. Harris, Introduction to Natural Language Processing, Reston Publishing Co., Reston, VA. (1985).

[55] M. Vallez, R. Pedraza-Jimenez, Natural language processing in textual information retrieval and related topics. <http://www.upf.edu/hipertextnet/en/numero-5/pln.html>.

CHAPTER Z

Recent Trends in IOD

Z.1 INTRODUCTION

With the ushering in of digital era and emergence of Internet, there have been several new developments that have made a great impact on information organization and dissemination activities. Such developments have been briefly described in the following sections.

Z.2 E-INFORMATION SERVICE

The increasing application of electronic or digital technology in rendering information services in recent decades has given rise to the concept of electronic or digital information services. Basically all library services are information services. Even circulation of documents is also an information service in the sense that documents bear information and through circulation a document bearing information pertinent to the user concerned is supplied to him or her. This may, at the best, be called indirect information service. However, reference service and documentation service can be called direct information services. In the digital era, some more services have come into vogue, such as Internet searching service or database searching service, which are in fact varieties of documentation service/information service. It may be pointed out that e-information service (EIS) can be provided only when the information are available in digital format. That is why EIS is defined as "one where maximum use is made of electronically held information" [1]. There are two aspects of electronic information services, viz., availability of information in electronic format and provision of service through electronic medium. EIS can also be given on the basis of information sources available in print form, but that will involve a lot of efforts and costs making the proposition unrealistic. Obviously, a fully digital library will only be in a position to provide totally electronic information services.

Elements of Information Organization and Dissemination
DOI: http://dx.doi.org/10.1016/B978-0-08-102025-8.00026-0
527

Z.2.1 Modes of EIS

EIS can be organized locally through intranet set up for the purpose and mounting the locally compiled digital information sources and/or those available on CD onto the server or through the Internet/World Wide Web, especially when the users are located remotely. Both the modes can also be used simultaneously for providing the service.

Z.2.2 Types of EIS

Though any of the traditional information services may be converted into EIS, normally EIS involves:
- Providing access to e-books, e-journals, and other electronic information products;
- Providing access to bibliographic databases, including abstracting services;
- Providing access to full-text databases (with hyperlink facilities);
- Providing e-alerting service (about availability of required information/document);
- Providing Internet searching (institutional and government websites, bulletin boards, etc.) service.

EIS may also include conditional and limited downloading facilities. The Internet-based EISs have been discussed in a subsequent section.

Z.2.3 Characteristics of EIS

The main characteristics of EIS are:
- The services are mainly generated on the basis of digital information resources that are available online or offline;
- The services are provided in digital medium, either offline or online;
- The services may be obtained by the users directly sitting at home;
- The services may be available in the form of access only or access and limited downloading; and
- Some services may be available commercially to the users, without the intervention of any library/information center.

Z.2.4 Organization of EIS

The following steps may be followed while organizing any EIS [2]:
- *Initiation*: Before planning any EIS in a library, some preliminary tasks have to be undertaken so as to assess the availability of information

and existence/nonexistence of the users' need for the proposed service. These tasks are:

- *Establishing goals and objectives:* Starting of EIS improves the overall performance of the library and helps in achieving the goals and objectives of the library itself. The specific goals of EIS are [3]: expansion of personalized information service to the users; improvement of quality of research, decision-making, etc., undertaken by the users; broadening the scope of the library resources; integrating the new service with the existing information services rendered by the library; increasing the effectiveness and efficiency of the information retrieval process; and acquainting the users with electronic services to enhance lifelong information gathering skills.

- *Information audit:* Information audit finds out what information exist and where in an organization, what information are needed, and the information flows and gaps.

- *Assessment of users' needs:* Assessment of users' needs may be undertaken as a part of information audit itself. "The exercise should provide a clear understanding on the ways that users currently access information, and the types of information that they use" and should reveal "what kind of information is needed, who needs it, and the range of topic that must be covered" [1]. (See Chapter-C)

- *Planning and Preparation for EIS*: Once information audit and assessment of users' needs are complete, planning of different aspects of the intended service needs to be undertaken and some preparatory tasks will have to be accomplished.

  - *Planning:* This will involve deciding the details of product or service to be started; the space required for organizing and providing the service; the financial requirements; and the staff requirement, including the skills to be possessed by them. It will also involve preparation of a proposal for starting the new service and obtaining approval for the same and setting up a timetable for implementation of the proposal.

  - *Preparation:* This will involve securing necessary funds, building of basic infrastructure, building of adequate information resource base, building of technological capability, recruitment/training of staff, and training of users.

- *Provision of EIS*: Finally for introducing the EIS, the required information resource/product has to be created and/or mounted on the Internet/Intranet; a trial run has to be organized to assess its effectiveness and the service has to be introduced after necessary modifications, if required.

- *Marketing of EIS*: Though an EIS is started only after assessing the needs of the existing users, the service may be helpful to many potential users and even nonusers. The service should be properly marketed among all types of users and even non-users through usual marketing channels.
- *Evaluation, monitoring, and measuring of EIS*: There is need to constantly assess, evaluate, and monitor the EIS after it is started. Many new and competing services and products are constantly arriving on the scene. It is necessary to consider them for their potential impact on the EIS being run by a library. Each part of the service should be examined in detail and evaluated.
- *Continuation/discontinuation/replacement of EIS*: The evaluation of the utility of the service will enable the library to decide if the service should be continued or discontinued; if it should be continued whether it should be in the same format or in a changed format. If the evaluation gives negative results the service may be discontinued or replaced by a new service. In that case the whole process of creating the service may have to be repeated.

Z.3 INTERNET/WEB-BASED INFORMATION SERVICE

Advent of Internet, which is also known as information superhighway, has been a revolutionary development in the field of information dissemination. The Internet is a global network of computer networks utilizing a suite of protocols called TCP/IP (Transmission Control Protocol/Internet Protocol) that supports interconnection of a number of different computer networks. The Internet covers large, international Wide Area Networks (WANs) as well as smaller Local Area Networks (LANs) and individual computers connected to the Internet worldwide. The Internet supports communication and sharing of data and offers vast amount of information through a variety of services and tools [4]. Internet is not only a great source of information, but also a very effective and efficient medium for speedy dissemination of information. Through Internet, it has been possible to replace the concept of "fixed-time-fixed-place" information service to "anytime anywhere" information service. As a source of information, Internet hosts a large number of websites, bogs, online public access catalogs (OPACs) and other databases, digital libraries, and even primary e-information sources, such as e-books and e-journals. These sources have been described in Chapter-B.

Z.3.1 Facilitating Tools

Internet has several tools and services that can facilitate rendering of online information services to the users remotely. The major Internet tools and services that can help in this regard are:

- Email: Email or electronic mail is a method of exchanging digital messages from one person to another or more recipients. This is often used by libraries and information centers to provide current awareness service (CAS) and selective dissemination of information (SDI).
- Telnet: The Terminal Emulation protocol or Telnet allows one computer to access another computer by enabling a user to exchange data and issue commands on the other computer. This is mainly used by libraries and information centers to allow access to information stored in their computers.
- File Transfer Protocol (FTP): FTP is a standard language of Internet that facilitates transfer of files from one computer to another. This can be used by libraries and information centers to transfer a required file to the computer of a user.
- WWW: Invented in 1991 by Tim Berners-Lee and based on HTML (Hypertext Markup Language), WWW is a system that transfers text, graphics, and sound files through the Hypertext Transfer Protocol (http). Innumerable websites are available on WWW, which can be accessed by client programs known as web browsers. Library websites and OPACs are also available on WWW.
- TCP/IP: It is the core Internet protocol, which allows computers to communicate and exchange information by using the different Internet tools.

Other Internet tools and services include Gopher, WAIS, Archie, Veronica, Usenet, and other online Internet forums.

Z.3.2 Searching Tools

Search engines are available for searching information available on the web, but search through them often leads to a huge number of websites, most of them being irrelevant and it becomes difficult and time-consuming for a user to retrieve the relevant sites. To obviate this difficulty and make the search more relevant and pinpointed, some search tools have been devised, mainly by librarians, such as library portals and subject gateways.

Z.3.2.1 Library Portals

The term "portal" describes a variety of web-based interfaces, everything from a relatively static homepage with general product and contact information to a dynamic one-stop homepage where users can customize the content to meet their needs [5]. According to Joint Information Systems Committee of the United Kingdom, a portal is "a network service that brings together content from diverse distributed resources using technologies such as cross searching, harvesting and altering, and collates this in to an amalgamated form for presentation via a web browser to the user" [6]. Thus, a library portal is an interface to access library resources and services through a single access and management point for users [5]. Many libraries/information centers have created such portals individually or by collaborative efforts, e.g., *The European Library Portal* (http://www.theeuropeanlibrary.org/tel4/), which provides access to the collections of the 48 National Libraries of Europe and leading European research libraries. Portals can be subject-based too, e.g., *Social Welfare Portal* of the British Library (http://socialwelfare.bl.uk/about/).

Z.3.2.2 Subject Gateways

Subject gateways are the Internet search tools to help people find different types of resources available on the net on a specific subject area, such as electronic journals, software, data sets, e-books, mailing lists/discussion groups (and their archives), articles/papers/reports, bibliographies, bibliographical databases, organizational home pages, educational materials; news, resource guides, etc. [7]. Subject gateways facilitate location of high-quality information available on the web. They are typically databases with detailed metadata records describing the resources and providing hyperlink to the resources [8]. Subject gateways are characterized by two key factors: (1) they are selective, pointing only to Internet resources that meet with quality selection criteria and (2) they are built by subject and information specialists—often librarians. In the field of Library and Information Science, *BUBL* (http://bubl.ac.uk/link) is a well-known subject gateway.

Z.3.2.3 Internet Resource Guides

The Internet resource guides or directories are basically lists of relevant and useful websites with hyperlink either in a specific subject field or in a wider field arranged category-wise or subject-wise. Examples of some such well-known guides are *Internet Resource Guide*, compiled by

Infoplease (http://www.infoplease.com/ipa/A0777781.html), *Zorg Web Directory* of quality Internet resources (http://www.zorg-directory.com/), *Internet Directory for Botany* (http://www.ou.edu/cas/botany-micro/idb-alpha/), and *India-Yahoo Directory* (http://dir.yahoo.com/regional/countries/india/).

Z.3.3 Online Information Services

As indicated above, online EISs can be provided using appropriate Internet tools and services. Some major Internet-based or web-based services are briefly described below.

Z.3.3.1 Access to Databases

Several publishers today offer web-based, Intranet solutions for providing local access to their databases, such as Silver Platter, Cambridge Scientific Abstract, and Institute for Scientific Information (now known as Thomson ISI). A library can also subscribe to bibliographic and full-text databases of users' interest and allow the users to access them remotely through Internet.

Z.3.3.2 Access to OPACs/Web OPACs

Online public access catalogs of many libraries are now available on the Internet, which can be accessed by anybody. A library can also upload its OPAC, which can be accessed by its users remotely. Web OPAC, which is interactive in nature and serves as a gateways to resources held not only by the concerned library but also by other linked libraries, can be accessed through a link on a library's web page. In addition to searching and browsing the library catalog end users can transmit orders or request directly from the Web OPAC as well as view their own borrower accounts.

Z.3.3.3 Online Reference Service

Online electronic reference services are rendered to the users mainly in two ways [9]:

- *Asynchrony:* Through this system, the user puts an email request to the library or fill in a specific web form from the library homepage with specific request and in due course answers are provided by email.
- *Synchrony:* In this service, there is a two-way communication between a user and the librarian using chat software or video technique. As in this method the user gets direct answer from the librarian, it is also known as real time, live, or interactive online reference service.

There are also some useful Internet sites or services, which provide reference service in their own way. Two such websites/services are:

- *"Ask A" Services:* These refer to the websites like "Ask A Librarian," "Ask An Expert," "Ask A Question" (http://talonline.ca/askaquestion), and "Ask ERIC" (http://askeric.org), in which users' questions are referred to and individually answered by concerned people [10].
- *Online Pathfinders:* Pathfinders are guides to help users find information on a particular topic. Some such pathfinders are: LibraryU (http://www.libraryu.org), Netlibrary (http://www.netlibrary.com), and Internet Public Library Pathfinders (http://www.ipl.org/div/pt/) [11].

Besides, now many ready reference sources, such as dictionaries, encyclopedias, directories, and yearbooks, e.g., Britannica Online (www.britannica.com), are now available online. A library can give link to free and subscribed reference sources on its web page for its users. Several virtual libraries of reference tools have also been created on the Internet, such as *Library Spot* (www.libraryspot.com/) and, *Infomine* (http://lib-www.ucr.edu). The users can get answer to their reference queries from these sites.

Z.3.3.4 Online CAS

There are several Internet sites providing CAS, such as *Bibliotech Review*, providing nascent information on library automation (http://www.gadget-server.com/bibliotech); *Current cites*, providing selected titles of books and e-documents on IT (http://sunsite.berkeley.edu/currentcites/); *Oxford Journals Table of Contents Service* (http://www3.oup.co.uk/jnls/tocmail/); and *Scholarly Article Research Alerting*, providing tables of contents of academic journals (http://www3.oup.co.uk/jnls/tocmail/). Several publishers of scholarly and scientific journals like Elsevier, Pergamon Press, Royal Society of Chemistry, etc., also send the content pages of the issues of journals published by them in advance to the registered individuals by email. A library can link relevant Internet sites to its web page or can also provide its own CAS using email facility.

Z.3.3.5 Online SDI

In many R & D organizations and academic institutions, electronic SDI service has been introduced to deliver current information of interests to the users directly on their computer terminals. In such systems, research interest profiles of users are matched with the latest literature on the subject at regular intervals and the results are communicated by email to the respective users.

Z.3.3.6 Online Clipping Service

In electronic newspaper clipping service, newspaper cuttings are converted into a suitable format by a library and transmitted to the respective users using email facility.

Z.3.3.7 Online Document Delivery Service

Email facilities are often used by libraries for document delivery service too. On receipt of the request from a user, the library scans the required documents and sends the scanned images to the user as an email attachment. Inter-library loan requests are also received by email. There are also some online document delivery services such as *UnCover* (http://uncweb.carl.org), *Ariel* of OCLC, *CitaDel*, and *Article Express* of University of Kentucky.

Z.3.3.8 Discussion Fora

A library can create its own discussion forum (Bulletin Board of News Group) for communication with its users as also discussion among the users. The users can post their views on the forum and also exchange information among themselves.

Z.3.4 Advantages of Web-Based Information Service

The main advantages of web-based information services are:
- The required information are available instantly or in shortest possible time;
- The users can access information directly, i.e., without mediation of any library staff;
- Information can be accessed remotely; and
- A user can access information on his/her own computer without physically visiting the library or information center.

Z.4 OPEN ACCESS MOVEMENT

Scientific and technical journals play a vital role in scholarly communication. Scholars need these journals for acquiring new knowledge and information and applying those in their own work. They also need these journals for publishing the results of their own research work. Scholarly communication has been facing some sort of a crisis in the recent decades

as the scholars faced problems in accessing requires resources. The problems that are responsible for creation of such a situation are:
- Continued increase in world production of published materials;
- Rise in costs of research publications at unprecedented rate;
- Non-rise in the acquisition budget of libraries commensurate with pace of inflation, particularly for journals;
- Acquisition of academic/society publications by more expensive commercial publishers; and
- Fast rise in electronic production, storage, and distribution of research information.

The idea of Open Access (OA) was mooted as a mechanism to overcome this crisis. Gradually, the concept has become very popular and has taken the shape of a movement. Both the scholars and the users have become part of this movement. The underlying philosophy of OA is that as most of the research is carried out through public funding, the research results should be available freely to the public.

Z.4.1 Concept of OA

The term "Open Access" has been in use in the library environment for long to indicate provision of unhindered access to the users inside the stack room for selection and consultation of their required information resources. In the digital and networked environment the term is used in at least two senses. To some, OA literature is digital, online, and free of charge. It removes price barriers but not permission barriers. For others, OA literature is digital, online, free of charge, and free of unnecessary copyright and licensing restrictions. It removes both price barriers and permission barriers. It allows reuse rights that exceed fair use. Scientists have agreed to use the term "weak OA" for the removal of price barriers alone and "strong OA" for the removal of both price and permission barriers [12]. OA is certainly a cost-effective way to access information available around the world. Of course sometimes a reader is required to register with the service in question, which, for instance, can be useful for the service providers in view of the production of readership statistics [13].

Z.4.2 Main Features of OA

The main features of OA are [14]:
- OA literature is digital, free of charge, and free of copyright;
- It is compatible with copyright, peer review, revenue, print, preservation, prestige, career advancement, indexing, and supportive services associated with conventional scholarly literature;

- Its campaign focuses on the literature that authors give to the world without expectation of payment;
- The literature is not free to produce or publish;
- It is compatible with peer review and all the major OA initiative for scientific and scholarly literature insist on its importance.

According to IFLA, an OA publication is one that meets the following conditions [15]:

- The author(s) and copyright holder(s) grant(s) to all users a free, irrevocable, worldwide, perpetual (for the lifetime of the applicable copyright) right of access to, and a license to copy, use, distribute, perform, and display the work publicly and to make and distribute derivative works in any digital medium for any reasonable purpose, subject to proper attribution of authorship, as well as the right to make small numbers of printed copies for their personal use.
- A complete version of the work and all supplemental materials, including a copy of the permission as stated above, in a suitable standard electronic format is deposited immediately upon initial publication in at least one online repository that is supported by an academic institution, scholarly society, government agency, or other well-established organization that seeks to enable OA, unrestricted distribution, interoperability, and long-term archiving.

Note: This definition of OA publication was adopted by IFLA from the *Position Statement in Support of Open and Unrestricted Access to Published Research* and was based on the definition arrived at by delegates who attended a meeting on OA publishing convened by the Howard Hughes Medical Institute, Chevy Chase, Maryland, USA, on June 20, 2003, which came to be known as Bethesda Statement.

Z.4.3 Objectives of OA

The main objectives of OA are:
- To remove all barriers to accessing information—financial, technological, legal, temporal; and
- To hasten research and development through free and speedy access to information.

Z.4.4 Mechanisms of OA

OA is achieved through various mechanisms. The two main ways of achieving OA are known as:
- "*Green*": the author self-archives his paper in an openly accessible repository at the time of submission of the publication (the "green"

route) whether the publication is gray literature (usually internal non-peer-reviewed), a peer-reviewed journal publication, a peer-reviewed conference proceedings paper, or a monograph [16].

- "*Gold*": either the journal is subsidized by interested parties [17] or the author or author's institution pays a fee to the publisher at the time of publication; the publisher thereafter makes the material available "free" at the point of access (the "gold" route). The two are not, of course, incompatible and can co-exist [16].

The specific mechanisms are [18]:

- OA periodicals providing complete and unrestricted access to web-based OA journals, such as *D-lib, PLoS Biology*.
- Domain-specific, subject-specific institutional, and digital repositories where the authors or authors' institutions or institutions administered by an organization or scholarly society make publications available free online, e.g., *Arxiv*.
- Limited access, i.e., conventional journals that allow OA to certain sections of their issues, e.g., *Nature*.
- Delayed OA version, i.e., periodicals going OA after a specified period of time from the date of publication, e.g., *Highwire Press Journals*.
- Dual mode subscription-based print on paper edition along with OA online edition, e.g., *British Medical Journal*.
- State of economy-based access where conventional periodicals are made available as OA periodicals to countries based on economic criteria, e.g., *HINARI, AGORA*.

Besides, another mechanism may be self-posting by authors in their blogs.

Z.4.5 Search Tools for OA Resources

Several directories of open source resources are now available that helps in easy and speedy access to such resources. The most well-known such directory is *Directory of Open Access Journals (DOAJ)*. This was created by the efforts of Lars Bjornshauge of the University of Lund, Sweden, in 2003 (http://www.doaj.org). Currently, about 700 journals are searchable through this directory at article level.

Z.4.6 Barriers to OA

The major barriers to OA are:

- *Copyright:* As the author holds the copyright of any intellectual creation, OA to copyrighted materials is not possible unless the copyright of that material expires after the stipulated period;

- *Business Interest of the Publisher:* A publisher of scholarly journal may not agree to put his publication on OA as it threatens his business viability;
- *National Interest:* Putting some research results on the OA may go against national interest, such as research in the field of defense.

Z.4.7 Advantages of OA

The advantages of OA are:
- It helps libraries to better cope with subscription costs and provides more stability to budgeting;
- It provides researchers wider access to relevant literature;
- It allows wider dissemination of scientific and technical information in shortest possible time;
- It helps authors to receive instant and worldwide readership;
- It helps in cutting the delay in dissemination of information inherent to the print medium;
- It removes both the price barrier and permission barrier that undermine access to current literature; and
- It results in more access, citation, and impact.

Z.4.8 Progress of OA Movement

It is reported that one of the Mahatma Gandhi's earliest publications, *Hind Swaraj*, which was published in Gujarati in 1909 and is recognized as the intellectual blueprint of India's freedom movement, and was translated into English the next year, with a copyright legend that read "No Rights Reserved" [19], indicating that no copyright was claimed for this work and hence could be used by anybody freely. However, the modern OA movement (as a social movement) traces its history at least back to the 1960s but became much more prominent in the 1990s with the advent of the digital age. With the spread of the Internet and the ability to copy and distribute electronic data at no cost, the arguments for OA gained new importance [20]. Today it is possible to publish a scholarly article and *also* make it instantly accessible anywhere in the world where there are computers and Internet connections [21]. The first online-only, free-access journals (eventually to be called "open access journals") began appearing in the late 1980s. Among them were *Bryn Mawr Classical Review*, *Postmodern Culture*, and *Psychology*. The first free scientific online archive was arXiv.org, started in 1991, initially a preprint service for physicists, initiated by Paul Ginsparg. In 1997, the US National Library of Medicine (NLM) made *Medline*, the most comprehensive index to medical literature on the planet, freely available in the form of *PubMed*. Usage of this database increased tenfold when it became free, strongly suggesting that prior limits on usage were impacted by lack of access. While indexes are not the main focus of the OA movement, free *Medline* is important in that it opened up a whole new form of the use of scientific literature—by the public, not just professionals. The *Journal of Medical Internet Research* (*JMIR*), one of the first OA journals in medicine, was created in 1998, publishing its first issue in 1999. In 1998, the American Scientists Open Access Forum was launched (first called the "September98 Forum"). In 1999, Harold Varmus of the NIH proposed a project, "E-biomed" (now called "PubMed Central"), intended as an OA electronic publishing platform combining a preprint server with peer-reviewed articles. It was also in 1999 that the Open Archive Initiative and its OAI-PMH protocol for metadata harvesting was launched in order to make online archives interoperable. In 2000, *BioMed Central*, a for-profit OA publisher, was launched by the then Current Science Group (now known as the Science Navigation Group). In 2001, 34,000 scholars around the world signed "An Open Letter to Scientific Publishers," calling for "the establishment of an online public library" that would provide the full contents of the published record of research and scholarly discourse in medicine and the life sciences in a freely accessible, fully searchable, interlinked form." Scientists signing the letter also pledged not to publish in or peer-review for non-OA journals. This led to the establishment of the Public Library of Science, an advocacy organization. However, most scientists continued to publish and review for non-OA journals. PLoS decided to become an OA publisher aiming to compete at the high-quality end of the scientific spectrum with commercial publishers and other OA journals, which were beginning to flourish [20].

Z.4.8.1 International Initiatives

The first major international statement on OA was the Budapest Open Access Initiative in February 2002, launched by the Open Society. This provided the first definition of OA and has a growing list of signatories. The Budapest Open Access Initiative stated that OA would permit users "to read, download, copy, distribute, print, search or link to the full texts of works, crawl them for indexing, pass them as data to software, or use them for any other lawful purpose, without financial, legal, or technical barriers other than those inseparable from gaining access to the Internet itself" [22]. This statement clarified the spirit of OA. The Bethesda Statement on Open Access Publishing released in June 2003 endorsed the principles of OA model and delineated some significant and concrete steps that all relevant parties connected with scientific research and publishing and librarians and others who depend on access to such materials can take to promote the rapid and efficient transition to OA publishing [23]. The Berlin Declaration on Open Access to Knowledge in the Sciences and Humanities signed and issued in October 2003, outlined concrete steps to promote the Internet as a medium for disseminating global knowledge [24], and the World Summit on Information Society held in Geneva in 2003, included OA in its Declaration of Principles and Plan of Action [25]. Furthermore, the Slavador declaration made in September 2005 stressed on providing high priority to OA in national science policies and the role of developing countries in shaping OA worldwide, while the Bangalore declaration of 2006 proposed a model National Open Access Policy that could be offered to governments, and their funding organizations, as a practical tool for driving OA forward.

IFLA Initiatives

IFLA Governing Body adopted "A Statement on Open Access to Scholarly Literature and Research Documentation" in December 2003, wherein it suggested some OA principles and advocated their adoption "in order to ensure the widest possible availability of scholarly literature and research documentation" [15]. These principles are [15]:

- *Acknowledgment* and defense of the moral rights of authors, especially the rights of attribution and integrity.
- *Adoption* of effective peer-review processes to assure the quality of scholarly literature irrespective of mode of publication.
- *Resolute opposition* to governmental, commercial, or institutional censorship of the publications deriving from research and scholarship.
- *Succession* to the public domain of all scholarly literature and research documentation at the expiration of the limited period of copyright protection provided by law, which period should be limited to a reasonable time, and the exercise of fair use provisions, unhindered by technological or other constraints, to ensure ready access by researchers and the general public during the period of protection.
- *Implementation* of measures to overcome information inequality by enabling both publication of quality assured scholarly literature and research documentation by researchers and scholars who may be disadvantaged, and also ensuring effective and affordable access for the

people of developing nations and all who experience disadvantage including the disabled.

• *Support* for collaborative initiatives to develop sustainable OA publishing models and facilities including encouragement, such as the removal of contractual obstacles, for authors to make scholarly literature and research documentation available without charge.

• *Implementation* of legal, contractual, and technical mechanisms to ensure the preservation and perpetual availability, usability, and authenticity of all scholarly literature and research documentation.

UNESCO Initiatives

UNESCO also "promotes OA, with particular emphasis on scientific information (journal articles, conference papers, and data sets of various kinds) emanating from publicly funded research. Working with partners, UNESCO works to improve awareness about the benefits of OA among policy makers, researchers, and knowledge managers. Through its global network of Field Offices, Institutes, and Centers, UNESCO facilitates the development and adoption of OA-enabling policies. In addition, UNESCO engages in global OA debates and cooperates with local, regional, and global initiatives in support of OA" [26]. It has also developed a Global Open Access Portal (http://www.unesco.org/new/en/communication-and-information/portals-and-platforms/goap/), which depicts the status of OA to scientific information in 158 countries worldwide and has brought out *Institutional Repository Software Comparison* that provide guidelines for comparing institutional repository software and can be downloaded online [27].

Supportive Initiatives

Some important supporting initiatives at international level are creation of DOAJ, Directory of Open Access Repositories (OpenDOAR), Registry of Open Access Repository Mandates and Policies (ROARMAP), and Directory of Open Access Scholarly Resources (ROAD). DOAJ was launched in 2003 at Lund University, Sweden, with 300 OA journals, and at present it lists 9000 OA journals covering all areas of science, technology, medicine, social science, and humanities [28]. OpenDOAR, maintained by the University of Nottingham, United Kingdom, is an authoritative directory of academic OA repositories. It now has over 2600 listings [29]. ROARMAP was created by EPrints at University of Southampton in 2003. It is "a searchable international registry charting the growth of OA mandates and policies adopted by universities, research institutions, and research funders that require or request their researchers to provide OA to their peer-reviewed research article output by depositing it in an open access repository" [30]. ROAD, which has been developed with the support of the Communication and Information Sector of UNESCO, "provides free access to a subset of the ISSN Register. This subset comprises bibliographic records which describe scholarly resources in Open Access identified by an ISSN: journals, monographic series, conference proceedings and academic repositories" [31]. Besides, a database named MELIBA: Directory and estimator policies for OA to scientific production (http://www.accesoabierto.net/politicas/default.php) has been launched with an aim to "identify and analyze the existing policies that encourage, request, or require OA to scholarly outputs that arise from projects, in whole or in parts, supported by public funds." ROARMAP mandates are classified in terms of strength and effectiveness in MELIBEA [32].

Z.4.8.2 National Initiatives

OA scenario in some countries where OA has made considerable progress is briefly described below on the basis of information available in UNESCO OA portal [33].

OA in North America

The United States embraced OA principles in the 1960s developing ERIC and MEDLINE. Initiatives, e.g., PubMed Central, continue and offer repository facilities and access to international medical scholarship. As of May 2015, there are 469 OA repositories registered in OpenDOAR and 1053 OA journals from the United States indexed in DOAJ, making it the world's largest OA publisher. ROAD currently lists one scholarly blog from the United States. As of February 2015, 127 OA policies are registered in ROARMAP. As of May 2015, the United States has four funding mandates registered in ROARMAP and over 50 institutional mandates at public and private institutions, research universities, and liberal arts colleges. In February 2013, the US government announced its new OA policy that mandated all publications arising from taxpayer-funded research to be made free to read after a 1-year embargo period. This policy was earlier being applied only to the biomedical publications. An Open Access Working Group has been initiated by Scholarly Publishing Academic Resources Coalition (SPARC) in 2003, to build a framework for collective advocacy of OA to research. As of May 2015, OpenDOAR lists 72 Canadian OA repositories, the majority of which are hosted by universities or research institutions. DOAJ indexes 260 Canadian OA journals. The 2013 study by Science-Metrix estimated OA availability of articles at 49% for Canada. Currently, 27 OA policies are registered with ROARMAP.

OA in South America

Brazil is the most active country of the region in OA implementation. This is also the first country to have a bill presented in 2007 to parliament proposing a national mandatory policy for OA. Around 97% of all Brazilian journals are OA journals. In 2013, Scientific Electronic Library Online (SciELO) made all its journals available on Web of Science in a move to improve international visibility. Salvador Declaration on Open Access (2005), Brazilian Manifesto in support of Open Access to Scientific Information and Carta de São Paulo (2005), the letter of St. Paul, a manifesto in support of OA to scientific literature signed, by scientists, teachers, and librarians of some public and private universities, have raised interest on the potential benefits of OA. As of June 2015, there are 16 OA policies registered in ROARMAP. Since 2013, nine new institutional OA policies have been registered in MELIBEA database.

OA in Europe

In Europe, the United Kingdom has a strong history in the development and implementation of OA. The first institutional repositories were developed in the United Kingdom, and it has also been the home for several major OA publishing developments. The Wellcome Trust, one of the world's largest biomedical charities, alongside the government Medical Research Council, has been a consistent leader in requiring its funded researchers to make publications OA and was the major original driver behind Europe PubMed Central. UK government and charitable research funders have some of the strongest OA policies. UK universities are leaders in the provision of OA infrastructure. This has made OA a mainstream issue for UK researchers in a way that it is often not in other countries and awareness is extremely high. There are currently 608 OA journals published in the United Kingdom, which are indexed in DOAJ and 228 OA repositories registered in OpenDOAR. In June 2013, UK government developed an Open Data Charter consisting of principles and minimum technical standards for countries releasing Open Data. Research Council UK (RCUK), a consortium of seven research councils in UK, which funds research in 170 educational institutions, have established an OA policy effectively requiring all funded researchers to adopt OA in conjunction with three major academic publishers Macmillan, Blackwell, and Elsevier. In Germany, there is strong OA awareness. As of July 2015, OpenDOAR has 172 OA institutional repositories of Germany registered with it. The German Initiative for Network Information (DINI) is supporting a national repository infrastructure. DOAJ indexes 354 German OA journals. ROAD currently lists highest number of scholarly blogs in Germany (49). The big research organizations and many institutions of higher education have OA policies. ROARMAP has 22 German OA policies on its register. The Netherlands also has strong OA awareness and actively promotes OA through institutional mandates, funder mandates, the establishment of OA repositories, and OA publishing agreements. As of June 2015, 28 OA institutional repositories in the Netherlands are registered with OpenDOAR, while DOAJ indexes 103 Dutch journals. Eight OA policies are register in ROARMAP. Several Netherland-based well-known publishers, like Elsevier, Kulwer, and Brill, participate in OA publishing in various degrees. In Poland systematic work of OA advocates has resulted in steady growth in number of OA journals (as of June 2015, 293 indexed by DOAJ) and OA repositories (87 in OpenDOAR). Even the general public also supports OA which is indicated by the petition for Open Mandate initiated at the beginning of 2012 signed by over 10,000 people of which substantial amount did not claim academic affiliation. There are currently two OA policies registered in ROARMAP. Spain also has a strong community of OA Institutional Repositories. Currently there are 56 institutional repositories across the country, which means that 80% of the Spanish Universities have their own institutional repository. Spain also participates in European and International OA projects and initiatives. As of July 2015, there are 500+ OA journals published in Spain, which are indexed in DOAJ. Currently, 27 OA policies are registered in ROARMAP, 24 of which are institutional and three of which are funders' OA mandates. In Russia, one of the main steps towards OA movement has been the Belgorod Declaration. The main goals of this declaration include stimulation of development of OA to scientific knowledge and cultural heritage. According to DOAJ statistics, the number of OA publications in Russia is increasing every year. As of July 2015, there are 15 OA journals published in Russia, which are indexed in DOAJ. Twenty-four OA digital repositories are recorded in OpenDOAR. OA movement has also been initiated in other countries of Europe.

OA in Africa

In Africa, South Africa is the leading country in terms of OA policies on the governmental level and grass-root OA initiatives in universities and research organizations. As of June 2015, there are 30 OA repositories registered in OpenDOAR. The momentum to embrace OA initiatives in Egypt has been building up. As of June 2015, DOAJ lists 531 journals mostly published by Hindawi Publishing Corporation—a rapidly growing academic publisher with more than 300 OA journals covering all major areas of science, technology, and medicine. Five OA repositories from the country are registered in OpenDoar. OA movement in other countries of the region is at various stages of progress.

OA in Oceania Region

There is high level of awareness of OA in communities of information professionals in Australia. OpenDOAR reports a total of 53 OA repositories from Australia. As of April 2014, there are 31 OA policies from various research organizations in Australia registered in ROARMAP. During 2013–14, four Australian universities adopted new repository mandates. The Australian research Council (ARC) requires any publication arising from ARC-funded projects to be deposited into an OA institutional repository. As of May 2015, there are 118 OA journals published in Australia, which are indexed in DOAJ. In New Zealand, currently, there are 116 OA journals that are indexed in the DOAJ and 145 OA journals that are indexed in ROAD. Furthermore, a total of 12 OA repositories are indexed in OpenDOAR. Although the New Zealand Government has not announced its position on OA to scholarly research, a growing number of institutions have policies encouraging or mandating OA publication. There are currently six OA policies registered in ROARMAP.

OA in Asia

In Asian region, Japan has one of the high density of repositories—184 institutional repositories—in its fold (OpenDOAR). Having made considerable OA progress, Japan continues its mission to facilitate global access of its research outputs with variety of outreach programs and initiatives with funding from societies, government, and through international liaison. As of May 2015, there are 98 OA journals published in Japan, which are indexed in DOAJ. OA movement in India has also made good progress. As of July 2015, DOAJ indexes 576 OA journals from India. Sixty-nine

OA digital repositories are registered in OpenDOAR. Fourteen OA policies are registered in ROARMAP. In December 2014, the Department of Biotechnology (DBT) and the Department of Science and Technology (DST), the nation's two top most scientific departments, functioning under India's Ministry of Science and Technology, released a new OA Policy, under which researchers who receive or have received funding since 2012 or use resources from these departments are mandated to deposit, within 2 weeks after acceptance by a journal, copies of the final papers and supporting data in institutional repositories where the information can be accessed by the public. There are two other notable developments which are worth mentioning in this regard. Firstly, Dr. D.K. Sahu, a medical practitioner and publisher of medical journals, being influenced by the idea of OA, has started publishing many of his journals as OA journals through his publishing house MedKnow and currently publishes 150 journals of which 148 are OA journals. Secondly, Informatics India Pvt. Ltd., a Bangalore-based company, which had already developed a subscription-based online current awareness database called J-Gate, released Open J-Gate, the world's largest OA e-journals portal on February 27, 2006. Besides, an important international workshop on Electronic Publishing and OA was held in Bangalore in the first week of November 2006, where a model National OA Policy for Developing Countries was drafted [34]. OA movement in other countries of the region is at different stages of progress.

Z.5 DIGITAL REPOSITORY DEVELOPMENT

Another significant development has been the development of digital repositories. A digital repository is a mechanism for managing and storing digital content [35]. A digital repository is also known as "digital archive." Digital repositories may be subject or discipline based, type-of-document based and institution based. There may be also repositories that are limited by more than one characteristic. A subject repository or disciplinary repository is an online store or archive of research or scholarly publications in a particular subject area. It is not limited by affiliation of the authors. Subject repositories provide one of a number of alternative channels for provision of scholarly OA literature, the primary alternative being the OA journals [36]. There are many subject-based repositories, such as *PubMed Central*, *CiteSeer*, *RePEc*, and *SSRN*. Type-of-document-based repositories specialize in some specific type or types of documents, such as journal articles, conference papers, and preprints. An example of type-of-document-based repository is ar.Xiv, which is a repository on electronic preprints of scientific papers in mathematics, physics, astronomy, and computer science. Institutional repository that covers materials related to a particular institution or a group of institutions is the most common type of digital repositories, and there are now hundreds of such repositories. Different aspects of this type of repository are discussed below.

Z.5.1 Institutional Repository (IR)

An institutional repository is an online locus for collecting, preserving, and disseminating—in digital form—the intellectual output of an institution, particularly a research institution [37]. According to Scholarly Publishing and Academic Resources Coalition (SPARC) of the United States, "an institutional repository is a digital archive of the intellectual products created by faculty, research staff, and students of an institution, with few, if any, barriers to access" [38]. A repository supports mechanisms to import, export, identify, store, and retrieve digital assets [39]. Setting up of institutional repositories is an outcome of OA movement, and hence most of the institutional repositories are OA repositories.

Z.5.1.1 Characteristics of IR

An institutional repository is expected to have the following characteristics [40]:
- institutionally defined (as opposed to discipline-focused or subject-focused);
- scholarly (containing the products of faculty, research staff, and students);
- cumulative and perpetual (the content will be preserved on a long-term basis); and
- open and interoperable (attentive to the Open Archives Initiative—Protocol for Metadata Harvesting);

According to Gibbons, the main characteristics or core features of IR are [41]:
- *Digital Content:* Institutional repositories are supposed to have only digital resources, independent of physical collection. It can be supplementary to physical collection.
- *Community-driven and Focused:* It is the community that creates an IR. It is a collective effort, where every individual of the concerned community is expected to contribute by way of depositing his/her

intellectual contribution in the repository. It is created by the community for the community and eventually it belongs to the global community.

- *Institutionally Supported:* Digitization or creation of IR involves a lot of capital expenditure and also requires recurring expenditure to run it, which needs institutional support and patronage.
- *Durable and Permanent:* An IR is a permanent asset, whereas other digital materials may not be available permanently.
- *Accessible Content:* IRs are expected to be accessible to all within the institute and to all globally, except those resources that have limited or restricted access for some specific reasons.

Z.5.1.2 Objectives of IR

The main aim of an IR is to build a full-text database of the intellectual creations of the members of an institution to enable anyone within the institution or any other interested person from outside the institution to access it in his or her intellectual endeavor. However, the specific objectives of having an institutional repository are [37]:

- To provide OA to institutional output by self-archiving it;
- To maximize the visibility of an institution's scholarly research;
- To collect content in a single location; and
- To store and preserve other institutional digital assets, including unpublished or otherwise easily lost literature (i.e., gray literature), such as theses or technical reports.

Z.5.1.3 Scope and Coverage of IR

The scope of institutional repositories can be limited to a single organization or multiple institutions. Broadly speaking, an IR may have any such digital resources that may be useful to the institutional community. Besides scholarly publications, such as papers published in journals and/or presented at seminars/conferences, book chapters, and theses and dissertations, an IR may also cover unpublished/gray research materials, such as working papers of continuing education programs, various types of internal reports, and other materials that may be of value to the institution and its beneficiaries at local as well as global level such as Acts, statutes, curricula, teaching materials, and serial publications. Other materials that an institutional repository may cover are [16]:

- *Preprints:* Preprints are articles that are pre-peer-reviewed;
- *Postprints:* These are articles that are post-peer-reviewed;

- *E-prints:* These can be either preprints or postprints but in electronic form;
- *White Literature:* These are peer-reviewed published articles;
- *Gray Literature:* These are preprints or internal "know-how" materials.

It may not only cover text materials but also materials in other forms or formats, such as graphic materials, audio or video recordings, photographs, data sets resulting from research projects, models, computer programs, software, and simulations. An IR may not limit itself to its own resources and may like to augment them with other such e-resources that may be useful to the academic and/or research community of the institution concerned. However, priorities relating to coverage of an IR will have to be fixed by the concerned institution. And while doing so, usability of the material and/or easy availability of the material in other national and international databases should be considered. It may be pointed out that an institutional repository should not contain any content for which suitable copyright or licensing arrangements have not been made [42]. It may be pointed out here that "an effective repository will not only have the bibliographic reference to the work in question, but wherever possible, the actual digital work publicly accessible" [17].

Z.5.1.4 Functions of IR

The core functions or stages of an institutional repository are [41]:

- *Material Submission:* An institutional repository must have some means by which an author can submit content or document to the system. And this should be a simple one so that anyone with little or no training can make the submission without any hassles. Presently, the document submission function is often accomplished through file upload feature in the website. There may be editors who can judge the quality and appropriateness of the document's inclusion to the collection and enhancing metadata.
- *Metadata Application:* Each document within an IR requires some level of metadata. Usually a set of basic identification metadata, such as title and author, is required as part of the submission process. Abstracts, keywords, and other descriptive metadata fields also are common, although usually optional. The system itself adds administrative metadata, including date and time of the deposit and identity of the depositor.
- *Access Control:* Access control is also referred to as digital rights management. An IR system must have controlled access to the content. This may be accomplished by integrating an organization's

authentication or identity management system with the IR. Access control ensures that only appropriate people obtain an IR's content.

- *Discovery Support:* An institutional repository must have a discovery mechanism by which users can ascertain its content. Most commonly, this mechanism is a search engine although the search engine's sophistication can vary from just a few searchable metadata fields to full-text searching of the documents themselves.
- *Distribution:* Closely intertwined with access control and discovery mechanism is an IR's distribution function. Once an authorized user locates the desired content, the IR system must then have a mechanism by which a copy of the digital file can be provided or displayed to the user.
- *Preservation:* An institutional repository is based on the assumption that the documents will be retrievable in the short and long term. To assist with short-term preservation, an IR system supports some means by which its content and metadata can be backed up. For long-term preservation, the system may include ways to identify and isolate files by type to assist in their migration.

Z.5.1.5 IR Creation of IR

Creation of an institutional repository entails careful planning and execution. There are also some prerequisites for successfully creating an IR.

Step in Creation of IR

The major steps in building an IR are [43]:

- Learning about the process by reading about and examining other institutional repositories;
- Developing a Service Definition and Service Plan;
  - Conducting a needs assessment of the institution;
  - Developing a cost model based on this plan;
  - Framing a schedule and timeline;
  - Developing policies regarding content acquisition, distribution, and maintenance.
- Forming a working team
- Selecting and installing suitable hardware and software
- Marketing the IR
- Launching IR service
- Running IR Service

It may be mentioned that the selection of technology—hardware and software—should reflect the requirements outlined in service planning.

Tools for IR Creation

Besides suitable hardware, an appropriate software is required for creating a good IR. A number of open source and proprietary software packages are available for developing and running an institutional repository, Some well-known software are:

- *DSpace*: Developed by DuraSpace and written in Java, it was first released in November 2002. It runs on Linux, Solaris, Unix, Ubuntu, and Windows platforms and is completely customizable to fit user needs [44].
- *EPrints*: Developed by University of Southampton and written in Perl, it was created in 2000. It runs on Linux, Solaris, and Mac OS X platforms. A windows version has been released in 2010 [45].
- *Fedora Commons*: Fedora (or Flexible Extensible Digital Object Repository Architecture) is a digital asset management architecture upon which institutional repositories, digital archives, and digital library systems might be built. Developed by DuraSpace and written in Java, it was first released in 2003 [46].
- *MyCoRe*: MyCoRe (acronym for My Content Repository) is an open source repository software framework for building disciplinary or institutional repositories, digital archives, and digital libraries. Since the release of the first public version of MyCoRe in October 2001, the software was developed by the MyCoRe team. Written in Java, JavaScript, XSLT, it runs on Linux, Solaris, Unix, and Windows platforms [47].
- *Opus*: OPUS (originally an acronym for the Online Publikationsverbund der Universität Stuttgart) was developed with the support of the Deutsches Forschungsnetz in 1997 and 1998 at the University of Stuttgart. Written in PHP, XSLT, JavaScript, it works on several platforms.
- *Greenstone*: Greenstone was produced by the New Zealand Digital Library Project at the University of Waikato and developed and distributed in cooperation with UNESCO and the Human Info NGO. Greenstone runs on all versions of Windows, Unix/Linux, and Mac OS X. Its reader's interface is available in over 60 languages [49].

Prerequisites of IR Creation

The success in building of an IR depends of the following eight "C"s [50]:

- *Comprehension:* Comprehension means that all members of institution community must share common vision and understanding of the purposes and scope of the repository.

- *Collaboration:* Collaboration involves thinking and working together, with different people contributing their different talents, working with others to solve problems and making important decisions.
- *Context:* Context is each person's world view and working environment. Each person has a unique mind-set based on background, education, and experience. Thinking and working together in a nonthreatening atmosphere helps people integrate other contexts into their own.
- *Change:* Repositories involve change in the way research is disseminated, preserved, and published. This change requires the concerned people to deposit their intellectual products to the repository.
- *Caring:* Caring motivates the desire to share research results and joint scholarly endeavors, preserve history, and provide knowledge and information needed for future generations to learn.
- *Commitment:* Caring leads to the commitment to deposit one's scholarly work in the repository, encouraging others to do likewise by contributing ideas and energy.
- *Creativity:* Creativity involves imagination and the ability to visualize a new way of doing things.
- *Competence:* Competency means knowing how to make the repository work for all its constituents.

Z.5.1.6 Advantages of IR

The advantages of IR are:
- IR makes the collective intellectual output of an institution available online from one source;
- It facilitates scholarly communication;
- It makes sharing of intellectual products among different institutions possible;
- It helps in long time preservation of scholarly materials produced in an institution in digital format;
- It showcases research activities of an institution; and
- It increases visibility and impact of the works available in the depository.

Z.5.1.7 Current Scenario

Institutional repositories are now being created almost in every country, but the pace is certainly not same. An indication about the current scenario of IR creation in different regions may be found in the section dealing with OA movement.

Z.6 OTHER DEVELOPMENTS

Other major developments in the field of information organization and dissemination, which have taken place in recent decades are spread of information literacy movement and community information service. These developments have been discussed in detail in some earlier chapters.

REFERENCES

[1] S. Pantry, P. Griffiths, Creating Successful E-Information Service, Facet Publishing, London, 2002.
[2] A. Chatterjee, Organizing e-information services in library and information centres in India: some important issues, in: Library Profession in Search of a New Paradigm: Paper presented at the National Seminar of IASLIC, Kolkata, (2008), 281–290.
[3] J.F. Sieburth, On-Line Search Services in the Academic Library, ALA, Chicago, 1988.
[4] The Internet as an information resource (PPT. presentation). <http://www.google. co.in/url?sa=t&rct=j&q=&esrc=s&frm=1&source=web&cd=8&sqi=2&ved=0CF4 QFjAH&url=http%3A%2F%2Fwww2.unescobkk.org%2Felib%2Fpublications%2Fict lip%2Fmodule5%2FLesson1.ppt&ei=jcJcUqeSCIaQrQfbkYDoAw&usg=AFQjCNG Y5x_YekRqN3S-8Vbhdvxu0uPCdg&bvm=bv.53899372,d.bmk>.
[5] P.V. Konnur, U. Kacherki, Library portal: role of librarian, in: Proceedings of the 4th CALIBER International Convention, Gulbarga, 2006.
[6] Joint Information Systems Committee (UK), Portal. <http://www.jisc.ac.uk/upload-ed_documents/tsw_02-03.pdf>.
[7] P.K. Das, Subject gateways: the clever way to information. <http://ir.inflibnet.ac.in/ bitstream/handle/1944/107/cali_26.pdf?sequence=1>.
[8] S.R. Hatua, Web based library and information services. <http://shatua.tripod.com/ DRTCseminar.html#semi3.7>.
[9] S. Sen Bandyopadhyay, Transformation of L & I services in digital environment, in: Library Profession in Search of a New Paradigm: Papers presented at National Seminar of IASLIC, Kolkata, (2008), 215–220.
[10] L. Berube, Digital reference overview. <http://www.ukoln.ac.uk/public/nsptg/ virtual/>.
[11] A.K. Sinha, Digital reference services: an overview for user's satisfaction, in: Library profession in search of a new paradigm: Papers presented at National Seminar of IASLIC, Kolkata, (2008), 303–311.
[12] E. Canessa, M. Zennaro, (Eds.), Science Dissemination Using Open Access, ICTP Science Dissemination Unit (2008), http://sdu.ictp.it/openaccess/book.html.
[13] C. Bjork, Open access to scientific publications: an analysis of the barriers to change. (2004). <http://www.informationr.net/ir/9-2/paper170.html>.
[14] P. Suber, Open access overview. <http://www.earlham.edu/~peters/fos/overview.htm>.
[15] IFLA, A statement on open access to scholarly literature and research documentation, December 2003. <http://archive.ifla.org/V/cdoc/open-access04.html>.
[16] K.G. Jeffery, Open access: an introduction, ERCIM News 64 (January 2006). http:// www.ercim.eu/publication/Ercim_News/enw64/jeffery.html.
[17] C. Jones, Institutional Repositories: Content and Culture in an Open Access Environment, Chandos Publishing, Oxford, 2007.
[18] R.S. Bist, V.P. Mohanty, Open access movement and open access initiatives in India, in: Paper presented at PLANNER Convention, (2006), Aizwal.

[19] Mahatma Gandhi (1869-1948). <http://www.indiaonline.in/About/Personalities/Freedom-Fighters/Mahatma-Gandhi.aspx>.

[20] Open Access-History. <http://www.liquisearch.com/open_access/history>.

[21] F. Guimaraes (Ed.), Research:Anyone Can Do It, Pedia Press GmbH, Boppstrasse, 2011

[22] Budapest Open Access Initiative. <http://www.budapestopenaccessinitiative.org/read>.

[23] Bethesda Statement on Open Access Publishing. <http://legacy.earlham.edu/~peters/fos/bethesda.htm>.

[24] The Berlin Declaration on Open Access to Knowledge in the Sciences and Humanities. <https://openaccess.mpg.de/Berlin-Declaration>.

[25] World Summit on the Information Society. Declaration of Principles. <http://www.itu.int/net/wsis/docs/geneva/official/dop.html>.

[26] UNESCO. Communication and Information. Open Access to Scientific Information. <http://www.unesco.org/new/en/communication-and-information/access-to-knowledge/open-access-to-scientific-information/>.

[27] UNESCO. Communication and Information. Institutional Repository Software Comparison. <http://www.unesco.org/new/en/communication-and-information/resources/news-and-in-focus-articles/all-news/news/unesco_publishes_guidelines_to_compare_institutional_repository_software/#.V57Vffl97IU>.

[28] DOAJ: Directory of Open Access Journals. <https://doaj.org/about>.

[29] OpenDOAR: Directory of Open Access Repositories. <http://www.opendoar.org/about.html>.

[30] ROARMAP: Registry of Open Access Repository Mandates and Policies. <https://roarmap.eprints.org/>.

[31] ROAD: Directory of Open Access Scholarly Resources. <http://www.issn.org/the-issn-international-is-pleased-to-introduce-road/>.

[32] Registry of Open Access Repositories Mandatory Archiving Policies. <https://en.wikipedia.org/wiki/Registry_of_Open_Access_Repositories_Mandatory_Archiving_Policies>.

[33] UNESCO. Global Open Access Portal. <http://www.unesco.org/new/en/communication-and-information/portals-and-platforms/goap/>.

[34] S. Arunachalam, M. Muthu, Open Access to Scholarly Literature in India—A Status Report (With Emphasis on Scientific Literature), Centre for Internet and Society, Bangalore, 2011.

[35] What is a repository? <http://www.rsp.ac.uk/start/before-you-start/what-is-a-repository/>.

[36] P. Suber, Open Access, MIT Press, Boston, 2012, http://cyber.law.harvard.edu/hoap/Open_Access_(the_book.

[37] Institutional repository. <http://en.wikipedia.org/wiki/Institutional_repository>.

[38] The Scholarly Publishing and Academic Resources Coalition (USA). The case of institutional repositories: a SPARC position paper, prepared by Raym Crow. (2002). SPARC, Washington, 16.

[39] B.K. Roy, et al., An analytical study of institutional digital repositories in India, Library Philosophy and Practice (2011). http://unllib.unl.edu/LPP/.

[40] R.K. Johnson, Institutional repositories: partnering with faculty to enhance scholarly communication, D-Lib Magazine 8 (11) (2002). http://www.dlib.org/dlib/november02/johnson/11johnson.html.

[41] S. Gibbons, Establishing an institutional repository: library technology reports, No.4, July–August (2004). <http://www.techsource.ala.org/>.

[42] A.S. Chandel, F.R. Sumer, Institutional repository, in: A.S. Chandel (Ed.), Knowledge Management in Digital Era, Westville Publishing House, New Delhi, 2011, pp. 191–205.

[43] M.R. Barton, M.M. Waters, Creating an Institutional Repository: LEADIRS workbook, The Cambridge-MIT Institute (2004).
[44] DSpace. <https://en.wikipedia.org/wiki/DSpace>.
[45] EPrints. <https://en.wikipedia.org/wiki/Fedora_Commons>.
[46] Fedora_Commons. <https://en.wikipedia.org/wiki/Fedora_Commons>.
[47] MyCoRe. <https://en.wikipedia.org/wiki/MyCoRe>.
[48] Opus. <https://en.wikipedia.org/wiki/OPUS_(software)>.
[49] Greenstone wiki. <http://wiki.greenstone.org/doku.php>.
[50] M. Drake, Institutional repositories: hidden treasures, Searcher 12 (5) (2004). http://www.infotoday.com/searcher/may04/drake.html.

INDEX

Note: Page numbers followed by "*f*" and "*t*" refer to figures and tables, respectively.

Printed in the United States
By Bookmasters